RENOIR
LANDSCAPES
1865–1883

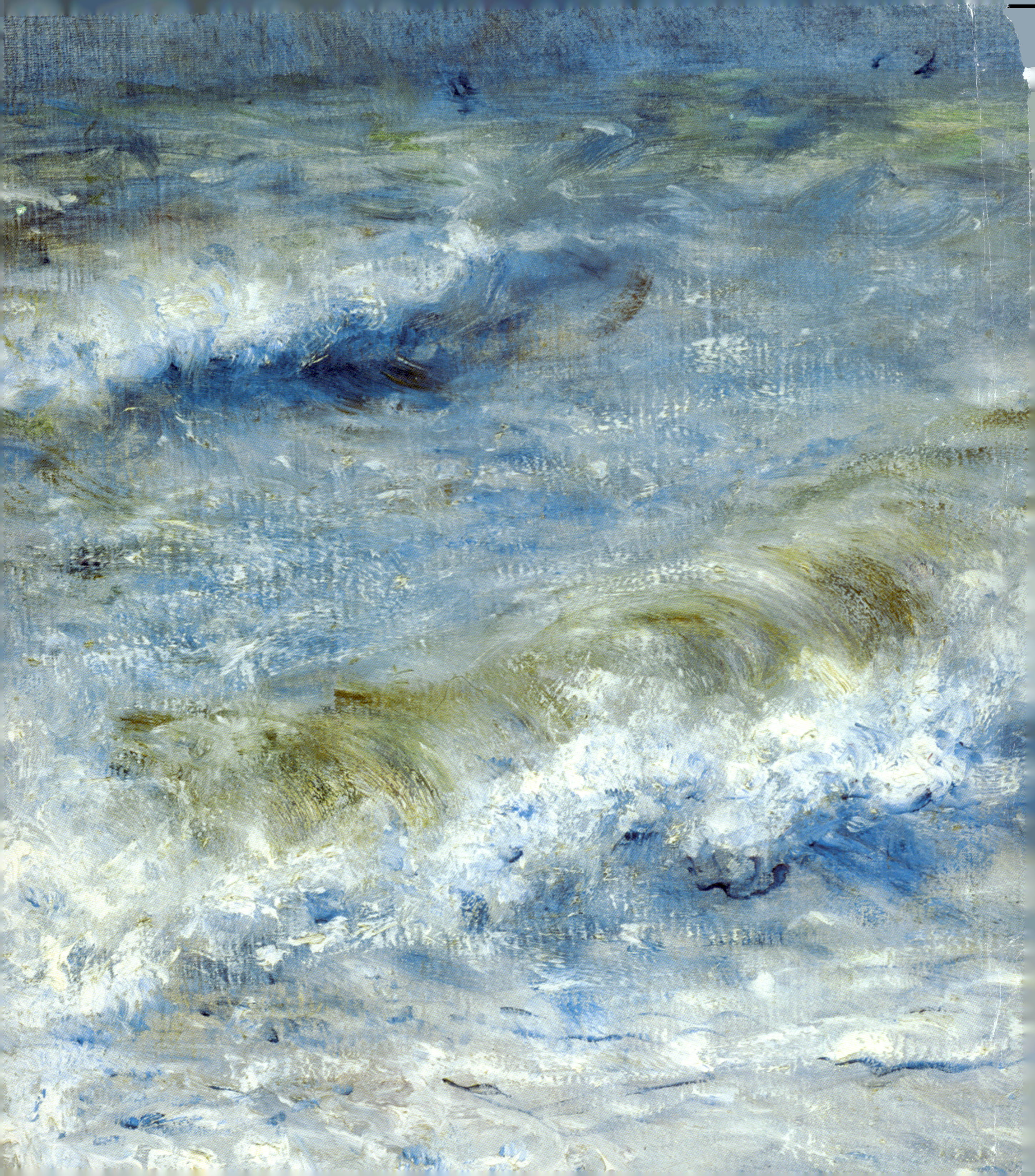

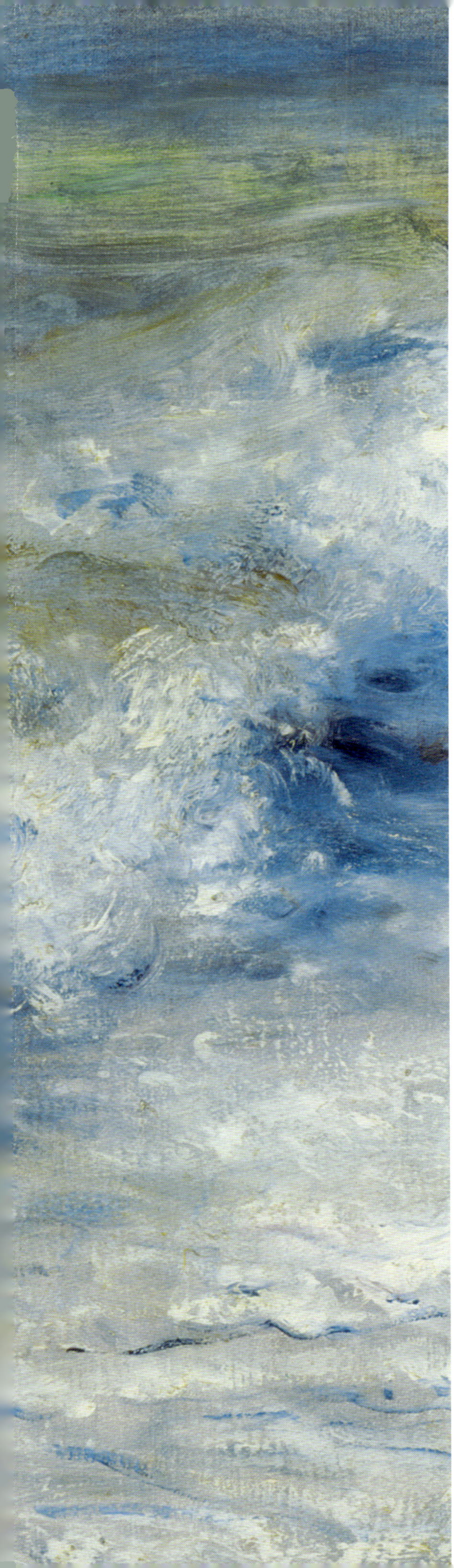

RENOIR
LANDSCAPES
1865–1883

Colin B. Bailey and Christopher Riopelle
John House, Simon Kelly, John Zarobell
with contributions from Robert McDonald Parker

Published to accompany the exhibition
Renoir Landscapes
1865–1883

The National Gallery, London: 21 February – 20 May 2007
The National Gallery of Canada, Ottawa: 8 June – 9 September 2007
Philadelphia Museum of Art: 4 October 2007 – 6 January 2008

First published in Great Britain in 2007 by
National Gallery Company Limited
St Vincent House
30 Orange Street
London WC2H 7HH
www.nationalgallery.co.uk

ISBN 9781857093179 paperback 525488
ISBN 9781857093223 hardback 525489

British Library Cataloguing-in-Publication Data
A catalogue record is available from the British Library
Library of Congress Control Number: 2005939207

PUBLISHER Kate Bell
PROJECT EDITOR Claire Young
EDITOR Paul Holberton
EDITORIAL ASSISTANCE Lise Connellan, Elizabeth O'Reilly, Davida Saunders
DESIGN Libanus Press
PICTURE RESEARCHER Suzanne Bosman
PRODUCTION Jane Hyne and Penny Le Tissier
Printed and bound in the United Kingdom by Westerham Press

All measurements give height before width
It has not been possible to confirm all exhibition loans before the final stages of catalogue production.
Some artworks shown here might not travel to all venues.

Front cover/jacket: Pierre-Auguste Renoir (1841–1919), *Garden in the Rue Cortot, Montmartre*, 1876 (detail of cat. 39).
© Carnegie Museum of Art, Pittsburgh. Acquired through the generosity of Mrs. Alan M. Scaife (6535).

Frontispiece: Pierre-Auguste Renoir (1841–1919), *Seascape*, 1879 (detail of cat. 45).
© The Art Institute of Chicago, Illinois. Mr and Mrs Potter Palmer Collection (1922.438).

CONTENTS

Sponsor's Foreword 6
Directors' Foreword 7
Authors' Acknowledgements 9

The Public Face of Renoir as a Landscapist 10
JOHN HOUSE

'The Victory of Modern Art': Landscape Painting in Mid-Nineteenth-Century France 18
SIMON KELLY

Renoir in the City 32
CHRISTOPHER RIOPELLE

'The Greatest Luminosity, Colour and Harmony': Renoir's Landscapes, 1862–1883 50
COLIN B. BAILEY

CATALOGUE 82
COLIN B. BAILEY
JOHN HOUSE
CHRISTOPHER RIOPELLE
JOHN ZAROBELL

Topographical Chronology: 1860–1885 268
ROBERT McDONALD PARKER

Appendix: Landscapes in the Salon 280
NELDA DAMIANO

Bibliography 281
Lenders 291
Photographic credits 292
Index 293

SPONSOR'S FOREWORD

Sun Life Financial is honoured to be the Presenting Sponsor of *Renoir Landscapes, 1865–1883*, the National Gallery of Canada's extraordinary presentation of the first major exhibition devoted to landscape paintings by the renowned Impressionist Pierre-Auguste Renoir.

As *Renoir Landscapes* comes to Ottawa, Canadians from all walks of life will have the rare opportunity to see for themselves magnificent paintings that have been treasured in the finest galleries and private collections around the world. Ottawa is privileged to be the sole Canadian venue for this international exhibition, which will also travel to London, England, and Philadelphia in the United States.

In keeping with our long-standing support of the arts in Canada and our ongoing commitment to make the arts accessible to all, Sun Life Financial welcomes the opportunity to partner with the National Gallery in presenting this unique show. As an international financial services organization, we seek out and celebrate excellence in all its forms, and believe we can find no better example of it than in Renoir's masterpieces. We are pleased to know that *Renoir Landscapes* will be not only a celebration of beauty, colour, and light, but a living tribute to the genius of the artist, as well.

We commend the National Gallery for co-organizing this tour de force with the National Gallery, London, and the Philadelphia Museum of Art, and for bringing it to Canada. In doing so, the Gallery enhances and enriches our own cultural landscape.

Sun Life Financial

Donald A. Stewart
Chief Executive Officer
Sun Life Financial

DIRECTORS' FOREWORD

The paintings of Pierre-Auguste Renoir (1841–1919) have long enjoyed near universal popularity. The rooms in which they hang in galleries and museums are usually thronged with visitors who take delight in his colourful scenes of urban, suburban and country life on an apparently endless summer's day: the boaters and imbibers, the young lovers, the beautiful young women who populate his world all are meant to please and charm us, and they do. A particular kind of French conviviality animates such scenes, to which anyone who has ever visited France, or longs to do so one day, cannot help but respond. What is sometimes forgotten in the pure pleasure that Renoir can evoke in his viewers, however, is how radical and provocative an artist he once was, and was seen to be. The indefatigable Philadelphia collector, Dr Albert C. Barnes, rated him at the very apex of innovation in modern art, a greater colourist even than Matisse. Barnes, who conceived of his collection as a body blow to conventional thinking, went on to acquire more paintings by Renoir than by any other artist and to build the great Foundation that bears the Barnes name around his works and those of the three artists whom he felt were Renoir's only equals: Cézanne, Picasso and Matisse. If we can know these four artists well then we can know the lineaments of modern art; Matisse and Picasso in turn were fervent admirers of Renoir and over and again turned to him for inspiration as they broadened the characteristics of painting in the early twentieth century.

It seems to us that one aspect of Renoir's art has been given too little study and appreciation. When we examine his work as a painter of landscapes in the first two, most enthusiastically experimental decades of his career, we rediscover once again that greatly daring innovator to whom avant-garde artists and collectors responded so powerfully decades ago. It was in landscape painting during the 1860s and 1870s, working side-by-side with his friends and colleagues Monet, Sisley and Cézanne, that Renoir achieved some of his most startling Impressionist effects and his most arresting colouristic discoveries. So completely is form dissolved in some of his paintings that Renoir comes closer to pictorial abstraction than any other artist of his time. Landscape was also an area in which he felt a particular freedom to improvise with touch and application of paint, moving from a surface of thick impasto on one canvas to a watercolour-like application of thinned-down oil paint on another.

Renoir Landscapes: 1865–1883 is the result of several years' fruitful collaboration between the National Gallery, London, the National Gallery of Canada, Ottawa, and Philadelphia Museum of Art. As well as being a stunning presentation of a major artist's work, *Renoir Landscapes: 1865–1883* is an invaluable reappraisal with many new discoveries. For this, we owe a great debt of thanks to the venue curators and catalogue authors, Colin B. Bailey, Christopher Riopelle and John Zarobell. Through their energy and tenacity in securing wonderful loans from around the world, including many rarely seen treasures from private

collections, we are able to present a remarkable exhibition. We also thank the other catalogue authors for enhancing this catalogue with their expertise: John House, Simon Kelly and Robert McDonald Parker.

We are indebted to all the lenders for agreeing to let their precious works join this tour, enabling us to create this impressive display. We also acknowledge the support of our sponsors: Ernst & Young in London; Sunlife Financial in Ottawa; GlaxoSmithKline, the Robert Lehman Foundation and the Annenberg Foundation in Philadelphia.

CHARLES SAUMAREZ SMITH, *Director, The National Gallery, London*
PIERRE THÉBERGE, *Director, The National Gallery of Canada, Ottawa*
ANNE D'HARNONCOURT, *Director, The George D. Widener Director and CEO, Philadelphia Museum of Art*

AUTHORS' ACKNOWLEDGEMENTS

Colin B. Bailey: I am most grateful to Anne Poulet, Director of The Frick Collection, for allowing me to continue my work on Renoir while acquitting my duties as Chief Curator of the Collection, and thus bring to fruition a project initiated at the end of my tenure at the National Gallery of Canada, several years earlier. It is a pleasure to thank members of the curatorial department at The Frick Collection, Margaret Iacono, Michael Bodycomb, Mary Lydecker, David Pullins and Esther Chadwick, whose support and assistance have been constant and unfailing. Colleagues at The Frick Art Reference Library were also unstinting in placing the unique resources of that institution at my disposal. At the National Gallery of Canada, I thank Pierre Théberge and David Franklin for inviting me to pursue my interest in Renoir in the form of a second exhibition devoted to a specific aspect of his production. I have received the strongest possible support from many members of the National Gallery of Canada, notably Daniel Amadei, Claire Berthiaume, Karen Colby-Stothart, Marie-Claire Morin, Christine La Salle, Christine Sadler, Lise Villeneuve, Diane Watier and Nelda Damiano, the last-mentioned a superb research assistant. The successful realisation of this exhibition in Ottawa is due to Alan Todd, Ellen Treciokas, Christine Feniak, Stephen Gritt, Monique Baker-Wishart, Serge Thériault, Joanne Charette and Alain Boisvert.

Among the many friends, specialists and colleagues who have responded so generously to my requests, I must mention Marc Le Coeur, Paul Durand-Ruel, Caroline Durand-Ruel Godfroy, Anne Distel, Robert McDonald Parker, Walter Feilchenfeldt, Lukas Gloor, Christine Jenny, Gary Tinterow, George Shackelford, Richard Shone, Susan Grace Galassi, Ann Dumas, Pierre Georgel, Carol Togneri, Bruno Jansem, Manuel Schmitt, Joseph Baillio, Ay-Wang Hsia, Charles Moffett and Guy Bennett. I am indebted to Judy Sund for her meticulous review of my introductory essay, and to Alan Wintermute for his forbearance, encouragement and constant support.

Christopher Riopelle: I would like to thank Sarah Herring, Nancy Ireson and Anne Robbins, Assistant curators of post-1800 paintings, Sarah Rimmo-Toure in the Curatorial Department, and the Exhibitions team at the National Gallery, London. I am also very grateful to Dr Johannes Nathan for his advice and assistance.

John Zarobell: For her essential help with research, I would like thank my intern Emma Chubb. I would like to thank my fellow authors, Martha Lucy, Robert Herbert and Joseph Rishel for all their assistance in making sense of the complexities of this artist and his works. I would like to thank Claire Young for her managing of the catalogue project and Paul-Louis Durand-Ruel for his invaluable assistance with provenance research. For their logistical support, I am very grateful to Miranda Stacey, Suzanne Bosman, Jennifer Vanim and Deniz Turker.

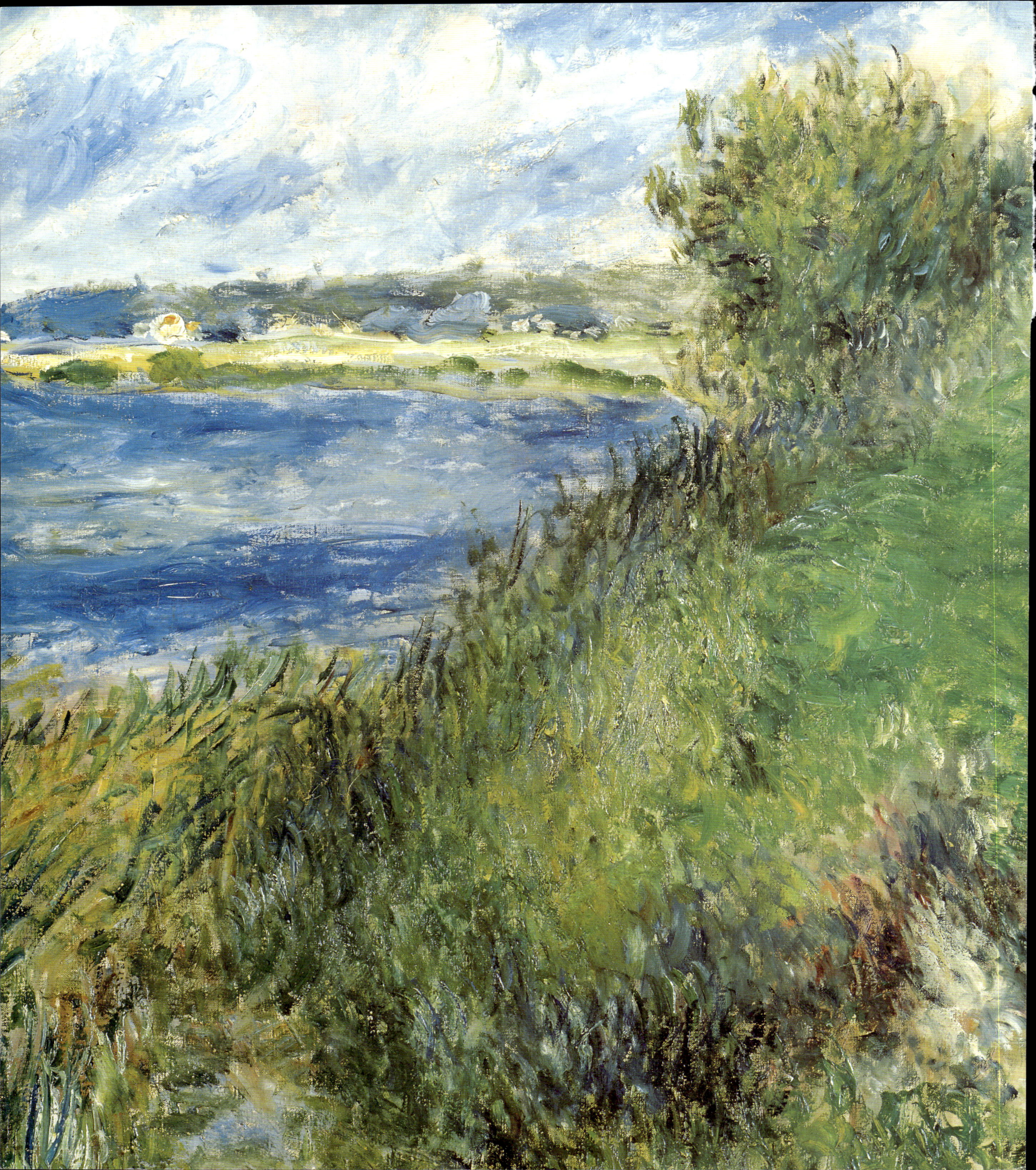

THE PUBLIC FACE OF RENOIR AS A LANDSCAPIST

JOHN HOUSE

In December 1883, Renoir and Monet made a brief trip together along the French Mediterranean coast. For Monet, it was his first exposure to the problems of painting the light of the South, whereas Renoir had recently been painting in Algeria and Italy and with Cézanne at L'Estaque. Within three weeks of their return to Paris, Monet left again for the South, enjoining their dealer Paul Durand-Ruel not to let Renoir know about his departure: 'I have always worked better in solitude and from my own impressions'.[1] Within a few weeks of his departure, though, he wrote to tell Renoir of his trip, and received a warm letter in response that reassured him that his friend had no plans to join him: 'I am stuck in Paris, where I am thoroughly fed up, running after the [perfect] model that cannot be found; but I am a figure painter! Alas! This is sometimes very enjoyable, but not when one can only find figures that are not to one's taste.'[2]

This moment, in January 1884, marks the end of the present survey and the beginning of a brief phase when Renoir concentrated his efforts on the problems of figure painting, culminating in the display of his *Bathers: Essay in Decorative Painting* (now Philadelphia Museum of Art, Tyson Collection) at the fashionable Paris gallery of the dealer Georges Petit in 1887.[3] But to what degree was this focus on the figure something new in Renoir's career? And what role did landscape play in his oeuvre in the years up to 1884? The present exhibition demonstrates that he was very active as a landscapist; but what significance did landscape hold for him, alongside his paintings of figure subjects? An approach to this question must begin by studying the ways in which he presented himself and his work in public, and specifically his exhibition strategy through these years.

Exhibiting at the Paris Salon was the most visible means by which an artist might reach the public and potential buyers: with annual attendance figures in the 1870s of around 500,000 during its six-week run, it was overwhelmingly the single most significant outlet for an artist's work, and the forum where reputations were made. The Salon was Renoir's primary focus throughout the period covered by this catalogue, apart from the four years,

FIG. 1 Detail of cat. 36.

1874–7, of the first three Impressionist group exhibitions and the two auction sales organised by members of the group.

The majority of Renoir's Salon submissions up to 1873 that can be identified were scenes of figures in the open air, whether nudes, such as *Diana the Huntress*, rejected by the jury in 1867 (National Gallery of Art, Washington), and *Bather with a Griffon*, exhibited in 1870 (Museu de Arte, São Paulo), or figures in contemporary dress, like *Lise with a Parasol*, shown in 1868 (Folkwang Museum, Essen), and *Riding in the Bois de Boulogne*, rejected and included in the Salon des Refusés in 1873 (Kunsthalle, Hamburg). This sequence displayed his consistent interest in effects of outdoor light, but in all of them the setting is subordinated to the figures and is treated more as a backdrop than as a landscape in its own right.

His two submissions of 1866 cannot be definitively identified, but they were described at the time in a letter from a friend of Renoir's as 'a landscape with two figures' and a canvas executed in a fortnight at Marlotte, in the Fontainebleau forest, that Renoir himself characterised as a *pochade* – a quick sketch. The former – the larger canvas – was rejected by the jury, and Renoir seems to have withdrawn the *pochade*, presumably because he felt that it could not stand alone.[4] It has been suggested that this larger picture was the canvas (of which only a fragment survives) depicting a nude and a clothed figure that can be seen on the wall of Frédéric Bazille's *Studio in the rue de la Condamine* of 1870 (fig. 55, p. 84);[5] the predominance of the figures in this might suggest that it is unlikely to have been characterised as a landscape; it is very possible, though, that the *pochade* was indeed a landscape.

In the years of his return to the Salon, 1878–83, Renoir used the forum primarily to promote his developing practice as a fashionable portrait painter, but in 1880 he exhibited the large and ambitious *Musselfishers at Berneval* (fig. 44, p. 63), where again the figures are dominant, but set against a delicate and atmospheric background of rocks and sea.

Viewed in terms of his Salon paintings alone, Renoir was indeed primarily a figure painter throughout his career. But there were other crucial strands in his career in these years – his participation in the Impressionist group exhibitions and auctions, and his sales to commercial art dealers, particularly Durand-Ruel. All of these outlets catered specifically for smaller and more informal pictures, canvases that were suitable for the walls of private collectors and did not need to attract attention in the big halls and the crowded walls of an exhibition like the Salon. In these venues, landscape played a significant role in Renoir's self-promotion.

In his exhibits at the first and third Impressionist exhibitions Renoir gave a place to landscape. Of the six oils he included in the first show, in 1874, three, it is true, were ambitious figure paintings, among them *La Loge* (Courtauld Institute of Art Gallery, London); but the one landscape scene that he displayed, with the title *The Harvesters* (*Les Moissonneurs*; cat. 16), presented his art in a wholly different light. The harvesters themselves, the subject indicated by the title, are relegated to the right side of the canvas and treated in the most summary way; the third figure, in the middle of the corn, is notated in a few deft but seemingly casual smears of paint. The informal composition and multiple points of focus, together with the sketch-like execution, are a far cry from the stock images of harvest-time that appeared every year on the walls of the Salon, with their statuesque female figures and their emphasis on the fruitfulness of *la France profonde.*

In the second group exhibition, in 1876, Renoir included three figure paintings in outdoor settings, but no canvases that can be categorised as landscapes. However, at the next show, in 1877, he included five landscapes, which served much the same function as *The Harvesters* had in 1874, as a demonstration of a very different facet of Renoir's art from the portraits and genre paintings that formed the bulk of his display. Only one of these can be confidently identified, *The Seine at Champrosay* (cat. 36). Both of the critics who noted the picture in their reviews of the show focused on the freely improvised brushwork that Renoir used to convey the wind that animates the water, clouds and foreground reeds. Renoir's close friend Georges Rivière celebrated it as 'a superb landscape, one of the most beautiful ever done. Nobody before has given so striking a sensation of a windy autumn day'.[6] The other critic to note the painting, writing under the name of Jacques, could not accept the technique: '. . . its nuances are quite brutal although they give an impression of truthfulness. It is the long grasses of the bank that ruin the river for me'.[7]

The two canvases that he exhibited with the title *Jardin* cannot be securely identified, but one of them may well have been the monumental *Garden in the rue Cortot, Montmartre* (cat. 39); the critic Bernadille described them as 'apocalyptic gardens',[8] while another, Descubes, equally startled by their colour, described them as 'coloured by a light similar to the light that passes through chemists' jars'.[9] Less controversial was a view of the *La Place St-Georges* (cat. 31), praised by both Rivière and Roger Ballu for its truthful light effect.[10]

Writing later in 1877 and viewing the exhibition in retrospect, Rivière summed up the overall tone of Renoir's work: 'To seek the gay and charming aspects of nature, the aspects that make us love it, that is [his] aim; his whole oeuvre has this as its goal'. He added a brief summary of the landscapes in Renoir's oeuvre: 'In Renoir's art, the landscapes are as varied in their technique as the figures.'[11] This emphasis on diversity is fundamental to understanding Renoir's art during the 1870s, and the roles that landscape played in it. Viewing his oeuvre as a whole, his paintings in these years show an absolute refusal to be typecast, whether in choice of subject-matter or in their treatment. His landscapes are especially varied, and he seems to have viewed landscape as the theme that allowed him the freest scope for technical experimentation. The paintings show a remarkably wide range of different types of informal mark-making, giving the appearance of carefree improvisation. The broad and quite opaque touches and accents in *The Harvesters*, the thinner, fluid sweeps of paint in *The Seine at Champrosay* and the dense mesh of variegated dabs and dashes of colour in *Garden in the rue Cortot, Montmartre* create startlingly diverse results, each appropriate for conveying the dominant effect of the chosen scene.

We have little information about Renoir's sales through art dealers during the 1870s. Monet, Pissarro and Sisley made extensive sales to Paul Durand-Ruel in 1872–3, but not Renoir. However, the first of the few canvases that Durand-Ruel did buy from him was a landscape, the quite precise and delicately finished *Pont des Arts* of about 1867–8 (fig. 27, p. 44), with the dome of the Institut de France, the symbolic home of academic values, played off against the crowd of fashionable figures walking down the quayside from the landing stage.[12]

By contrast, landscapes played a major role for Renoir in a different type of self-promotion, through auction sales. Individual artists and groups of artists regularly presented their works for sale at the Hôtel Drouot in Paris, and the brief periods of display before these sales were regarded as a significant form of exhibition, and as one of the few means, apart from the Salon, by which an artist might gain a reputation and attract clients.[13] Members of the Impressionist group organised two sales, in 1875 and 1877, and Renoir was involved in both, on both occasions putting landscapes up for sale. Fuller details survive of the first sale, in which, judging from the titles in the sale catalogue, he included no less than eight landscapes;[14] among these were *The Gust of Wind* (cat. 13), listed as *Grand vent*,[15] and a work titled *Paysage d'été* (*Summer Landscape*) the size of which, as indicated in the auction records, suggests that it might be identified as the canvas now known as *Path rising through Tall Grass* (*Chemin montant dans les hautes herbes*; fig. 2). Both of these paintings represent Renoir's art at its most informal; in *The Gust of Wind*, the seemingly amorphous succession of loose dabs, dashes and broader swathes of colour coalesce to evoke with remarkable precision the effect of wind sweeping through trees and banks of foliage. Landscapes played a lesser role in Renoir's submissions to the 1877 sale – only two out of 16 works.[16]

Landscape reappeared as part of Renoir's public repertoire in 1882, in the seventh Impressionist group exhibition. This cannot be regarded as deliberate policy on the artist's part, since the display was mounted by Durand-Ruel (the 25 works by Renoir all came from his own stock) and indeed Renoir did not want his work included; he was not in Paris at the time of the show, which took place while he was convalescing from pneumonia on the French Mediterranean coast and in Algeria. The presence of landscapes in the show is, however, significant. After a fresh injection of capital, Durand-Ruel had begun to buy large numbers of paintings from Renoir early in 1881, among them a considerable number of landscapes: ten of these were included in the exhibition – two views of Algiers, deriving from his first visit to the town in spring 1881; two views of Venice, the first port of call in his Italian trip of autumn 1881; five views of the Seine in the environs of Paris, and one Normandy landscape. Those of the Seine views that can, tentatively, be identified were also all recent works.[17]

As a group, they are extremely varied. Some of the Seine scenes, such as *The Seine at Chatou* (cat. 58) retain the informality of the landscapes of the 1870s, but treated on a larger scale and with a fuller and more fluent touch and a greater richness of colour. Of the Algerian scenes, *Field of Banana Trees Near Algiers* (*Le Champ de bananiers près d'Alger*; cat. 55) is very unconventionally composed, the lower two thirds of the composition filled with a dynamically decorative mass of foliage, with the city beyond depicted as a white silhouette shimmering in the distance, as if suspended above the palm fronds. By contrast, *The Jardin d'Essai, Algiers* (cat. 56), though lavish in execution, is a more conventional view, very comparable to the topographical prints and photographs of this celebrated site.[18]

The two Venice views that were exhibited in 1882, *Venice, The Doge's Palace* (cat. 62) and *The Grand Canal, Venice* (cat. 63), both present famous and wholly conventional tourist subjects, vividly coloured but treated with a smaller, more refined touch than his other landscapes in the show. At first sight it is surprising that it was these Venice views that attracted the most hostile responses from the critics in 1882: Paul Leroi described them as 'the most outrageous series of ferocious daubs that any slanderer of Venice could possibly imagine'.[19] Several other critics compared the two pictures unflatteringly with the work of Félix Ziem, well known for his Venetian scenes, loosely painted in Turner-like rainbow hues.[20] It seems likely that these negative criticisms arose in part from the hallowed cultural associations of the Venetian subjects that Renoir chose; the Impressionist palette was more acceptable when applied to the environs of Paris or the exotic landscapes of Algiers than to the Grand Canal or the Doge's Palace.

The figure paintings on display in the 1882 show also stressed Renoir's preoccupation with the effects of open-air light and colour. Several of his scenes of Seine-side terraces were included, most notably *Luncheon of the Boating Party* (*Le Déjeuner des canotiers*; Phillips Collection, Washington, DC); but most interesting in the present context is *Woman gathering Flowers* (*Femme cueillant des fleurs*) of about 1874 (fig. 3); its treatment reveals Renoir's acute awareness of the social and cultural meanings of the subjects and sites he chose. The background clearly indicates the environs of Paris, with a villa at far right and a church and river bridge at far left, though the precise site has not been identified. The young woman stands stiffly amid a flowery meadow, a bunch of flowers in her hand and her fashionable Japanese-style parasol at her feet; her costume shows that she is a parisienne, while the awkwardness of her stance suggests that she feels ill at ease amid the lavish natural growth of the meadow. Rather than following the conventional association of 'woman' and 'nature', the picture seems actively to highlight the discomfort felt by the young woman as she leaves her habitual urban surroundings and seeks to immerse herself in the 'natural' world – a part of the 'natural' world that is itself compromised by the proximity of the city.

Since Renoir did not choose his own exhibits for the 1882 show, a clearer idea of his own attitude to his landscapes can be formed from the list of paintings that he sold to Durand-Ruel in these years – paintings that he knew would be presented by the dealer to prospective buyers as representative examples of his art.

Landscapes played a major role in these sales – canvases painted in Normandy during his visits to Paul Berard's house near Dieppe in 1879 and 1880;

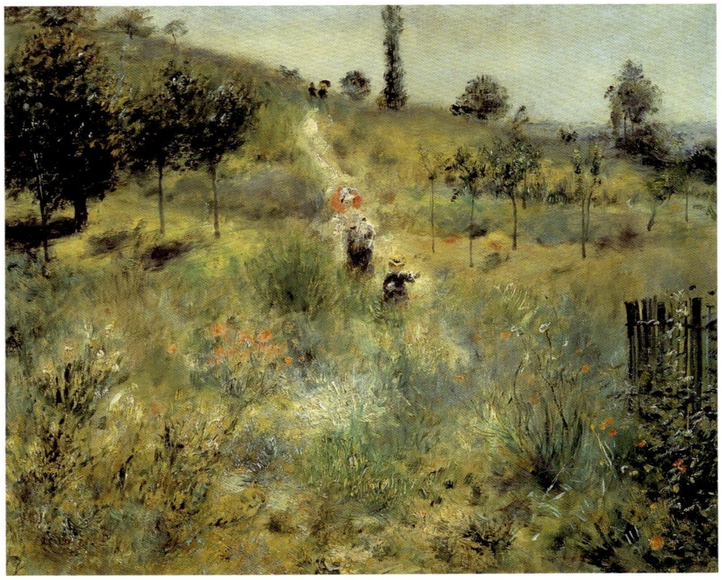

FIG. 2 *Path rising through Tall Grass* (*Chemin montant dans les hautes herbes*), 1873. Oil on canvas, 60 × 74 cm; 23⅝ × 29⅛ in. Musée d'Orsay, Paris (RF 2581).

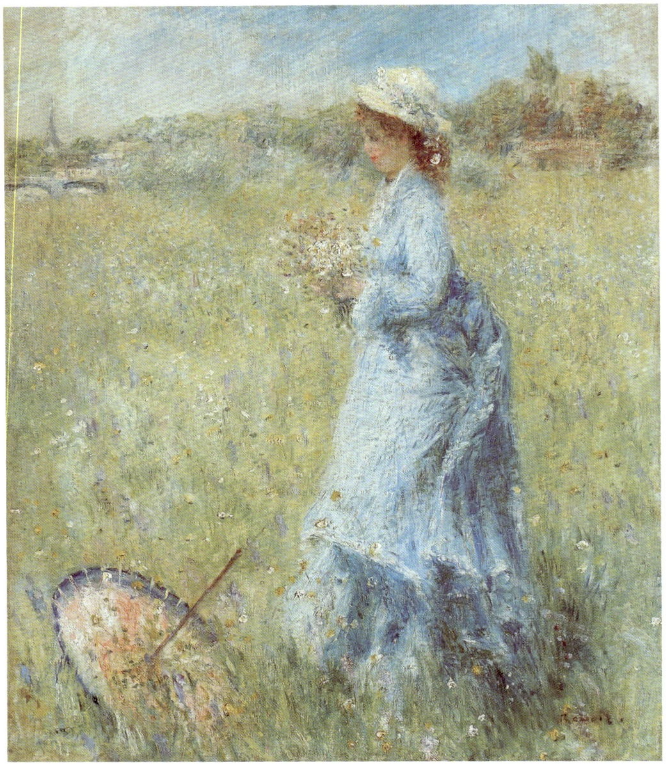

FIG. 3 *Woman gathering Flowers* (*Femme cueillant des fleurs*), about 1874. Oil on canvas, 65.4 × 54.5 cm; 25¾ × 29⅛ in. Sterling and Francine Clark Art Institute, Williamstown (1955.907).

on the banks of the Seine; in Algeria; in Italy; on the French Mediterranean coast – alongside still lifes and the figure subjects that continued to be the focus of his most ambitious projects. It is clear that he and Durand-Ruel regarded landscape as one key element in his production, and sought to market it accordingly.

At the end of the period covered by this exhibition and catalogue, Renoir summed up the position of landscape painting in his oeuvre by the choice of works included in the one-artist show that Durand-Ruel mounted in April 1883 as part of a sequence of monographic exhibitions of the Impressionist artists with which he sought to raise their profile.[21] This exhibition, unlike the 1882 group show, was not merely a presentation of the dealer's stock; over half of the seventy paintings included were loans from private collectors, intended to highlight the number of fashionable people who had already begun to collect Renoir's work. Of the seventy, only thirteen were landscapes. And Théodore Duret's preface to the exhibition catalogue emphasised Renoir's credentials as a figure painter, contrasting him to Monet: 'Among the Impressionist painters, I take M. Claude Monet as the quintessential landscapist, and M. Renoir as the quintessential figure painter. In the former's work, I find notated the most varied and fugitive appearances of sky, water and fields; the latter focuses on all the nuances to which the human figure is subject, all the reflections that the play of light can create across garments or flesh.'[22]

As an overall verdict on Renoir's career to date, this emphasis was accurate; but, as we have seen, Renoir did consistently seek to demonstrate his skills as a landscapist, alongside the figure paintings for which he was best known. Moreover, the present exhibition vividly shows that it was in this genre, subsidiary within his oeuvre, that he often felt able to parade the most informal and improvisatory aspects of his art; if landscape was primarily a recreation for him, alongside the serious business of figure painting, it was a pastime that encouraged him to produce some of his most immediate and unconventional works.

NOTES

1 Letter from Monet to Paul Durand-Ruel, 12 January 1884, in Venturi 1939, II, pp. 267–8.
2 Letter from Renoir to Monet, late January 1884, in Geffroy 1924, II, p. 25.
3 On this, see Riopelle 1990 and House 1992.
4 See letter from Marie le Coeur to Jules le Coeur, 6 April 1866, in Anon., 'L'Eternel Jury', 1921, between pp. 100 and 101; on the use of the term *pochade*, see House 2004, pp. 45–50.
5 See House and Distel 1985, pp. 179–80.
6 Georges Rivière, in Berson 1996, I, p. 180.
7 Jacques, 'Menus propos: exposition impressionniste', *L'Homme libre*, 12 April 1877, reprinted in Berson 1996, I, p. 157.
8 Bernadille, in Berson 1996, I, p. 130.
9 Descubes, in Berson 1996, I, p. 144.
10 Rivière, as cited in note 6; Roger Ballu, 'L'Exposition des peintres impressionnistes', *La Chronique des arts et de la curiosité*, 14 April 1877, reprinted in Berson 1996, I, p. 125.
11 Georges Rivière, 'Les Intransigeants et les impressionnistes: Souvenirs du salon libre de 1877', *L'Artiste*, November 1877, reprinted in Berson 1996, I, p. 186.
12 Details of Durand-Ruel's dealings with Renoir, here and throughout this essay, are derived from the Archives Durand-Ruel; I am deeply indebted to the late M. Charles Durand-Ruel for granting me access to the Archives, for research in preparation for the 1985–6 Renoir retrospective exhibition.
13 See House 2004; for a detailed study of the sales organised by Diaz and Rousseau, see Kelly 2003.
14 Bodelsen 1968, pp. 335–6; Renoir's landscapes were the following, listed by their number in the *procès verbal* of the sale: *#9, Vue de Paris [Institut]; #20, Bateau [Argenteuil]; #21, Grand vent [paysage]; #32, Le Pont Neuf; #44, Jardin aux dahlias; #45, Champ de rosiers; #59, Paysage d'été; #63, Le Lavoir de Bagneux.*
15 For this identification see Anne Distel's entry in House and Distel 1985, p. 202.
16 Bodelsen 1968, p. 336; they were *#29, Paysage. Automne; #30, Paysage. Printemps.*
17 See Berson 1996, II, pp. 210–12, 229–33; the '*verger normand*' was not listed in the exhibition catalogue, but was mentioned in a review by Charles Flor (reprinted in Berson 1996, I, p. 388).
18 See Benjamin 2003, pp. 64–70.
19 Paul Leroi, 'Salon de 1882', *L'Art*, 1882, reprinted in Berson 1996, I, p. 401.
20 The comparisons with Ziem were made by Jacques de Biez, A. Hustin and Armand Silvestre; reprinted in Berson 1996, I, pp. 381, 396, 413.
21 Durand-Ruel mounted five successive exhibitions, from February to June 1883, of Boudin, Monet, Renoir, Pissarro and Sisley; on these, see Ward 1996, pp. 22–6 and House 2004, p. 194.
22 Duret, reprinted in Duret 1998, p. 69.

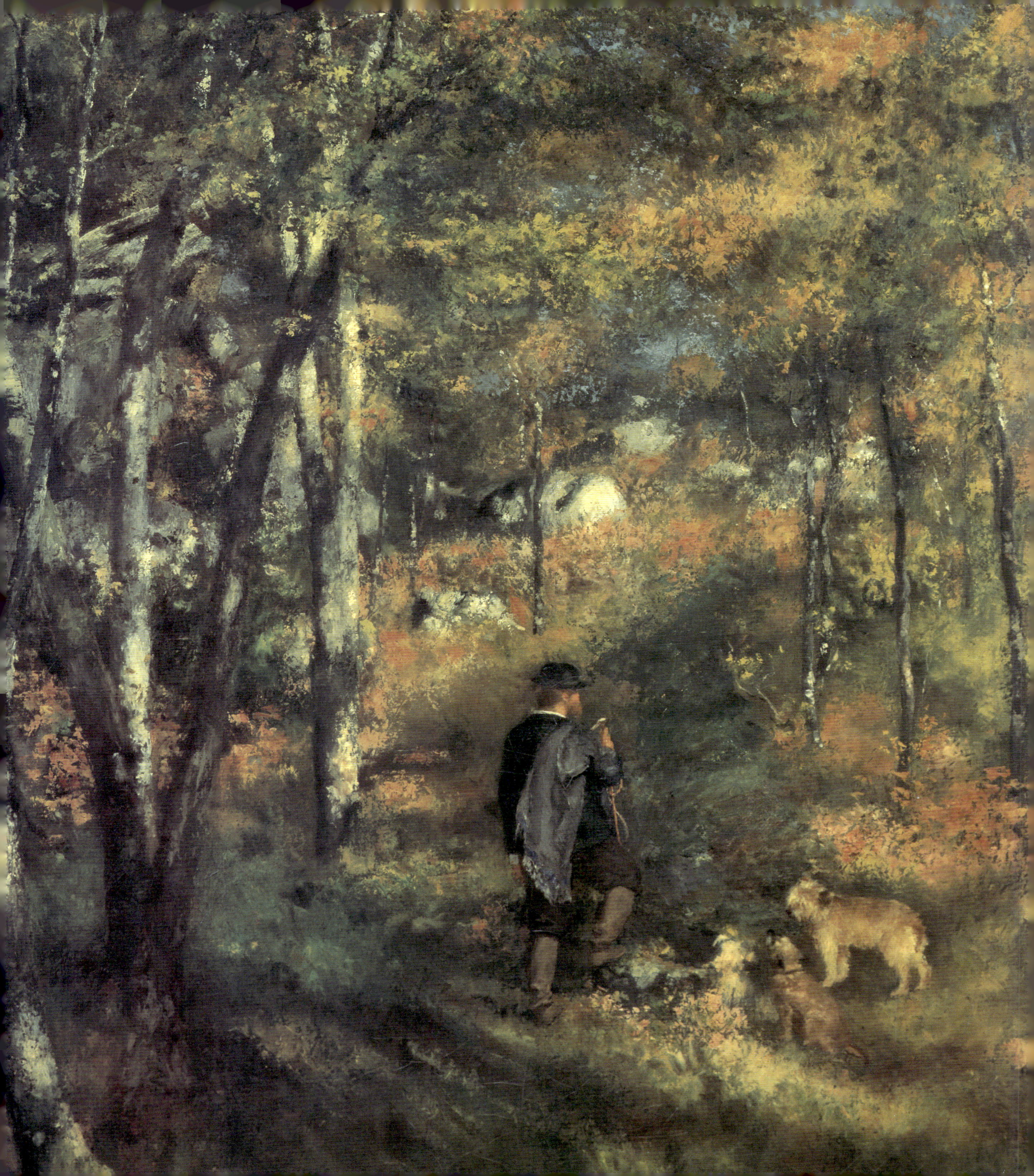

'THE VICTORY OF MODERN ART': LANDSCAPE PAINTING IN MID-NINETEENTH-CENTURY FRANCE

SIMON KELLY

By the time of the Exposition Universelle in 1867, critical consensus in France identified landscape painting as the strongest element in the national 'school'. Maxime Du Camp claimed, 'It is superfluous to state that our landscape painting is unrivalled in the world. It's a well-known fact that no longer needs to be proven'.[1] The Goncourt brothers had previously affirmed that landscape was 'the victory of modern art'.[2] Théodore Duret, future supporter of the Impressionists, praised the Naturalists 'where one finds the truest and most clearly defined originality of the modern French School'.[3] The young critic, Théodore Pelloquet, remarked that France had rivals in every other genre with the sole exception of landscape painting, since 'our landscapists are the best of all'.[4] Théophile Thoré, for his part, noted that 'in all conscience, it is landscape painting which will illustrate the French School of the nineteenth century'.[5] Such critical agreement among a wide range of commentators reflected the emergence of a remarkable range of landscape types in mid-century France – from the 'poetic' imagery of Jean-Baptiste-Camille Corot to the lyrical river scenes of Charles-François Daubigny and from luminous paintings of the forest of Fontainebleau by Théodore Rousseau to innovative marines on the Normandy coasts by Gustave Courbet. The output of these artists and their colleagues provides an essential context for our understanding of Impressionist landscape in general and that of Renoir in particular.[6]

Reflecting a new sense of nationalism, French landscape artists of the mid-nineteenth century travelled round the country, often taking advantage both of an expanded rail network and of new pigments and the newly invented paint tube, which facilitated their study of motifs on the spot and outdoors.[7] They painted above all in the forest of Fontainebleau some 40 miles to the south-east of Paris, forming a colony in the village of Barbizon – hence the term 'Barbizon School' that is frequently used to describe them as a group.[8] But they produced their images of rustic retreat for a very urban, newly modern market. They painted at a time of rapid urban expansion, as Paris was transformed during the Second Empire into the modern city of grand boulevards that we know today.[9] As we shall see, the Barbizon

FIG. 4 Detail of cat. 3.

artists not only produced work for the traditional space of the Salon but also for new exhibiting venues – dealer galleries, auction rooms and artistic societies – that transformed the nature of the Parisian, and French, art world in the mid-nineteenth century. It was in these diverse spaces that the rise of landscape was ultimately effected.

The Salon

The Barbizon artists remained loyal to the traditional venue of the Salon. Corot was perhaps the most devoted to the official space, exhibiting regularly between 1827 and 1875. Théodore Rousseau, although his work had been repeatedly refused by the Salon jury during the July Monarchy, exhibited consistently from 1849 until his death in 1867. Daubigny, for his part, exhibited at the Salon over a 40-year period from 1838 to 1878, and Millet from 1844 to 1870. Gustave Courbet, too, recognised the importance of the Salon from an early age, exhibiting landscapes from the late 1840s.[10] His large-scale *Demoiselles de Village*, an image of his sisters in the hilly landscape of his native Franche-Comté, was given prominent place in the Salon Carré in 1852 (fig. 5). Two small landscapes by Rousseau hung on the rail beneath.[11]

The Salon paintings of the Barbizon artists reflected a wider shift away from the representation of Italy and towards that of France. Images of the forest of Fontainebleau appeared particularly frequently, reflecting the centrality of this location for the school.[12] River paintings were also common, particularly of the Seine and Oise.[13] Daubigny, in particular, specialised in river subjects and took the practice of *plein-air* painting further than any of his Barbizon colleagues by constructing a studio on his boat, *Le Botin*, in 1857. His silvery

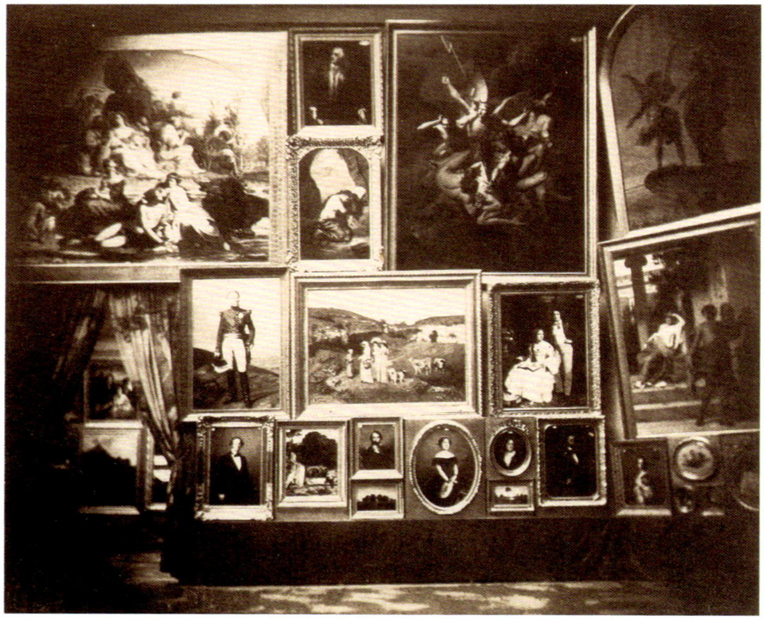

FIG. 5 Gustave Le Gray (1820–1884), *Interior of 1852 Salon (North Wall, Grand Salon)*, 1852. Photograph, Musée d'Orsay, Paris (PHO 1984-104-2).

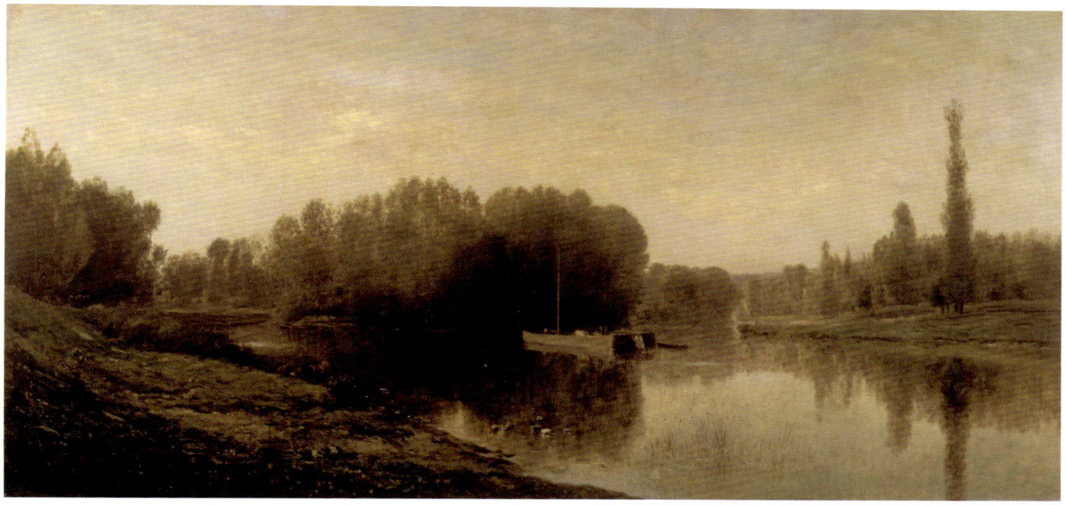

FIG. 6 Charles-François Daubigny (1817–1878), *The Banks of the Oise*, 1859. Oil on canvas, 90 × 182 cm; 35½ × 71⅝ in. Musée des Beaux-Arts, Bordeaux (M6230).

The Banks of the Oise (fig. 6) attracted praise at the 1859 Salon for its frank naturalism. Gautier described the artist as 'the first among objective landscapists' and went on: 'He makes no choices, he does not compose, he neither adds nor removes, he does not confuse his own feelings with the reproduction of the site; he paints the selected view with a charming naiveté, leaving the spectator free with his own impression; his paintings are pieces of nature cut out and set into frames of gold'.[14]

Gautier emphasised the informality of Daubigny's composition in contrast to the established academic tradition of structuring landscape with *repoussoirs* and *coulisses*. A similar critical discourse surrounded the landscapes of Jean-François Millet. Although he is known today principally as a painter of peasant life, Millet's correspondence reveals his profound sensitivity to nature.[15] In the final years of his life, from 1866 to 1870, he exhibited a major group of landscapes at the Salon, including *Winter* (fig. 7), shown in 1867. Here he represented the brooding expanse of the plain of Chailly beneath a sky dynamically animated by a wheeling flock of crows.[16] Millet's minimalistic composition disregarded established academic formulae for landscape while his rugged touch evoked the harsh surfaces of the cold soil. Millet's supporter, Théodore Pelloquet, described the work thus: 'Winter is certainly the least complicated subject that can be imagined. An expansive ploughed plain, crows pecking at manure, a hill in

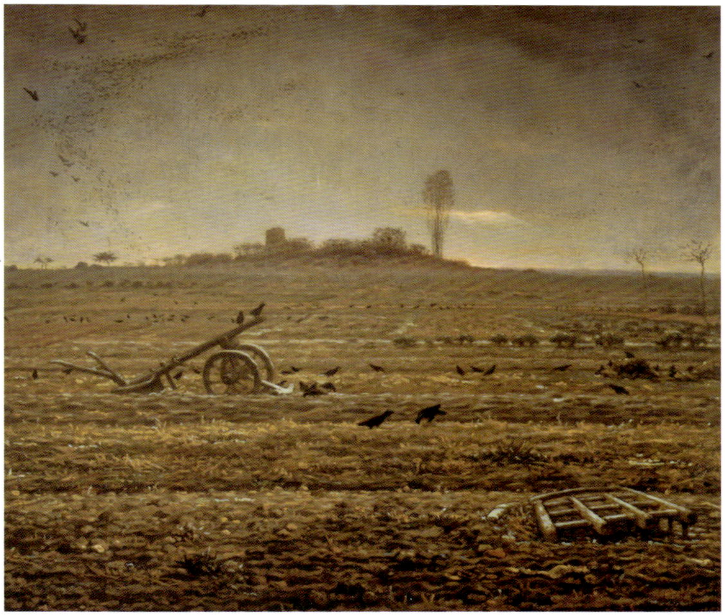

FIG. 7 Jean-François Millet (1814–1875), *Winter*, 1862. Oil on canvas, 60 × 73 cm; 23⅝ × 28¾ in. Oesterreichische Galerie Belvedere, Vienna (89).

the distance with trees stripped of leaves and with their thin branches silhouetted against a grey, heavy and black sky: this is a long way from the ambitious compositions of the pupils of Rome. But what a melancholic impression, at the same time full of poetry and reality, this painting produces on the attentive and competent onlooker!'[17]

Three years later, Millet exhibited an even larger work, *November*, his largest ever landscape (now lost) with a similarly reductive composition.[18] This again represented an empty field in winter, now enlivened by a single figure firing a gun to frighten off crows. Duret felt that there was nothing 'greater' than this painting not only at this Salon but in the whole of the modern school.[19]

Alongside their 'informal' compositions, the Barbizon artists also developed pioneering techniques of painting which confounded academic methods, in which the traces of artistic presence were generally self-consciously effaced. Their innovative painterly touch was evident not only in their private studies but also in their Salon works. Théodore Rousseau, for example, exhibited at the 1851 Salon a group of large-scale paintings of the forest of Fontainebleau painted with considerable abandon and with rough textures mimicking the ruggedness of natural surfaces.[20] The radical critic François Sabatier-Ungher referred to his 'whipped facture'[21] while the more conservative commentator Etienne Delécluze criticised his 'system . . . of only creating sketchy *ébauches*, instead of paintings'.[22] Throughout his career Corot attracted criticism for his lack of '*fini*' as well as for his supposed '*gaucherie*'.[23] *Solitude, Souvenir of Vigen, Limousin* (fig. 8), exhibited at the 1866 Salon, demonstrates the characteristic

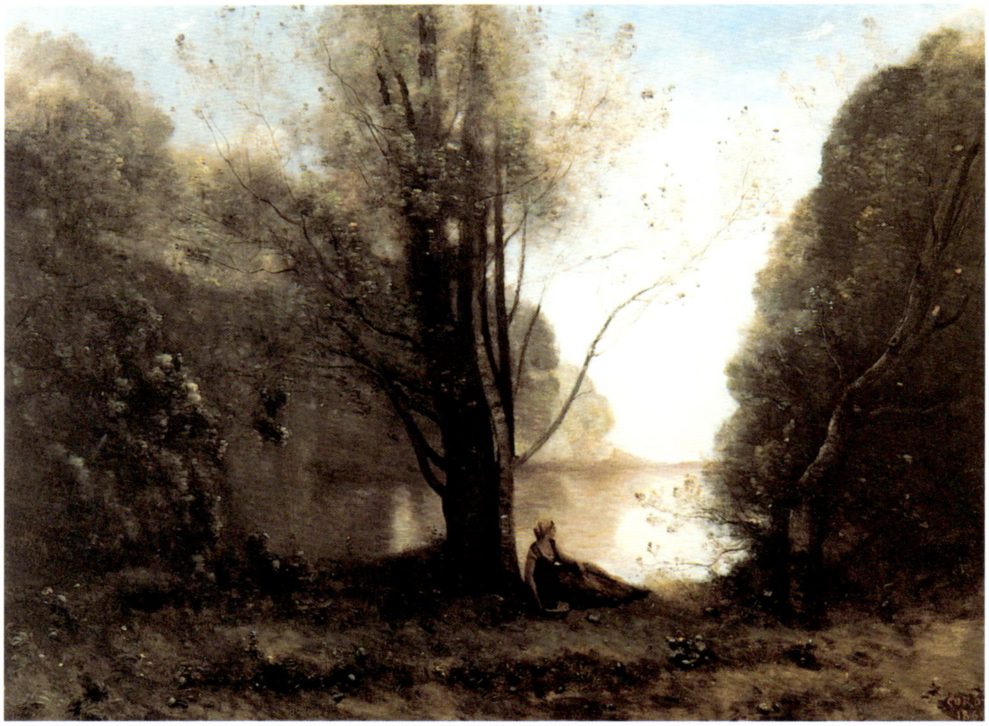

FIG. 8 Jean-Baptiste-Camille Corot (1796–1875), *Solitude, Souvenir of Vigen, Limousin*, 1866. Oil on canvas, 95 × 130 cm; 37⅓ × 51⅛ in. Carmen-Thyssen-Bornemisza Collection, on loan to Museo Thyssen-Bornemisza, Madrid (CTB 1999.27).

feathery touch with which Corot achieved effects of silvery, blurred foliage within a composition of delicately balanced symmetry. Inspired by a study made on a journey to Limousin in central France some 15 years previously,[24] the work also highlights Corot's fascination later in life with producing '*souvenirs*' of his many travels in France and Italy.[25] A solitary woman, holding a lyre, sits by the side of a lake, evoking a sense of melancholy comparable to the Romantic literature that Corot loved.[26] In reviewing this work, Charles Blanc noted that the 'poetry' of this painting saved the artist from the usual criticism of his lack of finish. Blanc noted the vogue for Corot's work among younger artists: 'M. Corot had his imitators who, seeing him succeed, thought they ought to focus on the harmonies of the *ébauche* and make do with "rendering the impression". It's the all important word among a certain group.'[27] Daubigny's work also regularly attracted criticism for its 'sketchiness'.[28] It is notable that the Barbizon School were supported by many of the young critics, such as Philippe Burty and Théodore Duret, who would later support the Impressionists.

Despite criticism of their works, the Barbizon artists won important patronage at the Salon. Corot received major support from the Emperor, who acquired three of his '*souvenir*' paintings. Among these was *Solitude, Souvenir of Vigen, Limousin* mentioned above, for which the Emperor paid the enormous sum of 18,000 francs, six times more than he paid for Corot's far better known *Souvenir of Mortefontaine* (Musée du Louvre, Paris). In 1865 the Emperor also acquired Courbet's *Entrance to the Puits-Noir Valley; Twilight Effect* (Musée d'Orsay, Paris). During the course of the Second Empire, Daubigny's often large-scale works also attracted state patronage, to an exceptional degree compared to his Barbizon colleagues.[29] Rousseau, in contrast, received no state or imperial patronage during the Second Empire and instead relied on private patrons such as the Alsatian textile industrialist Frédéric Hartmann. The provincial exhibitions that first developed in France in the early part of the nineteenth century also offered new opportunities for sales.[30] Rousseau, Millet, Troyon and Diaz all regularly sent their work round the provincial exhibition circuit, in which Corot, in particular, enjoyed considerable success.[31]

Commercial Galleries: 'a Kind of Permanent Salon'

Alongside the Salon, the Barbizon artists exhibited and sold their works in the commercial galleries that expanded greatly as a sector during the Second Empire.[32] Théophile Gautier described the rue Laffitte as an enticing world of spectacle where Parisians could promenade at night past illuminated windows.[33] Corot here displayed his naturalistic paintings, which attracted critical praise for their *naïf* freshness in contrast to his more formal Salon paintings.[34] Among his works in this vein was a view of a canal near Rotterdam, produced in 1854 (fig. 9) during a brief three-week trip to Holland. Painting outdoors in several sessions from 7 to 11 September, Corot evoked the silvery reflections across the water while enlivening his scene with the rich colour accents of red roofs.[35] The painting demonstrates

FIG. 9 Jean-Baptiste-Camille Corot, *The Banks of a Canal near Rotterdam*, 1854. Oil on canvas, 29.8 × 46 cm; 11¾ × 18⅛ in. Museum of Fine Arts, Richmond, Virginia. Gift of Count Cecil Charles Pecci-Blunt (59.31).

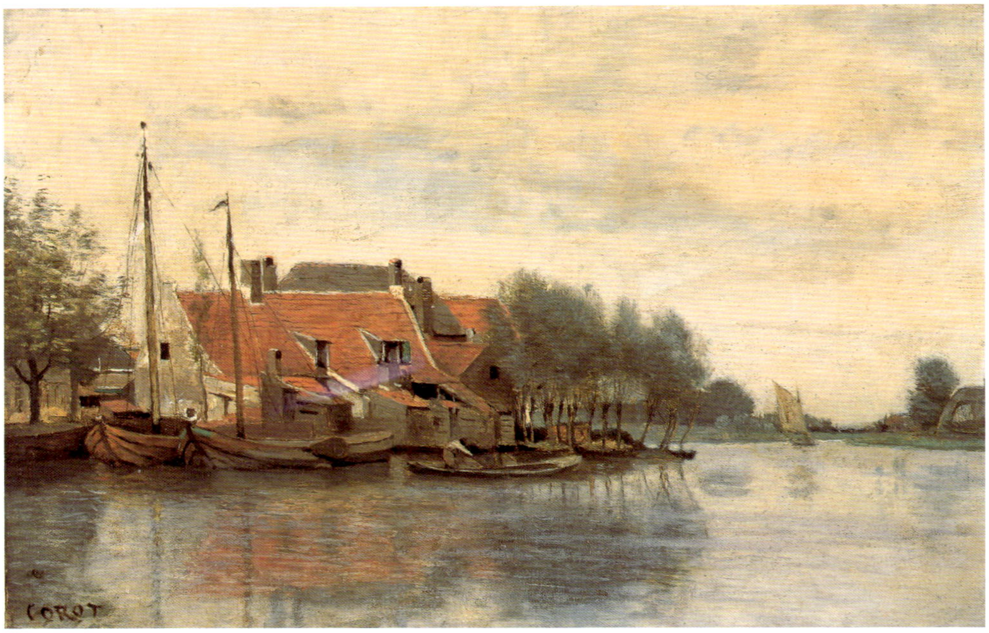

FIG. 10 Eugène Boudin (1824–1898), *On the Beach, Sunset*, 1865. Oil on panel, 38 × 59 cm; 15 × 23¼ in. The Metropolitan Museum of Art, New York. The Walter H. and Leonore Annenberg Collection. Bequest of Walter H. Annenberg, 2002 (2003.20.2).

his pioneering technique of '*peinture claire*', whereby he added areas of white to his shadows in an attempt to give his work an overall blondness in contrast to traditional chiaroscuro methods.[36] Théodore Rousseau also enjoyed success with a range of rue Laffitte dealers from the 1850s. Most spectacularly, he sold 91 of his paintings to the dealers Hector Brame and Paul Durand-Ruel for the enormous sum of 100,000 francs in 1866.[37] Daubigny's surviving account books – a useful comparison to those of Monet in the 1870s – also indicate his success in selling his naturalistic works to a wide range of dealers.[38] Variants of his *Banks of the Oise* enjoyed particular commercial success.[39] Daubigny even moved to a new, richly decorated Parisian studio on the advice of Hector Brame in order to cultivate patrons. By the early 1870s, Barbizon painters – particularly Corot, Rousseau, Dupré, Millet and Courbet – increasingly predominated in the stocks of Durand-Ruel.[40]

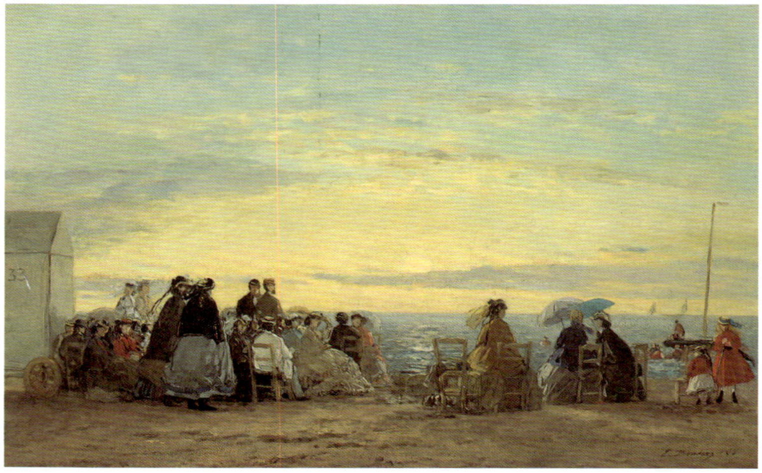

Constant Troyon enjoyed, too, enormous commercial success and was said to earn more than 300,000 francs a year. Significantly, he also nurtured the early career of the marine painter Eugène Boudin, whose images of Normandy coastal tourism enjoyed a vogue in the 1860s.[41] *On the Beach, Sunset* (fig. 10) represents a group of holidaymakers assembled close by the water's edge at dusk. The

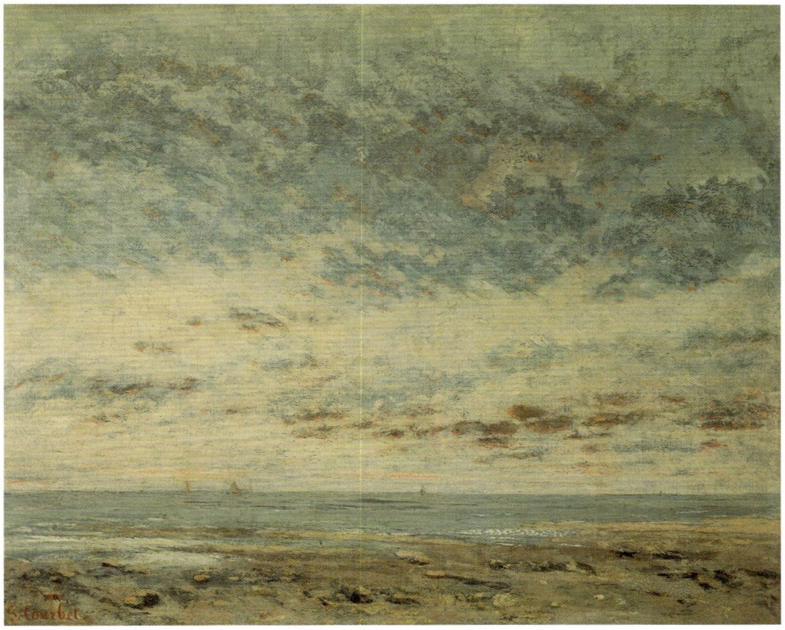

FIG. 11 Jean-Desire-Gustave Courbet (1819–1877), *Low Tide at Trouville*, 1865. Oil on canvas, 59.6 × 72.6 cm; 23½ × 28⅝ in. Walker Art Gallery, National Museums Liverpool (6111).

bathing wagons have been pulled back although a few swimmers remain in the sea. In his 1859 Salon review Baudelaire had praised Boudin's ability to capture transient weather effects.[42] Here the artist captures the moment the sun is about to meet the sea and turn the sky from yellow to orange. In contrast to Boudin's capturings of modern life, Courbet's radically minimalistic marines from his 1865 Normandy campaign at Trouville often showed no sign of human presence. Both artists, however, showed their seascapes successfully in the gallery of Alfred Cadart and Jules Luquet on the boulevard des Italiens.[43] Among the works exhibited in Courbet's one-man show in March 1866 was probably *Low Tide at Trouville* (fig. 11). The palette of colours moves from foreground brown tones through salmon pinks over the horizon and then to blues and grey in the sky above. The artist's signature palette-knife technique is clearly apparent. For Champfleury, Courbet's marines represented a challenge to established seascape conventions.[44]

The Auction House

Like the commercial galleries, the auction house enjoyed new prestige during the commercial prosperity of the Second Empire. In 1852, a new auction space, the Hôtel Drouot, opened in the most affluent area of Paris, close to the rue Laffitte. The Barbizon artists benefited from this by organising auctions of their paintings. Rousseau held three auctions in 1850, 1861 and 1863, while Corot and Boudin each held a single sale. Narcisse-Virgile Diaz de la Peña pioneered the strategy and used it most effectively, organising 11 sales of his works

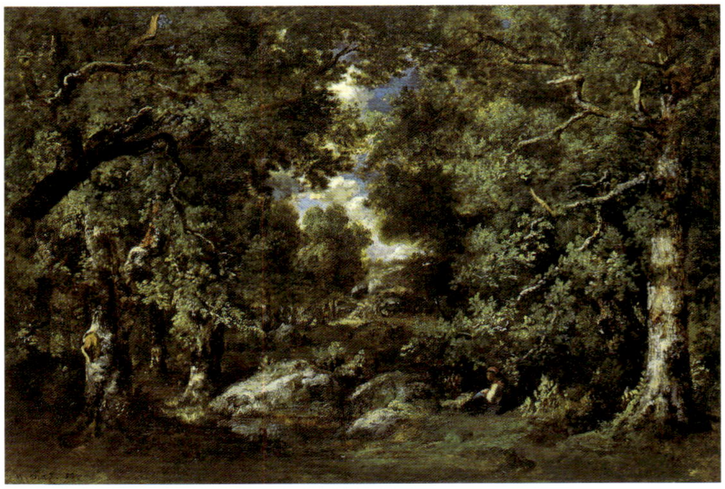

FIG. 12 Narcisse-Virgile Diaz de la Peña (1809–1876), *Forest of Fontainebleau*, 1858. Oil on canvas, 50.5 × 73.6 cm; 20 × 29 in. Toledo Museum of Art, Ohio (22.27).

between 1849 and 1868.[45] The auction house provided a space for the display and sale of *études d'après nature* and *esquisses* rather than more 'finished' works.[46] At the same time, the Barbizon painters also included more ambitious, studio works in their auctions. Rousseau's sale of 25 studio paintings in the spring of 1861 was the product of three years' work and, for Thoré, was his 'true exhibition' of the year, exceeding in importance his display at the Salon.[47] Corot's 1858 sale contained five ambitious studio pieces, including *Le Concert* (Musée Condé, Chantilly), although the artist's naturalistic views attracted greater collector interest.[48] Diaz, for his part, favoured richly coloured and carefully composed '*sous-bois*' compositions such as *Forest of Fontainebleau* (fig. 12).[49] Diaz was always a rich colourist: here light animates the sparkling greens of the foliage and the silvery-grey rocks and tree trunks around the foreground pool, complemented by the artist's usual picturesque, neo-rococo staffage.[50] Diaz, like Rousseau, conspicuously screened out all signs of the increasing levels of tourism in the forest in the 1850s and 1860s.

Diaz's affluence as a result of his sales is suggested by an image of his studio on avenue Frochot in northern Paris (fig. 13). The artist stands before his easel, on his wooden leg, while one of his '*sous-bois*' hangs on the wall behind.[51] A patron carefully examines the finish of a picture with a magnifying glass while, to the right, a female model poses for the artist. Diaz, like Renoir, aspired above all to success as a figure painter and most spectacularly exhibited an enormous painting of nudes at the 1855 Exposition Universelle.[52] Such work, however, only attracted critical ridicule and it was as a landscape painter that the artist received the most critical praise.[53] The considerable prices that Diaz received for his landscapes contrast markedly with the minimal sums received by Renoir at the 1875 Impressionist auction.

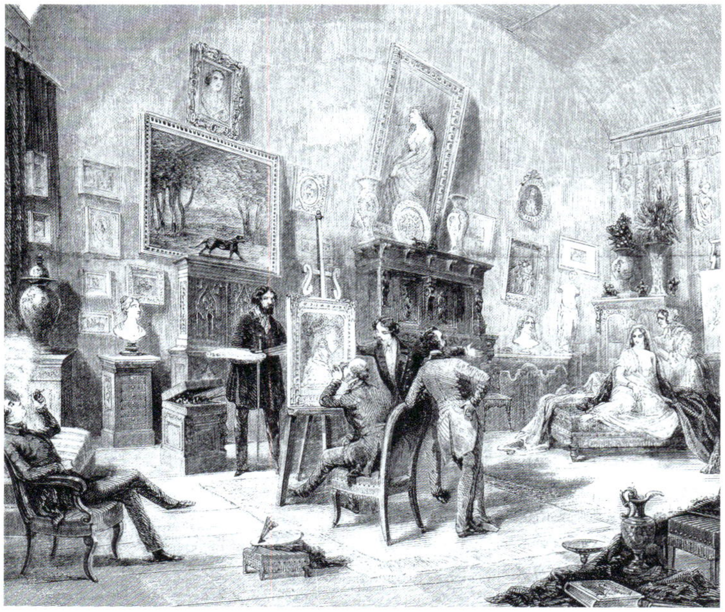

FIG. 13 Narcisse-Virgile Diaz de la Peña, *View of Diaz's Studio*, wood engraving in *L'Illustration*, 19 March 1853. Bibliothèque Nationale de France, Paris.

The 'Cercle des Arts': an 'Intimate' Venue

From the early 1860s, the Barbizon artists were provided with a new exhibiting venue, the Cercle des Arts on the rue de Choiseul, a private all-male arts club that offered a more intimate setting than the official Salon. As Martha Ward has noted, this space offers the closest precedent for the Impressionist exhibiting space in 1874.[54] Artists associated with the colony of artists at Barbizon all exhibited in group shows at the Cercle from 1862, sometimes showing works of a considerable scale.[55] Yet the venue seems to have been particularly conducive to the display of small-scale paintings. The critic Léon Lagrange praised its 'intimate' space in 1866 and went on, '. . . here at least one can see the paintings without seeing a bewildered crowd, one can have a discussion with a friend without fear of holding up the flow of people. It is landscape painting above all that benefits from this intimacy. As one of our collaborators has said, landscape is a hole in the wall of our houses . . . What would happen to the *Stream* of M. Dupré if it were placed below the enormous glass screens of the annual exhibitions? Hang this piece of canvas, smaller than a handkerchief, on the wall of your home and there you are immediately in the countryside'.[56] Lagrange's words are particularly apt in view of Rousseau's one-man show of 80 '*études*' held at the Cercle in 1867 at the same time as the Exposition Universelle. The show of these paintings recently acquired by Brame and Durand-Ruel attracted widespread critical praise.[57] Most of the works were small-scale and undoubtedly benefited from the intimate circumstances of the venue. The exhibition included a luminous view of the Gorges d'Apremont, dating from the early 1850s (fig. 14).[58] Rousseau was always accomplished at representing transient weather effects and here he renders the effects of falling rain in the distance while his gestural impasto conveys a sense of movement and flux in the clouds. This work, like many other *études* on display, was probably painted wet-into-wet in one or two sessions outdoors. In his introduction to this show Philippe Burty described the studies on display as 'really the key to his whole oeuvre'.[59] These often spontaneously rendered works, he argued, provided an essential background to Rousseau's more composed studio paintings. The records of the Durand-Ruel stockbooks highlight the degree to which these works enjoyed commercial success.[60]

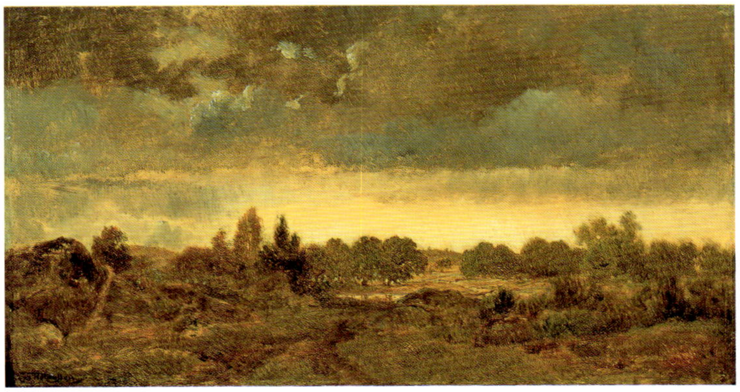

FIG. 14 Théodore Rousseau (1812–1867), *Fontainebleau*, about 1850. Oil on panel, 28.9 × 51.6 cm; 11⅓ × 20⅓ in. Taft Art Museum, Cincinnati, Ohio. Bequest of Charles Phelps and Anna Sinton Taft (1931.423).

The Trend for the Future

An overview of the diverse spaces in which the Barbizon artists displayed their works highlights the increasing prestige and commercial value of their landscapes at mid century. Renoir's artistic practice, particularly in his early years, was deeply affected by their example and principally by their method of working *en plein-air*, the increased informality of their compositions and the 'sketchy' finish of their exhibited paintings. As a student, he was an admirer of Rousseau and, by his own admission, painted pastiches of Rousseau's landscapes for the Parisian market.[61] He was also much impressed by the river scenes of Daubigny that represent an important precedent for his own river views around Paris.[62] In the early 1860s, he established a friendship with Diaz de la Peña, whom he had first met at Chailly in the forest of Fontainebleau in 1862. The elder artist seems to have mentored Renoir, allowing the young, impoverished painter to purchase colour supplies and canvases on his own account and even advising Renoir to lighten his palette.[63] Renoir himself later remembered his admiration for Diaz's '*sous-bois*', which evoked for him 'the smell of mushrooms, of rotting leaves and moss' and which undoubtedly informed his own early forest scenes (see cat. 3).[64] Renoir seems to have enjoyed the closest association with Diaz of all the Barbizon painters.[65] Both had trained as porcelain painters while both also shared a fascination with French eighteenth-century art.[66]

Renoir also met Courbet while working out-of-doors at Marlotte in the forest of Fontainebleau. He was encouraged by the elder artist – 'the idol of the young painters'[67] – and, for a brief period in the mid-1860s, employed Courbet's palette-knife technique (see cat. 3), although he had abandoned it by 1867. Subsequently his marines indicate his awareness of Courbet's vocabulary of expansive vistas as well as close-up views of single waves.[68] Of all the Barbizon artists, Renoir seems to have had the most substantial and long-standing respect for Corot, whom he later described as the 'greatest landscape painter who ever lived'.[69] He admired above all the naturalistic strain to Corot's work, rather than the more 'poetic' *souvenirs*, and his early forest views reflect the influence of the elder artist's blond palette and tonal subtlety.

By the late 1860s, Renoir had begun to turn away from the example of the Barbizon artists as he explored luminous colour effects in areas of light and shadow and an iconography of modern life. His landscapes, however, continued to reflect an awareness of Barbizon compositional strategies.[70] Even as late as 1884, he was inspired to visit La Rochelle by Corot's luminous view of this port (Yale University Art Gallery, New Haven). Shortly before his death, he humbly noted that, for all his lifelong study of nature, he had never been able to equal the work of Corot.[71] Renoir's landscape output – as he himself undoubtedly would have acknowledged – cannot thus be fully appreciated without an awareness of those Barbizon painters for whom he felt such deep respect.

NOTES

1 Du Camp 1867, p. 343.
2 Goncourt 1855, p. 18.
3 Duret 1867, p. 21.
4 Pelloquet 1867, 5th article, 29 June.
5 Thoré 1870, II, p. 354.
6 See Pomarède 2002. For an overview of 'realist landscape', see Loyrette and Tinterow 1994, section 3.
7 Callen 2000, p. 106.
8 The term was coined by the Scottish art historian and dealer David Croal Thomson in 1890 and was never used by the artists themselves.
9 Nearly 44,000 houses were demolished in Paris from 1852 to 1869 to make way for the *grands boulevards*. It has often been argued that the commercial popularity of landscape during the Second Empire was, in part at least, a response to the disorientating effects of the transformation of Paris. See Wagner 1981.
10 On 21 March 1847 Courbet wrote to his parents of the Salon, '*Pour se faire connaître il faut exposer et malheureusement il n'y a que cette exposition-là*'; Chu 1996, p. 67.
11 The image to the right can be identified as the *Effet de matin* now in the Cincinnati Art Museum (1954.25).
12 See J. Whiteley, Salon Index, Art History Department, Oxford University.
13 *Ibidem.*
14 Gautier 1992, p. 192.
15 On 1 December 1866, for example, Millet wrote to his patron Émile Gavet, '*J'ai vu, il y a quelques jours, un soleil couchant d'une nature très particulière et bien de saison. Je vais m'efforcer de rendre l'impression que j'en ai reçue*'; Chillaz 1997, aut. 2839.
16 Characteristically for Millet, he also produced variant compositions in pastel (Fogg Art Museum, Harvard, and Burrell Collection, Glasgow).
17 Pelloquet 1867 in Sensier 1881, p. 304.
18 This major work was lost during World War II. A black-chalk study is in the Louvre (RF 5776).
19 Duret 1870 in Duret 1998, p. 47: '*. . . il nous semble que, non seulement au Salon de cette année, mais que dans toute l'école moderne, il n'y a rien de plus grand que les deux Millet.*' See also the *Batteuse de beurre* exhibited at the same Salon (Yamagata Museum of Art, Japan).
20 See, for example, *Lisière de forêt, soleil couchant* (Musée du Louvre) or *Plateau de Bellecroix* (private collection).
21 F. Sabatier-Ungher, 'Salon de 1851', p. 13: '*. . . la touche carrée, la facture fouettée . . .*'.
22 E. Delécluze, 'Exposition de 1850', *Journal des Débats*, 25 February 1851.
23 Shiff 1999, pp. 120–38.
24 Robaut 1905, no. 844, for the study (private collection).
25 One-fifth of Corot's exhibited works between 1855 and 1875 include the word '*souvenir*' in the title – 14 exhibited at the Paris Salon and 13 in provincial exhibitions.
26 Corot had a particular admiration for the poetry of Alfred de Musset. His *Evening Star* (1864, Musée des Augustins, Toulouse) was specifically inspired by Musset's poem 'Le Saule'.
27 Blanc 1866, p. 40. It is notable that Camille Pissarro, Berthe Morisot and Alfred Sisley all identified themselves as pupils of Corot in the Salon *livrets* of the mid-1860s.
28 Gautier 1861, pp. 119–20: '*Il est vraiment dommage que M. Daubigny, ce paysagiste d'un sentiment si vrai, si juste et si naturel, se contente d'une première impression et néglige à ce point les détails. Ses tableaux ne sont que des ébauches, et des ébauches peu avancées.*'
29 The State acquired from Daubigny *La Vanne d'Optevoz* (Musée du Louvre) for 3,000 francs in 1854 and *Le Printemps* (Musée du Louvre) for 3,000 francs in 1856. Further commissions followed in the 1860s. In November 1852 the State purchased from Millet *Scène champêtre, gardeuse de vache* (Musée de Bourg-en-Bresse) for 1,000 francs. See Angrand 1968, p. 337.
30 See Brunner 1980.
31 Corot's *Effet de matin* (also called *La Compagnie de Diane*; Musée des Beaux-Arts, Bordeaux) was purchased by the city of Bordeaux for 5,000 francs at the Exposition de la Société des Amis des Arts, Bordeaux, 1858. At the 1864 Exposition de l'Union Artistique de Toulouse, *The Evening Star* (Musée des Augustins, Toulouse) was bought by the city of Toulouse for 3,000 francs.
32 Green 1989.
33 Gautier 1858, p. 10: '*La rue Laffitte est une sorte de salon permanent, une exhibition de peinture qui dure toute l'année. Cinq ou six boutiques offrent derrière leurs vitrines de glace des tableaux sans cesse renouvelés sur lesquels, le soir, de puissants reflecteurs concentrent la lumière.*'
34 Henriet 1854, p. 115: '*Une des plus agréables surprises qui attendent le flâneur, dans la rue Laffitte, c'est la rencontre imprévue de ces précieuses toiles de Corot, humides, embrumées. Blanchâtres, toutes frissonnantes encore de l'air vif du matin . . . Aux expositions dites annuelles, on ne voit que le styliste ingénieux, le Corot du Pausilippe ou de Tivoli. Mais c'est rue Laffitte seulement que l'on peut goûter le côté intime, familier de son talent, et que l'on apprend à aimer le naïf et bon Corot de Ville d'Avray, de Bougival et du Bas-Meudon.*'
35 Robaut noted it was painted over this five-day period. The work appeared in the artist's posthumous studio sale, at which it sold for 5,600 francs – one of the top prices of the sale. Corot is known to have produced several studio '*répétitions*' after this painting. See Robaut 1905, no. 744.
36 In his introduction to the catalogue of the May 1875 Corot retrospective at the Ecole des Beaux-Arts, Philippe Burty noted, '*Corot aura entraîné l'Ecole, avec une force irresistible vers la peinture claire, vers l'étude en plein air, vers ces horizons voilés qui laissent à l'imagination un champ illimité*'; Burty 1875A. As early as the 1830s Corot was using complementary colours and adding violet to his shadows – as, for example, in *View of Avignon* (National Gallery, London).
37 See Durand-Ruel stockbooks, Archives Durand-Ruel, Paris.
38 Daubigny kept a careful record of the titles, names of purchasers and year of sale of his paintings while also producing a small schematic pen-and-ink drawing of each work sold. Ten landscapes were commissioned, for example, by the dealer Goupil in October 1871 for a combined total of 32,500 francs. See 'Copie du Carnet de Ventes de Daubigny', Aut. 367b. Cote AR16, in Chillaz 1997.

39 Durand-Ruel, in Venturi 1939, p. 186: '*Daubigny . . . faisait encore de charmants paysages et surtout ces "Bords de l'Oise" que les amateurs préféraient à tous les autres motifs et qui se sont vendus très cher plus tard. Il m'en a donné une assez grande quantité et toujours à des prix très modérés, de* 800 *francs à* 1,000 *et* 1,500 *francs.*'

40 Silvestre 1873. 27 etchings after works by Millet, 27 after Dupré, 27 after Corot, 20 after Rousseau and 7 after Courbet appeared in this catalogue of Durand-Ruel's stock.

41 Boudin was well aware of the commercial attractions of his subjects and noted: '*On aime beaucoup mes petites dames sur la plage, certains prétendent qu'il y a là un filon d'or à exploiter*'; Boudin to Martin, 12 February 1863, in Jean-Aubry and Schmit 1968, p. 50.

42 Baudelaire 1992: '*Ces études* [pastels] *si rapidement et si fidèlement croquées d'après ce qu'il y a de plus inconstant, de plus insaisissable dans sa forme et dans sa couleur, d'après des vagues et des nuages, portent toujours, écrits en marge, la date, l'heure et le vent: ainsi, par exemple, 8 octobre, midi, vent de nord-ouest.*'

43 On 6 April 1866 Courbet wrote to his friend Urban Cuénot of the vogue for his Normandy marines, noting that each had taken him only two hours to paint but each had brought him 1,200 francs to 1,500 francs; cited in Chu 1996, p. 247. Courbet encouraged this vogue when he included 23 '*paysages de mer*' in his 1867 retrospective.

44 Champfleury 1861, p. 261.

45 Kelly 2003, pp. 33–48.

46 See 'Catalogue d'une jolie collection d'esquisses peintes, sujets de figures et études d'après nature, par M. Diaz', Paris 1849, and 'Catalogue d'une collection de tableaux et études peints [sic] d'après nature par M. Théodore Rousseau', Paris 1850. Diaz specialised in close-up paintings of tree trunks, several of which appeared in his 1849 sale.

47 See 'Salon de 1861' in Thoré 1870, p. 48.

48 *Le Concert* was bought in. The sale of 38 works included views of Ville d'Avray, Rosny, Dunkerque, Le Tréport, Domfront, Luzancy, Nanteuil-les-Meaux, Marcoussis, Geneva, Dardagny and Rotterdam. It raised 14,233 francs. See Robaut 1905, I, p. 186.

49 The location may be the Vallée de la Solle. A work with this title and very similar composition appeared in Diaz's 1858 one-man sale.

50 Diaz always insisted on his distance from contemporary 'realist' trends. According to his early biographer Théophile Silvestre, he remarked: '*Ma peinture . . . fait bien dans les salons et les boudoirs; les tableaux de Courbet resteront dans les antichambres et dans les cuisines . . .*'; Silvestre 1857. In another '*boutade*', he apparently told Millet, '*tu peins les orties, moi les roses*'.

51 Silvestre described Diaz's wealth thus: '*Son atelier est encombré de meubles, de tableaux, de tapisseries . . . Il a non seulement la passion des belles choses, mais la fureur du luxe, de la magnificence et du faste . . . Cinquante mille francs gagnés à coups de pinceau tombent tous les ans de ses mains comme l'eau qui s'écoule à travers les mailles d'un panier*'; Silvestre 1857, p. 230.

52 Gautier 1856 described this work (*Les Dernières Larmes*; private collection) thus: '*Cinq femmes d'une blancheur blafarde s'élèvent dans un ciel grisâtre, symbolisant nous ne savons trop quoi, mais si exsangues, si vides, si cotonneuses, qu'on reste stupéfait . . .*'

53 Silvestre 1857.

54 Ward 1991, pp. 605–8.

55 Corot, for example, showed a version of his *Evening Star* at the Cercle exhibition in 1864. Millet also exhibited a version of his *Sheepfold, Moonlight*. Dupré regularly showed works there, as did Troyon.

56 Lagrange 1866, p. 398.

57 Du Camp 1867, p. 344: 'There were some masterpieces there, not only in execution but also in impression, in strength of feeling, in intimacy, in frankness and in sincerity.' The show also included 29 '*tableaux*' that had been acquired by Brame and Durand-Ruel.

58 It has been suggested that the site represented was the Plaine de Chamfroy in the forest of Fontainebleau (Sullivan and Meyer 1995, p. 261). The work can, however, be identified with some certainty as no. 76 in the 1867 exhibition catalogue, in which it was described as follows: '*. . . éclaircie pendant la pluie, dans les gorges d'Apremont. L'eau, à gauche, tombe encore; le bas du ciel est déjà traverse par le soleil. 1853 – L. 49c; H. 26c. Peint sur panneau*'; Burty 1867. The description and measurements correspond to the Taft picture. The catalogue was written by Philippe Burty with Rousseau's collaboration so we may assume that the identification of the Gorges d'Apremont is correct. The work is listed in the Durand-Ruel stockbooks as no. 10,000, with the following record: '*46 ème affaire des 10,500. Juin '67. Acheté 1,000 francs. Vendu 2,800 francs, Decembre, 1868*'; Archives Durand-Ruel. Thanks to Caroline Durand-Ruel Godfroy for allowing me access to these archives.

59 Burty 1867: '*. . . vraiment la clef de tout son oeuvre . . . ces notes recueillies à toutes les heures, dans tous les milieux, par un esprit toujours attentive, une âme toujours vibrante, une main jamais fatigué.*'

60 See Durand-Ruel stockbooks, Archives Durand-Ruel, Paris.

61 In 1895, Renoir told Julie Manet that, as a young man working in the forest of Fontainebleau, '*il était logé pour 50 sous et Diaz qui se trouvait avec lui vendait ses tableaux comme des Rousseau. Il en faisait une huitaine par jour*'; Manet 1979, p. 66 (19 September 1895).

62 '*Rousseau m'épatait et aussi Daubigny*'; Renoir 1962, p. 73. Daubigny was one of the few on the Salon Jury in 1866 to support Renoir's work and apparently complimented the young artist on his refused painting: '*Il y a de grandes qualités dans son tableau*'; Corot was another jury member to support Renoir; Venturi 1939, I, p. 30.

63 After scaring off a group of passers-by heckling Renoir, Diaz apparently told the young artist: '*Pourquoi peignez-vous si noir? . . . même les ombres des feuillages ont de la lumière . . . regardez donc ce tronc de hêtre! Le bitumen est une convention. Ça ne durera pas . . .*'; Renoir 1962, p. 75.

64 *Ibidem*, p. 73. Renoir also remembered: '*Mon amour allait à Diaz. Il restait à ma portée. Je me disais que si j'étais peintre, j'aurais voulu peindre comme lui et que peut-être j'aurais pu le faire . . .*'

65 Morel (1883) makes the observation that Renoir's earliest manner followed Diaz as a genre painter as well as a landscapist: '*A cette époque Renoir faisait du Diaz. On pourrait retrouver des toiles qu'il a signées où figurent jusqu'à trois cents personages . . .*

De là des empâtements de bitumen, des touches noires près de tonalités tendres qui rappellent la manière du peintre des nymphes et des baigneuses des sous bois.'

66 In contrast, the one Barbizon artist for whom Renoir expressed dislike was Millet. He objected to the 'sentimentality' of Millet's peasant scenes: '*Je détestais Millet. Ses paysans sentimentaux me faisaient penser à des acteurs déguisés en paysans*'; Renoir 1962, p. 73. He may, however, have been more interested in Millet's 'pure' landscapes. The high horizons of his 1870s paintings (such as *The Watering-place*, cat. 15) suggest an awareness of the elder artist's example.

67 Renoir 1879: '*C'est là où mon frère rencontra Courbet, qui était l'idole des jeunes peintres.*'

68 See Rishel in Wilson-Bareau and Deneger 2003, p. 243–6.

69 Gimpel 1963, p. 13: '*Ce fut le grand génie du siècle, le plus grand paysagiste qui ait jamais vécu.*'

70 Renoir's woodland scenes (for example, cat. 41) continue to have an overall format similar to the over-arching forest interiors favoured by Rousseau and Diaz.

71 Gimpel 1963, p. 13: '*On l'appelle un poète. Quelle erreur! Ce fut un naturaliste. Je l'ai étudié sans pouvoir jamais parvenir à son art.*'

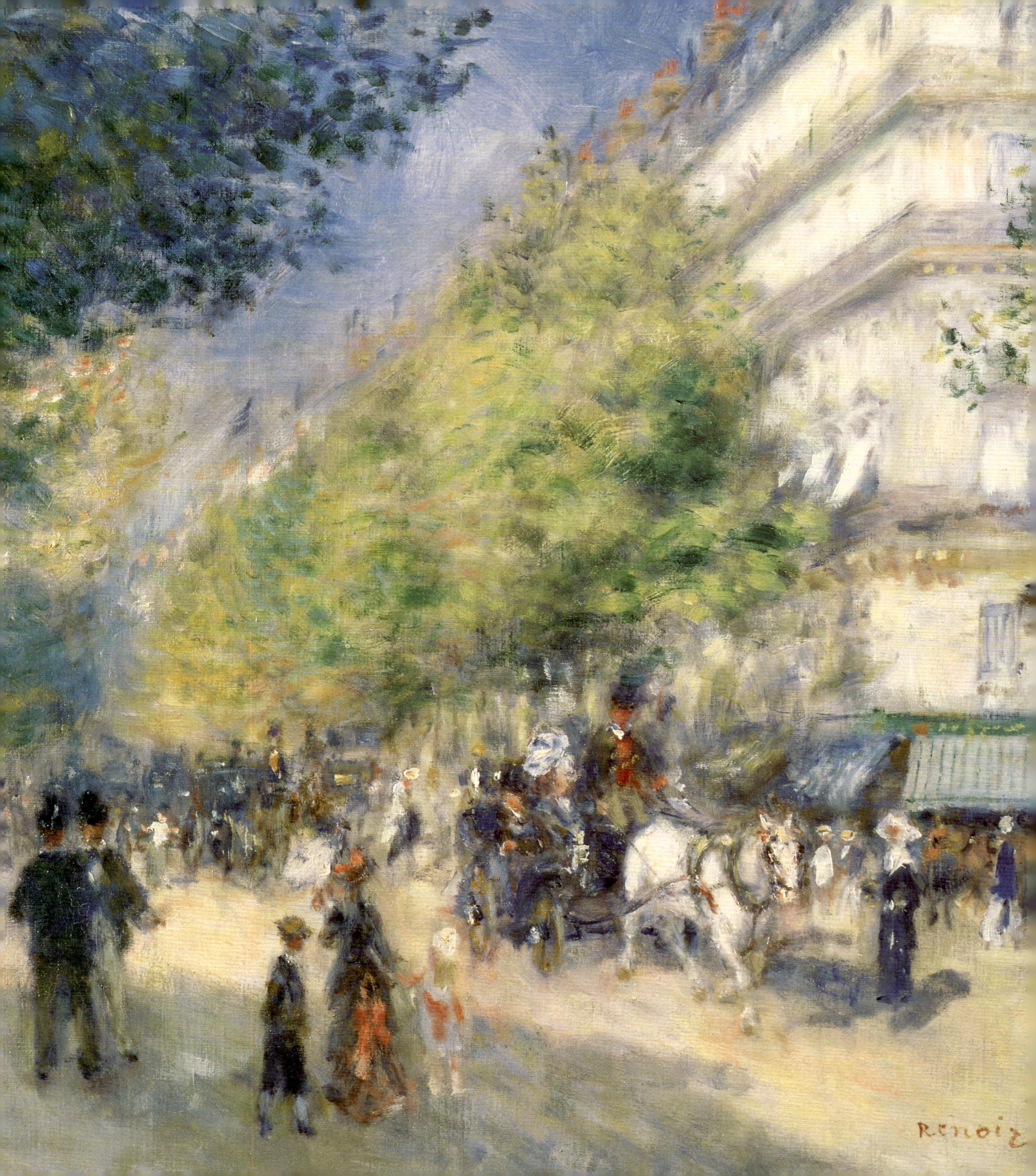
Renoir

RENOIR IN THE CITY

CHRISTOPHER RIOPELLE

Late in life Renoir recalled the pleasure he had taken in the Paris of his youth. 'In the streets of Paris I felt at home,' he declared.[1] He had not been born there but in the provincial manufacturing city of Limoges, in 1841, moving to the capital with his family at the age of four. From childhood, however, Renoir considered himself to be a Parisian, his character formed by the life of the vibrant, crowded city, his aesthetic principles shaped by what he saw there. He painted some ten views of the city during the 1860s and 1870s, not a large number but the subject was important enough to him that he returned to it every few years. The first painting he ever sold to the dealer Durand-Ruel, in 1870, was a Paris cityscape. During these same years, cityscape painting was taken up by his closest artist colleagues and allies as well, including Edouard Manet and Claude Monet; beginning in the 1860s, the young Impressionists can be seen to have launched a revival of a genre which had last flourished in France almost a century before. Renoir needed no further incentive to carry on painting his vivid and animated, depictions of bustling Paris streets, quais, bridges and squares, which capture the rushed but convivial charm of the place, its pulsing energy. In addition, a handful of paintings, while not depicting the city per se, but its parks and private gardens away from the noise of the street, suggest Renoir's fascination with a Paris in which, in pockets at least, nature lay close at hand, ready to be discovered amid the flow of urban life. Germane, too, are depictions (from 1881) of Algiers, Venice and Naples, the first foreign cities Renoir ever saw, each of them exotic, splendidly situated, and calling forth novel responses in the painter as his pictorial experiments grew bolder. Together, these works trace Renoir's emerging mastery of cityscape painting, and a deepening understanding of the dynamics of city life.

The revival of cityscape painting coincided with vast changes in Paris itself. From the mid-1850s the city had been undergoing the most radical and wide-spread transformation in its history. The Emperor, Napoléon III, and his Prefect of the Seine, Baron Georges Haussmann, were overseeing the reorganisation of what in many ways remained a medieval city of crooked streets and narrow lanes, turning it into a modern metropolis criss-crossed

FIG. 15 Detail of cat. 30.

by a series of grand boulevards lined with tall and uniform buildings faced in stone. Here and there, imposing new monuments such as the Académie de Musique, or Opéra, and the new Louvre punctuated the skyline and dramatically terminated carefully engineered urban vistas. By 1870, when Napoléon III fell from power, one fifth of the streets in central Paris were new; the number of trees had doubled; the sewage and street-lighting systems were immeasurably improved; the modern metropolis of boulevards, stone façades, imposing vistas, parks and public monuments that we see today was largely in place.[2]

Even as he painted beguiling images of a vibrant Paris, including depictions of several of these new streets and squares and buildings, Renoir was beginning to formulate a critique of what has come to be called 'Haussmannisation'. Specifically, he came to identify shortcomings in the architecture, ornament and craftsmanship of the modern city Haussmann was creating. Renoir would commit his ideas to paper in the later 1870s, and recent research by Robert L. Herbert has shown how complex, consistent and morally charged his thinking was about these issues.[3] They were topics of vital concern to him, not least because he himself had served an apprenticeship in the late 1850s as a craft worker, a fact of which he was always proud. It had given him a grounding in the French decorative tradition on which he would draw throughout his career. This tradition, he came to fear, was now fading away under the onslaught of mechanisation, and modern Paris was the prime example of the decline.

Cityscape painting can conjure up remarkably specific associations in viewers' minds. As one writer has phrased it, cityscapes become 'the geographical correlatives to . . . memories'.[4] It is a reason why, for example, so many wealthy British visitors of the eighteenth century

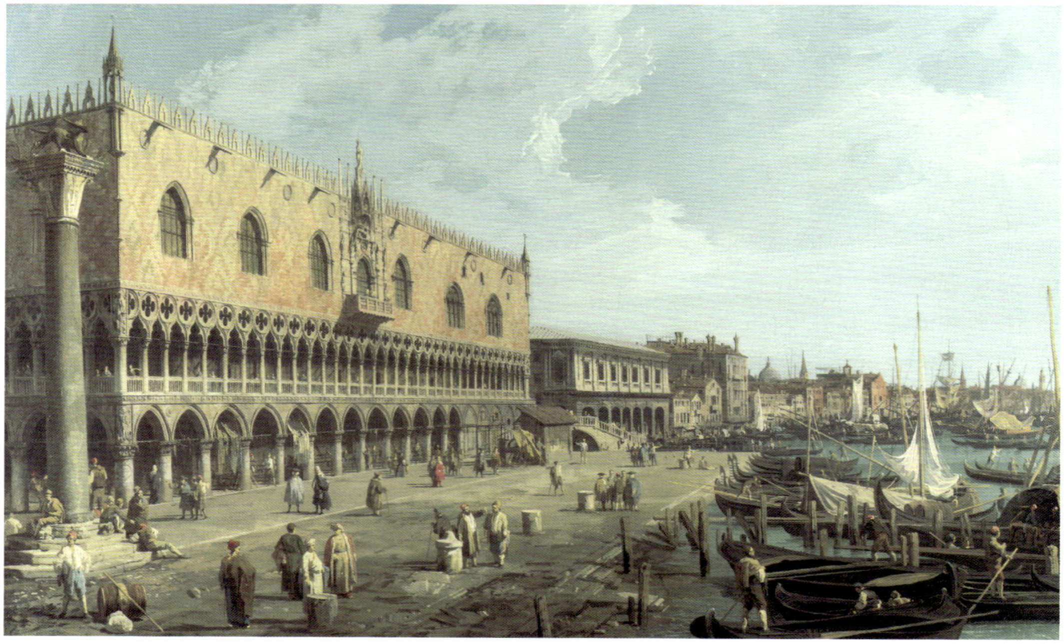

FIG. 16 Canaletto (1697–1769), *Venice: The Doge's Palace,* 1730s. Oil on canvas, 61.3 × 99.8 cm; 24⅛ × 39⅓ in. The National Gallery, London (NG 940).

returned from Venice with *vedute* by Canaletto (fig. 16); such urban scenes often represented the sites of the significant moral, emotional or aesthetic growth for which the Grand Tour had been undertaken. We can assume that the Paris scenes Renoir chose to depict called up such associations for him as well. In what relation, then, do Renoir's cityscape paintings stand to his thinking about modern Paris? Do the images themselves hold clues to Renoir's aesthetic and moral attitude to the city he called home, and to the changes taking place there?

Growing up in Paris

Among the Impressionists, Renoir's youthful experience of Paris was unique in that, unlike his contemporaries, he was brought up in a poor family in the densely populated heart of the city. His father was a tailor, his mother a seamstress, and when the family first arrived in 1845 they found housing in a working-class district known as the quartier du Louvre, a teeming warren of streets situated between the Palais Royal and the Louvre and Tuileries palaces in the 1st arrondissement. Specifically, their first home was near the Temple de l'Oratoire, adjacent to the north façade and Cour Carrée of the old Louvre. The long northern wing of the new Louvre, the so-called *aile Richelieu*, did not yet exist; it would begin to rise, cutting through the jumble of streets, only in the mid-1850s. Rather, the humble dwellings of workers lay cheek-by-jowl with the grand royal residences at the physical and symbolic centre of Paris – indeed of France, as it was from a point nearby that all distances in the realm were measured. Moreover, the neighbourhood had not always been a working-class enclave; many of the houses had been built centuries earlier for officials of the royal court and high-ranking soldiers and retained, here and there, dusty vestiges of former grandeur. Little had changed from a century and more earlier, when the richly detailed Turgot map of Paris had been drawn up in 1720–30s (fig. 17). As it suggests, the boy Renoir would have wandered among what remained of medieval and Renaissance Paris, through narrow streets and sometimes fetid lanes where Gothic turrets tilted precariously overhead and sewage flowed in open gutters. Behind many portals, however, lay tumbledown, sweet-smelling gardens, and every now and then, as Renoir remembered, he might catch a glimpse of a member of the royal family silhouetted in a nearby palace window.[5] Whether this latter recollection, almost cinematic in its emphasis on the moving eye, is strictly accurate or a happy embellishment by the artist's *cinéaste* son, Jean, who wrote it down, is perhaps less important than what is surely true, that Renoir in his later years insistently idealised pre-Haussmann Paris.

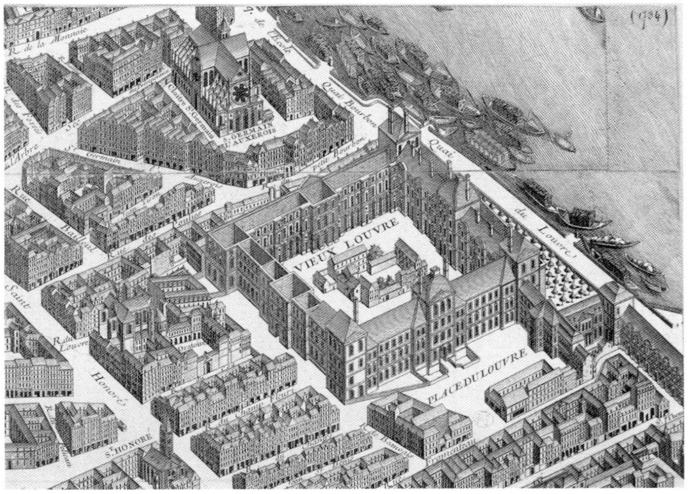

FIG. 17 Antoine Coquart and Claude Lucas, after Louis Bretez, detail of *Perspectival Map of the City of Paris* (*Le Plan Turgot*), etching and engraving, 1736–9. Musée Carnavalet, Histoire de Paris.

With the ascent to power of the Prince-Président, later Emperor Napoléon III, at the coup d'état of 1851, the quartier du Louvre's days were numbered. Soon after, he and Haussmann would begin their massive campaign of urban modernisation, expansion and rationalisation. Almost immediately after the coup, even before he appointed Haussmann to oversee the rebuilding programme, the Prince-Président intimated the breadth of his ambitions for his capital by reviving plans to restructure the area immediately adjacent to the Louvre in a radical manner – the first Napoleon had originally proposed the scheme – by cutting the rue de Rivoli and building the new north wing of the palace along it. There were inevitably delays but by 1855 the ancient neighbourhood in which Renoir had lived for some ten years no longer existed. Edouard Baldus photographed the massive undertaking that same year, showing the rubble that remained after the houses closest to the Tuileries Palace had been razed (fig. 18). They would be replaced by a vast ceremonial square framed by the two imperial palaces.

As swathes of the city disappeared, thousands of poor and working-class Parisians who formerly had inhabited the centre were displaced to the periphery of Paris (where, by and large, they remain today). Renoir's family was luckier than most. Perhaps because they were among the first to experience dislocation as the rebuilding project got underway, the Renoirs were able to find new lodgings that allowed them to stay in the centre. By 1855 the family had removed to 23 rue d'Argenteuil, also in the 1st arrondissement and directly north of the *aile Richelieu*, now under construction. Until as late as 1865, Renoir would periodically list this as his home address. The old street ran in a north-westerly direction more or less parallel to one of the most imposing new streets that Haussmann was beginning to cut through the fabric of the city, the broad Avenue de l'Opéra. The new avenue would culminate

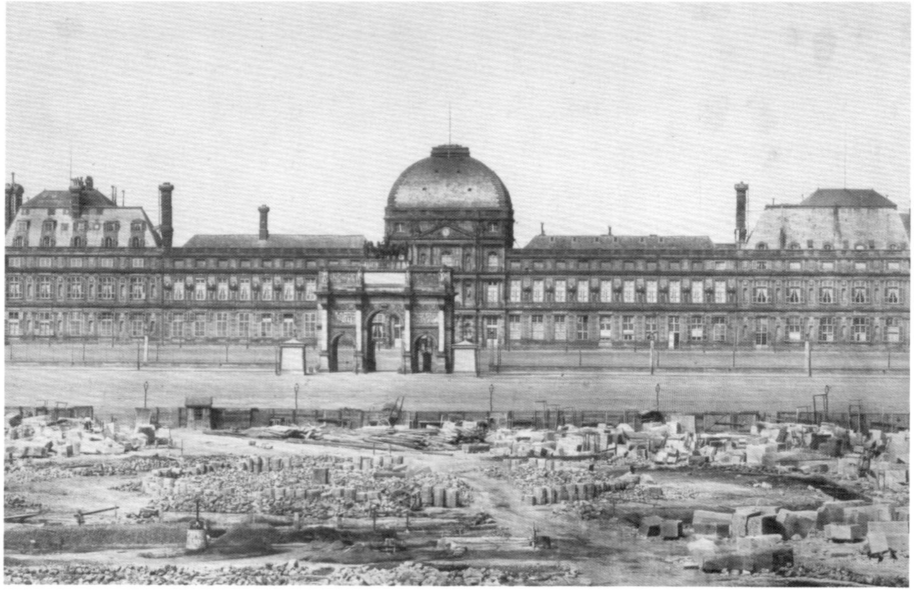

FIG. 18 Edouard Baldus (1813–1889), *Tuileries Palace, Paris*, 1855. Salted paper print from glass(?). Private collection, courtesy Galérie Michèle Chomette, Paris.

in one of the largest building projects and most imposing monuments of the modern city, the Opéra, or opera house, designed by the architect Charles Garnier in an ostentatious neo-Baroque style which, some 20 years in construction, finally would open in 1875. Thus Renoir, having known old Paris intimately as a child, had as a young man a front-row seat from which to witness, and assess, the most radical and ambitious aspects of its transformation.

Developing Ideas on Architecture

Renoir's opinion of 'Haussmannisation' evolved over the years. As a boy of 14 in 1855 he probably would have been far more thrilled by the wonders on view at Paris's first Universal Exhibition, held that year, than troubled by any sense of dislocation involved in moving house. The bustle of construction all around would have added to a general sense of change and expanding horizons, the promise of which might have intrigued the clever, inquisitive youth. Years later, however, Renoir had come to recall the quartier du Louvre with nostalgia, for two reasons. Old Paris, he opined, might have been decrepit but it was quaint and charming and brimming with life. What replaced it was cold and sterile and, especially along the spider-web of vast new boulevards, dominated by repetitious and characterless architecture.[6] Perhaps as important, the dislocations of 'Haussmannisation' represented a rupture of the traditional French social order. The easy intermingling of the social classes that had characterized life in the quartier du Louvre, especially the spontaneous relationship of trust and sympathy that, as Renoir remembered it, existed between the poor and their royal and aristocratic neighbours, was sacrificed to make way for a more bourgeois and banal state of affairs, and Paris was the worse for it. Writing about strolling in the streets of nineteenth-century Paris, Rebecca Solnit has argued: 'The real complaint against Haussmann seems to be . . . that in tearing down so much of the old city, he obliterated the delicate interlace of mind and architecture, the mental map walkers carried with them.'[7] Even in old age, Renoir could hark back to that mental map of Paris etched in his mind in his early years as he explored the streets of the quartier du Louvre.

To this it can be added that as a young artist in the later 1860s Renoir and his painter friends, including Monet and Frédéric Bazille, had begun to adopt a stance of opposition to the artistic policies of the government of Napoléon III.[8] The government showed little support for their work, they realised they had little chance of official purchases or commissions – quite the contrary – and they needed to explore ways to fend for themselves artistically and financially. The year 1867 saw a second Universal Exhibition in Paris, a symbolic coming-out party for Haussmann's new city. Renoir and his friends looked admiringly on the initiatives of older colleagues, Gustave Courbet and Edouard Manet, well-known for their disdain for the government, which was returned, who were holding intentionally provocative private exhibitions of their works in pavilions near the grounds of the Universal Exhibition. Such alternative exhibitions, which would grow in strategic importance over the following decades as a means of career advancement outside the spheres of official patronage, signalled the growing distance between the new directions in art these artists represented and establishment taste. Rejected from the official Salon as well, Renoir and his colleagues, under the enthusiastic encouragement of Bazille, were themselves planning their first independent group exhibition that year; lack of funds impeded them – they would not show together until 1874 – but the circumstances of the moment strengthened a sense of alienation from officialdom and official taste among them all.

It might well have been at this time, too, that Renoir began to develop his aesthetic doubts about modern Paris. These he first articulated in public in 1877 with two brief essays in successive issues of the journal *L'Impressionniste*. The first of the 1877 essays, couched in the form of a letter to a 'dear friend', begins, 'You have asked me to note down the conversations we have so often had on architecture . . .'[9] – a turn of phrase that suggests his concerns were by that time of long standing. In these essays Renoir compared the sorry state of contemporary Parisian architecture and the insipid decoration of its newest buildings with the glorious craftwork traditions, especially of the Middle Ages and Renaissance, which they had replaced. 'There is no modern building that can stand comparison with Notre-Dame, the Hôtel de Cluny, or the old Louvre,' he declared.[10] Garnier's Opéra came in for particular criticism, as did the ornamentation of the new Louvre, dismissed as 'heavy, banal, and made by workers chosen at random, whereas that of the old building is light and made by artists'.[11] Renoir expressed antipathy for the most prominent and ambitious monuments of the new city, favouring instead older forms of architecture and ornamentation, and artistic craftwork over modern machine-made building practices. He particularly objected to the sham historicism in which so much contemporary architecture was steeped, comparing such ostentatious works with the comparatively simple iron market sheds of Les Halles, 'the only buildings with a really original character and a look appropriate to their purpose'.[12] Renoir largely restricted his criticisms to the way the buildings looked and the way they were made, remaining silent on the obvious improvements to sanitation and circulation that Haussmann had also brought to Paris; it was what the eye could see as it scanned the city that most troubled him. He also proposed a novel solution. Until a new and better generation of architects should come to the fore, he suggested, 'it is painters who should be put in charge of constructing public buildings. I am persuaded that they will provide an originality, even a unity that one can only expect of the person who is at the same time both the brains and the arms'.[13]

Here the artist ascribes a high duty to the modern painter, to accept responsibility for shaping important aspects of the modern city. The painter is himself a craftsman forging unique objects with colour and canvas, and these are imbued with a personal sensibility. It is this uniqueness, and combination of intelligence and manual dexterity, that the medieval or Renaissance craftsman once brought to his labours, and which the painter can restore to the task of building the city. Thus he would supersede the bureaucrats, the drearily historicist architects such as Garnier, the machine workers 'chosen at random' who saw to such matters today. Robert Herbert has traced the roots of Renoir's thought to the works of John Ruskin with their celebration of craft traditions and commitment to workers' spiritual ownership of their labours. Renoir would continue to develop and refine this line of thought, and his appreciation of the hand-made, the natural, and what he came to call the 'irregular', over many decades, culminating in his preface to a 1910 edition of Cennino Cennini's medieval treatise on the arts.[14] Indeed, late in life he returned to the theme once more, in order to insist on the human dimension that must be evident in architecture and decoration. 'What was vital was to be able to recognise in the stone, wood or fabric the human being who had conceived and executed the work,' he told his son.[15] Renoir knew perfectly well that painters were not about to be put in charge. As he painted his views of Paris, however, he would have brought to the task a developing, lively sense of the way in which the artist's personal touch, the series of subtle aesthetic decisions he made, the skilled craftsmanship he brought to bear, could animate a scene and imbue it with character. Among many other things, the thought may have dawned on him that his canvases could function as a corrective, a subtle, utopian statement of what, at its best, the city ought to be like.

The Paris Cityscape Tradition

A long tradition, dating from the sixteenth century, of painting and print-making takes the French capital as its subject.[16] Parisians themselves, then as now, were fascinated by the city they inhabited and enjoyed seeing it depicted in art. Traditionally, the focus of the Paris cityscape was the river Seine which traverses the capital, the bridges that span it and the monuments such as Notre-Dame de Paris and the Palais du Louvre to be seen along its banks. Jacques Callot's etching of *The Pont Neuf and the Tour de Nesle* of 1630 (fig. 19) is not unrepresentative of the type. Hubert Robert in the eighteenth century had been the

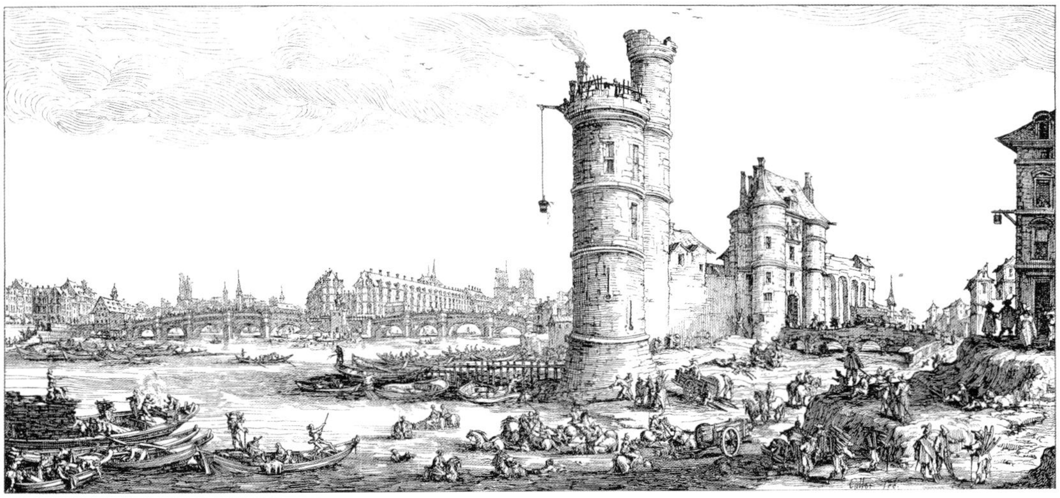

FIG. 19 Jacques Callot (1592–1635), *The Pont Neuf and the Tour de Nesle*, 1630. Etching. Private collection.

most accomplished exponent of Paris cityscape painting, while Joseph Vernet's monumental series of views of the ports of France, commissioned by the state in the 1750s, briefly raised the status of the genre as a whole. The practice had fallen somewhat into abeyance in the early nineteenth century, however, few Neo-Classical or Romantic masters taking up the theme, but by the mid-century the first intimations of a revival were seen. The etchings of Paris that Charles Meryon executed in the 1850s, again focusing on the Seine and the bridges that cross it, were much admired by fellow artists for their technical virtuosity and the sinister mood they imparted (fig. 20). By the 1860s, painters such as Stanislas Lepine and Johann-Barthold Jongkind were finding approval for their more conventional Paris cityscapes, not least at the Salon. The latter's *The Seine and Notre-Dame de Paris* of 1864 (fig. 21) adopts a traditional formula for depicting the sights, with the Seine, busy with boat traffic, serving as the city's principal thoroughfare, the cathedral a picturesque adornment to the skyline.

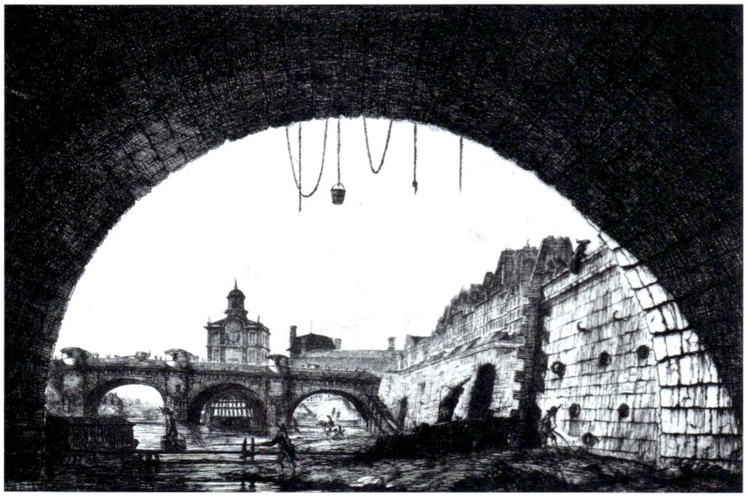

FIG. 20 Charles Meryon (1821–1868), *The Pont Neuf and the Samaritaine*, 1855. Etching. Bibliothèque Nationale de France, Paris (RES EF-397 BTE5).

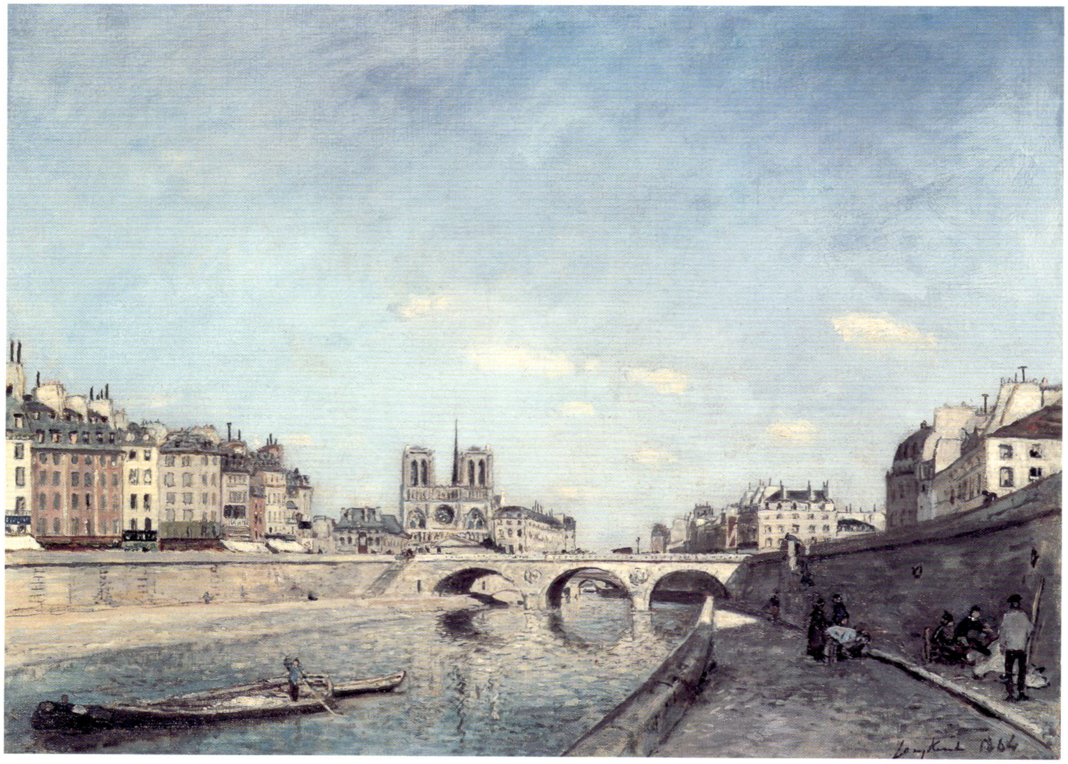

FIG. 21 Johann-Barthold Jongkind (1819–1891), *The Seine and Notre-Dame de Paris*, 1864. Oil on canvas, 42 × 56.5 cm; 16½ × 22¼ in. Musée d'Orsay, Paris (RF 1972-20).

The impetus for the first wave of Paris cityscape painting by the Impressionists seems to have been the Universal Exhibition of 1867 itself. The city was *en fête*, animated by countless foreign and provincial visitors there to admire the fruits of progress. It was under worldwide scrutiny as the model of urban modernisation and rationalisation. Parisians were only just beginning to acquaint themselves with their new surroundings, to inhabit the city again in a familiar way. For artists like Renoir and his Impressionist colleagues, committed to the depiction of modern life, Paris itself was suddenly a compellingly contemporary subject for investigation. It practically invited them to dare to break with convention and find novel ways to depict the new city rising around them. Three of them, Renoir, Monet and Manet, seem to have determined to paint cityscapes almost simultaneously that year. (A fourth artist, the German Adolph Menzel, visiting that summer, returned to the genre – he had first painted views of Berlin in the late 1840s – painting two Paris scenes, which inaugurated the ambitious series of crowded, anecdote-laden city views that punctuate his late career.)[17]

Manet turned to the subject of the Universal Exhibition itself in his first cityscape, painting a panoramic view of the fair grounds and the Parisian skyline beyond from the heights of Chaillot (fig. 22). The scene is populated by Parisian and foreign 'types', suggesting the cosmopolitan air of Paris at this particular moment. Such works confirm the topicality of the Parisian cityscape, that it could address contemporary events with the immediacy of a newspaper report. Indeed, the photographer Nadar's balloon floats in the sky at upper right, a motif Manet might have borrowed from a Meryon print.[18] Manet was always a leader to his younger colleagues but in this instance he does not seem to have been the first among them to turn to cityscape, his view of the Universal Exhibition probably having been painted by late June of 1867.[19]

While the chronology is complicated, the first artist to take up the challenge was probably

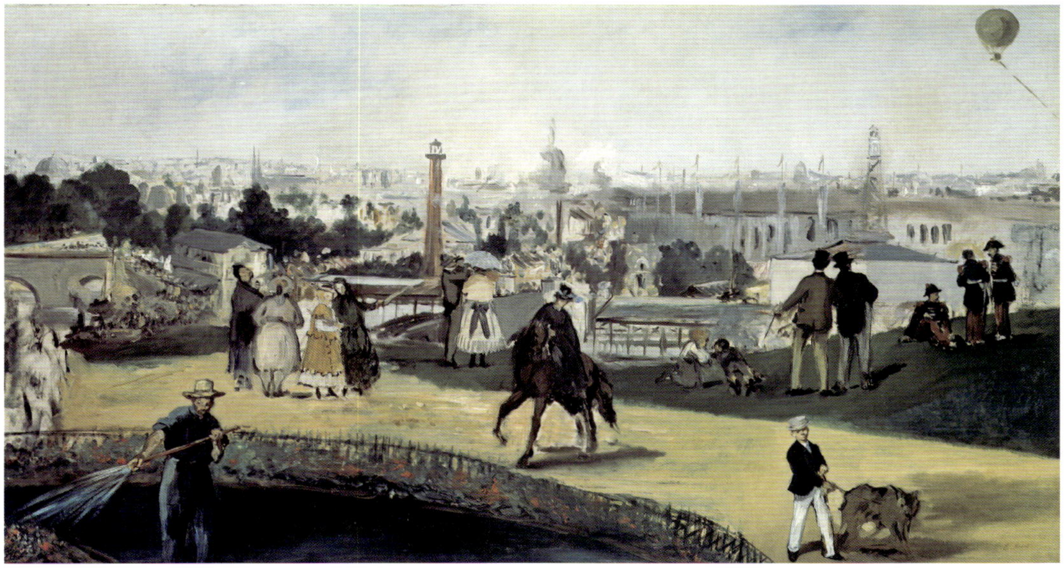

FIG. 22 Edouard Manet (1830–1883), *View of Paris at the Time of the Universal Exhibition of 1867*, 1867. 108 × 196.5 cm; 42½ × 77⅜ in. Oil on canvas, National Museum, Oslo (NG.M. 01293).

Monet, with Renoir soon following. On 27 April, Monet requested official permission to paint Paris views from an elevated vantage point on the east façade of the Louvre. On 20 May he reported in a letter to his friend Bazille that he and Renoir were 'still at work' on cityscape paintings.[20] Monet painted three Paris views that spring, including *The Garden of the Princess* (fig. 23), a vertically disposed composition – rare for a cityscape – in which the viewer looks down to the lawn in front of the Louvre and then up, across a busy street and the river partially hidden by trees, to the Left Bank dominated at the top of the canvas by the familiar dome of the Panthéon. It is like a cross-section of the sedimentary layers of Parisian society – church, state, commerce, leisure.

Monet also painted *St-Germain l'Auxerrois* (fig. 24) showing the Gothic church – traditionally the parish church of the kings of France – which stood directly opposite the east façade of the Louvre. With their brilliant colours and bold brushwork, these canvases announce the important role that cityscape painting would play in Monet's art for the next decade, as they also announce the artist's predilection for views from high above looking down into the streets of the city. And yet Monet's choice of motif in his depiction of the Gothic church is curious. The picture is cut off crisply at the left edge of the building. As he stood high on the east façade of the Louvre, however, this is not all that Monet would have seen. The church no longer stood alone. A neo-Gothic belfry had recently been constructed to the designs of Ignace Hittorff to its right, and the Mairie of the 1st arrondissement, designed by Théodore Ballu in a neo-Renaissance style, to the right of the belfry (fig. 25). The church was now part of a balanced, symmetrically disposed three-part architectural composition facing a recently cleared place, an element in the regularisation of the area around the Louvre that Napoléon III had initiated some 15 years earlier. As Herbert has noted,[21] Monet simply ignored the new architectural elements imposed on the site by the Emperor, ignored the pastiche modern architecture of the type that Renoir would come to criticise so severely, in favour of the vestige of old Parisian architecture that remained. This is a first indication that some kind of commentary about 'Haussmannisation' is somehow implicit in these paintings.

In the spring of 1867 Renoir was living in the absent Bazille's apartment in the rue Visconti near the Ecole de Beaux-Arts, where Monet was a frequent visitor. Almost certainly they would have compared notes on the new subject-matter they were both exploring, for Renoir seems to have undertaken two cityscapes at this time, *The*

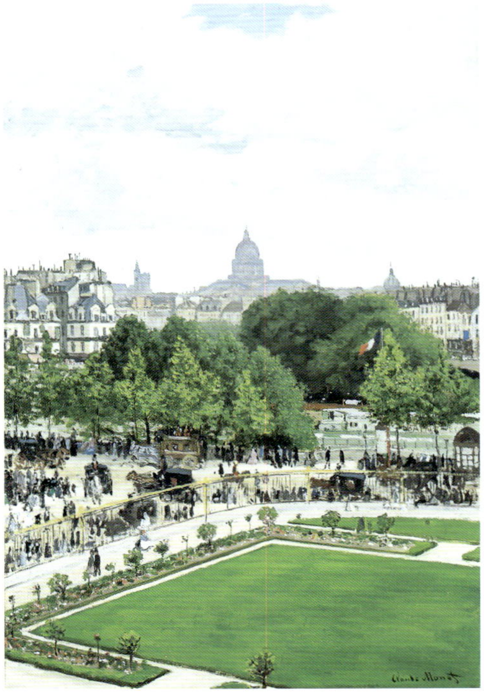

FIG. 23 Claude-Oscar Monet (1840–1926), *The Garden of the Princess*, 1867. Oil on canvas, 91.8 × 61.9 cm; 36¼ × 24⅖ in. Oberlin College, Ohio. R.T. Miller, Jr. Fund 1948 (1948.296).

FIG. 24 Claude-Oscar Monet, *St-Germain l'Auxerrois*, 1867. Oil on canvas, 79 × 98 cm; 31⅛ × 35⅜ in. Nationalgalerie, Staatliche Museen, Berlin (NG 998).

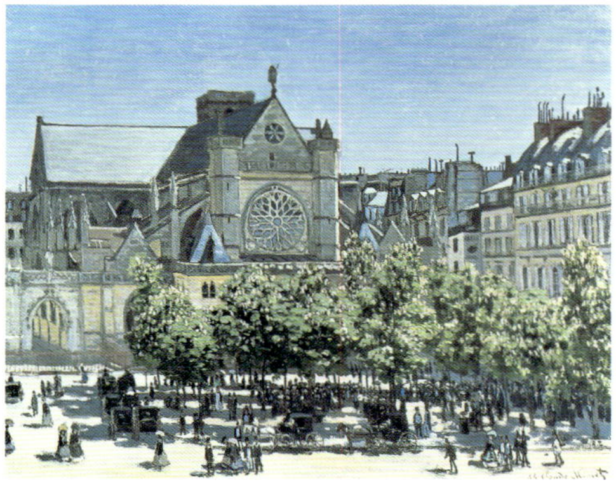

Champs-Elysées during the Fair of 1867 (fig. 26) and *Le Pont des Arts* (fig. 27). As Manet's painting would be, they are both highly topical in alluding to the Universal Exhibition. In the former painting, Renoir adopted the point of view Monet also was exploring. He placed himself high up above the street in a building near the Place de la Concorde in order to look down into the eastern, park-like precinct of the Champs-Elysées. Elegant revellers stroll and picnic among freshly planted, carefully maintained flowerbeds. At the right is the Café des Ambassadeurs, at the left, just glimpsed through the treetops, the Palais de l'Industrie built for the earlier exhibition of 1855 and called into service again now. Renoir's more conventional panoramic composition does not approach the audacity of the collision of broad urban vista and specific, identifiable figural motifs in Manet's painting of the Exhibition. With its brilliant colour, however, delight in the play of sunlight, and deft painterly characterisation of Parisian crowds, it expresses pleasure in the panoply of contemporary Paris. It is a Watteau-like *fête galante* transported to a park in the heart of the city from which the noise and cares of city life have been banished.

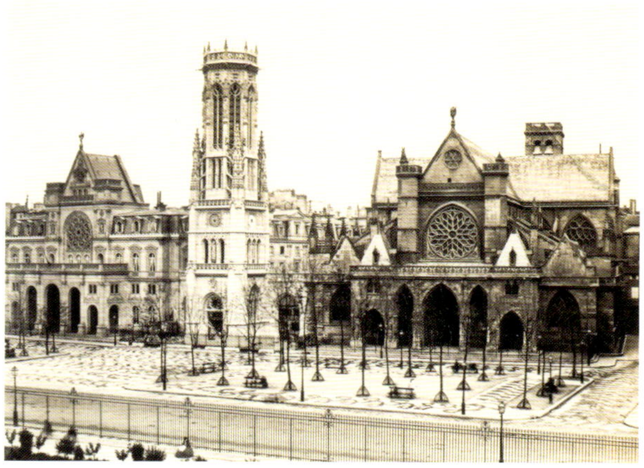

FIG. 25 Edouard Baldus (1813–1889), *Church of St-Germain l'Auxerrois*, 1861 or later. Albumen silver print from glass negative. Canadian Centre for Architecture, Montreal (PH1977-0058).

Renoir adopted a similar approach the following year when he depicted *Skaters in the Bois de Boulogne* (cat. 4). We are on the western edge of the city in one of the most successful schemes associated with 'Haussmannisation', a great public park brought up to date beautifully in recent years. A crowd has gathered in the wintry landscape to skate and chat. Deft licks of the artist's brush capture the animation of the scene, intensified in that the figures are seen against the blinding white of the snow. Nature has been allowed to play its vital role

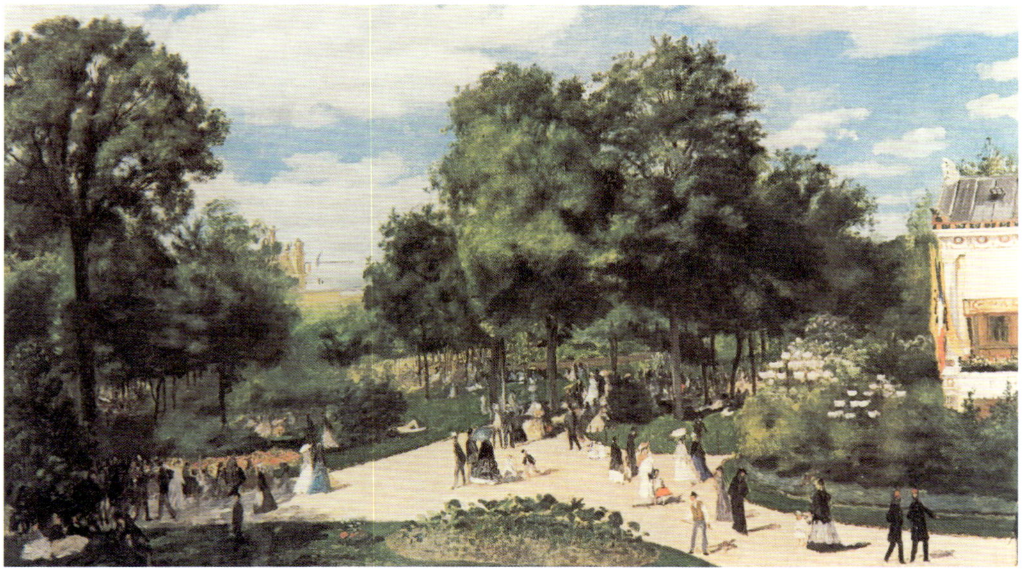

FIG. 26 *The Champs-Elysées during the Fair of 1867*, 1867. Oil on canvas, 66 × 81 cm; 25 × 31 7/8 in. Private collection.

in tempering the harsh edges of city life. A few years later, in the mid-1870s, Renoir was again drawn to the edge of the city when he rented a studio, and then a second one, in the rue Cortot on the Butte Montmartre to the north of central Paris. The area was still only partially urbanised and the artist installed himself in an old folie which gave on to an overgrown garden. The garden became a favourite subject for paintings in these years (cat. 39). Within walking distance of his home in the rue St-Georges, Renoir depicted a world of effulgent, sun-dappled beauty where flowers of varied and exotic hue grew in abundance and without restraint, and where neighbours passed the time in amiable chat. That such an ostentatious display of nature's almost untamed profusion should flourish within hailing distance of central Paris, that such islands of privacy and peace were still to be found in the metropolis, was, for Renoir, a beguiling feature of city life.

A good deal more of the city can be seen in *Le Pont des Arts* (fig. 27). Indeed, it seems at first glimpse to hark back to the tradition of Paris cityscape in which the Seine as the city's principal artery plays a dominant role. Down by the riverside along the quai Malaquais on the left bank, crowds disembark from a *bateau-omnibus*, part of a boat service that had been introduced recently to carry visitors to the Exhibition up and down the river. This was stop no. 8 on the boat route, giving passengers access to the treasures of the Louvre directly opposite on the right bank. The artist has situated himself in the shade of a bridge – we know where Renoir stands because we see the shadows of pedestrians passing overhead; a recent writer has characterised this as the 'embodiedness' in the picture of both the artist and the viewer [22] – and looks up from the *quai* to the ribbed dome of the Institut de France, formerly the Collège Mazarin, the seventeenth-century masterpiece of the architect Louis Le Vau that today houses the Académie de France. One third of the way up the picture the

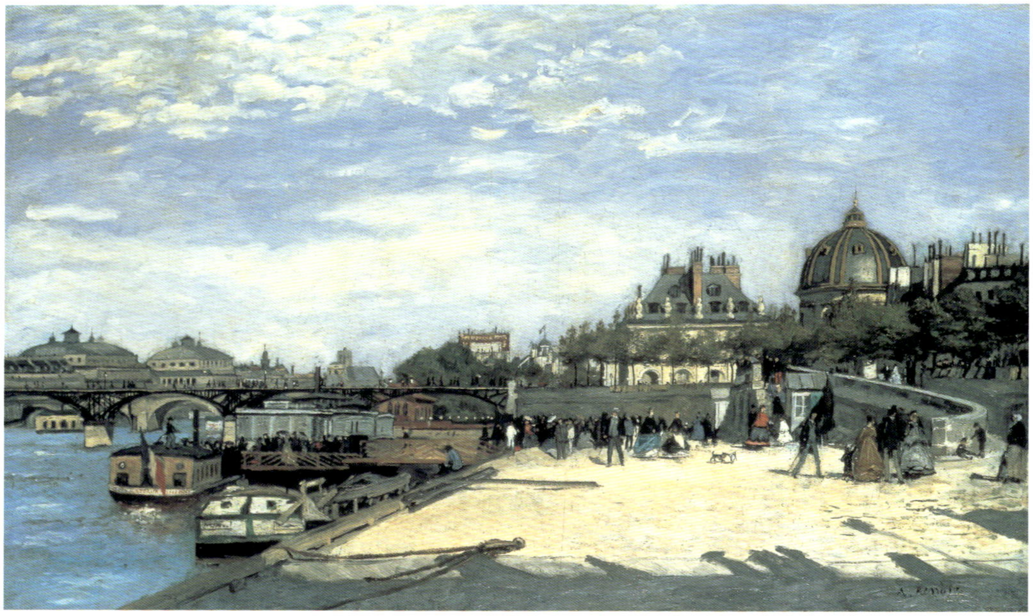

FIG. 27 *Le Pont des Arts*, 1867. Oil on canvas, 62 × 103 cm; 24½ × 40½ in. Norton Simon Museum, Pasadena (F.1968.13.P).

horizontal line of the pedestrian Pont des Arts cuts across the canvas and there we see people making their way from the Institut to the Louvre. In the distance are the recently completed theatres at Châtelet. Jane Mayo Roos was the first to note that the painting is notable for what it excludes, for what the artist chooses not to show the viewer.[23] At the right of the canvas the Institut de France is one of those monuments of old Paris that Renoir so admired. Below, visitors cross the bridge in the direction of the Louvre but the Louvre itself is conspicuously absent from Renoir's pictorial field, crisply cut off at the left. The long line of the Grande Galerie running along the right bank of the Seine, which one might have expected to see, is not there. Roos ascribes the omission to Renoir's growing opposition to the artistic policies of the government of Napoléon III, opposition being signalled by his refusal to depict the seat of imperial power. The choice may be more specific than that. In fact the Grande Galerie, originally constructed in the sixteenth century to link the Louvre along the river with the 'suburban' Tuileries Palace further to the west, had been razed earlier in the 1860s and was in the process of reconstruction in a new, more ornately pompous style, part of the larger project of the new Louvre. (Baldus was there to photograph it in 1865; indeed, his photographic record of the construction of the new Louvre was one of the most important projects of his career; see fig. 28.) What Renoir is declining to depict here is the Louvre not only as a symbol of imperial power but also as a building project central to the Emperor's ambitions for a new Paris, designed in an historicising style of a kind Renoir detested. Thus Renoir was employing the same strategy as Monet did when he painted St-Germain l'Auxerrois omitting the adjacent new Mairie and belfry, simply declining to turn his artistic attention to the new architecture.

As Colin B. Bailey shows elsewhere in these pages, Renoir's response to 'Haussmannisation' was nuanced. He approved of, indeed celebrated anything that added to the animation of Paris, its sense of liveliness and humanity. The *bateau-omnibus*, the pedestrian bridge, the bustling *quais*, skating rinks in the Bois de Boulogne – these were worthy of the artist's attention. It did not matter if they were innovations by Haussmann or of ancient lineage, it was their role in humanising and ameliorating city life that made the difference. But architecture was Renoir's particular concern and the banal, machine-made and lifeless buildings now being imposed on the city were to be shunned. The same is true of what is perhaps Renoir's most beguiling image of Paris, *The Pont Neuf* of 1872 (cat. 12). This

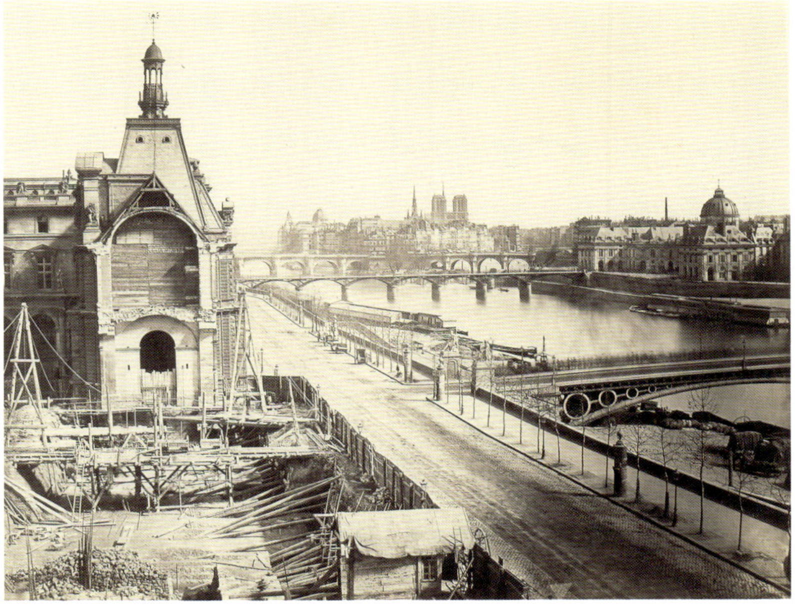

FIG. 28 Edouard Baldus (1813–1889), *Destruction of the Grande Galérie*, about 1865. Albumen silver print from glass negative. Musée d'Orsay, Paris (PHO 1988-11-8).

is a celebration of the return to civility and urbanity in Paris in the wake of the devastations of the Franco-Prussian War and the Commune that followed. On a brilliantly sunny day, crowds pour across the most ancient of Paris bridges from the right bank to the Ile St-Louis. The equestrian statue of Henri IV, a symbol of the continuity of French history, rises benignly in the middle distance. Of all the monumental buildings that Napoléon III erected in Paris, the one that Renoir detested the most, about which he wrote most scathingly as both mechanical and fussy and unbearably monotonous – 'by far too grotesque . . . deformed'[24] – was the Palais de Justice, the west façade of which had been designed by Joseph Louis Duc and constructed between 1857 and 1868. It stands directly behind the row of houses along the quai of the Ile St-Louis on the left side of the painting. Painting from a second-storey window, Renoir carefully situated himself in such a way that not a vestige of that enormous pile is to be seen across the river. In effect, he edited it out.

Herbert has shown that the upheavals of 'Haussmannisation' 'had their share in Renoir's . . . dislike of modern urban rationalism and the machine'.[25] In his second essay of 1877 Renoir criticised several recent Paris buildings by name: 'The Trinité, the Opéra, the Palais de Justice, the new Louvre, the Tribunal de Commerce, the Hôtel-Dieu are all Baroque, full of reminiscences of an art long since dead.'[26] Of these buildings, only one – this in itself may be significant – makes so much as an appearance in one of Renoir's cityscapes, and then glancingly. In 1875 he painted *Le Square de la Trinité* (cat. 29) showing on the far right side of the canvas a sliver of the façade of the first building Renoir lists, the church of La Trinité, designed by Théodore Ballu in a fussily French Renaissance-cum-Italianate style and built in 1867 in a fashionable area of the 9th arrondissement. So cursory is Renoir's depiction of the church, a few licks of paint, that it hardly catches our attention. Rather, interest focuses on the new square in front of the church where fountains gurgle and trees and flowers grow, and on the elegant strollers who traverse it. The square represents a pastel caesura in the sometimes harsh, new urban fabric of Paris; here, nature invades the city to soften façades and create a pastoral ambiance. Again, it is as if a *fête galante* by Watteau has been updated and brought to town.

The year 1875 saw Renoir's only campaign of cityscape painting, during the period covered by this exhibition, in which he directly depicted buildings erected in Paris under 'Haussmannisation'. In a second view of the *Place de la Trinité* (private collection, fig. 86) he turns his back on the church entirely, focusing on the convergence of streets on the square. The stone façades of the buildings surrounding it are almost entirely obscured by chestnut trees, however, and what we see of them seems to melt into limpid blue skies. Attention centres instead on the animation at street level, on a horse-drawn carriage and crowds of pedestrians making their bustling way. (Some 18 years later, probably in 1893, Renoir painted two more pictures of the square, in both of which the façade of La Trinité now figures prominently; by that time, perhaps, its novelty and the triteness of its architecture were less offensive to him. Or at least he was inured to them.)[27] Similarly, in the best known of Renoir's Paris views of that year, *Les Grands Boulevards* (cat. 30), he paints a generic view

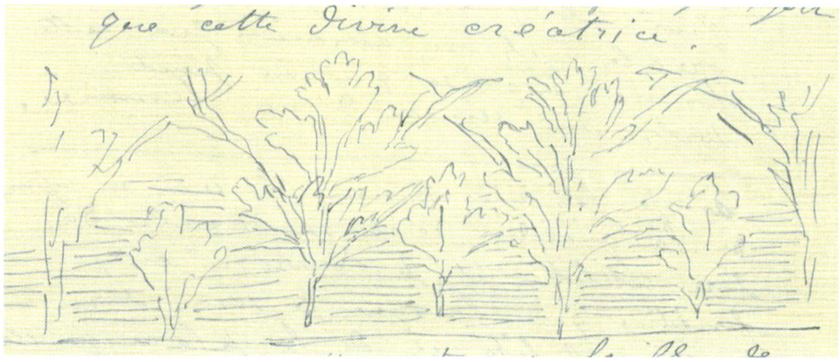

FIG. 29 Sketch of a frieze, about 1883, from the manuscript *Grammar*. Private collection (F 140–42).

– at least the specific avenue has not yet been convincingly identified – of one of the long arrow-straight boulevards that now traversed Paris. Renoir's pictorial strategies are the same. The role of the imposing stone buildings that line the boulevard is minimised. Only the canted corner of one such building can be seen to the right. Far more space is given over to the trees that line the boulevard, their leaves obscuring the buildings, and to the crowds who populate the scene, including a remarkably tall nun who glides through the traffic. Everything is bathed in sunlight. It dissolves the harsh angularity of the city in a beneficent glow.

Renoir addresses Haussmann's Paris, to be sure, but he seeks to minimise the role of the imposing new buildings and monuments. Rather, he focuses on those places where nature – trees, flowers, pedestrians wandering every which way – soften and obscure the outlines of the modern city so recently imposed on Paris. Indeed, Renoir specifically compared trees and buildings. 'It's God who made the first architecture,' he wrote. 'Look and see if everything is alike and monotonous. Do you see all the trees as being alike, do you see all the leaves of any one tree as having the same form?'[28] Renoir believed that artists should imitate divine creativity with its infinite variety, advising that they use the eye rather than the compass to guide them. In about 1883 he offered an example of how the process worked. Coming by chance upon various types of parsley in his kitchen, he spontaneously employed sprigs of the herb to create the prototype for a decorative frieze, pinning the splayed and overlapping fronds to a piece of cardboard. He sketched the results in the manuscript of his *Grammar*.[29] The frieze evokes classical decorative forms from antiquity but retains the irregularity of nature Renoir so valued (fig. 29). His sketch, however, also strikingly resembles the painting *Field of Banana Trees near Algiers* of 1881 (cat. 55), one of his most audacious formal inventions, where the entire foreground of the canvas is given over to a frieze of criss-crossing banana fronds and Algiers itself is seen through the interstices, glistening white across the bay. In Algiers he observed and recorded an exotic natural phenomenon; a few years later he perhaps unconsciously evoked it as he intuited the decorative possibilities latent in a few sprays of greenery and set about inventing an ornamental motif. That unpremeditated movement between nature and art, and the easy transformation of one into the other, lay at the heart of Renoir's aesthetic. The mechanical repetitions of the architecture along Haussmann's boulevards were inimical to it.

Renoir Abroad

The Algerian visit of 1881 was Renoir's first trip abroad and was soon followed by a visit to Italy as well. For the first time he was seeing cities different in kind from those with which he was familiar in France – Paris in particular, with its cool, grey light. At Algiers he saw a city in an intimate relationship to the brilliant blue sea, a blazing sun burning down and exotic plant life growing in profusion in close proximity. A timeless earthen architecture of domes and minarets and cool, dark interiors spread across the landscape in an almost haphazard manner. The ways of life and types of sociability he witnessed bore faint resemblance to the bourgeois conventions of Paris. Renoir responded in a series of complex paintings. His *Arab Festival* (cat. 54) evokes the chaos and splendour of the place. In *The Jardin d'Essai, Algiers* (cat. 56), in which the central *allée* lined by tall palms resembles nothing so much as a Gothic nave, he found a visual correlative anticipating his later conceit that trees are God's architecture. In fact, it seems to have rained heavily a good deal of the time he was there, hindering Renoir's ability to work.[30] Of this the artist gives no hint, but perhaps that is not surprising. He had come for the novelty, and there was nothing new to a Parisian in sheets of rain. Moreover, a disciple of Delacroix, he had been prepared for what he would see there in part by the master's own vivid Orientalist scenes (see fig. 105). For Renoir, too, North Africa was intrinsically a place of brilliant colour and sunlight and passion and it was on these he focused his dazzled attention.

In Italy as well, the artist responded powerfully to the distinctive natural settings of the cities he visited. In Naples the great sweep of the bay busy with sleek boats and dominated by Vesuvius beyond inspired the most panoramic of all Renoir's cityscape paintings (cat. 65). The wisp of smoke the volcano emits is a reminder that here city and nature do not simply co-exist; the former is uniquely at the mercy of the latter. In Venice, he painted sparkling images of famous landmarks such as the Doge's Palace and the Piazza of San Marco as seen from across the Bacino (cats. 62, 63, 64). Such pictures were conventional in conception and Renoir knew it, joking in a letter to a friend that the motif had never been done before, adding ruefully that 'we were at least six in a row'.[31] Such pictures, he also knew, might find ready buyers. He also painted far more experimental works, almost monochromatic images not unlike Whistler's paintings, in which the city is shrouded in fog, gondolas loom out of the mist and the domes of distant churches are mere blurs against the sky. Similarly, his *Piazza San Marco* (cat. 64) is audaciously abbreviated in execution, a brilliantly economical view in which no brushstroke is wasted; the Piazza is populated by a flock of pigeons, each one a single blue lick of paint. As he painted Venice, however, tellingly enough Renoir was thinking about Paris. Enumerating the monuments of the city, he added in an aside, 'I prefer St-Germain l'Auxerrois'.[32] Paris was the city that mattered to him most deeply and, confronted with new cities, new architecture, new conditions of light, his thoughts wandered back to it.

If Renoir always sought to soften the harsh new edges of Haussmann's Paris, Monet in contrast, in works such as *Boulevard des Capucines* of 1873 (Pushkin Museum, Moscow), analysed the rigid geometry, seemingly receding to infinity, of the modern boulevard. Gustave Caillebotte, too, was relentless during the 1870s in his pictorial dissection of the geometry of the Parisian street, often bleakly treeless. These artists would gradually retreat from the city, spending more and more time in suburban towns and the countryside. Monet, famously, would come to cultivate his garden at Giverny in Normandy, rarely venturing into town. But Renoir stayed on. In 1896 he was living on Montmartre in a tumble-down eighteenth-century estate, half countryside, half city. He painted the Sacré-Coeur under construction at the turn of the century. He maintained a Paris residence through the Great War, only at its conclusion as a very old man retreating to his house at Cagnes-sur-Mer in the South of France, where he died. For him, Paris remained alive, flawed to be sure but his ideal of city life nonetheless. It had been, from childhood, a realm of infinite possibility.

NOTES

1 Renoir 1962, p. 27.
2 On the rebuilding of Paris, D.P. Jordan, *Transformation of Paris: The Life and Labours of Baron Haussmann*, New York and London 1995.
3 Herbert 2000. See chapter one, 'Renoir's Writings, 1877–1884', pp. 1–24.
4 Solnit 2000, p. 205.
5 Renoir 1962, p. 20.
6 Herbert 2000, p. 3. Renoir described the new arrangements as 'cold and lined up like soldiers on parade'.
7 Solnit 2000, p. 205.
8 The fullest account is given by J. M. Roos, *Early Impressionism and the French State*, Cambridge and New York 1996.
9 Herbert 2000, p. 93.
10 *Ibidem*, p. 97.
11 *Ibidem*, p. 93.
12 *Ibidem*, p. 97.
13 *Ibidem*, p. 99.
14 For various states of this text, see *ibidem*, pp. 158–82.
15 Renoir 1962, p. 28.
16 A suggestion of the range of such depictions is provided in *Paris: Sous le ciel de la peinture*, Hôtel de Ville de Paris, Paris, 14 September – 17 December 2000.
17 *Afternoon in the Tuileries Gardens*, 1867 (National Gallery, London) and *Weekday in Paris*, 1869 (Kunstmuseum, Düsseldorf).
18 The fifth state of Meryon's etching *Le Pont-au-Change* of 1854 shows a balloon inscribed SPERANZA (Hope) at upper left. It should also be noted that issues of topicality and its relationship to easel painting were very much on Manet's mind at this moment. A few months earlier he had launched a stinging critique of Emperor Napoléon III's failed foreign policy when he began work on his *Execution of the Emperor Maximilian* paintings, themselves based on newspaper reports on the recent tragic events in Mexico. For an in-depth analysis of that work, see J. Wilson-Bareau, J. House and D. Johnson, *Manet: The Execution of Maximilian: Paintings, Politics and Censorship*, exh. cat., (National Gallery) London 1992.
19 M.B. Mena Marqués, *Manet en el Prado*, exh. cat. (Museo Nacional del Prado) Madrid 2003, cat. no. 74, p. 255.
20 Letter from Monet to Bazille, 20 May 1867, cited in White 1984, p. 26.
21 Herbert 2000, p. 15.
22 Forgione 2005, p. 666.
23 Berson 1996, p. 98.
24 Herbert 2000, p. 96.
25 *Ibidem*, see chapter two, 'Renoir, Ruskin, Morris and the Arts and Crafts in France', pp. 25–40.
26 *Ibidem*, p. 98.
27 *Church of the Holy Trinity in Paris*, 1892–3, oil on canvas, 65.3 × 54.2 cm, Hiroshima Museum of Art, Hiroshima. Fezzi no. 663, 1972, p. 119.
28 Herbert 2000, p. 139.
29 *Ibidem*, p. 149 and fig. 7.
30 Letter from Renoir to his wife, Aline, undated (about 1881–2), *Pierre-Auguste Renoir 1841–1919: Personal Artefacts and Archives Collection*, lot 59, Hantmans, Potomac, Maryland, 14 May 2005, p. 41.
31 White 1984, p. 112.
32 *Ibidem*.

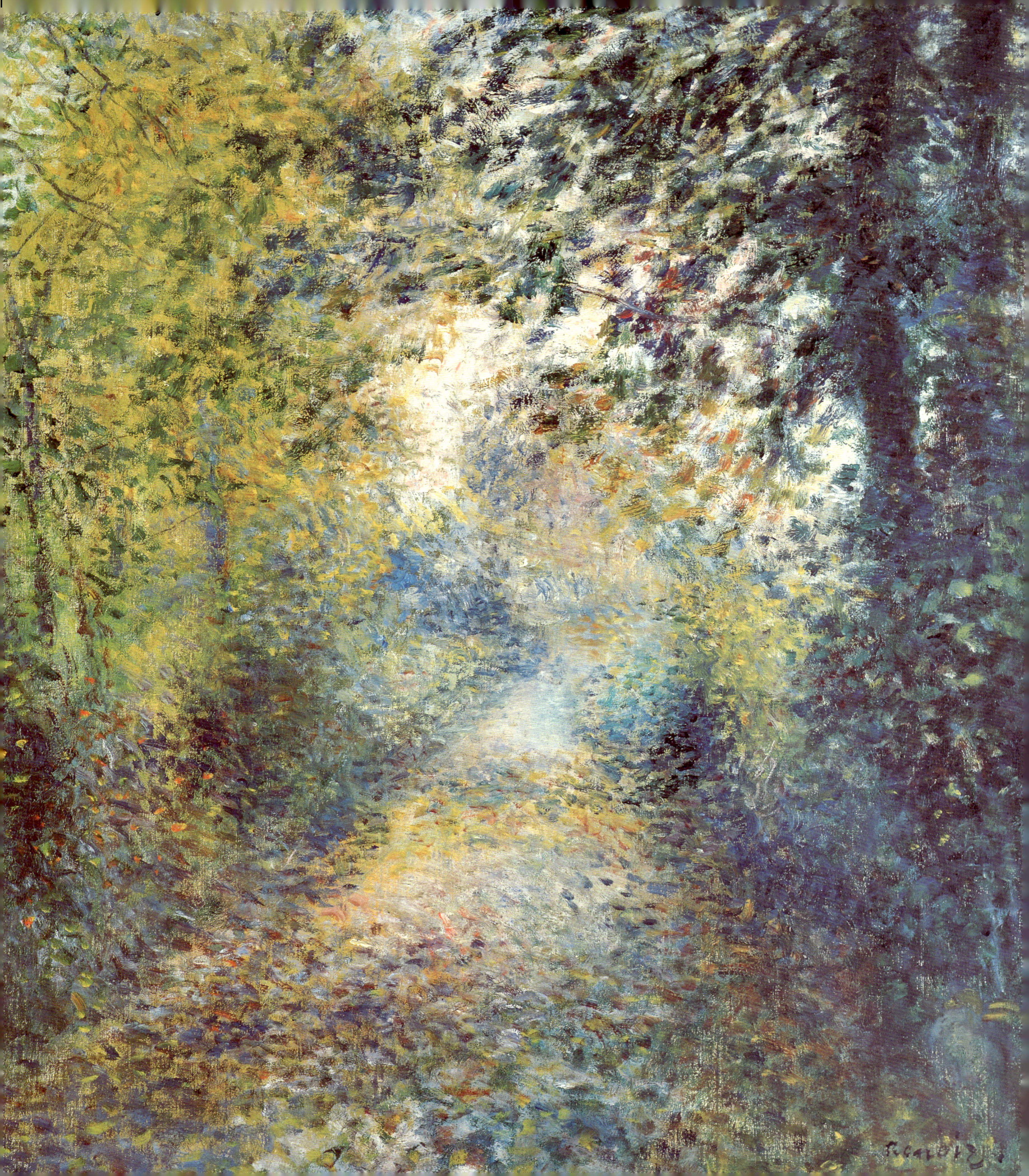

'THE GREATEST LUMINOSITY, COLOUR AND HARMONY': RENOIR'S LANDSCAPES, 1862–1883

COLIN B. BAILEY

> 'I'm taking advantage of a few days of fine weather to paint landscapes, as it will make a change from what I have been doing and will enable me to return to the figure with greater pleasure', Renoir to Théodore Duret, 15 October 1878
>
> 'But I am a figure painter!' Renoir to Monet, January 1884
>
> 'Clearly, it's the only way to learn one's craft a little, but to plonk myself down like a street entertainer, this is something I can no longer do', Renoir to Berthe Morisot, September 1892

As a very rough estimate, almost a quarter of the works Renoir produced in the two decades that saw the evolution of his Impressionist language were landscapes, or figures in the landscape.[1] A remarkable number of these are what Pissarro would have called '*paysages purs*' – works in which the human figure is entirely absent or plays an incidental role at most.[2] Like Monet, Renoir tackled every aspect of the Impressionist landscape – 'seascapes, snowscapes, cityscapes, paintings of flowering gardens, elegant leafy bosquets, and the great trees of the forest of Fontainebleau, reproduced in all the vivacity of their many-coloured effects'.[3] After his 'crisis' of 1883–5, landscape would remain a component of Renoir's production, but the landscapes of the last three decades of his career, with their roseate, liquid handling and calm generalisations, offer a corpus that is relatively unified, both stylistically and in subject-matter. In them details of site and setting were of less interest to Renoir than the creation of an Arcadian vision, timeless, natural and unchanging.

The present study of the development of Renoir's proto-Impressionist and Impressionist landscapes has, at its core, a series of works that are often extremely audacious in composition and handling. Their chronology is problematic; there is little agreement on exactly when or even where many of these works of the 1870s were painted. In certain cases, their

FIG. 30 Detail of cat. 41.

status – whether they were finished works made for exhibition and sale, or developed studies not intended for immediate consumption – remains to be established. Remarkably varied, spatially complex and surprisingly experimental in facture and colouration, Renoir's domestic landscapes of the late 1860s and 1870s invariably reject the picturesque or anecdotal.[4] Those painted in Normandy and abroad between 1881 and 1883, while often of conventional sites and views, are executed in such striking (and occasionally strident) tonalities that when first exhibited they alienated even the artist's most supportive critics.

From the mid-1860s on, Renoir's commitment to painting in and from nature was matched by his ambitions as a figure painter and his conventional attitude towards the 'lesser genres' – still life, genre and landscape. In the same way that flower painting allowed him to 'rest his brains', as he later explained to Georges Rivière, so landscape was 'also useful for the painter of figures. In the open air you are inspired to use colours that would have been unimaginable in the attenuated lighting of the studio'.[5] Ironically, by the 1860s landscape painting was generally considered to be the 'true strength of the French School', as well as 'the most important branch of contemporary art'.[6] Barbizon artists had established certain procedures that would influence their successors: working *en plein air*, greater informality of sites and compositions, a more sketch-like manner in paintings finished in the studio (see Simon Kelly's essay in this catalogue).[7] Critics supportive of the renewal of the French school (and of Courbet and Manet in particular) identified the Barbizon masters as godfathers of the modern movement – heirs to Delacroix who had created a heightened pictorial language that broke with academic conventions of decorum and finish.[8] Renoir's acquaintance with Monet, Sisley, and Bazille, all students in Charles Gleyre's studio, gave him immediate access to the most ambitious and innovative young landscapists.[9] Additionally, his early training as a decorator of porcelain would have predisposed him to practise as a landscapist when he progressed from the applied to the fine arts.[10] By his own admission, early in his career Renoir painted pastiches of Rousseau's landscapes for the Parisian market.[11] He is documented as having spent several summers working out-of-doors at Marlotte in the forest of Fontainebleau, encouraged by Diaz and Courbet.[12] And towards the end of the 1860s, he would paint cityscapes and landscapes of suburban leisure in Monet's company.[13]

Yet Renoir was also a student at the Ecole des Beaux-Arts – trained to master the precepts of history painting and hence the figure – who copied in the Louvre and in the print room of the Bibliothèque nationale and competed in annual drawing and painting competitions until 1864.[14] His ambitions as a figure painter are manifest in his Salon submissions between 1863 and 1873. In this decade, Renoir exhibited only one landscape – the lost *Soirée d'été* at the Salon of 1865. In keeping with the long-established hierarchy of the genres, a ranking system that lay at the heart of academic theory and practice, Renoir considered landscape to be of lesser status than history painting, portraiture and even genre painting. This assumption, shared, in fact, by many of the more progressive critics during the 1860s, was quite explicitly rejected by Monet and Pissarro towards the end of that decade.[15]

Renoir consciously chose to present himself at the Salon as a figure painter and a portraitist (even though his submissions were painted in an uncompromisingly modern idiom). Thus, in 1866 when his very large *Women bathing* was rejected by the jury,[16] he immediately withdrew his second entry – a landscape painted in Marlotte in about two weeks – which had been accepted for the Salon.[17] It is not surprising that among Manet's so-called acolytes represented in Fantin-Latour's *Atelier in the Batignolles* (fig. 31), Renoir was given pride of place. While Monet, a greater threat to the master, struggles to keep his footing at the edge of the canvas, Renoir, assuming a posture of solemn veneration, stands beside the figure with whom his ideals and ambitions were much more closely aligned, his head auspiciously 'framed by the secular halo of the gilded but empty picture frame' that hangs on the studio wall.[18]

By contrast, Renoir's attachment to Monet and his pioneering ambitions for landscape painting – and outdoor painting in general – would be affirmed only during the organisation of the first Impressionist exhibition of April 1874 and in a series of portraits and landscapes commemorating the artist and his household in Argenteuil made around that time.[19] Monet's influence was absolutely crucial to the evolution of Renoir's pictorial language after 1873. In their quest to capture the effects of daylight in nature – what Mallarmé would later term 'the natural light of day penetrating and influencing all things'[20] – both artists developed a shared synoptic handling and liberated colour that fully rejected traditional chiaroscuro. For the first time, light and shadow were rendered in a spectrum of colours given equal value, with half-tones systematically suppressed; this was by far the most disquieting aspect of the 'New Painting' for its early audiences.[21]

Between 1863 and 1873 – notwithstanding their joint experiments at La Grenouillère in the summer of 1869 – Monet's influence on Renoir was episodic and intermittent. Jules Le Coeur and the colony of landscapists at Marlotte offered Renoir an alternative milieu, with the extended Le Coeur family providing patronage and material support as well.[22] (Later on, Monet would expressly discourage Renoir from joining him in painting the landscapes of southern France, confiding to Durand-Ruel, 'I've always worked better on my own, following my own impressions. It's a bad idea to work in pairs.')[23] During this time Renoir was most committed to producing large-scale figure paintings to be seen at the Salon. Despite his attachment to Le Coeur and Marlotte, and to Monet and Sisley, landscape painting was a secondary endeavour for him. His ambitious, panoramic cityscape, *The Champs-Elysées during the Fair of 1867* (fig. 26), inspired by Manet's early morning *View of Paris at the Time of the Universal Exhibition of 1867* (fig. 22), may well have been intended as a companion to the figure painting *Lise with a Parasol* (Museum Folkwang, Essen) that he

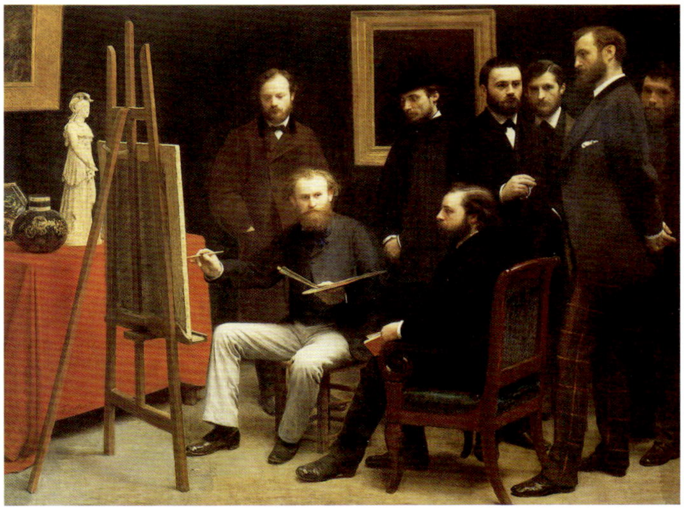

FIG. 31 Henri Fantin-Latour (1836–1904) *Atelier in the Batignolles* 1870. Oil on canvas, 174 × 208.3 cm; 68½ × 81⅞ in. Musée d'Orsay, Paris (RF 729).

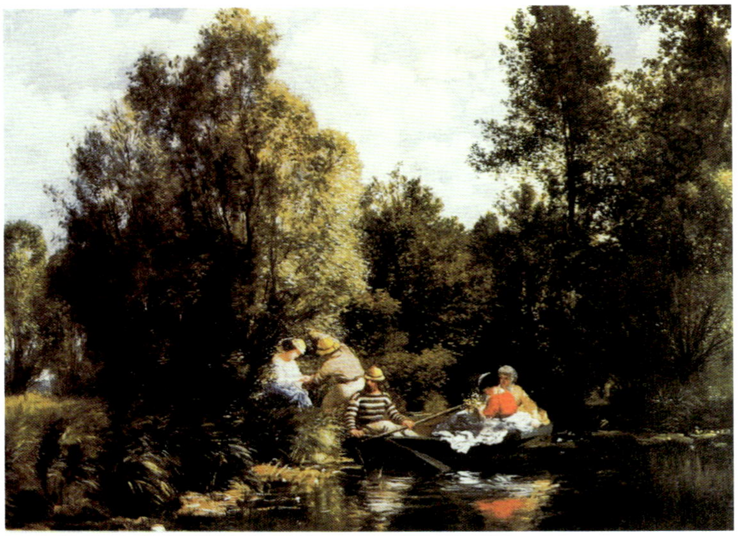

FIG. 32 *La Mare aux Fées*, 1866. Oil on canvas, 68 × 90.5 cm; 26¾ × 35⅝ in. Private collection.

exhibited at the Salon of 1868, even though it seems not to have been submitted after all.[24] Even Renoir's strikingly experimental pictures of boats and bathers at La Grenouillère, painted in Monet's company in the summer of 1869, were conceived as sketches in preparation for a larger 'tableau', never undertaken. This was Monet's reasoning, too: he thought of his own views as studies for the painting that he dreamed of making, as in themselves only '*quelques mauvaises pochades*'.[25] None of Renoir's paintings of La Grenouillère was exhibited at the time of completion; they were regarded as elaborate 'studies' and signed only when sold more than 30 years later.[26]

Landscapes scaled for the domestic market had good chances of selling, however, and outside the context of the Paris Salon Renoir appears to have been prepared to offer them occasionally – for example, at the provincial exhibition of the Sociéte des amis des arts in Pau. At Jules Le Coeur's encouragement, in January 1866 Renoir joined Monet and Sisley in sending there three works, all landscapes, to which he attached relatively high prices.[27] Nothing sold at the time, but in August of that year the Le Coeur family was pleased to note that Renoir's *La Mare aux Fées* (fig. 32), the most ambitious of the group, had been bought by a German banker for 500 francs.[28] 15 years later, Durand-Ruel was still paying Renoir about the same price for his landscapes.

It may well have been because he refused to identify himself as a landscapist that Renoir – in contrast to Monet, Pissarro and Sisley – did not find an early supporter in Paul Durand-Ruel (1831–1922). Given Durand-Ruel's commitment to the '*école de 1830*' and his large supply of Barbizon landscapes (see the essay by Simon Kelly in this catalogue), it is noteworthy that not a single work by Renoir was included in the illustrated survey of his stock that was prepared for publication by the summer of 1872.[29] Renoir had turned in fact to others in the largely fruitless attempt to sell his art – notably Armand-Auguste Deforge (1802–1886) and his associate and eventual successor Marie-Charles-Edouard Carpentier (1830–1883), colourmen and dealers on the boulevard Montmartre who had shown his recent work as early as December 1865.[30] Renoir routinely consigned work to them (*Sisley and his Wife*, *Riding in the Bois de Boulogne*), and he continued to buy his supplies and canvases from them until 1873, at least.[31] It is noteworthy that Durand-Ruel's first acquisition from Renoir, in March 1872, was an urban landscape for which he paid the meagre sum of 200 francs – the luminous *Le Pont des Arts* (see fig. 27; p.44), painted in the summer of 1867 and still without a buyer five years later.[32]

In abandoning the Salon in 1873 (for the next five years at least), and in putting monumental figure painting to one side, Renoir gravitated once again towards Monet's orbit. In the spring of 1873, Renoir is not mentioned in Pissarro and Monet's plans to organise a group exhibition in defiance of the Salon (*'il n'y a que Manet contre'*), nor was his name included in the list of potential participants that appeared in *L'Avenir national* in May of that year (Cézanne, Degas and Morisot were also absent).[33] But with his megalomaniacal *Riding in the Bois de Boulogne* (Hamburger Kunsthalle, Hamburg) hanging at the Salon des refusés that very month, Renoir apparently reconsidered his position, as his earliest Argenteuil pictures elegantly attest. In the summer of 1873, Renoir had also had a traumatic rupture with the Le Coeur family at Fontenay-aux-Roses and it is surely not coincidental that the artist subsequently came to spend more and more time with Monet and his wife Camille in Argenteuil.[34] *Claude Monet painting in his Garden at Argenteuil* (cat. 19) is an affectionate homage to Renoir's new host, the 'strongest of the group', whose flickering impasto and high chroma have now infiltrated Renoir's more suave and glistening manner.[35] And Renoir's two versions of *Duck Pond* (cats. 20, 21) may be dated quite precisely to the autumn of 1873, when he and Monet once again set their easels in front of the same motif.[36] By December 1873, Renoir's commitment to an artist's co-operative that would boycott the Salon and show works in an alternative space (with neither jury nor prizes) was complete. The bylaws of the Société anonyme were drawn up in his apartment on the rue St-Georges on 27 December 1873 and it was there, too, that the ailing co-operative would be dissolved a year later.[37]

In boycotting the Salon, however, Renoir did not relinquish his commitment to figure painting, and it was primarily as such a painter that he appeared at the four Impressionist exhibitions in which he participated.[38] In keeping with the subordinate status he assigned to the genre, he included only one landscape among the seven works sent to the inaugural exhibition of 15 April 1874. So it is somewhat ironical that the blond *The Harvesters* (cat. 16), signed and dated 1873 (and so probably executed that summer) was Renoir's only painting to find a buyer during the run of the show. It sold for the more than respectable sum of 1,000 francs to the music publisher Georges Hartmann (1843–1900), an early promoter of Jules Massenet and the founder of the Concert National (later the Concerts Colonne). Hartmann went on to commission a rather overblown full-length portrait of his wife from Renoir that same year (fig. 33). The heavily framed painting behind the grand piano in that portrait may well be the lower left-hand corner of *The Harvesters* itself.[39] Renoir returned to Argenteuil in the summer of 1874, when he again painted in tandem with Monet: two works from that campaign, *The Seine at Argenteuil* (cat. 23) and *Regatta at Argenteuil* (cat. 24), exemplify his commitment to the newly forged Impressionist style.

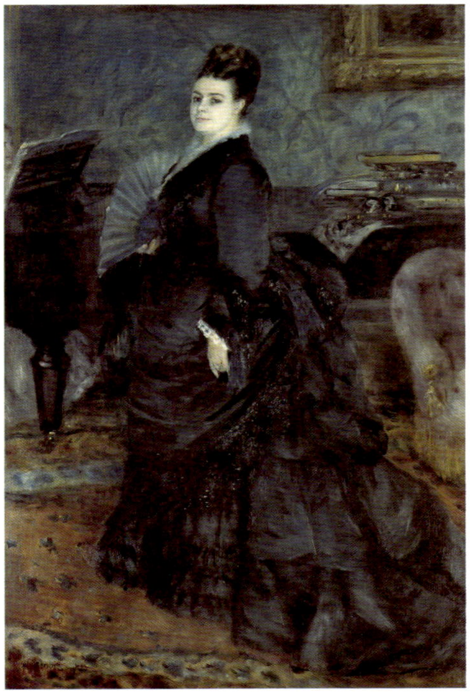

FIG. 33 *Portrait of Madame Hartmann*, 1874. Oil on canvas, 183 × 123 cm; 72 × 48⅜ in. Musée d'Orsay, Paris (RF 2792).

Renoir subscribed to Manet's 'habitual aphorism' that 'no one should paint a landscape and a figure by the same process, with the same knowledge, or in the same fashion'.[40] As his younger brother Edmond would note in June 1879, 'in none of his works, perhaps, is his manner of painting the same'.[41] In looking at the paintings he made in 1874, it is useful to consider the variations in Renoir's manner, and to note a distinction, in works of comparable dimensions, between 'pure' landscapes and the genre of 'figures in the landscape' – the latter, in some ways, works of greater ambition.

Woman with a Parasol (fig. 34, cat. 26), generally dated to between 1874 and 1876, was surely painted at the same moment as *Madame Monet and her son Jean* (fig. 35), securely documented to late July 1874.[42] Both paintings, fully 'Impressionist' in their sketchy handling and heightened palette, are painted with opaque, largely unblended strokes of colour, often applied wet on wet; the brushwork is svelte, somewhat oily, and quite different from the encrusted surfaces and flickering effects that characterise the landscapes Renoir made in Argenteuil in 1874 and 1875. Such dualities persist throughout the decade, but most notably in pictures made in 1879–80: silken, diaphanously handled and purple-hued views of the Normandy coast and countryside, painted during Renoir's residence at the château de Wargemont near Dieppe, present a marked contrast with the more densely hatched, syncopated handling of boating scenes made at the Parisian suburb of Chatou, in which the colouration tends towards green, orange and blue.

On only one occasion did Renoir promote himself as a landscape painter. Ten of the 20 works he contributed to the first Impressionist auction at the Hôtel Drouot in March 1875 were views.[43] The results were fairly disastrous, with most of his pictures fetching less than 100 francs. But while Durand-Ruel paid just 105 francs for *The Seine at Argenteuil* (cat. 23), the signed and dated *The Pont Neuf* (cat. 12) went for 300 francs, among the highest prices paid for any work in the sale.[44] Lampooned in the press, but widely reported on

FIG. 34 & CAT. 26 *Woman with a Parasol and a Small Child on a Sunlit Hillside*, 1874. Oil on canvas, 47 × 56.2 cm; 18½ × 22 in. Museum of Fine Arts, Boston. Bequest of John T. Spaulding (48.593).

FIG. 35 *Madame Monet and her son Jean*, 1874. Oil on canvas, 50.4 × 68 cm; 19⅞ × 26¾ in. National Gallery of Art, Washington, Ailsa Mellon Bruce Collection (1970.17.60).

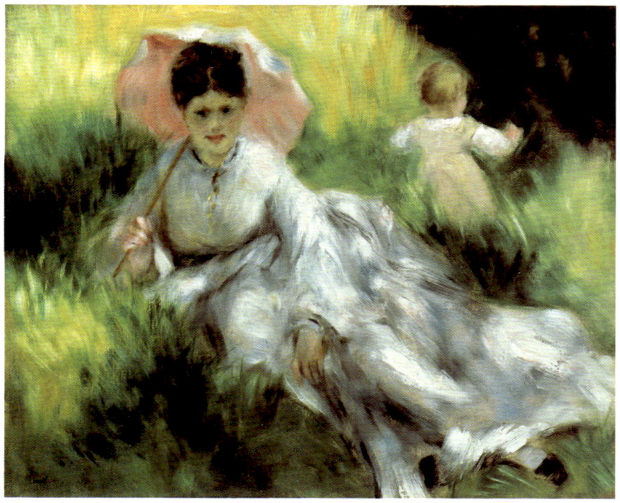

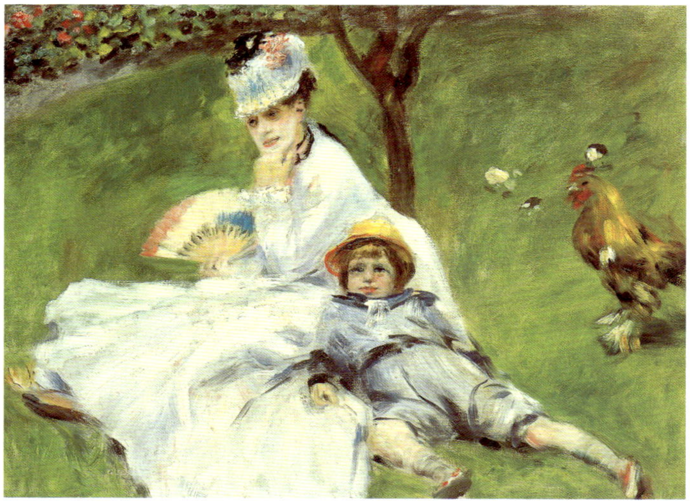

nonetheless, this auction seems to have enraged the Impressionists' fellow artists above all.[45] Thanks to Merete Bodelsen's pioneering research into the auctioneers' records, a sizeable group of Renoir's landscapes can now be dated. Thus, the '*Vue de Paris, Institut*' which sold to Monet's brother, Léon, for 70 francs is securely identified as *L'Institut au quai Malaquais* (fig. 36), which, with its pendant, *Le Quai Malaquais* (cat. 25), probably dates to the autumn of 1874.[46] It was at this auction that his patron Georges Charpentier made his first acquisition of Renoir's work, *The Fisherman* (*Pêcheur à la ligne*; private collection), a river scene of 1874 for which he paid 180 francs – and it should be noted that the seated woman in this picture wears the same white dress and hat resplendent with poppies as the protagonist of *Confidences* (cat. 27), most recently dated to 1872–3 (but the pictures are surely contemporaneous).[47] Charpentier also acquired a '*Jardin aux dahlias*' for 120 francs; this picture may tentatively be associated with the so-called *Garden at Fontenay-aux-Roses* (fig. 37), probably painted in the summer of 1873.[48]

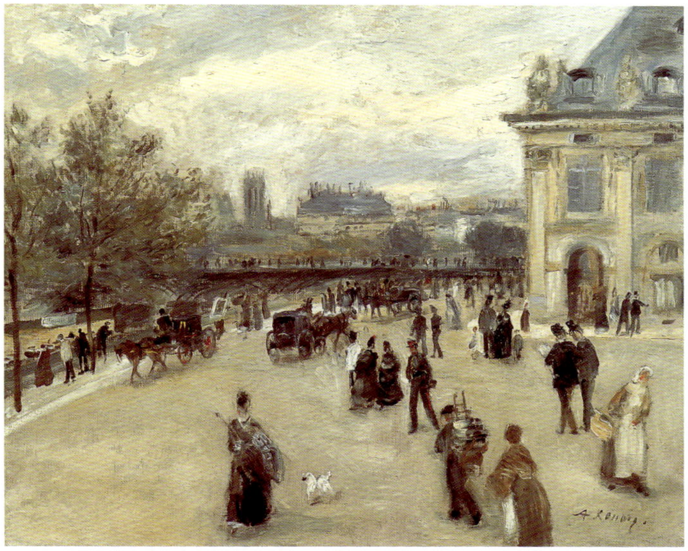

FIG. 36 *L'Institut au quai Malaquais*, about 1874. Oil on canvas, 46 × 56 cm; 18⅛ × 22 in. Private collection, Paris.

Most significantly, the auction records allow us to provide a *terminus ante quem* (and thus firmer dating) for one of the masterpieces of Impressionist landscape, *Path rising through Tall Grass* (*Chemin montant dans les hautes herbes*; fig. 2). Incorrectly assigned to 1876–7,[49] this painting appeared in the sale as '*Paysage d'été*' and was purchased for 105 francs by a certain 'M.G. Thomas', probably the 21-year-old Gabriel Thomas (1854–1932), a cousin of Berthe Morisot's and the future founder of the Musée Grevin.[50] With its vertiginous pathway propelling a well-dressed mother and her young daughter into view – the mother carrying the red-lined parasol beloved by Renoir at this time[51] – the composition repeats the energetic design of *The Watering-place* (*L'Abreuvoir*; signed and dated 1873; cat 15). It is also very close to Monet's contemporaneous *Poppies at Argenteuil* (*Les coquelicots à Argenteuil*, Musée d'Orsay, Paris) with which Renoir was surely familiar. In Renoir's luminous canvas, an inky, electric touch defines the fence at the right, the grasses scattered across the foreground, and the wispy trees to the right of the figures; this touch is repeated in the dabs of bright red that enliven the canvas throughout. Whether *Path rising through Tall Grass* dates from the beginning of Renoir and

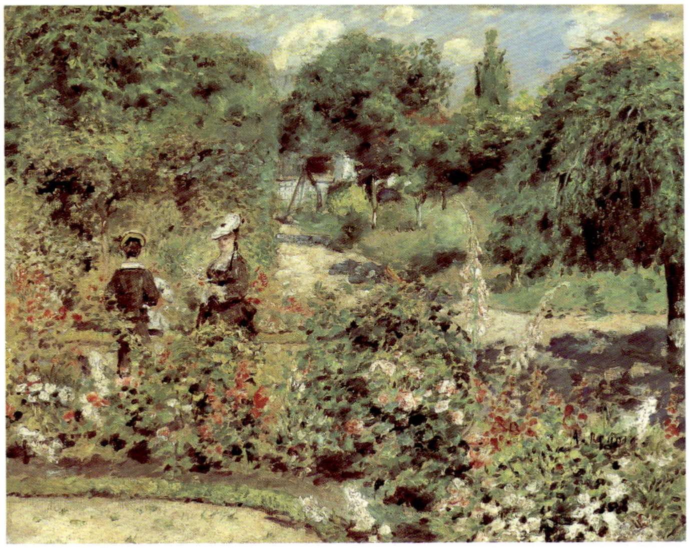

FIG. 37 *Garden at Fontenay-aux-Roses* 1873. Oil on canvas, 51 × 62 cm; 20 × 26¾ in. Oskar Reinhart Collection 'am Römerholz', Winterthur.

Monet's renewed collaboration in the summer of 1873, or from the summer of 1874, when Renoir had become a regular visitor to Argenteuil, thereby offering another stylistic variant for that year, remains something of an open question.[52]

Renoir's single submission to the Salon of 1875 was apparently rejected, and his participation in the second Impressionist exhibition, in April 1876, was dominated by figures and portraits. As Zola noted, and Duret would confirm two years later, Renoir was 'first and foremost a figure painter [*M. Renoir est surtout un peintre de figures*]'.[53] Among Renoir's 17 paintings, however, were several genre scenes of 'figures in a landscape', one of which, as we shall shortly see, helps to identify a series of works associated with Chatou but consistently dated too late in the decade (Renoir began to depict scenes in this 'prettiest of all the Paris suburbs' in the summer of 1874).[54] Certain of Renoir's landscapes of 1875 – those painted in Paris (see cat. 30) and Chatou, in particular *The Bridge at Chatou* in the Sterling and Francine Clark Art Institute, Williamstown (cat. 32) – have a soft, velvety brightness and delicately blended surfaces that are technically different from the paintings done in Argenteuil during the summer and winter of that year, with their granular, active brushwork. One finds this same allusive and atmospheric quality in *Luncheon at La Fournaise* in Chicago (fig. 38 and cat. 34), which hitherto has generally been dated *c.*1879 but which is again very similar in its coloration to the 1875 *The Bridge at Chatou*.[55]

FIG. 38 & CAT. 34 *Luncheon at La Fournaise* (also known as *The Rowers' Lunch*), 1875. Oil on canvas, 55.1 × 65.9 cm; 21½ × 25½ in. Art Institute of Chicago, Illinois. Potter Palmer Collection (1922.437).

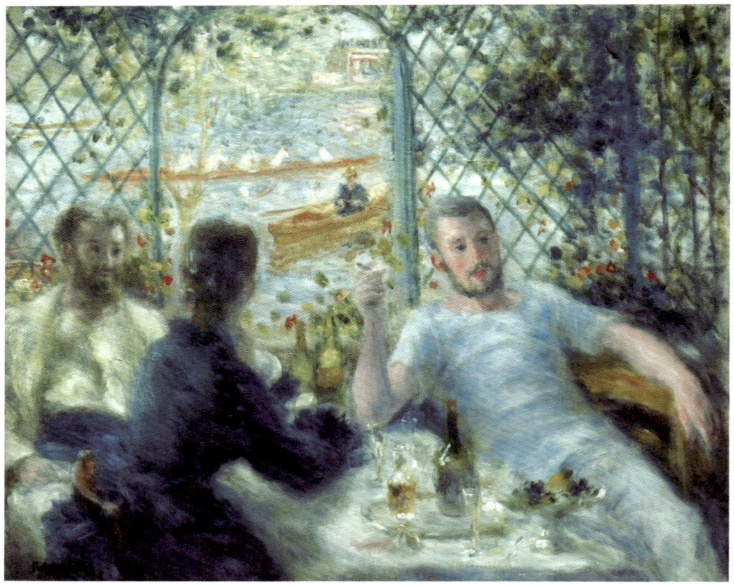

Despite the generic titles, absence of dimensions and the brevity of the critics' discussions of individual works, a comment on Renoir's '*Déjeuner chez Fournaise*', no. 221 in the second Impressionist exhibition, allows us to identify it securely as *Luncheon at La Fournaise.* In a hostile review in *Le Soleil*, Emile Porcheron railed against 'la *Tonnelle des Canotiers* sans jambes' or 'the *Arbour of the Rowers* who have no knees'. The bower or arbour of his title corresponds to the setting of the painting, and Renoir's otherwise unremarkable cropping does indeed leave his rowers without knees (Ruth Berson was the first to associate the picture in Chicago with that shown in the second Impressionist exhibition).[56] Once *Luncheon at La Fournaise* is redated to the summer of 1875 it is possible to assign a similar date to the exquisite *Luncheon* in the Barnes Foundation (fig. 39) – a larger canvas, but a pendant of sorts – in which two of the same models partake of a tender and intimate meal indoors.[57] A third picture of riparian conviviality in Chatou, painted at the same time, is the National Gallery's *The Skiff* (*La Yole*) (fig. 40, cat. 33), known since it first appeared at auction in July 1899 under the misleading title of *La Seine à Asnières*, and now routinely assigned to 1879–80.[58] Not only is *The Skiff* (*La Yole*)

related in style and subject-matter to *Luncheon at La Fournaise* – as has frequently been noted – but its glorious cobalt-blue water, with inflections of orange, pink and white, is also comparable in handling and hue to that of *The Bridge at Chatou*, a view taken from a different section of the river.[59] Of the four pictures in this group, three were signed by Renoir at the time of their completion – suggesting that they were sold or placed on exhibition fairly soon after that date (as indeed was the case with *Luncheon at La Fournaise*). The first owners of the Clark Institute and National Gallery paintings were among the select band of collectors who responded to the Impressionists in the mid-1870s. Ernest Hoschedé was obliged to sell *The Bridge at Chatou* in his bankruptcy sale of June 1878, where it was acquired by the homeopathic doctor Georges de Bellio for a derisory 42 francs.[60] *The Skiff* (*La Yole*), now redated to 1875, may have been among the first works by Renoir purchased by Victor Chocquet, the artist's most discerning early patron and collector, who commissioned a portrait of his wife from the artist in the spring of that year.[61]

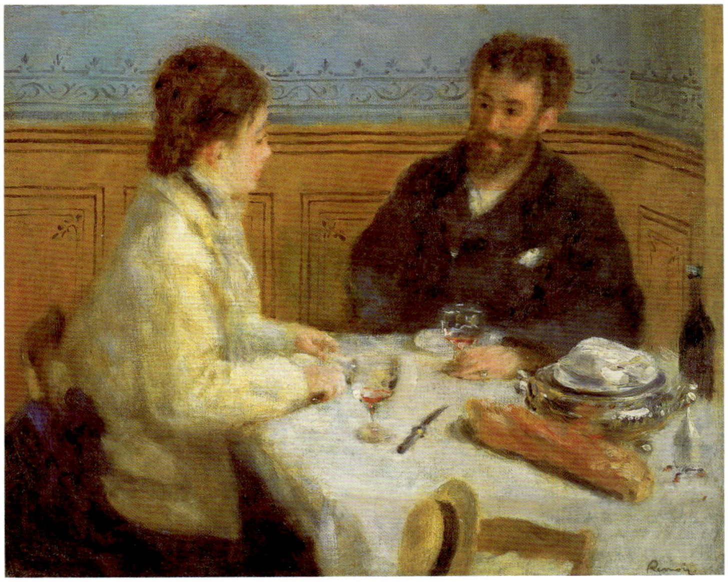

FIG. 39 *The Luncheon*, 1875. Oil on canvas, 48.9 × 58.4 cm; 19¼ × 23 in. The Barnes Foundation, Merion, Pennsylvania (BF 45).

Dominated by the *Ball at the Moulin de la Galette* (Musée d'Orsay, Paris) – Renoir's '*tableau historique*' – the third Impressionist exhibition was the last in which Renoir would participate of his own accord. Consistent with the priorities of a history painter, his 21 submissions included examples in all genres – six landscapes this time – but portraits and figures accounted for the lion's share. Like *Moulin de la Galette*, several of Renoir's landscapes had an urban feel.[62] Thanks to Rivière's poetic description of 'a May morning sun that burns the budding horse-chestnut trees' and 'the fresh scent of the large green trees that break loose from their gardens',[63] it is now possible to identify *La Place St-Georges* (cat. 31) as no. 196, one of the four paintings lent by Caillebotte to the exhibition and one of the two Renoirs that would be rejected by the State when Caillebotte's donation entered the Musée du Luxembourg in 1896.[64]

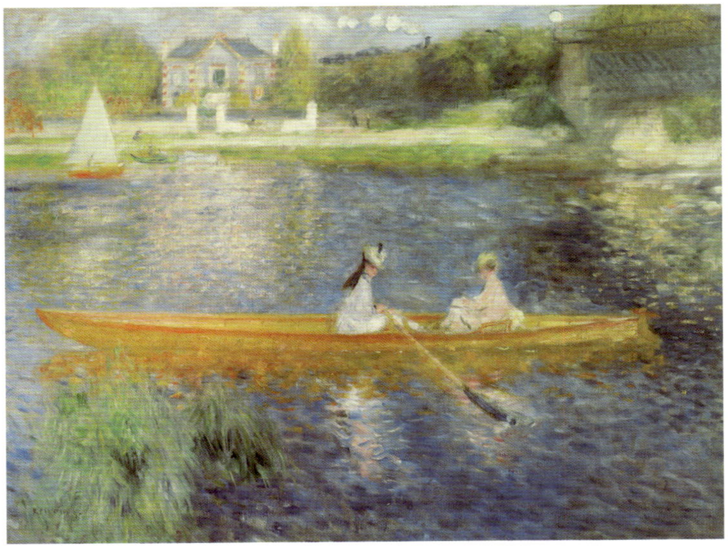

FIG. 40 & CAT. 33 *The Skiff* (*La Yole*), 1875. Oil on canvas, 71 × 92 cm; 36¼ × 28 in. The National Gallery, London (NG 6478).

Perhaps Renoir's most remarkable cityscape on display at the third Impressionist exhibition was the lost *Coucher de soleil* (no. 197), which Rivière called '*Le soleil couchant à Montmartre*' and described in considerable detail. His account, given here in full, may yet help identify this landscape, which otherwise remains unknown:

> With its atmosphere of gold and diamonds, [this picture] is ravishing to behold. While the sun still casts its rays on the valley, the foreground, hidden by a row of hedges, slowly takes on the mantle of evening. In departing, the sun seems to double in intensity; the brick roofs explode, the leaves sing out on their exalted branches, the cracks in the white walls turn metallic, and the horizon disappears from view behind the dazzling dust. Here and there, patches of shadow from the hills of which the summits are engulfed in gold struggle to break free, like fading dreams. The colouring of this landscape is more forceful than anything yet attempted.[65]

Renoir's fascination with Montmartre, a working-class quarter on the northern fringes of Paris, was celebrated in his other landscapes as well. Relying once again on Rivière, it is possible to associate '*The Dahlias*', exhibited as no. 204 in the third Impressionist exhibition, with Pittsburgh's *Garden in the rue Cortot, Montmartre* (fig. 41, cat. 39).[66] This unusually large landscape appears to have started out as a genre scene. X-radiography has revealed the head and chest of a moustached figure in the top right-hand corner of the canvas, a scarf around his neck, his face looking down on the garden below (fig. 42). Whether this bohemian figure

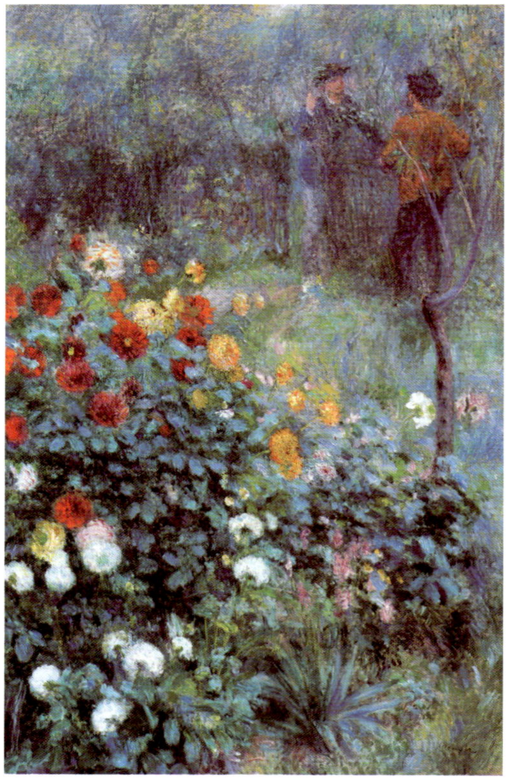

FIG. 41 & CAT. 39 *Garden in the rue Cortot, Montmartre*, 1876. Oil on canvas, 151.8 × 97.5 cm; 59¾ × 38⅜ in. Carnegie Institute, Museum of Art, Pittsburgh. Acquired through the generosity of Mrs Alan M. Scaife (65.35).

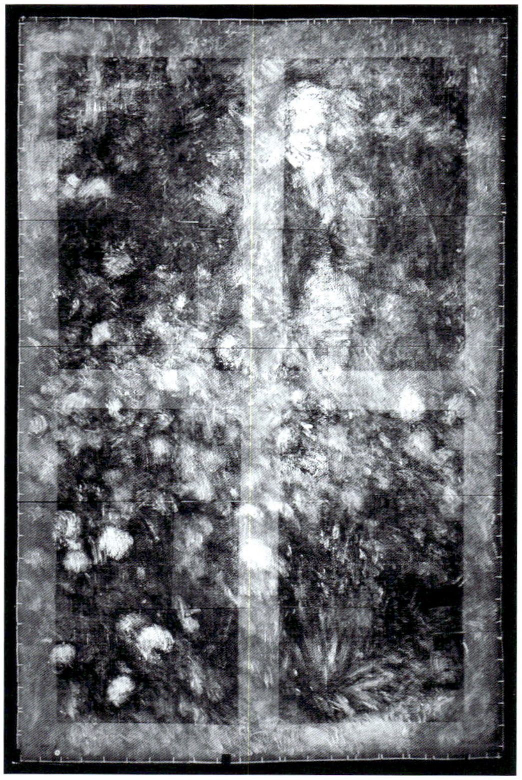

FIG. 42 X-radiography of *Garden in the rue Cortot, Montmartre*.

was intended to be part of the final composition is hard to say, since there is nothing painted beneath the rest of the canvas. Rivière ends his review of Renoir's entries with mention of 'the large panel with its magnificent red dahlias amidst the jumble of grass and creepers'.[67] Surprisingly, no other critic mentioned this over-scaled work – which makes a positive match problematic – but Rivière's comment that 'this large painting is a splendid decoration [*ce grand tableau est une splendide décoration*]' adds weight to the identification. Anne Distel has noted an affinity between *Garden in the rue Cortot*, executed in the summer of 1876, and the group of landscape decorations Monet made for Hoschedé's country house at Montgeron around the same time – one of which, *Les Dindons* (Musée d'Orsay, Paris), dominated the second room of the 1877 exhibition.[68]

The dating of the Pittsburgh canvas to 1876 has not been at issue for some time. Rivière was unusually precise in assigning Renoir's tenancy at 12 rue Cortot (the present-day Musée de Montmartre) to between March and October 1876 – an assertion confirmed early on by the artist's brother, who in 1879 noted that Renoir moved to Montmartre for six months in order to work on the *Ball at the Moulin de la Galette*.[69] Assuming that the Pittsburgh canvas does indeed represent a corner of this apparently enormous garden, which Rivière compared to 'a fine, abandoned park' with its 'vast, uncut lawn dotted with poppies, convolvulus and daisies',[70] its style and subject have consequences for the dating and locating of a group of related works. The composition of *Garden in the rue Cortot* is unexpectedly kinetic, with the brilliantly impastoed dahlias dominating both foreground and middle ground and dividing the canvas into two diagonal quadrants of unequal vibrancy and texture. Renoir's handling is rough and exuberant, the expansiveness of this Parisian garden conveyed with absolute assurance. At some distance in the background, two artists are engaged in conversation. The bearded figure, seen from behind, has a portable easel tucked under his arm and bears more than a passing resemblance to Monet; the figure on the other side of the fence looks very much like Renoir himself.[71]

In facture, coloration and spatial organisation *Garden in the rue Cortot* relates to a group of resplendent garden landscapes that are similarly daring in design and unfettered in handling. In these works, the elegant figure of a parisienne appears – shaded by a parasol, in conversation with a casually attired suitor, or even giving orders to a gardener – but as an ancillary motif, overwhelmed by the burgeoning flora. In what is perhaps the earliest picture in this group, *The Garden (in the Park)* (fig. 43), a female figure, barely discernible in the distant background, is accompanied by a child in straw boater and white smock.[72] Here we are presented with a grander garden, more formally laid out, of which the steps and white urns evoke

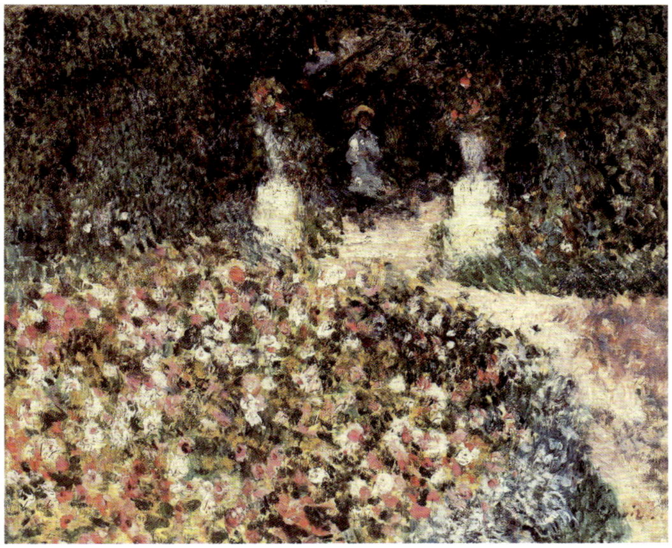

FIG. 43 *The Garden (in the Park)*, 1875–6. Oil on canvas, 54.6 × 65.1 cm; 21½ × 25⅝ in. Private collection.

Monet's residence on the boulevard St-Denis at Argenteuil, which Renoir surely continued to visit in 1875 and 1876. A more untamed garden, surrounded by trees that cast shadows of violet filigree, is the subject of *Women in a Garden* (cat. 40), customarily dated to 1873. One of the two women who converse at the end of the path, shaded by a white parasol, is dressed in a similar toque and tailored outfit as that worn by the model of *Nini in the Garden* (Metropolitan Museum of Art, New York).[73] The same figure and parasol reappear in the middle distance of the Thyssen Collection's *Woman with a Parasol in a Garden* (cat. 37), which Götz Adriani was the first to associate with the related work in Washington, *Picking Flowers* (cat. 38), generally dated 1875.[74]

Stylistic similarities among all of these works, and their mutual relationship to the Pittsburgh canvas, strongly argue for a dating around 1875–6. Indeed, it is possible that the garden canvases now in Washington and Madrid (or works very much like them) appeared alongside *Garden in the rue Cortot* at the third Impressionist exhibition of April 1877. Two of its reviewers made disparaging references to Renoir's *Gardens* (nos. 198 and 199), noting their 'apocalyptic' appearance – 'one certainly sees something, even if one has no idea what it is'– and likening them to objects 'seen through chemists' jars'.[75] For a less than sympathetic viewer in the late 1870s, the reference to a certain wildness and lack of clarity in these canvases might seem an appropriate response.

As John House has recently noted, it was during the final years of President MacMahon's repressive regime of moral order in France, and at a time when material support for the New Painting was at its most precarious, that the Impressionists' handling, colour and subject-matter became increasingly experimental and controversial.[76] As an example, consider Renoir's *In the Woods* (cat. 41), painted around 1877, a virtuoso display of dashes and dabs of pigment that create a vortex of light radiating outward from a central vanishing point. At first glance, this is a subject-less picture, almost an abstract one. Only the edges of a fence in the foreground at lower right, hints of the autumnal trees lining the pathway, and the suggestion of a building in the far distance establish that this is a forest scene in some proximity to the entrance of a country residence. The signature at lower right, which dates from this time, further confirms that *In the Woods* was intended for exhibition or sale.[77] Perhaps because landscape painting was of only 'secondary importance' to Renoir, as Duret noted in May 1878, it was an arena in which he allowed himself the greatest freedoms.[78]

It was also at this time, however, that Renoir sought to establish for himself a basis of support beyond the venues of alternative exhibitions and group auctions, neither of which was particularly congenial to him. As the only one of Duret's '*peintres impressionnistes*' 'with the eye and the paw of a portraitist',[79] between 1877 and 1881 Renoir was gradually taken up by wealthy patrons such as the Charpentiers and Berards, whose portrait commissions of family members, friends and public figures of their acquaintance gradually transformed his economic situation. This did not happen overnight: throughout 1877 and 1878 Renoir remained chronically short of money, despite having been 'pushed' and 'launched' by the Charpentiers.[80] As Duret noted many years later – and it was Duret who introduced Renoir in 1878 to Charles Deudon (1832–1914), heir to an English mining fortune and the artist's essential conduit to the Berard family – 'Remuneration from these portraits would in time provide him with a sizeable income . . . initially they enabled him to make a living.'[81]

The portrait commissions Renoir undertook in these years – the most prestigious of which enabled him to return to the official Salons – paved the way, to some extent, for his large-scale, multi-figured compositions of modern-day subjects for which there was, as yet, no established market (Durand-Ruel would only renew his financial backing of the Impressionists after February 1881). Here, as I have noted elsewhere, Renoir was following a course traditionally recommended to history painters, who were expected to turn to portraiture 'to subsidise the production of pictures of which the eventual ownership is uncertain'.[82] From this perspective, an artist painting landscapes was akin to a musician practising scales; Renoir would later claim that 'it was the only way to learn one's craft'.[83] In October 1878, having just completed the full-length *Portrait of Mlle Samary* (State Hermitage Museum, St Petersburg), and with *Mme Charpentier and her Children* (The Metropolitan Museum of Art, New York) almost finished, Renoir told Duret that he 'was taking advantage of a few days of fine weather to paint landscapes, as it will make a change from what I've been doing [*histoire de changer*] and will enable me to return to the figure with greater pleasure'.[84]

In 1879, Renoir's introduction to the seigneurial Berards led to an invitation to summer at Wargemont, their country estate eight kilometres east of Dieppe, next to the coastal village of Berneval-sur-mer (where they owned part of the shoreline).[85] As a guest at Wargemont, Renoir returned, in some respects, to the regime that he had followed in the late 1860s and early 1870s: he painted in all the genres, but structured his work around his submission to the forthcoming Salon. Thus the most significant product of Renoir's first contact with the Normandy coast was a monumental genre painting intended for the Palais de l'Industrie the following year. With its picturesque allusions to Normandy life, Renoir's least appreciated Impressionist figure painting, *Musselfishers at Berneval* (fig. 44), may have been conceived as a 'vacationer's picture'.[86] It shows a group of well-shod, healthy children on the top of a cliff overlooking the English Channel, with tiny yachts in the distance. Jacques-Emile Blanche, whose family spent the summer in Dieppe (and whom Renoir visited when he came into town on market-day), noted that Renoir's models might 'look like little Norwegians' but were in fact the children of local fishermen whom the artist had posed in the grounds of Berard's estate.[87]

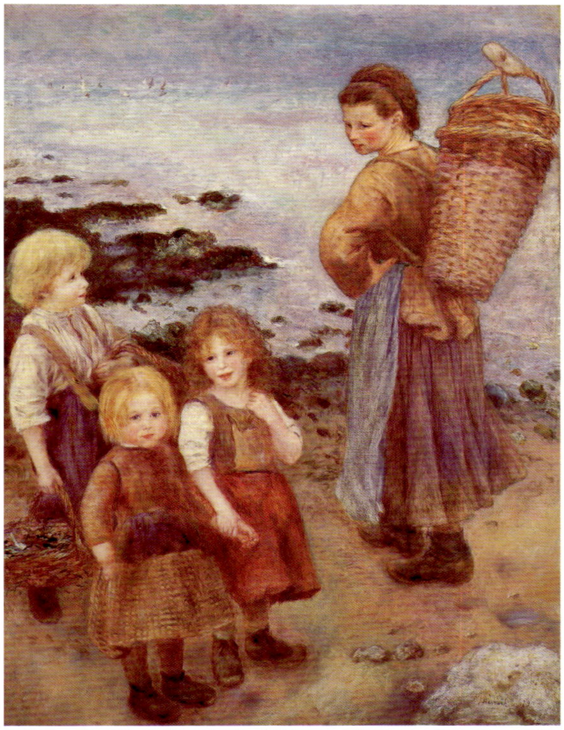

FIG. 44 *Musselfishers at Berneval*, 1880. Oil on canvas, 176.2 × 130.2 cm; 69⅓ × 21½ in. Barnes Foundation, Merion, Pennsylvania (BF 989).

When Renoir turned to landscape in Normandy – the magnificent panorama southwest of Wargemont (cat. 43), the resplendent 'portrait' of the château and its rose garden (fig. 45), orchestral seascapes with waves crashing against the shore (cats. 45, 68) – his range was remarkable, his manner unhesitatingly experimental. Blanche, recalling half a century later his summer meetings with Renoir, evoked the artist working with marten-hair brushes on canvases 'plastered white', his palette kept so clean that one could see one's reflection in it.[88] In his estimation, Renoir approached these summer landscapes as a form of relaxation ('*pour se délasser*'), painting in a spectrum dominated by 'a reddish violet, which we likened to redcurrant jam'.[89] In the magisterial *Landscape at Wargemont* (cat. 43), signed and dated 1879, Renoir applied layers of thin washes over the white priming to create a dynamic luminosity throughout.[90] Traces of his brush are visible and Renoir's handling here, 'terribly silky [*terriblement 'soyeuse'*]' in Blanche's memorable phrase,[91] evokes wind, height, and speed – as if we were taking the view from a passing carriage.[92] This extraordinarily animated scene nonetheless retains a complex topographical structure: the sinuous road through the hills dotted with trees and bushes leads the eye to the valley beyond; the panorama is taken from a vantage point high above the hedges in the right foreground, which bend before the coastal winds.[93]

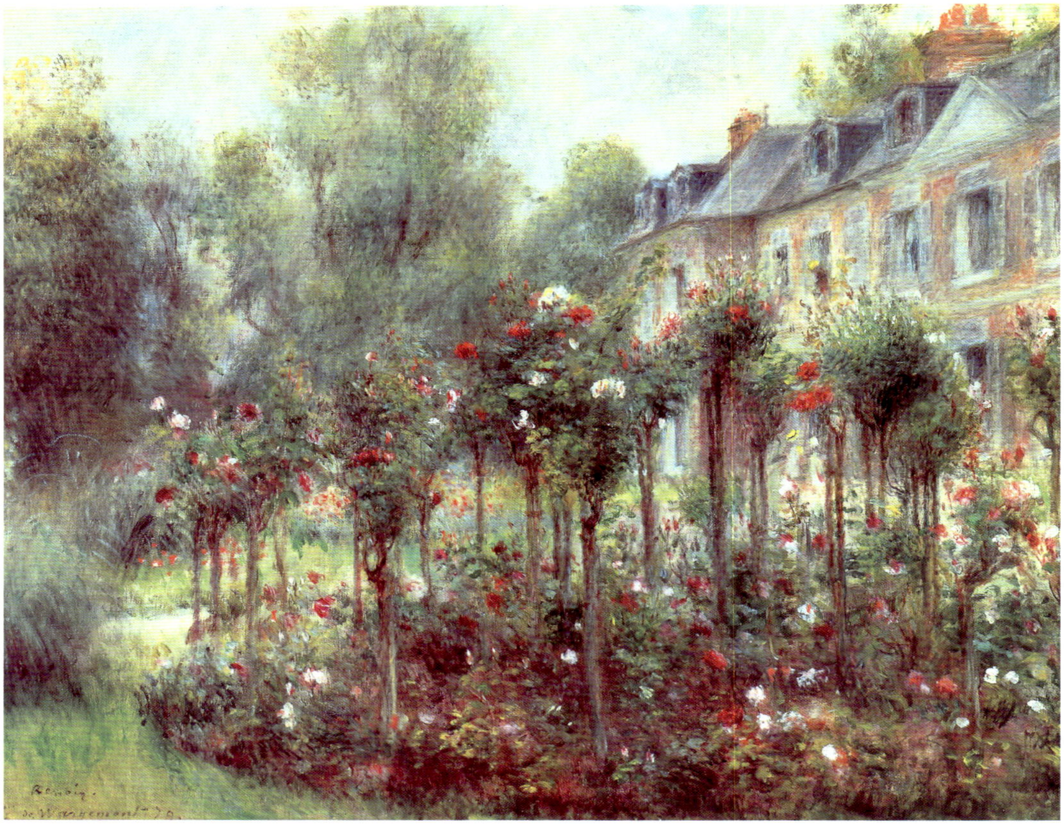

FIG. 45 *Château and its rose garden*, 1879
Oil on canvas,
65 × 81 cm;
25⅝ × 31⅞ in.
Private collection.

Renoir's touch changed again in the seascapes painted that summer, his palette now tending towards cobalt and emerald green, and his execution, while diaphanous in the sky, becoming more impasted in describing the crests of the waves as they crash on to the shore. The seascape in Chicago (cat. 45), with its turbulent sea and animated sky, evokes the same coastal vista that was to move Oscar Wilde a few years later: 'The sea and sky one opal, no horrid drawing master's line between them, just one fishing boat going slowly and drawing the wind after it'.[94] *The Wave* of 1882 (cat. 68) is even more audacious, a work that may be said to have been sculpted in paint, with the whites applied directly from the tube.[95] This extraordinary painting dates from August 1882, when Renoir was Durand-Ruel's guest in Dieppe, there to paint a series of peerless family 'portraits in the sunshine' in a style of which his dealer did not altogether approve (see below).[96] The energy, grandeur and recklessness of *The Wave* may reflect something of Renoir's temporary liberation from the confining formality of his host's summer house. Certainly this was a work, in Blanche's words, that would 'turn the heads of connoisseurs of the future'.[97]

In the landscapes painted at Wargemont and Berneval between 1879 and 1882, Renoir depopulated the modest resort town and its environs, wilfully omitting the chalets and bungalows that dotted the coast in ungainly clusters, and refining his palette to a register dominated by madder and violet. Free now to 'roam the countryside and the beaches',[98] enjoying the company of the elegant Berard and his *mondain* guests (Deudon, Ephrussi, Cahen d'Anvers and, occasionally, Victor Chocquet), taken up by the young Jacques-Emile Blanche and his friends in Dieppe, passionate for Manet and Whistler – during these Norman summers Renoir's robust, Impressionist technique underwent a subtle re-evaluation. However, once he found himself back in the suburbs of Paris, among denizens of less rarified sensibilities, and at the side of his new mistress, Aline Charigot – whom he discouraged from visiting him in Dieppe [99] – Renoir returned to a more robust manner.[100] For it was in the summers of 1879 and 1880 that Renoir painted two of his radiant Chatou boating scenes (cats. 49, 50), and devoted himself to 'the picture of Boaters which has been gnawing away at me for such a long time'.[101] In the spring and early summer of 1881 Renoir closed his cycle of suburban recreation with such masterpieces as *Chestnut Trees in Bloom* (cat. 60), *The Railway Bridge at Chatou* (cat. 61), and *Two Sisters* (*On the Terrace*) (see fig. 102; 212)[102] – the result of his 'struggle with trees in bloom and women and children'.[103]

Between March 1881 and January 1884 Renoir virtually abandoned Paris. Having never previously been abroad, indeed having travelled previously no further than Normandy, during this period Renoir went twice to Algeria, made a three-month journey to Italy, and visited L'Estaque, the Channel Islands, and the French Riviera.[104] This was in addition to a proposed visit to London in Duret's company, postponed twice (in March and April 1881) and eventually abandoned;[105] annual trips to Wargemont and Dieppe; and a brief stay at the *maison* Aubourg in nearby Yport in August 1883, to paint portraits of the Nunès children.[106]

At one level, travel was a sign of Renoir's very recent (and still relative) affluence; it may also have been encouraged by his involvement with Aline, whom he allowed to accompany him abroad. At yet another level, travel provided a means of escape, allowing Renoir to leave unresolved the conflicts he faced as a founding Impressionist still determined to make his mark at the Salon.

Not only could Renoir now rely upon the lucrative commissions brokered by Berard and his circle (portraits of the Cahen d'Anvers, the Foulds, the Grimpels) but also, thanks to Durand-Ruel and his associates, his subject pictures were beginning to find a respectable market. In November 1880, Durand-Ruel acquired Renoir's Salon submission, *Musselfishers at Berneval*, from Dubourg for 2,500 francs; in January 1881, Renoir received the same amount for *Girl with a Cat* (Sterling and Francine Clark Art Institute), the other picture he sent to the Salon of 1880; the following month, Durand-Ruel paid him the princely sum of 6,000 francs for the recently completed *Luncheon of the Boating Party* (The Phillips Collection, Washington, DC), acquired as '*Déjeuner champêtre*'.[107] At the same time Durand-Ruel was establishing exclusive agreements with the other Impressionists. In January 1881, Pissarro joyfully informed his niece that 'one of the most important dealers in Paris . . . has proposed to take whatever I paint. This offers me tranquillity for the foreseeable future, and the means to make important work.'[108]

Just months before, while labouring over *Luncheon of the Boating Party*, Renoir had confided his anxiety to Berard regarding the 'enormous costs' involved in painting such a picture – even though many of the models were friends who must have given their services free of charge.[109] With his financial situation now secure, Renoir might have been expected to devote himself to similarly ambitious multi-figured subject pictures, 'important work' of the kind to which Pissarro alluded. This was not to be the case, however. On some level, Renoir found the immediate consequences of material security highly destabilising. In spite of Durand-Ruel's support, he remained committed to the official Salon and to 'portraits only'.[110] Increasingly suspicious of group exhibitions, he had refused to participate in them in 1880 and 1881, and vehemently resisted Durand-Ruel's suggestion that he relent in 1882, declaring, '. . . *rester avec l'Israélite Pissarro, c'est la révolution*'.[111] He reluctantly conceded, however, that his dealer was free to lend paintings from his own holdings and thus Durand-Ruel sent 25 Renoirs to the seventh exhibition of the '*artistes indépendants*' the following month.[112]

Both Renoir's travels to North Africa in 'search of the sun' and his first acquaintance with the museums and sites of Italy led him to question his method of working out-of-doors – an interrogation that would continue for the next six years. During the winter of 1881–2 he was propelled into a '*maladie des recherches*', as he sought to privilege 'the larger harmonies' over 'those small details which extinguish the sun instead of kindling it'.[113] Renoir's efforts to infuse his portraits with such luminosity did not, however, meet with his patrons' approval. Durand-Ruel disliked the sunlit portraits of his children Renoir painted in Dieppe in August 1882, and that autumn the painter's *Portrait of Mme Clapisson* was returned to him as 'too audacious'. Renoir produced an appropriate replacement, and recycled the rejected portrait as a genre painting, now entitled *In the Rosegarden* (fig. 46).[114] As late as December 1883 Berard confided to Deudon that Renoir was in poor spirits, overwhelmed by the size (and rent) of his new studio, and demoralised 'by the difficulty of having his painting accepted'.[115]

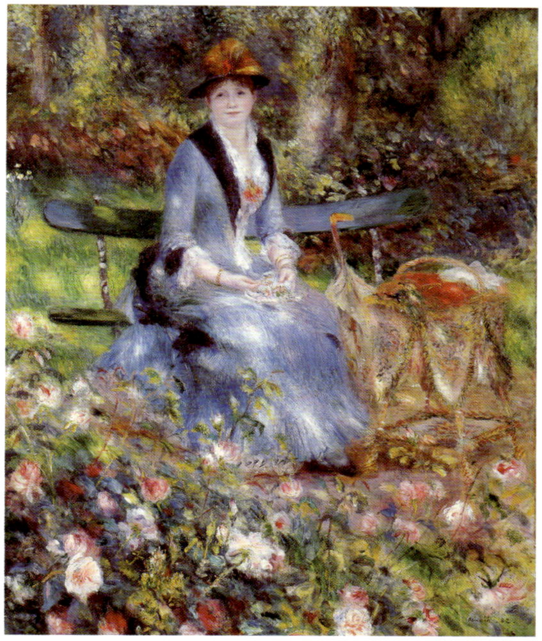

FIG. 46 *In the Rosegarden*, 1882. Oil on canvas, 100 × 81 cm; 39⅜ × 31⅞. Private collection, Las Vegas.

As he travelled in these years, Renoir – however much consumed by his ambitions as a figure painter – worked primarily as a landscapist, seeking out the picturesque tourist sites already made familiar by lithographers, photographers and other painters (and this is as true of Algeria as it is of Venice, Naples, Guernsey and Monte Carlo).[116] Although he yearned to paint living models, and was now in a position to hire them, on his first trip to Algeria in March 1881 Renoir limited himself to landscapes, overwhelmed as he was by '*une richesse de nature extraordinaire*' (even though it did not stop raining for the first week of his stay).[117] He was also intimidated by the Arab women, whom he could not understand and 'found unapproachable'.[118]

For the first time in his career Renoir was painting canvases (other than portraits) of which the purchase was assured. Immediately upon the artist's return to Paris, on 7 April 1881, Durand-Ruel acquired a group of five Algerian views for prices that ranged from 200 francs (*Field of Banana Trees Near Algiers*, cat. 55 and '*The Ravine of the Wild Woman*', cat. 57,) to 700 francs (*The Jardin d'Essai, Algers*, cat. 56). These were modest sums, certainly, but at the high end of the prices that any of Renoir's landscapes had garnered in the 1880s.[119] In keeping with his somewhat guarded approach to Durand-Ruel, Renoir chose not to offer him the most daring composition from this first North African visit. The complex, but highly controlled *Arab Festival* (cat. 54) shows five Arab musicians performing before a mixed audience within the ruined Turkish ramparts. The teeming spectators (and there are hundreds of them) are captured at various sites in this dizzying bird's-eye panorama which leads the eye to the battlements and the sea beyond.[120] This painting was only deposited with Durand-Ruel seven years later, in December 1888, and was finally acquired by him in February 1892 for the relatively modest sum of 500 francs.[121]

For all Renoir's delight in capturing the tourist spots – in Venice he was one of six painters in front of the Doge's Palace, and joked with Deudon and Mme Charpentier that such a view had never before been attempted[122] – his Italian journey of November 1881 to mid-January 1882 had something of the flavour of a belated Prix de Rome. Renoir delighted in seeing the Raphaels, particularly his frescoes – 'I bet they'll say I've been influenced' – and in visiting the museum at Capodimonte in Naples (he later advised Deudon to 'spend his life there').[123] Hence also his anxiety that 'his lengthy investigations' had reduced him to a schoolboy who, at 40 years of age, was still blotting his copybook.[124] Such concerns,

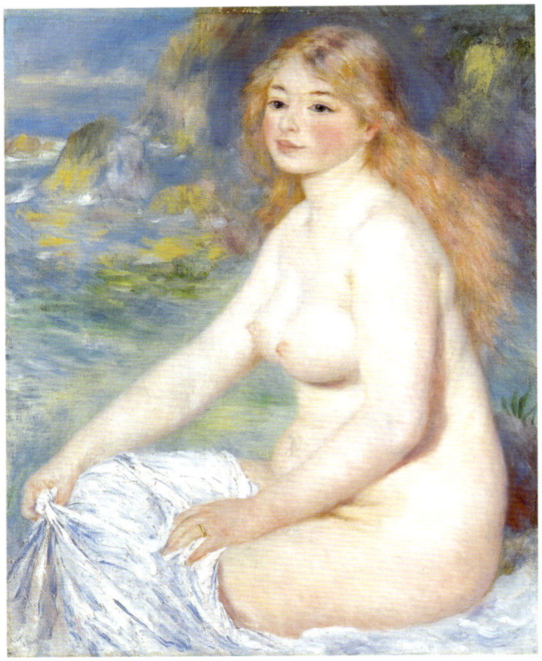

FIG. 48 *Blonde Bather I*, 1882. Oil on canvas. 81.8 × 65.7 cm; 21¼ × 27⅞ in. Sterling and Francine Clark Art Institute, Williamstown Massachusetts (1955.609).

unrelated to landscape painting, were generated by Renoir's decision to return to the female nude, a decision that caused him to 'waste a lot of time', as he put it, because, while numerous, his Italian models 'sickened him' as soon as they 'sat down and posed in three-quarters, with their hands on their knees'.[125] His companion Aline Charigot may have solved the dilemma by modelling for the surpassing *Blonde Bather I* (fig. 47), Renoir's most ambitious work from this period.[126]

Despite his appreciation of Raphael's 'knowledge and wisdom' and a renewed respect for Ingres, Renoir in Italy (as in Algeria earlier that year) largely confined his production for Durand-Ruel to landscapes – or, more properly, to cityscapes (*Blonde Bather* was not offered to the dealer). In May 1882, upon the artist's return to Paris after an absence of six months, Durand-Ruel acquired two views of Naples for 700 francs each (including fig. 48, cat. 65), one of Sorrento for 600 francs, two of the Grand Canal (including cat. 63) for 500 francs and views of Calabria and Capri for 400 and 300 francs respectively.[127] He also took *Mother and Child* (*La Soeur aînée*; fig. 49), the single genre painting to emerge from this campaign, for the sum of 2,500 francs.[128] Putting to one side the differences in size between Renoir's landscapes and this

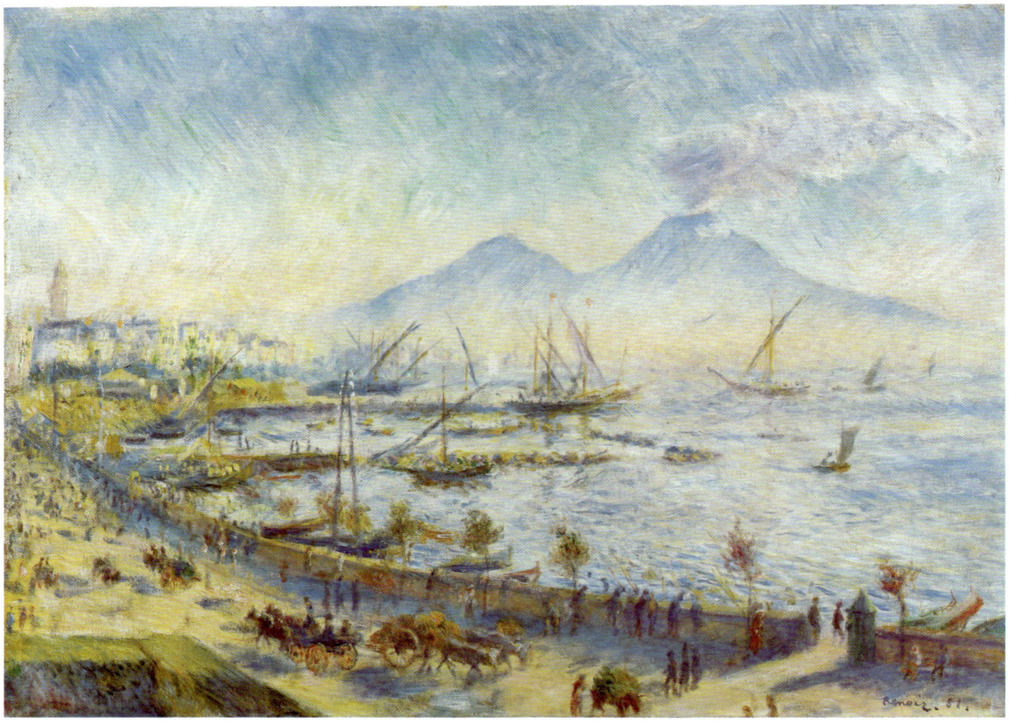

FIG. 48 & CAT. 65 *The Bay of Naples* (*Morning*), 1881. Oil on canvas 59.7 × 81.3 cm; 23½ × 32 in. The Metropolitan Museum of Art, New York. Bequest of Julia W. Emmons, 1956 (56.135.8).

genre scene, the considerable discrepancy in the prices they commanded reflects still the traditional hierarchy of subject-matter, persisting even in this most progressive of markets. Renoir himself considered his more informal landscapes as little more than '*documents*' or studies, and he priced them accordingly. *Venice, Fog* (fig. 50), signed and dated 1881 – with its reticent, Whistlerian touch – was dispatched to Berard from Naples towards the end of November for a mere 100 francs. And Berard, Renoir wrote, was not to hesitate to give it back 'if it turned out not to be to his liking'.[129]

In keeping with Renoir's Italian 'investigations', his second trip to Algeria (mid March to late April 1882), this time undertaken in Aline's company, was devoted above all to figure painting.[130] It was also made under very different circumstances, since Renoir, recovering from the severe pulmonary infection that he had contracted in L'Estaque, was in considerable anguish over Durand-Ruel's decision to support the seventh Impressionist exhibition. Once he had made his peace with his dealer, Renoir informed him that he was 'negotiating with Arabs for models, which is not easy', and expressed the hope that he would 'succeed in bringing you back some figures,

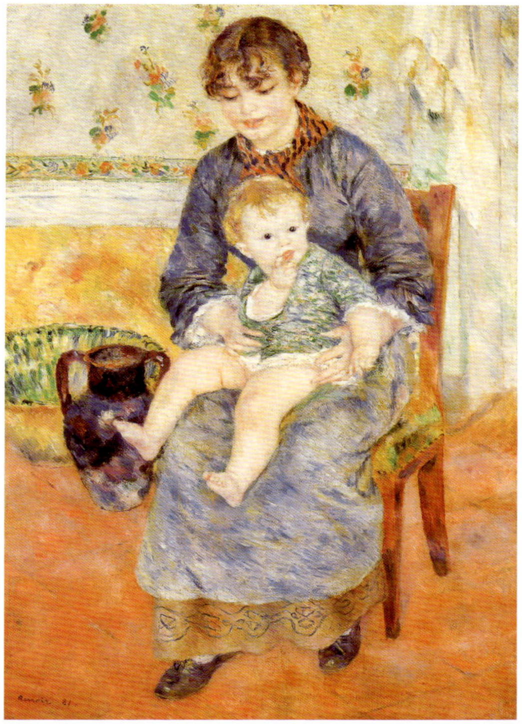

FIG. 49 *Mother and Child* (*La Soeur aînée*), 1881. Oil on canvas, 121.3 × 85.7 cm; 47¾ × 33¾ in. The Barnes Collection, Merion, Pennsylvania (BF15).

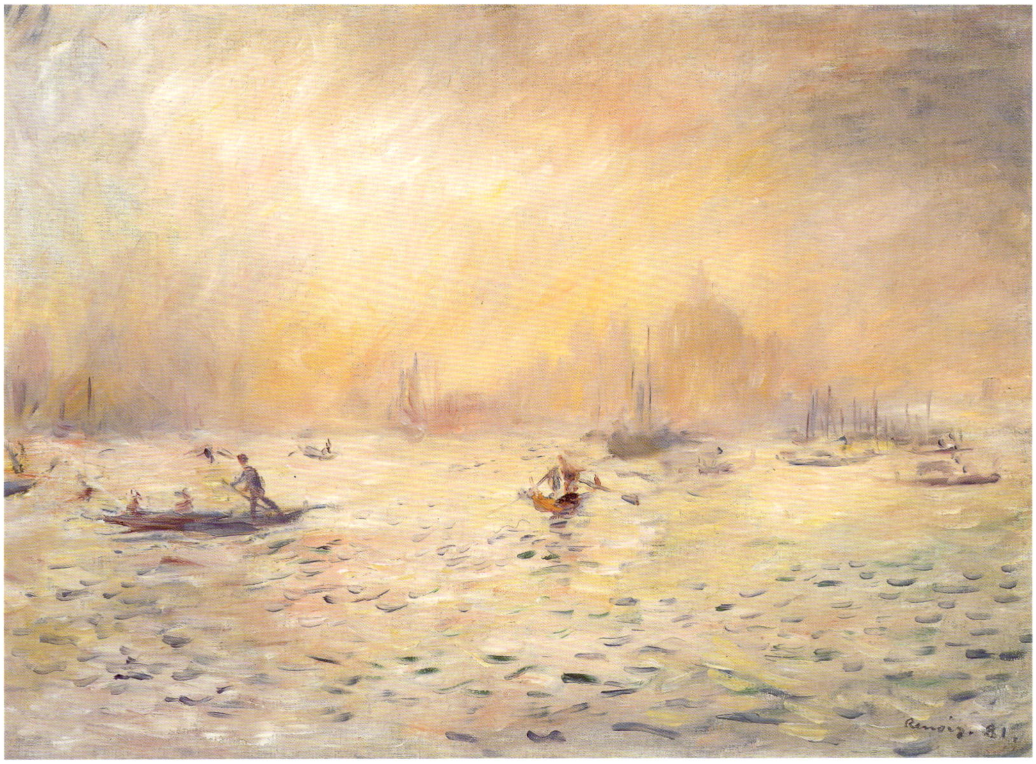

FIG. 50 *Venice, Fog,* 1881. Oil on canvas, 45.5 × 60 cm; 17⅞ × 23⅝ in. Kreeger Museum, Washington, DC (1962.11).

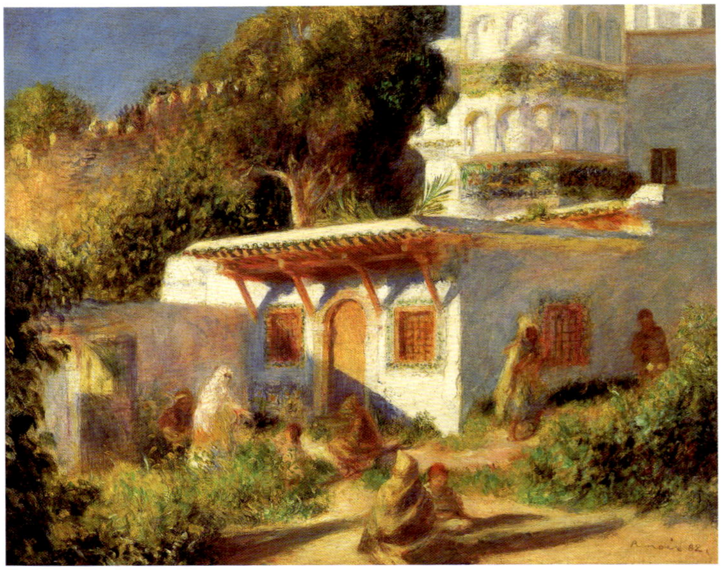

FIG. 51 *The Mosque at Algiers*, 1882. Oil on canvas, 49.5 × 67.3 cm; 19½ × 26½ in. Private collection.

which I was unable to do on my last visit'.[131] Renoir's canvases from the second Algerian stay included only one finished view, *The Mosque at Algiers* (fig. 51), a dignified close-up of the Mosque Sidi-Abd-er-Rahman, built in 1696, and already something of a cliché in the visual iconography of Algiers.[132] It was acquired by Durand-Ruel on 22 May 1882 for the considerable sum of 1,000 francs, and sold two days later for double that amount to Léon Clapisson, who would commission his wife's portrait from Renoir later that summer.[133] True to his word – '*Je veux faire le plus possible de figure*' – Renoir made several figure paintings during his second visit to Algiers, ranging from costumed genre scenes for a Parisian clientele (much appreciated by Durand-Ruel), to more experimental studies of indigenous models (held back from the dealer), in which the softer handling and caressing tonalities created a more memorable sensuality.[134]

In March 1882, as Renoir and Aline were preparing to leave L'Estaque for Algiers, Durand-Ruel showed 25 canvases by Renoir at the seventh Impressionist exhibition, including *Luncheon of the Boating Party* (exhibited as '*Un Déjeuner à Bougival*') and several recently acquired genre paintings of appealing parisiennes – *Girl with a Cat* (Sterling and Francine Clark Art Institute), previously shown at the Salon of 1880; *The Two Sisters* (Art Institute of Chicago); *A Loge at the Opera* (Sterling and Francine Clark Art Institute).[135] In a departure from previous displays of his work at the *indépendants*' exhibitions, not a single portrait by Renoir was on display; instead, ten landscapes painted during the last two years presented the artist at his most current and most experimental. Five views of the Seine at Chatou shared the company of resplendent landscapes from Algiers and Venice.

Critical reaction to Renoir's landscapes – and particularly his 'foreign' landscapes – was almost universally hostile. Even those who liked his monumental *Luncheon of the Boating Party* were at something of a loss before his scenes of 'sunny climes'. Philippe Burty, invoking Renoir's 'crisis', envisioned an artist rendered feverish by the sun;[136] Eugène Manet, while admiring a 'successful landscape of palm trees', found the views of Venice 'detestable';[137] Armand Silvestre, enraptured by the *Luncheon of the Boating Party*, dismissed the Venetian scenes as a 'sorry compromise between Ziem and Monticelli'.[138] Pissarro, who found everything Renoir painted 'admirable', labelled his Algerian views 'studies' – a curious choice of term, given that all three paintings were signed and dated – and considered them odd, 'full of pigment [*plein de pigment*]'.[139]

Renoir, monitoring the reception of his works from Algiers, received such criticism with good-natured resignation, but he rebuked Durand-Ruel for his over-eagerness in showing the most recent work, 'unsaleable' in the painter's opinion. In a letter written in mid-March 1882, Renoir told his dealer: 'I am very pleased that I did not send you my latest paintings' – referring perhaps to landscapes done at L'Estaque the month before – 'as you would have put them into the exhibition. I share Wolff's opinion, which reflects bourgeois taste in general, that you should not show my paintings until they have been bottled away for a year. In three or four years' time, Wolff will find my views of Venice quite beautiful.'[140]

Both Renoir and Durand-Ruel underestimated the degree to which the artist's recent landscapes disconcerted even the most ardent supporters of the New Painting. For the retrospective exhibition of Renoir's works the following year (1–25 April 1883), organised by Durand-Ruel and held in sumptuously decorated rented rooms on the boulevard Madeleine, some 70 works were assembled, among which several of Renoir's most masterful narrative paintings and no fewer than 21 portraits.[141] In his preface to the catalogue Duret wrote, 'Among the Impressionists, I consider Claude Monet to be the archetypal landscape painter, just as M. Renoir is the archetypal figure painter.' He had special praise for Renoir's 'grasp of woman's grace and delicacy, which has led him to excel particularly in portraits'.[142]

This 'mid-career retrospective' (to use a thoroughly anachronistic term) included 14 landscapes, the earliest of which, *The Seine at Champrosay* (cat. 36), painted in 1876 and acquired by Caillebotte, had been shown at the third Impressionist exhibition. The remaining works were much more recent (but nothing less than a year old!), and this time Renoir encouraged lenders to participate. Two landscapes painted at L'Estaque (cats. 66, 67) in February 1882, and which Renoir had left in Cézanne's possession, were sent to Paris at his request.[143] Although neither picture was mentioned in the press, in August Durand-Ruel purchased *Rocky Crags at L'Estaque* (cat. 67) – a luminous panorama of the barren ravines behind this picturesque sea-bathing resort – for the considerable sum of 1,000 francs, the most that he had paid for a landscape by Renoir, and a tacit recognition of the picture's extraordinary structure and cohesion.[144] Renoir's travels, at home and abroad, were once again well represented by landscapes painted at Chatou, Wargemont and L'Estaque, and port-of-call scenes from Italy and Algeria. But the more familiar the site, it seemed, the more incensed the review, and this was especially the case for critics well disposed towards Renoir. Philippe Burty, a long-time comrade-in-arms who had written the preface for the catalogue of the first Impressionist auction of May 1875, was even more outspoken now than he had been in his criticism of the seventh Impressionist exhibition the year before:[145]

> Renoir fails completely as a landscapist. It seems that the open air throws him off balance. He sees only patches of light, splashes of sunbeams instead of the unity that prevails in nature even when showers burst through the clouds or shafts of light dart between leaves and branches. The viewer's eye will never become accustomed to those circles of light that stain his lawns and pathways – and even appear on the faces and clothes of his figures. In nature such effects are too fleeting, and artists should not

attempt to immobilise the blinding sensation they produce. Furthermore, Renoir's rocks, hillocks, bushes and tufts of grass are no more than blurred iridescences that call to mind balls of wool strewn on the ground or heaped together in a large basket. From Naples and Venice we have studies by him that prove, once and for all, that landscape is not his province.[146]

Similar sentiments, reminiscent in tone of the earliest attacks on the Impressionists, were voiced by a young critic at the start of his career, who would later become a champion of Monet and Cézanne. 28-year-old Gustave Geffroy (1855–1926) saw in Renoir the failure of a fine figure painter who failed to 'triumph' in the 'landscape of the impression':

> His views of Naples and Algeria, his banks of the Seine all appear as more or less the same multi-coloured sketches, random notes in which nothing is logically structured, with planes lacking exactitude and tones lacking truthfulness. From my point of view, such iridescences, such illuminations, such flickerings of light may well be acceptable for Algeria and Italy, but they cause me considerable concern when used in such abundance for the sky, leaves and waters of our own suburbs. M. Renoir is at fault in wanting to squander the joys of his palette over everything he sees: he succeeds only

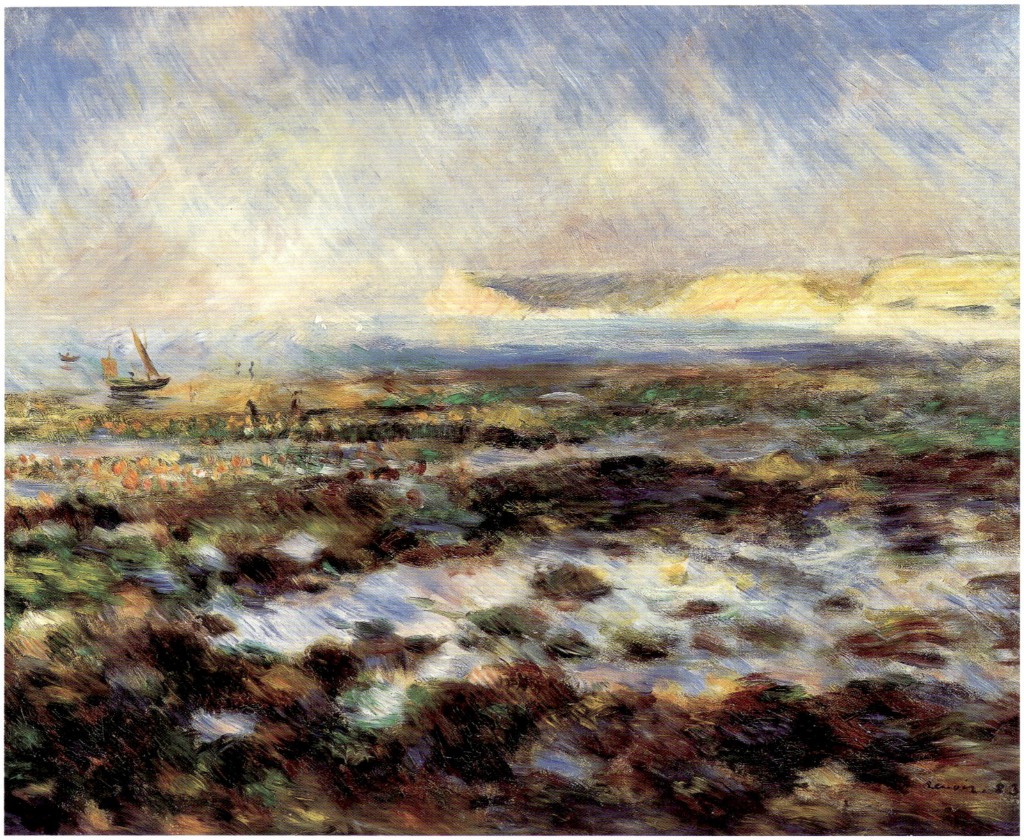

FIG. 52 *Low Tide at Yport*, 1883. Oil on canvas, 54 × 65 cm; 21¼ × 25⅝ in. Sterling and Francine Clark Art Institute, Williamstown, Massachusetts (607).

in violating the mysteries of the half-tone, and in falsifying the true colour of objects and the quality of our atmosphere.[147]

Other critics either ignored Renoir's landscapes altogether or identified them as objects of hilarity. Yet the incomprehension of partisans must have given the artist and his dealer a certain pause for thought.

In spite of self-admonitions that he had already travelled too much – 'I can't wait for winter so that I can remain in my studio. Outdoors has not been a success this year'[148] – in September 1883 Renoir added a three-week visit to his annual sojourn in Normandy. In the company of Aline and Paul Lhote, he stayed in furnished rooms that were but a short walk from the Bay of the island of Moulin Huet, its most 'famous resort for artists'.[149] As Renoir noted on 27 September, in an often-quoted letter to Durand-Ruel, he looked forward to returning 'with several canvases as well as documents for pictures to be made in Paris'.[150] Although the *Bathers* pictures for which he had made sketches in Guernsey never materialised, his experiences of the Normandy coast and the Channel Islands inspired both *At the Coast* (The Metropolitan Museum of Art, New York) and *Seated Bather* (Fogg Art Museum, Cambridge, Massachusetts), the most important figure paintings undertaken in Paris after his return.[151]

Recalling Edmond Renoir's insight – 'in not one of his works, perhaps, does he adopt the same manner of painting' – it is worth examining the group of landscapes produced in Yport and Guernsey during the summer and early autumn of 1883, in view of their remarkable variety of tonality, handling and atmospheric effects. Renoir worked on them *in situ* between 21 August and 10 October, finished them in his new studio on the rue Laval, and delivered them to Durand-Ruel on 15 December 1883, the day before he left for the Riviera.[152] The earliest in this group are a pair of coastal scenes from Yport, of which the most spectacular, *Low Tide at Yport* (fig. 52), was long thought to show the sea at Guernsey.[153] Aglow with iridescent tones of orange and purple, this assured landscape is admirably constructed: parallel hatchings in the sky recede before the rocky beach, which dominates both foreground and middle-ground. Far out at sea, tiny sailboats bob in the wind; close up, pools of water flecked with emerald green and sky-blue glisten among the seaweed and rocks that seem to rest at the viewer's feet.[154]

Crossing the Channel, *View at Guernsey* (fig. 53), *Fog on Guernsey* (cat. 70) and *The Bay of Moulin Huet through the Trees* (private collection) are painted in a different language altogether, devised in and for a different place. The brushwork is open, and delicate dabs and dashes of colour flicker against an

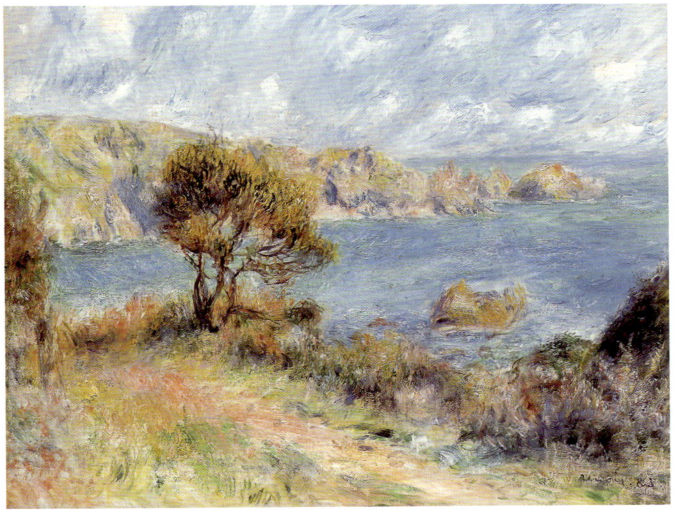

FIG. 53 *View at Guernsey*, 1883. Oil on canvas, 46 × 55.9 cm; 18⅛ × 22 in. Sterling and Francine Clark Art Institute, Williamstown, Massachusetts (1955.601).

abundance of white pigment. The sense of air and wind in these unpopulated scenes is palpable. *Hills around the Bay of Moulin Huet* (cat. 69) is a more structured, densely worked view, in which Renoir's meticulous handiwork and interlocking forms recall the tightly-knit hills and ravines of L'Estaque that he painted the year before. Quite different again is the unfinished *Marine, Guernsey* (fig. 54), in which unblended colours and summary notations capture Renoir's initial responses to the motif, and suggest the degree of elaboration required before he was ready to sign and date his landscapes.[155]

During the summer and winter of 1883, Renoir continued to re-evaluate the Impressionist idiom that rendered form through the dissolving lens of ambient light. He undertook 'investigations' that fostered a gradually emerging classicism (Renoir's '*nouvelle manière*') – one that sought structure and solidity above all, but retained luminosity and colouristic richness. Such investigations depressed him – 'I'm in a slump [*Je suis dans le marasme*]' is a phrase that reappears in his correspondence – and in December 1883 Berard spoke of Renoir experiencing '*une crise de découragement*'.[156] Symptomatic of this distress, perhaps, was the decision to travel with Monet to the Riviera – a trip undertaken at Renoir's urging as a prelude to a future, extended campaign of landscape painting.[157] As Renoir informed Durand-Ruel: 'We have decided that it is preferable to study the countryside carefully so that when we return we will know where to stop'.[158] His 'poor palette', he complained, was not up to the 'extraordinary colours' of the Mediterranean coast, and 'the sea's beautiful hues turn heavy on our canvases. But it is more for seeing than for working that I have

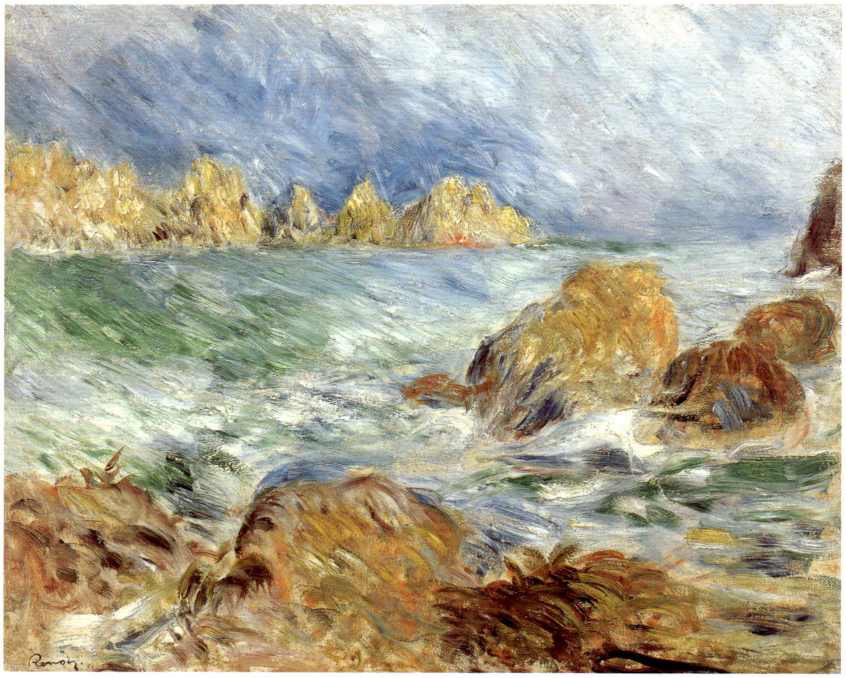

FIG. 54 *Marine, Guernsey*, 1883. Oil on canvas, 46 × 56cm; 18⅛ × 22 in. Musée d'Orsay, Paris (RF 1973-22).

come'.[159] Indeed, while Renoir could not refrain from putting paint to canvas, he was in no hurry to part with the works he produced. In keeping with his belief that his paintings should be bottled for a year – and acknowledging that he also required time in his studio, away from the motif, to transform his 'documents' into paintings – it was only in December 1884 that he sold two 'Menton landscapes' to Durand-Ruel, dating at least one of them from the previous year (cat. 72).[160]

Indicative of Renoir's turmoil at this time was his inability to resolve the different requirements of working on site and in the studio, of painting from the model in nature and refining the experiential through more rigorous analysis. Thus evolved the 'crisis of Impressionism' to which Vollard devoted a chapter in his biography of Renoir written at the end of the artist's life.[161] In January 1884, back home and as yet unaware that Monet was planning to travel to Bordighera without him, Renoir lamented his stature as a figure painter ('*Mais je suis peintre de figures! Hélas!*'), 'stuck in Paris, where I am thoroughly fed up, running after the [perfect] model that cannot be found'.[162] Preoccupied by his 'investigations' and labouring on *Children's Afternoon at Wargemont* (Nationalgalerie, Berlin) – a masterpiece of polychromy that he would finish in the summer of 1884 – Renoir, for the first time, came to question his calling.[163] Almost on a whim (and with little money in his pocket) he travelled to La Rochelle, inspired by Corot's radiant landscape of the port painted in 1851 (Yale University Art Gallery, New Haven): 'The last picture by Corot that I saw made me want to see this port more than anything.' Bad weather prevented him painting a view of the town, but his experience of the rainy port conjured vivid memories of Corot's picture, its half-remembered tonalities impressing him all the more.[164]

Memory and recollection; the guidance of the past; nature mediated, its particularities expunged ('those small details which extinguish the sun instead of kindling it') – the visit to La Rochelle did indeed signal the end of Renoir's Impressionism, even if the artist was at first unaware of its consequences:

> This is the first trip that has been of any use to me. Precisely because the weather is so bad, it has enabled me to think and to see, rather than to do any real work. I realise that I have lost a great deal by confining myself to the four square metres of my studio. Had I followed Monet's example, I would have been ten years further ahead.[165]

NOTES

I am particularly grateful to Judy Sund for her meticulous reading of this essay, to which she has made numerous improvements. Thanks are also due to Alan Wintermute and John Zarobell. For their assistance with research, it is a pleasure to acknowledge Mary Lydecker, Margaret Iacono, Nelda Damiano, and Robert McDonald Parker.

For the essay title see Signac 1978, p. 33: '. . . un maximum de luminosité, de coloration, et d'harmonie'. The letter quoted in the first of the opening quotations is in the Tabarant collection, Pierpont Morgan Library, New York. For the second quotation, see Baudot 1949, p. 58; for the third, Rouart 1951, p. 170.

1 Fezzi 1985 catalogues 568 works between 1861 and 1883, 131 of which are landscapes. In the absence of the volume of the late François Daulte's catalogue raisonné devoted to Renoir's landscapes, these figures are a most approximate guide at best.

2 The term is coined by Pissarro in a letter to Duret, informing him of the reaction of his fellow citizens in Pontoise to the Hoschedé sale of January 1874, in which one of his landscapes fetched 950 francs: '*Un Monsieur a même dit que c'était étonnant pour un paysage pur*'; Bailly-Herzberg 1980, *Correspondance*, I, p. 90.

3 Duret 1998, p. 66; from his preface to the catalogue of the exhibition *Le Peintre Claude Monet*, held at the gallery of *La Vie Moderne* in June 1880.

4 For recent general introductions to the Impressionist landscape that have sought to refine and extend Rewald's pioneering study, see Herbert 1988, esp. pp. 195–264, and House 2004. On Renoir's landscapes until 1883, Schneider 1985.

5 Rivière 1921, p. 81.

6 Du Camp 1859; Castagnary 1892, p. 71, cited in Loyrette and Tinterow 1994, p. 15.

7 Adams 1994, esp. ch. 5; Loyrette and Tinterow 1994, sections 3, 5 and 8.

8 See also Duret 1998, p. 30: '*Le gloire de l'école moderne est surtout dans la manière dont les peintres qui la composent ont su voir et rendre la nature. C'est dans la donnée naturaliste que se sont révélés tant de maîtres de premier ordre, les Rousseau, Corot, Troyon, Millet. C'est dans cette branche particulière de l'art que l'école moderne a montré le plus de grandeur*'; 'Le Salon', *L'Electeur libre*, 12 May 1870.

9 Rewald 1973, pp. 71–6, although it has long been recognised that he overstated the notion of a pioneering band of brothers. Renoir, a year ahead of Monet and Bazille, was absent from Gleyre's studio on Monet's arrival in the winter of 1862, and is not recorded as painting at Chailly with him and Bazille the following spring. Only after the winter of 1866 does Renoir seem to have worked occasionally in tandem with Monet, Bazille and Sisley.

10 Between 1854 and 1858 Renoir worked as an apprentice to a porcelain painter in the Marais, and '*sa grande ambition était d'entrer à la manufacture de Sèvres*'; Rivière 1921, p. 6. Adams (1994, p. 59) has noted that 'the careers of many Barbizon painters began in the ateliers of porcelain manufacturers', citing as examples Troyon, Dupré, Cabat and Diaz.

11 In 1895 Renoir told Julie Manet that as a young man working in the forest of Fontainebleau: '*Il était logé pour 50 sous et Diaz qui se trouvait avec lui vendait ses tableaux comme des Rousseau. Il en faisait une huitaine par jour*'; Manet 1979, p. 66, 19 September 1895. A similar anecdote is recounted by Arsène Alexandre (1892, p. 12). Early on Renoir had been supported by a dealer '*qui lui prenait de bitumineux payages, en échange des couleurs, de toiles, et de maigres sommes, suffisantes pourtant pour payer le séjour en campagne*'. The dealer in question may have been Diaz's colourman and promoter, Armand-Auguste Deforge (see note 30).

12 Renoir 1879: '*C'est là où mon frère rencontra Courbet, qui était l'idole des jeunes peintres.*' Morel (1883) makes the interesting observation that early on Renoir followed Diaz as a genre painter as well as a landscapist: '*A cette époque Renoir faisait du Diaz. On pourrait retrouver des toiles qu'il a signées où figurent jusqu'à trois cents personnages . . . De là des empâtements de bitume, des touches noires près de tonalités tendres qui rappellent la manière du peintre des nymphes et des baigneuses des sous bois.*' Renoir told Vollard (1918, p. 20) that the one-legged Diaz was his '*grand homme*', who, having scared off a group of passers-by heckling him as he painted, advised the young artist to lighten his palette ('*Pourquoi diable, peignez-vous donc si noir?*').

13 Their Paris views can be dated precisely to May 1867: '*Renoir et moi travaillons toujours à nos vues de Paris*'; Monet to Bazille, 20 May 1867; Wildenstein 1974–91, I, no. 423. They are of different motifs since Renoir, unlike Monet, had not applied for permission to paint his view from within the Louvre. The two painters worked together on the same site for the first time at La Grenouillère in August and September 1869.

14 Renoir first enrolled as a copyist at the Louvre on 24 January 1860, on the recommendation of Abel Terral (1811–1886), a history painter who had been a student of Paul Delaroche. He renewed his card annually until June 1864: see Archives des Musées du Louvre, *LL 16. It was Gleyre who provided him with an introduction to the Cabinet des Estampes of the Bibliothèque nationale on 8 November 1861, probably shortly after Renoir entered his atelier: B.N., Autographes, Demandes de cartes, Y. 118. Details of Renoir's participation in the Ecole's drawing competitions, the last of which took place on 5 April 1864, are to be found in the excellent chronology in House and Distel 1985, pp. 294–5.

15 'No matter how sceptical or independent the critic, each had assimilated the hierarchy of subjects ordained by the state's art establishment, which gave pre-eminence to the depiction of noble subjects in a noble style'; Loyrette and Tinterow 1994, p. 55. While the hierarchy of the genres may have been respected by Manet, Degas and Renoir, traditional terminology was not; Manet commented that to be called a history painter '[*était*] *la plus sanglante injure que l'on pût adresser à un artiste*'; Proust 1897, p. 21.

16 Submitted as '*Paysage avec deux figures*', Renoir's large composition of two female figures in a landscape – one seated and fully clothed, the other naked – was inspired by Courbet's *Women bathing* of 1853

(Musée Fabre, Montpellier). Renoir's rejected Salon picture, which he later cut into pieces, is the enormous painting in a gold frame that towers over the artists in Bazille's *Studio in the rue Condamine 1870* (Musée d'Orsay, Paris): see House and Distel 1985, pp. 179–80, and Le Coeur 1998.

17 '*L'autre a été fait à Marlotte en 15 jours, il appelle cela une pochade*', *Cahiers d'aujourd'hui*, 1921; as a candidate for the Salon it is unlikely to have been too small or sketchy. As Marie Le Coeur explained to her brother on 6 April 1866 (*ibidem*), Renoir '*ne l'a envoyé à l'exposition que parce qu'il en avait un autre qui avait plus de valeur, sans cela il en aurait trouvé qu'il ne fallait pas l'exposer*'.

18 House 2004, p. 6; Tabarant (1947, p. 175) noted that Renoir was '*le mieux placé et Manet lui-même en avait décidait ainsi*'. Renoir returned the compliment the following year with his *Still Life* of 1871 (Museum of Fine Arts, Houston), in which each item pays homage to the painter of *Olympia* and the *Portrait of Zola*; see Faison 1973.

19 Bailey 1997, pp. 122–32.

20 Mallarmé, 'The Impressionists and Edouard Manet' (1876), in Moffett 1986, p. 30.

21 The abandonment of traditional chiaroscuro and reliance on colouristic modelling to replicate the effects of daylight were by far and away the most radical of the Impressionists' formal innovations. As Cézanne noted to Pissarro in June 1874 à propos of a conversation he had had with the director of his local museum: '*Lorsque je lui disais . . . que vous remplaciez par l'étude des tons le modelé . . . et que je tâchais de lui faire comprendre sur nature, il fermait les yeux et tournait le dos*'; cited in House 2004, p. 149.

22 Cooper 1959, Le Coeur 1996. Renoir's frequent stays at Le Coeur's house on the rue de la Cheminée Blanche (the current 30 rue Delort) began in May 1865; in August 1866 he and Sisley spent two weeks in Berck with the Le Coeur family. In April 1868 Renoir was commissioned by Charles Le Coeur to present sketches for the decoration of the Hôtel Bibesco, a *chantier* upon which he would be involved, intermittently, until early 1872. In August 1868 Renoir and Jules Le Coeur established temporary residence in Ville d'Avray with their mistresses, Lise and Clémence Tréhot, both in the final stages of pregnancy. Renoir's first illegitimate child by Lise, Pierre Tréhot (whose paternity he did not recognise), was born at 38 rue de St-Cloud on 4 September 1868, the same day as Françoise Le Coeur, Jules's daughter by Clémence; see Marc Le Coeur's excellent essay in São Paulo 2002, pp. 203–5.

23 Monet to Durand-Ruel, 16 December 1883; Wildenstein 1974–91, II, p. 232.

24 For Manet's unfinished panorama, see Loyrette and Tinterow 1994, pp. 293, 412–13. Renoir told Vollard (1919, p. 38) that the Exposition Universelle of 1867 had provided him with '*le sujet d'une étude de plein air que je terminai en 1868. Ce tableau, si peu audacieux pourtant, fut jugé d'une hardiesse inacceptable. Il resta, pendant de longues années, roulé dans un coin, à Louveciennes, où habitait ma famille*'. The juxtaposition of paintings representing town and country would have been an appropriate Salon submission for a young *actualiste*.

25 '*J'ai bien un rêve, un tableau, les bains de la Grenouillère pour lequel j'ai fait quelques mauvaises pochades, mais c'est un rêve*': Monet to Bazille, 25 September 1869; Wildenstein 1974–91, I, no. 427.

26 Herbert 1988, p. 219. As noted in House and Distel 1985, p. 192, the paintings now in Moscow and Stockholm (cats. 5, 6) were both in the possession of Renoir's brother, Edmond, and were probably 'signed' when he divested himself of them before 1903. Brettell (2000, p. 156) is in error when he argues that the 'signatures at the base of these paintings, applied so confidently and so legibly' served to show that they were considered to be finished works.

27 Le Coeur 1996a, p. 68. At Pau, Renoir exhibited a '*Baigneuses* (*paysage*)' valued at 600 francs; *La Mare aux Fées* (fig. 32), 800 francs; and '*Nymphe se mirant dans l'eau*', valued at 200 francs (see Daulte 1971, no. 3, where the picture is dated four years too early, to 1860).

28 '*Renoir a vendu hier un tableau qu'il rapportait – 500 f., c'est gentil, une partie de bateau au bord de la forêt . . . Hier Jules a vu Mr . . . un grand banquier allemand, celui qui a acheté le tableau de Renoir*'; letter from Louise Le Coeur to Marie Fouqué, 15 August 1866, Paris, private collection, partially cited in Le Coeur 2002, p. 220, note 90. *La Mare aux Fées* reappeared most recently at Christie's, New York, 11 May 1995, lot 105.

29 Silvestre 1873. Durand-Ruel's three-volume *Recueil* included five works by Pissarro, four by Monet and three by Sisley. The dealer acquired 25 landscapes from Sisley in 1872 and 29 the following year; from Monet he bought 29 paintings in 1872 and 34 in 1873; see Godfroy 1992, p. 50, and Stuckey 1995, pp. 196–8.

30 On 9 December 1865 Le Coeur noted to his mother: '*Si tu vois Renoir, parle-lui de l'exposition de Pau, il y pourrait mettre son tableau de l'année dernière . . . ainsi que son dernier qui est chez Deforge*'; Le Coeur 1996, p. 31, no. 6. On Deforge and his associate Carpentier, who operated from 1865 as Carpentier-Deforge, see Davenport 1983 and Distel 1990, p. 33. Kelly (1999, p. 420) notes that Deforge was the first dealer to acquire works by Rousseau; in the 1869 Salon *livret* Pissarro gave his address as 'Carpentier, 8 Bd Montmartre': Bailly-Herzberg 1980, *Correspondance*, I, p. 62. Carpentier died at his home on 37 rue de Moscou, in the 8th arrondissement, on 5 May 1883, aged 53, see Archives de Paris, Actes de décès, 5 Mi 3/1199.

31 In October 1869 Renoir informed Bazille: '*J'ai exposé Lise et Sisley chez Carpentier. Je vais tâcher de lui coller pour une centaine de francs*'; Poulain 1932, p. 156. In the Archives du Louvre is a receipt of 1873 from 'M. Carpentier Deforges, 62 rue Legendre, Batignolles' for Renoir's '*Amazone*' (*Riding in the Bois de Boulogne*) and '*Femmes en Algériennes*' (*Parisian Women in Algerian Dress*), large Salon paintings being stored in the firm's warehouse.

32 Archives Durand-Ruel, stockbook 1872, no. 1131, *Vue de Paris, Pont des Arts*, March 1872, 200 francs; the painting was sent to London on 8 October 1872 and returned, unsold, on 10 March 1873.

33 Letters of 22 April 1873 and 7 May 1873; Wildenstein 1974–91, I, p. 438.

34 On Renoir's breach with the Le Coeurs, after his love letter to the 15-year-old Marie was intercepted by her father Charles, see, most recently, São Paulo 2002, p. 214.

35 Bailey 1997, pp. 122–6.

36 Rewald 1973, pp. 284–6; Wildenstein 1974–91, I, no. 289.

37 Rewald 1986, pp. 200–1, 394–5.

38 As Zola noted of the second Impressionist exhibition: '*Renoir est un peintre se spécialisant dans les figures humaines . . . On dirait un Rubens éclairé par le soleil brillant de Vélasquez*'; Zola. *Ecrits sur l'art*, ed. by J-P Leduc Adine, Paris 1991, p. 354 ('Lettres de Paris', *Le Messager de l'Europe*, June 1876).

39 Distel (1993, p. 40) reproduces a page from a lost annotated catalogue of the first Impressionist exhibition, where Renoir's *Harvesters* is noted as '*vendu par la société à M. Hartmann*'. On Hartmann's career see Devriès and Lesure 1988, II, pp. 210–13. The *Portrait of Madame Hartmann* (Daulte 1971, no. 112) is most clearly reproduced in Brenneman 2002, p. 49.

40 Mallarmé, 'The Impressionists and Édouard Manet', in Moffett 1986, p. 29.

41 Renoir 1879: '*dans aucun de ses ouvrages, peut-être, on ne retrouve la même façon de procéder*'.

42 Shackelford and Wissman 2002, pp. 159, 267; Bailey 1997, pp. 130–1. *Woman with a Parasol* may also be associated with the '*Femme et enfant*' belonging to Victor Poupin and exhibited as no. 209 at the second Impressionist exhibition of April 1876; see Moffett 1986, p. 164.

43 Bodelsen 1968; traditionally, landscapists had taken the lead in organizing auctions of their own paintings, sketches and drawings, Diaz having done so annually between 1864 and his death in 1876; see Kelly 1999.

44 Bodelsen 1968, p. 335, p.v. 20, 32. From annotations in the Frick Art Reference Library's *Catalogue des Tableaux et aquarelles*, Hôtel Drouot, 24 March 1875, we know that Renoir's *Femme au chien noir* (Clore collection) elicited '*grande hilarité*' and that *La Source* (Barnes Foundation, Merion, PA) was greeted with '*applaudissements*'.

45 '*Tous les peintres chevalus étaient là au grand complet, et c'était au milieu de cris et de vociférations que M. Pillet a procédé à la vente*'; *Le Figaro*, 26 March 1875; *La République française* (26 March 1875) noted that interruptions to the sale had been '*le mot d'ordre des ateliers*'. This is confirmed in Morel 1883, who notes that '*la salle était littéralement envahi par les artistes protestants. Il y en avait dans les couloirs, dans l'escalier, dans la cour, sur les trottoirs extérieurs*'.

46 Bodelsen 1968, p. 335, p.v. 9; *L'Institut au Quai Malaquais* is thoroughly documented in Tajan, 12 June 2003, no. 5.

47 House 1994, pp. 62–3; redated to 1875 in House 1997, p. 73. *Pêcheur à la ligne* is reproduced in colour in Néret 2001, p. 81.

48 Bodelsen 1968, p. 335, p.v. 44; Reinhard-Felice 2003, pp. 436–7, where the painting's possible appearance in the auction of 1875 is not recorded.

49 Fezzi 1985, no. 299; Stevens 1984, pp. 292–3; Néret 2001, p. 120. In the *Catalogue sommaire* 1990, II, p. 393, the painting is dated to '*vers 1875?*'

50 Bodelsen 1968, p. 336, p. v. 47. The identification was first proposed in D'Ayala Valva 2005, pp. 86–7, and more tentatively in House 2004, pp. 153, 231. Gabriel Thomas, who also acquired Morisot's pastel *Blanche* for 255 francs, is listed in the *procès-verbal* as living at 119 rue de la Tour (Bodelsen 1968, p. 335, p. v. 29); on his patronage of Morisot, see Stuckey and Scott 1987, pp. 64, 181.

51 But is Renoir's handling of these staffage figures really 'a blatant affront to any notion of female elegance and propriety' as House (2004, p. 154) would have us believe?

52 Schneider (1985, p. 51) and House (2004, p. 155) date it to *c.*1873; Monneret (1989, pp. 49–50) and D'Ayala Valva (2005, pp. 86–7) to *c.*1874.

53 Zola 1991, p. 315 'Lettre de Paris', *Le Sémaphore de Marseille*, 30 April 1876.

54 For Renoir at Chatou, see Herbert 1988, pp. 246–54, and Rathbone 1996. The earliest work at this site is *The Seine at Chatou*, 1874, in the Reves Collection at the Dallas Museum of Art; see Brettell 1995, pp. 56–7. In September 1880 Renoir described Chatou to de Bellio as '*l'endroit le plus joli des alentours de Paris*'; *Autographes et documents historiques*, Librairie Henry Saffroy, Paris, June 1983, no. 118.

55 House and Distel 1985, p. 216; Herbert 1988, pp. 246–7; Néret 2001, p. 130; D'Ayala Valva 2005, p. 120.

56 Berson 1996, I, p. 103; II, pp. 44–5; see also Rathbone 1996, p. 32, and Druick 1997, pp. 26–7.

57 Wattenmaker 1993, p. 54, where the picture is dated to *c.*1879.

58 House and Distel 1985, p. 216; Bomford 1990, pp. 172–5.

59 The redating of the National Gallery's *The Skiff (La Yole)* to 1875 was first proposed in Rathbone 1996, p. 32, plate 41.

60 Bodelsen 1968, p. 340; Distel 1990, pp. 101–4; Adriani 1996, pp. 146–7.

61 Distel 1990, pp. 132–3; Bailey 1997, pp. 32–5.

62 On Renoir's immersion in Montmartre and the genesis of the *Moulin de la Galette*, see, most recently, Collins 2001.

63 Rivière in Berson 1996, I, p. 180. Rivière's article appeared on 6 April 1877 in the short-lived weekly *l'Impressionniste*, a review that he launched in collaboration with Renoir.

64 The painting was listed in Caillebotte's 'Tableaux légués à l'Etat' (in his *inventaire après décès* of 8 March 1894) as '*Coin de l'ancienne place St-Georges*'; see Anne Distel's illustrated checklist of the donation in *Caillebotte* 1994, pp. 31, 65.

65 Rivière, 'L'exposition des Impressionnistes', *l'Impressionniste*, 6 April 1877; in Berson 1996, I, p. 180.

66 First proposed in Herbert 1988, pp. 188, 312, note 52, and in the excellent entry in Gerstein 1989, p. 164.

67 Berson 1996, I, p. 180.

68 House and Distel 1985, pp. 209–10; see also Willsdon 2004, p. 163.

69 Rivière 1921, p. 129; Renoir 1879: '*Peint-il le Moulin de la Galette? Il va s'y installer pendant six mois.*' Vollard (1919, pp. 72, 75) complicated the matter by claiming that Renoir rented his second Parisian residence in the spring of 1875, after selling *Mother and Children* for the princely sum of 1,200 francs. (The Frick's *Promenade*, however, was probably painted in autumn 1875, before being shown at the second Impressionist exhibition in April 1876.)

70 Rivière 1921, p. 130.

71 The identification of these two figures has presented certain difficulties: see House and Distel 1985, p. 209; Gerstein 1989, p. 164. It should be noted that the same two figures in the garden reappear in the background of the tiny panel *Jeune femme assise dans un jardin* (Paris, Musée d'Orsay; Daulte 1971, no. 140), a genre scene that must date from 1876 as well.

72 The painting most recently appeared at Sotheby's, New York, 15 May 1984, lot 6.

73 For *Nini in the Garden* and its related pictures, see Bailey and Rishel 1989, pp. 32, 33, and House 2004, p. 167, for the related *Young Woman on a Bench*, there dated *c.*1876.

74 Adriani 1996, pp. 150–3.

75 Bernadille, 'L'exposition des Impressionnistes', *Le Français*, 13 April 1877, and Descubes, *Gazette des lettres, des sciences et des arts*, in Berson 1996, I, pp. 130, 144.

76 House 2004, pp. 141–2. Discussing Renoir's participation in the second Impressionist exhibition of 1876, Alexandre (1892, p. 18) noted that '*l'on eut acquis la conviction que la politique était dans l'affaire, et qu'il était impossible d'aimer la peinture claire sans avoir été pour le moins colonel de la Commune*'.

77 House 1994, pp. 72–3, where the picture is correctly redated to *c.*1877. *In the Woods* might possibly be associated with one of the two landscapes that Renoir put up for sale in the second Impressionist auction; see *Catalogue. 45 Tableaux par MM Caillebotte Pissarro Renoir Sisley*, Paris, 28 May 1877, nos. 29, '*Paysage. Automne*', and 30, '*Paysage. Printemps*'. The absence of dimensions in the catalogue (for which no annotated copy exists) makes a firm identification impossible.

78 '*Renoir, au contraire de Monet, Sisley et Pissarro, est avant tout un peintre de figures, le paysage ne joue dans son oeuvre qu'un rôle accessoire*'; Duret 1998, p. 58.

79 de Lora, 'L'Exposition des Impressionnistes', *Le Gaulois*, 10 April 1877, in Berson 1996, I, p. 162.

80 Bailey 1997, pp. 6–8.

81 Duret 1924, p. 70. On Deudon, see Distel 1989.

82 Bailey 1997, p. 13, quoting a comment made by Philippe Burty in his review of the Salon of 1879.

83 Renoir to Berthe Morisot, September 1892; Rouart 1951, p. 170.

84 Letter from Renoir to Duret, 15 October 1878, in Pierpont Morgan Library, New York, Tabarant collection.

85 Blanche 1937, pp. 34–6; Berard 1956; Bailey 1997, pp. 34–8. Oscar Wilde, who settled in Berneval on his release from Reading prison in May 1897, described it as 'a tiny place consisting of a hotel and about 20 chalets; the people who come here are *des bons bourgeois* as far as I can see. The sea has a lovely beach, to which one descends through a small ravine, and the land is full of trees and flowers, quite a bit like Surrey, so green and shady'; Wilde to Blacker, 12 July 1897, in Holland and Hart-Davis 2000, p. 911.

86 For *Musselfishers at Berneval*, see White 1984, pp. 86–97, and Wattenmaker 1993, p. 28. On Monet's Normandy landscapes and their calculated appeal as 'vacationer's pictures' see Herbert 1994; and for Dieppe's long history as a fashionable coastal resort popular with artists, Willett 1992.

87 Blanche 1931, p. 70: '*Il faisait poser des enfants des pêcheurs, en plein air; de ces blondins à la peau rose, mais hâlée, qui ont l'air de petits Norvégiens.*' Blanche (1937, p. 36) specified that Renoir posed his models 'not on the sea-shore – but in the park at Wargemont'.

88 Blanche 1921, p. 35: '*J'ai observé Renoir les 'tricotant' avec des pinceaux de martre, sur une toile blanche au plâtre.*'

89 Blanche 1931, p. 71.

90 For an analysis of Renoir's palette at this time, with its varieties of yellows, rose madder, and viridian green, see the list that he may have drawn up for Jacques-Emile Blanche's use reproduced in White 1984, p. 94.

91 Blanche 1921, p. 36.

92 With train travel in mind, Duranty (in *La Nouvelle peinture*, 1876) had urged landscapists to make more authentic views: 'Everyone has crossed 70 miles of countryside in the middle of summer and seen how the hillsides, meadows and fields disappear, as it were, into a single luminous reflection that they share with the sky . . . For the first time painters understand and reproduce these phenomena, or try to'; quoted in Moffett 1986, p. 43.

93 See the fine analysis in House 1995, pp. 250–1.

94 Wilde to Ross, 31 May 1897; Holland and Hart-Davis 2000, p. 868.

95 Brettell 2000, pp. 186–7.

96 Bailey 1997, pp. 190–7, 311: as Renoir noted to Berard that autumn, '*J'ai fait un four fort. Durand n'est pas je crois très content des siens.*'

97 Blanche 1949, p. 41.

98 *Ibidem*, p. 152.

99 Renoir sent Aline money in Chatou and Paris, advised her not to work too hard ('*ne t'éreinte donc pas dans cet atelier inutilement*'), and complains that the weather in Normandy is poor and his models '*horrible*'; see *Pierre Auguste Renoir, 1841–1919, Personal Artifacts and Archives Collection*, Hantman's, 14 May 2005, lots 23, 52, 57.

100 Rathbone 1996.

101 Renoir to Berard, September 1880; Berard 1968, p. 54.

102 Bailey 1997, pp. 186–9.

103 Renoir to Duret, 18 April 1881; Florisoone 1938, p. 40.

104 For Renoir's travels see White 1969, House 1988 and Benjamin 2003.

105 Invited to London by Duret, Renoir had started to learn English; in March 1881 he explained from Algiers that his curiosity to see '*ce qui c'était le pays du soleil*' had preempted the trip to London: Braun 1932, p. 11; from Chatou, on 18 April, he informed Duret that he had charged Whistler with explaining '*les milles raisons qui me font retarder mon voyage peut-être à l'année prochaine*'; Florisoone 1938, p. 40.

106 On Renoir in Yport, see Wattenmaker 1993, pp. 60–3 (entry by Christopher Riopelle). From his lodgings at the *maison* Aubourg, rue de l'Eglise, Renoir wrote to Aline: '*Il y a des jolies choses dans ce pays . . . J'ai presque envie d'y passer avec toi quelque temps, il y a des modèles, des enfants blonds, assez curieux, qui poseraient pour dix sous*'; see *Pierre Auguste Renoir, 1841–1919, Personal Artifacts and Archives Collection*, Hantman's, 14 May 2005, lot 50.

107 Archives Durand-Ruel, Journal 1880, 30 November 1880, purchased from M. Dubourg, '*Enfants des Pêcheurs*', 2,500 fr; Journal 1881, 3 January 1881, purchased from Renoir, '*Jeune fille au chat*', 2,500 francs; 14 February 1881, purchased from Renoir, '*Déjeuner champêtre*', 6,000 francs. This painting was sold immediately to a business associate, the banker Ernest Balensi, who returned it to Durand-Ruel at the end of the year.

108 Bailly-Herzberg 1980, I, p. 142, 4 January 1881.

109 '*Je n'ai pas voulu retarder cette petite fête dont je ne serais plus capable de faire les frais plus tard, c'est déjà très dur . . . quand même les frais énormes que je fais ne me feraient pas finir mon tableau*'; Renoir to Berard, September 1880; Berard 1968, p. 54.

110 '*Surtout pas de tableaux, des portraits*'; Renoir to Berard, March 1882. See Renoir's anguished correspondence

with Paul Berard over his participation in the Salon of 1882, in Bailey 1997, pp. 344–5.

111 Godfroy 1995, I, p. 30, for the letter written on Renoir's sick bed in L'Estaque and sent to Durand-Ruel by his brother Edmond.

112 Godfroy 1995, I, p. 27.

113 '*J'ai fini par ne plus voir que les grandes harmonies sans plus me préoccuper de petits détails qui éteignent le soleil au lieu de l'enflammer*'; Renoir to Madame Charpentier, L'Estaque, January 1882; Florisoone 1938, p. 36.

114 Bailey 1997, pp. 202–33. *In the Rosegarden* appeared at Sotheby's, New York, 6 May 2003, no. 18, and is now in The Wynn Collection, Las Vegas.

115 Berard to Deudon, 12 December 1883; Distel 1989, p. 62.

116 The most rigorous study of Renoir's sites and motifs as a 'port-of-call painter' is Benjamin 2003; Renoir's (predictable) inclination for the locally celebrated views in Guernsey and Monte Carlo has been studied in House 1988 and Robinson 1983 (entry by Lisa Simpson).

117 Renoir to Duret, from Algiers, 4 March 1881; Braun 1932, p. 11.

118 Berard 1968, p. 5.

119 Archives Durand-Ruel, Journal 1881, 7 April 1881, no. 954, '*Route de Bermandreys*' (*sic*), 200 ff; no. 955, '*Champs de bananiers*', 200 ff; no. 952, '*Jardin Desaix*' (*sic*), 700 ff.

12c Benjamin 2003, pp. 58–60.

121 Archives Durand-Ruel, Journal 1888, 14 December 1888, D 6636, deposited by Renoir as '*Escalier d'une mosqueé*'; Journal 1892, 3 February 1892, no. 1993, '*Mosquée*', purchased for 500 francs; sold to Monet on 31 January 1900.

122 Renoir to Deudon, Venice, November 1881, Schneider 1945, p. 97; Renoir to Madame Charpentier, Venice, November 1881, Florisoone 1938, p. 36.

123 Renoir to Deudon, Venice, November 1881, Schneider 1945, p. 96; '*Allez voir le Musée de Naples. Pas les peintures à l'huile, mais les fresques. Passez-y votre vie*': Renoir to Deudon, Monaco, December 1883, *ibidem*, p. 98.

124 Renoir to Durand-Ruel, Naples, 21 November 1881; Godfroy 1995, I, p. 15.

125 Renoir to Deudon, Naples, November 1881; *ibidem*, p. 97.

126 House and Distel 1985, p. 234.

127 Archives Durand-Ruel, Journal 1882, 12 May 1882, no. 2109, *Vue de Venise, Grand Canal*, 500 ff; no. 2110, *Vue de Venise*, 500 ff; 22 May 1882, no. 2390, *Naples*, 700 ff; no. 2391, *Naples*, 700 ff; no. 2392, *Sorrente, Capo di monte*, 600 ff; 25 May 1882, no. 2397, *Campagne en Calabre*, 400 ff; no. 2400, *Marine à Capri*, 300 ff.

128 *Ibidem*, Journal 1882, 22 May 1882, no. 2389, *La Soeur aînée*, 2500 ff; on this picture see Wattenmaker 1993, pp. 56–58 (entry by Christopher Riopelle).

129 Letter from Renoir to Berard, Naples, 26 November 1881; Vente Hôtel Drouot, Rive Gauche, 16 February 1979, lot 71.

130 Benjamin (2003, pp. 42, 150 note 6) has established that Renoir and Charigot crossed the Mediterranean on the 95-metre-long steamer *Moeris* (on which Gautier had travelled to Egypt in 1870). On 11 March 1882 the local newspaper, *L'Akhbar*, reported the arrival of '*Renoir et sa femme* [*sic*]'.

131 Renoir to Durand-Ruel, Algiers, March 1882; Godfroy 1995, I, p. 31.

132 Benjamin 2003, pp. 46–51.

133 Archives Durand-Ruel, Journal 1882, 22 May 1882, no. 2396, *Mosquée de sidi aderhamman*, 1,000 ff; sold to Clapisson, 24 May 1882 for 2,000 ff. On Clapisson as a collector, see Distel in Bailey 1997.

134 Bailey 2003, pp. 683–4.

135 Moffett 1986, pp. 373–95.

136 P. Burty, *La République française*, 8 March 1882, in Berson 1996, I, p. 382.

137 Letter of 2 March 1882 to Berthe Morisot; Rouart 1951, p. 104.

138 Silvestre, *La Vie Moderne*, 11 March 1882, in Berson 1996, I, p. 413.

139 Pissarro to de Bellio, 26 March 1882; Bailly-Herzberg 1980, *Correspondance*, I, p. 162.

140 Renoir to Durand Ruel, Algiers, March 1882; Godfroy 1995, I, p. 35. Albert Wolff (1835–1891), the German-born art critic of *Le Figaro*, was an implacable opponent of the Impressionists' exhibitions and auctions, though respected by Manet (to whom he had sat for his portrait in 1877).

141 Ward 1991, p. 617.

142 *Catalogue de l'exposition des œuvres de P.-A. Renoir*, 1883; Duret 1998, p. 69.

143 So Cézanne informed Zola on 10 March 1883; Rewald 1978, pp. 208–9.

144 Archives Durand-Ruel, Journal 1883, 9 March 1883, D. 3923, *La Montagne (L'Estaque)*, deposited by Renoir; 2 August 1883, 2991, acquired by Durand-Ruel for 1,000 ff; see also House and Distel 1985, p. 233.

145 Burty and Renoir had been friends for almost a decade. In April 1874 Renoir, occupied with hanging the first Impressionist exhibition, had been unable to accept Burty's invitation to '*bavarder du Japonisme*'; Archives du Louvre, Fonds Henraux Ms 310 (3). Two years later, Burty encouraged Edmond de Goncourt to see Renoir's portraits at the second Impressionist exhibition: '*J'ai diné hier avec un jeune intransigeant Renoir. Vous n'imaginez pas tout ce qu'il nous dit d'intéressant et pas en style de journaliste. En vrai style d'artiste – sur les qualités de votre oeuvre*'; Weisberg 1993, p. 196. In 1884 Renoir would receive the commission to paint the portrait of Burty's four-year-old grandson, Paul Haviland (Kansas City, The Nelson-Atkins Museum of Art); Bailey 1997, p. 206.

146 P. Burty, 'Les Peintures de M. P. Renoir', *La République française*, 15 April 1883.

147 Geffroy, 'P.-A. Renoir', *La Justice*, 16 April 1883.

148 Renoir to Berard, Trouville, 19 July 1883; Private collection.

149 House 1988.

150 Renoir to Durand-Ruel, Guernsey, 27 September 1883; Godfroy 1995, I, p. 40.

151 House and Distel 1985, pp. 239–40.

152 Archives Durand-Ruel, Journal 1883, 15 December 1883, no. 3121, *Baie du Moulin Huet*; no. 3122, *Brouillard Guernsey*; no. 3123, *Côtes du Moulin Huet*; no. 3124, *Marée basse Yport*; no. 3125, *Baie du Moulin Huet*. As no prices are attached, it is possible that these were only deposited by Renoir at this time.

153 House (1988, p. 19), was the first to question the traditional identification of the *Guernsey Seascape* in Williamstown, noting the resemblance of the cliffs to those in the background of the *Portrait of Robert Nunès* 1883 (Barnes Collection, Merion, Pennsylvania), painted at Yport in August 1883; see also Kern 1996, pp. 83–7.

154 The purple-orange palette and handling of the Williamstown picture, and its dense, oily hatching are close to *Low Tide at Yport* (Hermitage, St Petersburg), formerly in the Otto Krebs collection, catalogued in Kostenevich 1995, pp. 60–2.

155 House 1988, pp. 3–11. This brings to mind Renoir's apology to Durand-Ruel, made from Algiers in March 1882 for the delay in sending his

Italian landscapes of the previous December: '*C'est dommage qu'il y ait des retouches indispensables à faire*'; Godfroy 1995, I, pp. 31–2.

156 In June 1882, informing Berard of his difficulties with the portraits of the Durand-Ruel children and Mme Clapisson, Renoir uses the term for the first time, 'L'art est dans le marasme'; Wemaere-De Beaupuis, Vente inaugurale, Rouen, 13 May 1992, lot 86; it appears again in his letter to Berard of 19 July 1883 (cited note 148). For Berard's letter to Deudon, see Distel 1989, pp. 62–3.

157 On Monet's travels to the Mediterranean in 1884, see Pissarro 1997, pp. 13–46.

158 Renoir to Durand-Ruel, Genoa, December 1883; Godfroy 1995, I, p. 41.

159 Renoir to Berard, Monte Carlo, December 1883; Vente Hôtel Drouot, Rive Gauche, 16 February 1979, lot 76.

160 Archives Durand-Ruel, Journal 1884, 23 December 1884, no. 605, *Paysage Menton*, 500 ff; no. 606, *Paysage Menton*, 200ff; the former is likely to be the painting in Boston, see House and Distel 1985, p. 239.

161 Vollard 1919, ch. XIII, p. 127. The chapter opens with the memorable declaration: '*Vers 1883 il s'est fait comme une cassure dans mon œuvre. J'étais allé jusqu'au bout de l'impressionnisme et j'arrivai à cette constation que je ne savais ni peindre ni dessiner.*'

162 Renoir to Monet, January 1884; Baudot 1949, p. 58.

163 Bailey 1997, pp. 209–10.

164 Corot's *Port of La Rochelle* of 1851, shown at the Salon of 1852, had been in Durand-Ruel's possession since 1878 at least; see Pantazzi, Pomarède and Tinterow 1996, pp. 278–9 (entry by Michael Pantazzi).

165 Renoir to Durand-Ruel, Hôtel d'Angoulême, La Rochelle, summer 1884; Godfroy 1995, I, p. 43.

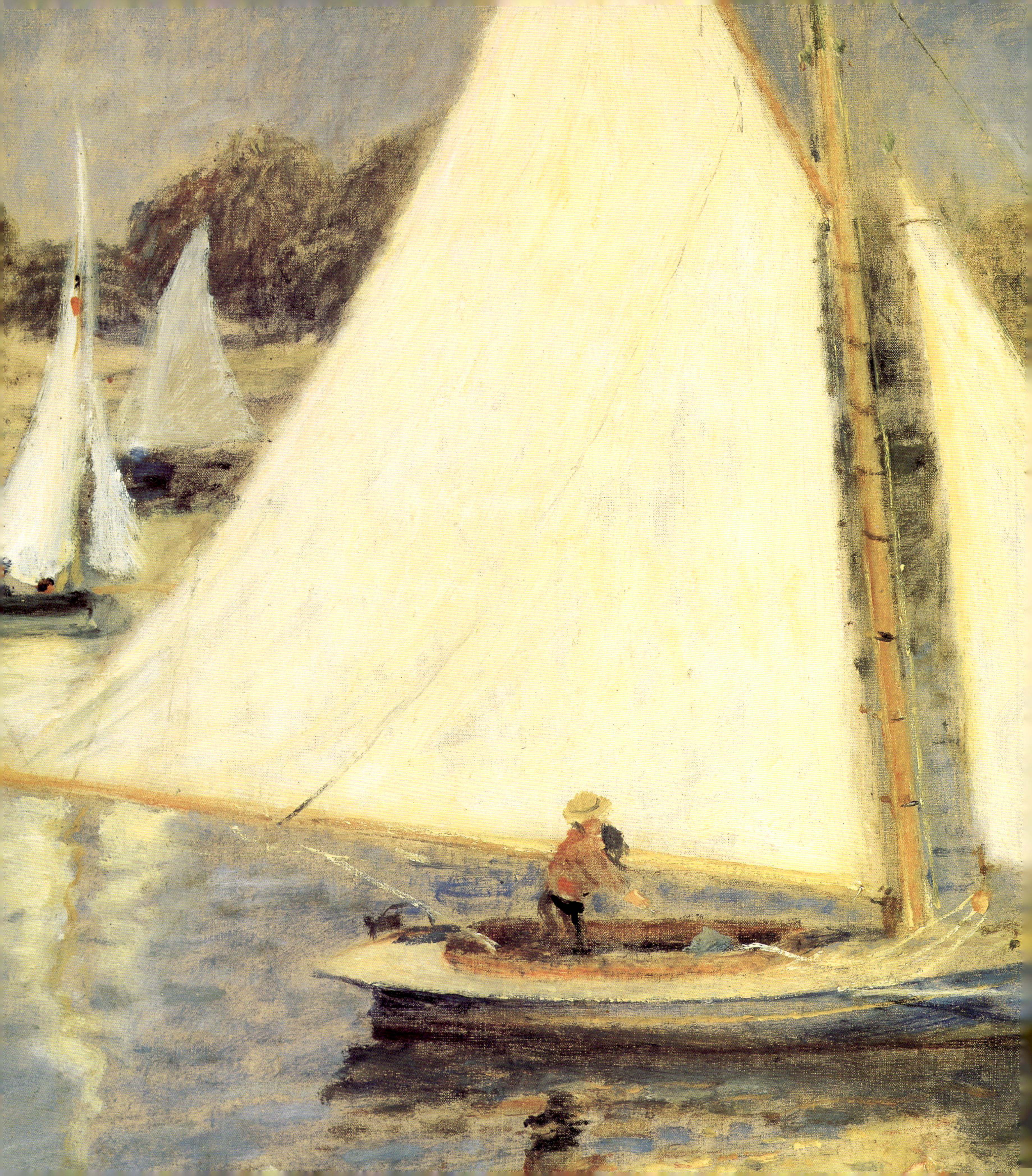

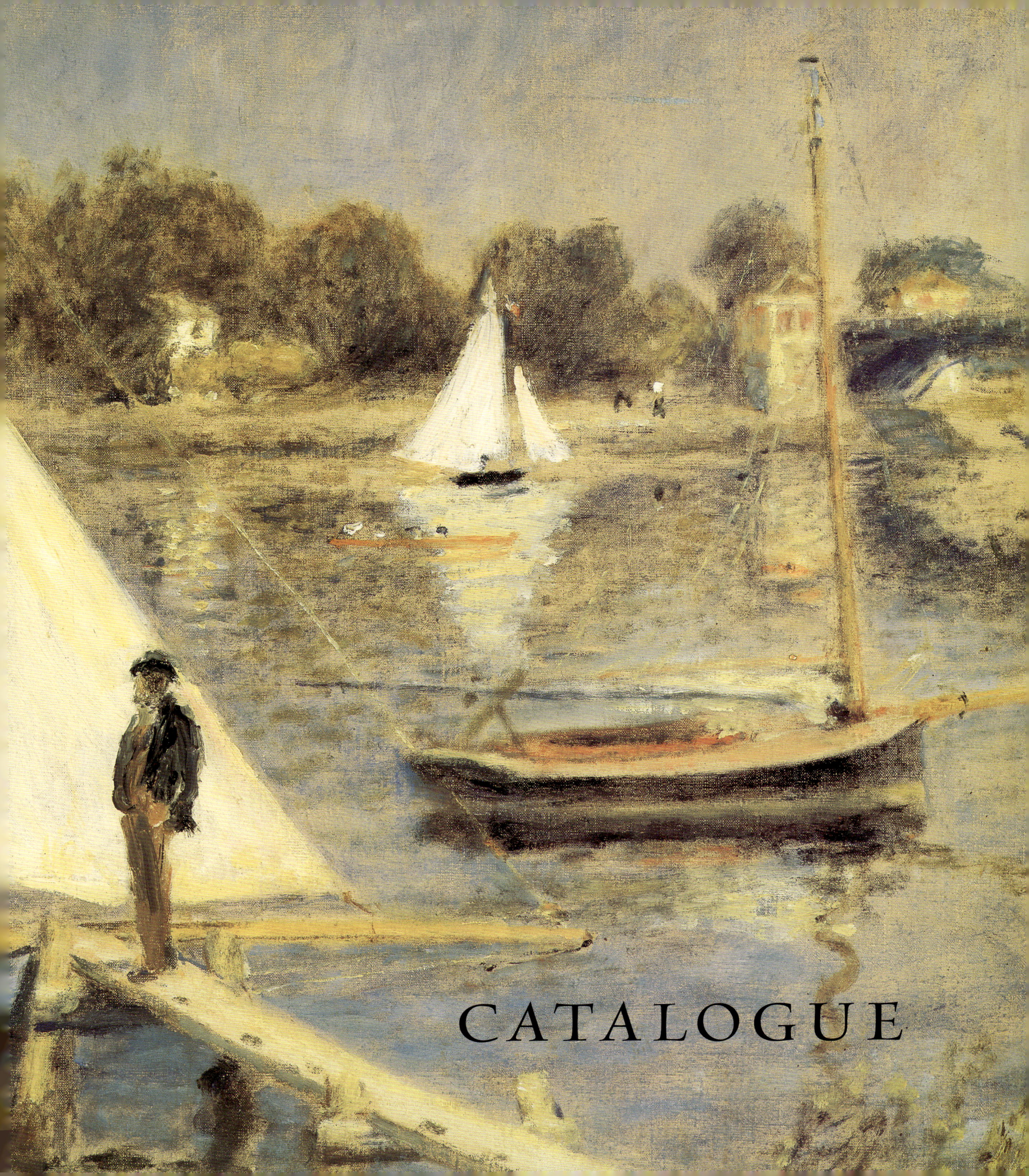

CATALOGUE

1 Country Road near Marlotte, about 1865–6

Oil on canvas
33 × 24.1 cm; 13 × 9½ in.
Private collection

PROVENANCE:
Given by the artist to Lise Tréhot and by descent; private collection

LITERATURE:
Cooper 1959, pp. 163–4, 325; Daulte 1971, p. 33; Champa 1973, p. 39; White 1996, p. 21; Néret 2001, p. 17

This diminutive painting was made, as Kermit Champa has noted, while Renoir was still very much under the influence of Corot, and the lightly brushed forms and strong light certainly recall the compositions of the elder artist. In the 1860s Corot was famous and established, one of the jurors of the annual Salon, yet he also had a reputation as an outsider whose art, though he had trained in the Academy, opened new avenues for experimentation, especially through *plein-air* painting. Corot was one of the group of artists who frequented the forest of Fontainebleau and came to be known as the Barbizon School, and Renoir was almost certainly in or near Fontainebleau when he made the present work, staying with the Le Coeur family in the village of Marlotte. He spent part of the spring there painting out of doors in 1865 and 1866.

This painting has been supposed to be the 'sketch [*pochade*]' to which Marie Le Coeur referred in a letter about the artist's difficulties in getting his pictures accepted for the Salon of 1866.[1] Apparently the jury had accepted a small painting of his, but Renoir withdrew it because his major submission, entitled *Landscape with Two Figures*, was rejected, and he felt that the small study could not stand on its own. Barbara White, reprinting the letter, followed Douglas Cooper in assigning the present painting the title *Landscape with Two Figures*, but, while this small painting might be the sketch described by Marie, it is not likely to be the *Landscape with Two Figures*, since it is not a major painting and contains more than the two most obvious figures.[2] Anne Distel has argued convincingly that *Landscape with Two Figures* is the work visible in the background of Frédéric Bazille's painting of the *Studio in the rue de la Condamine* (fig. 55), an atelier that he shared with Renoir.[3]

The picture is not ambitious but instead appears both natural and unpretentious. There are two figures strolling along a country lane with a dog at their feet, but a third figure is just visible behind them and another figure works under the tree on the right. The palette is composed of dark greens, warm browns and bright yellows. Taken together, these colours provide a sense that one is looking at the natural world unadorned, and modern life, a future source of visual interest for Renoir and his Impressionist colleagues, is nowhere in evidence. Rather, the image of the house nestled into the landscape and the figures who move along the path reflect the slow pace of unchanged country life on a summer afternoon, at one with the larger totality of nature. And yet it is a carefully constructed and balanced picture. It is instructive that Marie noted that Renoir completed his *pochade* in two weeks. While this would not be long enough for a young artist to work up a major composition, it seems too long to spend on a true 'sketch'. JZ

Shown in London and Philadelphia only

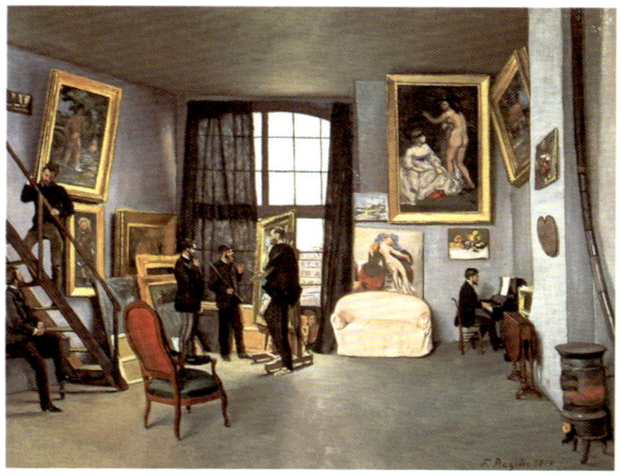

FIG. 55 Frédéric Bazille (1841–1870), *Studio in the rue de la Condamine*. 1870. Oil on canvas, 98 × 128.5 cm; 38½ × 50½ in. Musée d'Orsay, Paris (RF 2449).

1 Marie Le Coeur's letter was published in *Cahiers d'Aujourd'hui*, n.p.
2 Cooper 1959, pp. 163–4; White 1986, p. 21.
3 House and Distel 1985, pp. 179–80.

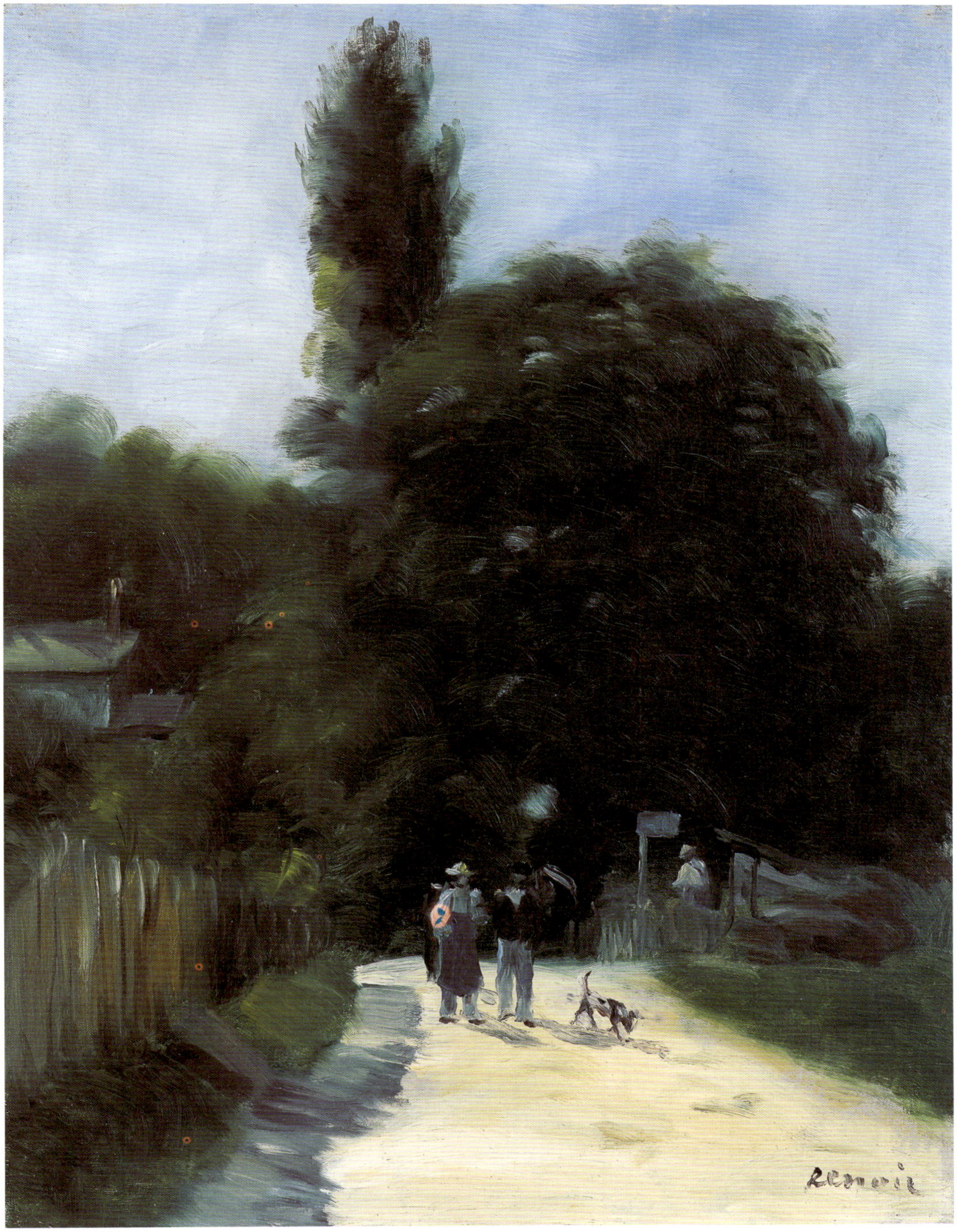
Renoir

2 A Clearing in the Woods, 1865

Oil on canvas
57.2 × 82.6 cm; 22½ × 32½ in.
Detroit Institute of Arts, Detroit, Michigan
Bequest of Ruth Nugent Head, in memory of her mother, Anne E. Kresge, and her husband, Henry W. Nugent (1985.25)

PROVENANCE:
Ambroise Vollard, Paris; Galerie Bignou, Paris and New York; Alex Reid & Lefevre Galleries, London, by 1946; Arthur Tooth and Sons, London, 1953–55; Colonel and Mrs Henry Nugent, New York, acquired 29 December 1955; bequeathed by Mrs Ruth Nugent Head in 1985

LITERATURE:
Champa 1973, p. 38–40; Champa 1991, pp. 207–8; Wissman 2000, p. 67

Although the signature in red at lower left was added long after Renoir painted this stately realist landscape, there is no reason to question the dating of *Clearing in the Woods* to the summer of 1865. In this unpopulated scene, the eye is drawn over the rocky, watery terrain – at least two small ponds are visible – towards a line of massive chestnut trees in full leaf. Renoir's handling, while forceful in the delineation of the open forest, is at times painstaking and fussy: red and yellow wild-flowers dot the foreground, sprigs of grass are clustered around the rocks, the foliage of the tree at upper left is meticulously described. The silvery palette and blond, even lighting are reminiscent above all of Corot, for whom Renoir had a lifelong veneration, as his son Jean recalled. Even as a young man, enthusiastic for Rousseau and Diaz, Renoir had 'realised immediately that the really great painter was Corot. His work is for all time.'[1] As has also been noted, the rugged character of the site, and the unyielding, planar construction of the landscape, evoke Courbet, 'the idol of the young generation'.[2]

Kermit Champa noted that the 'open foreground and horizontal emphasis' of this landscape recalled 'the contemporary work of Sisley as well'.[3] In fact, Sisley's activities in the summer of 1865 help identify the site and subject of Renoir's picture, which is catalogued as showing a part of the forest of Fontainebleau, and which Champa himself assumed was painted at Marlotte.[4] The closest cognates for *Clearing in a Wood*, however, are Sisley's two pictures of different scale (and function) of *The Avenue of Chestnut Trees in La Celle-St-Cloud* (fig. 56), the larger of which was probably intended for submission at the Salon.[5] Similar flat, rocky terrain and patches of water reappear in Sisley's canvases, in which the sense of a dry, hot summer's afternoon is more palpable than in Renoir's sylvan setting.

Situated between Bougival and Vaucresson, six and a half kilometres from St-Cloud, to the west of Paris, La Celle-St-Cloud was a village of some four hundred souls, not yet accessible by rail. Apart from the château de La Celle briefly inhabited by Madame de Pompadour, its chief attraction for visitors was 'the forest that surrounds it on three sides and which offers many charming promenades'.[6] The avenue of chestnuts trees, La Châtaignerie, was the most celebrated of these forest sites, accessible from the road that led directly to the château.[7] On 3 July 1865, Renoir – who was living at Sisley's studio at 31 avenue de Neuilly (in the west of Paris) – informed Bazille of a proposed group outing along the Seine as far as Le Havre: 'I'm going to bring my box of colours to make sketches of the spots that I like.' He also told Bazille that he was about to meet Sisley at La Celle, at the Tourne Bride – a restaurant just above the château, run by a certain Lamiot and noted in the guidebooks – inviting him to join them there.[8]

If Renoir and Sisley did indeed pitch their easels at the same edge of the woods at La Celle-St-Cloud, their views are markedly different. In Sisley's landscapes there is a struggle to be rid of Barbizon formulae, whereas Renoir's *Clearing in*

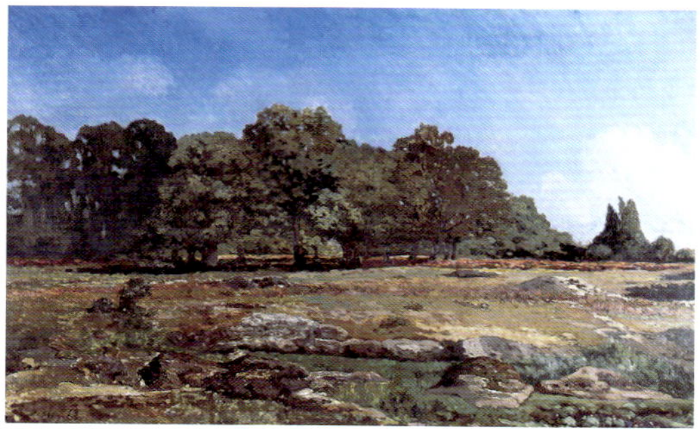

FIG. 56 Alfred Sisley (1839–1899), *The Avenue of Chestnut Trees in La Celle-St-Cloud*, 1865. Oil on canvas, 129 × 208 cm; 50¾ × 81⅞ in. Petit Palais, Musée des Beaux-Arts de la Ville de Paris (PPP0693).

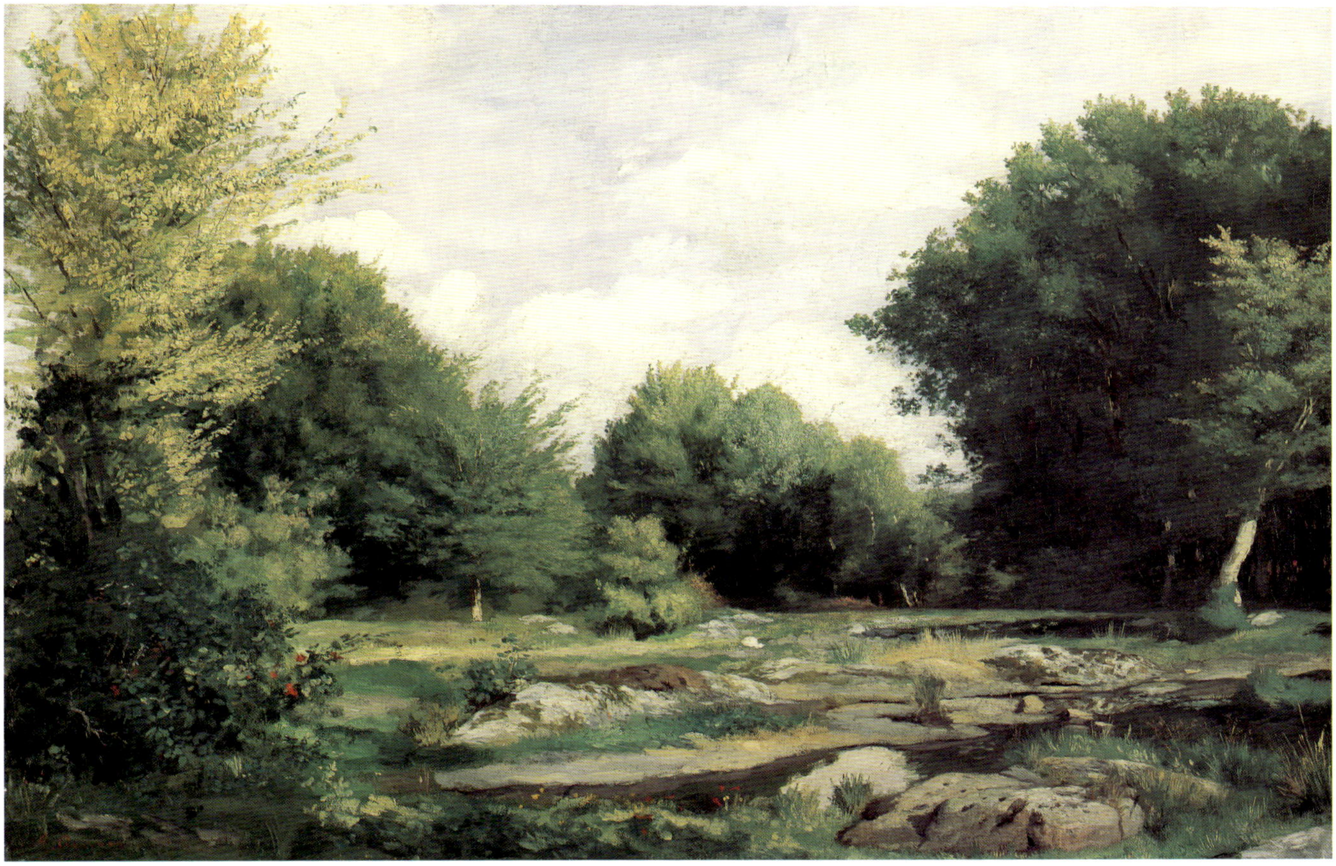

the Woods, even if a *pochade* or sketch of a spot that had caught his attention, remains fully dependent on these earlier models. As experiments in realist landscape, their work in the summer of 1865 shares certain affinities with Bazille and Monet's endeavours further away at Chailly in Fontainebleau.[9] In every case, we sense the grandeur (and challenge) of the enterprise in which each artist sought to 'see the forest with fresh eyes'.[10] CBB

1 Renoir 1962, p. 68; Renoir 1981, p. 81.
2 Cited Champa 1973, p. 39.
3 Champa 1991, p. 207.
4 Champa 1973, p. 39.
5 Stevens 1992, p. 86–9; Shone 1992, pp. 35–7; Loyrette and Tinterow 1994, pp. 73, 461–2. Tinterow's arguments for dating the larger canvas, signed and dated 1865, to 1866–7 seem unconvincing to me.
6 Joanne 1856, p. 326. By 1881 the population of the village had almost doubled to 560: see Joanne 1881, p. 181.
7 Joanne 1856, p. 329.
8 Daulte 1952, p. 47. The rest of the letter, not published in Daulte, notes that Renoir and Sisley are meeting at La Celle '*au Tourne Bride*' to paint and go swimming: '*Si tu viens, apporte ta boîte, si tu veux. Si tu sais nager, apporte un caleçon*'; Paris, Drouot-Richelieu, *Vente Autographe, Manuscrits*, 10 December 1991, no. 375. The restaurant is mentioned in Joanne 1856, p. 328.
9 The most pertinent comparisons are Bazille's *Landscape at Chailly*, 1865, Art Institute of Chicago, and Monet's *Pavé de Chailly in the Fontainebleau Forest*, 1865, Ordrupgaardsamlingen, Charlottenlund; see Loyrette and Tinterow 1994, pp. 77–9.
10 *Ibidem.*

3 Jules Le Coeur and his Dogs walking in the Forest of Fontainebleau, 1866

Oil on canvas
106 × 80 cm; 41¾ × 31¾ in.
Museu de Arte de São Paulo Assis Chateaubriand, São Paulo

PROVENANCE:
Jules Le Coeur, Paris; Paul Cassirer, Berlin; M. Kuthe, Berlin; his sale, Berlin, 2 December 1911, no. 47, purchased by Dr Georg Hirth, Munich, for DM 6,800; his sale, Düsseldorf, 12 November 1932, no. 142; M. Knoedler and Co., New York; acquired by the Museu de Arte de São Paulo in 1958

LITERATURE:
House and Distel 1985, pp. 185–6; Camesasca and Bardi 1989, pp. 132–6; Loyrette and Tinterow 1994, pp. 70, 453

A lone hunter and his two expectant dogs pause as they ascend a steep pathway in a rocky section of the forest, lined by trees. The majestic sweep of the view, its insistent verticality and centrifugal shadows, animate the composition but succeed in dwarfing the figure, who seems incidental to the landscape. It is not easy to determine the season, since hunting generally takes place in the winter and early spring, yet Renoir's russet tonalities suggest autumn. These are set off by the blacks of the hunter's apparel, the bark of the trees and the deep shadows in the foreground. The sky is merely glimpsed as patches of blue in the upper right hand quadrant of the canvas.

Jules Le Coeur and his Dogs walking in the Forest of Fontainebleau is an ambitious work, striking in size, format and technique: painted with the palette knife, it was doubtless worked on in the studio as well as before the motif.[1] Two preparatory studies are known, both made *in situ* and also executed with the palette knife – *In the Forest of Fontainebleau* (private collection), a close-up of sunlight and shadow on the trees and their overhanging foliage,[2] and *Young Trees in the Forest* (fig. 57), a composition virtually identical to the present canvas, but lacking both hunter and dogs.[3] Renoir's use of the palette knife – an instrument to which Pissarro and Cézanne also turned, quite independently, in the summer of 1866 – signalled the younger generation's admiration for Courbet, for whom it was a sort of signature.[4] The palette knife was not an altogether congenial tool for Renoir, however, since it did not allow him to rework his canvases, and he abandoned it within a year.[5]

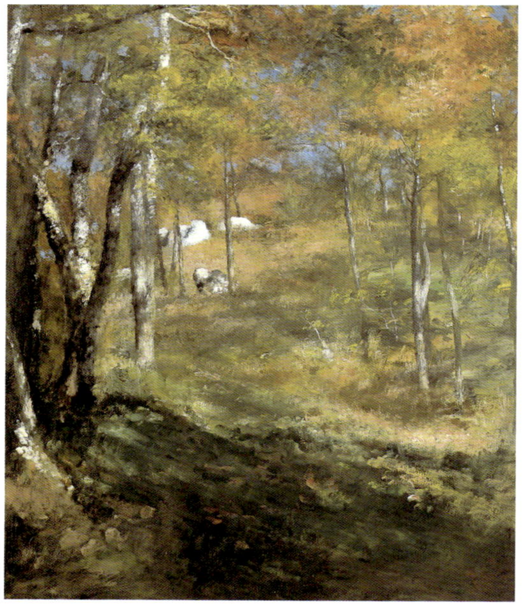

FIG. 57 *Young Trees in the Forest*, 1866. Oil on canvas, 73 × 59.5 cm; 28¾ × 23⅜ in. Private collection.

In no sense a portrait,[6] *Jules Le Coeur and his Dogs walking in the Forest of Fontainebleau* nonetheless relates to the firm friendship that Renoir had established with the 34-year-old architect turned painter, to whose house and studio in Marlotte he was a frequent visitor during 1865 and 1866.[7] In February 1866, Renoir and Sisley had joined Le Coeur on a walking and painting tour of the forest of Fontainebleau, stopping at Milly and Courances.[8] On 29 March, nine days after the deadline for consigning entries for the Salon, Renoir accompanied Le Coeur by train to Marlotte, returning to Paris four days later to enquire whether his works had been accepted.[9] Following the rejection of the larger of the two works he had submitted and his decision to withdraw the sketch made 'at Marlotte in two weeks',[10] in early May he announced to Le Coeur that he had discovered '*la vraie peinture*'.[11] During the summer Renoir continued to divide his time between Marlotte and Paris; and in mid-August he and Sisley spent a fortnight in Berck, as guests of Le Coeur and his family.[12]

It is within this chronology that *Jules Le Coeur*

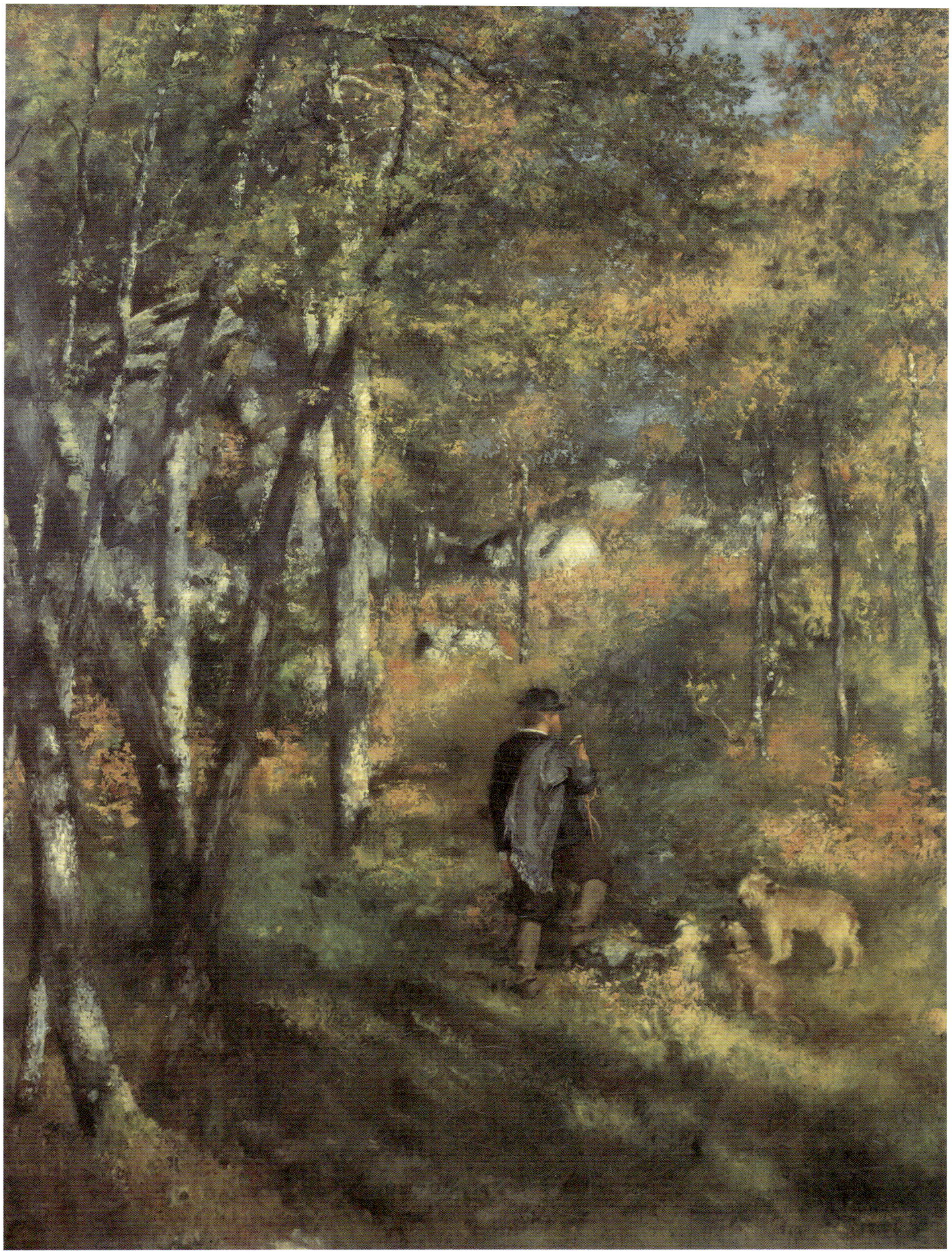

and his Dogs walking in the Forest of Fontainebleau should be situated. In claiming, much later, that the work was accepted at the Salon of 1865 Renoir clearly had a faulty memory,[13] but for a long time the date was not questioned. Recently the painting has been assigned to the winter of 1865, the summer of 1866, and the autumn of that year.[14] As Douglas Cooper and Marc Le Coeur both argued, Renoir's group of Fontainebleau forest scenes should be dated to late March and early April 1866 – before the rejection by the jury had led Renoir to question his manner of painting.[15] By mid-May, Renoir gives up the palette knife and returns to the brush ('*la vraie peinture*'), painting in quick succession a pair of fluid, suavely handled flower still lifes and his first monumental group portrait, *The Inn of Mère Antony* (Nationalmuseum, Stockholm).[16]

Despite its indebtedness to Courbet, signalling the end of his dependence on Barbizon examples, *Jules Le Coeur and his Dogs walking in the Forest of Fontainebleau* celebrates Renoir's early enthusiasm for Diaz. It was Diaz, after all, who had 'rescued' the young Renoir from a group of mocking bystanders while he was alone, dressed in workman's overalls, painting in the forest of Fontainebleau.[17] Diaz had encouraged Renoir to lighten his palette, introduced him to his colour man and dealer, and helped pay for materials.[18] The closely cropped, dense forest view – a motif also favoured by landscape photographers in the 1850s and 1860s[19] – was something of a cliché in Diaz's oeuvre (see the essay by Simon Kelly in this catalogue). 'In Diaz's paintings, you can almost smell the mushrooms, dead leaves and moss,' Renoir confided to his son; to Vollard he remarked that Diaz's landscapes were 'as sparkling as precious stones [*aussi éclatante que des pierreries*]'.[20] It is these sensory qualities – of touch, smell and light – that *Jules Le Coeur and his Dogs walking in the Forest of Fontainebleau* appropriates so masterfully. CBB

1 As noted in Champa 1991, p. 207, and Adriani 1996, p. 75.
2 Cooper 1959, pp. 164–5.
3 Fezzi 1985, no. 10; the painting most recently appeared at Christie's, London, 27 June 1988, lot 5. Another related work, unknown to Cooper, is the diminutive *Young Man in the Forest of Fontainebleau* (Milan, private collection): see Vallès-Bled and Sanfo 2002, p. 41.
4 In December 1865, Bazille had informed his brother that his forthcoming Salon submission '*m'a valu des compliments du maître Courbet qui est venu nous faire une visite pour voir le tableau de Monet, dont il a été enchanté*'; Vatuone 1992, p. 116. For Pissarro and Cézanne's use of the palette knife in 1866, see Loyrette and Tinterow 1994, pp. 89–91.
5 As recounted in Vollard 1918, p. 23: '*Ce tableau est peint au couteau, par exception; car c'est un procédé qui ne me va pas*'; Renoir's comment to Albert André that the palette knife was inimical to reworking is cited in Cooper 1959, p. 163. On 23 August 1867, Edmond Maître informed Bazille that Renoir '*faisait la dernière fois que je l'ai vu à Paris d'étrange peinture, ayant changé la térébenthine contre une sulfate infâme et quitté son couteau pour la petite seringue que vous savez*'; Daulte 1952, p. 64, my emphasis.
6 Champa (1973, p. 40) curiously approaches the work as a 'hunting portrait'.
7 On Le Coeur in Marlotte, which the Goncourts considered '*le pays d'élection de la paysage moderne*', see Cooper 1959, pp. 322–5; Le Coeur 1996, pp. 23–7; and São Paulo 2002, pp. 198–9.
8 Cooper 1959, p. 322, note 6.
9 *Ibidem*, p. 164.
10 *Cahiers d'Aujourd'hui*, 1921, n.p.
11 '*J'ai reçu une lettre de Renoir. Qu'il ne se presse pas de venir et surtout qu'il soigne bien ce qu'il fait là-bas . . . Il me dit avoir trouvé la vraie peinture: je l'en félicite*', Jules Le Coeur to his mother, Marlotte, 14 May 1866; Paris, Le Coeur collection, partially cited in Cooper 1959, p. 164.
12 Le Coeur 1996, p. 26.
13 Vollard 1918, p. 23; Duret (1924, p. 23) also dates the work to 1865.
14 Champa 1973, p. 40; White 1984, p. 21; Adriani 1996, p. 75.
15 Cooper 1959, pp. 164–5; São Paulo 2002, p. 199.
16 For the *Spring Bouquet* (Fogg Art Museum, Cambridge, MA) and *Flowers in a Vase* (National Gallery of Art, Washington, DC) see Wolohojian 2003, pp. 274–6 (entry by Christopher Riopelle), and for the dating of *The Inn of Mère Antony* to the summer of 1866, Bailey 1997, pp. 97–9.
17 Vollard 1918, p. 22; Loyrette and Tinterow 1994, p. 453.
18 Distel 1993, p. 20.
19 As examples, see Charles Marville's *View of Fontainebleau*, 1859, reproduced in Camesasca and Bardi 1989, p. 132, and Charles Famin's *Trees in Fontainebleau*, 1870, in Heilbrun 1986, p. 75.
20 Renoir 1962, p. 68; Renoir 1981, p. 81.

4 Skaters in the Bois de Boulogne, 1868

Oil on canvas
72 × 90 cm; 28⅞ × 36⅛ in.
Private collection

PROVENANCE:
Ambroise Vollard, Paris; Robert von Hirsch; his sale, Sotheby's, London, 26–27 June 1978, no. 717; Marquess of Northampton, Warwick; Richard L. Feigen and Co., New York

REFERENCES:
House and Distel 1985, pp. 48, 187; Herbert 1988, pp. 143–9; Moffett 1998, pp. 130–3, 212–13

'I have never been able to stand the snow. Even if you can bear the cold, why paint snow? It is a blight on the face of Nature.'[1] As Renoir recalled to Vollard,[2] Renoir's snowscapes can indeed be counted on the fingers of one hand: the present picture, the *Winter Landscape* of the same time (but of a far more modest village street),[3] and two beautiful wintry scenes, the '*effets de neige*' painted at Argenteuil in the mid-1870s (cat. 35).[4]

Skaters in the Bois de Boulogne can be documented quite precisely to the bitter winter of late December 1867/early January 1868, when the Seine stayed frozen for 11 consecutive days, and snow was recorded as far south as Nice.[5] In early January 1868 Renoir took his paints and canvas to the Bois de Boulogne's western lake, the Lac supérieur – reached by train from St-Lazare – which had been transformed into a '*grande fête du patin*', a great skating show.[6] In a bird's-eye view, he recorded in vignettes both remarkably synoptic and affectionate the flurry of warmly dressed bystanders at the edge of the lake and the participants (and workmen) who promenaded and skated on the ice itself. Framed by an oversized pine tree at left, the panorama recedes at a gently ascending angle to the trees, hills and clouds in the distant background – brushed in soft greys, russets and whites. Renoir's decisive signature and date in black at lower left indicate that he considered this to be a finished work, albeit of a radically abbreviated manner, and not merely a sketch or *pochade*. As Robert Herbert has noted, only the most enlightened dealer would have considered exhibiting such a picture in his shop window – as Latouche had done for one of Monet's city views the previous May – and there is no record of Renoir having been as fortunate in this regard.[7]

Renoir always claimed to despise the Haussmannisation of Paris (see the essay by Chris Riopelle in this catalogue), yet the parks, gardens, waters and entertainments of the Bois de Boulogne, created between 1852 and 1858, were among the Baron's most ambitious urban projects. The Bois quickly became the preferred setting for the '*haute gentry*', the winter promenading hour being from 3 o'clock to 5 o'clock in the afternoon. Ice-skating, normally possible only for a few days at any one time, was another élite pastime. In 1865 a new Cercle des Patineurs, with limited membership and regulations on dress, had established itself at the Lac pour le patinage, a rink illuminated by electric lights just south of the château de Madrid. Renoir's skaters, no less patrician, are shown at the frozen Lac supérieur to the west of the park.[8] In the foreground we see the wooden barriers and gas lamps at the lake's edge that in summertime demarcated the boat landing.[9]

Lilliputian in scale, speedily painted, with colours often applied wet on wet, Renoir's figures bring to life an entire society, with workers and officials at its margins. In the foreground to the left of the empty chair we see the gloved gendarmes with their golden buttons, and at right, with his back to us, an aproned street vendor. In the middle ground, at left and right, attendants dressed in low-hanging grey smocks are clearing the snow with large paddles.[10] Two soldiers in red trousers, with brandenbourgs on their jackets and officer's hats, stand together in the background at right. However, Renoir's skating populous is by and large a well- and warmly attired gathering that includes several children, a priest,[11] and many women in hats and fur-trimmed coats. Renoir, always sensitive to women's fashions, celebrates high life on the ice, with an enthusiasm that echoes that of the contemporary press: 'The Bois de Boulogne is one great skating party! As if the ballet from

FIG. 58 E. Roevens. *Le Club des Patineurs, établi sur le petit lac du Bois de Boulogne*, 1865. Engraving. Musée Carnavalet, Paris.

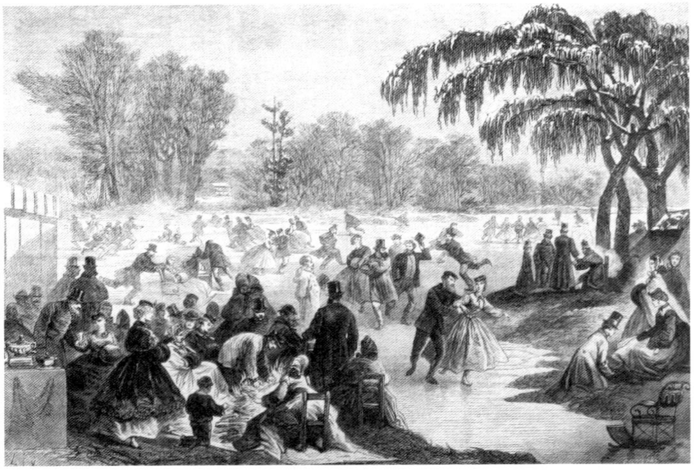

Meyerbeer's *Le Prophète* were being danced by those charming, noble ladies whose names are well-known to readers of the *Almanach de Gotha*. The Jockey-Club has turned Polish: furs of every kind, from black sable to white ermine, make an appointment to rendez-vous on the Lake.'[12]

Renoir draws from a variety of sources for his apparently spontaneous, vivid cityscape. Although the Louvre had yet to acquire winter scenes by Avercamp and Van Goyen, its seventeenth-century Northern collection included scenes of skaters on the canal by Van Ostade and Van de Velde.[13] Renoir surely studied Manet's panorama of *le beau monde* in *Music in the Tuileries Gardens*, 1862 (The National Gallery, London), when it was among the 50 paintings exhibited at his retrospective on the Pont de l'Alma in May 1867.[14] He may also have been inspired by Roeven's rollicking engraving that celebrated the newly formed *Le Club des Patineurs* of 1865 (fig. 58) – its lone chair and overhanging tree at right appear to have made their way into Renoir's painting.[15] Stylistically and conceptually, however, *Skaters in the Bois de Boulogne* relates most closely to Renoir's affectionate *Portrait of Bazille* (Musée d'Orsay, Paris), a similarly elegant exercise in greys, ochres and russets, painted in November 1867. In that portrait, Monet's barren snowscape of Honfleur from the winter of 1866–7 had hung like a nimbus above Bazille's head. In *Skaters in the Bois de Boulogne* it is as an absent godfather that Monet presides over Renoir's celebration of hibernal conviviality. CBB

Not in the exhibition

1 Vollard 1925, pp. 51–2 (translation slightly amended).
2 '*Aussi, en fait de paysages d'hiver, il n'y a que cette toile . . . Je me rappelle aussi deux ou trois petites études*'; Vollard 1919, p. 40.
3 Rewald 1973, pp. 209–10; Champa 1971, p. 58; the picture appeared most recently at Christie's, New York, 10 November 1987, lot 4.
4 For *Snowy Landscape*, see Sapporo 1999, pp. 70–1.
5 Moffett 1998, pp. 221–2.
6 De Andia 1991, p. 42; 'Courrier de Paris,' *L'Illustration*, 11 January 1868.
7 Herbert 1988, p. 149; Stuckey 1995, p. 194.
8 See the superb discussion in Herbert 1988, pp. 143–7. For the élite Cercle des Patineurs, see De Andia 1991, p. 44, and Vail 1886.
9 See the photograph in *Album Fiorillo*, no. 112 (*Biblio-thèque historique de la Ville de Paris*, vol. 4, no. 112).
10 Noted in Herbert 1988, p. 147.
11 The figure in the foreground at left, just behind the gendarmes, wearing a biretta and clerical collar.
12 'Courrier de Paris', *L'Illustration*, 11 January 1868.
13 Early nineteenth-century engravings of a large *Canal gelé avec couple patinant* (Frozen canal with skating couple) by Isaac van Ostade and *Rivière glacée avec patineurs et joueurs de hocquet* (Frozen river with skaters and kolf-players) by Adriaen van de Velde were also available.
14 Cachin 1983, p. 122–6.
15 For *Le Club des Patineurs, établi sur le petit lac du Bois de Boulogne*, see Musée Carnavalet, Cabinet des Arts Graphiques, p. 116 G bis.

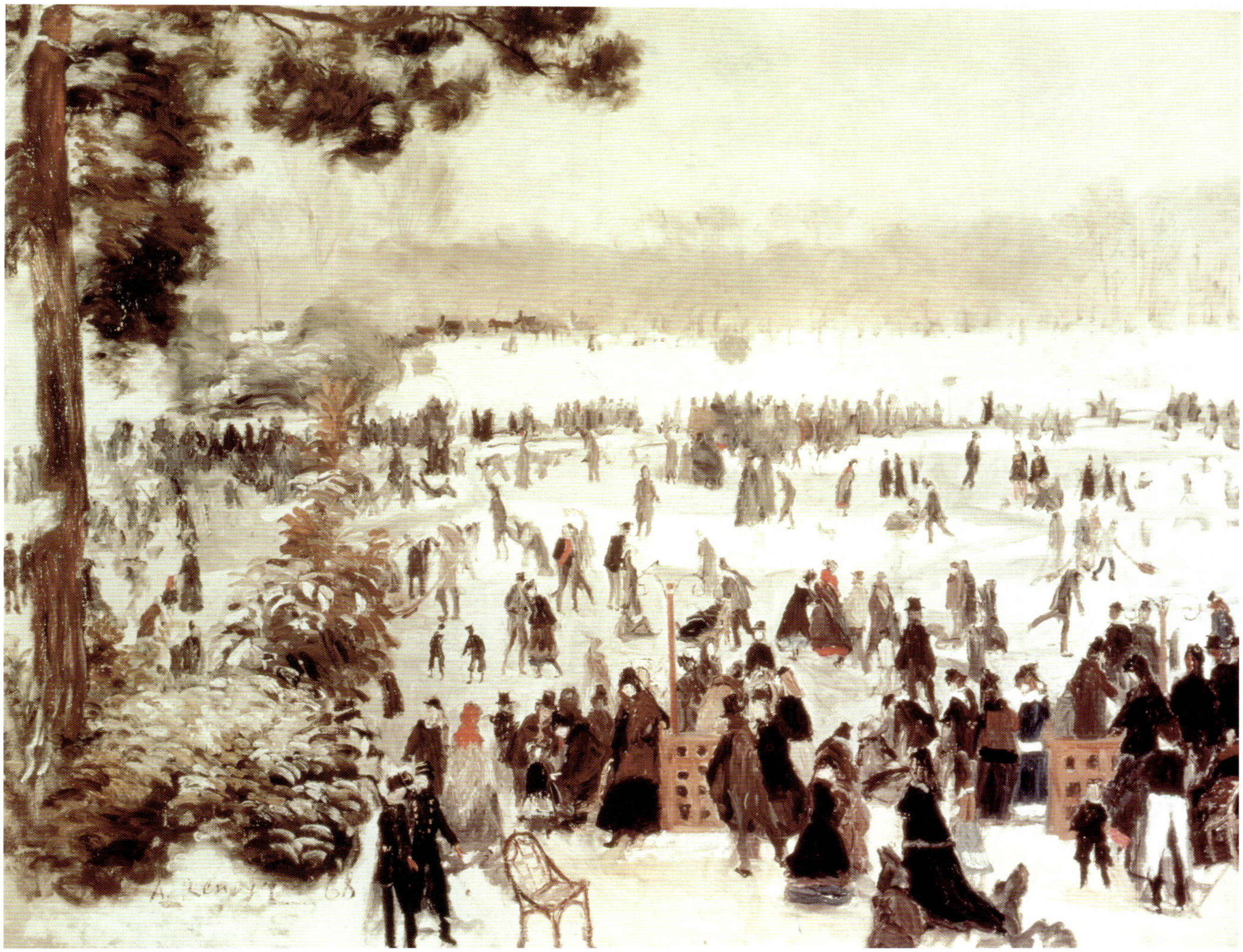

5 La Grenouillère, 1869

Oil on canvas
59 × 80 cm; 23¼ × 31½ in.
Pushkin State Museum of Fine Arts, Moscow

6 La Grenouillère, 1869

Oil on canvas
66.5 × 81 cm; 26⅛ × 32⅞ in.
Nationalmuseum, Stockholm (NM 2425)

PROVENANCE (CAT. 5): Edmond Renoir, Paris, until 1903; Ambrose Vollard, until 1908; purchased by Ivan Morosov, Moscow, 1908; his collection nationalised as the Second Museum of Western Painting, 1918; Museum of Modern Art, Moscow, 1923; Pushkin State Museum, 1948

PROVENANCE (CAT. 6): Edmond Renoir, Paris, until 1903; private collection; anonymous gift through the Friends of the Nationalmuseum, 1923

LITERATURE: Pickvance 1984; House and Distel 1985, pp. 191–2; Herbert 1988, pp. 210–19; Bomford 1990, pp. 120–5; Lay 1993; Loyrette and Tinterow 1994, pp. 252–9, 455–6

For two months in the summer of 1869, Renoir – staying with his parents at Voisins-Louveciennes, a suburb 17 kilometres west of Paris – painted in sustained collaboration with Monet, who had settled with his wife Camille and son Jean in the nearby village of St-Michel, just north of Bougival.[1] Having had both works he had submitted rejected from the Salon of 1869, Monet was in a fairly desperate state, and without money for food, light or art supplies. To Bazille he announced somewhat melodramatically that 'Renoir gave us bread from his home so that we would not starve'.[2] Renoir, who had shown one work at the Salon of 1869 but was no less impoverished, informed Bazille a few days later that he, too, was unable to work much because he 'did not have many colours'. His mood was ebullient, however: 'I am spending nearly all of my time with Monet . . . and I am more than happy, because when it comes to painting, Monet is very good company'.[3]

Towards the end of September 1869, with the fine weather over, Monet lamented that he had not been as productive as he had hoped in preparing for the next Salon: 'I have a dream, a painting of bathing at La Grenouillère, for which I did some bad sketches, but it's only a dream. Renoir, who has just spent two months here, also wants to do such a painting'.[4] This often-quoted letter to Bazille confirms the status of the La Grenouillère canvases as sketches, or studies ('*quelques mauvaises pochades*'), albeit of considerable complexity and ambition. Years later Durand-Ruel would also refer to two of Renoir's La Grenouillère canvases as 'studies [*études*]'.[5] As Robert Herbert has noted, their status as preparatory works, not intended for exhibition or sale, was liberating, and both artists seem to have been released from any inhibitions in forging a new pictorial language.[6] It is also noteworthy that these highly innovative proto-Impressionist masterpieces were conceived in the context of the Salon. Renoir never produced a finished composition of La Grenouillère: his experience of the river makes a tepid appearance as the background for his Courbet-like *Bather with a Griffon* (Museu de Arte de São Paulo), shown along with the bejewelled *Algerian Girl* (National Gallery of Art, Washington, DC) at the Salon of 1870.[7] Monet, true to his dream, apparently completed a painting of *La Grenouillère*, which may have been rejected at the Salon of 1870 (along with *The Luncheon*; Städel, Frankfurt): ironically, it is the one work in the series the whereabouts of which is no longer known.[8]

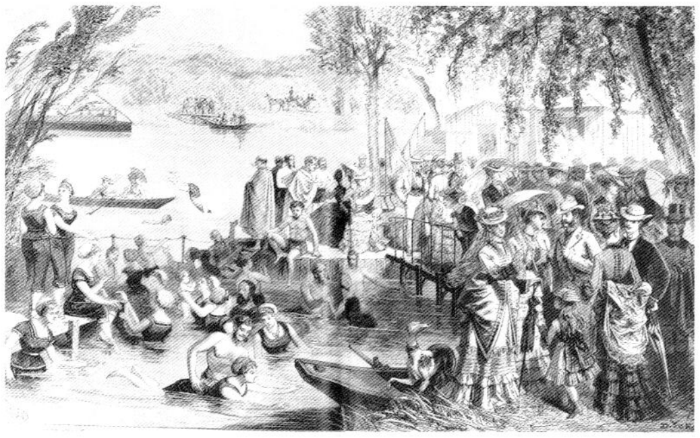

FIG. 59 Miranda, 'Les environs de Paris, La Grenouillère,' *L'Illustration*, 16 August 1873. Engraving. Bibliothèque Nationale de France, Paris.

In the summer of 1869, Renoir and Monet were engaged upon a series of elaborate, highly experimental *plein-air* studies. Their six paintings of La Grenouillère are an astonishingly direct and vibrant evocation of the summer landscape, in which an entirely new vocabulary has been created to convey 'the fleeting effects of rippling water, dappled sunlight, shifting boats and the constant movement of bathers and promenaders'.[9] It has been well said that Monet and Renoir's joint 'invention of a stenographic style of brushwork to render the choppy, sun-dappled river initiates the pictorial language of classic Impressionism'.[10]

This joint campaign was undertaken at the fashionable and somewhat raucous bathing and boating establishment of La Grenouillère on the Ile de Croissy, of which the proprietor, François-Joseph Seurin, was a carpenter and ferryman turned entrepreneur.[11] It was a popular spot for Sunday visitors from Paris, who took the twenty-minute train ride from St-Lazare to Reuil or Chatou; as temporary residents of the region, Renoir and Monet would have reached it easily on foot, crossing the bridge at Bougival. La Grenouillère was sufficiently well known to receive a visit from the Imperial family on 26 July 1869, and paintings of the site appeared at the Salons of 1869 and 1870.[12]

In June 1868 La Grenouillère had been written up by Raoul de Presles (and illustrated by Riou) in the weekly *L'Evènement illustré,* which catered to an affluent Parisian readership. His description suggests the fidelity with which Renoir and Monet crafted their compositions.[13] 'On a well-tarred old barge firmly moored to the bank . . . stands a wooden hut, painted green and white . . . Refreshments are on sale in a large room. To the left there is a boatbuilder's yard; the bathing huts are to the right. One reaches the floating house by crossing a series of highly picturesque but very primitive footbridges. One footbridge connects the island to a little islet with a surface area of no more than ten square metres or so. A tree stands in the middle of the islet; there is only one tree and, to tell the truth, it seems somewhat surprised

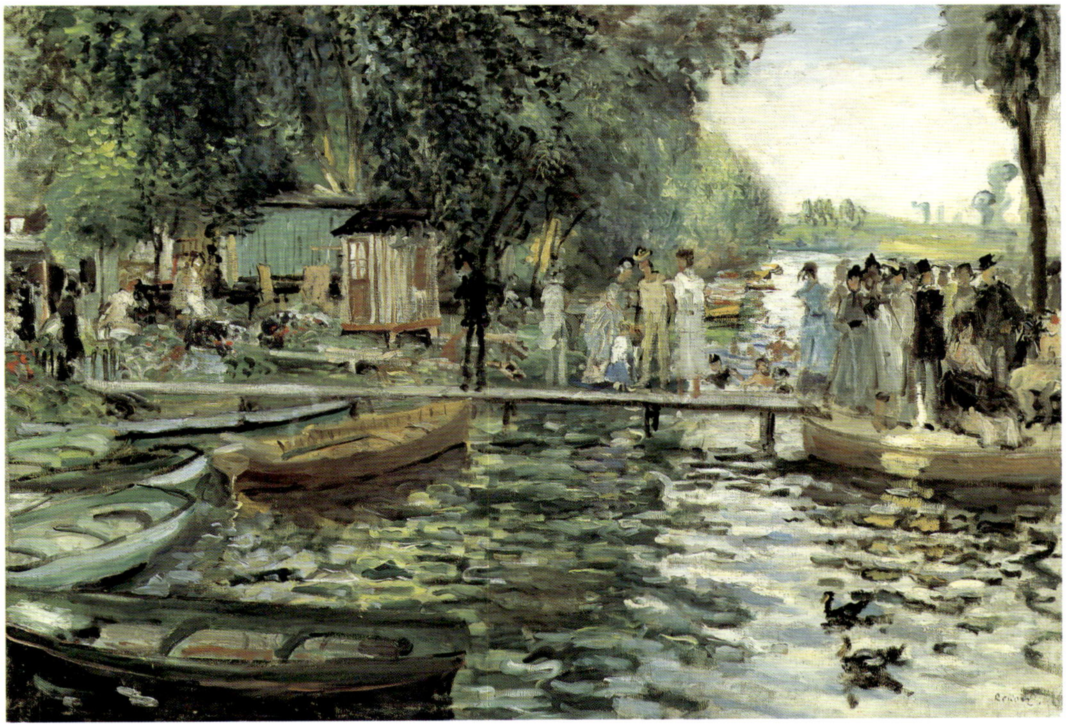

FIG. 60 *La Grenouillère,* 1869. Oil on canvas, 65 × 92 cm; 25½ × 36¼ in. Oskar Reinhart Collection 'am Römerholz', Winterthur (1931.4).

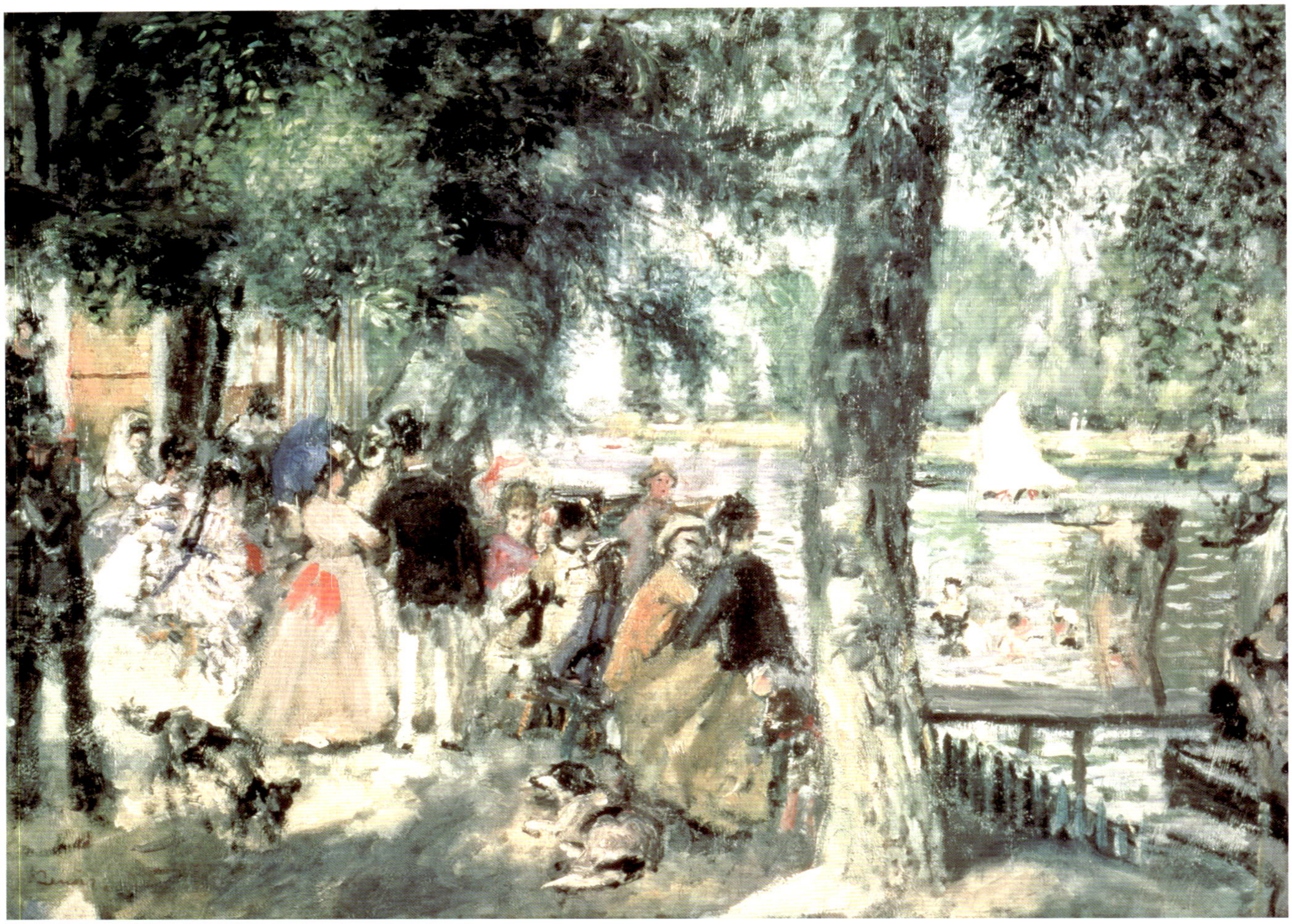

to be there. Most of the men and women who want to see the human race reduced to its most basic expression crowd on to this tiny islet. From this island, another bridge connects to the eating establishment. There is a small bathing area to the left, the river bed is of fine sand and the bathing area is roped off so that no one can get out of their depth . . . Boats are moored all around the island.'[14]

There are several similarly detailed accounts of La Grenouillère, and with these, and their accompanying illustrations (fig. 59) as guides, it is possible to identify the location, activities and *dramatis personae* of Renoir's various views of the site, each of which is meticulously described in this most abbreviated of pictorial languages.[15]

The canvas in Moscow (cat. 5), showing the river bank on arrival at La Grenouillère – a site not painted by Monet – is in all likelihood the earliest of Renoir's three paintings. Well-attired couples in the latest summer fashions sit and stroll under the shade of the overhanging willow trees, the occasional dog sleeping on the ground. The prow of a tiny boat at lower right; the spectral form of a half-painted waiter (?) on the wooden bridge, carrying a tray, a draped figure behind him; the male and female bathers bobbing in the water (the women in white caps and

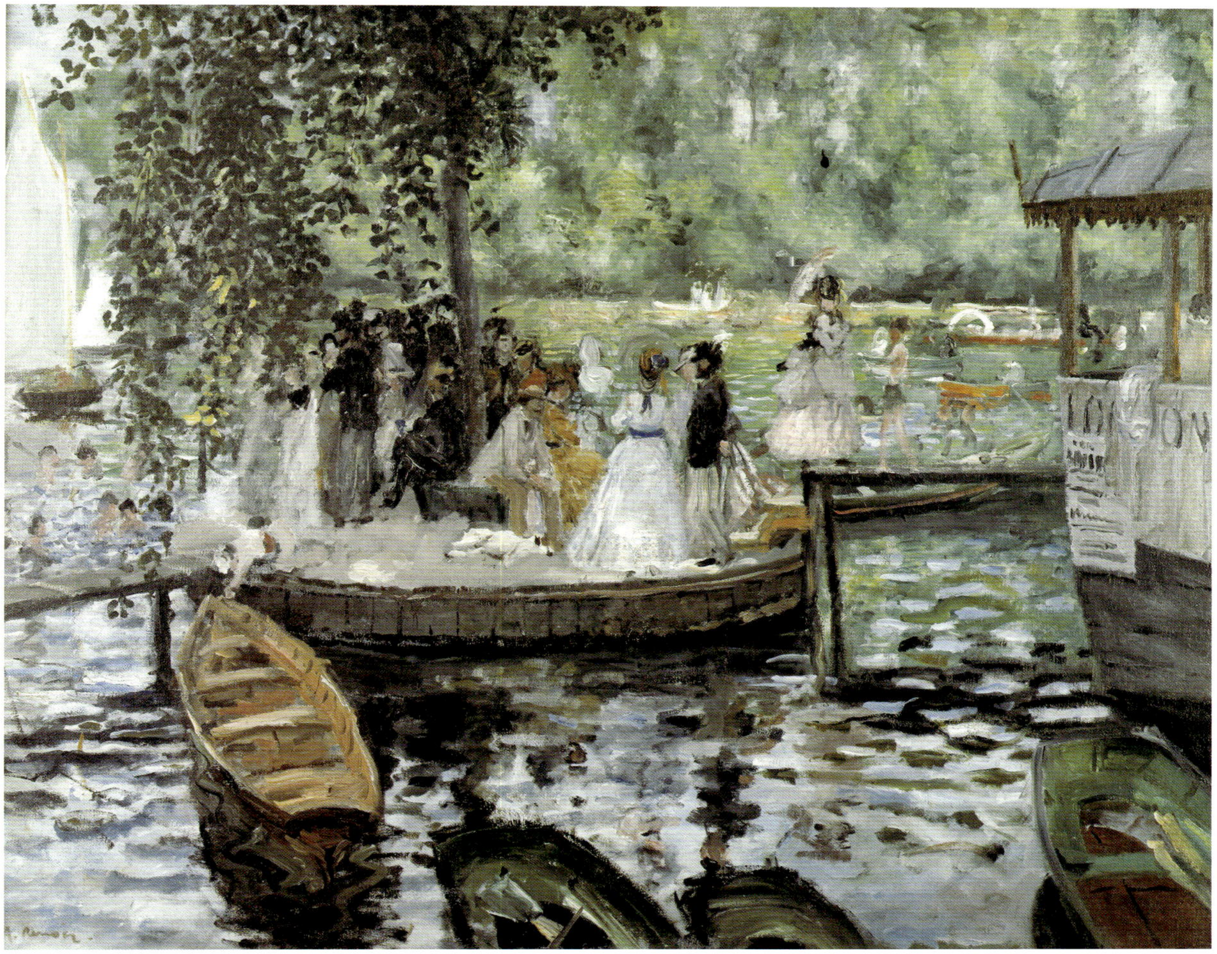

regulation black costumes), and the white sail of the skiff coming into view – these marginal motifs, all set in the gloriously dappled water, will assume greater prominence in the canvases to come. Despite Renoir's luminous, highly coloured touch, his composition maintains the priorities of the illustrated weeklies – pets, children (a tiny girl appears, bending forward, between the tree and the women seated with her back to us) and, above all, fashion. The women are dressed in bustles with brightly coloured bows at the back, carry parasols of striking hue, wear hats that tilt forward and tie up behind, 'real pieces of fashionable machinery'.[16] For his suburban Cythera, where the lovers have just begun their journey, Renoir creates a mood that is both ardent and decorous.[17]

In his second (cat. 6) and third (fig. 60) paintings of La Grenouillère, Renoir oriented his canvases to the same sites as Monet, to whose priorities and language (fig. 61) he became increasingly attentive. The artists must have set up their easels as far back from the river's edge as they could go, slightly uphill under one of the overhanging willows that lined the banks of this 'microscopic beach'.[18] For their first view, they tackled the islet in the middle, known as the 'Camembert' or as the 'flowerpot', which was only

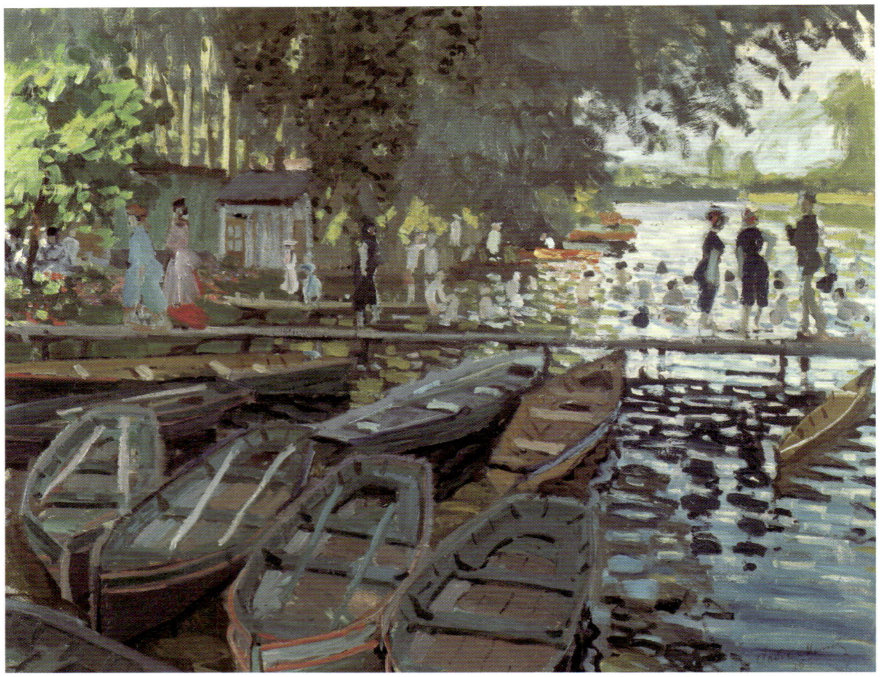

FIG. 61 Claude-Oscar Monet (1840–1926). *La Grenouillère*, 1869. Oil on canvas, 73 × 92 cm; 28¾ × 36¼ in. The National Gallery, London. Bequeathed by Mrs M.S. Walzer as part of the Richard and Sophie Walzer Bequest, 1979 (NG 6456).

five metres in diameter, and always crowded: Barbara White has counted as many as fifteen figures in Renoir's picture.[19] Guided by Monet, no doubt – whose inclinations as a marine painter could not be stifled – the artists described the boat-rental area, with the boats for hire resting in the shallow waters and the floating rental office, its sign partially obscured by a wet towel, anchoring the composition at right. As has been noted by all who have compared Monet and Renoir's canvases, Renoir privileges the denizens of the 'flowerpot', describing their costumes, attitudes, and activities with wit and affection. Examples of this would include the sleeping white dog, with his black snout and ears; the louche men in summer suits, one with his hands behind his back; the elegant parisienne, parasol in hand, looking back on the flirting couples and about to collide with the bather in green trunks who is crossing the footbridge in the opposite direction. Renoir also provides more information than Monet, showing two tiny yachts at left, various orange rowing boats at right, and a host of swimmers in the bathing area, demarcated with vertical posts and swaying ropes – all visible in the tiny patch of canvas above the footbridge at left. By comparison with Monet's supremely taut composition, in which the angled forms of the boats, building and footbridge compel the eye to the attend to the pontoon with its perfectly centred tree, Renoir's painting is unbridled and jaunty, almost chaotic at times.[20] Symmetries are eschewed (an early manifestation of Renoir's 'irregularity'), brushwork is busy and feathery, and the paint is applied more thinly than in Monet's insistent strokes. Renoir's *La Grenouillère* is also a supremely luminous composition, and in high key: by contrast, Monet's colourism is almost austere – even though in his picture in London (fig. 61) no fewer than 15 different pigments have been identified.[21]

Renoir and Monet's final pair of landscapes (figs. 60, 61) take as their subject the 'picturesque and primitive' footbridge that linked the 'flowerpot' to the riverbank, here shown laden with swimmers and promenaders. In his painting, it has been noted that Renoir followed Monet in giving priority to the water and its reflections, the rowing boats bobbing in the foreground, and the overhanging trees through which the view is screened (the most *japonisant* aspect of these compositions).[22] Fascinated now by the 'complex life of the water'[23] – into which two black ducks have strayed – Renoir pays less attention to the *dramatis personae* on the bridge, rendered in more summary terms. Nonetheless, we discern a black-suited man, lighting his cigarette, at left, and the family group next to him, attending to the little girl in white shawl and straw boater. Renoir's sociable instincts, never fully suppressed, may also have engaged Monet, whose largest (lost) painting of La Grenouillère paraded a group of well-dressed figures whose hats, parasols and cravats were all lovingly described.[24] Monet's discontinuities and Renoir's harmonies: 'One of those rare and marvellous periods of symbiosis between artists, when each is student and teacher of the other, spurred equally by rivalry and regard'.[25] CBB

Cat. 5 shown in Philadelphia only. Cat. 6 shown in London and Ottawa only

1 Loyrette and Tinterow 1994, p. 323; Stuckey 1995, p. 194.
2 Monet to Bazille, 9 August 1869; Wildenstein 1974–91, I, p. 426.
3 Renoir to Bazille, 13 August 1869; Daulte 1952, p. 35.
4 Monet to Bazille, 25 September 1869; Wildenstein 1974–91, I, p. 427.
5 '*Renoir a traité ce sujet plusieurs fois. Deux études de ce motif appartenaient à son frère qui les a vendues*'; letter from Paul Durand-Ruel, 13 July 1903, Archives Durand-Ruel; cited in House and Distel 1985, p. 192. Renoir's third sketch of *La Grenouillère* (fig. 60) was probably signed in blue at lower right when he sold it to Durand-Ruel in 1880; see Reinhard-Felice 2003, p. 431.
6 Herbert 1988, p. 214.
7 House and Distel 1985, pp. 193–4; House 1997, p. 46.
8 Loyrette and Tinterow 1994, pp. 439–40; Stuckey 1995, p. 184. Monet's lost *La Grenouillère*, last recorded in the collection of Eduard Arnhold in Berlin in 1909, and considered to have been destroyed in World War II, was not signed, and therefore is unlikely to have been the picture submitted to the Salon of 1870. House (2004, p. 49) also questions the identification of Monet's second Salon submission as *La Grenouillère*, citing descriptions that strongly indicate that the rejected picture was a seascape. He also notes that in February 1873 Durand-Ruel paid Monet the considerable sum of 2,000 francs for a canvas of *La Grenouillère*, a price that would have been inconceivable at the time for a sketch.
9 Bomford 1990, p. 122.
10 Stuckey 1995, p. 194.
11 Pickvance 1984, p. 42, and Lassalle 1992.
12 Herbert 1988, pp. 210–12; Loyrette and Tinterow 1994, pp. 455–6. At the Salon of 1869, Antony Morlon exhibited *La Grenouillère de l'Ile de Choisy, près Bougival*; at the Salon of 1870, François Heilbuth exhibited *Au bord de l'eau*, the site of La Grenouillère being identified by a critic who noted: '*Le site est fort beau; mais la population? Des hommes de mauvaise compagnie, des femmes déjà peintes*'; cited in House and Distel 1985, p. 192.
13 Isaacson 1982, p. 102; House and Distel 1985, p. 191.
14 House and Distel 1985 (French edition), p. 86.
15 For example, M.V., 'La Grenouillère. Bains froids de Croissy, à Bougival', *Le Monde illustré*, 25 July 1868, pp. 59, 61; Paul Parfait, 'La Grenouillère', *L'Univers illustré*, 31 July 1869; C.P., 'La Grenouillère', *L'Illustration*, 28 August 1869, p. 144; I am grateful to Marc Le Coeur for these references.
16 Clark 1985, p. 165.
17 While not yet the fleshpot described in Maupassant's *La Femme de Paul* (1881) and *Yvette* (1885), La Grenouillère's reputation for laxity and easy morals was well established in the late 1860s: '*O Grenouillère! Qui chantera tes échoes gouailleurs, tes ondes folles où fraternisent gaiement le sexe qui naît faible et celui qui le devient!*'; Parfait, 'La Grenouillère', *L'Univers illustré*, 31 July 1869. The courtesy (and affection) of Renoir's representation should be set against such discourse: for example, the often cited comment of Berthe Morisot's mother: '*C'est un petit-rendez vous très agreste d'un monde très léger et que, si l'on y va seul, on revient au moins deux*' (Rouart 1951, pp. 19–20), and Renoir's own comment to Vollard (1918A, p. 45): '*Là, Maupassant exagère un peu. On voyait bien, de temps en temps, à la Grenouillère, deux femmes s'embrasser sur la bouche; mais ce qu'elles avait l'air sain!*'
18 I have used the illustration by Crafty published in *Le Monde illustré*, 25 July 1868, to suggest the location. For Bomford (1990, p. 120) the artists set their easels on the floating platform looking towards the bathing area; Lay (1993, p. 282) has them on the gangway connecting the floating café to the shore; and Brettell (2000, p. 155) on the restaurant platform itself.
19 White 1996, p. 65.
20 See House 1986, pp. 51–3; Herbert 1988, pp. 214–6; Spate 1992, pp. 56–8.
21 Bomford 1990, p. 125.
22 House and Distel 1985, p. 192; Loyrette and Tinterow 1994, pp. 252–9, where the impact of Japanese coloured woodcuts on Renoir and Monet, at this early stage, seems overstated.
23 Spate 1992, p. 59.
24 See the illustration in Loyrette and Tinterow 1994, p. 439.
25 R. Gordon and A. Forge, *Monet*, New York 1983.

7 La Promenade, 1870

Oil on canvas
80 × 64 cm; 32 × 25½ in.
The J. Paul Getty Museum, Los Angeles (89.PA.41)

PROVENANCE:
Gustave Goupy, *c.*1890; his sale, Paris, Hôtel Drouot, 30 March 1898, lot 33, acquired by Durand-Ruel for 1,500 francs; sold by Durand-Ruel on 11 September 1908 for 12,000 francs to Galerie Paul Cassirer, Berlin; Bernhard Koehler, 1908–27; Bernhard Koehler Jr, 1927–33; Paul Rosenberg & Co.; Nate and Frances Springold, New York, 1957–76; Sotheby's, London, 29 November 1976, no. 22; Seito, Japan; British Rail Pension Fund; sale, British Rail Pension Fund, Sotheby's, London, 4 April 1989, lot 6

LITERATURE:
House and Distel 1985, p. 194–7; House 1997; Loyrette and Tinterow 1994, pp. 141–2, 231, 457

Set in bright afternoon sunlight, *La Promenade* shows a young man wearing the red-ribboned straw hat beloved of rowers helping his elegant companion to ascend the pathway at right. Almost crouching in the undergrowth, he holds back the branches that bar their access into this dense part of the forest. The demure parisienne, in a flawless white summer dress – not a spot of dirt in sight! – seems to be disentangling her skirts as she makes her unhurried way forward.

'He is trying to do what we have all so often tried to do: place a figure in the outdoor light.'[1] Morisot's comment of the previous year is the starting point for a consideration of Renoir's picture of two figures in the forest – part genre painting, part landscape – the modernity of which has been admirably investigated by John House.[2] Building on his experiences at La Grenouillère of the previous summer, Renoir now harnesses the brightness of his palette and the freedom and energy of his brushwork to convey the effect of filtered and direct light as it models the courting couple and establishes the steep, rough terrain in which they are posed.[3] Through a skein of rapid, abbreviated dabs and strokes – at times applied wet on wet and impasted (the girl's flowery hat, face, and dress), at times laid on with the slightest of touches (the undergrowth in the background, the shrubbery in the foreground) – Renoir, in full command of his medium, achieves for the first time a seamless integration of figures and setting. His brushwork has assumed the weight of academic drawing and is now the agent of authentic visual sensation.[4]

The prominent signature and date at lower left also remind us that this early Impressionist masterpiece was intended for exhibition and sale. Too small for the Salon, it was the sort of modern painting handled by dealers on the rue Lafitte, and occasionally shown in their shop windows. Renoir had exhibited the slightly larger *Engaged Couple* of 1868 (Wallraf-Richartz-Museum, Cologne) with his colourman and dealer Carpentier on the boulevard Montmartre in November 1869 (he was asking 100 francs for it), and was also considering the Hôtel Drouot as an outlet for *Lise* (Museum Folkwang, Essen), shown at the Salon of 1867, which had yet to find a buyer.[5] We do not know how Renoir marketed *La Promenade*, or even what he called it: the first recorded owner, Gustave Goupy, formed his collection of Impressionist pictures in the late 1880s.[6] But the signature in black confirms the status of *La Promenade* as a finished work and not a sketch (as is the case for the La Grenouillère canvases). In the final years of the 'liberal' Second Empire there was evidently some demand (small though it may have been) for such experimental, audaciously painted scenes of modern life.[7]

The date of 1870 also suggests that *La Promenade* was executed in the early summer of that year, before war against Prussia was declared on 19 July 1870. Renoir was living with his parents at Voisins-Louveciennes at the time, and, while there is no water in sight, the jaunty straw boater of the crouching male figure suggests that the Seine is not too far away. House has shown how Renoir's image of courtship in the suburbs – the '*canotier* and his *camarade*' – evoked associations that were less than innocent or decorous (this in addition to the assertive visibility of the brushwork itself). The appearance of a male figure in this sort of genre painting was in itself transgressive; his gesture towards the trysting place beyond suggests lovemaking as the conclusion of this promenade; and the 'emphatic highlight near the man's groin may be seen as a hint of the sexual dimension of the scene'.[8]

Renoir's debt in *La Promenade* to eighteenth-century French painting has also been noted:

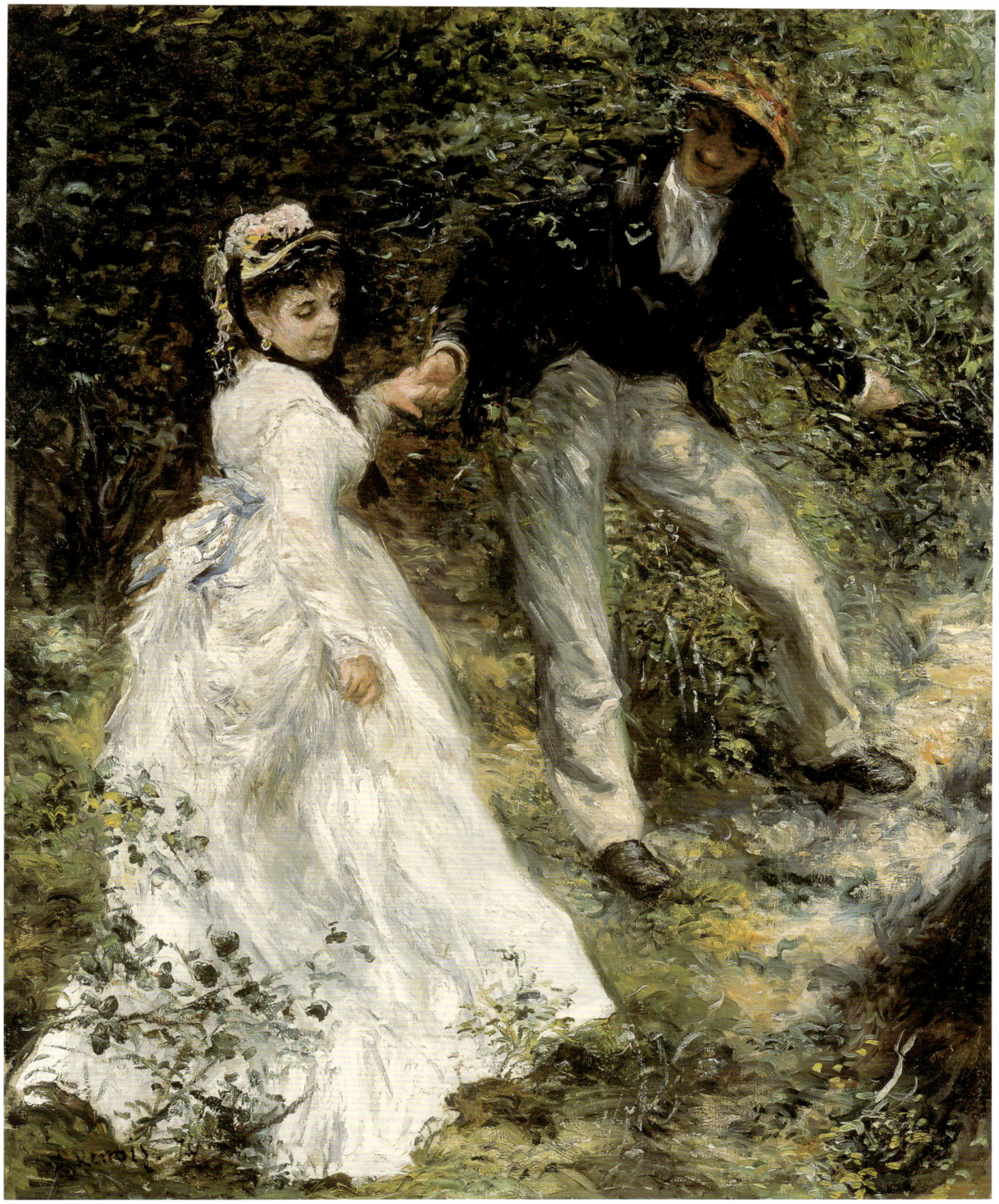

Herbert and House invoked Fragonard, Thomas Crow neatly characterised the protagonists as 'Harlequin and Columbine updated'[9] – but this too was part of the picture's modernity. Only very recently would Renoir have been exposed to the large number of works by Watteau, Chardin and Fragonard that had entered the Louvre as part of the La Caze donation. They were installed in the former Salle des Scéances de Louis XVIII, on the west side of the Cour Carrée, in February 1870.[10] The impact of the eighteenth-century French paintings in the La Caze donation on artists – rather than art historians and critics – remains to be studied, but such works as Watteau's *La Finette* and *Le Faux Pas* (both Musée du Louvre, Paris) are the Rococo antecedents for Renoir's single- and double-figure genre paintings of the 1870s.[11]

Finally, one needs to address the identity of the figures themselves. While in no sense a portrait, it is agreed that Renoir's dark-eyed parisienne was modelled for by the 22-year-old Lise Tréhot (1848–1922), daughter of a country postmaster and tobacconist who was Renoir's companion between 1866 and 1872 and who posed for no fewer than 16 of his figure paintings and portraits.[12] Her youthful swain, who is shown without a beard and lightly moustached, may well be a stand-in for the artist, but was in all likelihood modelled for by his younger brother Victor-Edmond (1849–1944), who was part of Renoir and Monet's circle at the time.[13] The delicacy with which Lise is portrayed as the hesitant parisienne – hardly Duret's 'woman whose demeanour and toilette leave one not knowing quite what to think'[14] – may have had something to do with her situation at the time. For in the early summer of 1870 Lise was pregnant with Renoir's second child: the first, a boy born in September 1868, had died in infancy, and Lise would give birth to Jeanne-Marguerite Tréhot on 21 July 1870.[15] No hint is given in *La Promenade* of Lise's advanced pregnancy, but in the light of such information the gesture of the helping hand and the unsullied frock take on new meanings. CBB

1 Morisot to her sister, commenting upon Bazille's *View of the Village* (Musée Fabre, Montpellier), exhibited at the Salon of 1869; see Loyrette and Tinterow 1994, pp. 125–47, 333–4.
2 House 1997.
3 Which Henri Loyrette has aptly characterised as 'a suburban jungle'; Loyrette and Tinterow 1994, p. 457.
4 For an appraisal of Renoir's aesthetic around 1870 see my discussion of *Woman with a Parrot* (Guggenheim Museum, New York) in Drutt 2001, pp. 206–11.
5 House 1997, pp. 17–22.
6 Goupy (often confused in the literature as Goupil) was a client of Boussod and Valadon who owned five paintings by Monet, three by Pissarro, and Manet's *Kearsage at Boulogne* (The Metropolitan Museum of Art, New York) and *In the Garden* (The Shelburne Museum, Vermont), the latter two paintings acquired in 1890.
7 This issue is taken up again in House 2004, pp. 51–3.
8 House 1997, pp. 64–7.
9 Herbert 1988, pp. 190–2; House 1997, p. 20; Crow 1986, p. 118.
10 F. Rieset, *Notice des Tableaux légués au Musée Impérial du Louvre par M. Louis la Caze*, Paris 1870. On the collection of Louis La Caze (1798–1869), see Laclotte 1989, pp. 243–4.
11 For the consequences of the Rococo revival on French painting and criticism of the 1850s and 1860s, see Haskell 1976, pp. 76–7, pp. 102–3; for the impact on contemporary painting of the Spanish Old Masters in the Louvre at this time, see Tinterow and Lacambre 2003, pp. 84–5.
12 Cooper 1959; Bailey in Drutt 2001, p. 208.
13 White (1996, p. 85) suggested that the models for the companions were Monet and Doncieux; this is rejected by House (1997, p. 81), who notes that 'Lise was the model for nearly all of Renoir's figures at this time'.
14 Duret 1998, p. 36, commenting on Alfred Steven's fashionable genre paintings at the Salon of 1870.
15 See Le Coeur pp. 203–4 and Gelineau pp. 223–7 in São Paulo 2002.

8 Road in Louveciennes, 1870

Oil on canvas
38.1 × 46.4 cm; 15 × 18¼ in.
The Metropolitan Museum of Art, New York. The Lesley and Emma Sheafer Collection
Bequest of Emma A. Sheafer, 1973 (1974.356.32)

'Are you an intrepid hiker? Is it one of those sunny days that makes you want to go into the fields? Would you like to discover the most picturesque and evocative of all the Parisian suburbs, a region that is justly famous? If so, get up early in the morning and go to Bougival, and after a hearty luncheon on the banks of the river, proceed to Marly-le-Roi by way of Louveciennes.'[1] Victorien Sardou's contribution to Lacroix's illustrated guide to Paris and its environs, published to coincide with the Universal Exposition of 1867,[2] might well describe the scene that Renoir painted in Louveciennes three years later, in the early summer of 1870, not far from his parents' home on the rue de Voisins[3] – except that Renoir's elegant day-trippers (a couple and their well-dressed daughter) are on their way back, leaving Louveciennes for Bougival, the remnants of Louis XIV's aqueduct at Marly visible high above at left, peaking through the trees behind them.[4]

On this small canvas – a size eight – Renoir captures the intense heat of a summer's afternoon, with long shadows falling on the unpaved road with its exuberant vegetation punctuated by a single modest dwelling. In the spring of 1870 Pissarro had painted a similar view to the north-west, from the route de la Princesse in Louveciennes (fig. 62), in which the aqueduct at Marly was more clearly demarcated.[5] Renoir did not set his easel on the very same stretch of road, however; his view is taken from a parallel street nearby, the rue St-Michel, site of the present day place de la Gare (Louveciennes was only incorporated into the Paris-Marly railway line in April 1885).[6] In Renoir's canvas the

PROVENANCE:
Ambroise Vollard, Paris; A.R. Ball, New York, until 1948; Lesley and Emma Sheafer, New York, 1948–73; bequeathed by Emma A. Sheafer to the Metropolitan Museum, 1973

LITERATURE:
Loyrette and Tinterow 1994, pp. 260–3, 456; House 1995, pp. 192–3; House 2004, pp. 79–82, 89–90

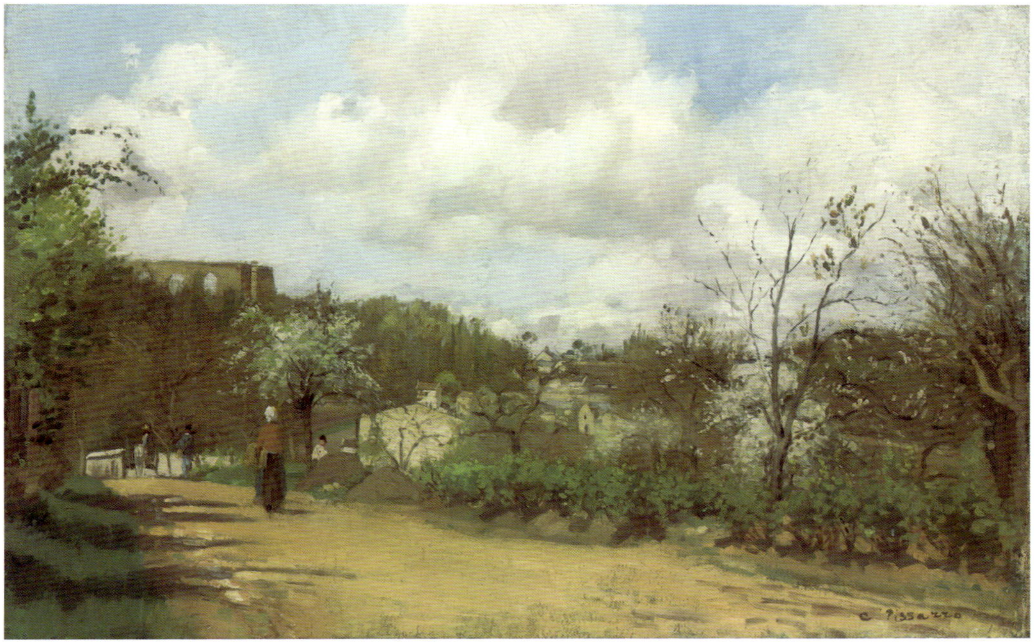

FIG. 62 Camille Pissarro (1839–1903), *View from Louveciennes*, about 1870. Oil on canvas, 52.7 × 81.9 cm; 20¾ × 32¼ in. The National Gallery, London (NG 3265).

historical marker of the Marly aqueduct dissolves into the afternoon light and is almost indistinguishable from the hills and trees that surround it.

Undated, and perhaps not intended for sale – the 'signature' at right is a much later addition – *Road in Louveciennes* is an admirable exercise in what Gary Tinterow has termed the 'aesthetic of the *pochade*'.[7] In this composition, an exercise in various tones of green, paint is handled in flickering dabs and strokes, as in *La Promenade* (cat. 7), with which it is strictly contemporaneous.[8] Since, in this instance, the figures are little more than staffage, Renoir unifies his landscape in broad, generalised lighting and with blended brushwork, both of which suggest the continuing potency of Corot's example. But a more assertive, 'modern' handling imposes itself in the nodules of impasto that describe the clouds and in the wavy strokes of cream and grey delineating the shadows on the road in the foreground.

As has been recently emphasised, Renoir's idyllic vision of a day in the country was for metropolitan consumption.[9] His Parisian day-trippers are fashionably attired: the man's cane, the woman's little red parasol, the girl's salmon bow and tiny black shoes are all scrupulously noted, with the eye (and hand) of a miniaturist. Yet the contrast between Renoir's 'sense of pleasurable escape' and Pissarro's commitment to the site as 'workplace' – the latter's *View from Louveciennes* shows a single peasant woman with local figures beyond – is arrived at a little too easily.[10] If one looks hard at the cluster of figures in the centre of Renoir's composition, it is possible to identify the back of an adolescent peasant boy in blue smock and serge trousers. Next to him, but more difficult to make out, is a woman on the back of a four-legged creature – a mule or a donkey? – which the boy seems to be leading. (He is shown listing slightly to his left, as if straining to pull the animal along). On this empty, sun-drenched road, town and country briefly encounter each other and pass by in quiet acknowledgement of their separate rituals. CBB

1 Sardou in Paris Guide 1867, II, p. 1455.
2 Brettell and Schaefer 1984, pp. 81–2.
3 From June 1868 until his father's death in December 1874 Renoir's parents lived on the rue de Voisins, no. 23 of the street as it stands today; information kindly provided by Marie Amynte Denis.
4 House 1995, pp. 192.
5 Herbert 1988, p. 205; Loyrette and Tinterow 1994, p. 448.
6 I am grateful to Jacques and Monique Laÿ for this information; see also *De Renoir à Vuillard*, 1984, p. 101, and *Louveciennes: Bulletin d'Accueil*, undated, p. 7.
7 Loyrette and Tinterow 1994, p. 260.
8 House 1995, p. 192; Loyrette and Tinterow 1994, p. 456, date the painting to '1869?', which seems unnecessarily fastidious given the strong stylistic similarities with the Getty *La Promenade*.
9 House 2004, pp. 79–83.
10 House 1995, p. 192.

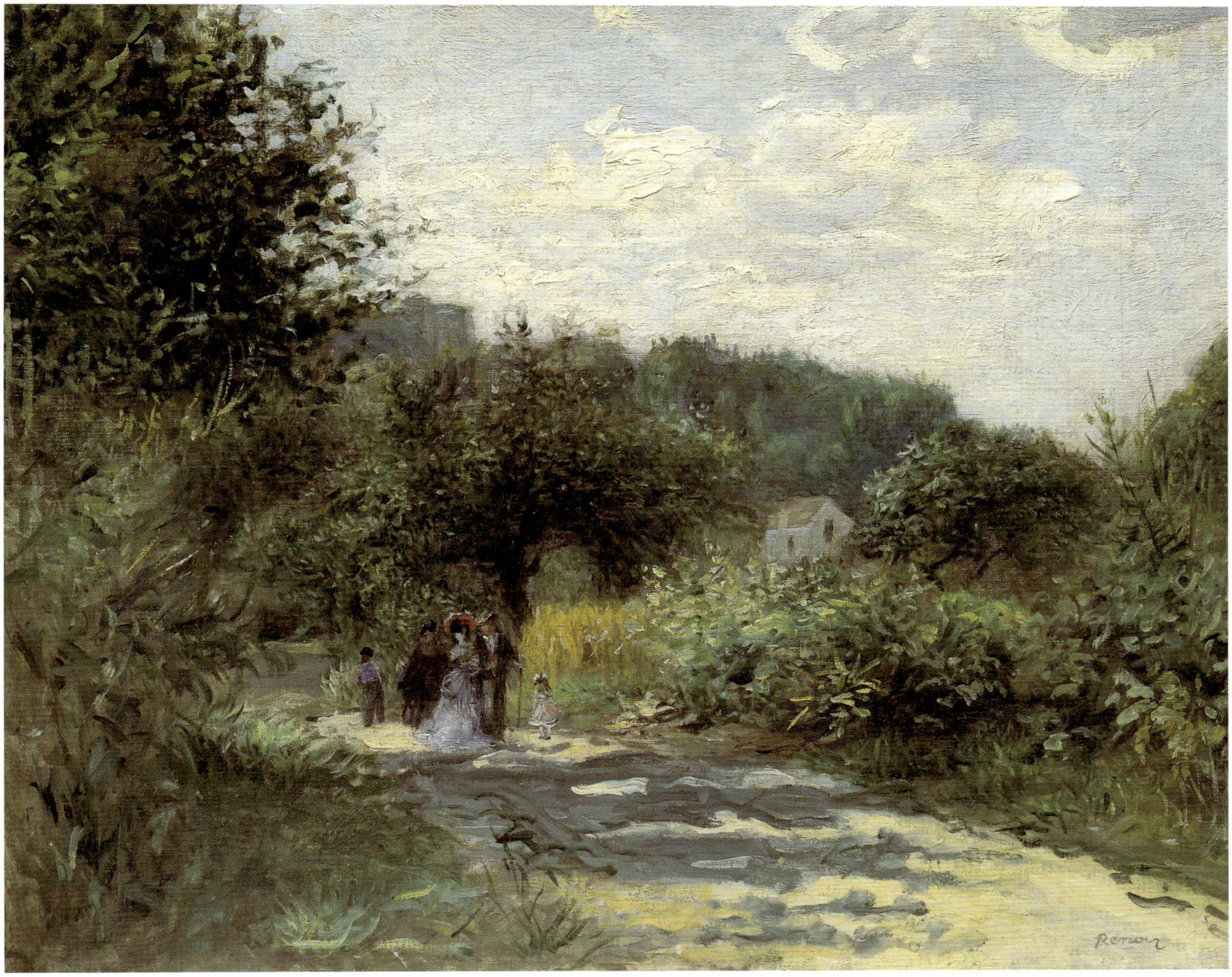
Renoir

9 The Seine at Chatou, 1871

Oil on canvas
45.7 × 55.9 cm; 18 × 22 in.
Art Gallery of Ontario, Toronto
Purchased 1935 (2304)

PROVENANCE:
Ambroise Vollard; Alex Reid & Lefevre Ltd, London; acquired by the Art Gallery of Ontario in 1935

LITERATURE:
House 1994, pp. 60–1; House 2004, pp. 153–5, 231

Were it not for the signature embedded in the lower-left hand corner of the canvas, indicating that Renoir considered the painting to be a finished work, *The Seine at Chatou* might well be taken for an exploratory sketch, abandoned in mid-stream (as it were).[1] As John House has eloquently argued, this view across the empty river, in which the central villa is shown in *contrejour*, conveys the immediacy of visual sensation through a remarkably audacious painterly shorthand. The patch of white impasto on the building just left of centre – perhaps the sunlight glinting from a glass roof – and the corresponding dabs of white in the river below (reflections of this structure in the water) are notations that consciously draw attention to themselves, but their function is not altogether clear. Renoir is attempting to convey the uncertainty of vision, the moment before recognition, when optical effects are registered but not fully processed. Hence a composition whose focal point is 'without any declared referent'.[2]

This was Renoir's first landscape of Chatou, a popular centre for rowing and fishing and a short train ride from Paris, which he would later refer to as 'the loveliest of all the Parisian suburbs'.[3] As House has also noted, *The Seine at Chatou* is almost wilfully anti-picturesque, as if Renoir were resisting the pleasure and sociability that would pervade his scenes of Chatou from mid-decade on.[4] Although the village was renowned for its 'delicious vistas and delightful views',[5] Renoir's picture is of a scrubby river bank, with a stunted sapling at left, that looks towards a distinctly lack-lustre and charmless group of villas (the largest of which has a gated entrance on the towpath), with the village's celebrated yew trees straining to be seen, and two tiny figures (one carrying washing on her head?) rendered in insignificant blobs of paint.

Terse in subject-matter, experimental in handling, Renoir's *The Seine at Chatou* can be associated with a group of riparian sketches which show Lise Tréhot seated alone in a rowing boat (fig. 63), or standing on the grassy banks, her white summer's dress edged in black.[6] These slight works have been variously dated to between 1867 and 1872, yet the bold description of water in them, with strokes of white doing little to remedy the 'sombre-hued' effect overall, is consistent with the mood and facture of *The Seine at Chatou*.[7] The entire group, surely part of the same campaign, must have been painted at Chatou in the summer of 1871. Renoir had been called up for military service in August 1870, returned to Paris after a seven-month absence in March 1871, and during the Commune would divide his time between the city and his parents' home at Louveciennes.[8] The 'summer holiday' he enjoyed with Lise at Chatou would thus have taken place in the months following the '*semaine sanglante*' of the Commune (21–28 May), which may in part account for the somewhat mournful air of these pictures. Lise continued to sit for Renoir and act as his model until the spring of 1872. On 24 April of that year she married the architect Georges Brière de l'Isle and communication between her and Renoir abruptly came to an end.[9] Tréhot is an absent figure in *The Seine at Chatou*, ironically the only completed work to emerge from this post-war 'day in the country'. CBB

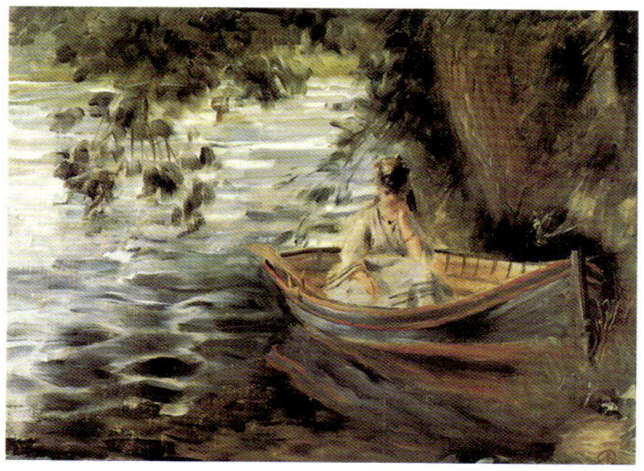

FIG. 63 *Boat at Chatou*, 1871. Oil on canvas, 25 × 34 cm; 9⅞ × 13⅜ in. Private collection.

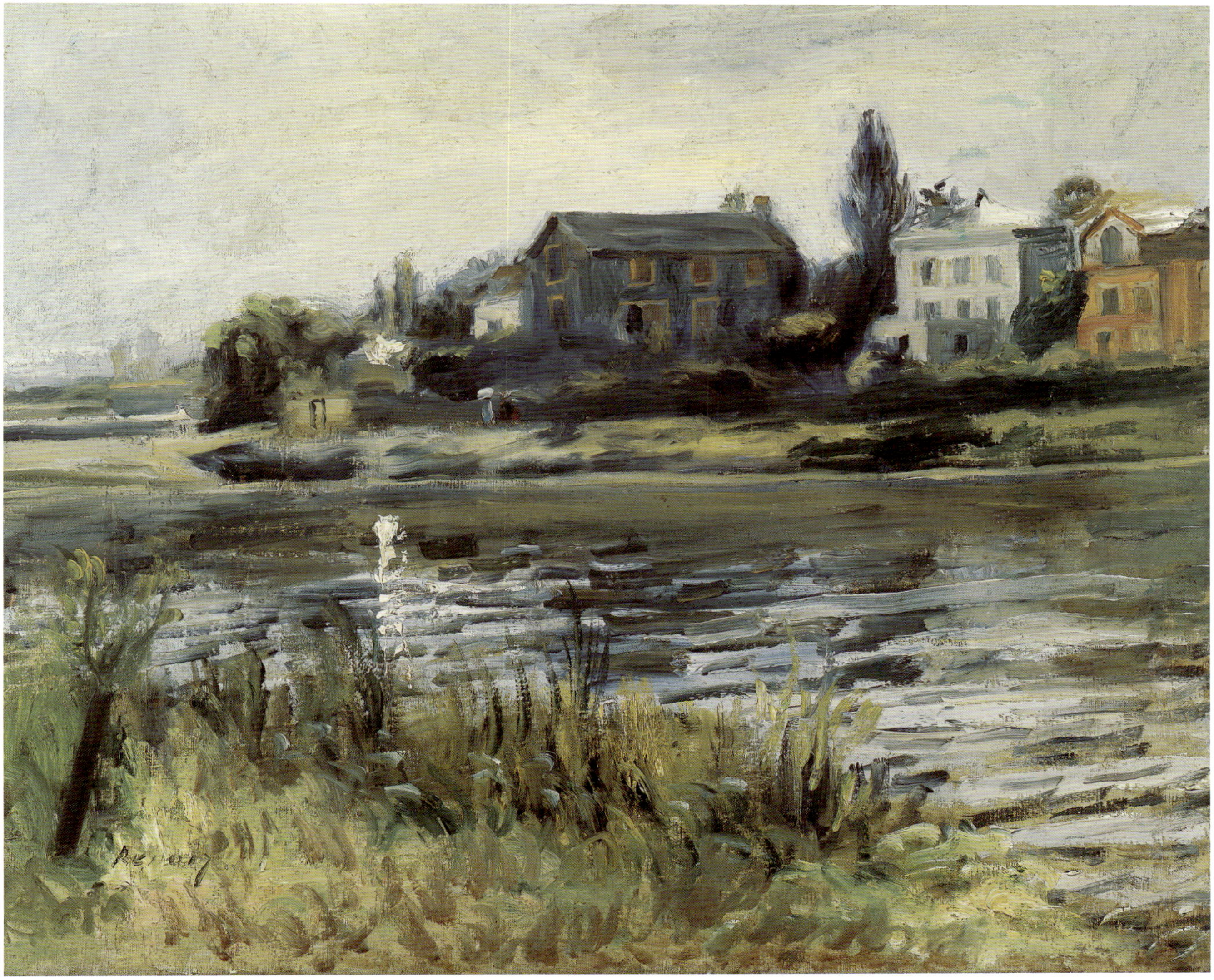

1 House (2004, p. 231, n. 26) points out that the form of the signature belongs to the early 1870s.
2 House 2004, pp. 153–5.
3 Renoir to de Bellio, September 1880, *Autographes et documents historiques*, Librairie Henry Saffroy, Paris, June 1983, no. 118. On Renoir at Chatou, see Herbert 1988, pp. 246–4, and Rathbone 1996.
4 House 1994, p. 60; on Renoir's later production at Chatou, see cats. 32, 33, 49, 50, 60, 61.
5 Larousse 1865–90, III, p. 1090.
6 Vollard 1918, I, p. 5 (plate 19), p. 6 (plate 21), where all are dated 1870; Fezzi 1985, pp. 48–50, 51 (all dated 1870). For *Boat at Chatou* (fig. 63), see Leymarie 1955, I, p. 78; Cooper 1959, p. 169; Fezzi 1985, p. 36, and, most recently 1988, pp. 38–9 (where the painting is variously dated 1867, 1869, and 1868–70).
7 Clement Greenberg 'Renoir and the Picturesque', *Art News*, Vol. XLIX (April 1950) and Maxon 1973, p. 11, also drew attention to the 'partially overcast sky'.
8 House and Distel 1985, pp. 196–7.
9 Cooper 1959, pp. 168, 171.

10 Village Street (Louveciennes), about 1871–2

Oil on canvas
38 × 46 cm; 15 × 18 in.
Private collection

PROVENANCE:
Ambroise Vollard; family of the current owner, to whom by descent

LITERATURE:
Vallès-Bled and Sanfo 2002, p. 42; Spadoni 2006, p. 118

In the spring of 1868, Renoir's parents moved from Paris to Louveciennes, a small town west of the city, on a hill above the Seine. This painting appears to have been created some time later than that, though not as late as 1876, as the work has been dated previously. On the basis of the technique employed in this work, the painting has been redated to *c.*1871–2. It is very close to *The Seine at Chatou* (cat. 9) in a number of respects, most visibly in its use of pastel colours as highlights on buildings and in the presence of rapidly rendered vertical strokes in the foreground. As in this landscape, the pigment is mixed with a high proportion of solvent, there is no impasto, and one finds in the buildings a transition of colours – for example, in the door on the right hand side, where the blue/green of the door changes to orange just above, then to lavender – that is otherwise unusual in Renoir's work. Renoir did not use this technique for long, turning soon after to a drier, more impasto style.

The image of a bend in the road is one of the most beloved clichés of nineteenth-century landscape painting, as it was also common in seventeenth-century Dutch precedents. Countless variations of this theme occur in the works of the Barbizon artists and also in the works of the Impressionists. In this exhibition, another example is the *Road in Louveciennes* (cat. 8) but other curving roads occur in works by Corot, Pissarro, Cézanne, Monet, and perhaps the best comparison to this painting is a work by Alfred Sisley, *Early Snow at Louveciennes* (fig. 64). This also focuses on the village of Louveciennes but the view is wider and there are a handful of figures walking along the road in both directions. Sisley's painting is larger and more finished but the basic principle is similar: a curving road leads one's eye into the distance, which is tightly bordered by small houses and provides a sense of an intimate space shared by the inhabitants of the village. Such rustic scenes held great meaning for viewers of paintings in the nineteenth century, suggesting the timeless ideal of peasants living in traditional enclosures and practising age-old activities that reflected the natural cycle of the seasons. Such romanticised, if sometimes authentic, views of the country found a ready market in the bustling modern capital, Paris, where the pace of change was rapid and the traditional quarters were being destroyed in order to make room for large boulevards and civic monuments. In fact, Renoir's parents moved to the village of Louveciennes because they were displaced by redevelopment from their home in Paris.

Village Street presents a timeless idealisation of village life and seems infused with a sense of stillness, except for the presence of a carriage, drawn by a single horse, that approaches the viewer. This element of action in the scene is depicted with no more than a handful of rapidly placed strokes of paint, so that the pace of the carriage is reflected in the speed of its representation. This centrally placed component animates this otherwise static composition and, like the flower in the window box at the right, makes the viewer realise that, though the scene appears rustic, time is not standing still. JZ

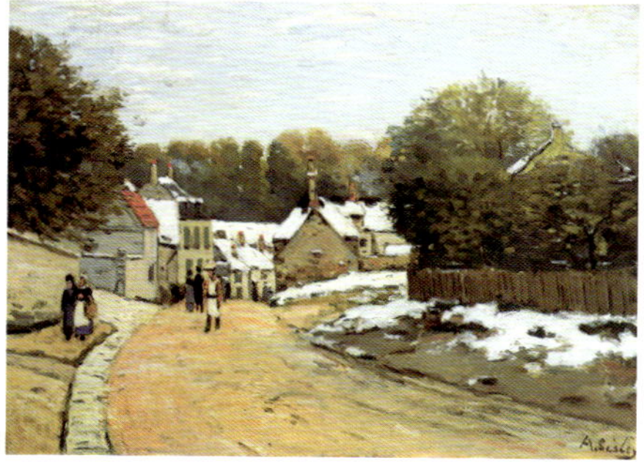

FIG. 64 Alfred Sisley (1893–1899), *Early Snow at Louveciennes*, about 1870–1. Oil on canvas, 54.8 × 73.8 cm; 21½ × 29 in. Museum of Fine Arts, Boston, Bequest of John T. Spaulding (48.600).

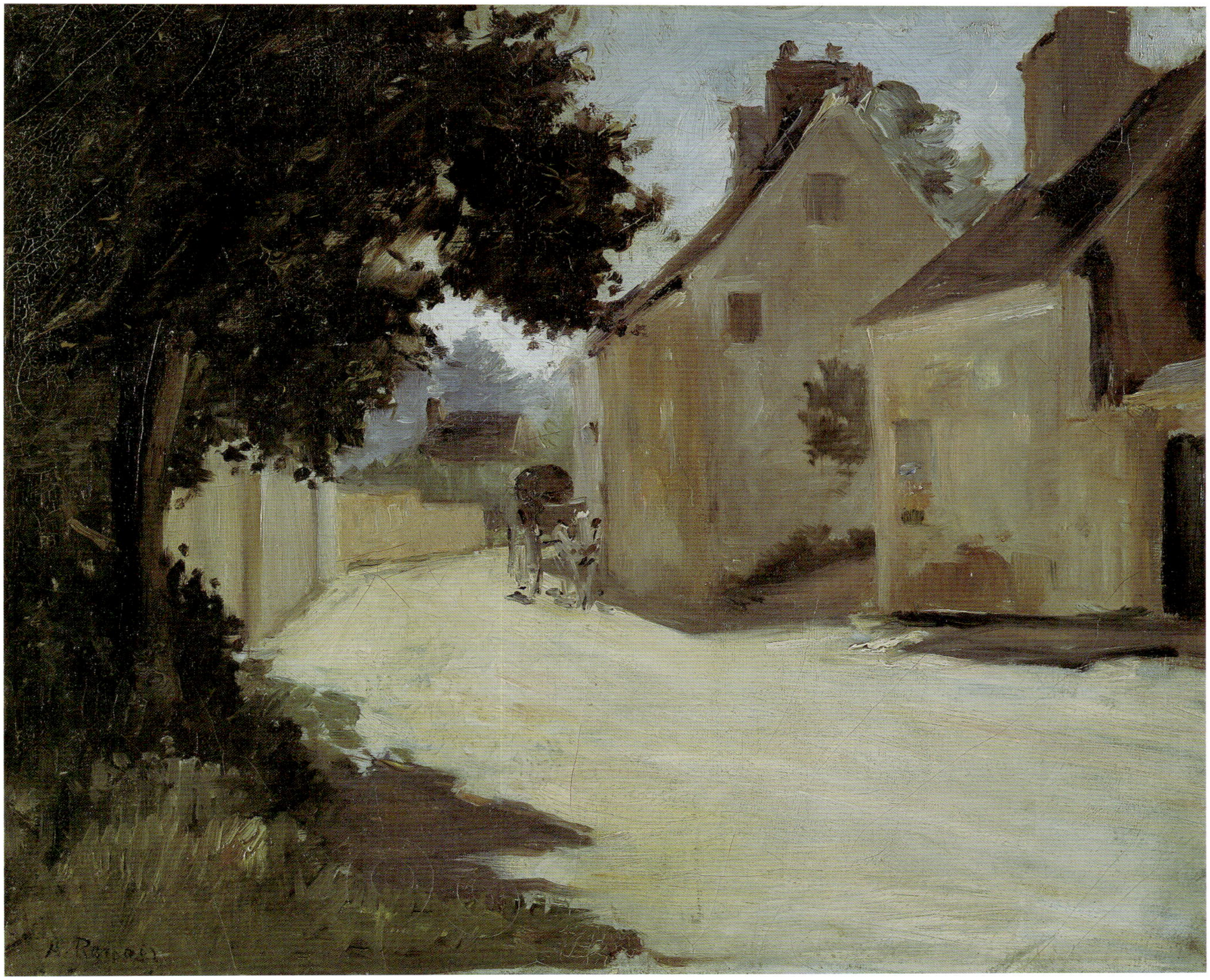

11 Laundry-boat on the Seine, Near Paris, 1871

Oil on canvas
46.4 × 55.9 cm; 18 × 22 in.
Morohashi Museum of Modern Art, Japan

PROVENANCE:
Family of the artist; Bruno Stahl, Berlin (stolen during World War II, returned to owner by 1946); Wildenstein, London, 1955; private collection, London; sold Sotheby's, New York, 1 May 1996; private collection, Japan

LITERATURE:
Los Angeles 1955, no. 3, p. 42

The year of 1871 was a bleak period in the history of Paris. Just after the nation's defeat at the hands of the Prussians, the brutal repression of the Commune in the spring of 1871 doubled the city's misfortunes. Renoir seems to respond to this dark mood in this work, perhaps the dreariest landscape he ever painted. The canvas is covered in greys and browns and the laundry boat that serves as the main motif casts a black shadow into the river below. On the right, a woman who carries a laundry basket is surrounded by several children and, in the middle distance, another figure labours under the weight of a parcel of laundry.

Unlike his earlier and later views of the quays and bridges of Paris (see cat. 12), this image features neither a sunny day nor a sense of bustling activity but more closely resembles another picture from 1871, *The Seine at Chatou* (cat. 9). In both works, Renoir depicts river landscapes with a patchwork of vivid brushstrokes in the foreground and a loosely composed spatial structure covered by vague and impenetrable skies. While *The Seine at Chatou* is rendered in subdued colours that provide a general richness to the scene, *Laundry-boat on the Seine* features an overcast sky that results in darker tones and murky reflections in the water. In the background, the industrial buildings that even today line the edges of Paris are visible but their faceless grey façades do not indicate any sign of life. Some sort of fence or barrier lines the painting's right edge and suggests the barricades which were a common feature of Paris throughout the rule of the Communards. For once, the cheery artist seems to have yielded to the bleakness of the world around him.

Emile Zola, the naturalist author who championed Manet and his Impressionist friends, would later make the washhouse into a symbol of modern labour in his novel *L'Assommoir*, published in 1876. 'A wan daylight penetrated the hot steam hanging like a milky fog . . . Everywhere a heavy moisture rained down, laden with the smell of soap, a persistent, stale, dank aroma sharpened at times by a whiff of bleach. A row of women stretched along the washing-boards down each side of the central passage; their arms were bare up to the shoulders, dresses turned down at the neck, skirts caught up, showing their coloured stockings and heavy laced boots.'[1]

Though Renoir would turn his hand to making illustrations for Zola's novel in 1878, it was well before Zola wrote *L'Assommoir* that Renoir chose to depict this most pedestrian of sites, in which working-class women gather to toil with scalding water, beaters, brushes and chemicals to remove the soil from garments in order to make others appear fresh and new. To make a painting of such a place was a radical gesture, not simply because no sense of beauty or inspiration could seemingly be derived from it but also because this so-called landscape is no pretty country lane. The picture stands as a form of pictorial recording of the bleak realities of modern urban life, a form of gritty naturalism that Renoir usually eschewed.

JZ

1 E. Zola, *L'Assommoir* (1878), trans. L. Tancock, London and New York 1970, p. 33.

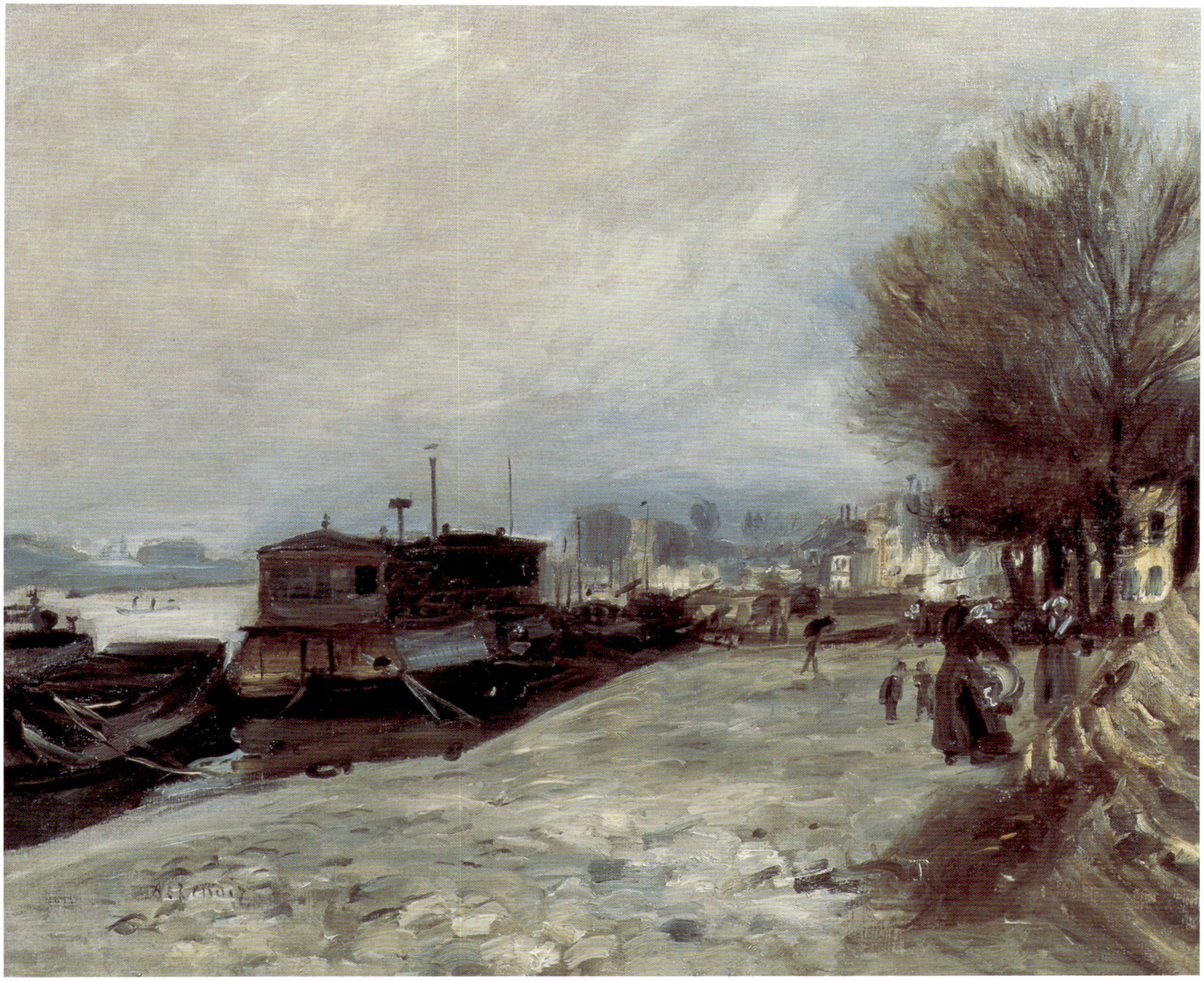

12 The Pont Neuf, 1872

Oil on canvas
75 × 94 cm; 29⅝ × 37 in.
National Gallery of Art, Washington, DC. Ailsa Mellon Bruce Collection (1970. 17. 58)

PROVENANCE:
Tableaux et Aquarelles par Monet, Morisot, Renoir, Sisley, Paris, Hôtel Drouot, 24 March 1875, no. 42, *Le Pont-neuf*, purchased for 300 francs by Durand-Ruel, Paris, on behalf of Nicolas-Auguste Hazard, Paris; sale of his widow, Paris, 1 December 1919, no. 206; purchased for 100,000 francs by Georges Bernheim, Paris; sold 1921 to Ralph M. Coe, Cleveland; on joint account with Carroll Carstairs, New York, and M. Knoedler & Co., New York, by 1935; probably from whom acquired by Marshall Field, New York, by 1937; Dr and Mrs Robert Boggs, New York; Mr and Mrs Peter Benziger; M. Knoedler & Co.; sold December 1966 to Ailsa Mellon Bruce; bequeathed in 1970 to the National Gallery of Art

LITERATURE:
Reff 1982, pp. 33–4, 42–5; House and Distel 1985, pp. 61, 200–1; Boime 1995, pp. 117–21; Rice 1997, pp. 69–76

Prominently signed and dated at lower left, Renoir's post-Commune cityscape is a paean to Haussmann's 'city of light' and the return to normality in the metropolis.[1] It is an elaborate, sun-filled view looking south across the Seine to the Ile de la Cité, and then to the Quai de Conti and the Quai des Augustins on the left bank beyond. Edmond Renoir's celebrated reminiscence, made to John Rewald some 70 years after the event, placed the artist on the mezzanine floor of a café at the corner of the quai du Louvre and the rue de la Monnaie, a spot visible just above the awning at lower left of Fichot's *Exterior View of the Grands Magasins de la Belle Jardinière* (fig. 65).[2] This may be identified as the *salle à boire* on the first floor of a wine merchant's establishment, run by a certain Noiron, whose premises between 1869 and 1875 were listed as at 2 Quai du Louvre and 1 rue de la Monnaie.[3] From here Renoir looked down on to a warm-water bathing establishment, the 'Bains de la Samaritaine' – marked by the sign and tricolour flag at lower right[4] – and across the wide entrance to the bridge, with its impeccable paving, rows of gas lamps, and bustling traffic, both pedestrian and horse-drawn.

Paris's oldest bridge, created by Henri III in 1577 and completed by Henri IV between 1599 and 1603, had been cleaned up early in Haussmann's administration. Between 1851 and 1854 all the shops had been removed from the semi-circular lunettes that protruded over the river, gas lighting was introduced (part of the campaign to install 15,000 street lamps in the city), and the pavement extended.[5] Now considered 'one of the most beautiful bridges' in the city, the Pont Neuf accommodated a huge volume of cabs, carriages and omnibuses; according to a survey conducted at the end of the century, it was crossed by as many as 18,000 vehicles a day.[6] Renoir chose not to dwell on the bridge's congestion, however, relegating the stream of traffic in both directions to the middle ground of his composition, and showing a small queue of pedestrians – two gendarmes at its head – waiting patiently for the next omnibus.[7] Renoir was more interested in human traffic, and he portrays a society of strollers, lovers, officials, workers, children and animals – each identified in remarkably faithful and affectionate detail.

In the foreground at right, for example, we see a man in a straw boater and cane, immersed in his reading, followed by a tiny dog (the same figure reappears, without the dog, at the far left of the composition).[8] On the pavement to his right, an elegant mother and her child pass in front of a trio of well-attired bourgeois. The woman with her back to us is shown with her chestnut hair almost to her waist; her companion, in a summer dress with a bustle, holds a red parasol to shield her from the sun. Lounging against the wall, at some distance from them, is a group of workers (two in their blue smocks), one of whom is peering into the water below. Next to him, a gendarme in cap and red epaulettes starts up a conversation with a girl, whose head is covered with a white bonnet and who carries a basket on her arm.

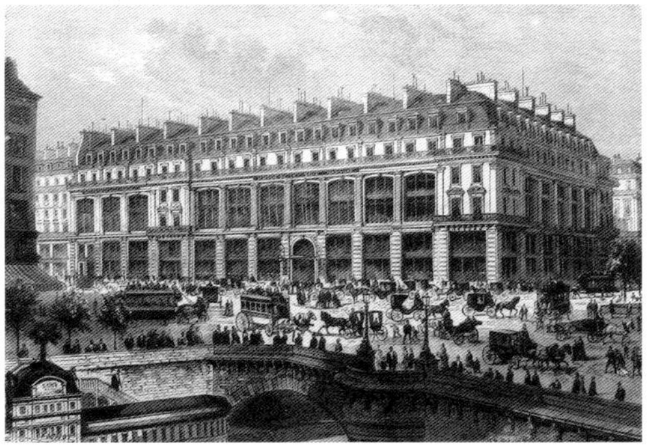

FIG. 65 Fichot, *Exterior View of the Grands Magasins de la Belle Jardinière*, 1867. Lithograph. Musée Carnavalet, Histoire de Paris.

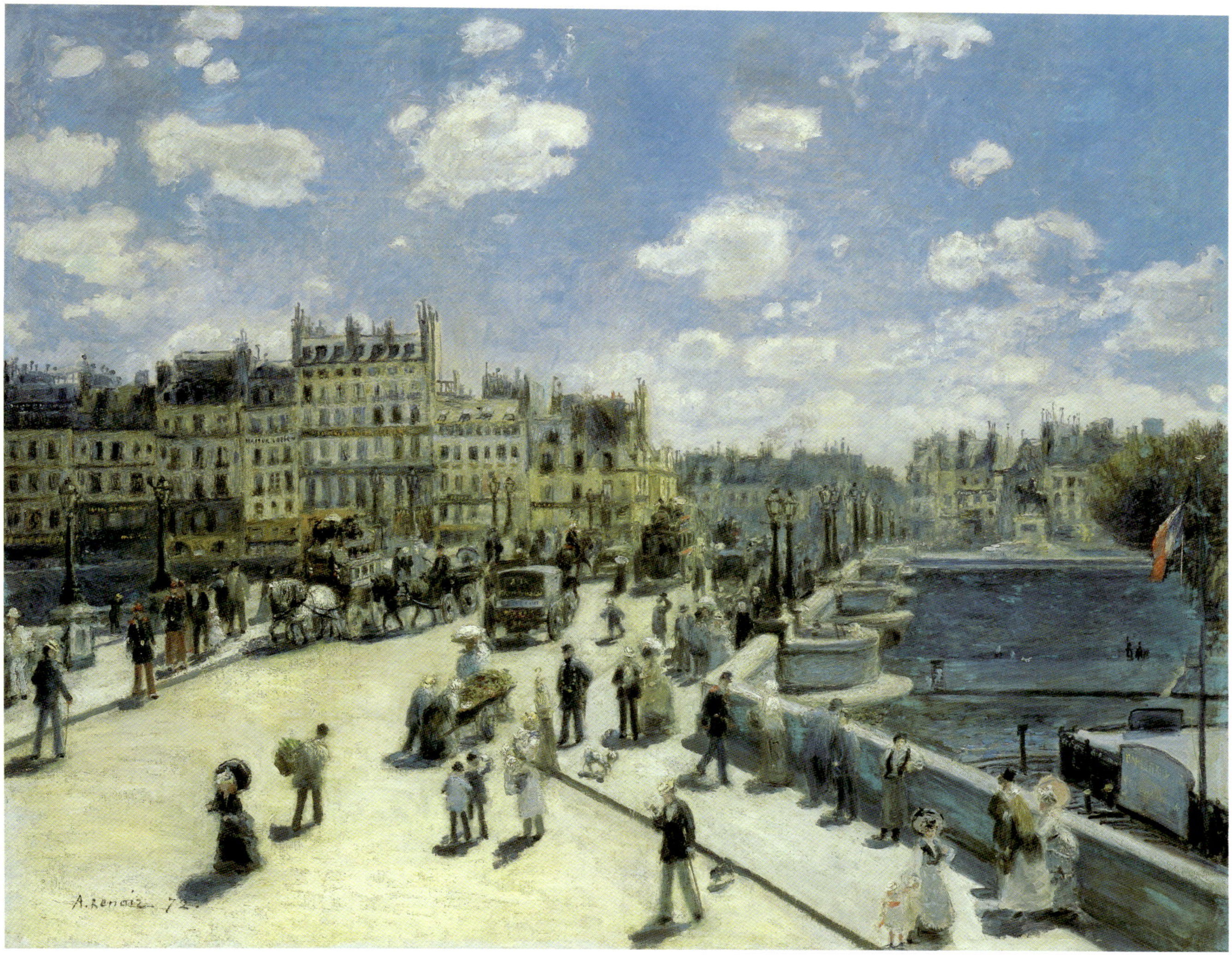
A.Renoir. 72.

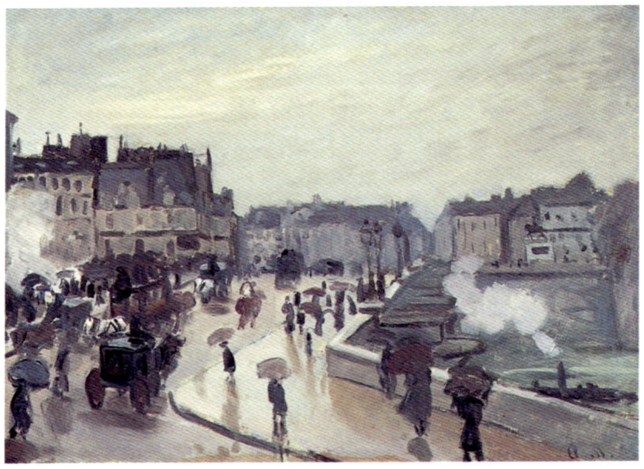

FIG. 66 Claude-Oscar Monet (1840–1926), *The Pont Neuf, Paris*, 1872. Oil on canvas, 53 × 72 cm; 20⅞ × 28½ in. Dallas Museum of Art, Texas. The Wendy and Emery Reves Collection (1985.R.38).

Renoir's street is for the *flâneur* and the labouring classes alike. In the middle of the foreground two working-class adolescents look up to inspect the wares of an aproned street vendor; behind them, an aged couple, in simple attire, push a barrow of provisions, while in front of them, to the left, a figure in blue carries a basket on his head. At some distance behind this group, a lone worker hauls a heavy bundle of vegetables on his back (their green stalks are just visible), while behind him a fashionably dressed woman, with white hat and black parasol, makes her way in the other direction – perhaps to visit La Belle Jardinière, one of the Grands Magasins specialising in ready-made clothing that had moved to impressive new quarters on the quai du Louvre in 1867.[9]

Given Renoir's frequently stated distaste for Haussmann's 'urbanism of regularisation',[10] his radiant panorama is unexpectedly optimistic, with little sense of the separate and impenetrable worlds that is to be found in Manet's street scenes of this period.[11] (Barnes and De Mazia aptly noted the 'Manet-like touches' of Renoir's handling).[12] Monet also painted this view from an identical vantage point, in a smaller, highly worked *esquisse* that has been dated variously to 1871, 1872, and 1873 (fig. 66), and shows a windy, rainy day quite unsuited for promenading.[13] Both Renoir and Monet were responding to the well-established tradition of the topographical print that captured the bridge and its users in a bird's-eye view.[14] They were also keenly aware of a new genre of street photography, the stereoscopic view, or stereocard (fig. 67), introduced in the 1850s, which cost little and catered to the tourist and the *flâneur* as its primary audience.[15]

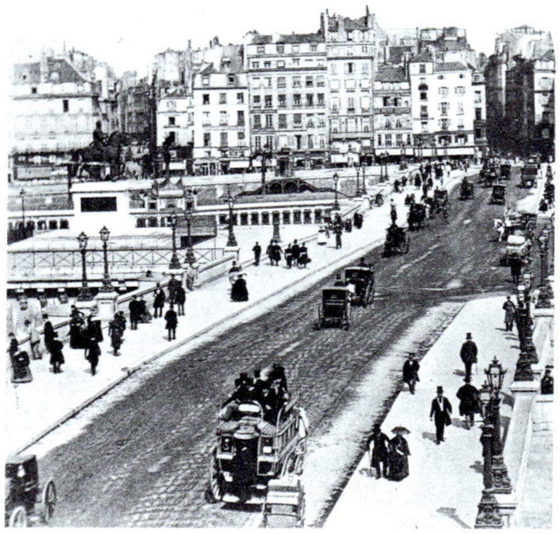

FIG. 67 Anonymous stereocard, *The Pont Neuf*, 1860s (?) The Metropolitan Museum of Art, New York. Gift of Weston J. Naef, 1975 (1975.514.2).

At the dawn of an age of commodification, with the urban environment emerging as a spectacle in its own right, for what sort of audience was Renoir's elaborate composition intended? As I have noted in my introductory essay, Renoir sold his first picture to Paul Durand-Ruel in March 1872, a cityscape painted in 1867; having had his Salon submission rejected in early May, he sold a second work, *Still Life with Peonies and Poppies*, to the dealer on 23 May for considerably more (300 as opposed to 200 francs).[16] It would seem reasonable to suppose that *Pont Neuf* was made with Monet and Pissarro's dealer in mind. Renoir's handling is less visibly sketchy and experimental than in his other summer landscapes (see the following cat. 13), and, even though his colouristic modelling is as audacious as it would ever be, his figures and buildings are crafted with considerable care and deliberation.[17] Edmond Renoir stated that his brother stayed at the café window for hours. He also noted that Renoir's method was to outline the architecture and then place his *dramatis personae* accordingly.[18] This is confirmed in the diagonal curb at lower right, which bisects the standing figures that are clearly painted over it. How ironic then, that *The Pont Neuf* – like the earlier *Pont des Arts* (see fig. 27) – would also have to wait several years before finding a purchaser, since, in contrast to Monet, Pissarro and Sisley,

Renoir sold only a handful of paintings to Durand-Ruel in the early 1870s. *The Pont Neuf* may well have been one of the unsold works that inspired Renoir to initiate the group auction of March 1875,[19] at which it was acquired by Durand-Ruel on behalf of the collector Nicolas Hazard (1834–1913) for the sum of 300 francs (the highest price paid for any work at the sale).[20]

Renoir's benign and hopeful vision of urban sociability has a romantic, even utopian quality about it[21] – an effect that was not lost on a picture dealer of a slightly later generation. Commenting on the price that the *The Pont Neuf* had fetched at the sale of Hazard's widow in December 1919, René Gimpel marvelled, 'It is blue as only Paris on the banks of the Seine can be; with something of Zola's realism and Baudelaire's poetry about it'.[22] CBB

Shown in Philadelphia only

1 For Haussmann's urbanism and responses to it in contemporary painting, see Clark 1985, pp. 23–78 *et passim*; for approaches to the interpretation of the Impressionist cityscape in the aftermath of the Commune, 'barely a year after the place was in flames and there were bodies on those very pavements', see Wood 1999, pp. 120–2.

2 Rewald 1945, p. 181.

3 Archives de Paris, D1 P4 / 659, '2, Quai du Louvre', 1862, notations for the rental of the 'Salle à boire', dating from 1869; *Annuaire du Commerce* 1871–2, 1611, Quai du Louvre, 2; *Annuaire du Commerce*, 1875, 1685, Quai du Louvre, 2; 1709, Rue de la Monnaie, 1; in all of these references, the proprietor is cited as 'Noiron, *vins*'.

4 The Bains de la Samaritaine offered a variety of amenities – '*Bains hydrothérapiques, douches variées, bains de pluie, salons et lits de repos*'. Adjacent was the 'Bain des Fleurs', offering swimming classes for women, which is perhaps the second structure visible at lower right of Renoir's painting; see Paris 1978, p. 46.

5 Albert-Montémont 1859, pp. 249–50.

6 Herbert 1988, p. 14, citing Gourdon de Genouillac's *Paris à travers les siècles*, which appeared in six volumes between 1893 and 1898.

7 'At almost any part of the lines, an omnibus passes every five minutes'; Baedeker 1878, p. 26.

8 Forgione (2005, p. 667) has suggested that this figure was posed for by Edmond Renoir, whom the artist would periodically send on to the bridge 'to speak with the passers-by to make them stop for a minute'; Rewald 1945, p. 181.

9 Hillairet 1963, II, p. 287.

10 Rice 1997, p. 39. See Christopher Riopelle's essay in this volume for the observation that Renoir has 'edited out' the new Palais de Justice, one of the buildings erected under Haussmann's direction that the painter most detested.

11 For example, the somewhat later *Rue Mosnier with Flags*, 1878, The J. Paul Getty Museum, Los Angeles; see Roos 1988.

12 Barnes and De Mazia 1935, p. 383.

13 Brettell 1995, pp. 46–7 (dated 1871); Reff 1982, pp. 44–5, and Boime 1995, pp. 117–18 (dated 1872); Rewald 1973, p. 281 (dated 1873).

14 For example, Moreau Le Jeune's *Vue du Pont Neuf et la Samaritaine*, 1778, reproduced in F. Boucher, *Le Pont-Neuf*, Paris 1925–6., I, p. i (frontispiece). For earlier views of the Pont Neuf, see also Reff 1982, p. 42. Crow (1986, p. 118) has pointed out that despite the modernity of Renoir's cityscape, 'this is as much Saint-Aubin's Paris as Haussmann's'.

15 Rice 1997, pp. 63–9; Frederick Scott Archer's invention of the wet collodion process, introduced in the early 1850s, had made possible the instantaneous view.

16 House and Distel 1985, p. 297.

17 The thinly applied pink ground is visible as a sort of silhouette around the outlines of the foreground figures, several of which have been painted over layers of impasto that have already dried. Both the foreground and sky show evidence of reworking, all of which suggests that the composition was elaborated over several campaigns. I am grateful to the National Gallery of Art for access to the technical notes in the curatorial files.

18 'Auguste … took pleasure, after having outlined the soil, the parapets, the houses in the distance, the Place Dauphine and the statue of Henri IV, in sketching the passers-by, vehicles and groups'; Rewald 1945, p. 181.

19 Vollard (1919, p. 75) has Renoir exclaim: '*Frappons un grand coup avec une vente à l'hôtel Drouot! Mes amis partagèrent, d'enthousiasme, cette idée.*'

20 Bodelsen 1968, p. 335, procès-verbal 32; Distel 1990, pp. 174–5; eighteen paintings, a quarter of all the works put up for auction, were acquired by Durand-Ruel.

21 For a different interpretation, which stresses the monarchical, 'recuperative' symbolism of Renoir's cityscape, see Boime 1995, pp. 117–19.

22 '*C'est le Paris bleu des bords de la Seine, avec du réalisme comme dans Zola, et de la poésie comme dans Baudelaire*'; Gimpel 1963, p. 235 (31 May 1923).

13 The Gust of Wind, about 1872

Oil on canvas
52 × 82 cm; 20½ × 32½ in.
The Fitzwilliam Museum, Cambridge (2403)

PROVENANCE:
Tableaux et Aquarelles par Monet, Morisot, Renoir, Sisley, Paris, Hôtel Drouot, 24 March 1875, no. 36, *Grand Vent (Paysage)*, sold for 55 francs to Auguste de Molins; acquired from his heirs by Durand-Ruel in 1899; sold to Alphonse Kann, St-Germain-en-Laye in 1908; L.H. Lefèvre & Son, London; sold to Frank Hindley Smith in 1923 and bequeathed by him to the Fitzwilliam Museum in 1939

LITERATURE:
House and Distel 1985, pp. 62, 202; Adriani 1996, pp. 110–11; Brettell 2000, pp. 163–4; Munro 2003, pp. 40–1

One of the boldest and 'purest' of Renoir's early Impressionist landscapes, *The Gust of Wind* is a *tour de force* of *plein-air* painting – a composition executed before the motif and probably completed in a single session.[1] Despite its rapid facture and sketchy appearance, it is also a finished work, signed in black at lower left on foliage whose paint was still wet. The title too – '*Grand Vent (Paysage)*' – is Renoir's own, since this was among the ten landscapes he put up for sale in the group auction held at the Hôtel Drouot in March 1875.[2] Sales of artists' work (organised by the artists themselves) were relatively commonplace by this time, but, as is well known, this event proved to be a fiasco, with many paintings fetching little more than the price of their frames.[3] Such was the case for *The Gust of Wind*, purchased for 55 francs by the painter Auguste de Molins (1821–1890), a fellow 'Indépendent' who had exhibited at the first Impressionist exhibition and was among those present at Renoir's apartment when the Société anonyme disbanded on 17 December 1874.[4] For ten francs more, Renoir himself bought back *After the Storm* (fig. 68), a slightly smaller landscape of similar bravura, which he had put up for sale as '*Temps d'orage*'. These two works surely date from the same moment, and may even be of the same site.[5]

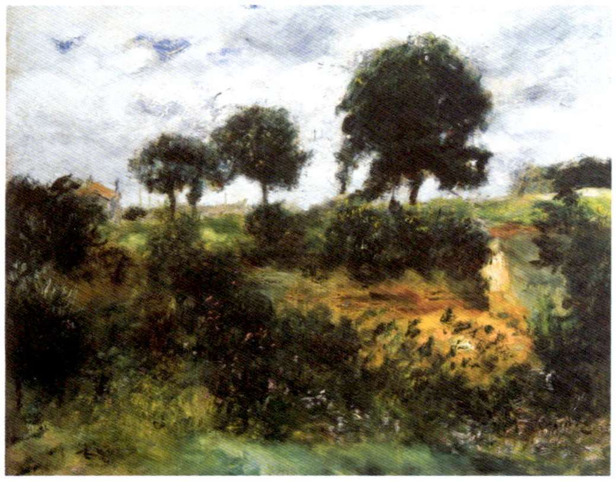

FIG. 68 *After the Storm*, about 1872. Oil on canvas, 45 × 55 cms; 17¾ × 21⅝ in. Private collection.

As Anthea Callen has recently shown, *The Gust of Wind* was painted on a standard canvas (a marine size 25), commercially primed with a biscuit coloured ground.[6] The active use of this reddish ground – which, having discoloured over time, is now less bright than when Renoir signed his picture – was one of the artist's most audacious technical experiments to date. The exposed ground provides a warm mid-tone for the grassy hills in the foreground and is also visible through the vigorously painted sky and clouds, formed by improvisatory strokes of grey, white and blue, applied wet on wet.[7] In the foreground of the composition Renoir's touch becomes gestural, with pulpy deposits of viridian green, chrome yellow and red lake creating the frieze of bushes and grass that sway in the wind.[8] Such is Renoir's action painting that blotches of white impasto are deposited in the sky, and touches of black and red punctuate the lower foreground, particularly the undergrowth at left.

Renoir's virtuosity is never gratuitous, however, and here it is placed at the service of an extraordinarily taut and solid composition, constructed of interlocking segments of land and sky. We are situated on one of the gentle slopes of this hilly terrain, and the eye is led along diagonal paths that stretch far into the distance – bushes to our left, a meadow to our right, and trees stacked in a row in the far horizon. While the wind does indeed activate every inch of the canvas, the impression is of a view glimpsed at great speed, with the vegetation in the foreground deliberately out of focus, and the tiny red-roofed building in the middle ground at right rendered impossibly small against the neighbouring tree. It is as if this sunny, windy panorama has fleetingly entered

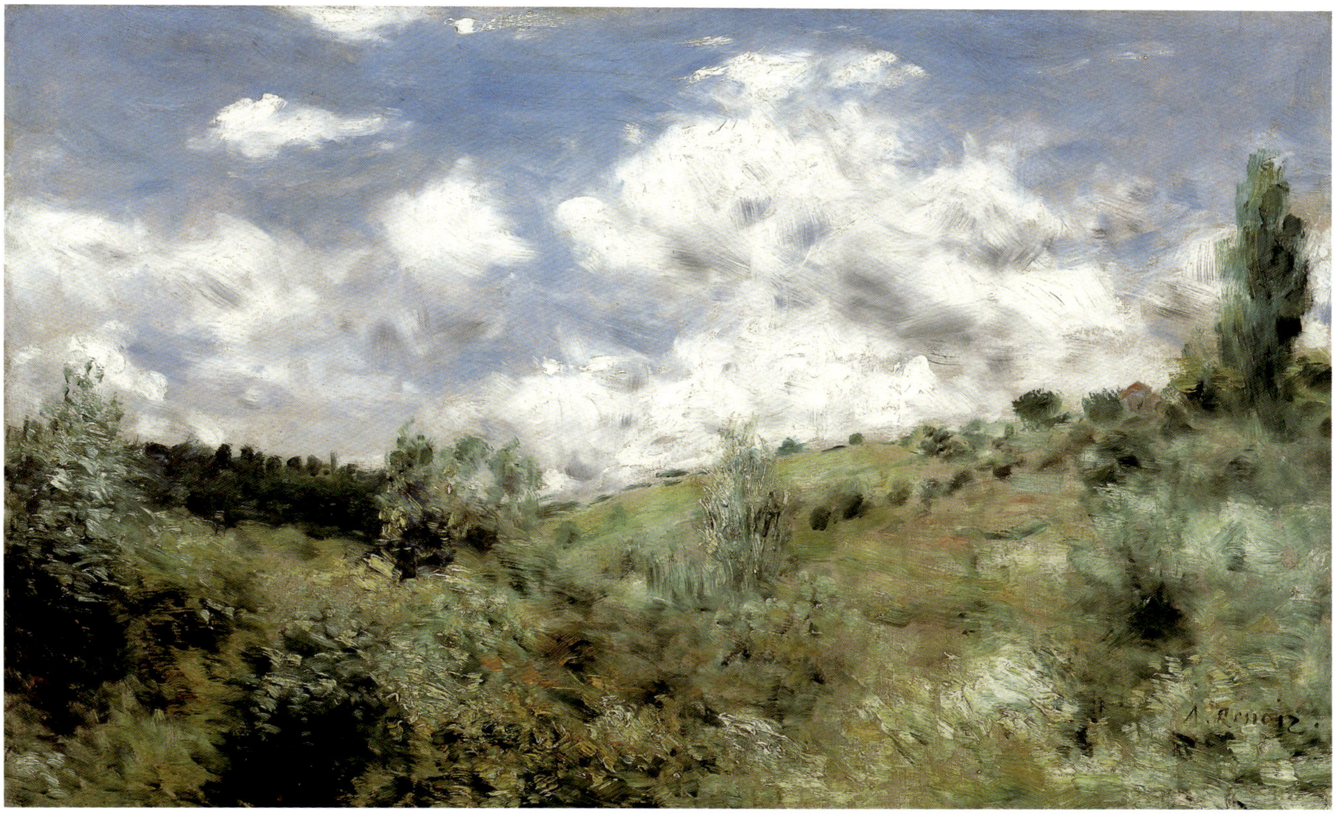

Renoir's frame of vision, and he has devised a language sufficiently animated to evoke a sensation of visual clarity, captured but for an instant. 'Everyone has crossed seventy miles of countryside in the middle of summer, and seen how the hillsides, meadows and fields disappear, as it were, into a single luminous reflection that they share with the sky.'[9] This passage from Duranty's *New Painting* of 1876, written a few years later, attests to the modernity of picturing the countryside through the window of a train (or a fast-moving carriage) – how else would one experience such 'vibration and palpitation of light and heat'? – a modernity enjoined by Renoir in *The Gust of Wind*.[10]

Yet if train-travel is a possible subtext in this landscape, we are at a loss as to which nearby countryside Renoir had journeyed. Despite the most painstaking scrutiny, historians have been unable to identify the topography of this hilly region. The mistaken notion that the view is of St-Cloud may derive from an overhasty reading of the auctioneer's records for the sale, which indicated that *The Gust of Wind* was to be sent to de Molins at his address in St-Cloud (and not Paris).[11] Fixing on the tiny 'villa' in the right middle ground, John House concluded this was 'a site within the orbit of urban impact'.[12] Yet, as in the related *After the Storm*, where one looks in vain to the (similar) red-roofed structure at far left and the tiny factory chimneys (?) beyond to help situate the composition, Renoir is deliberately parsimonious with this sort of information.

Equally vexing is the precise date of *The Gust of Wind*, for which the auction of May 1875 establishes no more than a *terminus ante quem* (several of the works Renoir put into this sale

FIG. 69 Jean-François Millet (1814–1875), *The Gust of Wind*, about 1872. Oil on canvas, 90.5 × 117.5 cm; 35⅝ × 46¼ in. National Museums Wales, Cardiff (NMW A 2475).

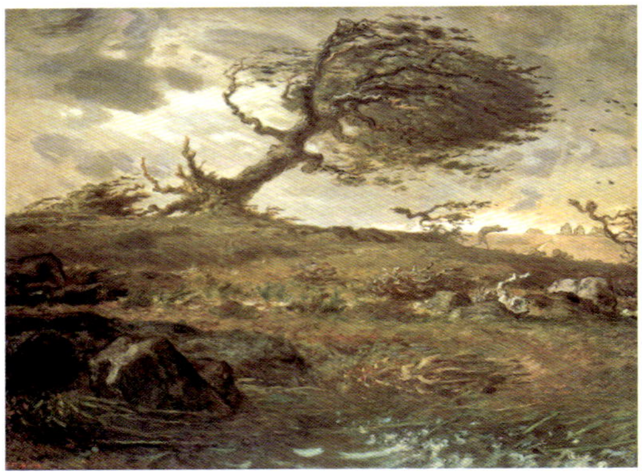

were three years old). If we consider the painting to have been made between the summer of 1872 and late spring of 1873, it is possible to place Renoir in Louveciennes, Bougival, La Celle St-Cloud or Marlotte (and possibly Chatou as well). More to the point perhaps, we know from the artist's earliest letter to Théodore Duret (which probably dates from the spring of 1873) that, when away from Paris at this time, Renoir was committing himself to a regime of *plein-air* painting. He would only come into town, he noted, 'on the first morning when the weather is grey'.[13]

Even the time of year evoked in *The Gust of Wind* is at issue. For certain writers, the season is apparent in 'the scorched summer grass' and the 'warm summer breeze'.[14] As Richard Brettell has pointed out, it is the 'unseeable wind of Barbizon painting' that guides Renoir's experiments out of doors here, and both the Fitzwilliam canvas and *After the Storm* relate to the tradition of the Four Elements, wind being represented as a manifestation of Air.[15] Yet as a comparison with Millet's closely contemporaneous *The Gust of Wind* (fig. 69) makes clear, Renoir has expunged all anecdote and melodrama from this trope. His *The Gust of Wind* is an example of what Burty termed the Impressionists' 'lofty assault' on tradition, and not for the faint of heart.[16] CBB

Shown in Ottawa and Philadelphia only

1 Renoir seems to have blocked in the sky and hillside simultaneously (some of the trees have been painted on top of the still wet clouds) and may have been using a travelling frame for working out of doors, since the paint stops quite abruptly on the edges of the canvas. Pin-holes around the edges of the canvas and stretcher may be evidence that corks were attached by pins to protect the canvas as it dried during transport. I am grateful to Jane Munroe for giving me access to Catherine Nunn's excellent report on the painting, dated 19 October 2004.

2 Bodelsen 1968, p. 335, procès-verbal 21; the association with the auction of March 1875 was first made in House 1974, p. 47.

3 In an interview many years later Durand-Ruel noted that he had taken care to frame the pictures, '*dans de superbes cadres*' and that as a result '*les tableaux furent vendus 50 ff à cause des cadres*'; Geffroy 1922, p. 46; see also Rewald 1973, pp. 351–4.

4 De Molins, a genre painter of hunt scenes, had shown *A Comming* [*sic*] *Storm* at the first Impressionist exhibition, in which a group of fashionable promenaders await their carriages as it starts to pour (illustrated in Berson 1996, II, p. 23). At the auction of March 1875 de Molins also purchased Renoir's *Femme en promenade* (private collection) for 50 francs; see Daulte 1971, p. 109. For the gathering at 35 rue St-Georges in December 1874, see Rewald 1973, p. 336.

5 Bodelsen 1968, p. 335, procès-verbal 10; Adriani 1996, pp. 112–13, where the association with the auction of March 1875 was not made.

6 Callen 2000, pp. 78–9.

7 Munro 2003, p. 40.

8 Pigments sampled by Catherine Nunn (see note 1).

9 Duranty 1876, in Moffett 1986, p. 43; *ibidem*, p. 481.

10 *Ibidem*, pp. 43, 481.

11 Munro 2003, p. 40; Bodelsen 1968, p. 335.

12 House 2004, p. 89, who notes that the site is 'otherwise unidentifiable'.

13 Undated letter from La Celle-St-Cloud, 'Maison de la Treille, par Bougival'; Florisoone 1938, p. 38. Duret, who had left Paris in May 1871 in the aftermath of the Commune and only returned from his travels in December 1872, was introduced to Renoir by Degas, probably in the early months of 1873; see Meier-Graefe 1912, p. 6, and Duret 1924, pp. 13–15.

14 Callen 2000, p. 165; Munro 2003, p. 40.

15 Brettell 2000, pp. 163–4.

16 Burty 1875: '*Le détail est supprimé avec une décision qui effarouche les âmes timides. L'ensemble aussi exprime les effets de lumière, les appositions de tons, les silhouettes et les masses par des attaques hautaines.*'

14 In the Parc de St-Cloud, about 1873

Oil on canvas
50 × 61 cm; 19¾ × 24 in.
Private collection

Ambitious, complex and unfinished,[1] Renoir's sketch of Sunday recreation on a glorious summer's afternoon continues the experiments began at La Grenouillère some four years earlier. His figures are now more fully absorbed into both the light and the landscape, however, making *In the Park de St-Cloud* a suburban cousin to the resolutely individuated (and completed) *The Pont Neuf* (cat. 12), painted the year before.

Under the sprawling canopy of a massive tree, four well-dressed adults and a child in red stockings take the shade. The man in a white jacket and his companion are viewed from behind; next to them, in profile, is a woman wearing an elaborate black dress and bustle, a straw bonnet of the latest fashion tipped precariously on her head. She has her back to the bare-armed woman in white, whose hat with blue flowers matches the colour of her parasol, held playfully by its tip. At some distance to the left of these figures, a bearded fellow in a dapper summer suit seems to gesture in their direction. Behind him are seated several figures at the tables of the outdoor restaurant that is nestled within the trees. The scene is bordered by the giant tree trunks at left, the sliver of water at right, and a low fence in the foreground, indicated by a single line parallel to the canvas's edge.

Until very recently, this landscape was still known by the title and date assigned to it by its first owner, Renoir's great friend Georges Rivière (1855–1943).[2] Rivière described the scene as representing 'a view of the *allée* at the water's edge in the Parc de St-Cloud', dated the work to 1866, and noted that it was unfinished.[3] While Rivière cannot be relied upon for the date, his assertion that the canvas is unfinished is incontrovertible, and there is equally no reason to doubt his designation of the site as St-Cloud. Renoir shows a spot in the *petit parc* or *bas parc* to the north-east of the domain, that 'stretched all the way along the Seine' and of which the *allées*, bordered by trees, were lined by 'little confectioners' shops, toy shops for children and cafés'.[4] Then, as now, the major attraction at the Parc de St-Cloud were the Grandes Cascades that fronted the palace, memorialised since the late eighteenth century by artists from Fragonard to Daubigny.[5] Renoir's

PROVENANCE:
Georges Rivière, Paris; Edmond and Hélène Rivière, Viroflay; sale, Sotheby's, London, 2 December 1981, lot 8; sale, Christie's, New York, 15 May 1985, lot 5; sale, Christie's, New York, 12 May 1993, lot 5; private collection

REFERENCES:
Rivière 1921, pp. 8, 13; Champa 1973, pp. 47, 57; Adriani 1996, pp. 98–9

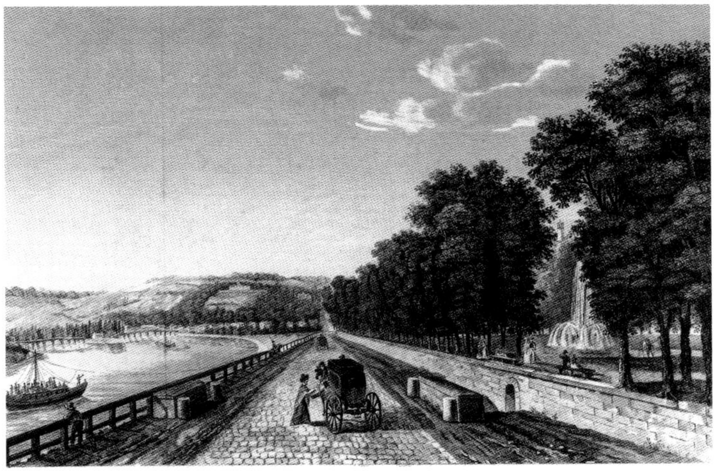

FIG. 70 Courvoisier, *Vue de la terrasse du Parc de St-Cloud*, 1870s (?). Engraving. Bibliothèque Nationale de France, Paris (VA-92B FOL).

FIG. 71 Jules Andrieu (1816–after 1876), *Désastres de la guerre; St-Cloud incendié après l'Armistice*, 1871, plate 5 of *La Guerre et la Commune*, Canadian Centre for Architecture, Montreal (PH 1985:0548:005).

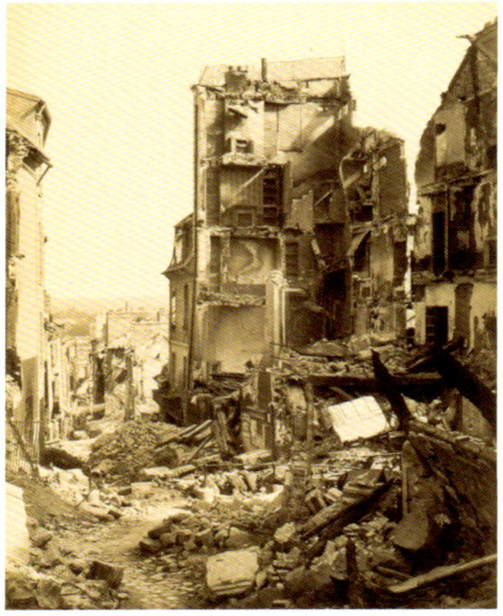

restaurant or *guingette* is situated at some distance from these fountains, and it is true that he represents the park's celebrated tall trees somewhat haphazardly. He does, however, include the low fence that bordered the river, just visible at right, here at least keeping faith with topographical tradition (fig. 70).

As Götz Adriani was the first to note, the freedom of handling, high chromatic scale and sketchiness overall place this landscape at a considerable remove from those executed in 1866.[6] Renoir's brushwork is vigorous and energetic; he applies his greens, yellows, blues and whites in thick, oily dabs, working wet on wet in the delineation of the figures and overhanging foliage. His creation of space is masterful, with the circular group and lush canopy of leaves anchored by the dappled sunlight on the grass below.

Redating the work to 1871 is not without its difficulties, however, for reasons that are both biographical and stylistic. Citing Renoir's earliest letter to Duret, written from La Celle-St-Cloud and customarily dated to August 1871, Adriani believed that this profession of working out of doors could reasonably be applied to Renoir's view of the nearby park.[7] As noted in the preceding entry, however, Renoir's letter in all likelihood dates from the spring of 1873, after Duret had returned to Paris from an 18-month absence abroad; in August 1871 he was travelling with Henri Cernuschi in the United States, *en route* to the Far East.[8] Although Renoir had lived through the Commune without any personal hardship, it is hard to imagine him painting such a scene at St-Cloud in the summer of 1871, with the former imperial residence 'a Pompeii of destruction', and many houses in the nearby town still in ruins (fig. 71).[9]

An interval of two years goes some way to resolve these issues. The dappled lighting, impasted figures and experimental touch of *In the Parc de St-Cloud* are more characteristic of landscapes painted in 1873, in the months before Renoir would join forces with Monet at Argenteuil. In mood, handling and subject-matter *In the Parc de St-Cloud* may be compared with *View of Bougival* (cat. 17), a finished picture and one with which it shares similarly resolute moral and pictorial values. CBB

Shown in London only

1 The work is neither signed nor stamped; it was probably given by Renoir, during his lifetime, to Rivière as a gift.
2 Rivière reproduced the work (in colour) in *Renoir et ses amis*, published in 1921. Rivière met Renoir in 1874 and was his most sympathetic apologist in the mid-1870s; having lost sight of him after 1882, he renewed his friendship in 1897 and the families grew very close when his daughter Hélène married Renoir's nephew, Edmond, in November 1909.
3 Rivière 1921, p. 13.
4 Joanne 1856, p. 163; the same text appears in Joanne 1881, p. 12.
5 Fragonard's *Fête à St-Cloud*, about 1775, is in the Banque de France, Paris; Daubigny's *Vue du Château de St-Cloud*, 1850, is in the Musée Condé, Chantilly.
6 Adriani 1996, p. 98.
7 *Ibidem*. See Florisoone 1938, p. 38, for Renoir's undated letter from La Celle-St-Cloud, 'Maison de la Treille, par Bougival'. Despite the similarity of place names, the Parc de St-Cloud was closer to Sèvres and Ville d'Avray; La Celle-St-Cloud was further to the west, near Louveciennes and Bougival.
8 Duret 1998, p. 11; see above, cat. 13, note 13.
9 See Luxenberg 1998 for contemporary photographs of the devastated palace and town.

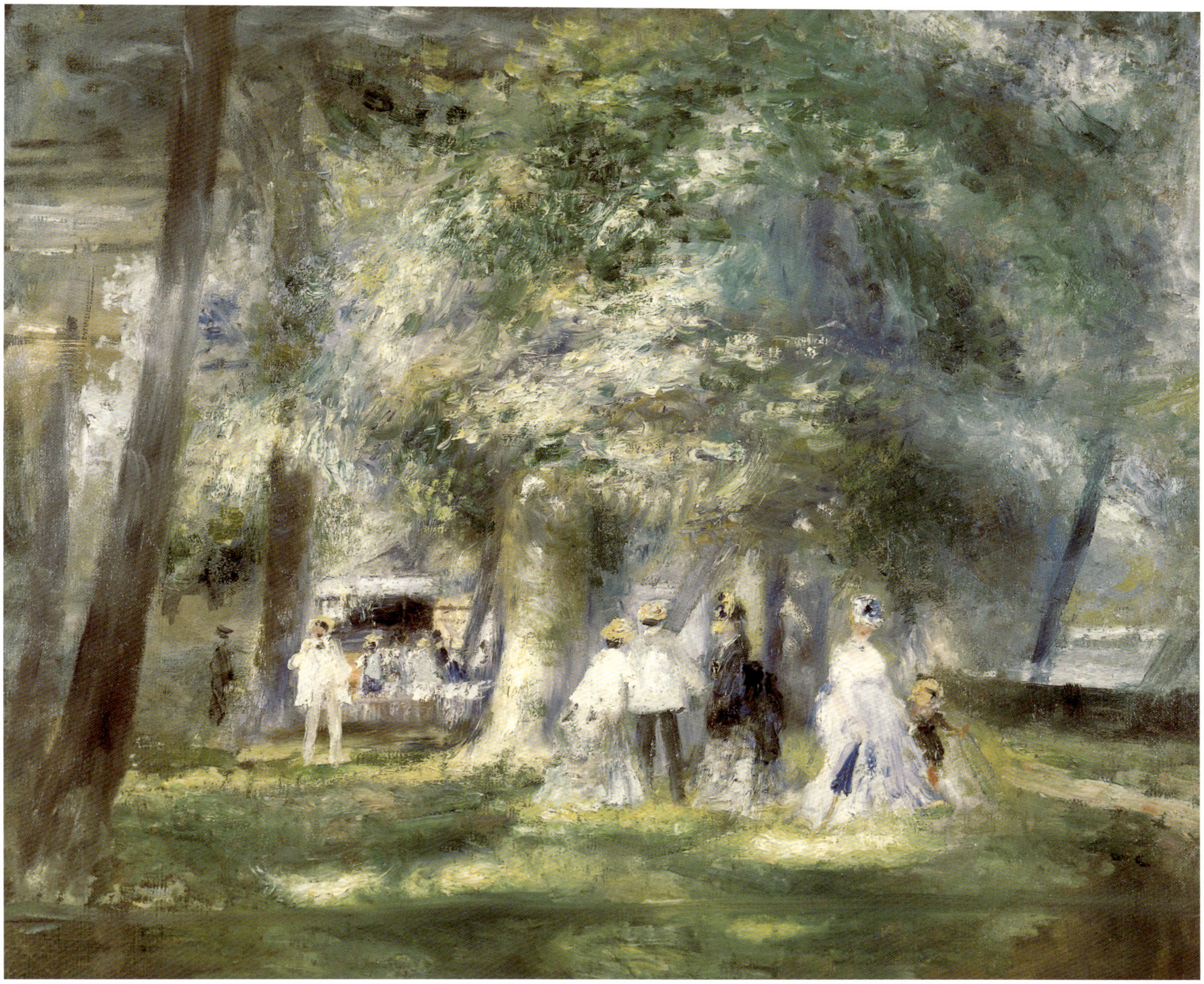

15 The Watering-place, 1873

Oil on canvas
47 × 61 cm; 18½ × 24 in.
Private collection

PROVENANCE:
Galerie Georges Petit, Paris; Paul Cassirer, Amsterdam; Siegfried Kramarsky, Amsterdam and New York; Rosenberg & Stiebel, New York; Dr Peter Nathan, Zurich; private collection

LITERATURE:
Fezzi 1972, no. 99; Wheldon 1975, pp. 56, 58, 63; Rouart 1985, p. 32; Monneret 1989, no. 23; Czynmek 1990, no. 150; Keyzer, 1995, no. 54; Adriani 1996, no. 22.

Two small figures climb a path through wheat fields on a hillside. On the undulating hilltop stands a humble animals' water trough made of wood, one end of which can be seen beyond the tree at right. Thick clouds roll across the sky and a breeze seems to be rustling the trees and plant life. It is a simple countryside motif entirely without striking visual incident. Increasingly, however, Renoir was drawn to such motifs, seeing in them possibilities for a daring new kind of landscape painting without traditional or even immediately apparent pictorial structure. Nothing here terminates the view to right or left; seemingly, the eye could continue to scan the horizon without interruption, and Renoir's decision to commit this particular patch of nature to canvas appears at first as breezily arbitrary. It soon becomes clear, however, that colour has been assigned an important role in structuring the composition internally. Renoir explores a wide and vivid range of green tonalities in this picture. Darker foliage bordering the path up the hill cuts a diagonal across the canvas from lower right until, turning into a thin and intermittent horizontal line, it outlines the horizon at upper left. This is countered by other patches of darker and lighter green indicating where parts of the hillside have been touched by sun or shadow. A second easy curve of dark foliage arcs up from lower left to meet the first. Thus, attention is drawn to the centre of the canvas and to the receding space that Renoir depicts with economy but without recourse to the *repoussoirs* and framing devices of earlier landscape traditions. The seventeenth-century landscape master Claude Lorrain would not, one suspects, have been able to recognise a true landscape painting in this seemingly spontaneous and artless image.

Renoir had tried something similar in his somewhat earlier *The Gust of Wind* (cat. 13) where the rounded forms of the intersecting hillsides and the white clouds that billow above the horizon are enough in themselves to create a thrillingly fresh image. He would address another featureless and largely monochromatic landscape made up of countless shades of green, like this, in *Springtime* (*in Chatou*) (cat. 28). Not least, brushstroke plays an important role in *The Watering-place*, and Renoir adjusts his touch across the surface of the painting to suggest the varying textures and density of the foliage. This ability to find equivalences between natural forms and painterly touch is a hallmark of Renoir's landscape achievement. CR

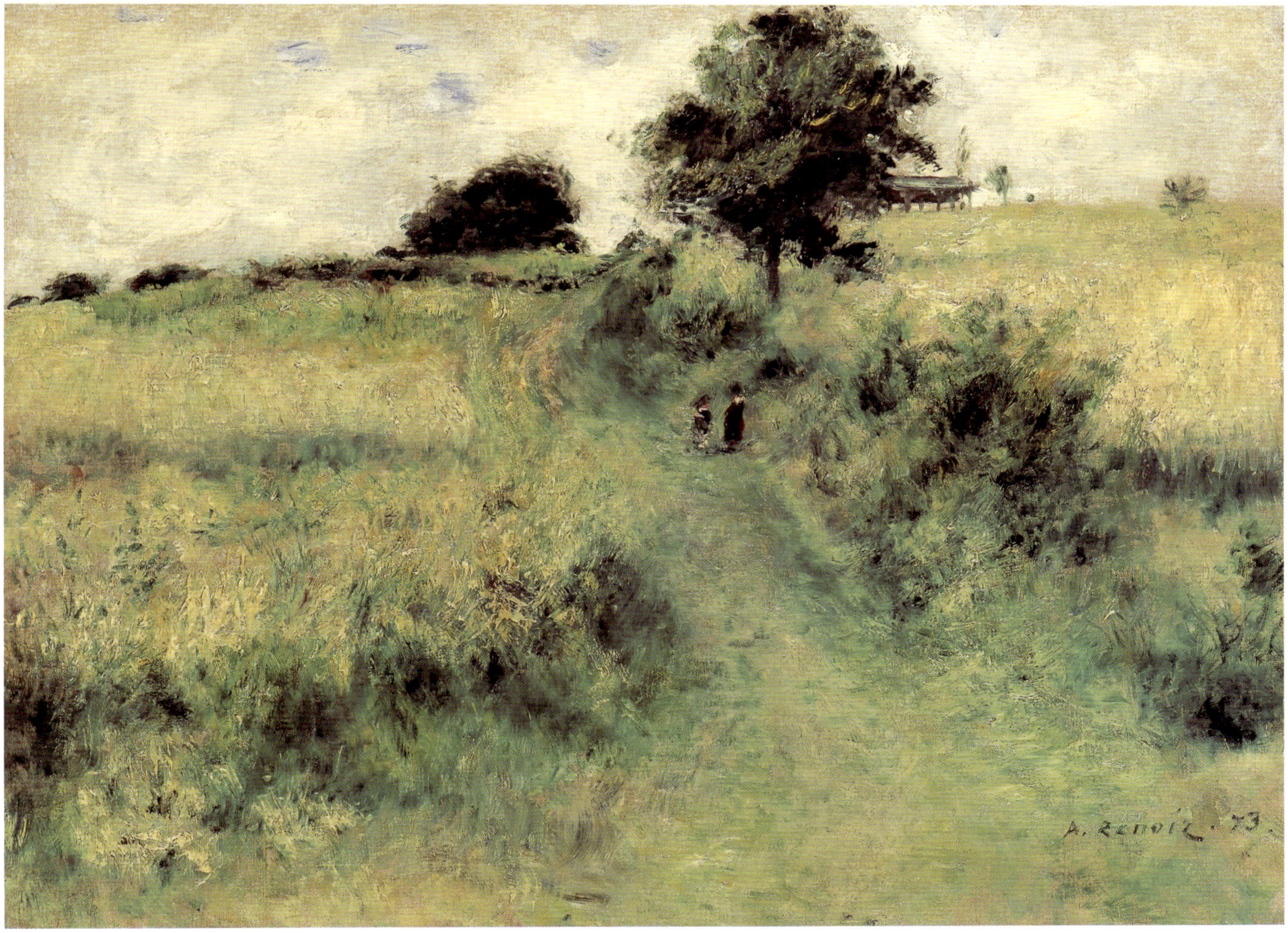
A. Renoir . 73.

16 The Harvesters, 1873

Oil on canvas,
60 × 74 cm; 23⅝ × 23⅛ in.
Private collection, Switzerland

PROVENANCE:
Acquired from the Sociéte anonyme coopérative des artistes peintres in 1874 for 1,000 francs by Georges Hartmann; Madame Carmona, Paris; sale, *Vente de tableaux modernes*, Paris, Hôtel Drouot, 30 March 1938, lot 27; Galerie Dr Fritz Nathan, Zurich; purchased by Emil Georg Bürhle (1890–1956) in 1951; private collection

LITERATURE:
Paris-New York 1974, 250–2; Washington-Montreal-Yokohama-London 1990, no. 50, p. 238; Berson 1996, II, p. 12; Adriani 1996, pp. 114–17; House 2004, pp. 55–6, 88–9, 153, 165

Renoir's *Harvesters* is a summer landscape showing 'one of the most hackneyed themes' in rural imagery.[1] In the middle of a large field, three men in peaked caps are cutting ripe grain. Furthest to the right, the labourer with his back to us – his left arm bare – is shown waist deep in wheat: his form is rendered by a few stabs of blue and white paint. In front of him, at the edge of the harvested field, a second figure unwittingly moons the viewer as he bends over to crop. The third male figure stands a little way back, just right of centre, his jacket discarded at his feet. He holds a scythe in his right hand – the preferred instrument for harvesting grain in this pre-industrial age[2] – and turns towards the two women who are arriving with provisions in a basket. Sheaths of cut wheat lie in neat rows to the right of the path; and on the other side we see a patch of root vegetables – or cabbages, perhaps – in orderly arrangement. The eye is led swiftly past the labourers and crops to the horizon line in the distance where sky and field meet, the two-storey house with its imposing roof at left balanced by a lone fruit tree, its branches swaying in the wind, at right.

Traditional the subject might well be: artists of an earlier generation, notably Millet and Daubigny (fig. 72), had treated the summer harvest in a variety of ways.[3] Yet Renoir's composition could not be more radical and experimental, his touch changing as it describes, with the greatest economy, the summer sky, the anonymous peasants and the bales of cut grain. The salmon-beige ground of this commercially prepared canvas is particularly active in the foreground, which is flecked with touches of red (a hallmark of Renoir's handling in the early 1870s). Here, craggy and summary deposits of yellow, white and blue pigment become the notations for

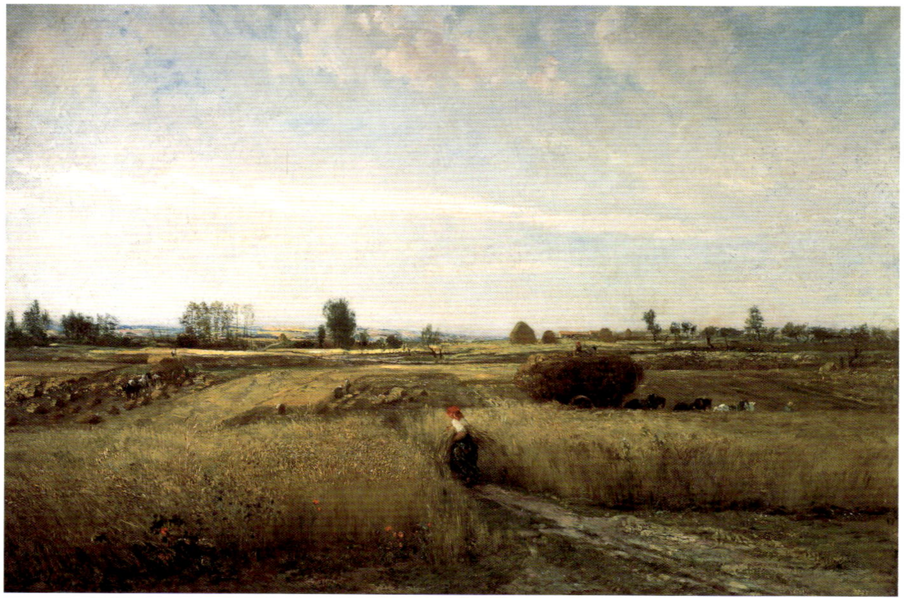

FIG. 72 Charles-François Daubigny (1817–1878), *The Harvest*, 1851. Oil on canvas, 135 × 196 cm; 19⅛ × 77⅛ in. Musée d'Orsay, Paris (RF 1961).

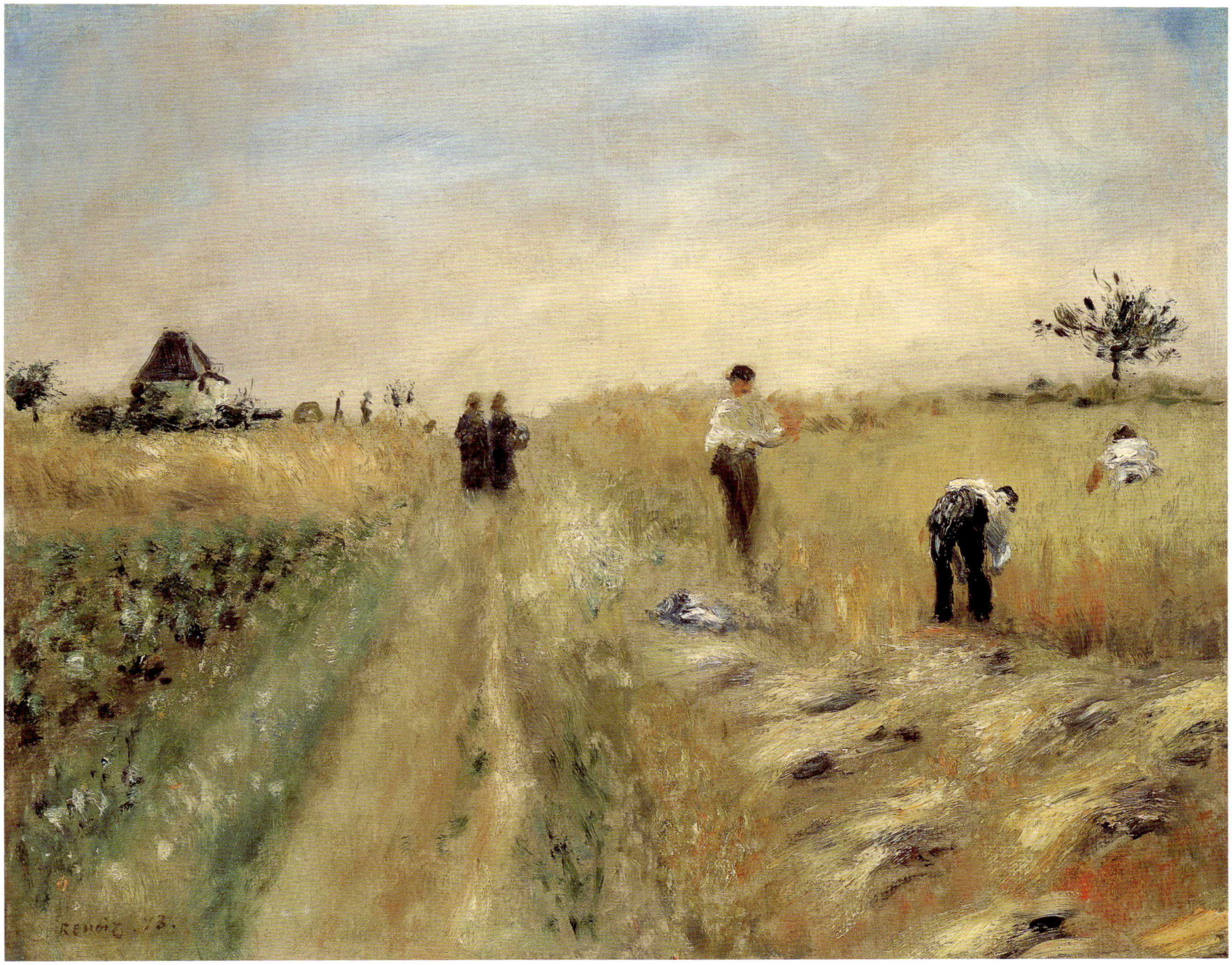

corn, cabbages and their shadows. The noon-day sky with its blustering clouds is painted more thinly, as is the endless field, the softness and depth of which are magisterially evoked. Sketchiness is a carefully contrived quality, however, as is the effect of instantaneity, brilliantly achieved.[4]

As the resolute signature implies, this was a picture for exhibition or commercial display. Indeed, *The Harvesters* was the only landscape – and 'a very loosely brushed one' at that – to be included among the six paintings that Renoir submitted in April 1874 to the first Impressionist exhibition, held on the top floor of Nadar's former studio on 35 boulevard des Capucines.[5] Despite the brevity of Renoir's handling in this composition – at its most destabilising in the depiction of the figures ('just look at those three touches of colour that are supposed to represent a man in the field!')[6] – critics were surprisingly receptive to the work's experimental qualities, even if Chesnau judged Renoir's research ill-considered, and Montifaud assumed that the harvesters were women.[7]

FIG. 73 Camille Pissarro (1830–1903), *A Morning in June*, 1873. Oil on canvas, 41 × 69 cm; 16⅛ × 27⅛ in. Staatliche Kunsthalle, Karlsruhe (2539).

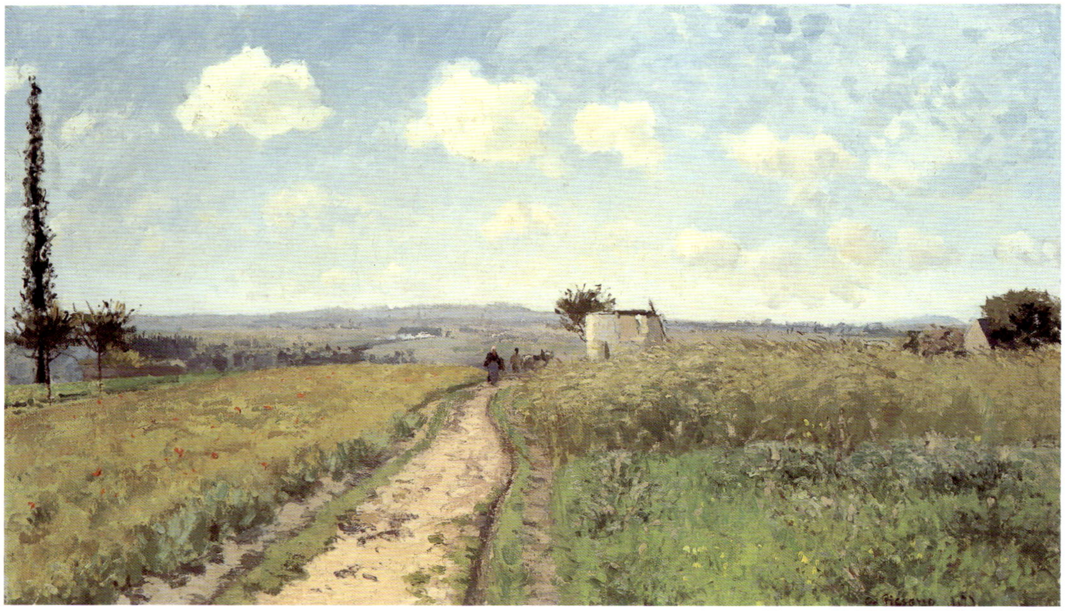

The most probing discussion of *The Harvesters* came from Philippe Burty (1830–1890), who would write the preface to the catalogue of the first Impressionist auction the following March. In the review that appeared (in English) in *The Academy* on 30 May 1874, Burty noted that 'M. Renoir, who presents some singular points of affinity to Turner, has given us some reapers in a field of ripe corn'.[8] Although he did not mention *The Harvesters* by name in his review for *La République française* (which predicted 'a great future for M. Renoir'), it was surely this canvas that prompted, once again, comparison with the English master: 'Renoir delights in the same iridescences and blond tonalities as Turner, even though his draughtsmanship is more assured'.[9]

The Harvesters' striking luminosity and dynamic perspective may have evoked Turner's late work for a select Parisian audience; thanks to Burty's protégé the engraver Félix Bracquemond, an unfinished etching after *Rain, Steam and Speed* was also on display at the first Impressionist exhibition.[10] No paintings by Turner could yet be seen in any public institution in France, and it was only during the run of the Société anonyme's exhibition that the first Turners to appear at sale in Paris were auctioned at the nearby Hôtel Drouot.[11] But in Naturalist circles at least, Turner's late work had become synonymous with unfettered colourism and 'virginal, primordial daylight', and Renoir was able to benefit by association.[12]

Thanks to the annotated catalogue of the first Impressionist exhibition, it is possible to establish the correct early provenance of *The Harvesters*, which has been confused in all previous publications.[13] Renoir's single landscape was the only work to sell during the run of the exhibition, and it was acquired for the very respectable sum of 1,000 francs by Georges Hartmann (1843–1900), an up-and-coming music publisher and impresario, whose modest offices on the boulevard de la Madeleine were but a short distance from the exhibition's galleries on the boulevard des Capucines.[14] Later in the year, Hartmann would commission from Renoir a somewhat grandiose full-length portrait of his wife (fig. 33), in the background of which a corner of this landscape, now elaborately framed, makes a sly appearance. *The Harvesters* remained in Hartmann's collection until his sudden death in April 1900, when it was inventoried among his effects and appraised for the modest sum of 500 francs.[15]

As to Renoir's landscape itself, there is one final question that remains to be raised. Previous discussions of *The Harvesters* have tentatively located the site as a field in Argenteuil, and Monet as the prime mover behind Renoir's synoptic handling and heightened colour.[16] There is no reason to associate this scene of rural labour with any particular suburb (indeed, Renoir offers no clues in this regard), and in handling and subject-matter this work predates the period in which Renoir again took up painting *en plein air* in Monet's company (by a matter of months, admittedly). If the traditional theme of the harvest, with its seasonal associations, had been a staple of the Barbizon landscapists, it was still of interest to certain of Renoir's future comrades-in-arms. His model here was not Monet, but rather the most rustic of the Impressionists, with whom he may have experienced a temporary falling out the previous year.[17] In both subject and structure *The Harvesters* shares an affinity with Pissarro's harvest landscapes of Pontoise, a superb example of which, *A Morning in June* (fig. 73), was also exhibited in Nadar's former studio as part of the inaugural Impressionist exhibition.[18] CBB

Shown in London and Ottawa only

1 House 2004, p. 87.
2 Considered 'vastly more efficient' than the sickle (*la faucille*), the scythe (*la faux*) enabled the labourer to work more quickly and crop closer to the ground; Weber 1976, pp. 123–4. In Renoir's day, scythes were manufactured in France (having formerly been imported from Germany), and some million and a half were in annual usage; Larousse 1865–90, VIII, p. 155.
3 For recent surveys, see Patin 1986 and Herbert 1995.
4 Here Renoir anticipates Mallarmé, who memorably characterised Impressionist landscapes as 'instantaneous and voluntary pictures' in which 'all is harmonious and would be spoiled by a touch more or less'; see 'The Impressionists and Edouard Manet' (September 1876), reprinted in Moffett 1986, p. 32.
5 House 2004, p. 55; on the exhibition, see Tucker in Moffett 1986, pp. 93–117.
6 Louis Leroy, 'L'Exposition des impressionnistes', *Le Charivari*, 25 April 1874, in Berson 1996, I, pp. 25–6.
7 Ernest Chesnau, 'A côté du Salon: II Le Plein Air', *Paris-Journal*, 7 May 1874, in Berson 1996, I, p. 18; Marc de Montifaud, 'Exposition du boulevard des Capucines', *L'Artiste*, 1 May 1874, in Berson 1996, I, p. 29.
8 Burty, 'The Paris Exhibitions: *Les Impressionnistes*', *The Academy*, 30 May 1874, in Berson 1996, II, p. 10.
9 Burty, 'Exposition de la société anonyme des artistes', *La République française*, 25 April 1874, in Berson 1996, I, p. 36.
10 Berson 1996, I, pp. 4, 17.
11 For Turner's reception in France and his possible influence on modern painting, see, most recently, John House's essay in Lochnan 2004, especially pp. 37–41. In *J.W.M. Turner*, (exh. cat, Grand Palais, Paris 1983, p. 50) Gage noted that in the John W. Wilson sale of 27 April 1874 at least one authentic early work by Turner appeared on the Paris market for the first time. After 1870, Turner occupied pride of place in the extended and reinstalled rooms at the National Gallery, London, where Berthe Morisot would admire his work in the summer of 1875; Renoir, never having visited London, would not have been familiar with Turner's paintings at first hand.
12 In the Goncourts' novel, the painter Coriolis, at the end of his career, is led astray by Turner's example of aspiring '*de s'élever, dans une toile, avec le rêve des couleurs, à un jour vierge et primordial*'; E. et J. de Goncourt, *Manette Salomon* (1867, p. 531), cited in Lochnan 2004, p. 38.
13 Published in Distel 1993, p. 40. Because of the similarity of their dimensions, *The Harvesters* has been misidentified as the *Paysage d'été* that Renoir consigned to auction on 24 March 1875 (lot 47), acquired by Gabriel Thomas for 105 francs; see Adriani 1996, p. 117. As I have noted in my essay in this catalogue, the *Paysage d'été* is now properly associated with *Path rising through Tall Grass* in the Musée d'Orsay (fig. 2, p. 15).
14 Devriès and Lesure 1988, II, pp. 210–13. The high-living Romain-Jean-François Hartmann, known as Georges, was an early supporter of Massenet, Bizet and Franck. From 1895 until his death, Hartmann subsidised Claude Debussy, whose score of *Pelléas et Mélisande* (1902) was dedicated to his memory; see S. Sadie, ed., *The New Grove Dictionary of Music*, London 1980, VIII, p. 266.
15 Paris, 'Inventaire après décès', 8 May 1900, Etude of Maître Granger: '*Mobilier: 1 portrait de Mme Hartmann, par Renoir, pour mémoire; une peinture de Renoir, 'La Moisson', prisée 500 francs.*' No other works by Renoir are recorded in this inventory.
16 Adriani 1996, p. 114.
17 In June 1872 Pissarro had apparently criticised Renoir's latest work to the dealer, Madame Latouche, and word may have got back to Renoir; in a letter of 27 June 1872 to an unnamed correspondent, Pissarro was trying to clear up the incident over '*ce que j'ai pu dire à Madame Latouche concernant le tableau de mon ami Renoir*'; Bailly-Herzberg 1980, I, p. 75.
18 Berson 1996, II, pp. 12, 27; Pissarro and Durand-Ruel Snollaerts 2005, II, no. 312; for another comparison, see *Wheatfield*, 1873 (*ibidem*, II, no. 316).

17 View of Bougival, 1873

Oil on canvas
49.5 × 57 cm; 23⅝ × 28⅞ in.
Milwaukee Art Museum, Wisconsin. Gift of Jane Bradley Pettit (M2001.161)

PROVENANCE:
Durand-Ruel, Paris, by 1891; Carlo Z. Thomsen, Hamburg, by 1911; Fine Arts Associates, New York; acquired in 1949 by Ralph and Mary Booth, Detroit; William and Virginia Booth Vogel, Milwaukee; Christie's, New York, 9 November 1994, lot 13; Sotheby's, London, 28 June 1999, lot 10; acquired by Jane Bradley Pettit and donated to the museum in 2002

LITERATURE:
Pickvance 1984; Adriani 1996, pp. 100–3; Noël and Hournon 2004, pp. 81–2

Formerly published as representing the bathing establishment of La Grenouillère (where Renoir and Monet had painted in 1869), and dated variously between 1869 and 1875,[1] Renoir's gallant, sun-filled landscape was first identified as a view of the Seine at nearby Bougival by Ronald Pickvance, and assigned quite precisely to 1873 on the basis of its stylistic similarities with *The Watering-place* (cat. 15).[2] Pickvance's intuitions were right on both counts. The designation of the site as Bougival was independently arrived at in a recent study of nineteenth-century images of the river and its communities, and the affinities in handling and composition to *The Watering-place*, signed and dated 1873, can be put to the test in the context of the present exhibition.[3]

On the river bank by a flotilla of empty orange rowing boats (and a single barge), a solitary couple, in fashionable city clothes, hurriedly embrace by the steps of a deserted shed. The dark-green hull that intrudes in the left foreground suggests that the lovers have come upon the dock of an absent boatbuilder, or a fisherman of means.[4] The woman, resplendent in a white and grey summer dress and tiny white tocque, is shown with her back to us. Such is her companion's ardour as he clasps her left hand that she loses control of her red-lined parasol, arrested in mid fall. Dominating the central foreground of the composition, a black and white dog basks comfortably in the sun, his red tongue panting with the heat.

Comparison with landscapes of the Seine at Bougival by Monet (fig. 74) and Sisley, painted in the early 1870s, confirms that Renoir set his easel on the Ile Gautier, just west of the Ile de la Chaussée, and within striking distance of La Grenouillère.[5] He chose a view upstream, with

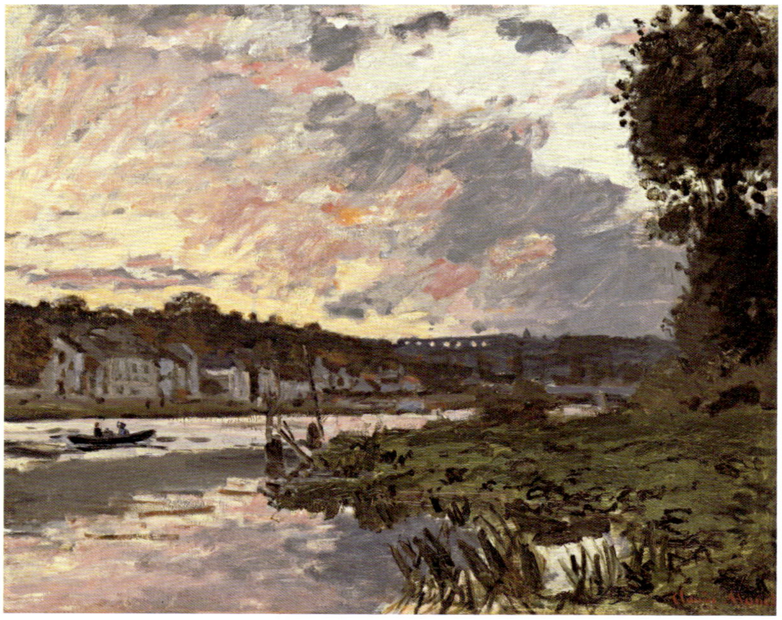

FIG. 74 Claude-Oscar Monet (1840–1926), *The Seine at Bougival*, about 1870. Oil on canvas, 60 × 73.3 cm; 23⅝ × 28⅞ in. Smith College Museum of Art, Northampton, Massachusetts (SC 1946:4).

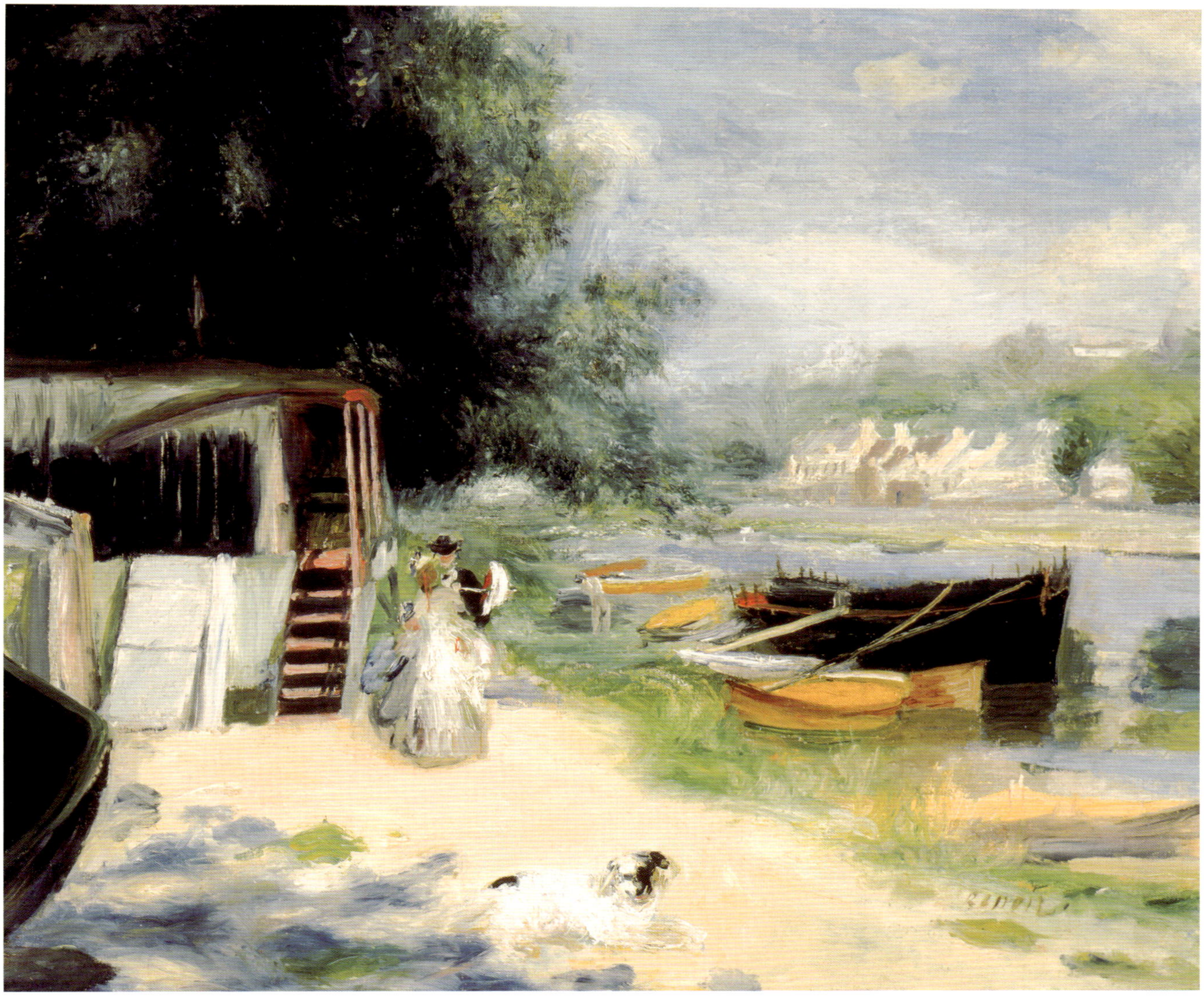

FIG. 75 Roger Jourdain (1845–1918), *Summer* (*Au Bal des Canotiers de Bougival*), 1894. Engraving, *Le Monde illustré*.

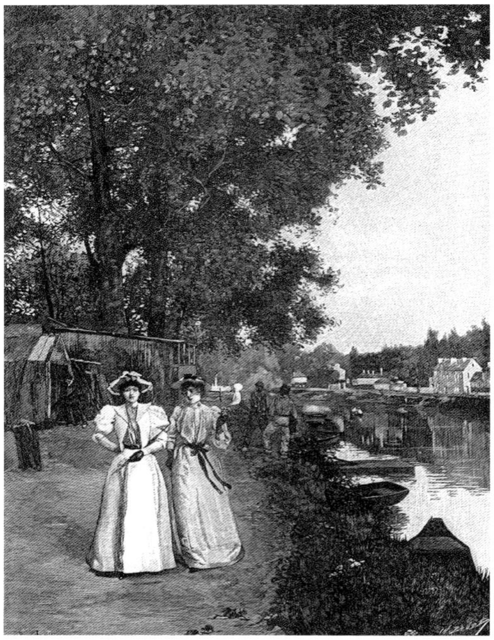

the unpictured Bougival bridge and Marly aqueduct behind him on the far side of the river, beyond the canvas at right. The cluster of houses on the far bank may be identified as the *auberge* Souvent, an inn beloved of landscapists of an earlier generation, and memorialised in song; there are also indistinct buildings, imposing in their scale, in the hills above.[6]

Renoir's dazzling palette, coloured shadows and rich, almost strident impasto (his hues are at times blended on the canvas itself) all suggest a nascent Impressionist manner. Meier-Graefe noted Manet's influence here; Barnes and De Mazia cited Corot.[7] Both dated the work to 1873, and I have suggested in the entry on *In the Parc de St-Cloud* (cat. 14) that in the spring and early summer of this year Renoir may have been experimenting in *plein-air* landscape painting, on 'days when the weather is not grey', from his temporary lodgings in La Celle St-Cloud, a few kilometres away.[8] That he considered this work to be a finished *tableau* is indicated by the resolute signature at lower right, beneath the orange skiff.

A 20-minute train ride from St-Lazare station, Bougival boasted a population of 2,086 inhabitants in 1873, and apart from tourism its economy was dependent on small-scale industry such as saw mills and sand extraction.[9] In the 1840s and 1850s it had gained renown as an artist's colony; by the 1870s it had become a fashionable weekend retreat. 'After artists, came the rowers and now, every Sunday, we have the railway to thank for a great number of day trippers [*promeneurs*].'[10] As in the *Parc de St-Cloud*, Renoir celebrates summer fashions, but lingers here on the amorous and frankly erotic associations of an afternoon in the country. A decade later, Maupassant would also explore the carnal possibilities of a Sunday outing by the Seine. The protagonists of his short story, *Le Père* (1883), take the train to Maisons-Lafitte, and as they walk to the river, 'The warm air softened both flesh and spirit; the sun shone brightly on the water, leaves and grass, infusing body and soul with myriad sparks of gaiety'.[11] After lunching at the river's edge, the couple returns along the bank and the inevitable seduction follows, in a field of lilacs.[12] Unlike Maupassant's Tessier and Louise, Renoir's couple seems equally complicit in their attraction, stealing a kiss in this strangely deserted corner, where all the boats lie dormant. The absence of milling promenaders is a feature common to Renoir's landscape and Maupassant's short story.

Not for Renoir the famed Sunday sociability of Bougival's 'Bal de Canotiers', a subject taken up in fashionable illustration (fig. 75).[13] Rather, with Watteau's example before him – a work such as *Le Faux Pas* (Musée du Louvre, Paris) that had recently entered the Louvre as part of the La Caze donation – Renoir captures momentary passion, its intimations of violence (the red lining of the parasol, the red bows and ribbons) mitigated by the presence of a knowing dog.[14] Despite the proper relocation of this landscape to Bougival, Renoir's *fête galante* in a sun-filled, suburban Cythera can be said to keep faith with La Grenouillère after all – 'A very rustic meeting place for a very frivolous society', as Berthe Morisot's mother famously described it, 'and if one ventures there alone, one is sure to return in the company of at least one other person'.[15] CBB

1 House and Distel 1985, p. 192 (dated 1869); Loyrette and Tinterow 1994, p. 456 (dated 1875, but with the location of La Grenouillère questioned); Adriani 1996, p. 100, and Rathbone 1996, no. 6 (1871–2).

2 Pickvance 1984, pp. 46, 51 (where the related painting is entitled *The Meadow*).

3 Noël and Hournon 2004, p. 61; Henri Bevan's photograph *Banks of the Seine*, taken in 1870, shows a site very similar to Renoir's landscape; see Brettell and Schaefer 1984, p. 86.

4 Adriani 1996, p. 100.

5 Monet's *The Seine at Bougival* (see fig. 75, Wildenstein 1974–91, II, no. 150), looks across the river on to the same cluster of buildings, but from the other direction; see Stevens 1992, pp. 116–17, for Sisley's bucolic *The Seine at Bougival*, 1872–3, Musée d'Orsay, Paris, where the buildings are just visible in the background at left.

6 Noël and Hournon 2004, p. 81: Houth 1972, pp. 136–46; the Souvent dynasty had established itself in the early nineteenth century; '*A Bougival, chez Souvent/Qu'il vous en souvienne.*'; Joanne (1881, p. 168) noted that in the 1840s, '*Une petite colonie de peintres vint, pendant la belle saison, s'y établir dans une auberge qu'elle faillit rendre célèbre, l'auberge de M. Souvent, sur le quai*'.

7 Meier-Graefe 1912, p. 58; Meier-Graefe 1929, p. 64; Barnes and De Mazia 1935, p. 53.

8 See cat. 13, note 13.

9 Houth 1972, p. 163; Stevens 1992, p. 116.

10 Joanne 1856, p. 325; the entry repeated in Joanne 1881, p. 168.

11 '*L'air tiède amollissait la chair et l'âme. Le soleil tombant en plein sur le fleuve, sur les feuilles et les gazons, jetait mille reflets de gaîté dans les corps et dans les esprits*'; the short story first appeared in *Gil Blas*, 20 November 1883.

12 Richard Brettell has drawn attention to the river outing as a theme of Naturalist literature; see his essay in Rathbone 1996, especially pp. 106–15.

13 Noël and Hournon 2004, pp. 63–82.

14 For the possible impact of the La Caze collection on Renoir, see cat. 7, notes 10, 11.

15 Rouart 1951, pp. 19–20; the comment was made around 1868.

18 The Seine at Argenteuil, about 1873

Oil on canvas
46.5 × 65 cm; 18½ × 25⅝ in.
Musée d'Orsay, Paris. Gift of Dr and Mme Albert Charpentier, 1951 (RF 1951–14)

PROVENANCE:
Durand-Ruel, Paris, 1922; Gift of Dr and Mme Albert Charpentier, 1951

LITERATURE:
Tucker 1982, pp. 89–96; Brettell and Schaefer 1984, pp. 146–54; House 2004, pp. 82–4

This delicately brushed, somewhat tentative river landscape has been identified as a view of the Petit Bras of the Seine, with the Ile Marante to the left and Argenteuil far in the background.[1] Renoir would have placed his easel on the sandy banks of the Seine at Colombes, a village of 1,800 souls served by the Chemin de fer d'Argenteuil since April 1851 and a favourite spot for Sunday fishing.[2] Despite Argenteuil's well-established reputation as a centre for sailing and yachting, Renoir gives no hint of the town's attractions for a visiting Parisian – it was a 20-minute train ride away – but lingers instead on the wide expanse of slowly moving water, on which a tiny rowing boat with two figures is just visible in the middle ground at left. Equally discreet is his depiction of a much larger barge, moored to the bank at right, and, in the far distance, an orange skiff with a single rower, minimally noted.

This may well be a view similar to those that Monet and Sisley painted in 1872.[3] Monet's *The Seine at Argenteuil* (fig. 76) captures a spot further upstream and closer to the centre of town, with the poplars of the Ile Marante reflected in the water, and the church spire at left and bright new villas at right anchoring the horizon line.[4] The poplars are absent from Renoir's view, and the cluster of buildings in the distance is indeterminate (though the spire is certainly visible), with the red-roofed villas indicated in the most summary of ways. Renoir's handling in *The Seine at Argenteuil*, with its lean washes of paint and gentle dabs of colour, is nothing like Monet's more emphatic touch in the related picture; it is closer to the softness and thinness in Monet's *View of the Argenteuil Plain* (fig. 77), in all likelihood done in the autumn of 1872, which shows the town from the hills of Sannois to the north.[5] It is not possible to date Renoir's earliest visits to Argenteuil with any precision: Monet

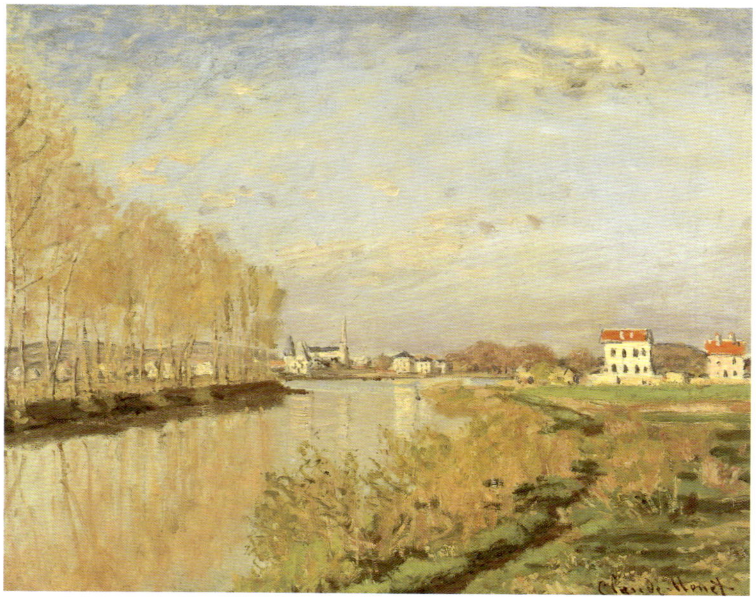

FIG 76 Claude-Oscar Monet (1840–1926), *The Seine at Argenteuil*, 1872–3. Oil on canvas, 50 × 61 cm; 19¾ × 24 in. Musée d'Orsay, Paris (RF 1951.13).

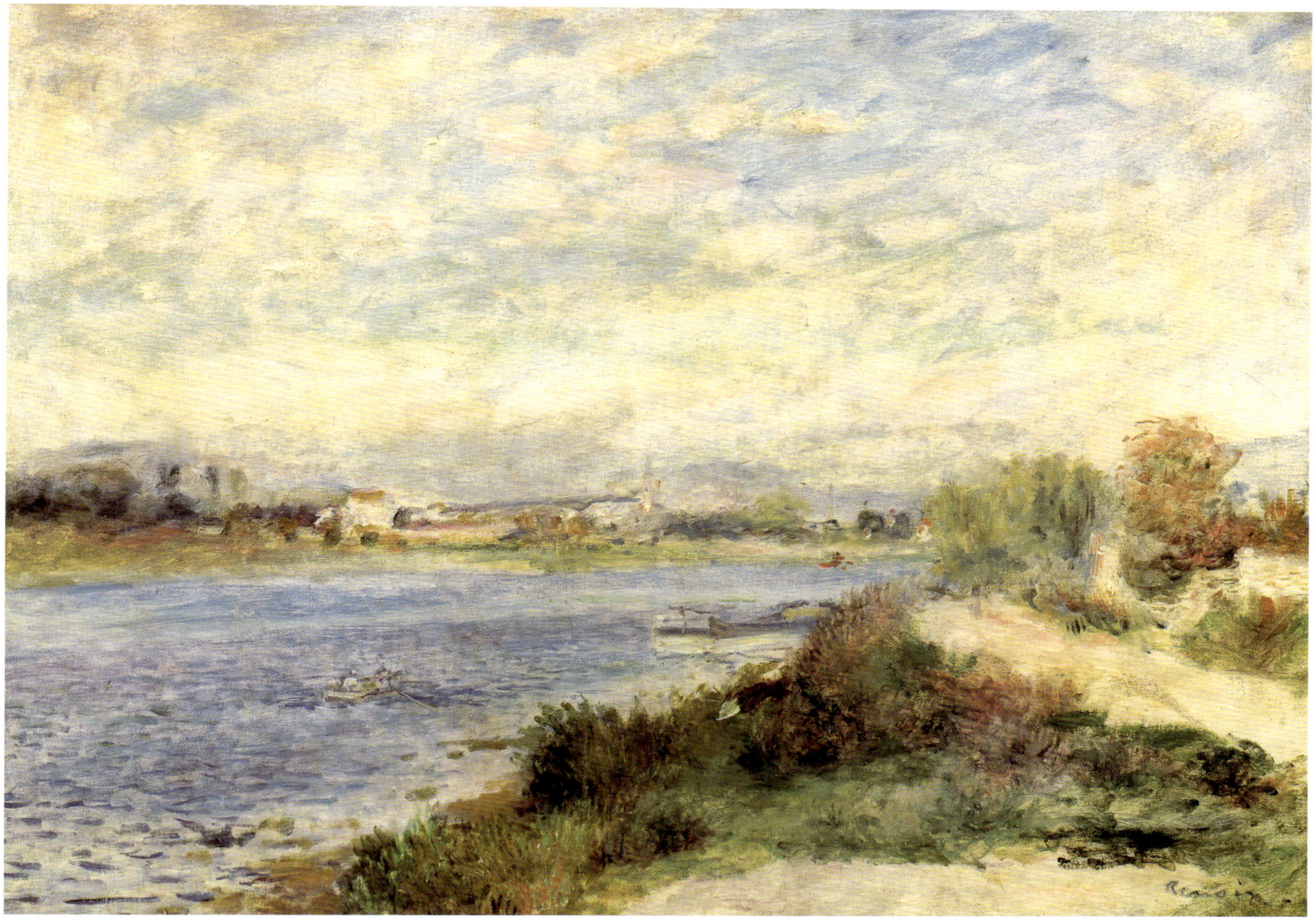

FIG. 77 Claude-Oscar Monet (1840–1926), *View of the Argenteuil Plain*, 1872. Oil on canvas, 52 × 72 cm; 20½ × 28¼ in. Musée d'Orsay, Paris (MNR 855).

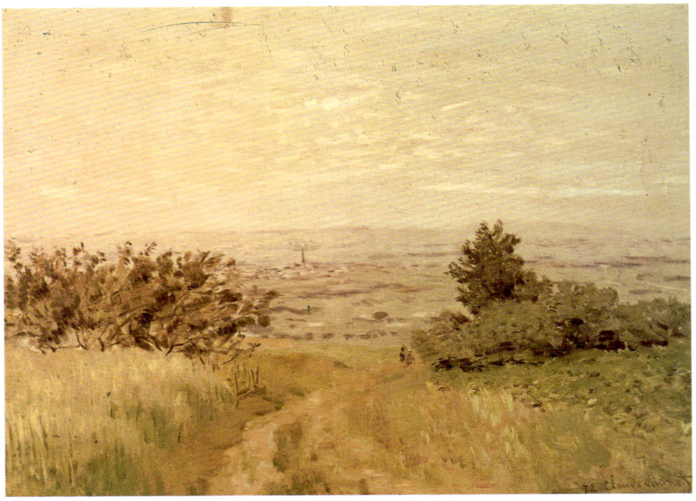

first mentions his presence there only in September 1873, but it is quite possible that he came to paint there on his own earlier in the year, or even during the previous year.

To Vollard, Renoir reported, 'That same year [1873] I made a number of studies [*études*] in Argenteuil, where I found myself in Monet's company.'[6] Renoir's use of the term 'study' is of significance, because *The Seine at Argenteuil*, in its sketchy, exploratory handwriting, is surely an unfinished work; the signature at left was added many years later. In its relatively subdued colours and understated generalities, *The Seine at Argenteuil* shares something of the unvariegated topographical view beloved of Daubigny and Jongkind; the latter had produced informal scenes of Argenteuil from almost the identical spot during the previous decade.[7] Between 1873 and 1876 Renoir would paint a variety of scenes at Argenteuil (cats. 23, 24) – he would return for one last painting campaign in the summer of 1888 – but *The Seine at Argenteuil* may well be the earliest of his landscapes there. As such it bespeaks Renoir's affection for the familiar *banlieue parisienne* – which also included Louveciennes, Bougival, and St-Cloud – in which he preferred to overlook the new industrial squalor.[8] As Rivière noted, the appeal of such towns was in 'the light skies, meandering rivers, leafy trees and low-lying hills, whose undulating lines vanished into the misty horizon'.[9]

CBB

1 Brettell and Schaefer 1984, p. 154.
2 Joanne 1856, pp. 372–3, noting that the left bank of the Seine was a kilometre from the centre of Colombes. In Maupassant's *Les Deux Amis* (1883), set during the Franco-Prussian war, two friends take the train to Colombes to repeat their peacetime habit of a day of fishing, with disastrous consequences.
3 Wildenstein 1974–91, II, no. 198 (dated 1872); Brettell and Schaefer 1984, no. 40 (dated 1873). Coincidentally, both Monet and Renoir's views of *The Seine at Argenteuil* found their way into the collection of the Parisian psychiatrist Dr Albert Charpentier (1872–1953), who donated ten paintings to the Louvre in 1937; see Laclotte 1989, p. 170. For Sisley's *The Seine at Argenteuil*, 1872, see Daulte 1959, no. 26.
4 House 2004, pp. 82–3.
5 Wildenstein 1974–91, II, no. 220; Tucker 1982, pp. 22–3.
6 Vollard 1918, p. 58.
7 Auffret 2004, p. 306, for Daubigny's *Bords de la Seine à Argenteuil*, 1864; for Jongkind's watercolour of the same site, dated 1869, see Tucker 1982, p. 68.
8 In Rivière's opinion, artists such as Raffaelli had chosen to belabour the impoverishment of the suburbs: '*Ils n'en ont noté que les terrains semés d'immondices, l'herbe galeuse foulée par les hôtes loqueteux, les bouges et les masures misérables, le ciel gris, coupé par les hautes cheminées d'usines crachant une fumée épaisse et noire*'; Rivière 1921, p. 182. The implications of Rivière's reminiscences are discussed in Clark 1984, pp. 182–5.
9 Rivière 1921, p. 182.

19 Claude Monet painting in his Garden at Argenteuil, about 1873

Oil on canvas
46 × 60 cm; 19¾ × 24 in.
Wadsworth Atheneum Museum of Art, Hartford, Connecticut. Bequest of Anne Parrish Titzell (1957.614)

Claude Monet painting in his Garden at Argenteuil probably dates from the autumn of 1873, the time of Renoir and Monet's *rapprochement* and the period at which the giant *dahlia imperialis* would have been at their most abundant.[1] It is the only painting done at Argenteuil that Renoir remembered in any detail,[2] and, as Anne Distel has noted, does more to evoke the friendship that existed between the two men 'than any commentary could possibly do'.[3] *Claude Monet painting in his Garden at Argenteuil* is a record of Monet's second summer at 2 rue Pierre Guienne, a villa with a spacious garden previously rented by the realist painter Théodule Ribot (1823–1891).[4] Known as the 'maison Aubry', this property lay near the railway station in the most picturesque section of Argenteuil, a town in which the population had doubled to 8,000 by the time that Monet and his family moved there, and which, fifteen minutes from the Gare St-Lazare, had replaced Asnières as a favoured sailing centre with Parisians.[5]

Renoir's affectionate testimonial is a work of extraordinary delicacy and detail. Wearing a round hat and dark-blue jacket with a black velvet collar, his cuffs and shirt collar indicated by the merest slivers of white, Monet is shown with nearly all the tools of his trade. His portable paint-box and folded parasol are placed on the ground by his feet; he balances a rectangular palette on his left arm, while holding several long paintbrushes in his left hand. On the lightweight easel, also portable, can be seen a canvas of landscape format, primed with a white ground. Monet is portrayed painting in front of a thicket fence which can barely restrain the tumultuous array of red, yellow, and white dahlias. Behind them, at left, is a two-storey house with an attic window, flanked by a tree in full bloom. In the background at the right of the composition are several of the older villas on the rue Diane and the rue Pierre Guienne to the south of Monet's property.[6]

Renoir seems consciously to have adopted Monet's flickering, variegated brushwork: his garden landscape shares obvious affinities with Monet's own *The Artist's Garden in Argenteuil* (fig. 78), signed and dated 1873 and probably painted at more or less the same time.[7] In Monet's composition the flowering dahlias are overwhelming: they obscure the two-storey house, now positioned just right of centre, and dwarf the properly attired figures – Camille and Renoir? – seen walking by the thicket fence on the far edge of the garden.

Similar only at first sight, the two paintings can be seen in terms of distinct polarities. Unlike their views of the duck pond (cats. 20, 21) or the railway bridge at Argenteuil, Monet and Renoir did not paint these canvases side by side, since in each the garden is recorded from a different angle. Monet's composition, with its absent fence and windswept vegetation, stresses the seigneurial

PROVENANCE:
Hôtel Drouot, Paris, *Vente de tableaux*, 17 April 1896, no. 87, bought for 800 francs by Durand-Ruel, who sold it to Edmond Decap the same day; Edmond Decap; Georges Feydeau (1862–1921), his sale, Hôtel Drouot, Paris, 14 June 1902, lot 17, bought by Durand-Ruel for 4,700 francs; Charles Albert Corliss, New York; Josiah Titzell, Georgetown, CT; bequeathed by Anne Parrish Titzell to the Wadsworth Atheneum in 1957

LITERATURE:
House and Distel 1985, pp. 201–2; House 1994, pp. 64–5; Bailey 1997, pp. 122–3, 278–9; Willsdon 2004, pp. 20–1

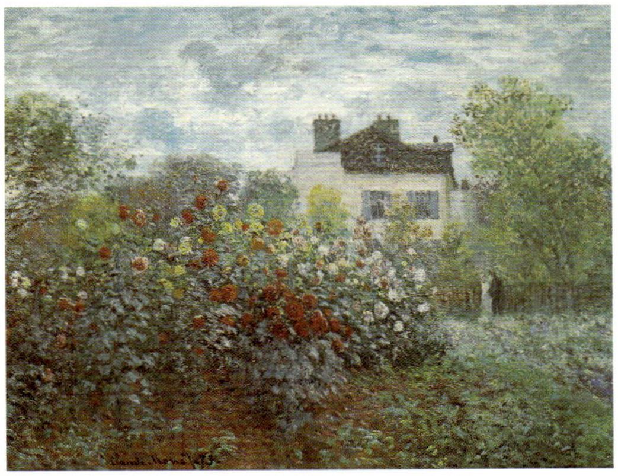

FIG. 78 Claude-Oscar Monet (1840–1926), *The Artist's Garden in Argenteuil*, 1873. Oil on canvas, 61 × 82.5 cm; 24 × 32½ in. National Gallery of Art, Washington, DC. Gift of Janice H. Levin, in honour of the 50th Anniversary of the National Gallery of Art (1991.27.1).

over the suburban; his *Artist's Garden in Argenteuil* is a modern *fête champêtre*, with the neighbouring villas ruthlessly excluded from view. Renoir, more faithful to the topography of Argenteuil, neither excises the surrounding architecture nor ignores the lack of privacy characteristic of suburban living, however gracious.[8]

Renoir and Monet have approached this corner of the garden with different expectations. Not only is there a staged quality in Renoir's portrayal of Monet working out of doors – he is equipped for a long day in the countryside, not a mere trip down the garden path – but it is also fair to ask whose garden is being painted. Monet's many garden views done at the maison Aubry between 1872 and 1874 invariably suggest an ordered, spacious realm, one that is protected by closed walls from the noisy suburb without. Renoir quietly punctures such a vision of gentility in the suburbs. Standing outside the garden, to which the thicket fence denies access, it seems reasonable to assume that he has shown Monet not painting his own garden, but that of a neighbour. The question must remain moot, since the maison Aubry at 2 rue Pierre Guienne was demolished in 1913, when the street was renamed boulevard Karl Marx, a change of address unlikely to have appealed to either Monet or Renoir.[9]

Claude Monet painting in his Garden at Argenteuil is also less spontaneous than Renoir's confident and shimmering brushwork would suggest. Preparatory to the painting, his pastel portrait of Monet in painter's costume, seen head on but without brushes or palette, suggests that Renoir worked out his composition beforehand, studying Monet from different angles before committing to the final *mise en scène*.[10] Less speculatively, it now known (as was first suggested by John House in 1994) that *Claude Monet painting in his Garden at Argenteuil* was painted over an entirely different composition.[11]
The ridges of paint underneath the present composition, visible to the naked eye, are the brushstrokes of an earlier painting, vertical in format, of Camille Monet wearing a summer bonnet, not unlike the one she wears in *The Reader, Springtime*, 1872 (The Walters Art Gallery, Baltimore).[12] Even with the evidence of X-radiographs of *Claude Monet painting in his Garden at Argenteuil*, the question first posed by House has yet to be answered conclusively. Was Renoir painting over a study by Monet of his wife that Monet had discarded, or did he replace his own close-up of Camille with a virtuoso performance of her husband at work?[13]

CBB

1 Willsdon 2004, p. 21. It should be noted that while *Claude Monet painting in his Garden at Argenteuil* is now consistently dated to 1873, Vollard (1918, I, p. 88, no. 351) and Daulte (1971, no. 131) both dated it to 1875. As a result, Daulte relocated the setting to Renoir's rented garden in the rue Cortot.
2 '*Je fis, cette même année* [1873], *nombre d'études à Argenteuil, où je me trouvais en compagnie de Claude Monet, notamment un Monet peignant des dahlias*'; Vollard 1919, p. 8.
3 House and Distel 1985, p. 201.
4 Moreau-Nélaton 1926, I, p. 22; Wildenstein 1974–91, I, p. 58.
5 Tucker 1982, pp. 10–19.
6 Walter 1966, p. 337.
7 The relationship between these two pictures is less straightforward than immediately apparent, and has been discussed by Rewald 1973, pp. 284–5; Tucker 1982, p. 143; Moffett in National Gallery of Art 1991, p. 166; and, most recently, Tucker 1995, pp. 86–7.
8 Tucker 1982, pp. 143–4.
9 Walter 1966, pp. 335, 342, n. 13.
10 See Daulte 1977, no. 126, p. 89, which follows Daulte 1971, no. 131, in which *Claude Monet painting in his Garden at Argenteuil* is dated to 1875, and moved to the garden in the rue Cortot.
11 House 1994, p. 64, and Bailey 1997, pp. 122, 279 and fig. 136.
12 Bailey 1997, p. 122. Camille Monet's distinctive oval face and rather gaunt features are also seen in *The Red Kerchief: Portrait of Camille Monet*, about 1872, Cleveland Museum of Art.
13 House 1994, p. 64; Bailey 1997, p. 123. In his account of Renoir painting *Camille Monet and her son Jean in the Garden in Argenteuil*, 1874, National Gallery of Art, Washington, DC, Monet told Marc Elder that Renoir had asked him 'for a palette, a brush and canvas', so the custom of using his host's materials was an established one; M. Elder, *A Giverny, chez Claude Monet*, Paris 1924, p. 70.

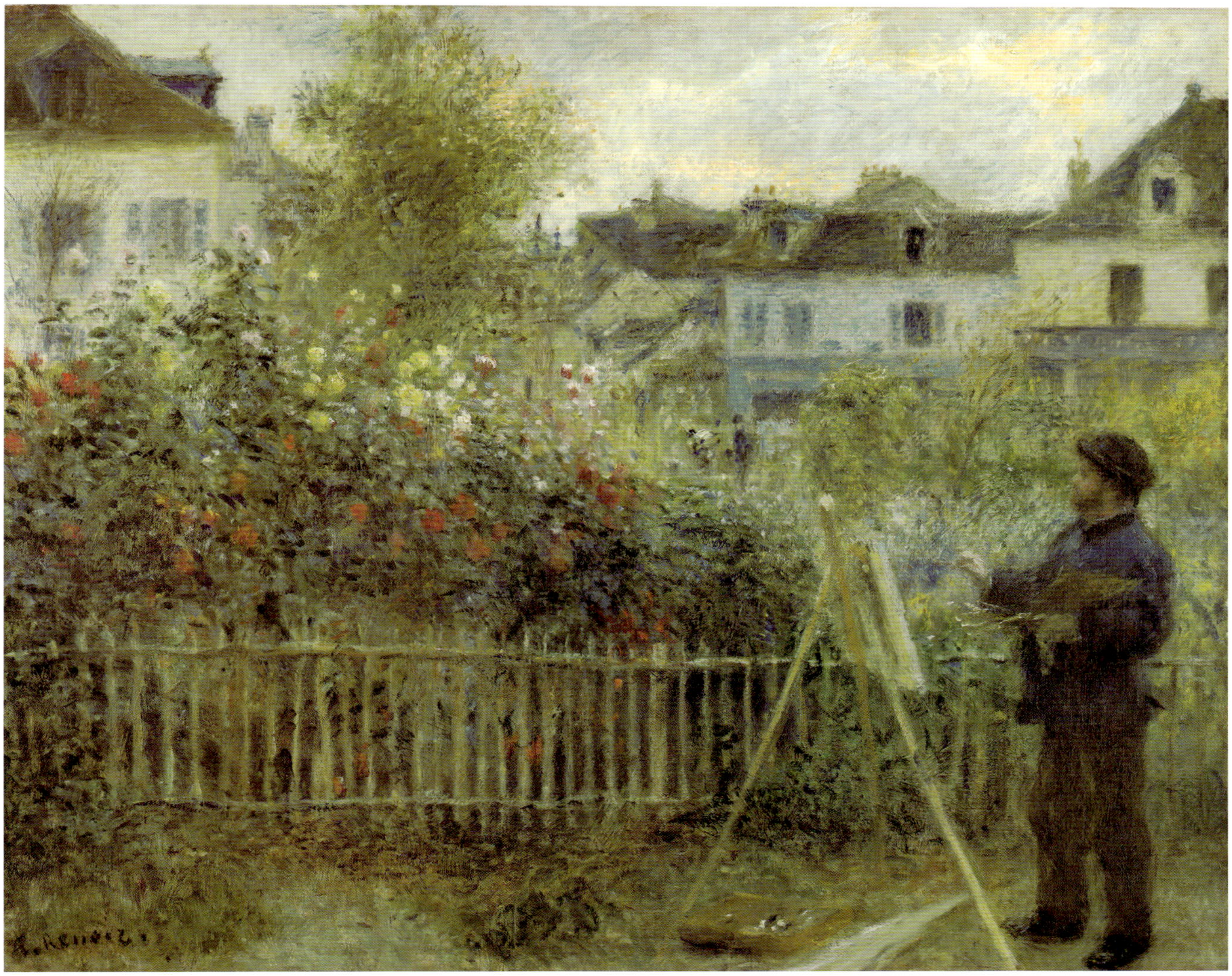

20 Duck Pond, 1873

Oil on canvas
50.8 × 62.2 cm; 20 × 24½ in.
Private collection

21 Duck Pond, 1873

Oil on canvas
50.2 × 61 cm; 19 × 24 in.
Dallas Museum of Art, Texas. The Wendy and Emery Reves Collection (1985.R.56)

PROVENANCE (CAT 20): Bought from the artist by Durand-Ruel, Paris, 1891; private collection; Valley House Gallery, Inc., Dallas, by 1986

LITERATURE (CAT 20): White 1984, pp. 47–8 and 1996, pp. 66–7; Tucker 2001, pp. 60–1

PROVENANCE (CAT 21): Durand-Ruel, Paris, 1891; Gertrude B. Whitmore, New York; Wendy and Emery Reves, France, March 1950; bequeathed to the Dallas Museum of Art, 1985

LITERATURE (CAT 21): Cognat 1950, p. 40; Laprade 1956, p. 38; Fosca 1961, pp. 29, 34; Rewald 1961, pp. 284–6, 307; Rouart 1985, p. 27; Brettell 1995, pp. 106–7; White 1996, pp. 66–7; Néret 2001, pp. 63–4

Renoir and Monet were artistic collaborators on several occasions, painting a site or a view side by side. While their campaign at the bathing spot La Grenouillère in 1869 generated the most paintings and is the most famous, in their paintings of a duck pond belonging to a farm near Argenteuil in 1873 they came closest together.[1] In these three paintings – two by Renoir, one by Monet (fig. 79) – the convergence of the artistic interests of the two men, if not their techniques, is clearly evident. Looking more carefully at Renoir's two paintings, one can come to understand what Impressionism meant to Renoir and what he would make out of it.

Both of his works are composed of blunt self-evident brushstrokes, but Renoir has produced from these patches a delicate view of the duck pond in Argenteuil, where he was staying at the home of Monet. The scene itself is not modern, in the sense that it does not depict a place that had recently been altered by the suburban intrusion into the French countryside around Paris. However, the motif could hardly be described as traditional. While artists of all stripes had followed the example of Jean-François Millet in depicting scenes of peasant life as subjects for paintings in their own right, these artists represented not peasants in the country

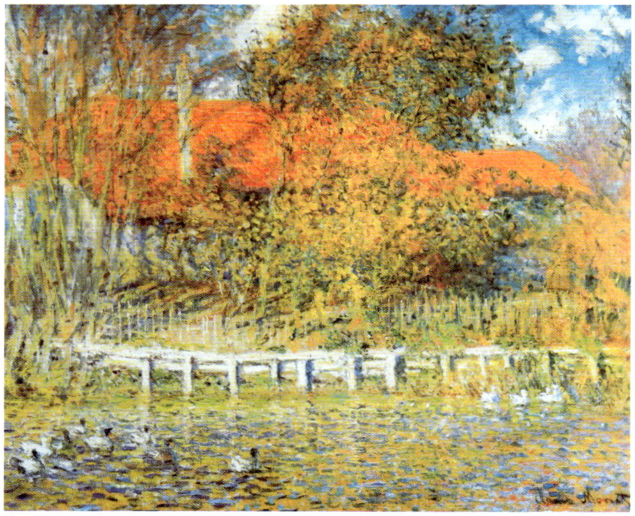

FIG. 79 Claude-Oscar Monet (1840–1926), *Duck Pond*, 1873. Oil on canvas, 54 × 65 cm; 21¼ × 25⅝ in. Private collection.

but the country itself, unadorned by humans except for the two polling boatmen visible at the right edge of the Dallas Museum version. In other words, these pictures feature a place, or setting, instead of representing a scene from country life, thereby eschewing all concerns about those who lived and worked in the country. The suppression of this kind of narrative content allowed the viewer to focus on these images as representations of place and the constituent elements of that place, such as light, colour, foliage and weather.

When these paintings were made, it was generally believed that art needed to be distinct from just the kind of prosaic details that are their visible focus. Art consisted not simply in the nature of the subject but in the composition that the artist created from the subject. But in these paintings, the viewer does not see the pond as an enclosed whole, rather as a band of water taking up roughly the lower third of each canvas, bordered by a low fence. The farm is almost completely obscured by foliage, ruining any picturesque character that the house may have had. What is left is a view of some ducks, fluttering leaves, reflections in the water, drifting clouds – all represented in the most vivid and direct method that painting could offer. Strong and subtle colour contrasts are built up with equal determination, individual marks are woven into shimmering prismatic wholes. Renoir's technique finds a new expression in these passionately wrought yet finely tuned chromatic experiments. The 'New Painting',[2] as Duranty would later dub it, resulted from these sessions, staged out-of-doors, in which the world was transformed into a collection of discrete chromatic elements that were recombined to produce a pictorial whole. Thus a painting needed no longer to be hinged upon the appropriate representation of the chosen subject, but instead upon the way that such a subject would be transformed through painting. It seems apposite that the very summer they made these paintings, Monet and Renoir, with their friend Camille Pissarro, began to plan their first group exhibition of what would come to be known as Impressionist art. JZ

1 John Rewald relates a story from Léon Werth that, when the Dallas Museum *Duck Pond* came to Durand-Ruel around 1913, neither Monet nor Renoir could determine which of the two artists had made the painting; Rewald 1961, p. 285, n. 13.

2 Edmond Duranty, *La Nouvelle Peinture*, Paris 1876.

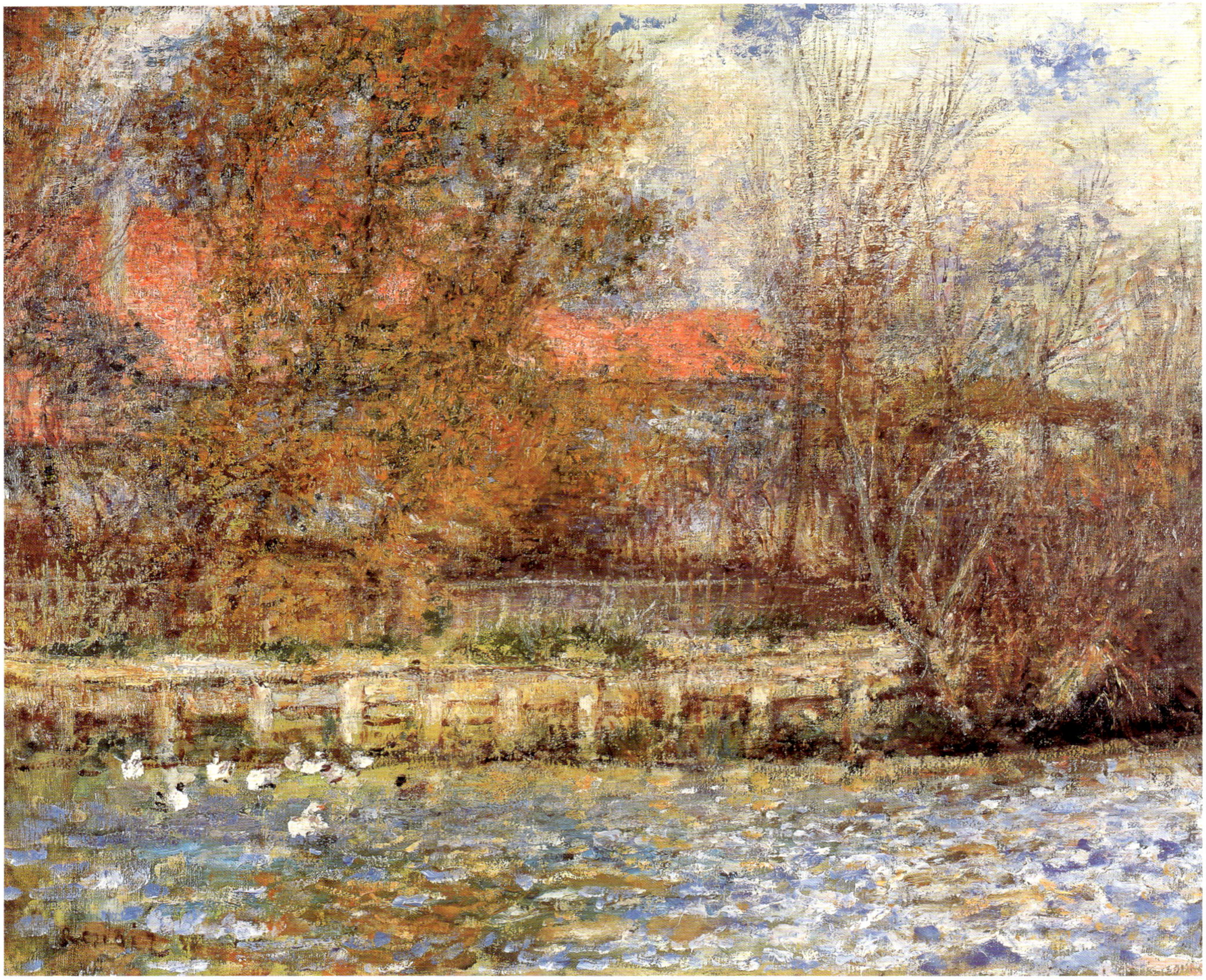

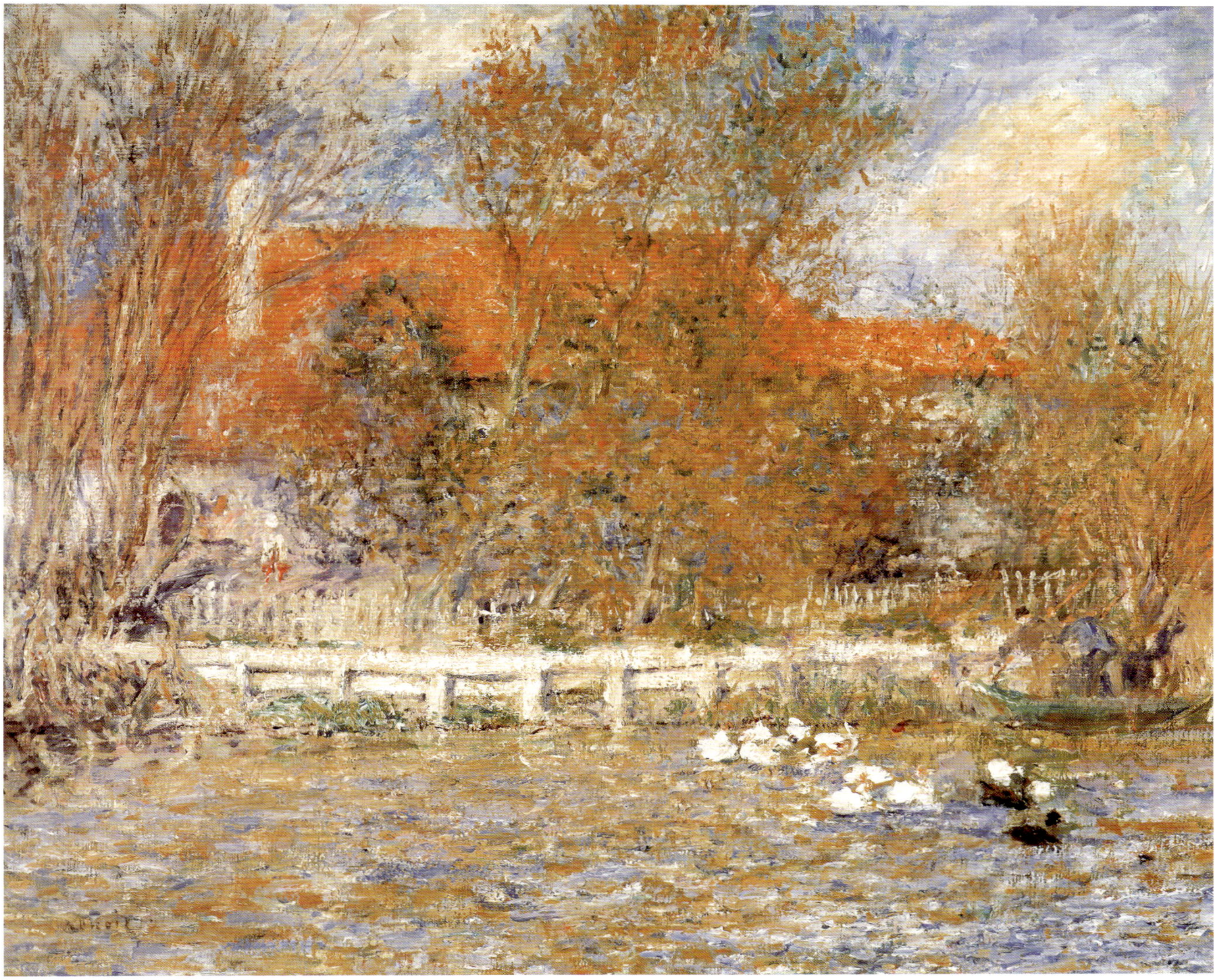

22 Rowers at Argenteuil, about 1873–4

Oil on canvas
50.2 × 61 cm; 19¾ × 24 in.
Joseph Hackmey, Israel

PROVENANCE:
Galerie Durand-Ruel, Paris, no. 1381; purchased by Sterling and Francine Clark, 5 April 1934; Clark Art Institute, Williamstown, MA, 1955; de-accessioned, 15 December 1970; private collection; Christie's, London, 3 February 2003, lot 60; private collection

LITERATURE:
Grafton Galleries 1905, no. 236; New York 1932, no. 12; Cabanne 1970, p. 52; Fezzi 1972, no. 97; Wildenstein 1974, no. 5; Fezzi 1985, no. 93; Kern 1996 pp. 28, 72–3, 106.

This painting of people boating on the Seine has usually been dated to the summer of 1873, which Renoir spent at Argenteuil with Monet and his family.[1] There once again the two artists worked side by side in the open air, as they had done in 1869 at La Grenouillère (see cats. 5, 6). Renoir's *Claude Monet painting in his Garden at Argenteuil* (cat. 19), from that summer, is evidence of the intimacy between the two friends. The closeness of their styles at the time also has been often noted, particularly regarding their *Duck Pond* paintings (cats. 20, 21). The small, dappled and intensely varied brushstrokes with which Renoir paints the water here can be compared with his technique in those two works, similarly detailed and intricate in their handling of separate touches of colour. At the time, Renoir and Monet were also busy discussing the establishment of an independent exhibiting society to promote their works and those of their artist friends. It would be founded at the end of the year; the first Impressionist exhibition would open on 15 April 1874. Thus, like the paintings mentioned above, the present work has been regarded as an example of the bold experiments in colour and painterly touch in which Renoir and Monet engaged at a vital and highly creative moment in the development of the collective painting style the Impressionists would put on public display a few months later.

Renoir was back at Argenteuil the following summer as well, however, soon after the first Impressionist exhibition had ended. He worked there with Monet, Sisley and Manet. Caillebotte was on hand, too. Under the impetus of their example, and as he grew more confident in his own technique, his painting was no less innovative than the previous year. The present work can also be compared to such paintings of 1874 as *The Seine at Argenteuil* (cat. 23), with which it shares a firm sense of composition and a mastery of the scintillating play of light on water.[2] Further, Steven Kern recently has wondered if the site depicted is Argenteuil at all. He suggests it might as well be Asnières or Chatou, both centres for rowing, while Argenteuil was better known as a sailing location (although a small sailing boat makes its appearance in this painting, too).[3] Juxtaposition in this exhibition of the painting with works from both years and of various sites along the Seine may help to answer such questions.

What is clear is that the present painting numbers among those works of the mid-1870s in which Renoir perfected his skill in depicting scenes of suburban sociability along the banks of the Seine. The pleasure to be derived from sunshine, open water, conversation and the quiet and informal rhythms of summer life all are manifest here. The painting style itself takes on a notable complexity in the intricate weaving together of colours, especially in the reflections cast on the water by the foremost boat. The seated female figure – she is almost the mirror image of the woman, also in a striped dress, in Monet's well-known *On the Bank of the Seine, Bennecourt* of 1868 (Art Institute of Chicago) – leads our eye from the riverbank, and the cool shade of a willow, to the sun-dappled expanse of water beyond. Renoir would further explore this movement from a more shadowy foreground to brilliant sunlight beyond in *Luncheon at La Fournaise* (cat. 34) of the following year.

CR

Shown in London only

1 See Fezzi 1985, no. 374, no. 93, and, most recently, sale catalogue, Christie's, London, 3 February 2003, lot 60.
2 This comparison was suggested by the author of the entry on the present painting in Christie's, London, 3 February 2003, lot 60.
3 Kern 1996, p. 106, note 6.

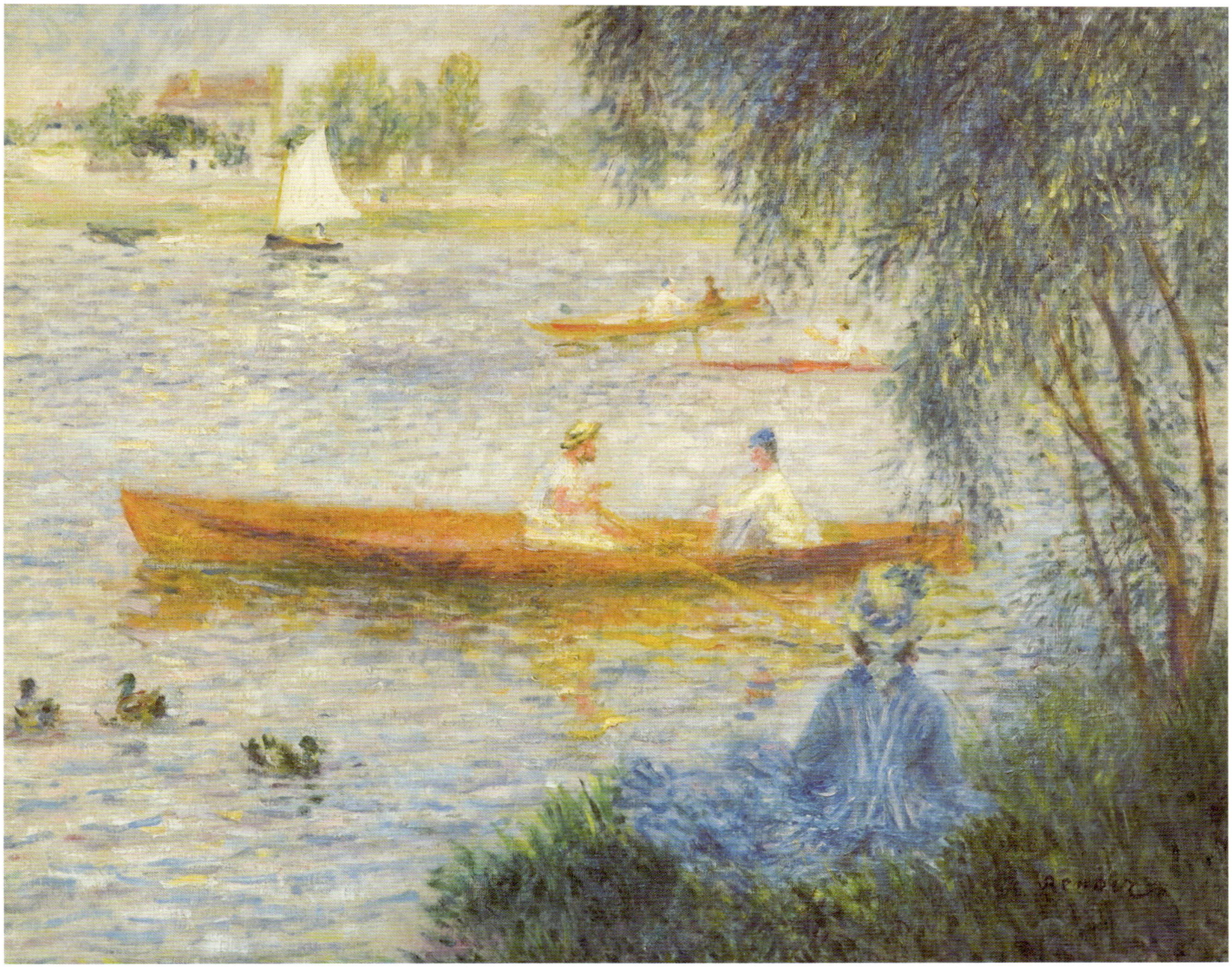

23 The Seine at Argenteuil, 1874

Oil on canvas
51 × 65 cm; 20 × 25⅝ in.
The Portland Art Museum, Portland, Oregon. Bequest of Winslow B. Ayer (35.26)

PROVENANCE:
Tableaux et Aquarelles par Monet, Morisot, Renoir, Sisley, Hôtel Drouot, Paris, 24 March 1875, no. 38, '*Bateau. (Argenteuil.)*', purchased for 105 francs by Durand-Ruel; sold by Durand-Ruel & Co. in 1926 to Winslow B. Ayer, Portland; bequeathed in 1935 to the Portland Art Museum

REFERENCES:
Tucker 1982, pp. 90–110; Clark 1984, pp. 173–85; House and Distel 1985, pp. 68, 205; House 1995, pp. 216–17; Tucker 2000, pp. 122–5

This resplendent boating scene is the most elaborate Impressionist landscape that Renoir painted at Argenteuil during the summer of 1874, when he and Monet were frequent visitors to this industrial suburb north-west of Paris that had been Monet's home since December 1871.[1] Renoir's view is from the banks of Petit Gennevilliers on the south bank of the Seine, looking across the river to Argenteuil's tree-lined promenade. Clearly demarcated in the background are the diminutive white- and pink-bricked tollhouse and the rebuilt highway bridge that linked Argenteuil to Gennevilliers, and to Paris beyond.[2]

Hands in his pockets, a bearded fellow in a black hat and jacket, dwarfed by the triangular jib, stands on the dock. He seems to be conversing with the skipper, shown standing in the sailing boat, who has let go of the ropes that manoeuvre the jib (they lie slack at the foot of the mast). The jib sways gently in the wind at an angle to the main sail as the boat approaches the dock. To the right, a second boat is shown at anchor, its sails unfurled.[3] On the far side of the basin three craft are in motion – two to the left of the main boat, one to its right – their sails reflected in the blue and orange water. Also visible (but just) is a tiny scull, manned by four rowers, indicated by a sliver of orange that punctuates the triangle of white in the background at right. On the leafy promenade of the Argenteuil bank we can make out the red roof and whitewashed walls of the former ferryman's house, now a thriving café-restaurant. Despite the activity on the water, there are few people in sight; only the ducks in the foreground bear animated witness to these nautical preparations.

As is well known, Renoir and Monet were in all likelihood working side by side on this summer's afternoon,[4] since Monet's very similar *Rowers at Argenteuil* (fig. 80) shows a slightly later moment in the proceedings, with the boat now cast off

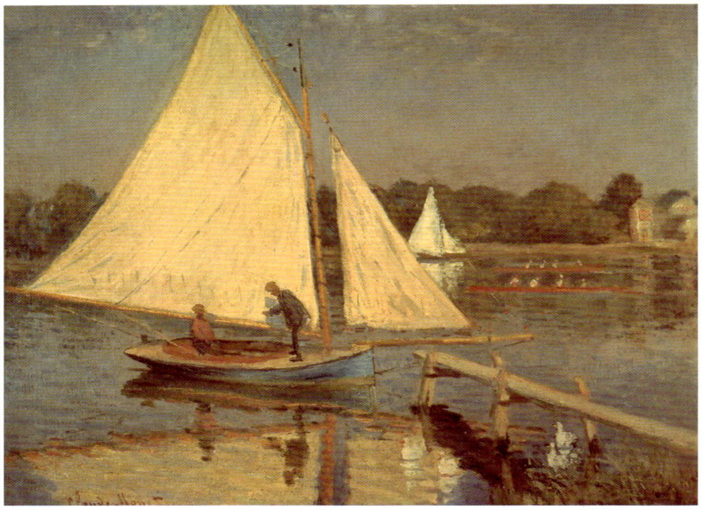

FIG. 80 Claude-Oscar Monet (1840–1926), *Rowers at Argenteuil*, 1874. Oil on canvas, 60 × 81 cm; 23⅝ × 31⅞ in. Private collection.

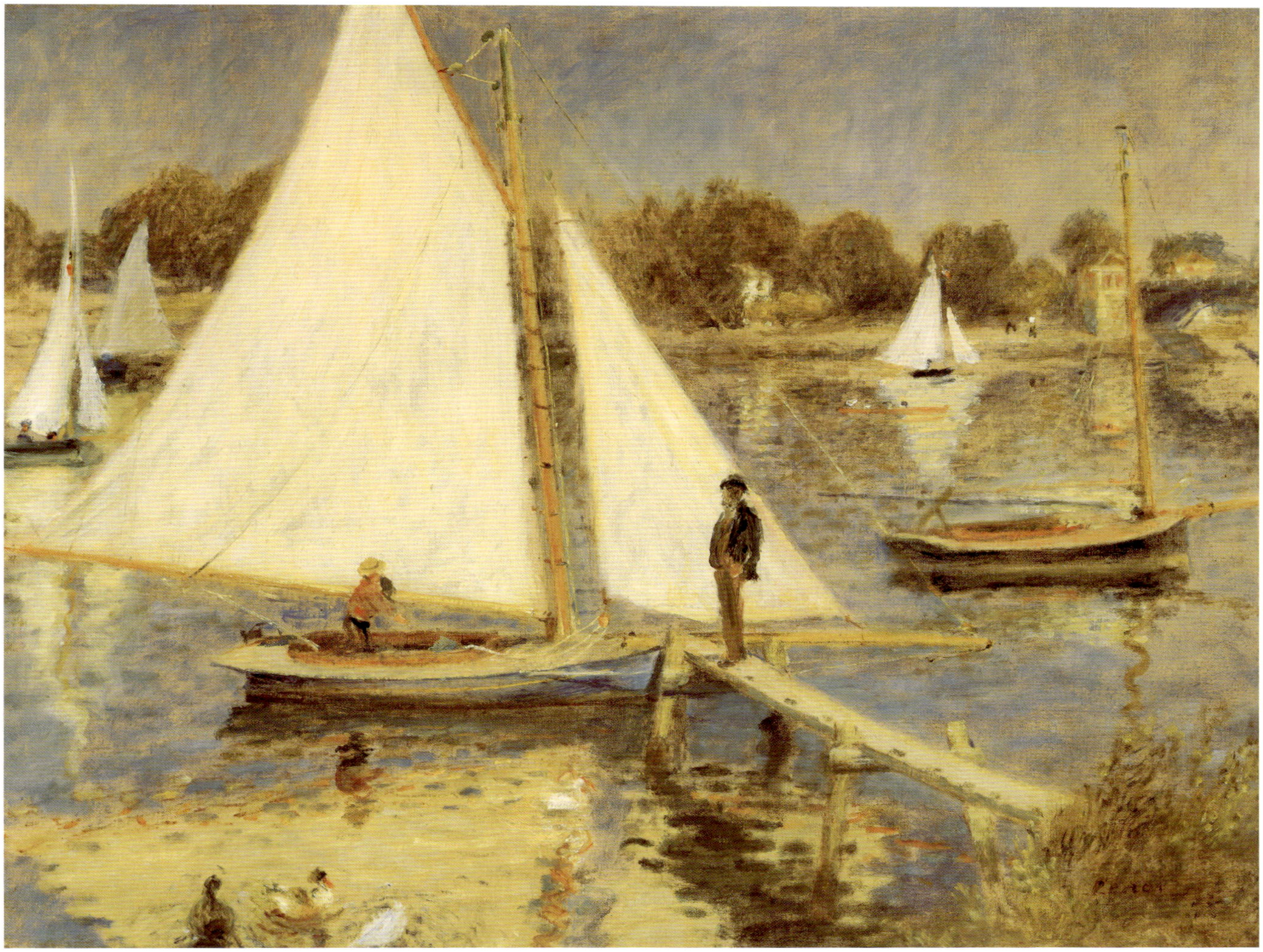

from the dock and both figures on board (though it might be noted that the figure in discussion with the skipper wears a blue smock and light cap, a different costume from that worn by Renoir's protagonist).[5] As has also been well observed, Monet's composition and handling are tauter and more controlled than Renoir's.[6] Monet's triangular sailing boat and its reflections, uninterrupted by any secondary vessels, are solidly anchored between sky and water; the pair of red sculls to the right reinforce the linearity of the horizon; even the ducks are paired in neat proximity to the diagonal dock. By contrast to such geometries, Renoir's *Seine at Argenteuil* appears energetic and spontaneous (even a little chaotic) – an early manifestation of his credo of 'irregularity', perhaps. In his virtuoso delineation of ropes, masts and sails, and with his brushwork conveying a river sparkling with movement and reflected sunlight, Renoir seems determined to 'out-Monet' Monet.

Renoir's dazzling chromatic harmonies and notational shorthand should not obscure the fidelity of his transcription of this corner of the Argenteuil basin, as comparison with contemporary photographs bears witness (fig. 81).[7] By contrast to a fairly well-established iconographical tradition, which cast Argenteuil as a lively, populous and fashionable centre for regattas and races, *The Seine at Argenteuil* finds its subject on the margins of suburban recreation.[8] We are not witnessing a regatta or race of any significance, since summer was inhospitable for yachtsmen (the winds were not high enough) and sailing competitions took place in spring and autumn.[9] Nor do Renoir and Monet celebrate the chief attraction of the regatta, the opportunity for well-heeled members of *Le Sailing-Club* to 'offer the public a fairy-tale glimpse of their equipment'.[10] Despite the brightness of its colour and the freedom of its brushwork, in terms of subject-matter *The Seine at Argenteuil* is something of a low-key affair.

However, as Renoir's signature at lower right reminds us, *The Seine at Argenteuil* was also a completed picture for Parisian consumption. As such, it may have been among the works that Renoir painted in the summer of 1874 in preparation for the second Impressionist exhibition, initially planned for the following autumn.[11] It was when this failed to materialise that Renoir (and his colleagues) may have decided to place some of their canvases for sale in public auction at the Hôtel Drouot. *The Seine*

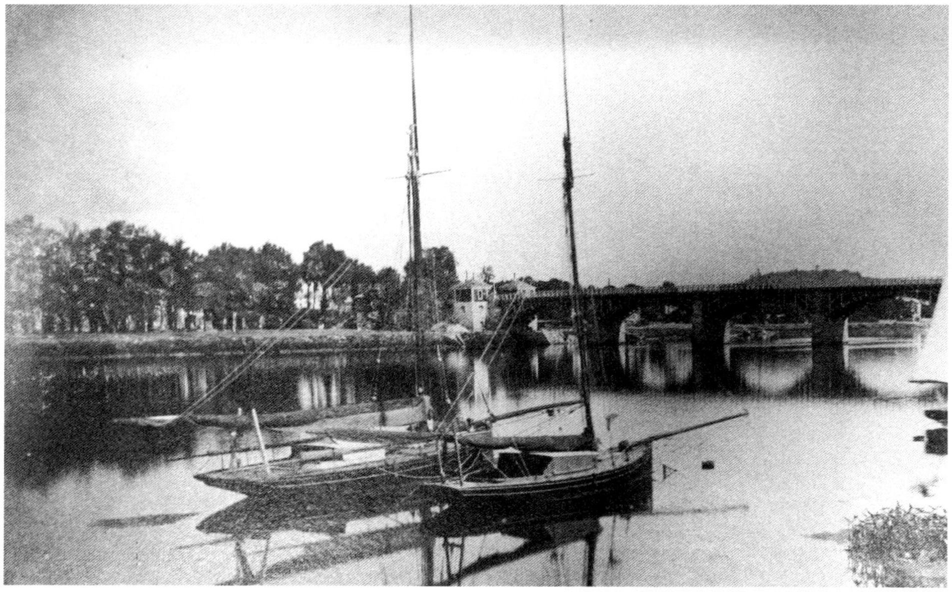

FIG. 81 E. Fiorillo (active 1879–1920) *Sailing Boats on the Seine*, 1880s (?). Photograph. Bibliothèque historique de la Ville de Paris (BhvP: Album 4 4. no. 13).

at Argenteuil was one of ten landscapes by Renoir to appear in the celebrated Impressionist auction of March 1875, where it was entitled simply '*Bateau. (Argenteuil.)*', and was acquired for the modest sum of 100 francs by Durand-Ruel.[12] For reasons that are not altogether apparent, it remained part of his stock for the next 50 years,[13] finding a first buyer only in November 1926, when it was acquired by Winslow B. Ayer (1860–1935), a businessman from Portland, Oregon, who donated it to his local museum nine years later. CBB

Shown in Philadelphia only

1 Rewald 1973, pp. 341–8; Tucker 1982. In nearly all publications prior to Tucker 1982, Renoir's *Seine at Argenteuil* is misdated 1873 or 1873–4.

2 For the clearest discussion of Argenteuil's topography see Wildenstein 1996, pp. 108–12, and also the maps in Tucker 1982, pp. 188–9, and Tucker 2000, pp. 15, 17.

3 For an expert nautical description, see Tucker 2000, p. 123, who notes 'in Renoir's picture the skipper stands, allowing the jib to luff and the ropes to lie on the deck by the mast'.

4 White 1996, pp. 70–2.

5 Tucker 2000, pp. 122–3; and see the entry in Christie's, *Impressionist & Nineteenth-Century Art*, New York, 18 November 1998, lot 13, where the intriguing suggestion is made that Renoir and Monet may have painted their landscapes from Monet's floating studio, moored near the foot of the dock shown in these pictures.

6 Tucker 2000, p. 123.

7 See also the photograph of the highway bridge at Argenteuil dated to 1875 in Wildenstein 1996, I, p. 111.

8 See the woodcuts reproduced in Clark 1984, pp. 177–8, and Tucker 2000, p. 16.

9 Larousse 1865–90, XIII, p. 840.

10 *Ibidem*, p. 840.

11 In his review of the first exhibition published in *La République française* on 25 April 1874, Philippe Burty noted: '*On peut compter sur une seconde tentative, plus complète, pour l'automne prochain*'; see Berson 1996, I, p. 37.

12 Bodelsen 1968, p. 335, procès-verbal 20; this reference to *The Seine at Argenteuil* has been overlooked in all previous publications.

13 Archives Durand-Ruel, stockbook, 25 August 1891, where the picture is re-inventoried (and retitled) 'no. 1297, *La Seine à Argenteuil*, photo 1315'.

24 Regatta at Argenteuil, 1874

Oil on canvas
32.4 × 45.6 cm; 12¾ × 18 in.
National Gallery of Art, Washington, DC. Ailsa Mellon Bruce Collection (1970.17.59)

PROVENANCE:
Edward Molyneux, Paris; Ailsa Mellon Bruce, 1955; bequeathed to the National Gallery, 1970

LITERATURE:
Rewald 1961, pp. 348–9; Fezzi 1972, p. 94; Wheldon 1975, pp. 64, 67; Monneret 1980, p. 150; Rouart 1985, pp. 26–7; Tucker 1982, pp. 106–8; Copenhagen 1996, no. 54; Tucker 2000, pp. 118–21

This small painting made in the summer after the first Impressionist exhibition in 1874 is an example of the kind of work that visitors might have found in the exhibition labelled simply *étude*, or 'study'.[1] The Impressionists disquieted some contemporary critics not only or simply by their willingness to present sketches and studies for exhibition or sale, but also because theirs were not sketches of the kind well-established in French tradition – made as part of the process towards creating a highly finished work – but works evidently to be regarded as an end product.

Regatta at Argenteuil captures a fleeting moment of suburban leisure with rapidly painted strokes that indicate the immediacy of the act of perception and lay bare the process of its depiction. Renoir has not covered the whole canvas with paint but used the ground showing through as a background colour. On top of this ground, the pigment was laid on very quickly, quite thickly in some areas, which results in a scintillating visual effect, still striking despite the ground having discoloured over time.[2] The figures on the shore and the reflections in the water are indeed nothing more than hastily placed daubs of paint, but, with these light gestures, Renoir successfully situated these boats in a believable space and provided all of the richness of a lively, and very fashionable, scene – a regatta that would have been attended by pleasure seekers from nearby Paris.[3]

The painting was probably created at the same time as Monet's larger and more structured *Regatta at Argenteuil* (fig. 82).[4] As Paul Tucker has noted, the Impressionists did not share the concerns of commercial illustrators who produced images of such events for illustrated journals.[5] Both artists passed over the details of the event itself and attempted rather to render such immediate visual effects as the wind in the sails of the boats and the reactions of visitors on the shore, in order to convey a sense of the moment witnessed. Unlike Monet in his painting, Renoir did not even convey a sense of the landscape, the wider space in which the action unfolds. Instead, he sought to translate the effects of light in the sky, water and sails into marks that allowed the viewer to perceive selected forms and to make out the subject by means other than clear pictorial organisation. JZ

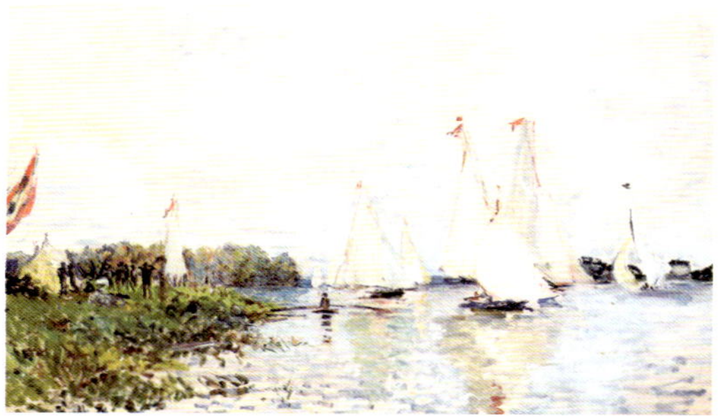

FIG. 82 Claude-Oscar Monet (1840–1926), *Regatta at Argenteuil*, 1874. Oil on canvas, 59 × 99 cm; 23¼ × 39 in. Private collection, Switzerland.

1 While Renoir did not exhibit any '*études*' in the Impressionist exhibition of 1874, he did exhibit a pastel '*croquis*', joining seven exhibited by Monet. Boudin exhibited six '*études*' – four of them sky studies. In addition, there were works exhibited without any traditional pictorial subject and in an experimental style, such as Pissarro's *Hoar Frost* (Musée d'Orsay, Paris)and Monet's *Impression, Sunrise* (Musée Marmottan, Paris).

2 In a discussion at the National Gallery of Art, Washington, DC, Ann Hoenigswald pointed out to me that the unique texture of tiny dots that shows through the background of this painting and gives it a darker appearance was the result of relining, and that recovering the original background of the work would be impossible.

3 See Herbert 1988.

4 Tucker 2000, p. 118.

5 *Ibidem*, p. 120.

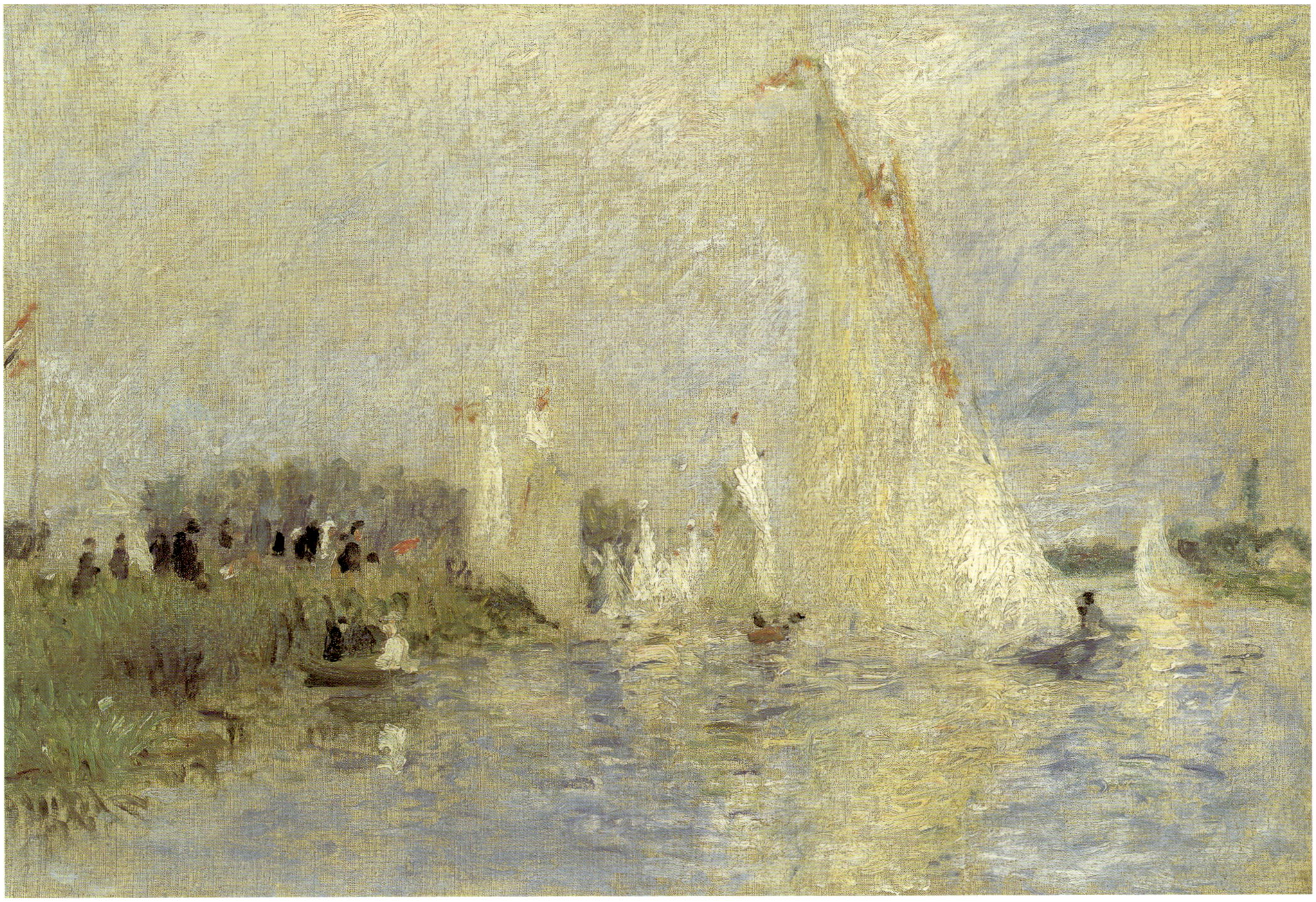

25 Paris, Le Quai Malaquais, about 1874

Oil on canvas
38 × 46 cm; 15 × 18 in.
Private collection, Paris

PROVENANCE:
Georges Viau; sale of Viau collection, Galerie Durand-Ruel, Paris, 4 March, 1907, lot 65; private collection; sale Piasa, Paris, 21 June 2002, lot 15; private collection, Paris

LITERATURE:
Drucker 1944, no. 21.
Galerie Charpentier 1945, no. 183

The Quai Malaquais on the left bank of the Seine is directly opposite the Louvre in the heart of the city. Its dominating landmark is the domed Institut, home of the Académie française, while the pedestrian Pont des Arts traverses the river at this point. Renoir had painted the site looking east from river level a few years earlier in 1867 (fig. 27, p. 44). To paint this animated scene he returned to the site but at the more elevated level of the *quai* itself. Here, he stood with his back to the Institut looking due west. The picture is structured around the two receding diagonals of buildings at left and a line of still young trees along the right, an urban improvement planted under the Haussmann administration. In the middle distance, glimpsed through the trees, is the Pont du Carrousel, in the shadow of which the artist had situated himself to paint the 1867 canvas.[1] It may be possible to recognise the distinctive round-headed mansard windows of the Ecole des Beaux-Arts among the buildings at left. In the far distance, the city dissolves into haze. The scene is richly animated with the comings and goings of ordinary Parisians, including soldiers, couples and top-hatted men riffling though the wares of the *bouquinistes*. Horse-drawn carriages move among the crowd and clouds billow in the sky. This was clearly a favourite corner of the city for Renoir, for here those aspects of Parisian life he appreciated most came together – the river, fine old buildings, green trees and the sociable animation of the street.

The present picture is one of two views of the site that probably were painted at around the same time. In the second, slightly larger work (fig. 83) Renoir looks in a north-easterly direction towards the Pont des Arts and the Place du Châtelet on the right bank. The westerly arm of the Institut cuts off the right side of the canvas. Here too, a crowd animates the scene with the bustle of Parisian life. The two works share a quick, sketch-like and improvisatory style of painting in which dabs of colour evoke forms with swift economy. The more autumnal colours of the second painting suggest that it may post-date the present, more summery work. That they both date from 1874 is suggested by the fact that the second painting was included in the generally unsuccessful sale of paintings by Monet, Morisot, Renoir and Sisley held at the Hôtel Drouot on 24 March 1875, where it was acquired by Monet's brother, Léon.[2] CR

Not in the exhibition

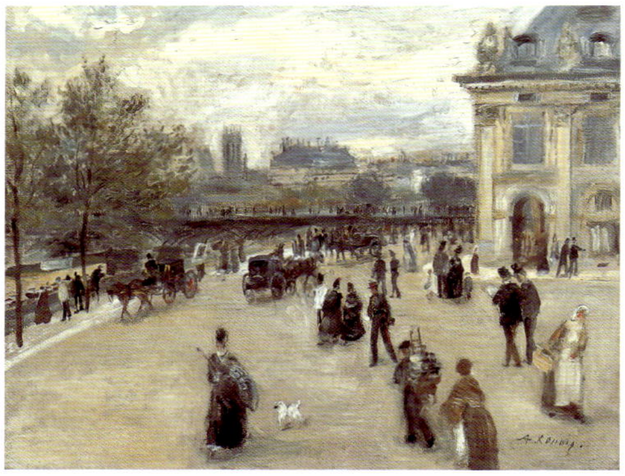

FIG. 83 *L'Institut au Quai Malaquais*, about 1874. Oil on canvas, 46 × 56 cm; 18⅛ × 22 in. Private collection.

1 Fezzi 1972, no. 94, mistakenly identifies the site depicted as the Quai Conti further to the east beyond the Institut, but if that were the case the Institut's dome would be visible at the upper left.
2 '*Paris, l'Institut au Quai Malaquais*' was lot 37 in that sale.

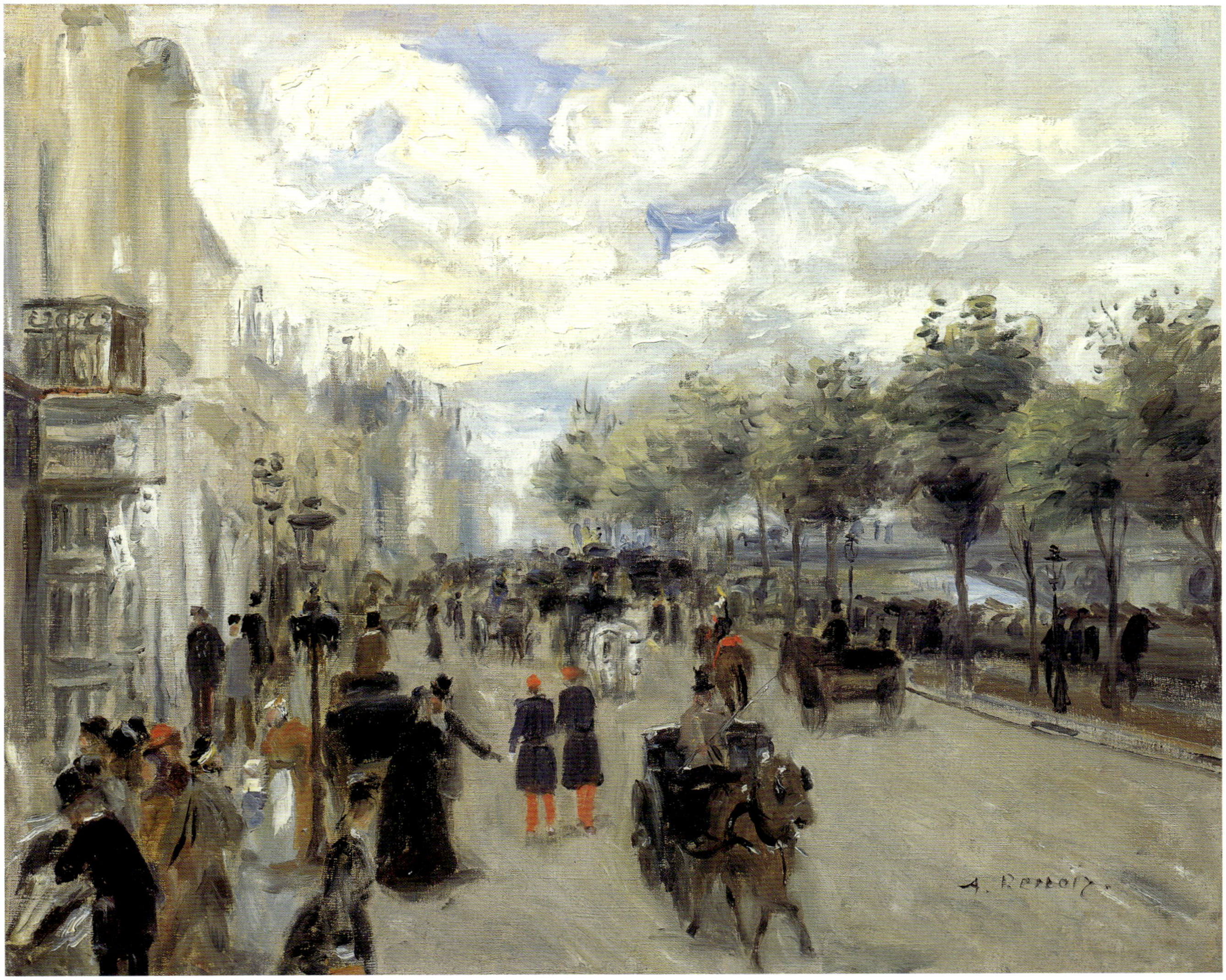
A. Renoir.

26 Woman with a Parasol and a Small Child on a Sunlit Hillside, 1874

Oil on canvas
47 × 56.2 cm; 18½ × 22 in.
Museum of Fine Arts, Boston, Massachusetts. Bequest of John T. Spaulding (48.593)

PROVENANCE:
Sold by the artist to Durand-Ruel, 1891; sold to Josef Stransky, New York, 1917; sold to Duncan Phillips, Washington, DC; sold to Durand-Ruel, 1926; sold to John Taylor Spaulding, 1927; bequeathed to the Museum of Fine Arts, 1948

LITERATURE:
Meier-Graefe 1929, p. 61, no. 52; Pope 1930, pp. 97, 121; Edgell 1949, pp. 63, 65; Constable 1955, p. 54; Daulte 1971, no. 260; Boston 1973, no. 70; Schneider 1985, p. 25; House and Distel 1985, no. 31; Monneret 1989, pp. 52–3; White 1996, pp. 94–5; Kern 1997, p. 16; Boston 1999, pp. 221–2; Rabinow 2000, p. 12; Néret 2001, pp. 82–3; Shackelford and Wissman 2002, pp. 157–9, 267

This picture is a quite magical composition of great tonal subtlety, owing a great deal to Manet's technique. It is dateable to 1874 because it is quite close both to Manet's *The Monet Family in their Garden in Argenteuil* (fig. 84) and Renoir's painting done at the same moment of Camille Monet and her son Jean in Monet's garden in Argenteuil of June 1874. The woman pictured in *Woman with a Parasol and a Small Child on a Sunlit Hillside* is probably Monet's wife Camille, but the identity of the child is unknown. In any case the image is effective because the artist left the features of the central figure in soft focus and thus allowed the general aspect of the painting, the contrast of dark and light tones modelled in overlapping thin layers, to provide an overall harmony.

This is a wonderful example of a landscape with figures. This is not an amorous pair, but a pair nevertheless and Renoir succeeds in providing a sense of human relation to the natural world in this light-filled image. The woman reclines on the ground, and the artist has positioned her diagonally across the surface of the painting. She looks back towards the viewer but her eyes are slightly averted. A parasol protects her creamy complexion. Her white dress catches the light of the sun and the strokes of white pigment that represent the highlights merge effortlessly with the golden and green light of the grass. In effect, she merges with the landscape visually but retains a sense of self-possession and even a hint of fashion in her presence. The young child, whose blond hair reflects the golden sunshine, has its back to the viewer. He or she is off to explore the world, unaware of our gaze.

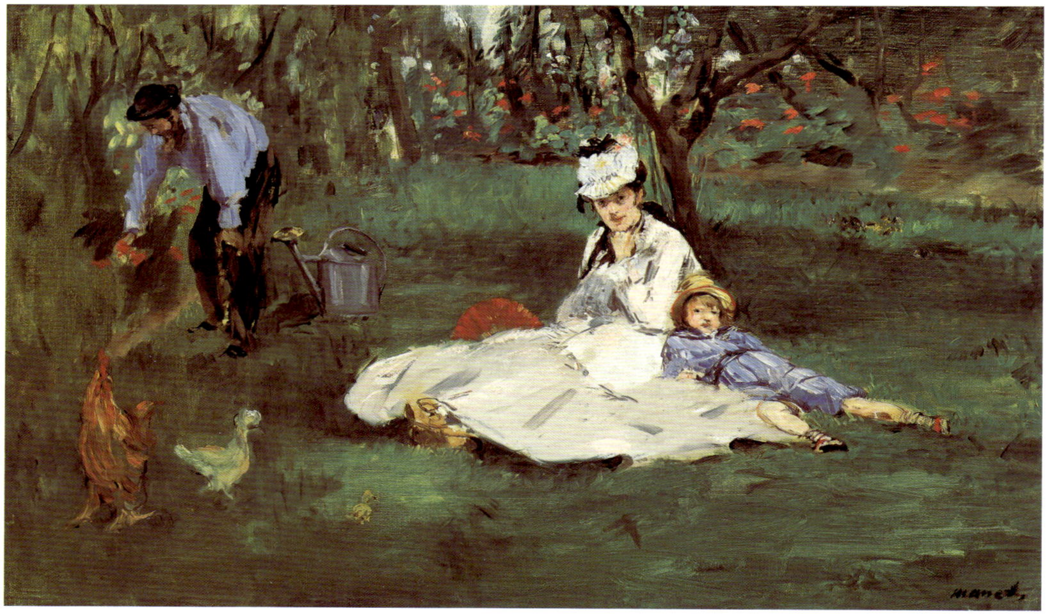

FIG. 84 Edouard Manet (1832–1883), *The Monet Family in their Garden in Argenteuil*, 1874. Oil on canvas, 61 × 99.7 cm; 24 × 39¼ in. The Metropolitan Museum of Art, New York. Bequest of Joan Whitney Payson, 1975 (1976.201.14).

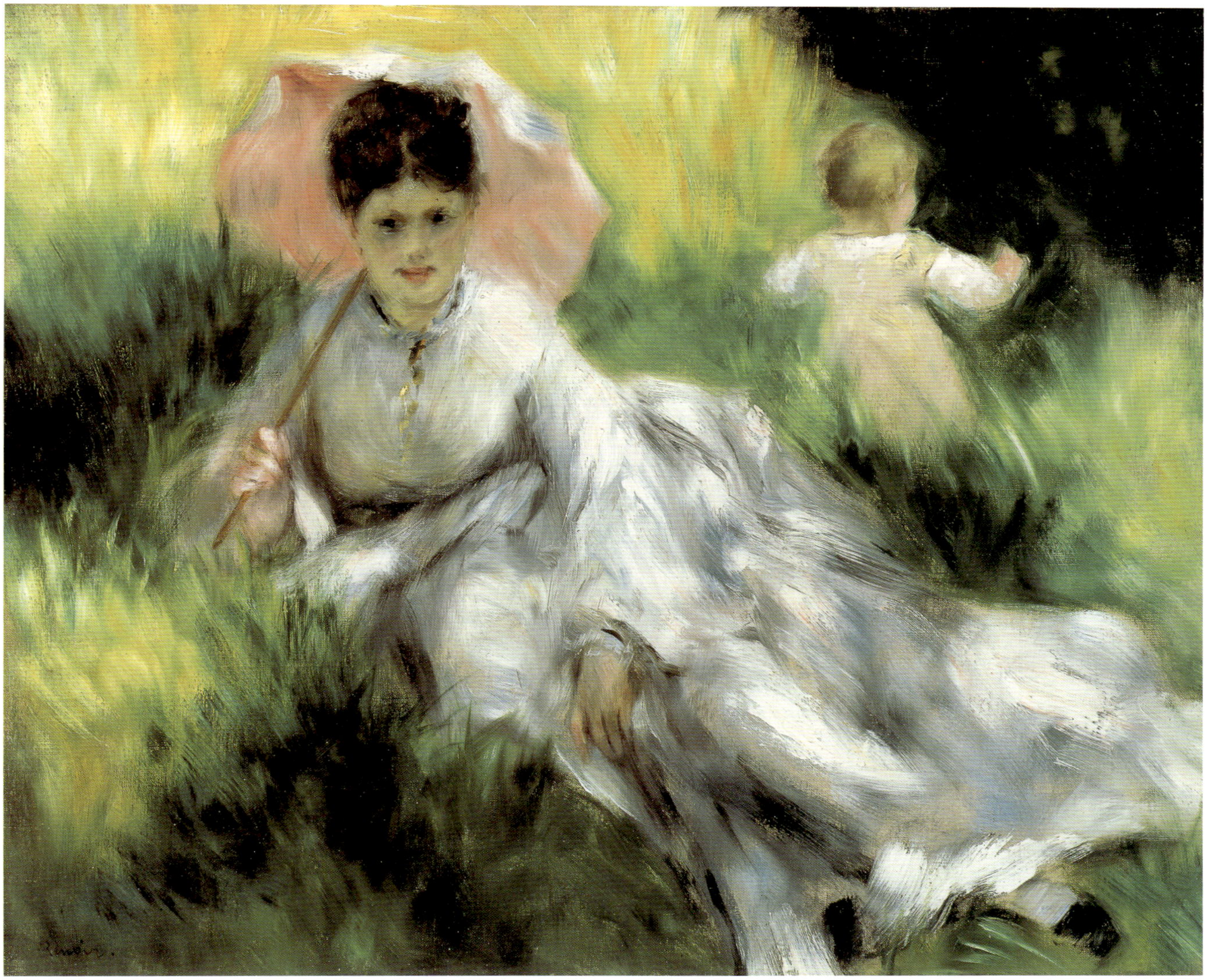

The image suggests a relationship of mother and child, but it expresses also the divergent means through which adults and children relate to the world. The woman is composed, presenting herself as a figure in a natural environment, at once immersed in and protected from it. This is a variation on a common theme for Renoir, whose images of women often align them with nature, a stereotype of the era that Renoir certainly did not challenge and indeed reiterated through his paintings. The child, on the other hand, is not self-conscious. Rather he or she relates to the environment in a manner that is direct and active – this world is not a backdrop against which to pose. The child sees and goes, exploring the immediate environment. JZ

27 Confidences (La Tonnelle), about 1874

Oil on canvas
81.3 × 60.3 cm; 32 × 23 in.
Portland Museum of Art, Maine. The Joan Whitney Payson Collection at the Portland Museum of Art, gift of John Whitney Payson (1991.62)

PROVENANCE:
Carl Reininghaus, Vienna; Knoedler & Co., New York; sold to Joan Whitney Payson (Mrs Charles S. Payson), 1928; The Joan Whitney Payson Gallery of Art, Westbrook College; gift to the Portland Museum of Art, 1991

LITERATURE:
Meier-Graefe 1929, p. 77, no. 51; Carstairs 1929, pp. 34–5; Drucker 1944, p. 184; Gotthard 1947, no. 16; Chamson 1949, no. 16; Wildenstein 1950, no. 18; Drucker 1955, p. 139; Daulte 1971, no. 128; Daulte 1977, p. 51; White 1984, pp. 51, 57; House and Murphy 1988, p. 235, no. 7; House 1994, pp. 62–3; White 1996, p. 85; House 1997, pp. 72–3; Portland 2004, pp. 54, 62

Among Renoir's landscapes are a group of paintings, made in the mid-1870s, that prominently feature figures in outdoor settings. In these, among them the present work, Renoir explored the traditional subject of the pastoral idyll with modern figures painted in an innovative manner. The importance of the La Caze bequest of eighteenth-century art to the Louvre has been noted as a source of inspiration for Renoir (see cat. 7), and this painting is largely derived, in terms of both subject and technique, from the idylls of Watteau and Boucher. The titles that have been assigned to the work over time reflect these associations. Yet there is more than a trace of Manet's influence here as well. Manet's *Déjeuner sur l'Herbe* (1863; Musée d'Orsay, Paris), with its uneasy cohabitation of references to canonical art and modern figures, left many contemporary viewers confused about the intent of the artist. Depriving the figures of the mythological references made the nudes in Manet's work seem vulgar to most viewers of his epoch.

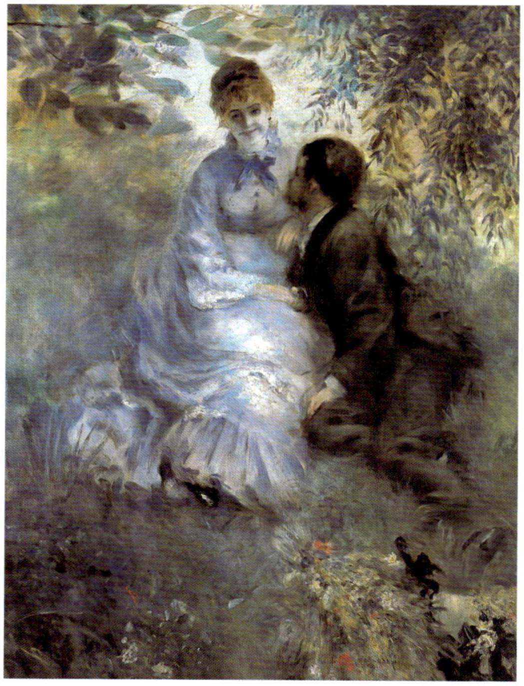

FIG. 85 *The Lovers*, 1875. Oil on canvas, 175.5 × 130 cm; 69⅛ × 51⅛ in. National Gallery, Prague.

While Renoir's figures are clothed, there would have been clear signs of impropriety in his painting for his contemporaries. This couple is young and unmarried and the woman is not chaperoned, which demonstrates that she is not bound by the inhibitions of respectability. She is leaning on the man's shoulder, reading the newspaper with her feet seemingly propped on his ankle and a white dog at her feet. Richard Thomson has suggested that such little animals would commonly have been associated with courtesans in that period.[1] In any case, the easy intimacy that these figures demonstrate, sharing a newspaper, sitting on a log, would have appeared to some critics of the day as too casual a subject for art. In the footsteps of Courbet and Manet, Renoir's depiction of a couple in the woods is a provocative image. However, in Renoir's hands the subject becomes light and gay and sheds any apparent conflict – even while retaining an intrinsic challenge to artistic conceptions of the day. This combination of the light-hearted and the revolutionary – both in subject-matter and in technique – is unique to Renoir.

Confidences is the smallest of a subset of three paintings made at the same time featuring figures arranged in a landscape setting. *The Lovers* (fig. 85) and *The Henriot Family* (Barnes Foundation, Merion, Pennsylvania) are both painted in an identical style, except that in the two larger works the features of the figures are more highly developed. In all three there is an incredible freedom of execution. Broad brushstrokes delineate foliage and costume, large sections of

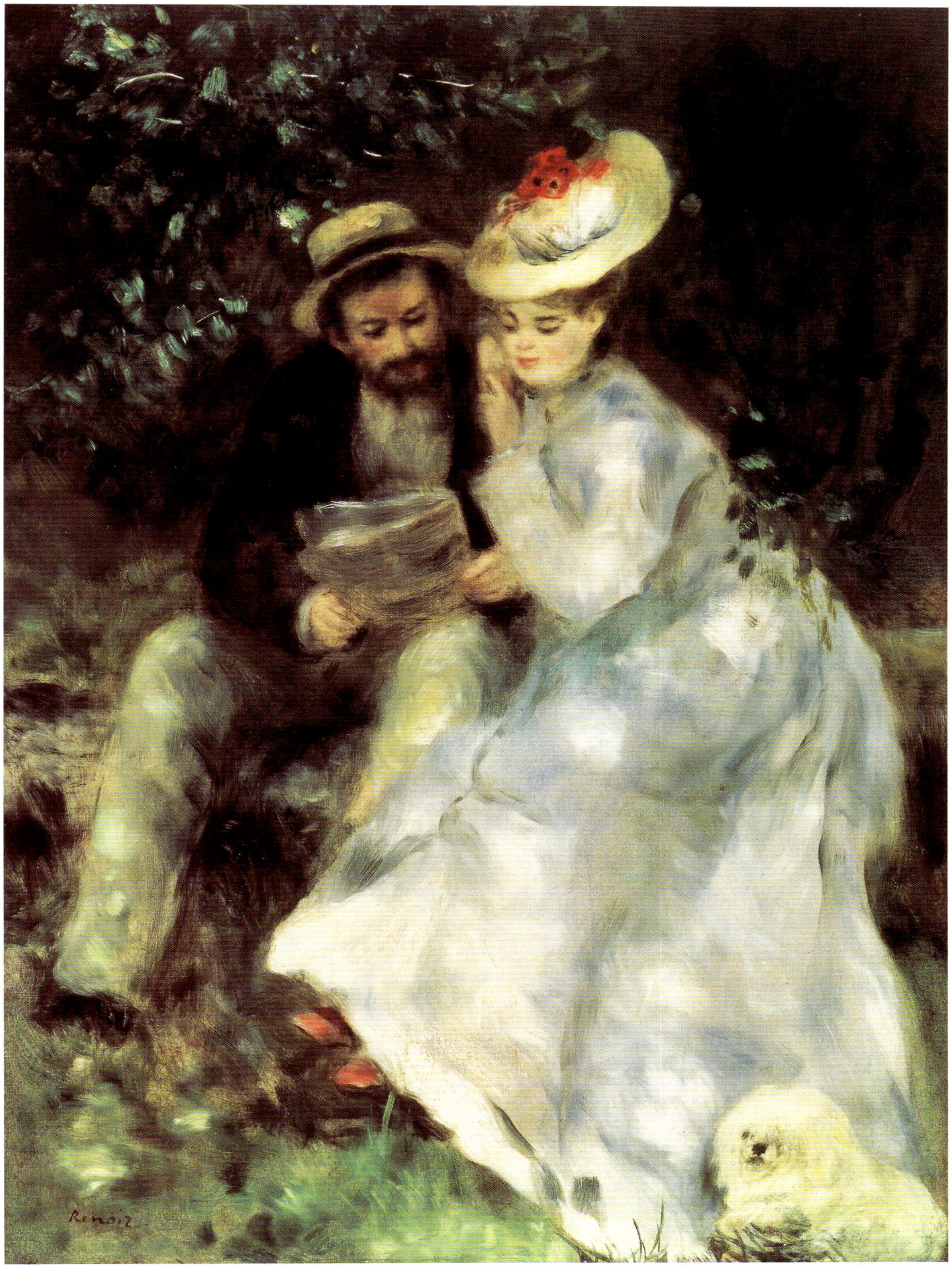

the canvas are left untouched, and the paint is laid on very thickly in some areas, resulting in the juxtaposition of thick impasto and almost bare canvas. While there are elements of all of these characteristics in Renoir's other paintings, in these works the alignment of such characteristics is unique. Further, there is an overlap of accoutrements in all of the paintings: the same white dress seems to appear in each work, and the same white dog appears in *Confidences* and *The Lovers*; even the figures in these two paintings could be the same, but the character of the features in *Confidences* is undefined. This suggests that *Confidences* was intended to function differently from the two larger landscapes. While these two paintings would have been major works demonstrating Renoir's ambition to make grand modern paintings, in the manner of Manet's *Déjeuner sur l'herbe* or Monet's attempt at a similar subject in the late 1860s, *Confidences* is freer and more modest. Probably the painting was made for private viewing, whether for a particular patron or even for one of its models.

The vagueness of the features makes the individuals hard to identify but it also makes the painting more suggestive. Whereas, in *The Lovers*, the narrative read through the features and poses of the figures seems to provide a definite point in a story, *Confidences* does not have such clarity. The woman's appearance is also decidedly more suggestive than in the other two similar paintings, even if the easy companionability of the figures seems to allow the viewer to interpret their gestures of intimacy at will rather than projecting a specific courting narrative on to their actions. The painter's indirectness adds to one's sense of the intimacy of this couple's conversation, and this is part of Renoir's brilliance as a painter.

JZ

Shown in London only

1 Thomson 1982, pp. 323–7.

28 Springtime (in Chatou), about 1875

Also known as *Spring at Chatou*
Oil on canvas
59 × 74 cm; 23¼ × 29⅛ in.
Private collection

At the end of a lush meadow, not far from the river's edge, a lone man is standing with his back to us, knee-deep in the grass. Without a jacket, he wears his straw hat at a jaunty angle and carries flowers over his right arm, their green stems visible against his thigh. The trees that are beginning to bloom cast deep shadows and, while sunlight fills the scene, only the tiniest patch of sky can be made out, in the upper left hand corner of the canvas. We seem to be taking this peaceful view from a vantage point at some distance from the figure, under the unseen tree whose shadows mark the foreground of the composition, which is also rich in wild flowers – rendered in dabs and dashes of red, white and blue. The scene is anchored by the slender trunks of the (fruit?) trees at left and right; between them in the background, just left of the standing man, is a sapling, barely in bloom, added as a finishing touch while the greens and reds of the grass and bushes were still wet.

This infinitely delicate, Corot-like landscape is fully Impressionist in handling: animated, pulpy deposits of white pigment enliven the composition throughout, and the shadows are handled colouristically. As John House has noted, nothing in this view links it with a specific site:[1] the designation of Chatou is a later addition, since the first record of the work in Durand-Ruel's stockbook lists it simply as '*Paysage*'.[2] In this carefully cropped composition, with its floating field of soft grasses and lambent, flickering sunlight, Renoir achieves a determined informality. He rejects illusionistic detail and pares narrative to the minimum (we are not encouraged to wonder for whom the flowers are intended). Yet the description of this patch of meadow attains a level of complexity new in his work.

Dated variously to between 1872 and 1878,[3] *Springtime* has a feathery handling and staccato brushwork that can be compared to that of landscapes such as *Fishing* (private collection), painted in the summer of 1874.[4] Its closest cognates, however, are a group of rustic views probably made in Louveciennes the following spring, and known only from early stock records and black and white photographs. Slightly larger (a size 25 as opposed to a size 20), and more prominently signed at lower left, *Orchard at Louveciennes* appears to portray a different part of the same meadow, dominated by an enormous pear tree, of which the branches bend in the wind. Three figures are just visible in the deep grasses and long shadows – the man at right, wearing the same straw hat and waistcoat as the lone promenader in *Springtime*; a peasant women at left, carrying a bale of hay on her head; and a second on the right, identifiable by her kerchief, collecting fruit at the foot of the tree.

Catalogued as having been painted in 1875,[5] *Orchard at Louveciennes* also relates to the lost *Almond Trees in Flower*, one of the three paintings by Renoir that Durand-Ruel sold to Count Armand Doria (1823–1896) on 18 July 1876,[6] and which was described (but not illustrated) in the catalogue of his sale of May 1899 as also having been painted in Louveciennes in 1875.[7] The second landscape that Durand-Ruel had sold to Doria for the meagre sum of 112.50 francs was simply entitled '*Paysage vert*'.[8] This work did not appear in the 1899 sale, and one wonders if *Paysage vert* and *Springtime* might not be one and the same painting, of which the subject would be an unidentified meadow in Louveciennes.[9] A green landscape indeed, instinct with spring and the promise of country pleasures. CBB

PROVENANCE:
Recorded in Durand-Ruel's stockbook, 25 August 1891; sold to Paul Cassirer, Berlin, 13 June 1910; Galerie Barbazanges, Paris; Percy Moore Turner, London, by 1922; bought by Samuel Courtauld for £5,500 in June 1927; Lady Aberconway; private collection

LITERATURE:
Cooper 1954, p. 110; House and Distel 1985, pp. 63, 202; House 1994, pp. 132–3, 223

1 House 1994, p. 132.
2 Archives Durand-Ruel, stockbook, 25 August 1891, no. 1499, '*Paysage*'. This is the date of an internal reordering of the dealer's records; we do not know when the landscape entered his stock.
3 Cooper (1959, p. 110) followed the catalogue of *Landscape in French Art, 1550–1900*, Royal Academy, London, 1949–50, in assigning the picture to Chatou and dating it to *c.*1878. Interestingly, when first exhibited at the Burlington Fine Arts Club in 1922 (before it entered Courtauld's collection), the picture was entitled *Spring* (*Le Printemps*) and dated 1875. House and Distel (1985, p. 202) dated it to '*c.*1872–1875'; House (1994, p. 132) dates it '*c.*1873'.
4 For the best recent illustration, see Néret 2001, p. 81.
5 *Tableaux modernes. Oeuvres importantes par Boudin, Courbet, Monet, Renoir . . . provenant de la Collection de M. Gustave Cahen*, Paris, 24 May 1929, no. 74.
6 Durand-Ruel, stockbook, 'Tableaux 1876', no. 518, '*Paysage vert*'; no. 519, '*Amandiers en fleurs* (*matin*)'; no. 520, '*Bouquets de Glaieuls*'; see House and Distel 1985, p. 27, note 23.
7 '*De grand matin . . . la brume qui envelope les choses d'une ambience grise. Pourtant sous la clarté du soleil qui s'annonce, les amandiers tendent vers le ciel bleu leurs branches chargées de fleurs. A gauche, deux paysannes en train d'en cueillir*'; Galerie Georges Petit, *Tableaux importants*, Paris, 4–5 May 1899, no. 211. This painting was the smallest of the group, a size 15, measuring 54 × 64 cm; 21¼ × 25⅕ in. Doria also owned *Les Grands Boulevards*, another landscape painted in 1875 (cat. 30).
8 Anne Distel (in House and Distel 1985, p. 27) noted the price of both landscapes as 112.50 francs, the *Still Life with Gladioli* selling somewhat higher for 150 francs.
9 Renoir regularly visited his recently widowed mother, Marguerite Merlet, at this time; she had lost her husband in December 1874, and remained a resident of Louveciennes until her death 22 years later.

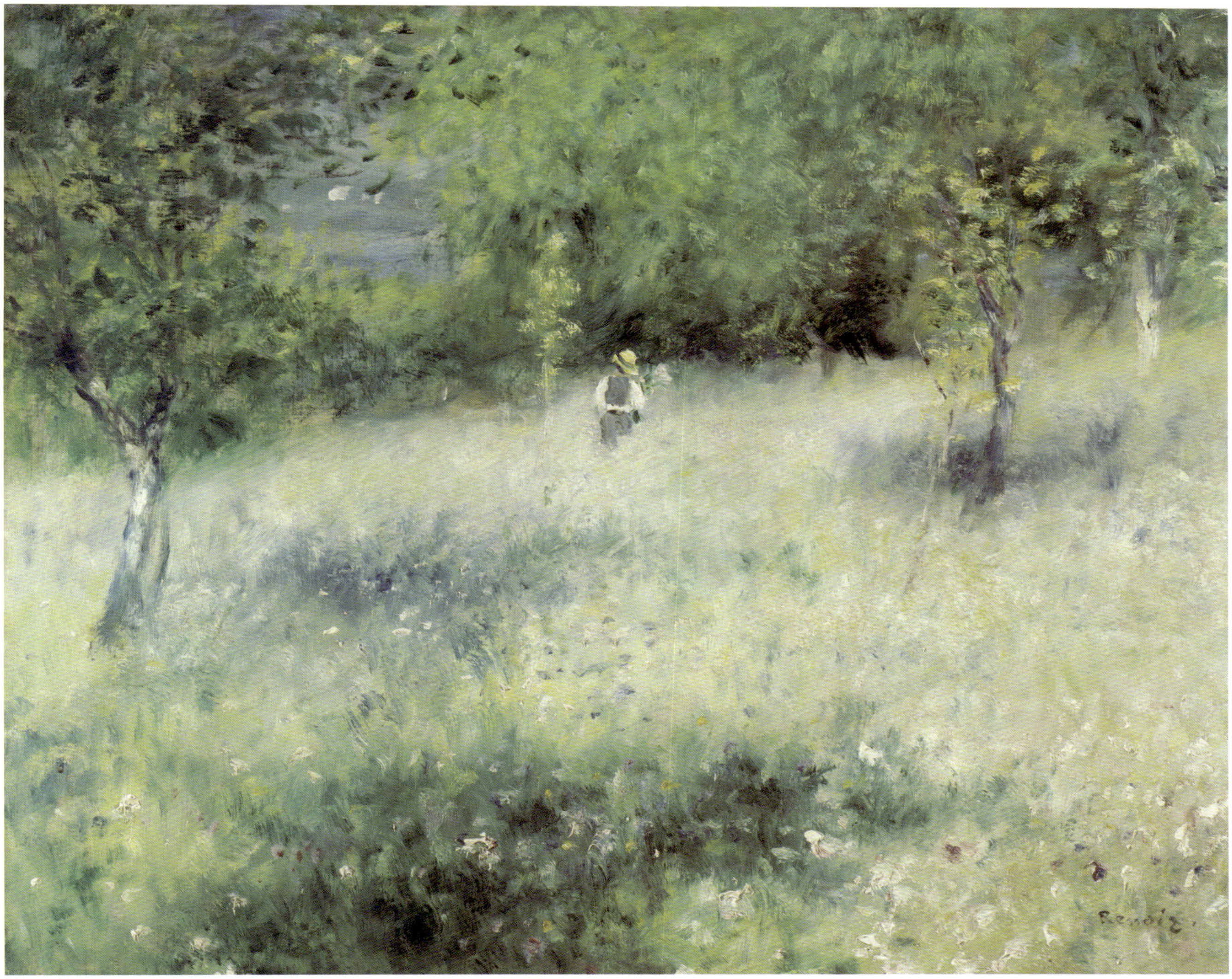

29 Le Square de La Trinité, 1875

Oil on canvas
54 × 65.4 cm; 21¼ × 25¾ in.
Museum of Art, Rhode Island School of Design, Providence. Private Collection (TL134.96)

PROVENANCE:
Sale, Hazard, Paris, December 1919, lot 207; Paul Rosenberg, Paris; Charles S. Carstairs; M. Knoedler & Co., New York; Carroll Carstairs, New York; M. Knoedler & Co., New York; private collection, New England; Sotheby's, New York, 8 November 1995, lot 28; private collection

LITERATURE:
White 1984, p. 202; Fezzi 1985, no. 622.

As a general rule, when he chose to paint Paris Renoir preferred to depict the old *quais* and bridges along the Seine in the heart of the city, areas which, though much enhanced under Baron Haussmann's regime of improvement, nonetheless contained visible vestiges of a more traditional city. His Paris would still have been recognisable to time travellers from the *ancien régime*. Only with a series of cityscape paintings of 1875, including the present work, a second depiction of the Place de la Trinité (fig. 87) and *Les Grands Boulevards* (cat. 30), did the artist specifically depict the newly created streets and squares that had altered Paris almost beyond recognition during the previous quarter century. Even here, however, as Robert Herbert has noted, Renoir tended to mask the regimented severity of the long rows of new buildings, softening their harsh outlines by focusing instead on the trees and flowers that filled the squares and lined the boulevards. Nature gave him the motifs with which to 'cover over the stark regularity of Haussmann's conception. They help expiate the crime of monotony with the aid of the picturesque'.[1] It is perhaps not surprising that Renoir waited until 1875 to take up such motifs. Only then, a decade or so after the new squares, boulevards and buildings had been completed, would the plantings that enhanced such sites have grown large and full enough to begin to obscure the raw novelty of the spaces.

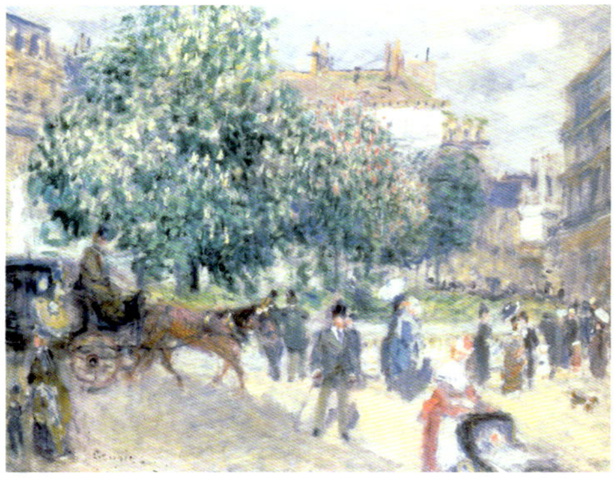

FIG. 86 *Place de la Trinité*, 1875. Oil on canvas, 51.5 × 62.8 cm; 24¾ × 28¼ in. Private collection.

The church of La Trinité had been erected to the designs of the architect Théodore Ballu between 1863 and 1867. An immense pile built on rising ground in a fussily detailed neo-Renaissance style, it stands facing south at the top of the rue de la Chaussée d'Antin, a fashionable street in the 9th arrondissement not far from the Gare St-Lazare. The church's spire makes it one of the landmarks of the neighbourhood. Renoir, in 1877, included the church on a list of new Parisian structures of whose architecture in various banal, historicising styles he did not approve.[2] La Trinité, however, is faced by a charming semi-circular *place* filled with trees to the right and left of the church façade, flowerbeds and three gurgling fountains. Amid the bustle of commercial Paris, it offered an oasis of calm and beauty in the urban fabric, and it was this park-like motif to which Renoir directed his attention. He situated his easel at ground level within the square but sharply to the east of the church. Seen obliquely, its spire is only summarily indicated at right; the modern apartment blocks beyond are thinly painted and largely obscured by trees; the broad boulevards that run into the square from several directions are simply invisible.

An early architecture critic had wittily dismissed the church of La Trinité as *'la petite maitresse des paroisses'* (the little mistress of parish churches), a sly dig at the reputation of the Chaussée d'Antin district, dating from the eighteenth century, as the Paris neighbourhood *par excellence* of expensively kept women.[3] It was, then, a site associated with love (of a kind) and dalliance. With the church all but invisible, Renoir too focuses attention on the square as a scene of

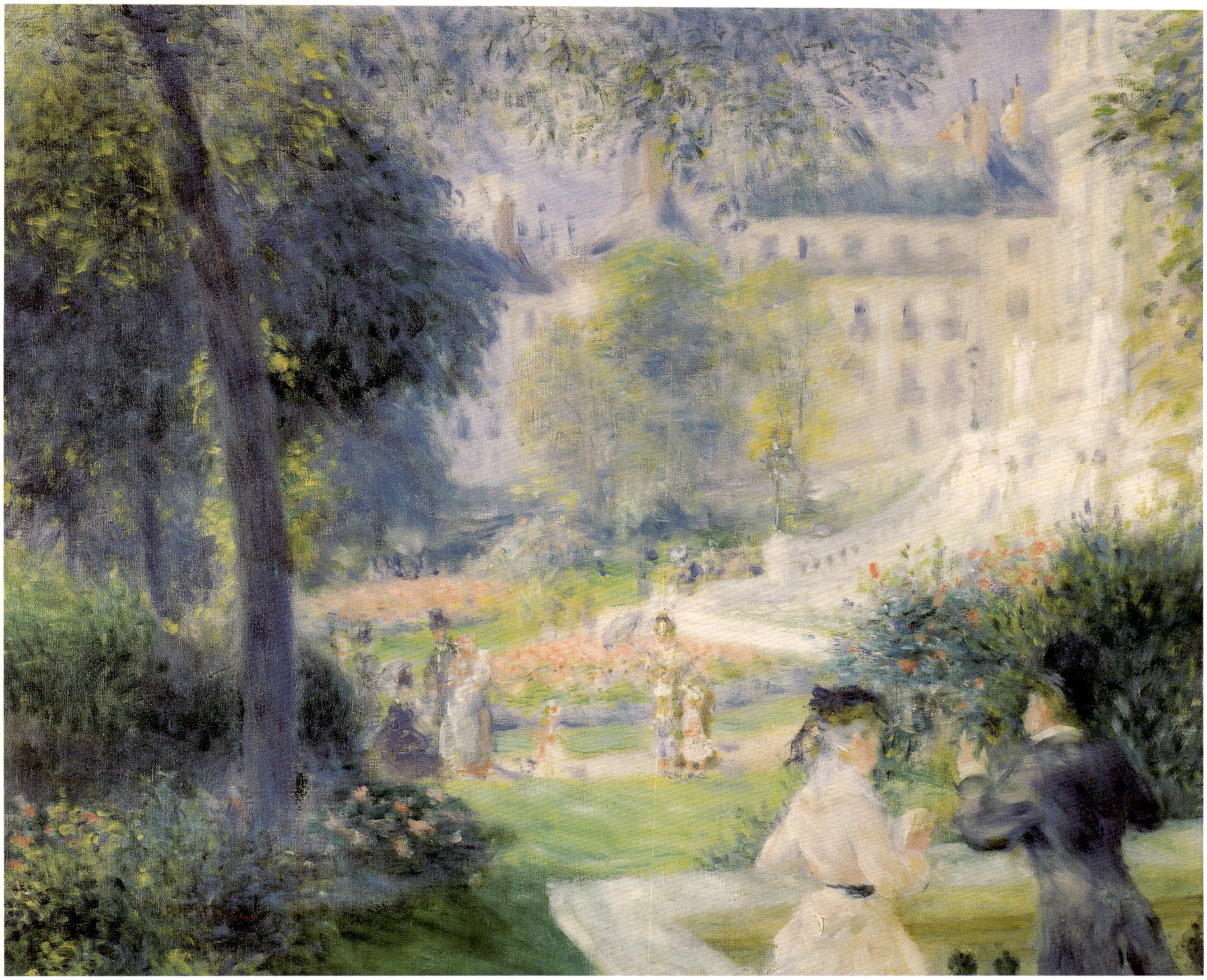

worldly social interaction. Primary attention falls on the fashionable folk strolling in the garden on a sunny day. A lady and gentleman standing in the shade converse at lower right. The man gestures towards the florid spaces beyond, as if to invite his companion to follow him into this idyllic realm. A Watteau-like *fête galante* has been transposed here to the heart of modern Paris. The very freedom of paint handling, with quick touches of colour, and longer, slower brushstrokes of luxuriant paint, along with the artist's evident delight in contrasting pastel and honey tones, emphasise the easy grace of the scene. Renoir here performs a feat of restitution, recuperating a corner of brash new Paris for the sensibilities of an older, more genteel time. Images such as this participate in the revival of interest in the Rococo period and its distinctive art forms that was gaining momentum in France in the 1870s, and of which Renoir would be a prime exponent. CR

1 Herbert 1988, p. 16.
2 Herbert 2000, p. 98.
3 Cited in Louis Hautecoeur, *Histoire de l'architecture classique en France*, IIIb, Paris 1963, p. 273.

30 Les Grands Boulevards, 1875

Oil on canvas
52.1 × 63.5 cm; 20½ × 25 in.
Philadelphia Museum of Art. The Henry P. McIlhenny Collection, in memory of Frances P. McIlhenny 1986 (1986-26-29)

PROVENANCE:
Count Armand Doria, Paris; Doria auction (4 and 5 May 1899), acquired by Durand-Ruel, Paris (stock no. 5197), and Bernheim-Jeune, Paris; Durand-Ruel sold his share to Bernheim-Jeune, 14 April 1900; Oscar Schmitz, Dresden; private collection, New York; Henry P. McIlhenny, Philadelphia

LITERATURE:
Fechter 1910, pp. 21, 24; Meier-Graefe 1911, pp. 64, 79; Vollard 1918, I, p. 88, no. 352; Meier-Graefe 1929, pp. 60, 91; Waldmann 1930, II, pp. 316, 320; Wildenstein 1936, pp. 112–13, 142; Drucker 1944, pp. 23, 184; Rewald 1946, p. 310; Fox 1953, no. 25; Rouart 1985, p. 29; Novotny 1960, p. 171; Feist 1961, no. 19; Fezzi 1972, p. 97, no. 105; Atlanta 1984, pp. 62–3; Shimada 1985, III; Wadley 1987, pp. 41, 121; Herbert 1988, p. 16; Arcangeli 1989, pp. 50, 155; Stevenson 1992, illus.; Distel 1994, fig. 9; Adriani 1996, pp. 141–3; Néret 2001, pp. 82–3

The transformation of Paris during the Second Empire under the direction of Baron Haussmann, Napoléon III's Prefect of Paris, was a complex historical event that generated a range of responses from contemporary journalists, authors, photographers and artists (see the essay by Christopher Riopelle in this catalogue). The present painting is Renoir's best-known view of one of the areas affected, that near the Gare St-Lazare and the Opéra, known as the Grands Boulevards as a result of the introduction of wide, tree-lined streets that encouraged strolling and provided a space for the modern experiences of traffic, leisure and consumption.

In Renoir's own lifetime, this painting was given two different titles suggesting two distinct locations, *Le Boulevard des Italiens* and *Place de la Trinité à Paris.*[1] Whichever is more correct, the aspect taken can reasonably be called an archetypical view of a grand boulevard. It is springtime and the city is filled with activity. Carriages proceed in line down the avenue, women and children stroll, men converse, a figure sits in the shade reading. The buildings along the street form a regulated row and the newly planted trees are turning from blossom to leaf. This view of the city would have appeared thoroughly modern to viewers of Renoir's era because it focused on the most fashionable and recently constructed part of Paris. Renoir's image makes the new Paris seem vivid and engaging, a location where the panorama of city life is available to all passers-by.

If one compares Renoir's *Grand Boulevards* to another roughly contemporary painting of this section of Paris by Jean Béraud (fig. 88),[2] the brilliance of Renoir's representation is evident. Béraud's naturalistic street scene depicts everyday life on the busy boulevard with numerous carriages and fashionably dressed Parisians. The time is autumn and the weather is rainy; the numerous details such as the street sweeper at left and pedestrians dodging puddles in the street provide a sense of particularity, which Renoir, for his part, is careful to avoid. Renoir also depicts figure types, but in such a way as to produce a sense of fleeting impressions rather than a moment frozen in time. *Les Grands Boulevards* is full of the pigment daubs and bright colours characteristic of Impressionist painting. Thus the sense of modern life in the city is transmitted through cues that enable the viewer to make a connection between the world passing by and the artist's practice of making a painting. This is the magic of Renoir's Paris. The world of the painting is truly historical – the modern city emerging – even though it is the subjective and poetic impression of the artist that is reflected on the surface of the canvas. JZ

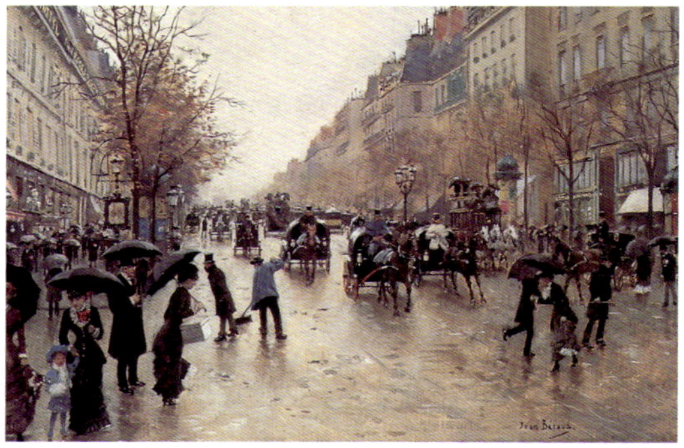

FIG. 87 Jean Béraud (1849–1935), *Les Boulevards*, 1880. Oil on canvas, 24 × 35.5 cm; 9½ × 13 in. Musée Carnavalet, Histoire de Paris (P1735).

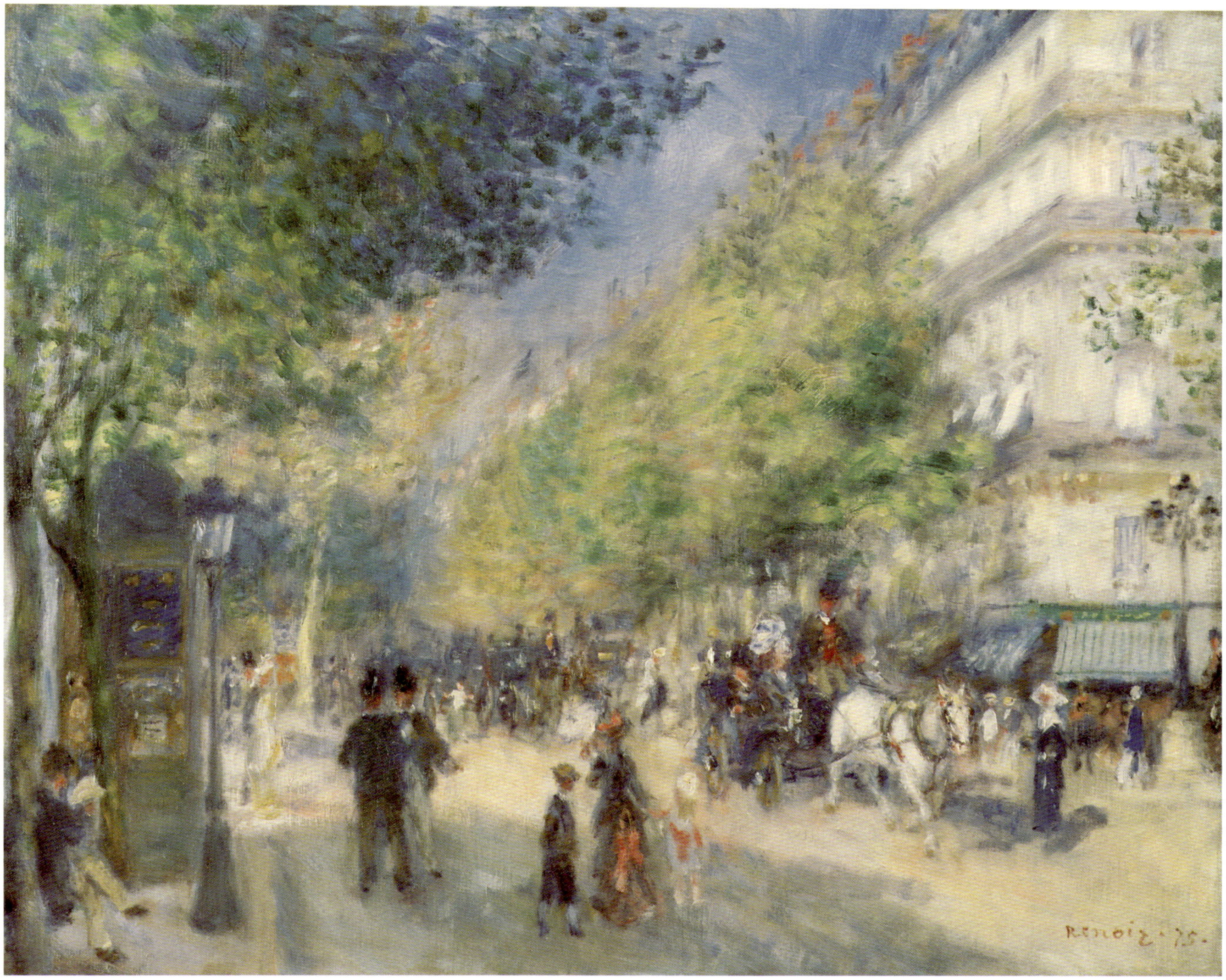

1 In *L'Art et la couleur. Les Maîtres contemporains*, no. 1, Paris 1905, n.p., Camille Mauclair titles the painting *Le Boulevard des Italiens* but does not justify or elaborate this description. In his 1918 catalogue of Renoir's works, Vollard transcribed the location from Renoir himself as *Place de la Trinité* and this has become a traditional title, but there is no Place de la Trinité in Paris, only the Square de la Trinité (see preceding entry), and this painting is not a view of a square in any case.

2 Herbert (1988, p. 17) compares Béraud's painting to Impressionist city scenes.

31 La Place St-Georges, 1875

Oil on canvas
65 × 54 cm; 25⅝ × 21¼ in.
Private collection

PROVENANCE:
Bought from the artist by Gustave Caillebotte, thence by descent in the family

LITERATURE:
Rivière 1877, reprinted in Venturi 1939, II, p. 311; Baudot 1949, pp. 20, 23; Wildenstein 1950, no. 14; Distel 1994, pp. 64–5

Renoir moved to the rue St-Georges in September 1873, taking a cheap room on a top floor. This part of town, nestled among the grands boulevards near the Gare St-Lazare, offered a number of open public squares for people-watching and Renoir took advantage of this opportunity to paint several urban landscapes in the years between 1874 and 1876. *La Place St-Georges* features a view of one such square, from above, in the full bloom of spring, with a flowering chestnut tree taking up almost half of the composition. Compared to *Les Grands Boulevards* (cat. 30), painted the same year, this view is more static and avoids a perspective view of the boulevard.

Renoir's friend, the writer Georges Rivière, described this picture in his review of the Impressionist exhibition of 1877, where the painting was featured alongside two of Renoir's best-loved masterpieces, *The Swing* and *The Ball at Moulin de la Galette* (both Musée d'Orsay, Paris). Rivière wrote: 'It's a morning effect, with the light of May scorching the flowering chestnuts. One can breath the fresh scents of the large green trees overflowing the gardens in this work.'[1] Rivière captures an essential aspect of Renoir's painting in this description – the ability to produce sensory effects through visual images. A fresh and vibrant picture by Renoir pleases not only the eye; his paintings seem to suggest pleasures available to the other senses as well. In this image of modern city life, the viewer can sense the warmth of the sun as the passers-by mill about in leisurely fashion, some standing to chat and others strolling along the boulevard. The shadow of the chestnut in the foreground only serves to enhance the brightness of the rest of the painting and the foliage itself appears to explode in colours. One can almost smell the heady odours that result when the heat of the sun touches those bright blossoms.

This painting was one of several works shown by Renoir at the third Impressionist exhibition of 1877, four of which were bought by the painter Gustave Caillebotte. Caillebotte played a central role in the organisation of the exhibition and clearly worked to make it a historic event.[2] Caillebotte loaned one painting that he already owned, *The Swing*, and he bought at least three more paintings shown by Renoir in that exhibition, *The Ball at the Moulin de la Galette*, *The Seine at Champrosay* (cat. 36) and *La Place St-Georges*. At his death in 1894, Caillebotte gave his collection of Impressionist paintings to the French nation for the Musée du Luxembourg, then the museum of contemporary art, with the intention of preserving the place of Impressionism in the history of the arts of France. Not all of Caillebotte's collection was accepted,[3] and, while many of the Impressionist paintings in the Musée d'Orsay most treasured today came from the Caillebotte bequest, some works, including the *La Place St-Georges*, remained in private hands. Owing to political machinations over a century ago, the public has not seen this wonderful city landscape for more than 50 years. JZ

1 Rivière (1877) 1939, II, p. 311.
2 See Brettell's article in Moffett, *The 'First' Exhibition of Impressionist Painters*, New York 1986, pp. 189–202.
3 See Distel 1994, pp. 21–30.

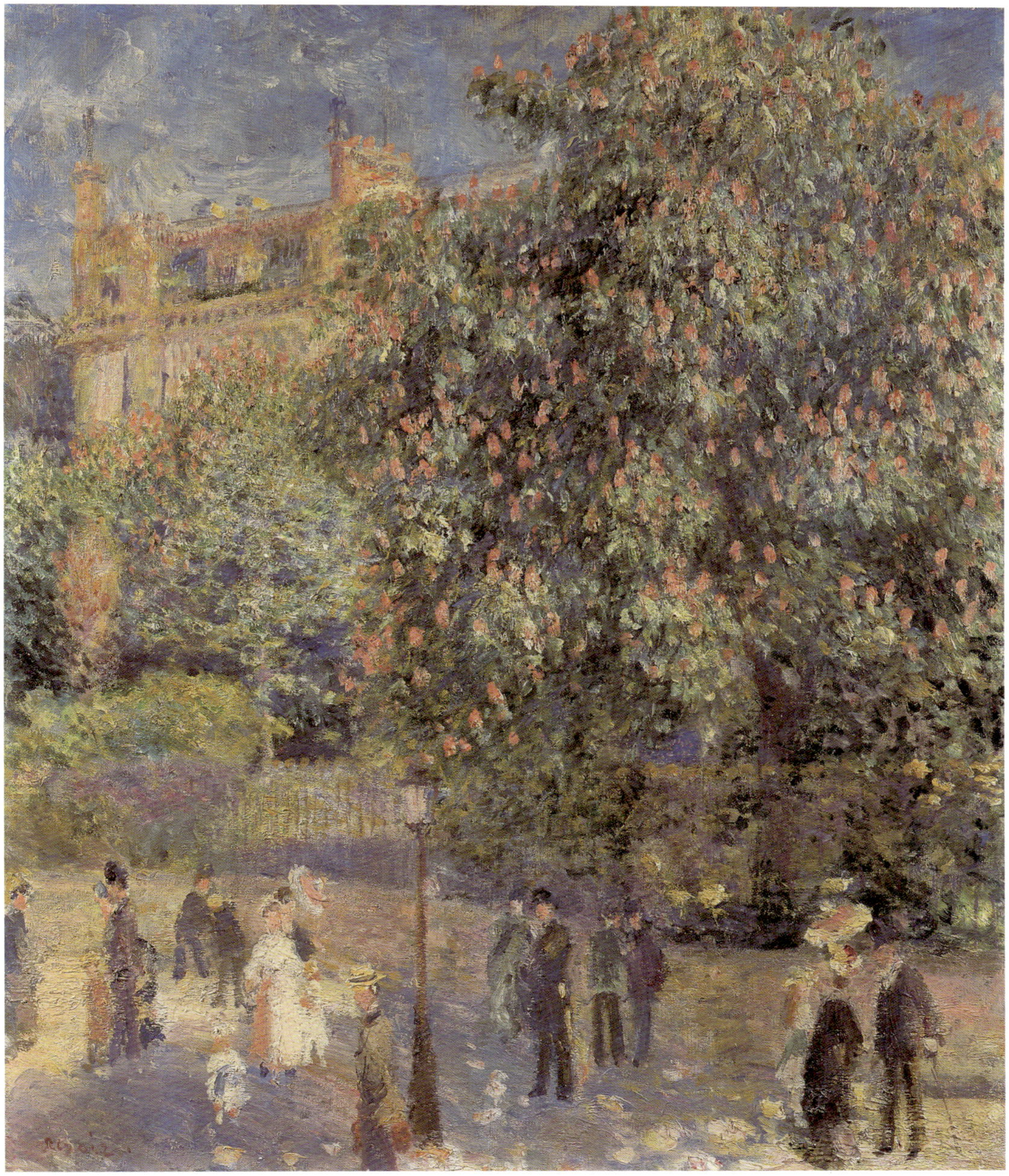

32 The Bridge at Chatou, about 1875

Oil on canvas
51 × 65.2 cm; 20⅛ × 25¾ in.
Sterling and Francine Clark Art Institute, Williamstown, Massachusetts (1955.591)

PROVENANCE:
Ernest Hoschedé, presumably purchased from the artist; Hoschedé sale, Hôtel Drouot, Paris, 6 June 1878, lot 74, bought by Georges de Bellio; Donop de Monchy; Hoentschel, Paris; Knoedler, Paris; sold to Robert Sterling Clark, 13 October 1925

LITERATURE:
Meier-Graefe 1912, p. 54 n.; Bodelsen 1968, pp. 339–40; Kern 1996, pp. 55–8, 72, 74

It seems to have been in 1875 that Renoir began to frequent the Restaurant Fournaise, on an island in the Seine alongside the village of Chatou, around nine miles west of Paris. His portraits of the proprietor Alphonse Fournaise (Sterling and Francine Clark Art Institute, Williamstown) and his daughter Alphonsine (Museu de Arte, São Paulo Assis Chateaubriand) are both dated 1875, and it seems very likely that *The Bridge at Chatou* was painted in the same summer. The canvas represents a view of the village from alongside the Restaurant Fournaise, with the road bridge that then ran across the river just to the north of the restaurant (the present bridge is sited further to the south). The terrace of Fournaise's restaurant was to provide the site for Renoir's very well-known *Luncheon of the Boating Party* of 1880–1 (fig. 89).

Writing in 1886, Louis Barron described the river crossing at the Chatou bridge as the transition between Paris's 'rough suburbs' and the 'civilised countryside' – between the realms of work and recreation, between factories and 'coquettish villas';[1] indeed, La Grenouillère, one of the most celebrated recreational sites of the surroundings of Paris, painted by both Renoir and Monet (see cats. 5, 6), was only a short distance downstream from Chatou. However, in *The Bridge at Chatou* Renoir presents a thoroughly urbanised view of the place, closing off the entire background of the canvas with rows of humdrum buildings, with no trace of the 'artificial paradise' that Barron found there. This is one of the landscapes in Renoir's oeuvre where the natural world plays the smallest part.

The Bridge at Chatou is very comparable to the views of the Argenteuil road bridge painted by Monet the previous year (see fig. 88); the resemblance is so close that in this instance Renoir was presumably deliberately following Monet's example. The bridge frames the composition on the right and leads the eye into the pictorial space, while the area of grass at bottom left gives the viewer a visual foothold. The brushwork throughout is lively and variegated, suggesting the diverse textures of the scene. However, Renoir paid less close attention than Monet to the detailed play of reflections in the

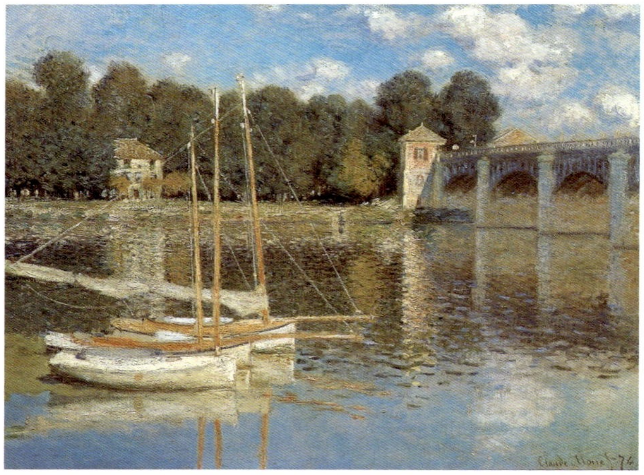

FIG. 88 Claude-Oscar Monet (1840–1926), *The Bridge at Argenteuil*, 1874. Oil on canvas, 60 × 80 cm; 23⅝ × 31½ in. Musée d'Orsay, Paris (RF 1937–41).

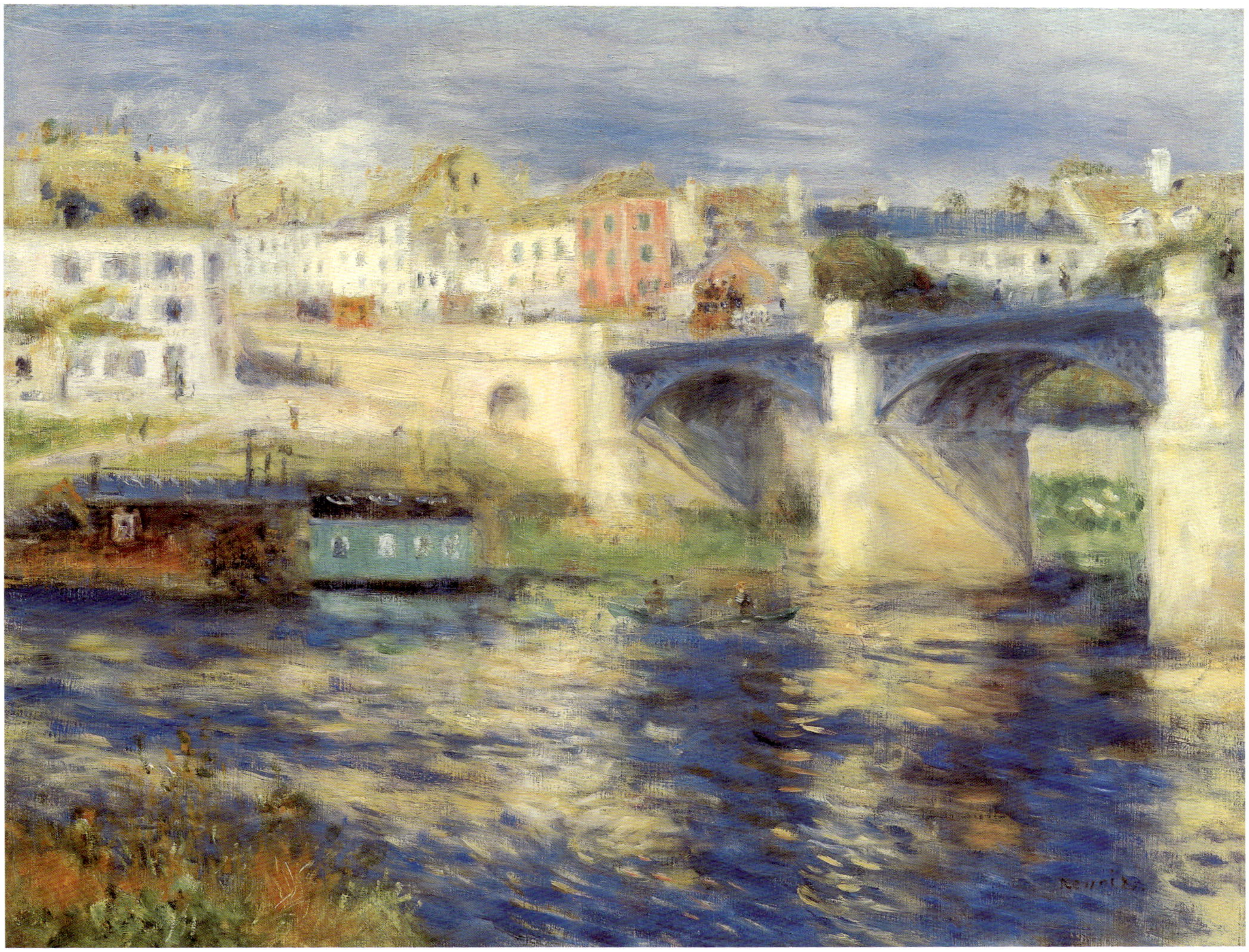

water; their forms in this picture do not closely match the positions of the structures above them, but seem, rather, to be arranged in such a way as to maximise the contrast between them and the intense blue of the open water. This contrast between blue and yellow is reiterated in the upper half of the canvas, with the single orange-red building at the far end of the bridge acting as a sort of pivot against which the remainder of the colour composition is played off.

The painting was bought, presumably directly from Renoir, by Ernest Hoschedé, proprietor of a company that made fabrics for women's clothing; at the auction sale following his bankruptcy in 1878, it was bought by another of the pioneer Impressionist collectors, Georges de Bellio, for the derisory sum of 42 francs.[2] JH

1 See L. Barron *Les Environs de Paris*, Paris 1886, pp. 493–4: '*la banlieue fruste*', '*la campagne civilisée*'.
2 See Bodelsen 1968, pp. 339–40.

33 The Skiff (La Yole), 1875

Oil on canvas
71 × 92 cm; 36¼ × 28 in.
The National Gallery, London (NG 6478)

PROVENANCE:
Victor Chocquet, Paris; Chocquet sale, Galerie Georges Petit, Paris, 1, 3 and 4 July 1899, lot 93; Galerie Bernheim-Jeune, Paris; Galerie Durand-Ruel, Paris; Reid and Lefèvre Gallery, London; Samuel Courtauld, London, bought 1929; Lady Aberconway; private collection; The National Gallery, London, 1982

LITERATURE:
Cooper 1954, no. 53; Pach 1973, pp. 93–4; Gaunt and Adler 1982, pl. 33; House and Distel 1985; no. 47; Roy 1985, pp. 15–16; Schneider 1985, p. 52; Herbert 1988, pp. 252, 313; Bomford 1990, pp. 172–5; House 1994, no. 41; Rathbone 1996, pp. 32, 73

The first owner of this signed but undated painting, Victor Chocquet, was one of Renoir's most enthusiastic early patrons. It is not known when he acquired the work and it was exhibited publicly for the first time only in 1899, at the posthumous sale of Chocquet's collection, at which it was titled *La Seine at Asnières.*[1] As John House remarked several years ago, the site does not seem to correspond to that western suburb of Paris, industrialised and relatively close to the centre of the city. He suggested that it was more likely to be Chatou, several miles further west and somewhat more countrified.[2] Noting that Renoir had painted in the Chatou region in the summer of 1880, he tentatively dated the work to that year, a slightly later date than that proposed by Douglas Cooper several years earlier: he had suggested it was from about 1879.[3] Today the picture is routinely dated 1879–80.[4] The present catalogue takes up a suggestion first made by Eliza Rathbone in 1996, that the site is indeed Chatou but that the painting was executed considerably earlier, in 1875. Rathbone also related the painting to *Luncheon at La Fournaise* (cat. 34), another work sometimes dated to around the end of the decade, and declared that both 'employ the soft feathery brushstroke and blurring of contours typical of Renoir's work of [1875]'.[5] Colin B. Bailey, in his essay in this catalogue, consolidates the argument by showing that *Luncheon at La Fournaise* must indeed date from 1875, as a reviewer noted on another occasion that it had been included in the second Impressionist exhibition the following year. Bailey also relates both paintings to *The Luncheon* (Barnes Foundation, Merion, Pennsylvania; fig. 39) and *The Bridge at Chatou* (cat. 32), thus constructing a fuller and far richer picture of Renoir's achievement in landscape and figure-in-landscape painting in the highly productive summer of 1875.

The Skiff is a beguiling image of leisurely sociability as two young women enjoy a sunny afternoon out on the water in a bright red-orange rowing boat. Part of the pleasure of the image resides in the strong contrasts of complementary colours, of red-orange and cobalt blue, part also in the diversity and energy of the brushstrokes Renoir employs in rendering such passages as the water, full of glittering accents, and the complex play of reflections cast on the water by the boat and its occupants. Particularly energetic is the depiction of green reeds in the foreground, and that colour note is picked up in the landscape beyond. Indeed, colours introduced in the foreground are consistently re-deployed here and there elsewhere on the canvas, thus almost imperceptibly weaving the image together. For example, the red-orange of the boat and white of the rower's dress reappear in the sailing boat at upper left and in the villa and wall further back. Among the many subtle colour accents is a wave-like, razor-thin line of brilliant white along the side of the boat, an accent the eye hardly registers at first but which adds that further bit of animation to the scene. Full of scintillating detail as it is, the painting is held in pictorial control by the strict architectonic structure that Renoir has imposed on the composition. As House has noted,[6] it is built up of a series of insistent horizontal forms including the boat, the shoreline and the white wall that lines it, and a railroad bridge at upper right. There, a train from Paris approaches. That bridge traverses the Seine, of course, but is seen here at such an oblique angle that it is made to function within the general horizontal patterning of the scene. As carefully layered as it is, the work is also open-ended, with nothing at the right or left side of the

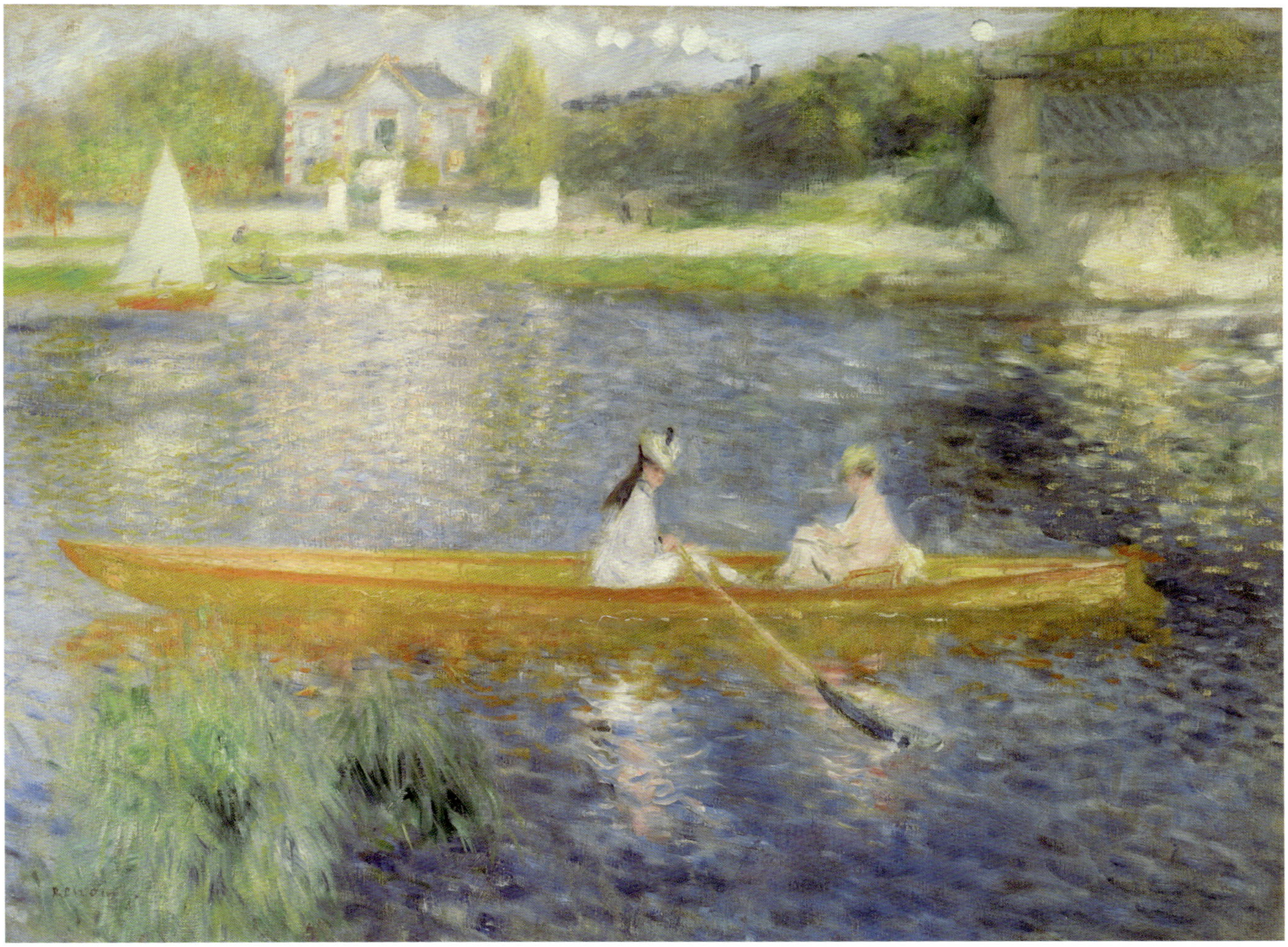

composition to bring our gaze to an end – like the skiff itself, our eye is free to continue drifting up or down the Seine – and with no traditional *repoussoir* elements to lead the eye deeper into the picture. Nonetheless, daringly, it is entirely convincing as a rendering of space. CR

1 *La Seine à Asnières*, Galerie Georges Petit (sale cat.) *Tableaux modernes, succession de Madame Chocquet*, 1, 3, 4 July 1899, no. 93.
2 House 1994, p. 138, no. 41.
3 Cooper 1954, p. 110, no. 54. The painting was dated 1880 when included in the 'Exhibition of French Art' at the Royal Academy of Arts, London, in 1932, but no source or reason was given for doing so.
4 The National Gallery, London, has used this date until only recently, as in Bomford 1990, p. 172.
5 Rathbone 1996, p. 32 and plate 41.
6 House 1994, p. 138, no. 41.

34 Luncheon at La Fournaise, 1875

Also known as *The Rowers' Lunch*
Oil on canvas
55 × 66 cm; 21½ × 25½ in.
Art Institute of Chicago, Illinois. Potter Palmer Collection (1922.437)

PROVENANCE:
Legrand; bought by Theo van Gogh 21 November 1887; bought Guyotin, 22 November 1887; bought Durand-Ruel, 21 March 1892; bought Potter Palmer, 9 April 1892

LITERATURE:
Meier-Graefe 1929, p. 124, no. 102; Maxon 1970, pp. 86, 285; Daulte 1971, no. 305; Fezzi 1972, pp. 108–9, no. 452; Art Institute of Chicago 1973, p. 24; Rewald 1973, pp. 13–14; Pach 1973, p. 115; House and Distel 1985, pp. 94, 216–17; Berson 1996, I, pp. 102–3, II, pp. 44–5; Herbert 1988, pp. 246–7 and frontispiece; Rathbone 1996, no. 40; Druick 1997, pp. 27, 30; Stolwijk 1999, no. 125

This painting is something of a hybrid between the landscape style Renoir developed after the first Impressionist exhibition in 1874 and the effortless, even suave, style he used for figure painting. It was first shown in the second Impressionist exhibition, in 1876, under the title *Déjeuner chez Fournaise*, here translated as *Luncheon at La Fournaise*.[1] The Restaurant Fournaise, frequented by Renoir (see cats. 32, 49) and eventually immortalised in the larger canvas *Luncheon of the Boating Party* (fig. 89), was a typical site of 'modern leisure', so often discussed by historians of Impressionism. Chatou was a popular spot for rowers and several of Renoir's landscapes between 1875 and 1881 feature them practising or relaxing with friends. Many writers have commented how Renoir's love of depicting pastimes enjoyed by robust youths is evident throughout his oeuvre, including *The Ball at Moulin de la Galette* (Musée d'Orsay, Paris) painted the following year, and *Luncheon of the Boating Party* painted some five years later, in which Renoir determinedly reprised this scene, but with greater complexity and monumentality.

Looking at the figure group that occupies the foreground of this composition, it is easy to see the similarities between these two paintings, but *Luncheon at La Fournaise* is a smaller, more freely painted picture: the figures sit in the foreground, framed by the interlacing threads of a trellis. The convivial atmosphere is evident in the dress and the composure of the three figures, and they are surrounded by a bounty of bright natural light. Renoir's brushwork is light and airy, suited to the relaxed atmosphere of the scene. The man in shirt sleeves at right, who smokes a cigarette while lounging in his chair is rendered in resplendent blue tones with notes of red highlighting his features; however, the woman with her back to the viewer is something of a unusual pictorial device in Renoir's compositions – an observer to this scene, like the viewer, but she cannot herself be engaged by the viewer. The figure on the left is lightly painted in yellow tones but the horizontal strokes of pigment beneath suggest that the artist added this figure after the other two.

In this image, landscape is less a site of natural beauty or visual interest than a modern Eden, where real men and women come to relax on their day off, leaving the chaos of Paris behind them. In the background are a skiff and two canoes, steered by figures in rowers' uniforms, the same as those that the figures in the foreground wear (the man's blue waistband and the woman's blue dress are typical team outfits for the respective sexes). The growing importance of exercise and leisure activities in the second half of the nineteenth century is shown as a topic worthy of a painter, though the activity in the background is juxtaposed to the relaxed attitude of the foreground figures. The trellis allows the light and the beauty of nature to enter and we gaze through the archway at the activity of the world behind. JZ

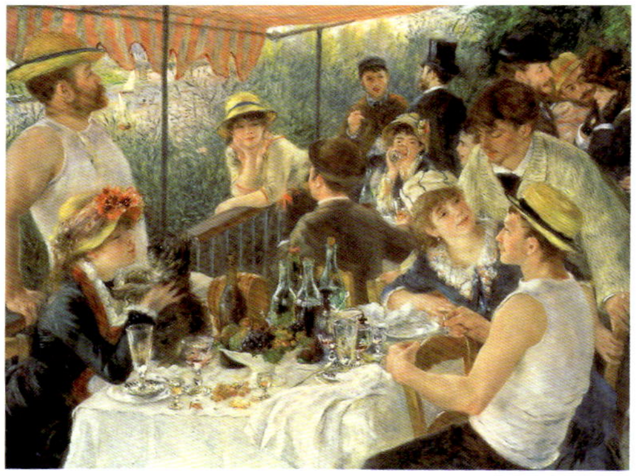

FIG. 89 *Luncheon of the Boating Party*, 1880–1. Oil on canvas, 129.5 × 172.7 cm; 51 × 68 in. The Phillips Collection, Washington, DC (1637).

1 Moffett 1986, p. 164.

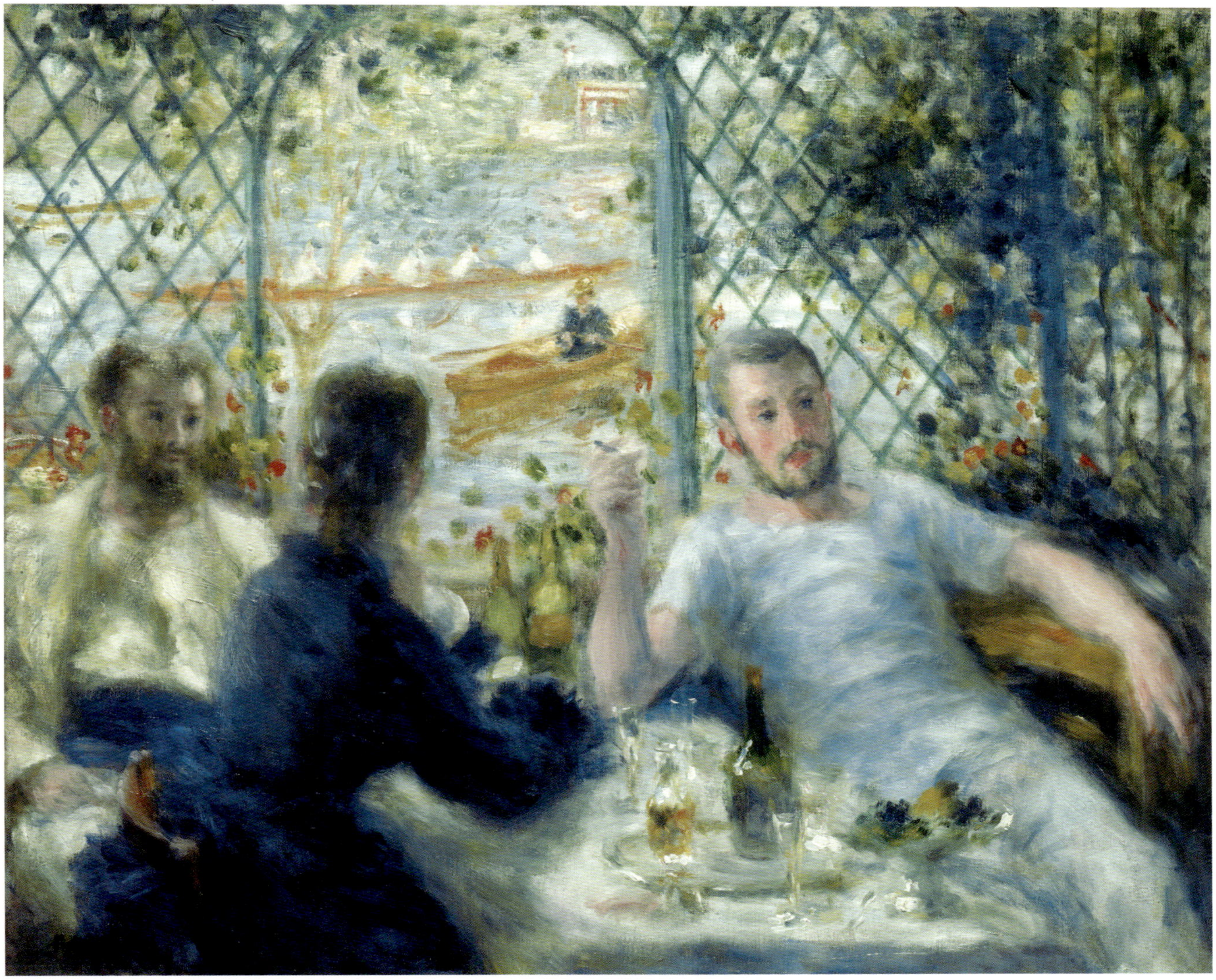

35 Snowy Landscape, about 1875

Oil on canvas
51 × 66 cm; 20½ × 26 in.
Musée national de l'Orangerie, Paris (RF 1960-21)

PROVENANCE:
Ambroise Vollard ?; Paul Guillaume; Mme J. Walter; gift to the Musée de l'Orangerie 1960

LITERATURE:
Vollard 1918; Galerie Charpentier 1943; Wildenstein 1950, no. 363; Drucker 1955; Hoog 1984; House and Distel 1985, p. 207

Snowy Landscape is a tour de force, a painting of great visual complexity demonstrating Renoir's exquisite skills as a landscapist and his unique contribution to Impressionist technique. It is one of the few winter landscapes Renoir painted (see also cat. 4), executed during the particularly snowy winter of 1874–5.

Renoir and Monet are generally said to have perfected the Impressionist method of painting while working side by side, first at the bathing resort La Grenouillière in 1869 (cats. 5, 6), and later at Argenteuil in 1873 (cats. 20, 21). *Snowy Landscape* might be another such landscape painted side by side with Monet; its viewpoint is very similar – among the quite large number of snow scenes painted by Monet that winter – to that of Monet's *Frost* (fig. 90). Although it has recently been claimed that *Frost* was painted in late January or February 1875 and features a view of the boulevard St-Denis in Argenteuil,[1] Paul Tucker has noted that many of Monet's landscapes painted during that winter were made close to his new home – probably just behind it[2] – which seems more likely to be the case for *Frost*, too. Renoir had been a regular visitor to Monet's home during the summer of 1874, and it is possible that he joined Monet again on one of his many painting campaigns the following winter.

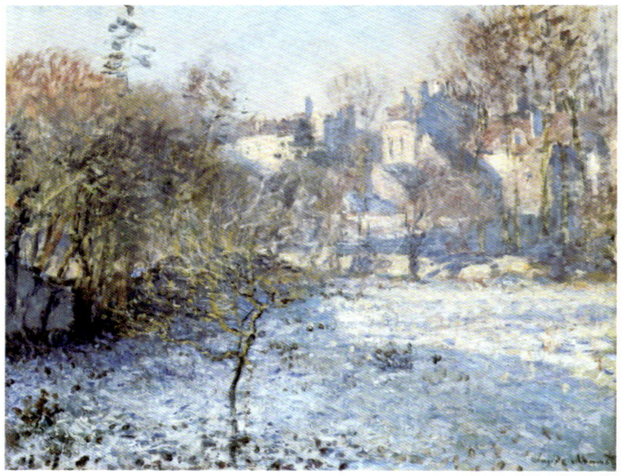

FIG. 90 Claude-Oscar Monet (1840–1926), *Frost*, 1875. Oil on canvas, 50 × 61 cm; 19⅝ × 24 in. Private collection.

While there is no documentary evidence to link the two pictures, when one compares *Snowy Landscape* to *Frost*, the similarities are immediately apparent. On the left, a stand of bare trees blocks the sunlight and casts a diagonal shadow across the composition. A small tree in the centre of the field catches the viewer's eye and, in the background, the buildings of Argenteuil are visible, bathed in winter sunlight. Capturing the light passing through bare branches is a major preoccupation of Renoir's picture and determines the overall texture of the canvas. The ground and sky are built up with many layers of strokes, creating a kaleidoscopic effect as contrasting and complementary hues are laid over one another, demonstrating that snow reflects all of the colours surrounding it and should never be depicted as white – an idea with which Renoir is usually credited.[3]

More important is the manner of execution. Renoir clearly came back to his painting and worked it up in a way Monet did not. In *Snowy Landscape* the forms converge into a unified effect, although it might be more accurate to speak of rhythms rather than forms. In Monet's *Frost*, the strokes provide a lively dynamic that animates the image, but in *Snowy Landscape* the landscape elements – though all present, like points of reference – blend into a mass of colours. Renoir's painting is not merely more detailed and richer in palette but is also more an interpretation, transposing his Impressionist taches into a vision of the world. JZ

Shown in Ottawa and Philadelphia only

1 Christie's, New York, 4 May 2005, p. 59.
2 Tucker 1982, p. 48.
3 Rewald 1961, pp. 210, 236, n. 28.

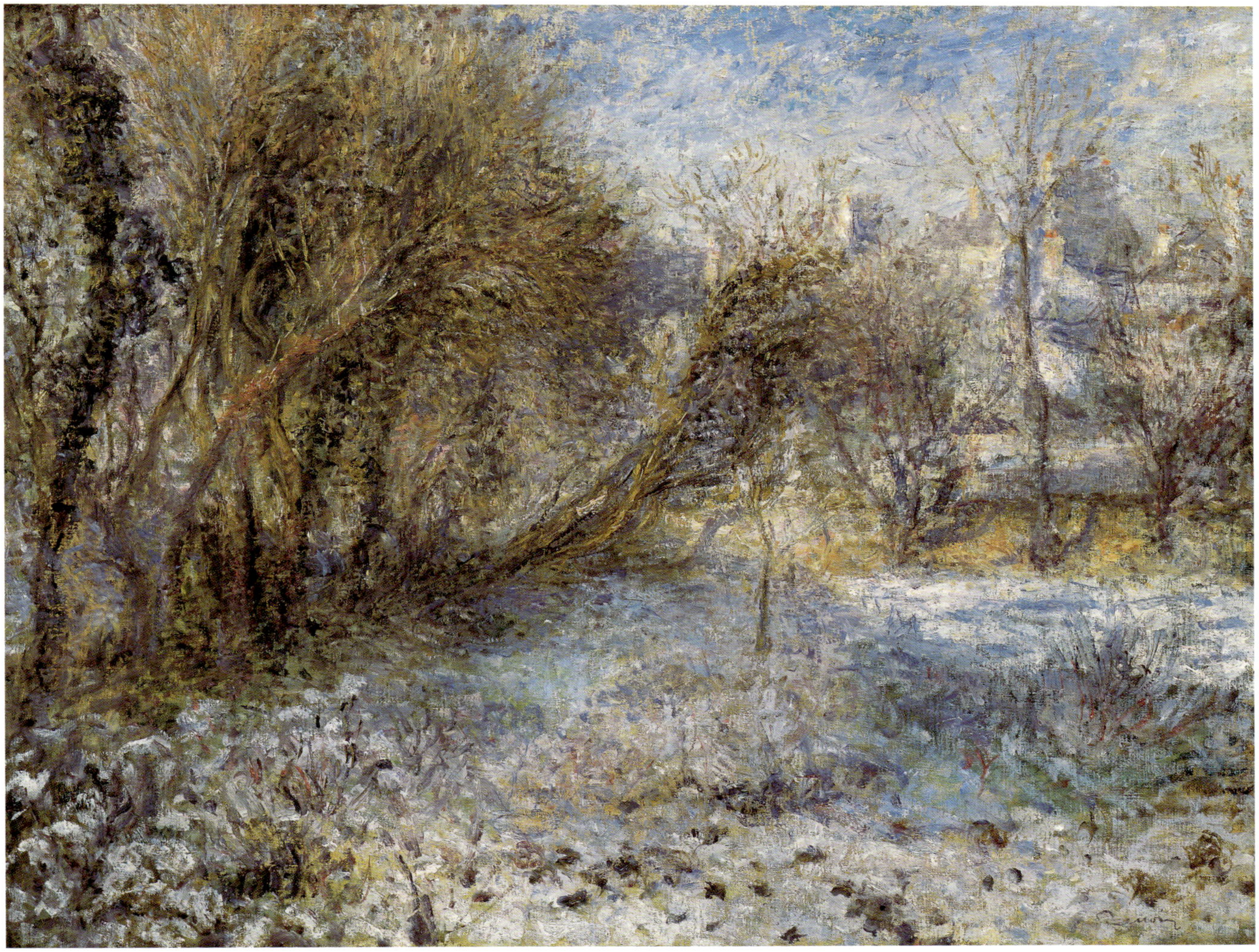

36 The Seine at Champrosay, 1876

Oil on canvas
55 × 66 cm; 21⅝ × 26 in.
Musée d'Orsay, Paris. Caillebotte Bequest 1894 (RF 2737)

PROVENANCE:
Purchased by Gustave Caillebotte (1848–1894) from the artist in 1876–7; Caillebotte bequest to the Musée du Luxembourg, 1894

LITERATURE:
Fezzi 1972, p. 100, no. 256; Adhémar and Dayez-Distel 1979, pp. 96, 168; White 1984, pp. 64, 73, 76–7; Compin and Roquebert 1986, IV, p. 174; Moffett 1986, p. 238; Distel 1994, pp. 63–9

This painting was one of five landscapes that Renoir submitted to the third Impressionist exhibition in 1877 (see also cat. 31). Renoir must have perceived the importance of landscape for his friends who had been labelled 'impressionists' and therefore, despite his growing reputation as a portraitist and figure painter, elected to exhibit a group of outdoor scenes. Of these, one was a city scene (cat. 31), two were gardens (see cat. 37, 38), and the other two were 'pure landscapes', to use a term employed by Camille Pissarro (see p. 51). One, the painting named *Sunset* ('*Coucher de Soleil*') cannot be positively identified now, but the other, *The Seine at Champrosay*, demonstrates that Renoir, no less than Monet, could produce a vividly brushed impression of a riverside scene with great clarity and force. Though it was his pair of masterpieces, *The Swing* and *The Ball at Moulin de la Galette* (both Musée d'Orsay, Paris), that attracted the great critical interest, one reviewer described *The Seine at Champrosay* as 'one of the most beautiful [landscapes] ever made'.[1]

This country setting to the south-east of Paris, accessible by a short rail trip, was not one of Renoir's regular haunts, though it was not a great distance from Barbizon and the forest of Fontainebleau, where Renoir had painted a decade before (see cats. 1, 2, 3). As Renoir knew, Champrosay was where Eugène Delacroix had bought a house where he could retreat from Paris and paint landscape and cloud studies.[2] This picture was made in September 1876, when Renoir was invited to Champrosay by the writer Alphonse Daudet to paint a portrait of his wife (now in the Musée d'Orsay, Paris),[3] a work that also featured in the third Impressionist exhibition.

The Seine at Champrosay is a dynamic *plein-air* painting that represents the height of Renoir's Impressionist landscape style. This view of the river on a windy day is crisply rendered through the autumnal tones of the foliage and deep blue hues of the sky and water. The composition possesses an overall harmony that results from a number of competing rhythms created by divergent methods of brushwork. In the foreground, the long thin strokes of the spiky grass alternate between the russet and blue tones to provide a sense of depth and texture, while also showing the effects of wind blowing through the basin. By contrast, the water in the middle ground is laid on with mostly flat strokes, reflecting the colours of the sky above, giving a sense of calm. The sky above is quite restive, rendered with broad expressive gestures of pigment that provide a sense of atmospheric agitation that echoes the windswept grass.

JZ

1 G. Rivière, *L'Impressionniste*, 6 April 1877, quoted in Moffett 1986, p. 238.
2 A. Sérullaz, V. Pomarède and J. Rishel, *Delacroix. The Late Work* exh. cat, (Philadelphia Museum of Art), New York 1998, p. 18.
3 White 1984, p. 64.

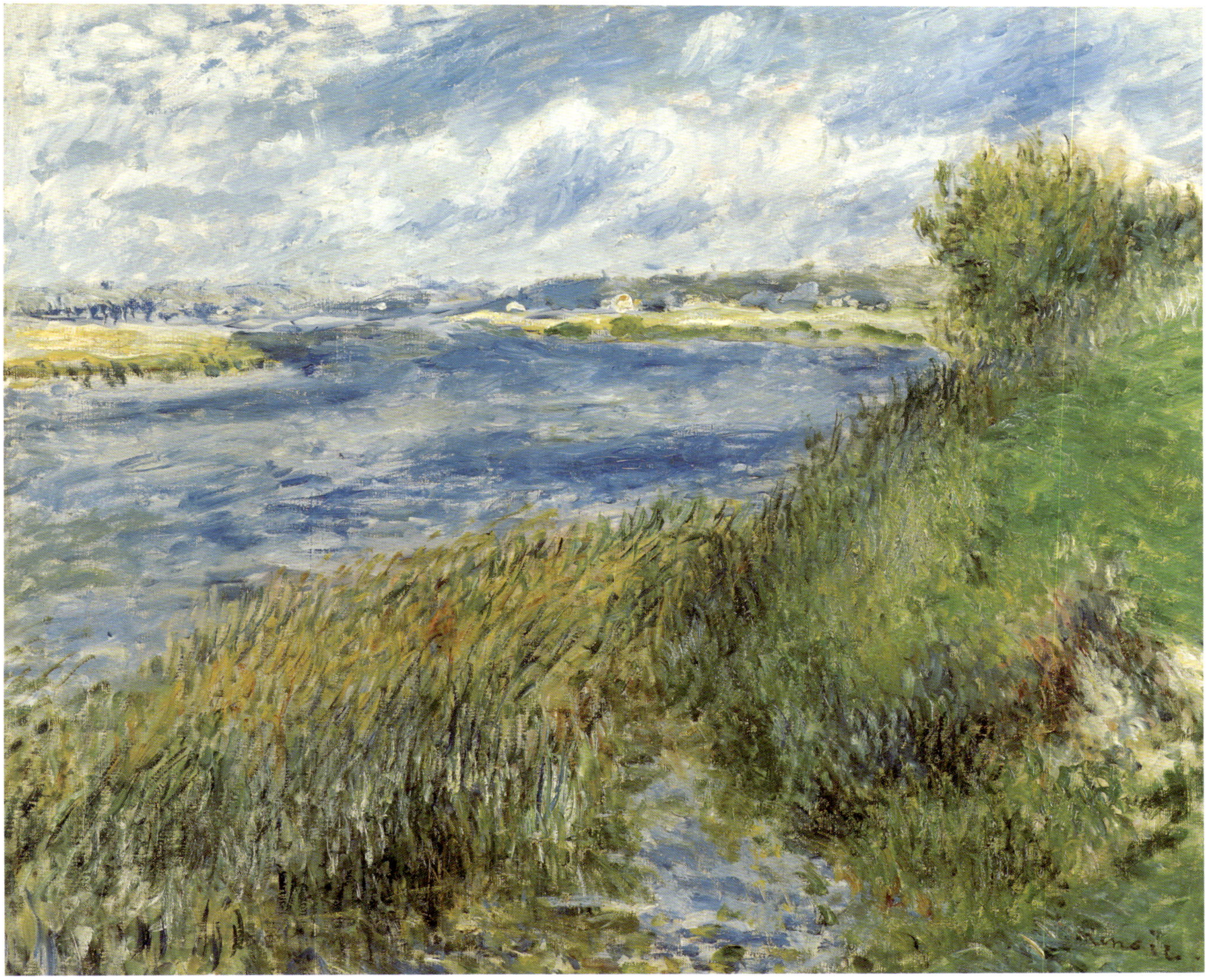

37 Woman with a Parasol in a Garden, 1875–6

Oil on canvas
54.5 × 65 cm; 21½ × 25⅝ in.
Museo Thyssen-Bornemisza, Madrid (1974.43)

38 Picking Flowers, 1875–6

Oil on canvas
54.3 × 65.2 cm; 21⅓ × 25⅝ in.
National Gallery of Art, Washington, DC. Ailsa Mellon Bruce Collection (1970.17.61)

PROVENANCE (CAT. 37): Durand-Ruel, Paris, by August 1891; Sam Salz, New York; Mrs Byron C. Foy, New York; her sale, Parke Bernet Galleries, New York, 13–16 May 1959, lot 13; Paul Rosenberg, New York; Lefèvre Gallery, London; Christie's, London, 1 July 1974, lot 14; Thyssen-Bornemisza Collection, Lugano; Museo Thyssen-Bornemisza, Madrid, 1993

PROVENANCE (CAT. 38): Durand-Ruel, Paris and New York; Sam Salz, New York; Howard Young, New York; Mrs L.L. Coburn, Chicago, by 1932; The Art Institute of Chicago, 1933–47; Carroll Carstairs, New York; sold 1 December 1947 to Ailsa Mellon Bruce (1901–1969), New York; bequeathed to the National Gallery of Art in 1970

LITERATURE (CAT. 37): House 1994, pp. 66–7; Adriani 1996, pp. 150–2; Dumas and Shapiro 1998, pp. 200–1, 246

LITERATURE (CAT. 38): Adriani 1996, pp. 150–2; Willsdon 2004, pp. 162–6

According to Vollard, in 1875 Renoir rented a second studio on the rue Cortot in the heart of Montmartre, in a house 'surrounded by a large garden'. He was in funds, for once, having sold 'a portrait of a mother with her two children' for 1,200 francs, a year's rent for the new studio.[1] Although Renoir retained his primary residence at 35 rue St-Georges, several streets south of the place Pigalle, it was in the studio and garden in Montmartre that he would work on his most ambitious narrative of modern life, *Ball at the Moulin de la Galette* (Musée d'Orsay, Paris), painted during the summer of 1876.[2] Georges Rivière, Renoir's good friend and apologist in the mid-1870s, dated Renoir's tenancy at 12 rue Cortot a year later, to between May and October 1876 precisely, and cited as the major works produced there the aforementioned *Ball*, *The Swing* (Musée d'Orsay, Paris) and *Leaving the Conservatory* (The Barnes Foundation, Merion, PA).[3] Rivière's account was confirmed early on by the artist's brother, Edmond, who, in commenting upon

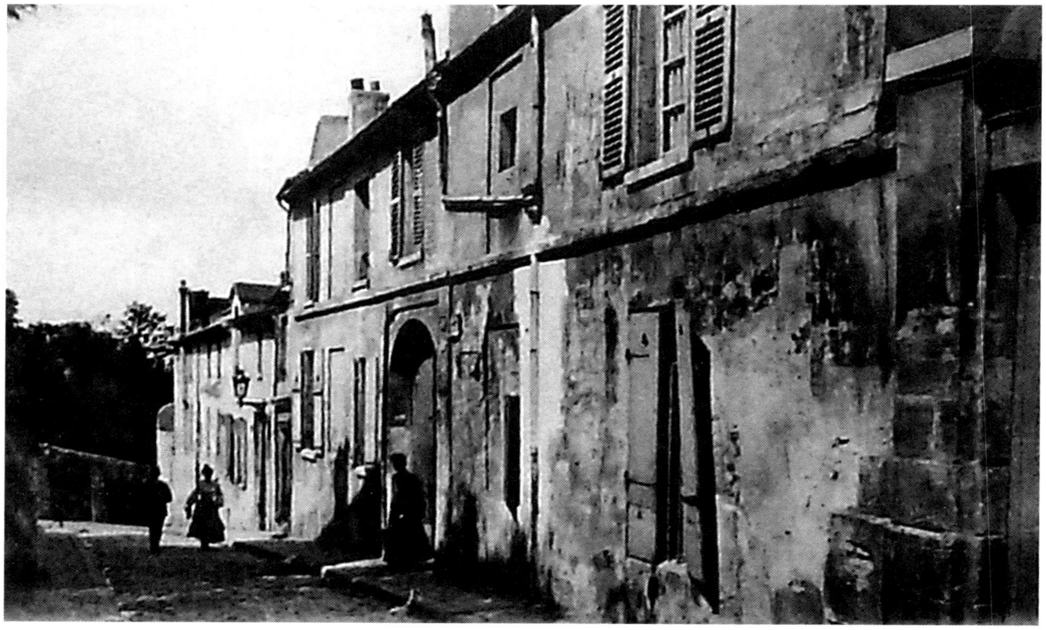

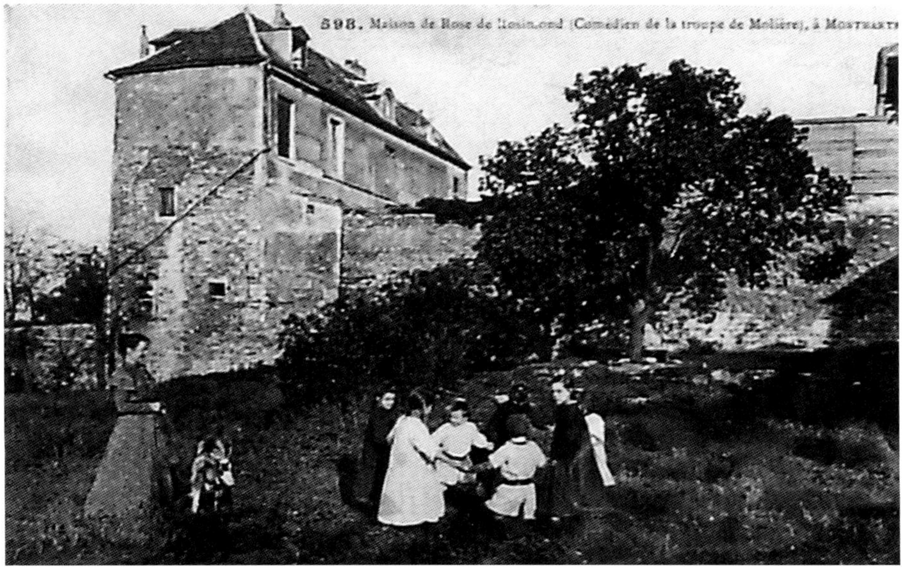

FIGS. 91 (p. 176) and 92 (left) 12–14 rue Cortot, about 1900. Photographs. Musée Carnavalet, Histoire de Paris.

Renoir's immersion in this working-class district, wrote that he 'settled in Montmartre for six months in order to forge his ties to this little world with its particular appeal'.[4]

Both Vollard and Rivière were writing more than 30 years after the fact, and their accounts, vivid and authentic though they are, are peppered with inaccuracies. The discrepancies in their dating of Renoir's tenancy of the dilapidated seventeenth-century house at 12 rue Cortot (figs. 91, 92),[5] would be of little consequence were it not for the group of garden landscapes most likely executed there, which have been assigned various dates between 1873 and 1878 and located to sites as far apart as Fontenay-aux-Roses and Wargemont.[6]

On one point Vollard and Rivière were in complete agreement. The chief attraction for Renoir in moving to this run-down quarter of the Butte Montmartre, a stone's throw from the basilica of the Sacré-Coeur (in the early stages of its construction),[7] was its large garden, 'with a magnificent view of the countryside as far as St-Denis'.[8] Rivière's account is the most vivid: 'As soon as Renoir entered the house, he was charmed by the view of this garden, which looked like a beautiful abandoned park. Once we had passed through the narrow corridor of the little house, we stood before a vast, uncultivated lawn dotted with poppies, convolvulus and daisies. Beyond, there was a pretty *allée* planted with tall trees spanning the full width of the garden, and, further still, an orchard, a vegetable patch, and thick shrubs with tall poplars, bending their leafy heads. We were enchanted.'[9]

This luxuriant garden, in various guises, is the subject of a number of Renoir's most experimental works, in which drawing and tonal contrast are rejected 'in favour of an art based on a network of coloured touches alone'.[10] John House's analysis of this 'process of dissolution' might well describe these verdant, exuberant landscapes, both painted on standard, commercially primed canvases – a size 15 – and both prominently signed in black at the moment of their completion, indicating that they were either intended for exhibition or for the (rare) collector interested in such work in the decade before Durand-Ruel became Renoir's primary vendor.

Woman with a Parasol in a Garden gives priority to the profusion of roses, poppies and irises that burst forth in the loose flower garden and divide the composition into two diagonal quadrants, weighted to the right. Energetic dabs and flecks of pigment, some blended on the

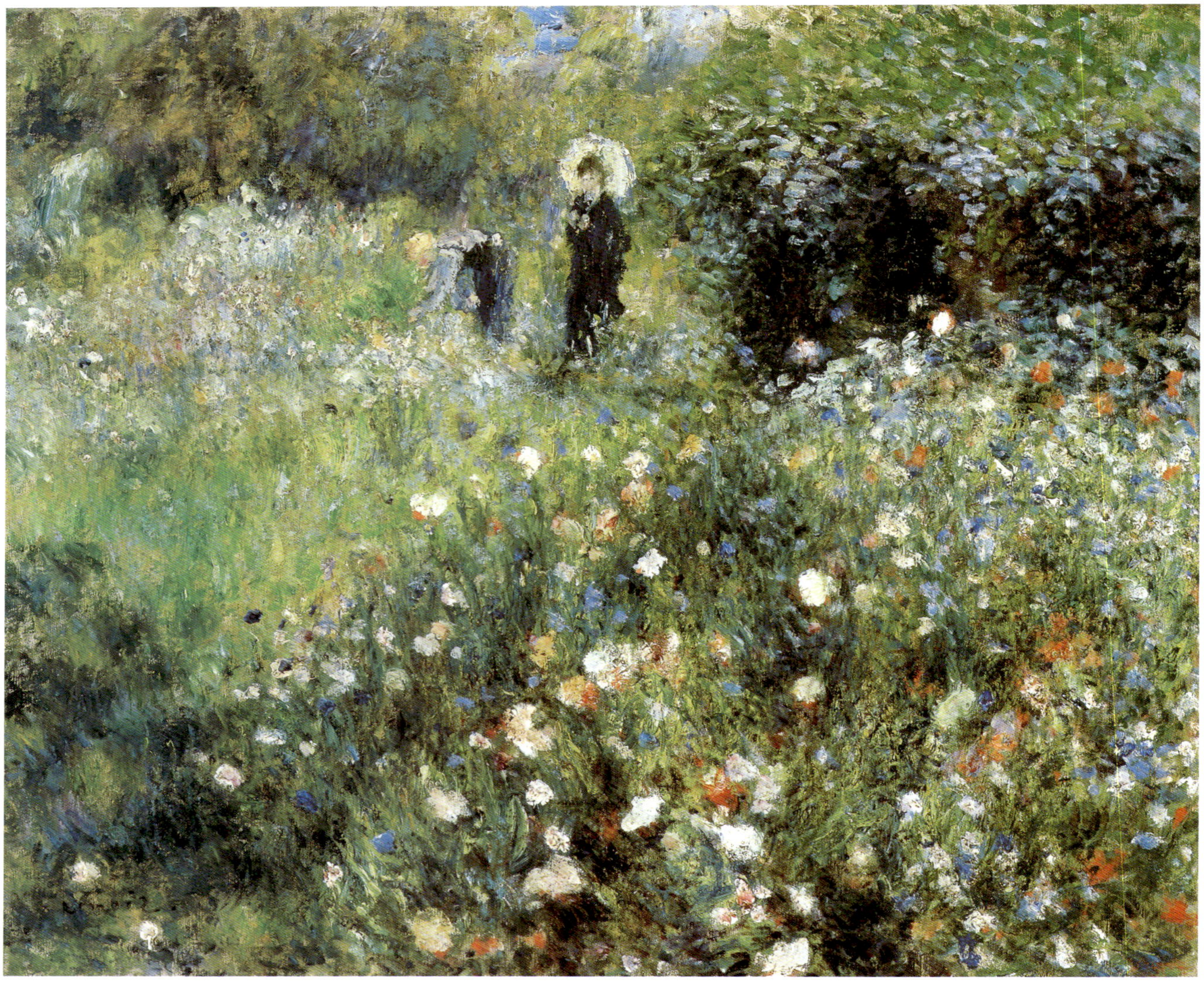

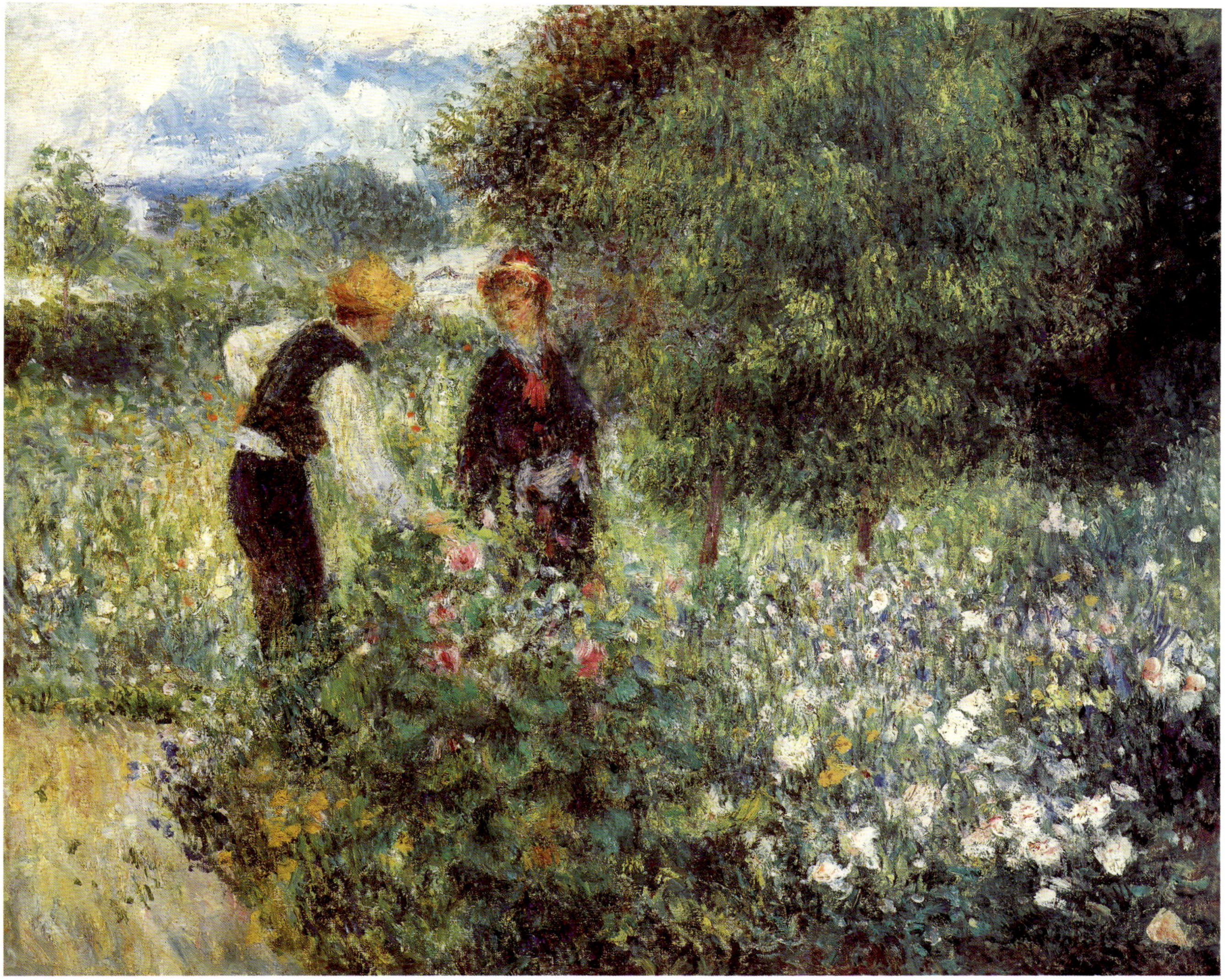

canvas itself, create a screen of flowers in the foreground, pulsating with energy. Relegated to the centre of the background, a properly attired parisienne protects herself with a white parasol, while next to her a man in working clothes and a straw hat bends over to attend to his blooms. Random and improvisatory only in appearance, the space of this verdant garden is carefully constructed – the banks of flowers at right, a less thickly planted meadow in the centre at left, and dense hedges in the background to the right of the standing figure. Only far off in the distance are the tiniest patches of sky to be seen, but light fills the canvas, and shadows in the foreground at left are rendered in strokes of the densest blue-black, cast by trees beyond the frame. Here is a truly 'instantaneous and voluntary' picture, in which 'all is harmonious and would be spoiled by a touch more or less', and of which Mallarmé would surely have approved.[11]

Previously assigned to *c.*1873 and *c.*1874, *Woman with a Parasol in a Garden* was first published as dating to 1875 by Götz Adriani, on the basis of its compositional and stylistic similarities to *Picking Flowers*, long considered a work of that year.[12] In this picture, a young man (also in gardening clothes) is showing roses to his companion, who wears the red-trimmed straw hat beloved of rowers and their consorts. While Renoir's handling here is no less informal and syncopated, this composition is a slightly calmer one, with the figures accorded greater prominence (although their relationship is not at all clear). A large (circular?) bed of flowers dominates the foreground – 'a virtual tide of blooms'[13] – with deep grasses behind, a pathway off to the left and (fruit?) trees marking the diagonal axis that leads the eye into the depth of the garden at right. The cropping of the trees, of which the 'leafy heads' are summarily truncated, and the abrupt emptiness of the path at lower left are precocious examples of Renoir's 'irregularity'.[14] The pulsating optical effects of pure whites mixed with reds, blues and yellows also bring to mind his comment to Rivière regarding the liberty he permitted himself in painting flowers: 'I can experiment boldly with tone and value without worrying about making a mess of the entire painting.'[15]

It must be noted that neither *Woman with a Parasol in a Garden* nor *Picking Flowers* makes any reference to their garden's location in Montmartre (figs. 91, 92) – one reason, surely, for their having been occasionally catalogued as representing the country estates of Renoir's well-to-do friends. It is their stylistic characteristics, and their relationship to the large, decorative *Garden in the rue Cortot, Montmartre* (cat. 39) – a view of yet another corner of this seemingly endless garden, presided over by clusters of *dahlia imperialis* – that form the basis for both their dating and their location. I have tentatively suggested that these two paintings may also have been exhibited at the third Impressionist exhibition of April 1877, where, entitled simply '*Jardin*', they were largely overlooked by the critics, one of whom, however, raged against their 'apocalyptic' appearance.[16] The fact that they are signed – a clear indication of their status as finished works and not sketches – encourages such conjecture. It should also be noted that in the reordering of Durand-Ruel's stock that took place on 25 August 1891, *Woman with a Parasol in a Garden* was given the title '*Jardin*'. The same stock number (1560) is to be found on a handwritten label that is still attached to this picture's stretcher. Next to the title, *Jardin* appears the year *1875* – another precious element in support of the redating and early exhibition history that are proposed here.[17] CBB

Cat. 37 shown in London and Philadelphia only

1 Vollard 1919, p. 72. The portrait to which Vollard refers is most likely to be *La Promenade* (Frick Collection, New York), probably painted in the autumn of 1875 and shown at the second Impressionist exhibition the following April.
2 House and Distel 1985, pp. 78, 211–12.
3 Rivière 1921, p. 129: '*Un matin de* ***mai*** *1876, nous partîmes de la rue St-Georges, Renoir et moi, dans l'espoir de trouver le local desiré*'; *ibidem*, p. 151: '*Il garda, cependant, la chambre de la rue Cortot jusqu'au milieu du mois d'****octobre***', emphases mine.
4 Renoir 1879: '*Peint-il le Moulin de la Galette? Il va s'y s'installer pendant six mois, lie des relations avec tout ce petit monde qui a son allure à lui.*'
5 Milner 1988, pp. 159–62; Willsdon 2004, p. 162. No cadastral records exist for the period of Renoir's tenancy; those for 1852 list the proprietors as the desmoiselles Virginie and Emilie Goubert (Archives de Paris, D1 P4, 1852, 12 rue Cortot).
6 Dumas and Shapiro (1998, p. 200) and Willsdon (2004, p. 159) have cited the summer residence of Charles Le Coeur at Fontenay-aux-Roses as the possible site for both *Woman with a Parasol in a Garden* and *Picking Flowers*, an identification that is erroneous since all relations between Renoir and this family had ceased in 1873; see Le Coeur in São Paulo 2002, p. 214. Until François Daulte reassigned *Picking Flowers* to *c.*1875, it had been published as having been painted on Berard's estate at Wargemont in 1878 (see letter to David Rust, 8 August 1972, in the curatorial files of the National Gallery of Art).
7 Collins 2001, pp. 58–61.
8 Renoir 1962, p. 180.
9 Rivière 1921, p. 130.
10 House 2004, p. 165.
11 Mallarmé's comments, published in September 1876, were directed towards the 'transcripts of nature' submitted by Monet, Sisley and Pissarro to the second Impressionist exhibition; see 'The Impressionists and Edouard Manet', in Moffett 1986, p. 32.
12 Adriani 1996, p. 150.
13 Willsdon 2004, p. 159.
14 Herbert 1988, pp. 188–90.
15 Rivière 1921, p. 81.
16 See further my essay above in this catalogue, pp. 51–81; for their possible listing in the *Catalogue de la 3e exposition de peinture* as '198, *Jardin*, 199, *Id.*', see Berson 1996, I, p. 120.
17 Archives Durand-Ruel, Brouillard, 25 August 1891, no. 1560, '*Jardin*', 54 × 64 (photo 1477). Both numbers are to be found on the stretcher; I am most grateful to Paloma Alarco and her staff for allowing me to examine the painting off the wall.

39 Garden in the rue Cortot, Montmartre, 1876

Oil on canvas
151.8 × 97.5 cm; 59¾ × 38⅜ in.
Carnegie Museum of Art, Pittsburgh. Acquired through the generosity of Mrs Alan M. Scaife (65.35)

PROVENANCE:
Eugène Murer, Paris (?); Galerie Durand-Ruel, Paris, by 1890; Durand-Ruel Gallery, New York, 1917; Sam Salz, New York; Carnegie Institute, Museum of Art, Pittsburgh, 1965

LITERATURE:
von Groschwitz 1966; Fezzi 1972 no. 238; Art Institute of Chicago 1973, no. 21; House and Distel 1985, no. 37; Milner 1988, pp. 159, 161; Distel 1993, p. 51

This exuberant depiction of an overgrown garden is linked to the creation of the most ambitious painting Renoir had attempted to that point in his career. In spring 1876 he was seeking a studio in Montmartre which would put him in proximity to the outdoor café where he planned to paint his large, multi-figure composition, *The Ball at the Moulin de la Galette* (Musée d'Orsay, Paris). There he would store the canvas overnight, enlisting the aid of friends to carry it the short distance to the Moulin to begin work each day. His friend Georges Rivière described how he and Renoir, exploring the neighbourhood, found such a studio in a run-down seventeenth-century property at 12 rue Cortot on the Butte Montmartre. They were delighted to discover that it came with a large, secluded garden, 'which resembled a beautiful abandoned park . . . strewn with poppies, convolvulus and daisies . . . . We were amazed.'[1] Renoir took possession of the studio – the rent was 1,000 francs a year[2] – and quickly put the garden to use. It became the setting for a number of important paintings executed over the next several months in which he pushed forwards with his analysis of the effects on the human figure of the play of sunlight filtering down through the leaves of trees. They include *The Swing* and *Study* (*Nude in Sunlight*) (both Musée d'Orsay, Paris). Renoir immediately put what he learned about such light effects to work as he painted his friends at the Moulin enjoying themselves under acacia trees on a sunny afternoon.

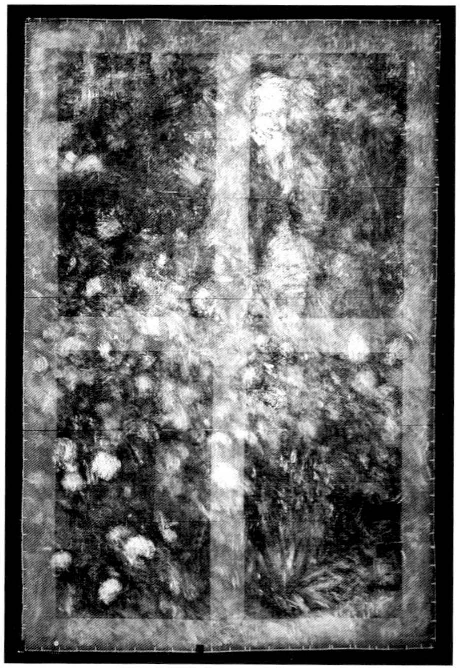

FIG. 93 X-radiograph of *Garden in the rue Cortot, Montmartre.*

The present painting also began as a figure study. A recent X-ray photograph has shown the head and chest of a moustached man at the upper right underneath the present composition. This would not, however, account for the areas of exceptionally thick paint on the canvas, and its complicated textures.[3] In the composition we see today the human figure plays less important a role, the garden itself capturing Renoir's primary attention. Two unidentified men[4] lean against a fence towards the rear of the garden, conversing amiably. Behind them, a wall of trees and shrubbery cuts off the horizon. The bottom two thirds of the canvas are given over to a wild profusion of flowers, principally dahlias in multiple brilliant hues. Such flowers are also seen in Renoir's *Claude Monet painting in his Garden at Argenteuil* of three years earlier (cat. 19), and Clare Willsdon has wondered if Monet perhaps might not have given Renoir some of his own dahlia tubers to plant in the rue Cortot garden; if so, and if Renoir had planted them in May or June, then the flowers would have been in full bloom, as here, by August, thus suggesting a

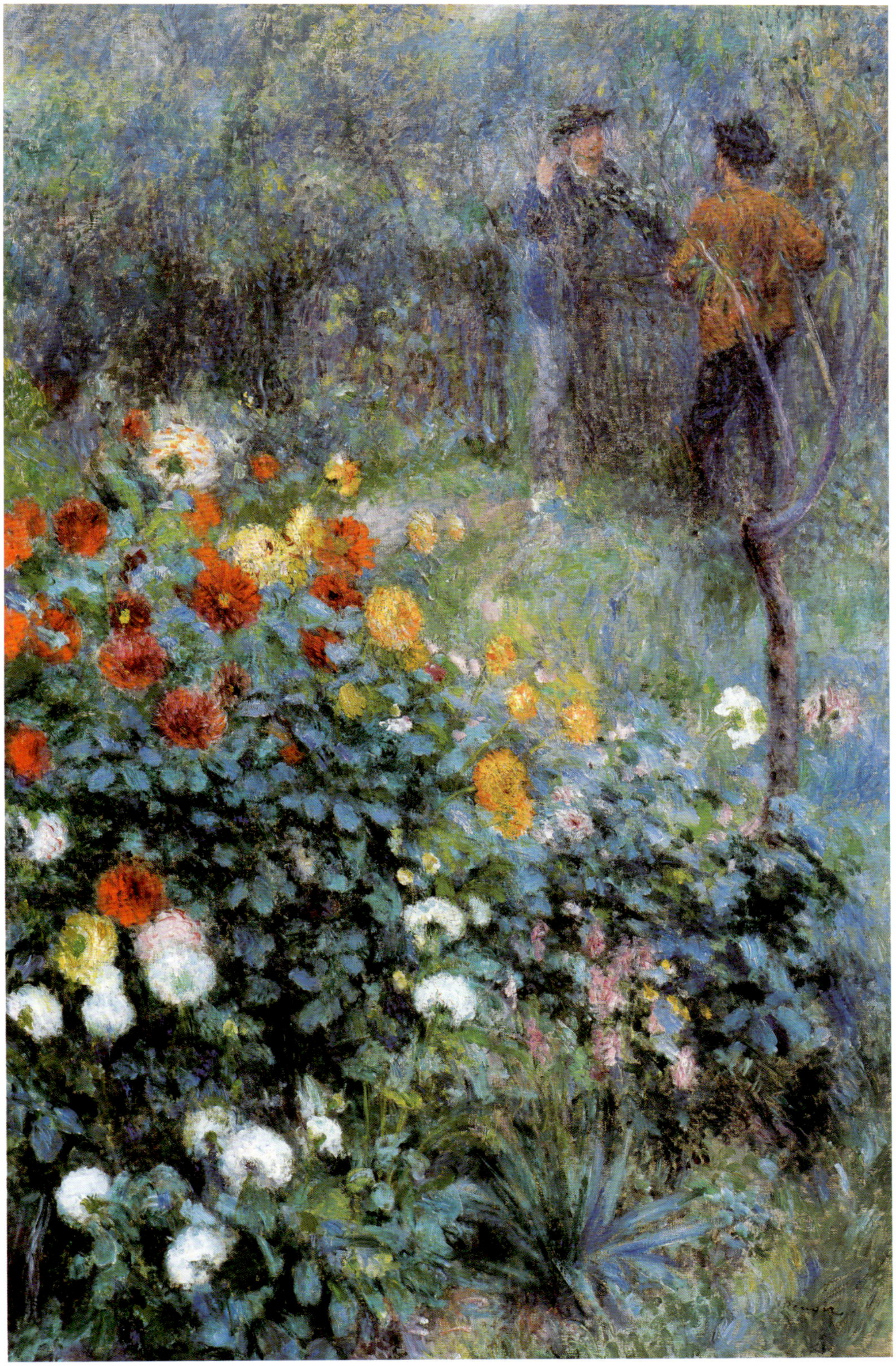

specific month in 1876 when the picture might have been painted.[5]

Monet's influence has also been detected in the painting's rich decorative effects. Specifically, it bears a relationship to the decorative panels featuring flowers that Monet was executing that same summer for Ernest Hoschedé's chateau at Montgeron.[6] Renoir looks down on the flowers from above, perhaps from a studio window, and then across at the men, surprisingly diminutive in relation to the dahlias. The result is the collapse of the space between foreground and middle ground. That spatial effect, along with the insistently vertical format of the canvas and the absence of horizon, also suggest a decorative intent not unrelated to such characteristics of Japanese prints as pictorial flatness. The fulsome, heavily worked quality of the painting, with its rich impasto, also serves to express the artist's delight in nature's fecundity. Secluded and tranquil but within hailing distance of central Paris, the garden in the rue Cortot was for several months in 1876 an oasis for Renoir and, in its lush splendour, a spur to his creativity at a vital moment of artistic development. CR

1 Rivière 1921, p. 130.
2 Milner 1988, p. 159.
3 As long ago as 1985 John House stated his conviction that a portrait would be found underneath the painting (Carnegie Institute curatorial file).
4 They have been variously identified as Monet and Sisley and as Monet and Renoir, but the first two were not living in Paris at the time, and there is no concrete evidence that Renoir intended to depict himself here. Moreover, a number of artists and writers who also might have served as models lived in the rue Cortot complex in 1876.
5 Willsdon 2004, p. 226, n. 36.
6 See Renoir 1981, no. 37.

40 Women in a Garden, about 1876

Oil on canvas
54.6 × 65.4 cm; 21⅜ × 25⅝ in.
Private collection

Related to the two previous garden landscapes (cats. 37, 38), *Women in a Garden* is set in yet another corner of Renoir's Montmartre residence, perhaps a spot giving on to 'the pretty *allée* with tall trees spanning its full width'.[1] Not only are the view and season slightly different than in the other works, with the riot of poppies and daisies suggesting a moment earlier in summer, but, even without a male figure, *Women in a Garden* has an urbane quality lacking in its more windswept companions. At the end of the sun-filled path, a well-attired parisienne, in a purple-blue pinafore dress with bows decorating the skirt, holds a white parasol in one hand and the flowers she has just picked in another. She is talking to a female companion in dark costume and hat on her right, almost invisible in the shaded depths.

As in Monet's garden pictures painted at Argenteuil that same summer (with which Renoir was surely familiar),[2] these diminutive figures function as *repoussoir* elements in reverse, establishing a scale for this luxuriant, sun-drenched garden which appears altogether grander than it must have been in reality.[3] Despite the profusion of red, yellow and white flowers, almost pounced in paint, and the riot of blues, greens and yellows that create the effect of a summer's sky seen through leafy branches, Renoir's fragmentary handling establishes space and depth with the utmost rigour. The eye is led with absolute assurance along the path that moves from shadow to full sunlight, bordered at right by the same fence that demarcates the edge of the property in *Garden in the rue Cortot* (see cat. 39).

It is in the description of the flowerbeds and trees to the left of the path that Renoir's urbanity gains full expression. The well-banked poppies and daisies line a pleached *allée*, the trees having been trimmed back and their trunks tied together to create a tiny arbour of sorts. By contrast, the trees on the opposite side of the path stand sentry-like in front of the wooden fence. The bourgeois flower garden – with or without an arbour – was a relatively recent phenomenon, and one whose popularity can be documented to the third quarter of the nineteenth century. According to a historian of French gardens writing in 1867, the century's greatest advance was 'to have restored to the garden its first and essential function – the cultivation of flowers'.[4] As a rule, Renoir was much less interested in garden design than Monet – he was more attentive to trends in women's hats and dresses – but in *Women in a Garden* he is properly respectful of recent horticultural fashion.

The violet-blue shadows on the pathway and splashes of light in the foreground are

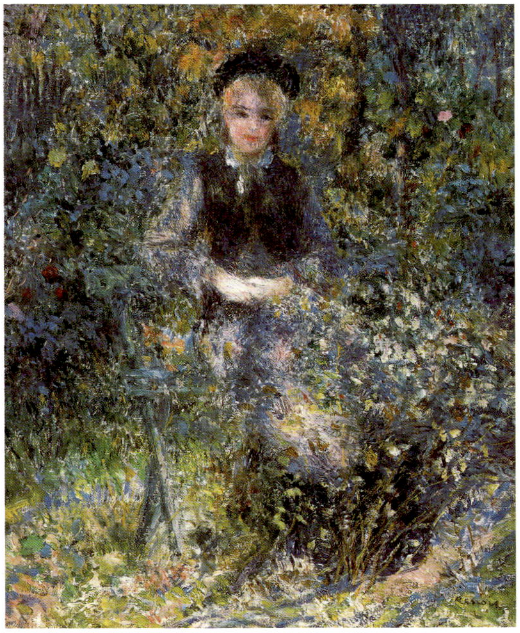

FIG. 94 *Young Woman seated in the Garden*, about 1876. Oil on canvas, 61 × 50 cm; 24 × 19⅝ in. Private collection.

PROVENANCE:
Durand-Ruel, Paris; Sam Salz, New York; Paul Rosenberg, New York; Mrs Thelma Chrysler Foy, New York; Sotheby's, New York, *Impressionist Paintings, Drawings and Sculpture*, 11 May 1993, lot 13; Phillips, New York, *Impressionist and Modern Art*, 6 November 2000, lot 9; Sotheby's, London, 19 June 2006, Lot 17; Private collection

LITERATURE:
House 2004, pp. 165–7; Willsdon 2004, pp. 162–6

characteristic of Renoir's handling in the mid-1870s. Indeed, although *Women in a Garden* has always been assigned to 1873, at the beginning of Renoir's Impressionist manner, it must surely date to the summer of 1876 and his tenancy at the rue Cortot.[5] At some remove from the unfettered garden scenes (cat. 37, 38) and the larger *Garden in the rue Cortot, Montmartre* (cat. 39), it belongs to a group of highly experimental paintings showing Nini Lopez or other young models from Montmartre seated outdoors (fig. 94), in which Renoir's technique reaches a new level of virtuosity and freedom.[6] In *Women in a Garden*, for example, the 'secular halo' of the standing figure's parasol is rendered simply as a triangle of thick white paint.[7] Renoir's brush works in a variety of modes here – thick dabs of pigment for the flowers at left; broader, wash-like strokes for the leaves and sky at upper right; thin, drawn lines of paint for the tree trunks on either side of the path.

As in all of his rue Cortot paintings, Renoir's experimental manner is at the service of an exuberant, sensuous vision – almost Baudelairean in its celebration of the 'perfumes, colours and sounds' of this sun-filled garden.[8] It has been noted that Renoir was at work on these garden scenes shortly after his neighbour from 21 rue St-Georges published *La Faute de l'abbé Mouret*, an overwrought novel about sexual awakening set in the south of France.[9] Central to this story is Le Paradou, the Edenic garden of an abandoned estate, in which an amnesiac priest is transformed by the love of an unrestrained, 'natural' young girl. Zola's garden – 'an orgy of greenery, a flood of exuberant grasses' – is complicit in the couple's lovemaking: it is described as being 'alive with the extravagance of a happy beast'.[10] However, although Renoir may have jokingly compared his rented Montmartre garden to Zola's Paradou, his fictions are gentle and decorous by comparison.[11] Abundant and sensuous certainly, this Parisian garden is rinsed in sunlight, and from the end of its single path a caparisoned (and chaperoned) figure demurely beckons. CBB

Not in the exhibition

1 Rivière 1921, p. 130.
2 For example, *Camille Monet in the Garden of the House in Argenteuil* (The Metropolitan Museum of Art, New York, Annenberg Collection) and *Gladioli* (Detroit Institute of Art); see Wildenstein 1974–91, I, nos. 410, 411, and Bailey and Rishel 1989, pp. 54–5.
3 See the photographs of the house and garden, dating from *c.*1900, in Léri 1983, pp. 156–8.
4 A. Mangin, *Histoire des jardins anciens et modernes*, Tours 1867, pp. 265–7.
5 Fezzi 1985, no. 101; Phillips, New York, *Impressionist and Modern Art*, 6 November 2000, lot 9; although the extensive entry notes the similarities with *Woman with a Parasol in a Garden*, it dates both canvases to 1873.
6 Bailey and Rishel 1989, pp. 32–3; House 2004, pp. 165–7; and see the examples illustrated in Christie's, London, *Impressionist and Nineteenth Century Art*, 29 June 1999, lot 14.
7 The term is taken from House 1994, p. 66.
8 Baudelaire, 'Correspondances', *Les Fleurs du mal* (no. 4), *Oeuvres complètes* (1857), Paris 1968, p. 46.
9 Willsdon 2004, pp. 161–4. Written during the summer of 1874, Zola's novel was published by Charpentier in the spring of 1875, and read straight away by Edmond de Goncourt who admired '*La sève fornicante et coïtante répandue dans le livre de Zola*'; *Journal*, II, p. 640, 4 April 1875.
10 '*Le grand jardin vivait avec une extravagance d'une bête humaine . . . c'était une débauche telle de feuillages, une marée d'herbes si débordantes*'; E. Zola, *La Faute de l'Abbé Mouret, Oeuvres complètes*, (1875), Paris 1967, III, pp. 109–10.
11 Renoir's son remembered him describing it as 'A mysterious, stately garden, like Zola's *paradou* [*sic*] – that was once part of a stately residence'; Renoir 1962, p. 180.

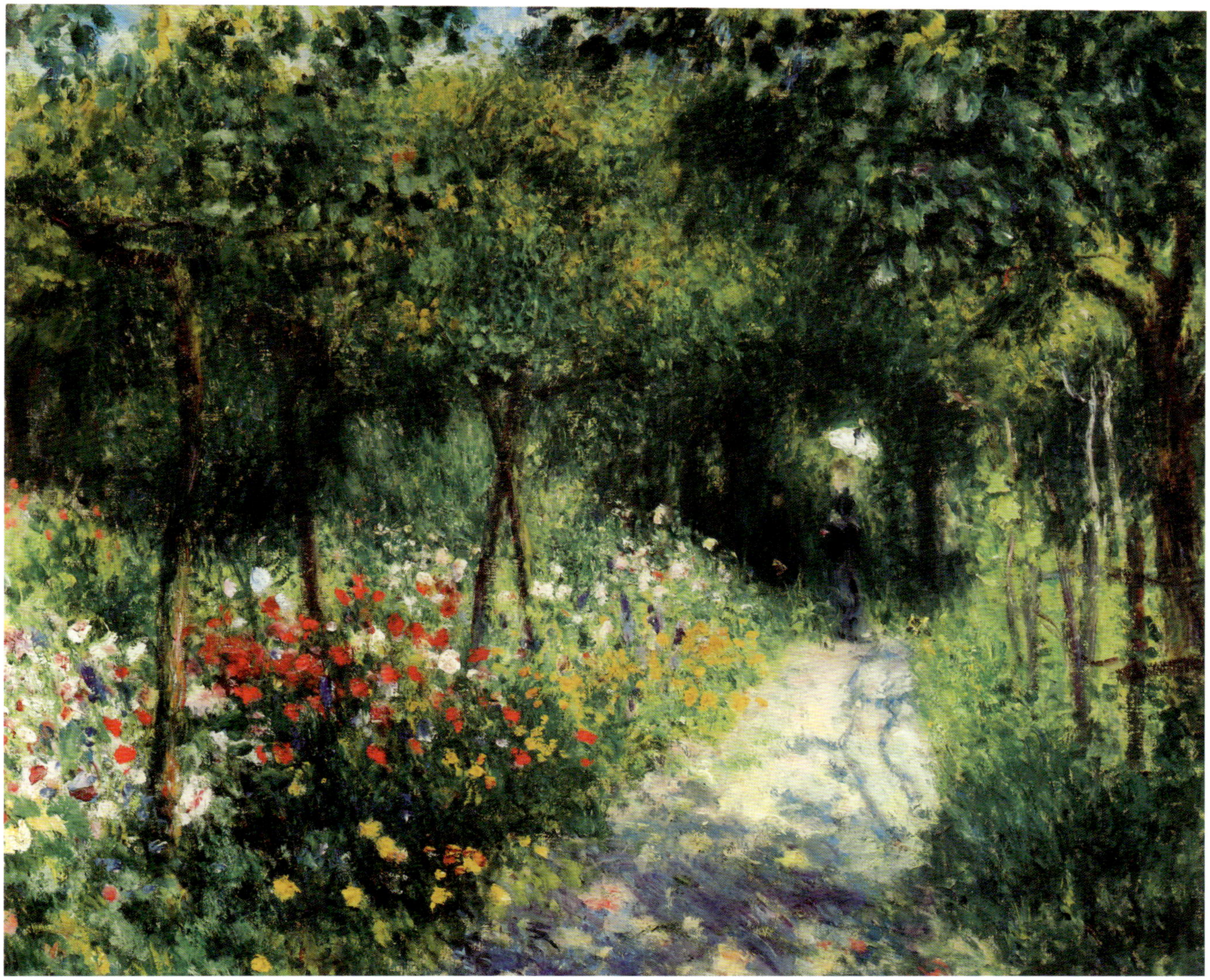

41 In the Woods, about 1877

Oil on canvas
55.8 × 46.3 cm; 22 × 18⅜ in.
The National Museum of Western Art, Tokyo, Matsukata Collection (P-1959-183)

PROVENANCE:
Kojiro Matsukata; sequestered by the French Government, 1944; returned to Japan, 1959; The National Museum of Western Art, Japan

LITERATURE:
Fezzi 1972, no. 400; Monneret 1980, no. 9; Fezzi 1985, no. 382; House 1994, no. 11

Sous-bois painting is the depiction of a forest interior with the sun filtering down through the leaves overhead to create variegated patterns of sunlight and shade on the forest floor. The Barbizon painters had made it a speciality and Renoir took up the motif in emulation as early as 1866, when he painted *Jules Le Coeur and his Dogs walking in the Forest of Fontainebleau* (cat. 3). It was a test the ambitious young artist set himself – how to capture the ambient atmosphere of a largely enclosed site. He returned to the motif periodically in later years, never more audaciously than here, in a painting that for John House represents 'the most extreme dissolution of form of any of Renoir's landscapes'.[1] The human figure is eliminated, although indications of a fence at lower right establish that we are adjacent to inhabited lands. The entire canvas is given over to a skein of mottled colours, most applied as small dots and dashes of pigment meant to represent leaves. Little beyond the tall, thin tree trunks at right suggests tangible objects in nature. Rather, the canvas dances with a thousand touches of disembodied pigment. The right side is comprised primarily of darker green and blue tones, the bottom features flashing red pigments, while the upper left side glows with golden highlights. These dominant tints merge in the centre of the canvas into a pastel haze as the road we seem to stand on disappears deeper into the woods.[2] Brushstrokes here are smaller and more blended. Nonetheless, a sense of space and place is vividly conveyed as our eye is drawn down the road, and as it also tries to trace a path up through the leaves to the source of the magical, enveloping light. The painting also conveys a single, specific atmospheric effect redolent of the moist, pungent mists of an autumn afternoon. Marx and Engels certainly were not thinking about landscape painting when they noted of the modern world, 'all that is solid melts into air',[3] but that is the impact and implication of this remarkable picture. Here Renoir explores the experience of pure colour more or less liberated from those objects in nature to which colours accrue. Only Monet would push further at this dissolution of form, in the monumental late landscapes painted at his garden at Giverny in the early decades of the twentieth century. And it would be mid century before Jackson Pollock achieved a dominant ambient atmosphere, similar to Renoir's, in paintings now fully divorced from the constraints of representation, such as *Lavender Mist* (*Number 1*), 1950 (fig. 95). An important aspiration of modern art announces itself here. CR

Shown in Ottawa and Philadelphia only

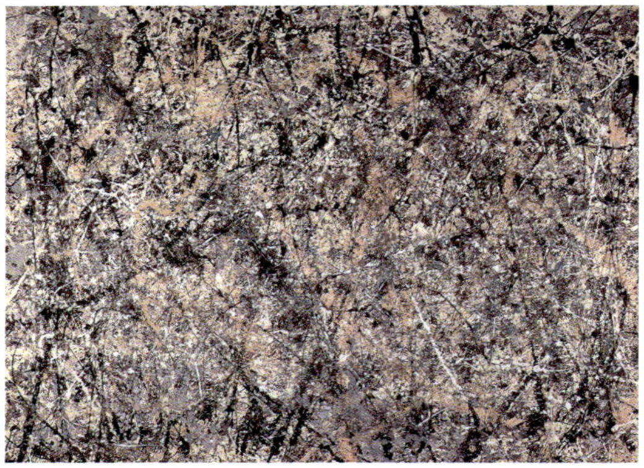

FIG. 95 Jackson Pollock (1912–1956), *Lavender Mist* (*Number 1*), 1950. Oil, enamel and aluminium on canvas, 221 × 299.7 cm; 87 × 118 in. National Gallery of Art, Washington, DC. Ailsa Mellon Bruce Fund (1976.37.1).

1 House 1994, p. 72, no. 11.
2 House (*ibidem*) points out that the straight lines of the receding road indicate that this is a man-made environment rather than the depths of the untouched forest.
3 K. Marx and F. Engels, *The Communist Manifesto* (1848), 2005, ch. 1, para. 17.

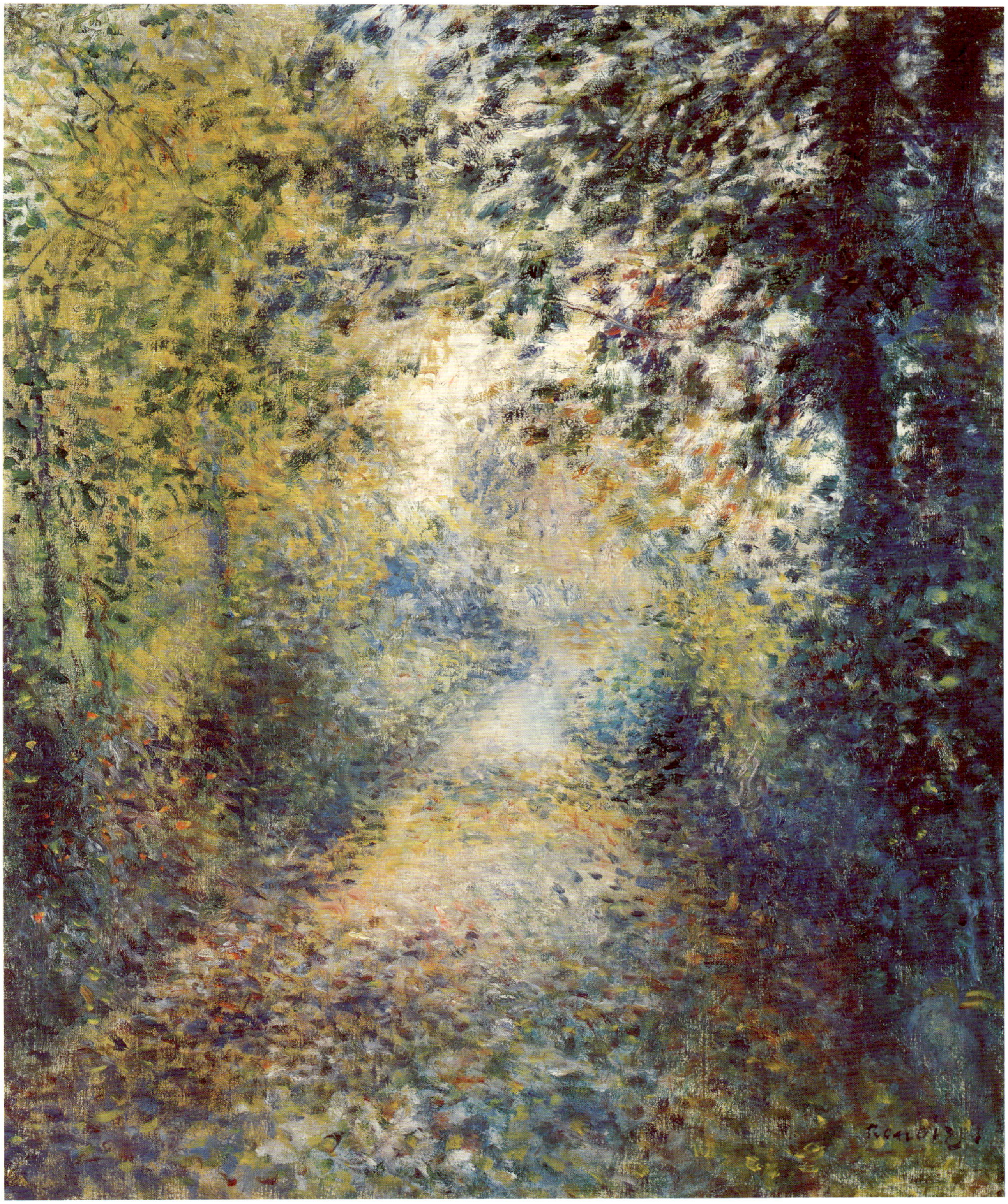

42 Allée in the Woods, about 1878–9

Oil on canvas
47.5 × 60 cm; 18¾ × 23⅝ in.
Private collection

PROVENANCE:
Private collection, England

In this work, painted perhaps a year or two after *In the Woods* (cat. 41), Renoir returned to his investigation of *sous-bois* light effects in a forest interior. As in the case of the earlier painting, the site is not known, but the artist's motivation is the same, to capture the effect of sunlight filtering down through leaves to the forest floor. He set himself such challenges periodically as a way to test and refine his skills, and indeed some years later would identify landscape painting as 'the only way to learn one's craft'.[1] That the picture is unsigned may suggest that Renoir saw it as a sketch rather than a picture for exhibition. He uses a wide range of green shades not only to differentiate among different kinds of foliage, including leaves of trees, grasses and shrubbery, but to carve out and define the space itself along the *allée* or pathway on which he stands. Thus, the darker boughs that hang down across the top of the canvas serve as a traditional *repoussoir* element creating an area of shade in the foreground and leading the eye towards the sunnier realms beyond. Other, less saturated greens line the path while the glowing pools of light on the forest floor are like stepping stones across a pond drawing us deeper into the space. The greens are accented with touches of russet, yellow and, very discreetly, cobalt blue, which add to the animation of the canvas. Brushstrokes serve both to differentiate between foliage, with quick, short touches of paint characterising some grasses, longer, more meandering strokes other forms of vegetal growth, and, to define space, the taller grasses at centre seeming to overwhelm the path as it disappears into the distance. The painting communicates an almost palpable sense of envelopment in the sensuous atmosphere of a summer's day, and the sense too that the play of dappled light is in constant flux as errant breezes cause boughs overhead to sway. CR

1 Renoir to Berthe Morisot, September 1892; Rouart 1951, p. 170.

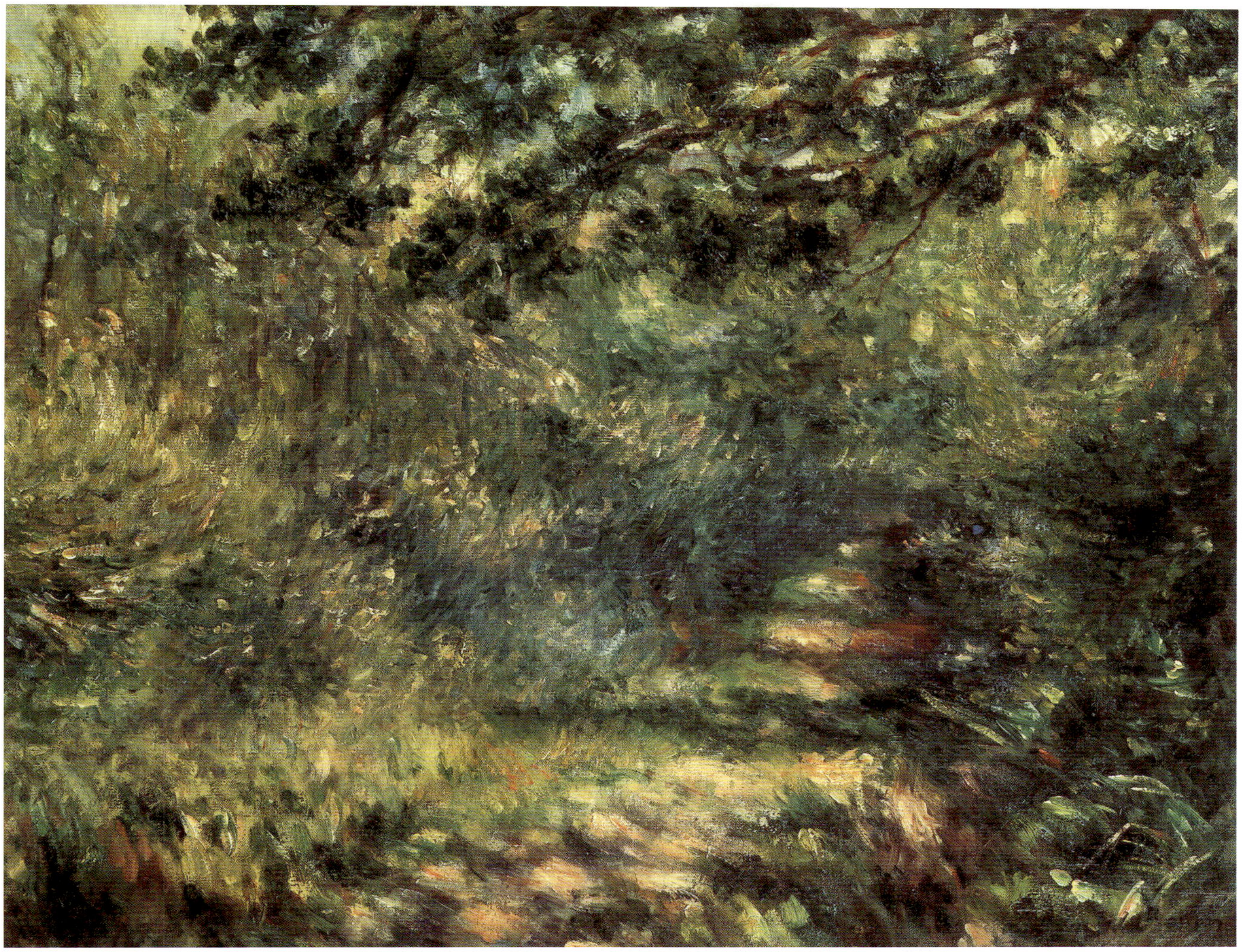

43 Landscape at Wargemont, 1879

Oil on canvas
80.6 × 100 cm; 31¾ × 39⅝ in.
The Toledo Museum of Art, Toledo, Ohio. Purchased with funds from the Libbey Endowment.
Gift of Edward Drummond Libbey (1957. 33)

PROVENANCE:
Possibly sold by Renoir to Durand-Ruel on 15 June 1882; recorded in Durand-Ruel's stock, 25 August 1891, as '*Paysage, Prairie à Wargemont, 1879*'; sold by Durand-Ruel to the Berlin collector Carl Steinbart (1852–1923), 30 May 1909; bought back on 14 October 1910; sold by Durand-Ruel to Conrad M. Pineus (1872–1945), Gothenburg, 10 December 1917; collection of Walther Halvorsen, Oslo, by 1929; with Nicolai Andresen, New York, by 1950; Wildenstein & Co., New York; purchased with funds from the Libbey Endowment, gift of Edward Drummond Libbey, 1957

LITERATURE:
House and Distel 1985, pp. 87, 215; Gerstein 1989, pp. 166–7; House 1995, pp. 250–1; Brettell 2000, pp. 180–1

One of Renoir's greatest landscapes – from any point in his career – *Landscape at Wargemont* has won the admiration of art historians as diverse as Kenneth Clark and Michael Fried, while inspiring in specialists some of their most sensitive analyses.[1] This large canvas – a size 40 –[2] has as its subject the sweeping countryside near the château de Wargemont, the seigneurial residence ten miles north-east of Dieppe that belonged to Paul Berard (1833–1905), who was Renoir's host for the first time in the summer of 1879.[3] Taken from on high, the view is of a road that snakes through a valley dotted with trees and bushes of acidic hue before finally disappearing behind the yellow trees and purple hills in the distance. The elements are in attendance, from the wind rustling through the grasses to the rain that threatens in the overcast sky above.

As has often been noted, this topographically complex, animated landscape is constructed through the most economical of means.[4] Renoir has carefully primed his fine-weave canvas with an opaque layer of white that establishes an almost porcelain-like surface on which to work and provides the basis for an all-over luminosity. Painting quickly, he applied his colours in thin, translucent veils, at times with the delicacy of watercolour. Traces of his brushwork are everywhere apparent, with the white ground revealed through silken layers of paint, and a tonal range that Jacques-Emile Blanche, a fellow guest of the Berards during this period (see cat. 45) likened to 'redcurrant jam'.[5] (Renoir's palette is an exquisite mixture of madder, emerald green, mustard-yellow and purple). Such is the speed and assurance with which Renoir worked that the beholder's eye takes in hill and valley with a dizzying velocity, the rows of trees and bushes – mere patches of hue – glimpsed as on the periphery of vision. Magisterial and sublime, *Landscape at Wargemont* is also experimental in technique, and anticipates Degas's idiosyncratic landscapes in pastel and monotype of the early 1890s.[6]

Much still remains to be discovered about Renoir's 'astonishing *tour de force*'.[7] Although prominently signed and dated at lower right, the painting was never intended for the patron whose sustenance and encouragement in the summer of 1879 provided Renoir with the ideal conditions in which to produce a body of surpassing work (notably, family portraits and Norman landscapes).[8] *Landscape at Wargemont* was not among the 30 or so paintings by Renoir in Berard's collection, nor, despite its size and signature, was it ever exhibited in Paris by Renoir (or his dealer). On only one occasion during Renoir's lifetime was the work on public display, and this in a survey of nineteenth-century French art in Copenhagen, organised by the Dansk Kunstmuseums Forening in May 1914, three months before the outbreak of the World War I.[9]

From Durand-Ruel's stock records, it is tempting to associate *Landscape at Wargemont* with the '*Route à Berneval*' acquired from Renoir for 500 francs on 15 June 1882, along with fourteen other pictures, including masterpieces from

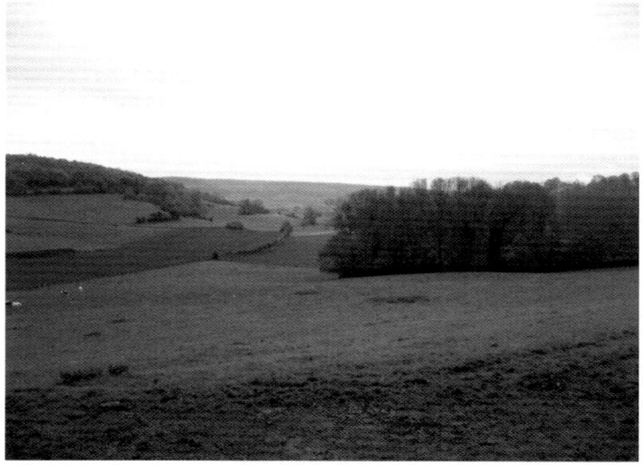

FIG. 96 Present-day view of the landscape at Wargemont.

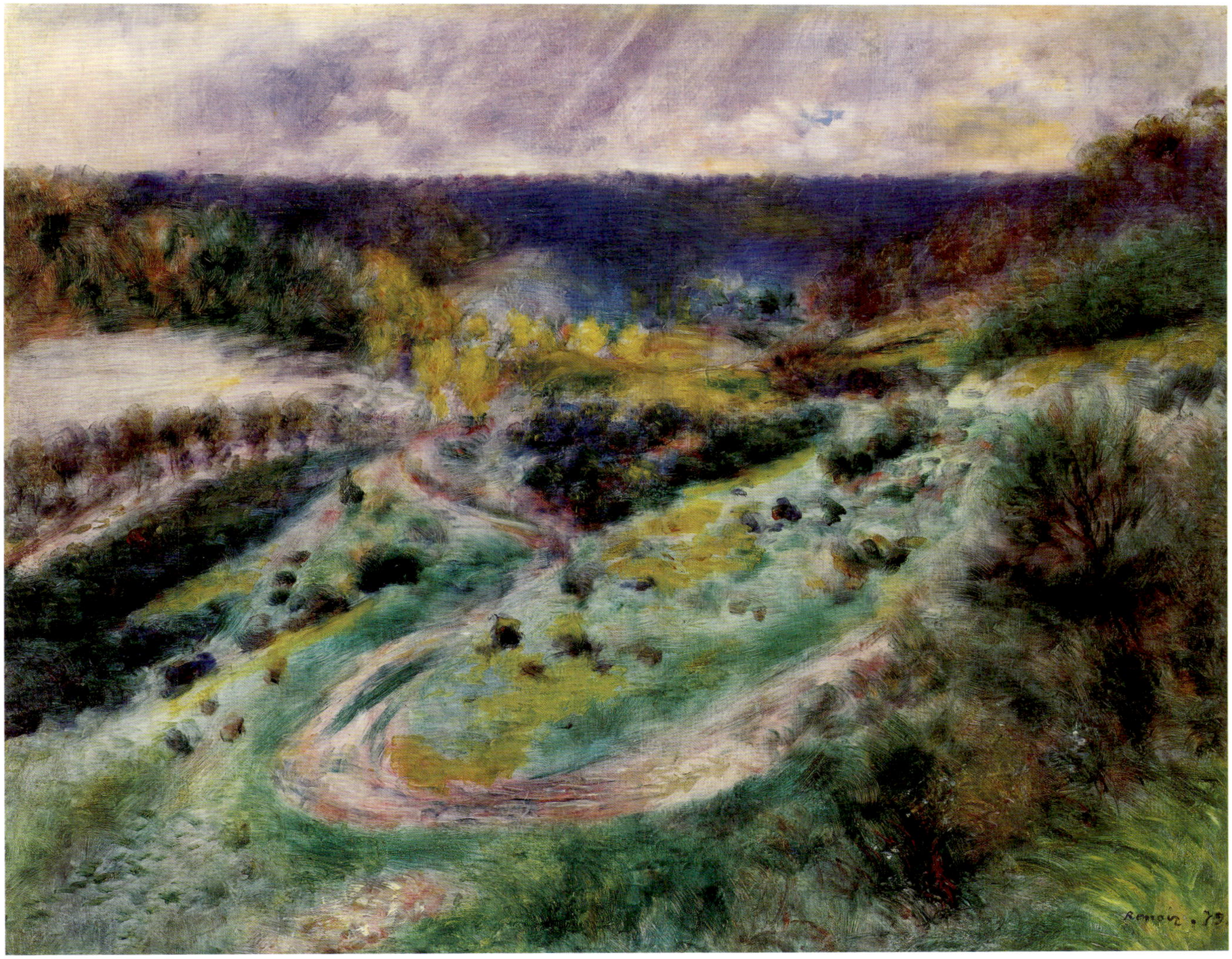
Renoir .79

the mid-1870s such as *Garden in the rue Cortot, Montmartre* (cat. 39).[10] It can be stated with absolute certainty that *Landscape at Wargemont* was in Durand-Ruel's possession by August 1891, when the dealer reorganised his records and assigned certain pictures new stock numbers (and occasionally new titles). The work was then listed as '*Paysage, Prairie à Wargemont, 1879*' and given the stock number DR 1584 and the photographic number 1672, both of which are still clearly visible in blue crayon on the back of the stretcher.[11] The painting remained with Durand-Ruel until it was sold in May 1909 to Carl Steinbart, a banker and collector from Berlin, who apparently returned it within a year and a half.[12]

Renoir's sweeping, unpopulated vista, with neither historical marker nor picturesque peasantry in sight, is the very opposite of the tourist picture made for Parisian consumption.[13] Although his activities as a guest of the seigneurial Berards are well documented in Jacques-Emile Blanche's vivid and affectionate reminiscence, we do not know exactly how Renoir went about creating his landscapes of the Norman countryside (on his portraits we are better informed).[14] As Renoir's decorations for the dining room at Wargemont attest, Berard and his guests hunted frequently during the late summer months.[15]

One has some difficulty imagining Renoir as an eager participant, but *Landscape at Wargemont* might relate to such an outing – a rather different sort of 'day in the country' from those usually associated with Impressionist landscape painting. Renoir's composition is also evocative of a view glimpsed through a carriage window, and, encountering Normandy for the first time, he was a most zealous visitor of its country. As Blanche recalled, the '*omnibus du château*' was always at his disposal.[16] To Madame Charpentier – whom he encouraged to rent a summer villa in nearby Puys – Renoir enthused upon the pleasures of a 'charming promenade' he had just made: 'From Dieppe you go to Ancourt via Martin-Eglise. Stop for a second at the Moulin d'Ancourt, which is adorable and not far away. If you have time, return via Sauchay-le-Haut, where there is the avenue of a château that is superb. You can return to Dieppe on the Envermeau road, and the entire journey takes only two hours.'[17] As Robert McDonald Parker and Francis Guého have very recently confirmed, *Landscape at Wargemont* is indeed the record of such a journey.[18] Renoir set his large canvas at the edge of the forest approximately one mile south-west of Berard's château – and so within walking distance of it – taking the view inland to the south, with the Channel far behind him. His panorama records the fields surrounded by the Bois de St-Quentin, with the lined *allée* – the Rideaux de Sauchay-le-Bas – shown as a band of purple in the distance. Such is Renoir's topographical honesty that the clump of trees that gently breaks the horizon at upper right can be identified as part of the forest surrounding the nearby village of Coquereaumont, where the Bois Gaillon and the Bois de l'Hirondelle eventually rise to become the Mont Blanc (fig. 97). CBB

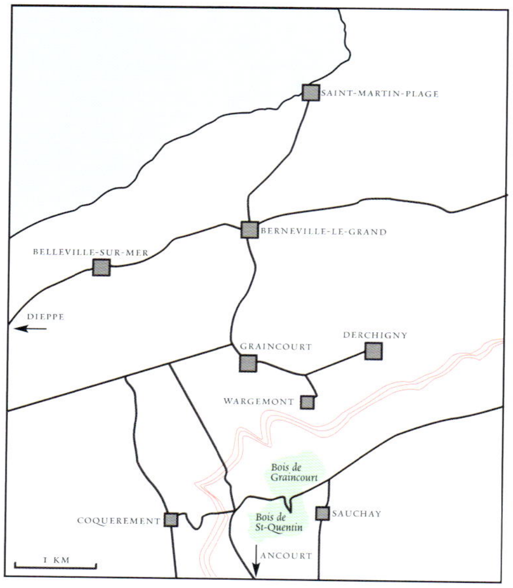

FIG. 97 Map showing Wargemont and its environs.

1 Clark 1935, pp. 3–4; Fried 1986, pp. 108–9; and see the entries by Maxon 1973, pp. 26–7; Gerstein 1989, pp. 166–7; House 1995, pp. 250–1; and Brettell 2000, pp. 180–1.
2 Bomford (1990, p. 46) provides a chart of ready-stretched, commercially prepared canvas sizes.
3 On Berard's patronage of Renoir, see Distel 1990, pp. 162–9, and Bailey 1997, pp. 34–8.
4 House 1995, p. 250.
5 Blanche 1931, p. 71: '*De la confiture de groseille, disait-on.*'
6 Kendall 1993.
7 House 1995, p. 250.
8 Although he owned six landscapes by Monet, Berard seems to have acquired only a single landscape by Renoir, the delicate *Venice, Fog* (fig. 50, p. 69), bought for 100 francs in November 1881.
9 See *Exposition d'art français du XIX siècle*, Royal Museum, Copenhagen, 15 May–30 June 1914, no. 179, exhibited by Durand-Ruel.
10 Archives Durand-Ruel, Journal 1882, 15 June 1882, no. 2463, *Route de Berneval*, 500 francs (*Garden in the rue Cortot, Montmartre* was acquired as *Grand Jardin* for 600 francs). This identification would account for the absence of *Landscape at Wargemont* in the seventh Impressionist exhibition of March 1882, but raises the question of why Durand-Ruel did not include it in the Renoir retrospective he organised the following year.
11 Archives Durand-Ruel, Stockbook, '*Tableaux achetés à Monsieur Durand-Ruel et mis en dépôt 35, rue de Rome*', 25 August 1891: 'No. 1584, *Paysage, Prairie à Wargemont, 1879*, photo 1672'. I am most grateful to Larry Nichols for examining the back of the stretcher and confirming these labels for me.
12 House and Distel 1985, p. 215. For Steinbart, the patron of the Berlin Secessionist Max Slevogt and a client of Cassirer's who supported Tschudi in his acquisition of French paintings for the Nationalgalerie, Berlin, see von Hohenzollern and Schuster 1996, pp. 90, 98.
13 Herbert 1994.
14 Blanche 1927, p. 62; Blanche 1937, pp. 35–40; Bailey 1997, pp. 170–2, 184–5, 209–11.
15 For Renoir's *trophées de chasse*, see the illustration in M. Berard, *Renoir à Wargemont*, Paris 1938. On 15 September 1877 Berard informed Deudon: '*Je n'ai pas interrompu mes courses en plaine et je suis recompensé par des sensations agréables de chasse. J'ai eu de beaux chiffres et des journées de chasse amusantes . . . Marguerite, André viennent souvent à la chasse*'; for this and other unpublished letters to Deudon, see *http://deudon.charles.free.art.htm*, nos. 1, 2.
16 Blanche 1949, p. 152.
17 Undated letter from Renoir to Madame Charpentier; Florisoone 1938, p. 37; the place names have been corrected with the aid of Robert McDonald Parker and Claude Féron.
18 The visit was made in May 2006, and followed upon an earlier field trip undertaken in the company of Claude Féron. Robert McDonald Parker and I are indebted to the kindness and expertise of these local historians.

44 Wheatfield, 1879

Oil on canvas
50.5 × 61 cm; 19⅞ × 24 in.
Carmen Thyssen-Bornemisza Collection, on loan to the Museo Thyssen-Bornemisza, Madrid (CTB. 1961.11)

PROVENANCE:
Possibly sold by Renoir to Durand-Ruel on 6 January 1881 for 300 francs; Paul Rosenberg and Co., New York; Stanley N. Barbee, Los Angeles; Thyssen-Bornemisza Collection, Lugano, by 1961

LITERATURE:
Whitfield 1990, p. 56; Pickvance in Llorens and Llombart 2002, p. 122; Kahn in Arnaldo 2004, II, pp. 36–7

Considerably smaller in scale than *Landscape at Wargemont* (cat. 43), but no less accomplished, *Wheatfield* was doubtless painted around the same time, when Renoir was a summer guest at the Berard's Norman estate.[1] As has been noted, both canvases share the same slightly acidic palette, white priming and translucency of paint, and are linked in visual, as well as technical, ways.[2] Renoir's view of a ripe wheatfield bordered by trees and gently rolling hills in the distance is captured as if from a passing window. The quality of instantaneity is such that we feel as if the scene has just entered our field of vision (and may soon be leaving it). For all his simplicity of means, in this seemingly 'uncomposed' vista Renoir creates a landscape of considerable depth and complexity, in which each formal element – field, trees, hills and sky – is perfectly individuated.

Most audacious is Renoir's handling of the frieze of wheat in the foreground, flecked with hatches of olive green, alizarin and yellow, and rendered in sharper focus than any other motif in the landscape (one can almost sense the wind rustling). As the golden field extends in the distance, Renoir's touch becomes softer and more generalised, and he establishes the rolling topography of the terrain with absolute assurance. The edge of the wheatfield is indicated by a few strokes of emerald green – a band of grass demarcating the transition to fallow land in the madder hills in the distance. Renoir's treatment of the sky in no less a *tour de force*. As Pickvance has noted, the touches of white, purple, yellow and green convey 'the distinctive light of a slightly overcast sky that speaks of the Channel coast'.[3] The dynamism of Renoir's handling throughout is all the more striking since it is at the service of a subject-less composition: this is the purest of landscapes, pared of any signifier, human or geographical.[4] If it is harvest season, Renoir pays no heed, and his earlier *The Harvesters* (cat. 16) is positively anecdotal by comparison. Yet this depiction of a rolling wheatfield, with scrubby trees and undemonstrative hills, has a lingering stillness and mystery. It is a landscape in which Degas's jockeys, on one of their eerie, meandering promenades, would have felt perfectly at home.

Renoir's resolute signature in blue, at lower right, reminds us that for all its brevity and sketchiness, *Wheatfield* was a finished composition, ready for sale and exhibition (neither of which was immediately forthcoming). Although the early provenance of this painting remains to be established, it seems likely that *Wheatfield* was part of the first group of canvases that Renoir sold to Durand-Ruel when the dealer started to back the Impressionists again in 1881. Among the nine paintings acquired by Durand-Ruel directly from the artist in January 1881 is a group of landscapes that can be related to those made at Wargemont eighteen months earlier. The *Wheatfield* might well be associated with the '*Champs de blé*' for which Durand-Ruel paid 300 francs and passed directly to Jules Féder, one of the directors of the Union générale bank (and his principal business associate at the time).[5] Féder's possession of the '*Champs de blé*' was short-lived, and the landscape returned to Durand-Ruel's stock soon thereafter.[6] Durand-Ruel may have included the picture – or a Normandy landscape like it – as an addition to the 25 Renoirs he lent to the seventh Impressionist exhibition in March 1882. Although not listed as such in the catalogue, an intriguing reference from Charles Flor in *Le National* to the variety of Renoirs on display suggests that the artist's time at Wargemont was commemorated

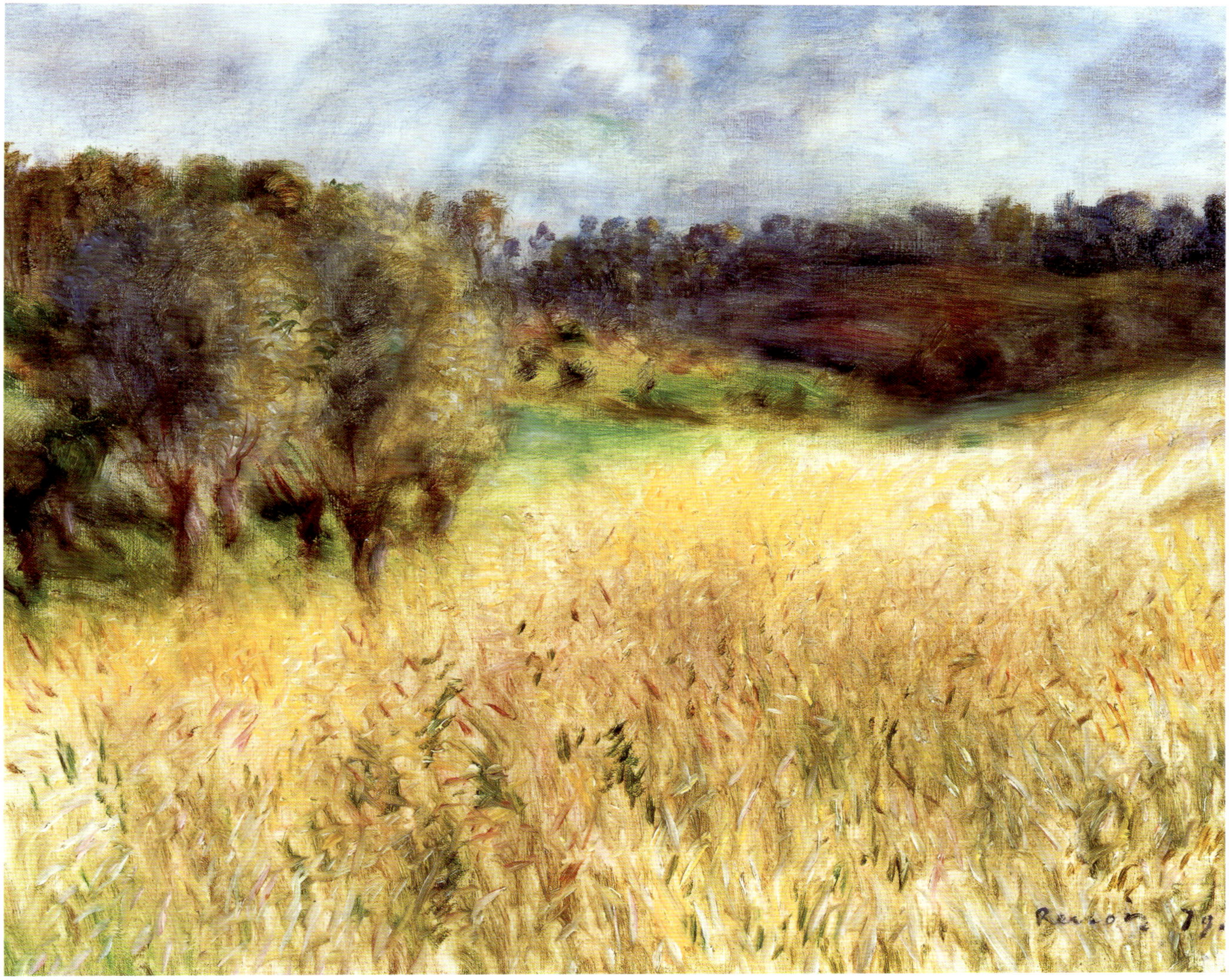

in at least one work: 'As a true artist, he is open to all of nature . . . with the same passion he shows us a view of Venice, a bouquet of geraniums, a group of rowers lunching at Bougival, the head of a woman, a garden in Algiers and an orchard in Normandy [*un verger normand*]'.[7] Might the critic have been thinking of the group of trees at lower left in *Wheatfield*?

CBB

1 See the references given under cat. 43; *pace* Pickvance (in Llorens and Llombart 2002, p. 122), the landscape cannot be documented precisely to July 1879, although it may well have been painted during that month.
2 Kahn in Arnaldo 2004, II, pp. 36–7.
3 Pickvance in Llorens and Llombart 2002, p. 122.
4 An insight culled from John House on Monet's *Wheatfield* of 1881 in the Cleveland Museum of Art; see House 2004, pp. 163–4. Unlike the so-called *Vintagers* (*The Mussel Harvest*; cat. 46) and *View of the Coast Near Wargemont* (cat. 52), which share certain architectural markers, *Wheatfield* is devoid of any identifiable topographical detail, although John Zarobell has suggested to me that the field might be the same as the one shown in the foreground of *View of the Coast Near Wargemont*, and as such locatable to the same coastal hamlet. However, like *Landscape at Wargemont*, *Wheatfield* would seem to portray a site further inland, in the vicinity of the Berard brothers' sprawling estates.
5 Archives Durand-Ruel, Stockbook, 6 January 1881, no. 726, '*Champs de blé*', 300 francs, to Féder. On Féder, whose financial backing of Durand-Ruel was over within two years, see Distel 1990, pp. 24–6.
6 Archives Durand-Ruel, 19 January 1883, no. 2733, '*Dans les blés*', bought from Féder (no. price given).
7 Berson 1996, I, p. 388; II, p. 283, HC 43, listing Renoir's *Verger normand* as one of the works shown *hors catalogue* at the seventh Impressionist exhibition.

45 The Wave, 1879

Oil on canvas
64.8 × 99.2 cm; 25 × 39 in.
The Art Institute of Chicago, Illinois. Mr and Mrs Potter Palmer Collection (1922-438)

'I was often present when Renoir painted in Normandy, in the region around Pourville, Berneval and the château de Wargemont, where he was Paul Berard's guest. Portraits, seascapes, geraniums, fruits, summer landscapes: I frequently observed him at work, "knitting" them with his sable brushes and plaster-white canvases.'[1] Jacques-Emile Blanche (1861–1942) was seventeen when he and Renoir first met, and in his reminiscences 40 years later he rightly accorded Renoir's seascapes – or 'coastscapes', as they have recently been called[2] – a place second only to portraiture in the body of work produced in Normandy. Both in terms of handling and composition, the small group of seascapes made in Normandy between 1879 and 1882 rank among Renoir's most audacious and experimental Impressionist landscapes (see also cat. 51).

The Wave, a signed and dated picture, is the largest of the group: a size 40, it is comparable in scale and achievement to *Landscape at Wargemont* (cat. 43).[3] The most Turneresque of all Renoir's landscapes, it is at first glance almost abstract in its composition, with its delicate lavender tonalities punctuated by bursts of white and cobalt. To use another anachronism, it is also Renoir's first 'action painting', with the blues and whites of the lower left hand quadrant applied wet on wet and blended on the canvas itself. In fact, as John House has noted of another work in this group, Renoir's 'highly informal and seemingly improvisatory' manner of painting creates a fully realised view of waves crashing on to the shore, on a turbulent, stormy sea. To

PROVENANCE:
Sold by Durand-Ruel to Berthe Honoré Palmer (1849–1918) on 14 December 1882 for $1,250; bequeathed to the Art Institute of Chicago in 1922

LITERATURE:
Maxon 1973, no. 27; Brettell and Schaefer 1984, pp. 288–9; Clarke and Thomson 2003, p. 165; Wilson-Bareau and Deneger 2003, pp. 243–7

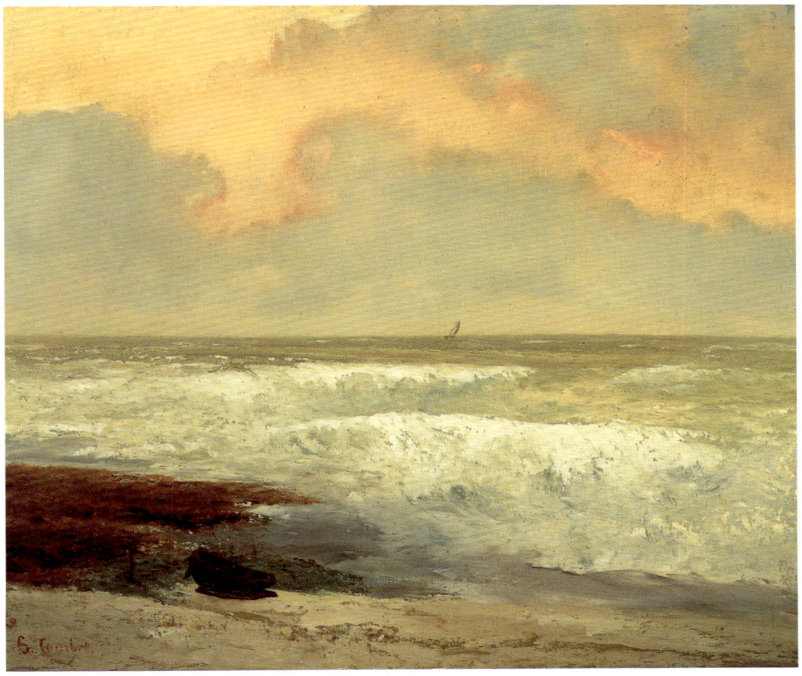

FIG. 98 Gustave Courbet (1819–1877), *Seascape*, 1869. Oil on canvas, 50.8 × 61 cm; 20 × 24 in. Private collection.

paraphrase House again, Renoir translates 'natural effects into paint' – here the violence and motion of sea and sky – 'quite without recourse to detailed illusionism', although in this instance the volume and weightiness of the foamy, rolling waves and the agitation of the tempestuous sky are constructed with care and conviction.[4] Renoir literally recreates in paint the bursts of foam that issue from the waves as they crash on to the shore; his touch changes altogether in the depiction of the rainy sky, which is more delicately and thinly painted. Only the triangular patch of beach at lower right and the microscopic purple sails on the horizon remind us that this elemental view was no doubt made in the environs of the holiday resort of Berneval.

Anticipating Monet's 'coastscapes' by two years, Renoir's *Wave* looked to realist painting and Japanese art as its models.[5] All recent commentators have made reference to Courbet's seascapes of the late 1860s, a particularly fine example of which (fig. 98) was included in Durand-Ruel's large survey of 'modern masters' held in his galleries in 1878 (which Renoir surely visited).[6] And although Vollard recalled Renoir dismissing Japanese prints in no uncertain terms, in the 1870s at least he had been sufficiently interested in them to engage in conversations on the subject with no less a connoisseur than Philippe Burty.[7] Hokusai's *Great Wave* from the series *Thirty-six views of Mount Fuji* stands as an *ukiyo-e* godfather to Renoir's entire series.[8]

It is Renoir's seamless integration of such sources in the service of a poetic naturalism that is so impressive here. More than anything else, *The Wave* conveys the sensation of sheer visual and emotional splendour inspired by the sight of the ocean, and it was probably on this summer visit to Wargemont that Renoir encountered the sea for the first time in over a decade.[9] In an undated letter to Aline, written during one of his Norman sojourns, Renoir recalled that he had learned to swim as a child in Paris, in an establishment where he progressed from jumping into the '*petit bain*' to swimming under the eye of the '*maître nageur*' himself.[10] In confronting the ocean, albeit the stretch of the Channel beloved by French and English holidaymakers alike, Renoir responded in appropriately ecstatic terms. In this he was not unlike a younger literary colleague, who, like him, also documented the pleasures of suburban recreation in Chatou.[11] As the setting for his first novel, the Normandy coast would inspire in Maupassant the same sense of awe as it seems to have evoked in Renoir. 'How terrible and beautiful the Ocean is', exclaims the aristocratic father of the heroine of *Une Vie*. 'The Mediterranean is like . . . the blue water of a pail of washing by comparison. Just look at how terrifying the Ocean is, with its crests of foam.'[12] CBB

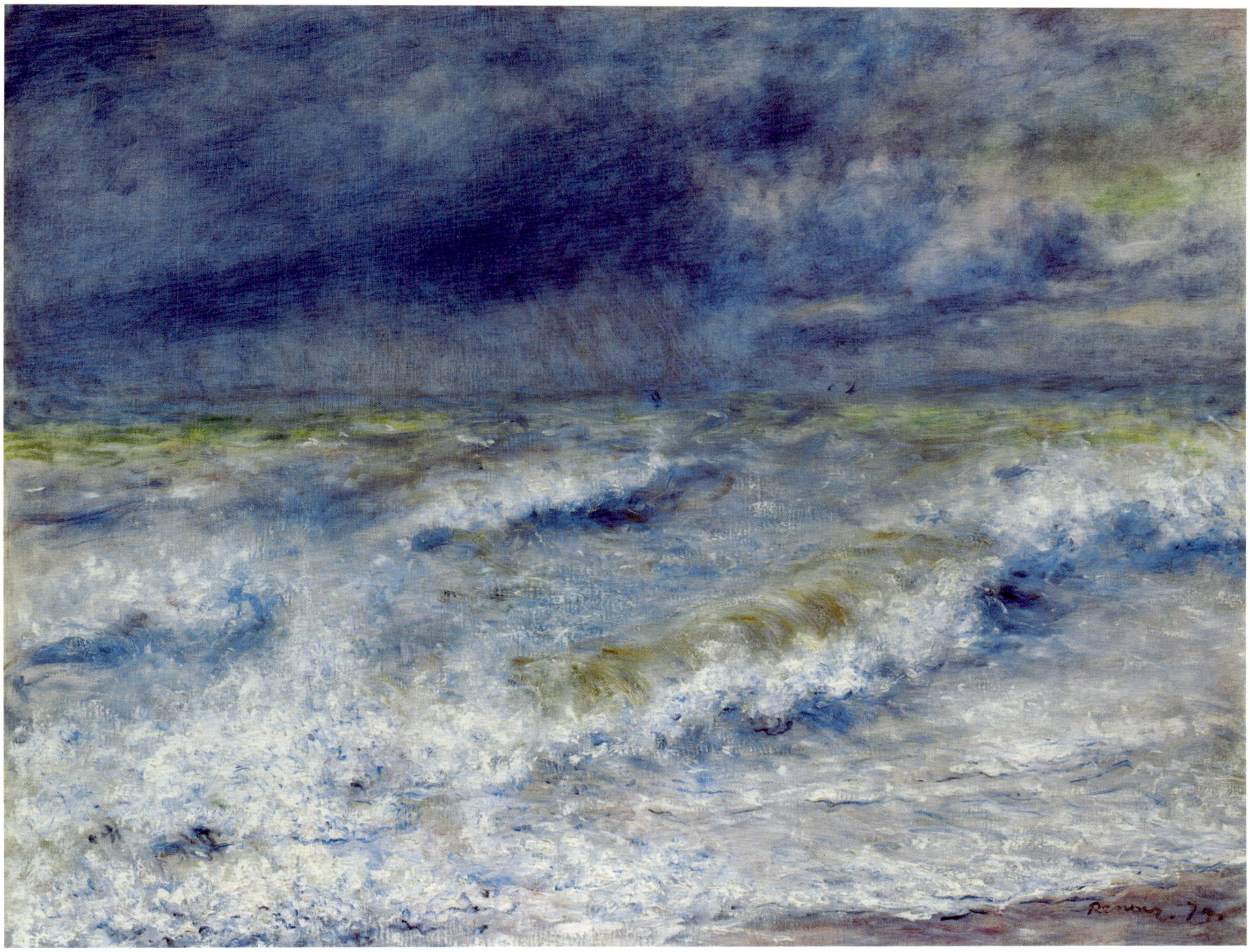

1 Blanche 1921, p. 35.
2 Stuckey 1995, pp. 204–5, a neologism of which neither Renoir nor Blanche would have approved.
3 It has not been possible to ascertain when (and for how much) Durand-Ruel acquired his painting. It is first recorded as no. 1011, selling from the New York branch on 14 December 1892, for $1,250 (information from Archives Durand-Ruel, in the curatorial files of The Art Institute of Chicago). I am most grateful to Paul Durand-Ruel for his timely assistance.
4 House 1995, pp. 76–7.
5 Stuckey 1995, pp. 204–5. Renoir's innovation in this work must modify the argument that his landscapes were a 'kind of weather vane indicating his relationships to those artists in his sphere'; see Rishel in Wilson-Bareau and Deneger 2003, p. 244.
6 *Exposition retrospective de Tableaux et Dessins de Maîtres modernes*, Galeries Durand-Ruel, Paris, 1878, no. 45, *Marine*; Fernier 1978, II, no. 702. My thanks to Sarah Faunce for her assistance.
7 'Japanese prints are very interesting, as Japanese prints – in other words, as long as they stay in Japan'; quoted in Howard 1991, p. 216. In April 1874, Renoir, in the middle of hanging the first Impressionist exhibition, had regretted missing Burty, but looked forward to seeing him the following week: '*ce sera toujours une occasion de vous dire bonjour et de bavarder un peu de Japonisme*'; Musée du Louvre, Fonds Henraux, Ms 310 (3).
8 Brettell and Schaefer 1984, p. 290.
9 In August 1866, Renoir (and briefly, Sisley) had spent a fortnight at Berck, a seaside resort on the Atlantic coast, staying with the Le Coeurs on a family holiday; see Le Coeur 1996, p. 26.
10 Renoir to Aline, from Dieppe, undated; *Pierre Auguste Renoir, 1841–1919, Personal Artefacts and Archives Collection*, Hantman's, 14 May 2005, lot 19.
11 Catinat 1952.
12 Guy de Maupassant, *Une Vie* (1883), Paris 1993, p. 105. '*Le baron, s'exultant devant l'Océan, murmura: C'est terrible et beau . . . La Méditerranée! . . . l'eau bleue d'un baquet de lessive. Regarde donc celle-ci comme elle est effrayante avec ses crêtes d'écume!*'

46 The Mussel Harvest, 1879

Formerly known as *The Vintagers*
Oil on canvas
54.2 × 65.4 cm; 21⅓ × 25¾ in.
National Gallery of Art, Washington, DC. Gift of Margaret Seligman Lewisohn in memory of her husband, Sam A. Lewisohn (1954.8.1)

Known as *The Vintagers* since it was first exhibited in May 1914,[1] and always published as such thereafter,[2] Renoir's delicately painted landscape actually shows a harvest of a different sort. It was entitled simply *Moisson* (Harvest) when acquired by Durand-Ruel from the artist in January 1881,[3] and a later entry in the dealer's stockbook identified the site as Berneval, a coastal village divided into Berneval-le-Grand and Berneval-le-Petit, just to the north of Berard's estate.[4]

The Mussel Harvest's thin, silken handling, overall luminosity and lime-purple tonalities are characteristic of the landscapes that Renoir painted at Wargemont in the summer of 1879 – an immensely productive summer, during which he embarked upon as many as 30 works.[5] With more picturesque detail than either *Landscape at Wargemont* (cat. 43) or *Wheatfield* (cat. 44), this view also strives to render the effect of the sea breeze coursing through the grassy terrain. The cluster of habitations at right are shielded by a group of trees whose branches sway in the wind.

With something of a *japonisant* bird's-eye view, we look down upon a group of fishermen (and a lone fisherwoman) who make their way up the narrow path from the beach below. The men, in red trousers, shoulder heavy baskets on their backs; the woman, in a white cap, carries a basket in each hand. They are headed for the low-roofed dwelling in the background at left, at the entrance of which they deposit the baskets' contents. The right-hand quadrant of the canvas shows a lush green field through which a serpentine path leads the eye to a low-lying cluster of buildings – a white-roofed house with a single chimney, and behind it a church of which the roof and steeple are just visible between the trees.

These architectural details allow us to identify the site as the one portrayed from a different

PROVENANCE:
Acquired from the artist by Durand-Ruel as "*Moisson*" in January 1881 for 300 francs; Galerie Levesque et Cie by 1914 (?); Adolph Lewisohn (1849–1938), New York, by 1921; Sam Adolph Lewisohn (1884–1951), New York; by inheritance to his wife, née Margaret Seligman, New York; bequeathed to the National Gallery of Art in 1954

LITERATURE:
Drucker 1944, pp. 53–4; Néret 2001, p. 122

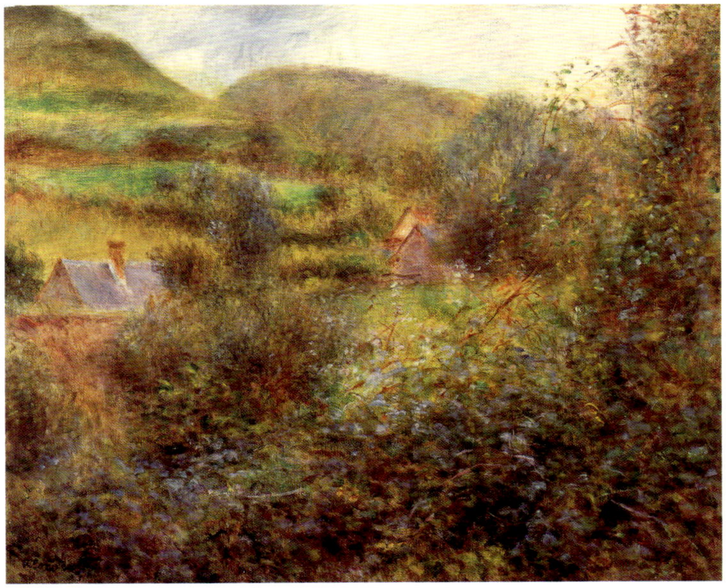

FIG. 99 '*Environs of Pourville*', 1879. Oil on canvas, 46 × 55.9 cm; 18½ × 22 in. Barnes Foundation, Merion, Pennsylvania (BF6).

FIG. 100 *Studies for Musselfishers at Berneval*, about 1880. Pen and ink. Whereabouts unknown.

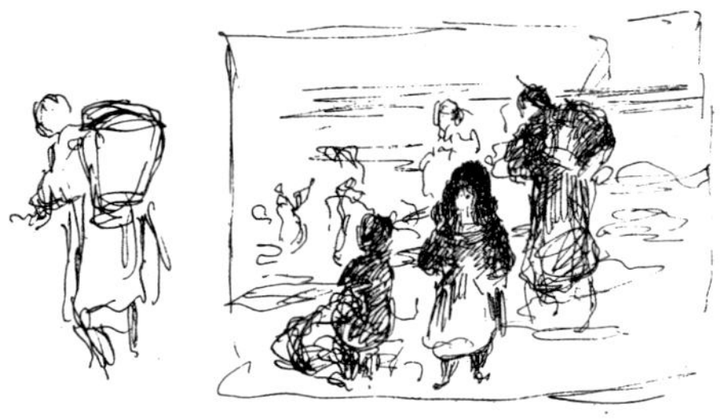

angle the following year in *View of the Coast Near Wargemont* (cat. 52), confirming the coastal location of *The Mussel Harvest*, in which the sea itself is nowhere visible. Comparing the two, it would appear that Renoir's musselfishers are shown ascending the path that leads from the beach to the house, with the church on their right. This same path can be seen cutting through the cliffs at right in the middle ground of *View of the Coast Near Wargemont*. Furthermore, as John Zarobell has indicated to me, the hills in the background of the *Mussel Harvest* are very similar to those in the so-called '*Environs of Pourville*' (fig. 99), signed and dated 1879, in which the same cluster of buildings can be seen through a frieze of bushes and trees.[6] All three canvases are thus of the same remote coastal hamlet, possibly on the outskirts of Berneval itself, which Oscar Wilde described as 'a tiny place consisting of a hotel and about twenty chalets'.[7] In *The Mussel Harvest* Renoir stands with his back to the sea, taking the view inland, probably to the south-west.

The barrel-like baskets, shown larva-like on the ascending figures' backs, are the key to the subject of Renoir's landscape. They confirm that the crop that is being harvested is not grapes, but mussels: the 'poor man's oyster' was an economic staple of the Normandy coast.[8] Throughout the summer of 1879 Renoir was engaged upon a large genre painting of *Musselfishers at Berneval* (see fig. 44, p. 63), which he exhibited at the Salon the following year. Numerous drawings of young women and children – the former carrying large wicker basket on their backs (fig. 100) – attest to his interest in the subject.[9] Upon close inspection of *The Mussel Harvest* it is clear that the fishermen carry heavy loads, and indeed Renoir's visit coincided with the height of the season, when the cultivation and harvesting of mussels were at their most intense. Renoir's canvas shows the final stage of the farming of stake-cultured mussels, when the shellfish – having been removed from the *bouchots* on which they are reared for at least a year – are harvested for immediate delivery to the fishmonger. Unlike oysters, it was noted that 'the low cost of mussels allows them to be consumed by the poorest sector of the inland population'.[10] Indeed, so thriving was the commerce of mussel fishing during the 1870s that demand in Paris could only be met by importing quantities of this shellfish from Antwerp.[11] CBB

1 *Exposition d'art français du XIXe siècle*, Royal Museum, Copenhagen, May–June 1914, no. 175, '*Vingaardsmaend – Les Vignerons*'.
2 See the complete bibliographic listing in Jane Becker's draft entry on this picture for the National Gallery of Art's systematic catalogue; I am very happy to acknowledge the generosity of the Department of Curatorial Records at the National Gallery of Art, which provided access to the unpublished entries on all the works lent to the present exhibition.
3 Archives Durand-Ruel, Journal 1881, 6 January 1881: no. 730, '*Moisson*', 300 francs.
4 Archives Durand-Ruel, 11 August 1888, no. 1721, '*Berneval*' (previously no. 730). Since Durand-Ruel had rented a summer house outside Dieppe in the summer of 1882, his designation of the site carries some weight. Blanche (1937, p. 36) recalled that the Berards owned part of the Berneval shore.
5 Berard 1956: as noted by Paul Berard's great-nephew, '*Renoir fit à Wargemont quelques-uns de ses plus beaux portraits et de ses plus subtils paysages.*'
6 Barnes and De Mazia 1935, pp. 256 (plate 80), 449. With John House and Martha Lucy, in March 2006 John Zarobell examined this landscape and established the date as 1879 (and not 1878 as had been previously published), thus confirming its association with Renoir's summer landscapes of that year. I am most grateful to John Zarobell for his timely assistance with this entry.
7 See my essay in this catalogue, p. 79, note 85.
8 Larousse 1865–90, XI, p. 630.
9 Baudot 1949, pp. 74–5; Bailey 1997, pp. 168–9.
10 Larousse 1865–90, XI, p. 630.
11 *Encyclopaedia Britannica*, 11th edn, 29 vols., Cambridge and New York 1910–11, XIX, p. 94.

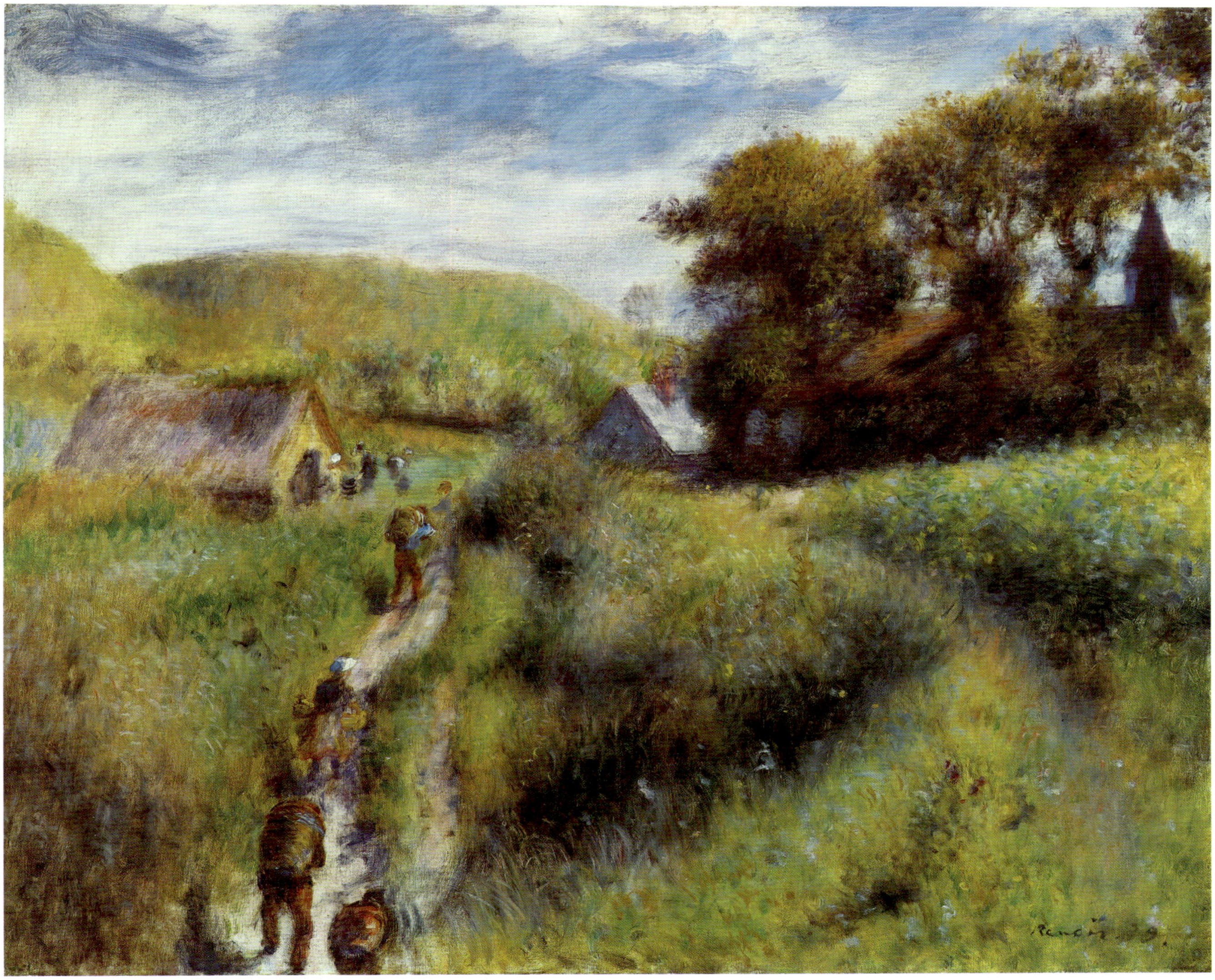

47 Cliffs at Berneval, 1879

Also known as *Cliffs at Pourville*
Oil on canvas
54 × 65 cm; 21¼ × 25⅝ in.
Private collection, courtesy of Nathan Fine Art Berlin/Zürich

PROVENANCE:
Victor Chocquet, Paris; Chocquet auction, Galerie Georges Petit, Paris, 1 July 1899, lot 92; Galerie Durand-Ruel, Paris; Hugo Nathan, Frankfurt am Main; Dr Fritz Nathan, St Gallen; private collection, Zurich

LITERATURE:
Drucker 1944, pp. 53, 201; Gaunt 1952, no. 46; Fezzi 1972, no. 359; Gaunt and Adler 1982, pp. 17f, ill. 5; Adriani 1996, no. 55

Renoir visited the diplomat and banker Paul Berard and his family at their château de Wargemont, near Dieppe in Normandy, for the first time in summer 1879, staying for some two months. He painted prolifically while there, including portraits, floral decorations and landscapes. These last, including the present work, tend to be subtle in colour and executed in particularly thin washes of paint. Renoir was seeking to capture the principal elements of the landscape as quickly and as simply as possible, without emphasis on detail. It is an impression of nature, abbreviated, generalised and given an overall muted tonal unity. The example of Whistler, who had painted tonal seascapes at Trouville in 1865, may have been on his mind.[1] Renoir found his motif in the chalk cliffs that tower above the beach and sea along the Norman coast.[2] He delighted in the juxtaposition of near and far the site provides, and in the vertiginous thrill of the plunge into deep space that occurs as one gazes warily over the edge. The German Romantic painter Caspar David Friedrich had often exploited such sublime effects in his cliff top and mountain scenes earlier in the century, although it is unlikely that Renoir had ever seen an example of his work. Besides, French travel literature and imagery would have provided examples enough of such picturesque motifs, and indeed had prepared the way for the growing tourist popularity of such coastal vistas. Here, the line of cliffs ripples down the right side of the canvas like a curtain caught in a sudden breeze. The Rococo flourish of that intensely graphic line – Renoir could not resist such decorative effects – contrasts with the calm, broad sea and sky dominating much of the rest of the canvas. Far below, a curving line of frothy waves meets the shore, where a few tiny figures stroll. In the foreground, a young man is seated in the grass gazing out across the water, enjoying the view rather than marvelling at nature's awesome grandeur, one suspects, his jaunty straw boater effectively undermining any hint of *terribilità* in the scene. Noting that Renoir was giving painting lessons that summer to young Jacques-Emile Blanche, Götz Adriani has speculated that the youth is Blanche himself, 18 years old in 1879, the painting an object lesson in landscape composition for the lad's instruction.[3] The suggestion may help to explain the hint of performance in the painting; it is a self-consciously bravura display of painting skill, quick, confident, controlled – and ravishingly pretty. CR

Shown in London only

1 Adriani 1996, p. 193, no. 55, has made this suggestion.
2 This work is traditionally titled *Cliffs at Pourville*, but Robert McDonald Parker believes that this is a view of cliffs at Berneval. See further in this catalogue pp. 276.
3 *Ibidem*, p. 192, no. 54.

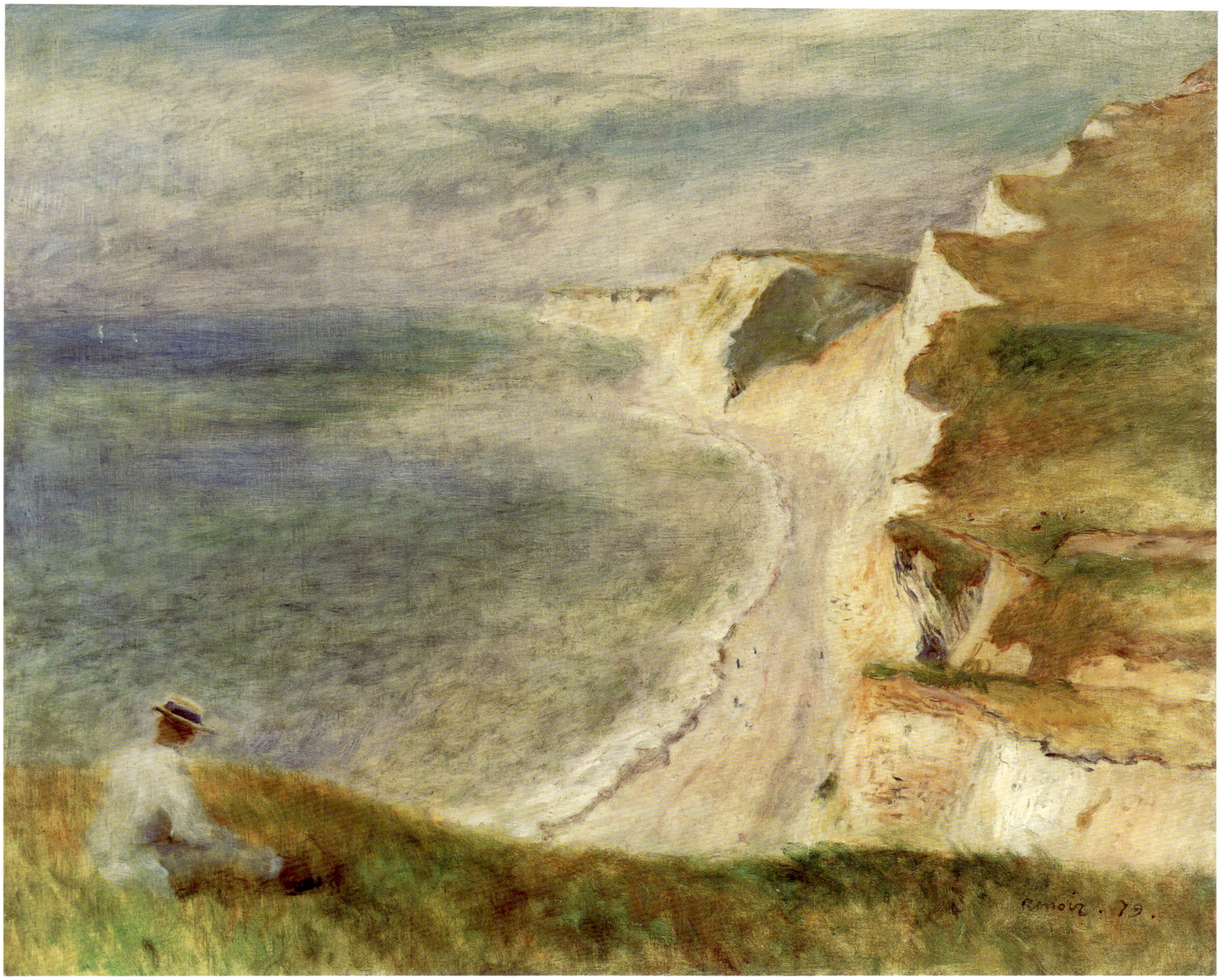
Renoir . 79.

48 Woman at the Seaside, Seascape, 1879–80

Oil on canvas
50.5 × 61.5 cm; 19 5/8 × 24 in.
Kunsthaus, Zurich (2634)

PROVENANCE:
Theodor Fischer, Lucerne; acquired by the Kunsthaus in 1943

LITERATURE:
Vollard 1918; Adriani 1996

The painting is not dated and has been ascribed both to 1879, the summer of Renoir's first visit to the Berard family in Normandy, and to 1880, the year of his second visit. It relates closely, however, to *Cliffs at Berneval* of 1879 (cat. 47) in style, technique and coastal motif, and this suggests that it is more likely to have been painted as part of the landscape campaign that first summer. The fluid application of paint, especially in the water where blue and green tones interweave, recalls not only *Cliffs at Berneval* but a third painting executed when Renoir was staying with the Berards in 1879, *Landscape at Wargemont* (cat. 43). There, swirls of thin, watercolour-like paint also weave around one another, and the greens of the foreground are similarly mottled. As in *Cliffs at Berneval*, the forms in the present work are simplified and pictorial incident is reduced to strong and simple contrasts, in this case between greensward, sea and sky arranged in three parallel, horizontally disposed bands across the picture plane. In both pictures, a solitary figure, in this case a woman, gazes out to sea, where tiny sailing boats pick up the breeze. The woman is surely sitting on a cliff-top high above the water. The artist, facing out to sea directly rather than looking obliquely along the coastline as in *Cliffs at Berneval*, does not see the chalk face of the cliffs, nor does he take in the sandy shore far below. Along this part of the Norman coast grass does not grow right to the water's edge. The transition between cliff-top grass and the sea beyond is abrupt and schematic, but it is the same contrast of near and far that Renoir explored in *Cliffs at Berneval*. The present canvas is an even more abbreviated and succinct image, a further step in the simplification of painting Renoir was exploring in landscape at this time but on which he would not linger long. CR

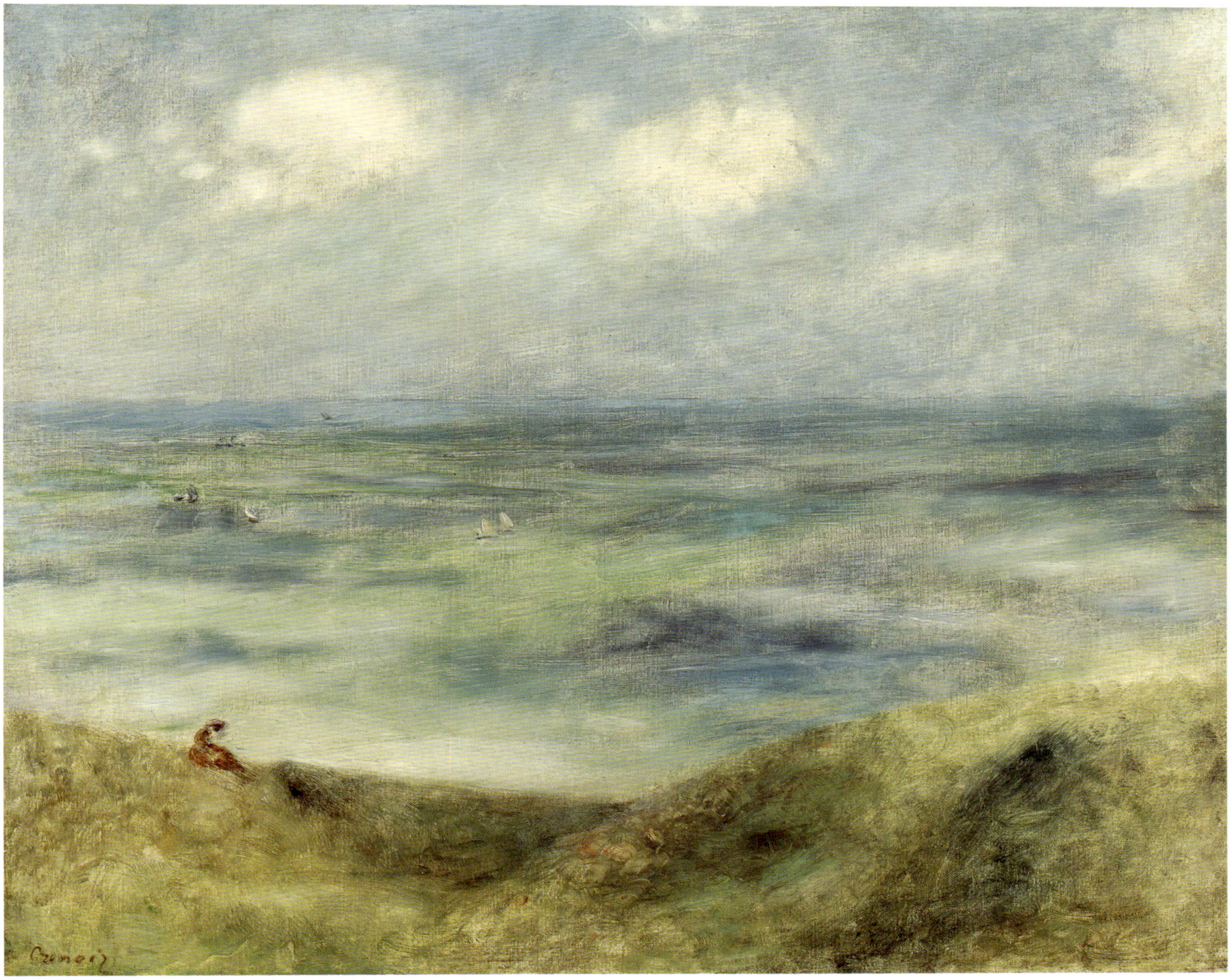

49 By the Water, 1879–80

Formerly known as *Near the Lake*
Oil on canvas
47.5 × 56.3 cm; 18 1/8 × 21 3/8 in.
The Art Institute of Chicago, Illinois. Mr and Mrs Potter Palmer Collection (1922.439)

PROVENANCE:
Bought from the artist by Durand-Ruel before 1887; Durand-Ruel, New York, by 1888 (no. 141); sold to Berthe Honoré Palmer, 2 March 1892; Potter Palmer Collection, Chicago; bequest to the Art Institute, 1922

LITERATURE:
The Art Institute of Chicago 1961, p. 396; Daulte 1971, no. 306; The Art Institute of Chicago 1973, no. 29; Rathbone 1996, no. 50; Druick 1997, pp. 47–8

Though the painting has been titled *Near the Lake*, this image of a couple in conversation on a terrace overlooking the water seems to depict a terrace like that of the setting for *Luncheon at La Fournaise* (cat. 34) and *Luncheon of the Boating Party* of 1880–1 (fig. 89, p. 170). A photograph of the proprietors of the Restaurant Fournaise taken in 1893 (fig. 101) shows the same terrace that is featured in the painting, with a balcony and roof trellis covered in vines.[1] Further, the figure on the right of the photograph, Jules-Alphonse Fournaise, strongly resembles the male figure on the left edge of the present painting, notably in the jacket and boating hat he wears. So it would seem that the water in the background does not depict a lake, but actually the river Seine at Chatou.

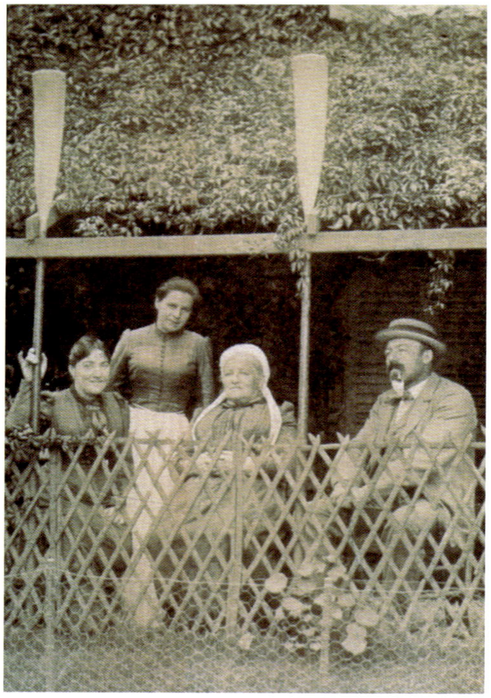

FIG. 101 *Alphonsine Papillon, née Fournaise, with her mother Louise and brother Jules-Alphonse and his wife Josephine Marchand*, 1893. Photograph. Les Amis de la Maison Fournaise, Chatou, gift of Mariette Fiant.

In the painting Renoir has directly interpreted the experience of looking out at a bright world from under a covered porch shielding the viewer from the sun. Unlike the two other terrace pictures mentioned above, the sun does not penetrate the trellis and infuse the figures in the composition. Rather, there is a strong contrast of light and dark, separating this intimate space from the world outside. The effect is achieved through the deployment of distinct tonalities, but also through the addition of a dark horizontal line at the top of the canvas that blocks the view of the sky and the world beyond.

With his usual creativity Renoir here experimented with his technique in order to create a painting unlike his other representations of the Restaurant Fournaise. The figures are rendered in fleshy, thick pigment that is broken into uncharacteristically small brushstrokes. The paint seems to swim across the canvas and only barely to coalesce into recognisable features. The intense chiaroscuro turns away from his more common technique of batheing his figures in light, but Renoir employed an incredible array of colours to achieve this general effect. The result is akin to a kaleidoscopic view of the world in which everything seems broken down into chromatic elements. Further, the strokes of pigment have an irregular character and seem to refer to a subjective apprehension of visual effects – a far cry from Georges Seurat's pointillist style which emerged later in the 1880s. Here, the natural world seems to be depicted as a sensation at once optical and physical. The viewer perceives the work as the embodiment of matter translated through the subjective sensations of a lover of nature. JZ

1 This photograph was unearthed by Colin Bailey. Bailey 1997, p. 305.

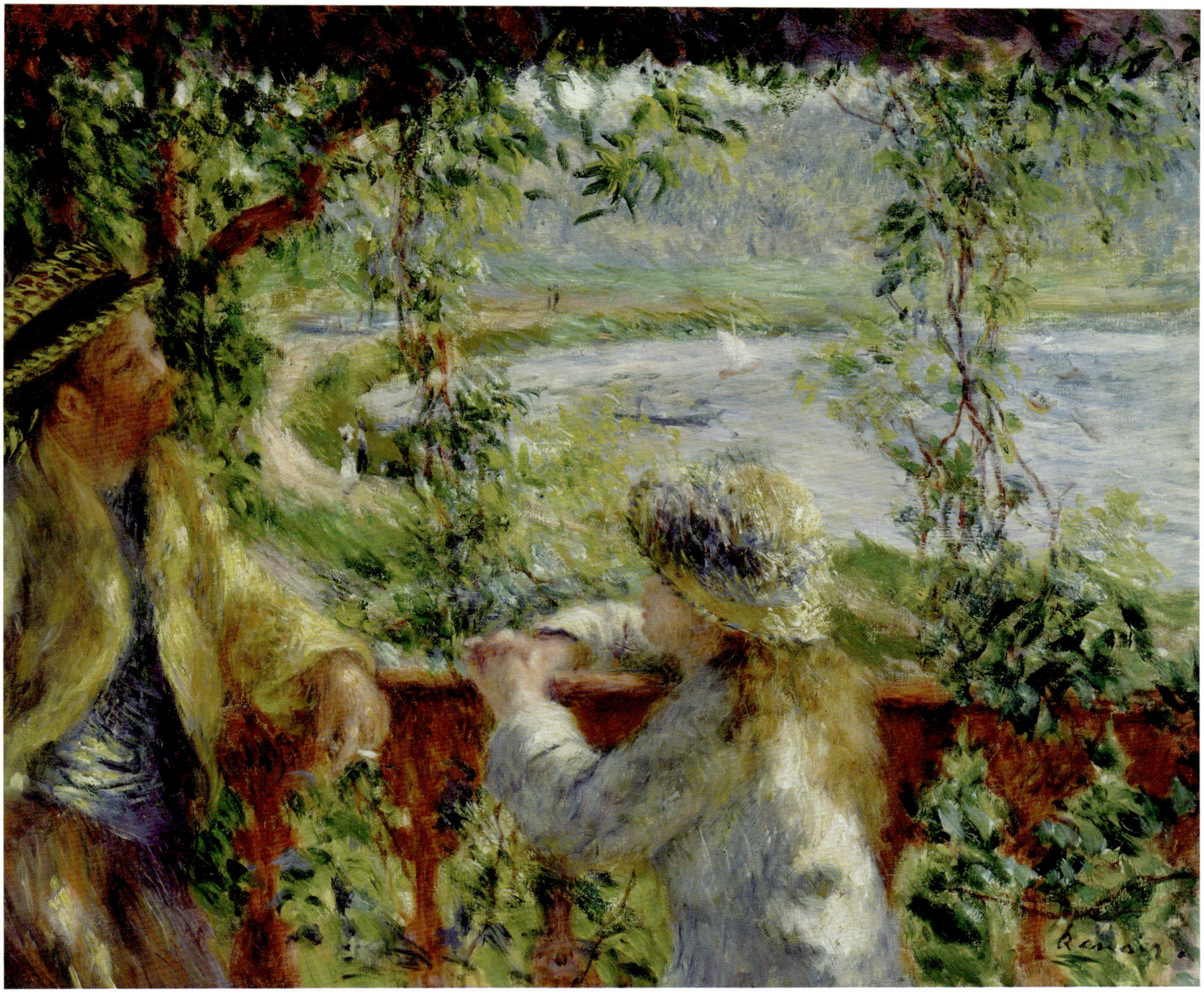

50 Rowers at Chatou, 1880–1

Oil on canvas
81.3 × 100.3 cm; 32 × 39½ in.
National Gallery of Art, Washington, DC. Gift of Sam A. Lewisohn (1951.5.2)

PROVENANCE:
Sold by the artist on 4 October 1911 to Durand-Ruel, Paris, for 10,000 francs; sold by Durand-Ruel on 24 May 1912 to Arthur B. Emmons, New York and Newport, for $18,000; his sale, American Art Association, New York, 14 January 1920, lot 47; purchased jointly by Durand-Ruel and M. Knoedler & Co. for $27,000; sold for the same amount in February 1922 to Adolph Lewisohn (1849–1938), New York; Sam A. Lewisohn (1884–1951), New York; bequeathed by him to the National Gallery of Art in 1951

LITERATURE:
Daulte 1971, no. 307; Brettell and Schaefer 1984, pp. 158–9; Herbert 1988, pp. 252–3; Noël and Hournon 2004, pp. 127–9

On a radiant summer's afternoon, a rower holds his gig steady at the river's edge as an elegantly attired couple – she in close-fitting, fashionable costume, he in more casual wear – approaches the craft. The pleasure gig accommodates only two people, the rower and, on the cushioned seat, a second person, who pilots the boat by manipulating the ropes attached to the rudder; the dainty posture of this demure parisienne suggests that she is the designated companion.[1] Various vessels ply the river. Two single-person skulls are shown at right, one of which is manned by a figure in white, with bare arms. A sailing boat enters the scene from left; and on the far bank a barge moves in stately procession, a small rowing boat moored by the grass to the right. The view is from Chatou looking south-east across the Seine to Reuil-Malmaison, and the white building with its red roof and tree-lined courtyard on the far bank has been identified as the inn of La Mère Franc, established by Emile-Louis Lefranc in 1860 and maintained by his widow until the 1920s.[2]

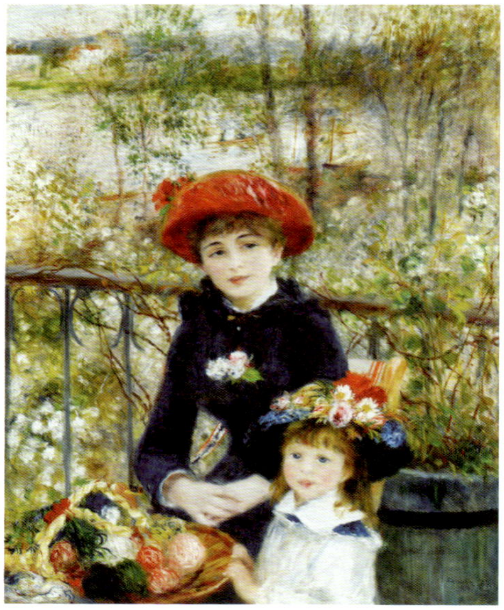

FIG. 102 *Two Sisters* (*On the Terrace*), 1881. Oil on canvas, 110.5 × 81 cm; 43½ × 31⅞ in. The Art Institute of Chicago, Illinois. Mr and Mrs Lewis Larned Coburn Memorial Collection (1933.455).

Renoir's strident palette of orange-reds, blues, whites and purples and his bravura, energetic handling are fiercely experimental. The colours are at times blended directly on the canvas: for example, in the sail at upper left and (more delicately) on the white blazer of the standing man left of centre. How summary, too, is his description of the foreground figure at far left, whose face and arms are left unfinished and whose right hand appears as little more than a claw. As Robert Herbert has aptly noted, eyes accustomed to Matisse's colour are initially less attentive to the brazen hedonism of Renoir's pictorial language, in which saturated oranges and orange-reds convey the effect of full sunlight 'penetrating and influencing all things'.[3]

Widely published, *Rowers at Chatou* (*Canotiers à Chatou*) is generally approached as an iconic Impressionist painting, treating the theme of middle-class leisure in the suburbs, with members of Renoir's immediate entourage (his family and future family) providing the *dramatis personae*.[4] Upon closer inspection, however, very little of what has been published on this picture turns out to be valid. Although this relatively large canvas – a standard size 40 – is signed *A. Renoir.* at lower right, it is not dated (as is routinely stated in the literature).[5] The date of 1879 seems to have appeared for the first time in Durand-Ruel's stockbook in October 1911, when the painting was acquired from Renoir, and presumably reflects the date assigned to the work by the artist (or the dealer) some 30 years after its execution.[6] Since *Rowers at Chatou* remained in Renoir's possession until 1911, it cannot have been among the 25 works that Durand-Ruel contributed – over Renoir's hysterical objections – to the seventh Impressionist exhibition of March 1882. Hence item no. 151 in that exhibition, entitled '*Les Canotiers*' and referred to briefly

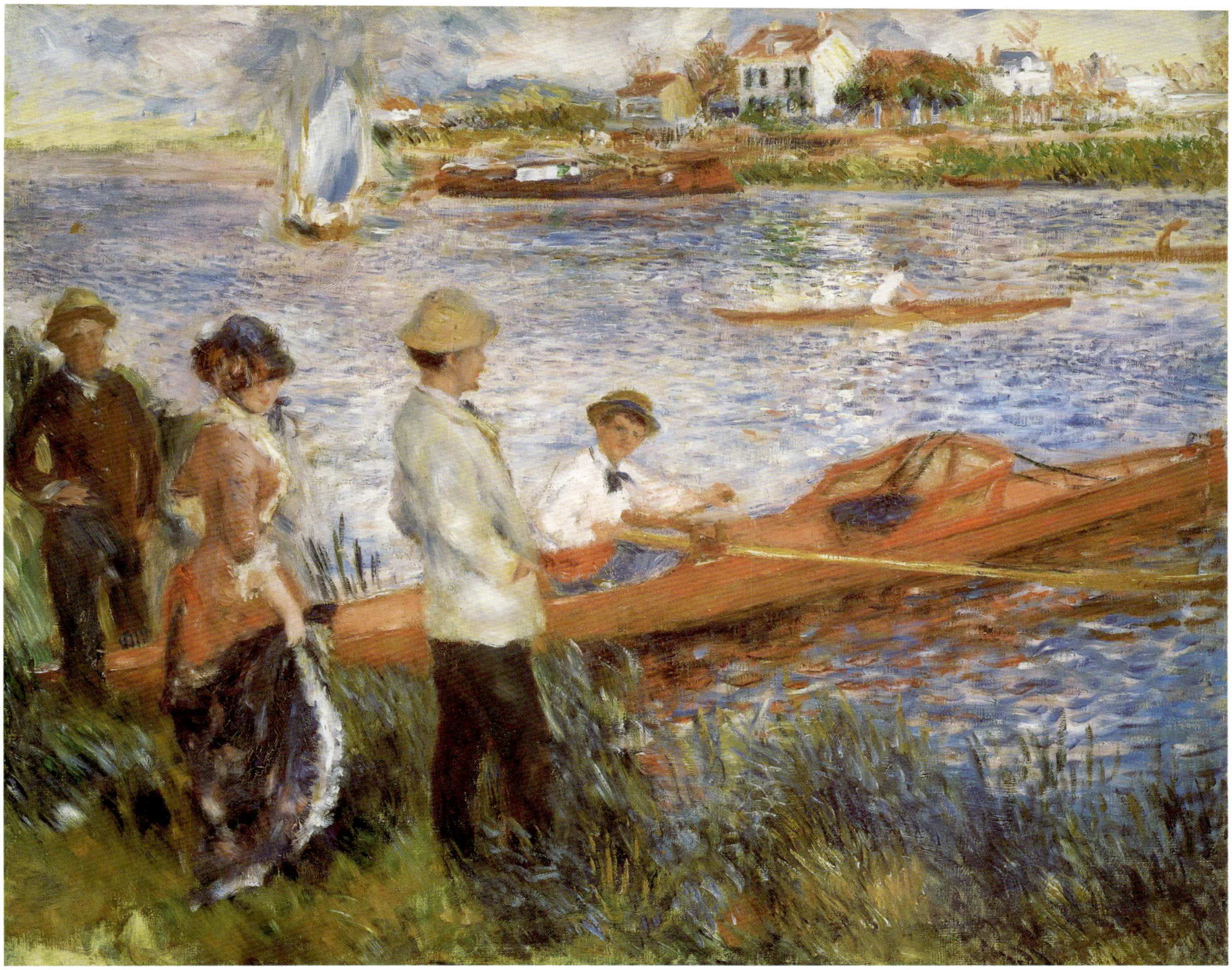

and disparagingly by a single critic,[7] should not be associated with the canvas in Washington.[8] Finally, the concordance of Durand-Ruel's stock and photograph numbers with numbers found on the back of the stretcher of *Rowers at Chatou* confirms with absolute certainty that this picture was not among the Chatou landscapes that Renoir sold to the dealer in July 1881, several of which were exhibited both in the Impressionist exhibition the following year and in Durand-Ruel's mid-career retrospective devoted to Renoir in April 1883 (see further cat. 60).[9]

When exactly was *Rowers at Chatou* painted, and what is its status? The work should surely be reassigned either to the period during which Renoir was immersed in *Luncheon of the Boating Party* (fig. 89, p. 170) – on which he laboured during the late summer and autumn of 1880[10] – or, better still, to the months immediately following his return from Algeria. Renoir is documented in Chatou (intermittently) from mid-April to early July 1881, engaged in a joyful 'struggle' with 'trees in bloom, women and children' and disappointing Duret yet again in postponing his visit to London: 'It is very good weather, and I have my models: that's my only excuse'.[11] Stylistically and in terms of its colour, *Rowers at Chatou* is close to genre paintings such as *Two Sisters* (*On the Terrace*) (fig. 102), signed and dated 1881, and sold to Durand-Ruel on 8 July of that year for the healthy sum of 1,500 francs.[12] By comparison, however, *Rowers at Chatou* is less fully composed, its brushwork at times more savage and its tonalities more dazzling. That Renoir withheld such a work from his dealer – to whom he happily sold landscapes of the region, as well as rowing pictures of a slightly earlier vintage (see cat. 34)[13] – is in keeping with his reluctance to part with his more experimental works, or those he considered to be less fully resolved. In a celebrated letter to Durand-Ruel written in March 1882, Renoir reminded the dealer that he should refrain from showing his most recent work, 'until it has been bottled away for a least a year'.[14] As it would turn out, *Rowers at Chatou* was laid down for the next three decades. CBB

Shown in London and Ottawa only

1 Herbert 1988, p. 252; he also notes that the gig is similar to the one piloted by two women in cat. 33. A related work, *Girl in a Boat*, 1877 (private collection), in which the companion rower is shown holding the ropes, is illustrated and discussed in Rathbone 1996, p. 34.
2 Catinat 1952, p. 39; Noël and Hournon 2004, p. 129.
3 Herbert 1988, p. 253; for Mallarmé's comment from 1876, made in connection with Manet's *Le Linge* (The Barnes Collection, Merion, Pennsylvania), see Moffett 1986, p. 30.
4 Jean Renoir first identified the female figure as Aline Charigot and the man standing next to her as Renoir's brother Edmond in 'My Memories of Renoir', *Life*, May 1952; see also Renoir 1962, p. 193. Daulte (1971, no. 307) identified the standing figure as Gustave Caillebotte, and this is retained in Brettell and Schaefer 1984, p. 158, and Herbert 1988, p. 252. Since these are staffage figures and not portraits, such correlations are somewhat beside the point. Renoir captures the slightly *louche* camaraderie similar to that evoked in the Goncourt brothers' *Manette Salomon*, where Anatole's rowing expeditions at Asnières are attended by '*des passants, des passantes, des camarades des deux sexes, des à peu près peintres, des espèces d'artistes, des femmes vagues dont on ne savait que le petit nom*'; cited in Grégoire 1993, p. 44.
5 I am grateful to Ann Hoeningswald at the National Gallery of Art for confirming this.
6 Archives Durand-Ruel, 4 October 1911, no. 9739, '*Canotiers à Chatou, 1879*'.
7 '*Mais je n'aime pas les canotiers*'; Armand Silvestre, *La Vie moderne*, 11 March 1882, in Berson 1996, I, p. 413.
8 First tentatively proposed in Moffett 1986, p. 395, and again, with greater certainty, in Berson 1996, II, pp. 211, 231.
9 Archives Durand-Ruel, 4 October 1911, stock no. 9739, photograph no. 7141. Both of these numbers reappear, inscribed by hand, on the back of the stretcher, photographs of which are in the conservation records at the National Gallery of Art.
10 Rathbone 1996; as noted in my essay in this catalogue, this painting was sold to Durand-Ruel on 14 February 1881.
11 Renoir to Duret, 18 April 1881; Florisoone 1938, p. 40.
12 Bailey 1997, pp. 186–9.
13 On 6 July 1881, Durand-Ruel purchased '*Les Canotiers*' from Renoir for 400 francs, which painting could possibly be *Luncheon at La Fornaise* in the Art Institute of Chicago (cat. 34), painted six years earlier; Archives Durand-Ruel, Journal, 6 July 1881, no. 1156, '*Les Canotiers*'. The numbering of Durand-Ruel's stock makes it clear that this does not refer to *Rowers at Chatou*.
14 Renoir to Durand-Ruel, Algiers, March 1882; Godfroy 1995, I, p. 35.

51 Harvest at Berneval, 1880

Oil on canvas
50.8 × 61 cm; 20 × 24 in.
Wendy and Leonard Goldberg Collection

In this little known, but well-documented, Norman landscape, Renoir's view is to the north towards the English Channel, taken from a verdant field near the coastline between the bathing villages of Belleville-sur-mer and Berneval – the latter within walking distance from his host's property at Wargemont.[2] Beyond a deep screen of flowers in bloom, three labourers – two men and a woman, each with their heads covered – are depicted in the middle of harvesting. At the centre of the composition, neatly stacked bales of hay gently lead the eye along the field as it rises to the right. In the background, several yachts bob on the blue and white sea, with a somewhat turbulent sky overhead. The site can be fairly well identified as the Val du Prêtre (fig. 103): Renoir reported accurately the way that the coast dips and descends to the sea, and he was equally scrupulous in his placement of the horizon line linking the hills on either side of the valley.[3]

Although *Harvest at Berneval* has generally been assigned to Renoir's first visit to Wargemont in the summer of 1879 (see cats. 43, 45),[4] it has little of the translucent, wash-like surfaces of the landscapes produced during that time.[5] Instead, the paint is applied in more richly impasted accents throughout – bright nodules of colour for the riotous flowers in the foreground and vibrant hatchings for the hay and cut grass in the middle ground (the harvester's smock a dab of pure white). A softer handling is apparent only in the cerulean sea in the distance. As such, *Harvest at Berneval* is closer in technique to *View of the Coast Near Wargemont* (cat. 52), signed and dated 1880 – one of the small number of landscapes produced during Renoir's second summer as Paul Berard's guest, when he spent the month of August at his Norman estate.[6] Of the same format as that landscape – a canvas size 12 – *Harvest at Berneval* is similarly rigorous in its structure of interlocking horizontal and triangular forms. The juxtaposition of these two works in the exhibition will determine whether this slight, but significant, refinement in dating can be sustained. CBB

Shown in London only

PROVENANCE:
Acquired from the artist by Durand-Ruel on 6 January 1881 for 300 francs; listed among Durand-Ruel's stock on 11 August 1888 as '*Paysage, Berneval*'; sold to A.W. Blake, Boston, on 1 January 1890; collection of Mrs F.L. Richardson, Charles River Village, MA; purchased from her by Durand-Ruel, New York, on 28 September 1929, with half share to Knoedler; Durand-Ruel's half share sold to Knoedler & Co., New York, on 12 December 1935;[1] Sir Frederick Hamilton; by descent in his family; Thomas Agnew & Sons Ltd; private collection

LITERATURE:
Fezzi 1985, no. 405

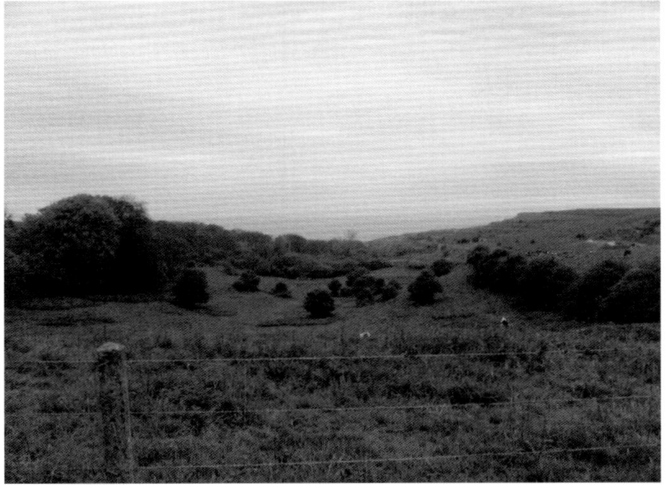

FIG. 103 Present-day view of the Val du Prêtre, Berneval.

1 I am most grateful to Paul-Louis Durand-Ruel for his assistance in compiling the early provenance of this painting.

2 Whereas the Berard family hunted on the land around Wargemont, they headed north (on foot) to Berneval to bathe: as Berard noted to Deudon in September 1877; '*Berneval a tort pour le moment . . . le vent a soufflé depuis quelques temps, de façon à compromettre les bains de mer. Il faudrait voire presence à Wargemont pour ramener à Berneval les promeneurs de la maison*'; see *http://deudon.charles.free.art.htm*, no. 1.

3 This identification was made by Robert McDonald Parker and François Guého in the course of two visits to Berneval in March and May 2006.

4 See Fezzi 1985, no. 405, and the correspondence between the late François Daulte and Alex, Reid & Lefevre Ltd, 28 June 1985.

5 For the differences in Renoir's technique over these two summers, see the entry on *View of the Coast Near Wargemont* in House 1994, p. 84.

6 For most of July 1880 Renoir had been retained in Paris working on commissions brokered by Charles Ephrussi, informing Berard that he wished 'only to finish these portraits as quickly as possible so that I can shake your hand and rest a little in the shades of Wargemont'; letter of mid-July 1880, reproduced in Distel 1989, p. 164. By September Renoir was back in Chatou working on *Luncheon of the Boating Party* (fig. 89, p. 170), the painting of *Rowers* that he had been 'itching to do for a long time'; Berard 1968, p. 54.

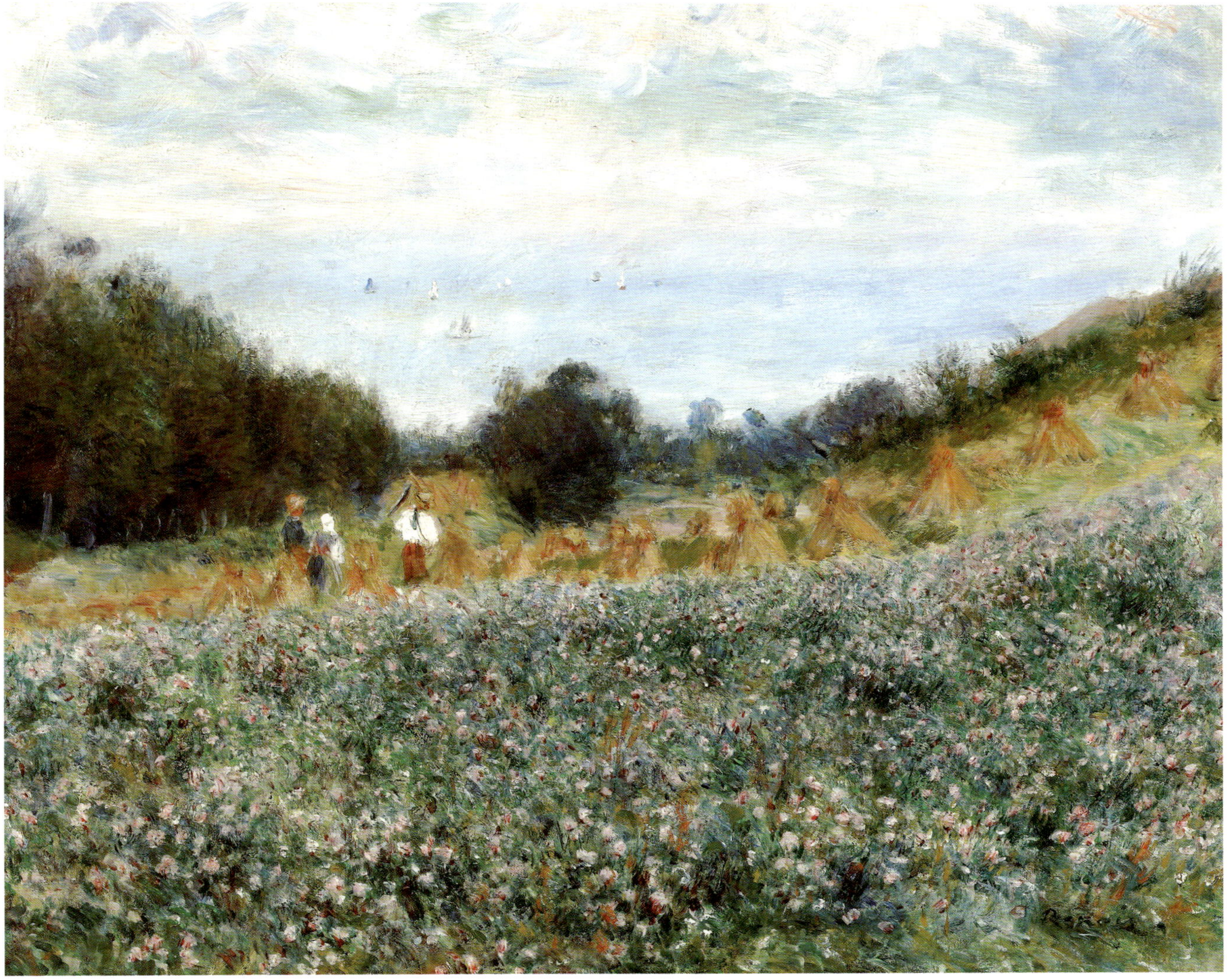

52 View of the Coast Near Wargemont, 1880

Oil on canvas
50.5 × 62.2 cm; 19⅞ × 24½ in.
The Metropolitan Museum of Art, New York. Bequest of Julia W. Emmons, 1956 (56.135.7)

PROVENANCE:
Sold by the artist to Durand-Ruel, 3 December 1890; sold to Durand-Ruel, New York, 7 January 1895; Arthur B. Emmons, Newport and New York, 9 February 1906; bequest of Julia Emmons, 1956

LITERATURE:
Sterling and Salinger 1967, p. 153; Fezzi 1972, no. 420; Bellony-Rewald 1976, pp. 68–9; Moffett 1985, p. 165; House 1994, pp. 21, 84–5; Adriani 1996, pp. 198–9

This coastal landscape, realised while staying at the Berards' villa in Wargemont, Normandy, in the summer of 1880, depicts a cliff-top farmhouse with a view of the sea behind. While staying with the Berards, Renoir took time away from his portraits and decorative paintings to make landscapes outdoors (see the essay in this catalogue by Colin B. Bailey). This work of the summer of 1880 is significantly different from his larger *Landscape at Wargemont* (cat. 43) of the previous year; in *View of the Coast Near Wargemont* the artist worked with thicker paint, producing the impression that the landscape is more substantial, composed of an opaque layer of pigment that suggests a dense materiality. Nevertheless, he has retained a sense of emanating light throughout – the scene is bathed in strong sunshine and the canvas practically glows.

The painting was definitely begun outdoors; however, on close examination of the painting, it is evident that Renoir could not have realised this view in one session. While the sea and sky are similar to other cliff-top scenes the artist painted (see cats. 47, 48), the rendering of wheatfields, trees and brush is quite different from the *plein-air* landscapes Renoir produced throughout the 1870s. Rather than compose the landscape with short, articulated strokes of colour, Renoir now loaded several colours on his brush which he laid on all in the single stroke. Notably, in the foreground, sheaves of wheat are rendered in white, ochre and red and these colours remain unmixed on the surface of the canvas. Not satisfied with the impression generated by this spectral effect, he later – in his studio – went over the masses of lighter tones with Naples yellow, which has darkened over time. Other areas of the canvas are built up similarly, using a thick pigment that contrasts with the lighter areas of sky and sea behind.

It is notable that Renoir signed and dated this small landscape; the picture is carefully worked and the artist must have perceived a considerable market for such intimate scenes.[1] Perhaps the view was insufficiently dramatic – he did not sell this work to his dealer, Durand-Ruel, until ten years after it was made. Durand-Ruel, in turn, took another 16 years to find a customer for it.

JZ

1 House 1994, p. 84

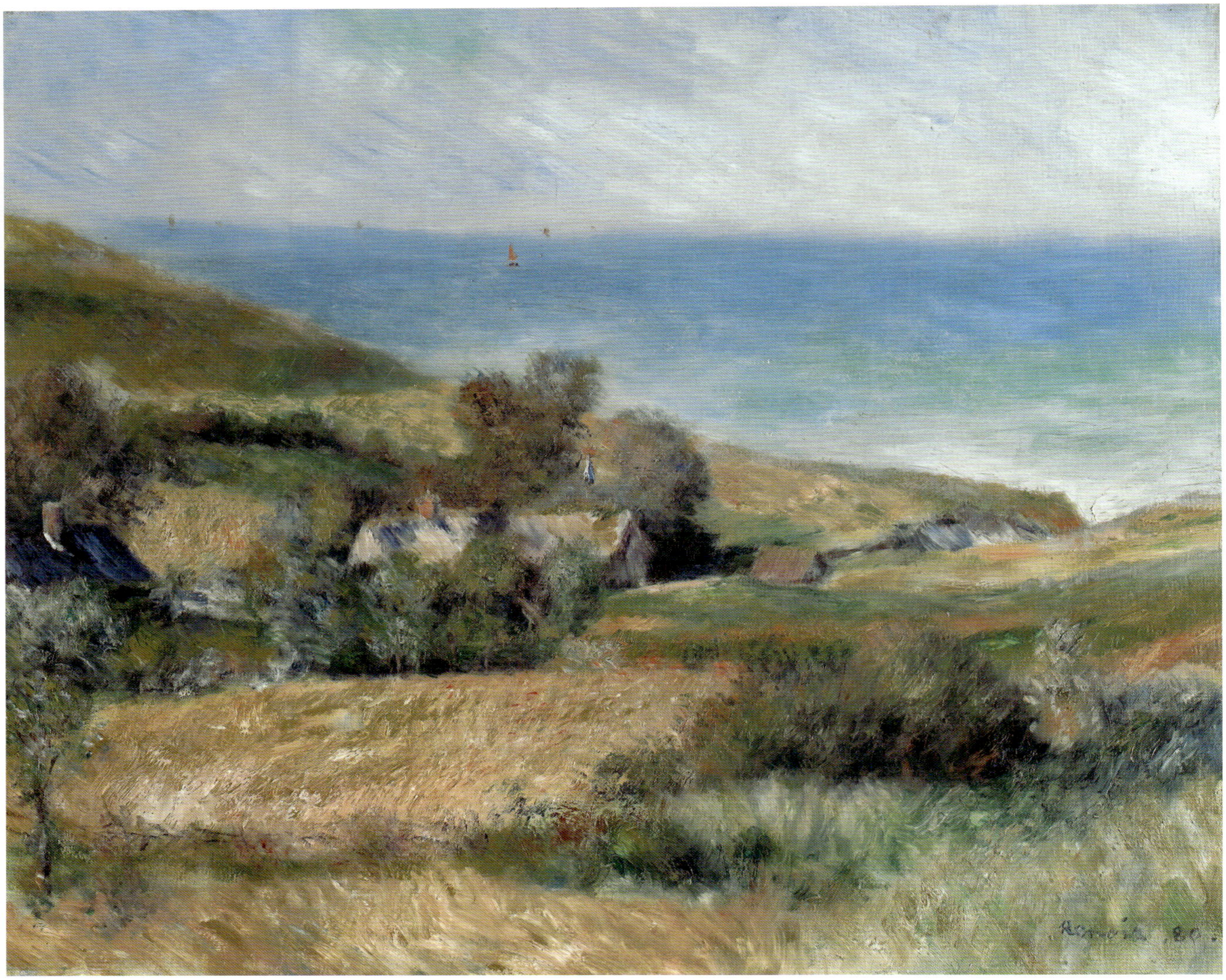

53 Madame Renoir with a Dog, 1880

Oil on canvas
32 × 41 cm; 12⅝ × 16 in.
Private collection courtesy of Durand-Ruel et Cie

PROVENANCE:
Picq; *Vente des Tableaux*, Paris, 7 May 1898, bought by Durand-Ruel; private collection, Paris

LITERATURE:
Durand-Ruel 1958, no. 11; Daulte 1964, p. 76; Durand-Ruel 1969, no. 9; Daulte 1971, no. 355, p. 44; Fezzi 1972, no. 407; Daulte 1973, p. 38; Durand-Ruel 1974, no. 47; Martini 1978, no. xv; Rouart 1985, pp. 52, 54; Néret 2001, p. 128

The figure in this painting, Aline Charigot, was a young woman of 20 years when Renoir painted her in a field with her dog. Renoir met Aline in a *cremière*, Chez Camille, across the street from his apartment on the rue St-Georges and she came to pose for him in his studio. On Sundays, they would go out to the country together and it was presumably on one of these trips that Renoir made this painting.[1]

Little has been written about this small picture although it has been exhibited numerous times. It represents a curious mixture of landscape and figure styles, though the work is remarkably distinct from Renoir's larger, more finished outdoor portraits made in this period such as *Portrait of Alfred Berard with his Dog* (fig. 104) made the following summer. The short sharp strokes that describe the grasses surrounding Aline are distinct from the softer, more subdued handling of the forest in which Alfred poses. However, the difference between the figures in these two works is notable. While the painting of Alfred and his dog is clearly a portrait staged out of doors, *Madame Renoir with a Dog* is more of a landscape with a figure who animates it.

The poses of both figures are conventional: Alfred leans against a tree with a hunting rifle in his hands and a hunting dog at his feet, while Aline sits on the grass with a bouquet of flowers in her lap and a small dog at her side. While Alfred's figure and features are carefully modelled and clear, Aline's figure seems to blend with its surroundings. This can partially be accounted for by the relative size of the works – the picture of Aline being a smaller sketch – and by the difference between a commissioned portrait and a study made on a visit to the country on a Sunday afternoon. Yet the flowers in Aline's hands (real) and the flowers in her hat (artificial) both seem to blend in with the textures of the surrounding landscape, and her hands and face are rendered in a loose, open manner like the grasses and trees around her. While her dress is modelled in a way that distinguishes its texture from the foliage around it, the material picks up the light that illuminates the scene and the form of the dress itself is lost in the tall grasses, making her figure indistinguishable from the landscape. The viewer cannot see her shoes or even where the hem of her dress ends and the shadow begins. Further, the dog is rendered in rapid strokes that provide no more than the clear identifying markings of her pet, such as its red face and white forepaws.

Just behind Aline on the right side of the painting, one can see the river passing behind the bushes. The placement of this figure near the river suggests that this work was made when Renoir was working at Chatou, on his now famous *Luncheon of the Boating Party* (Phillips Collection, Washington, DC; fig. 89, p. 170) and on a number of riverside landscapes (see cats. 50, 58, 59). JZ

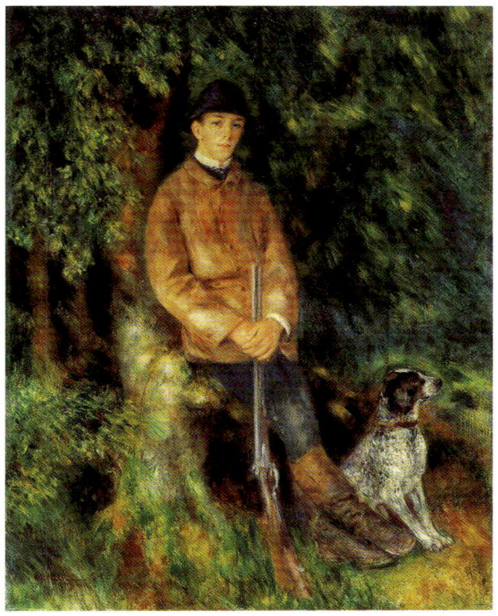

FIG. 104 *Portrait of Alfred Berard with his Dog*, 1881. Oil on canvas, 65 × 51 cm; 25¹¹⁄₁₆ × 20⅛ in. Philadelphia Museum of Art, The Mr and Mrs Carroll S. Tyson, Jr., Collection (1963-116-17).

1 Daulte 1973, p. 38.

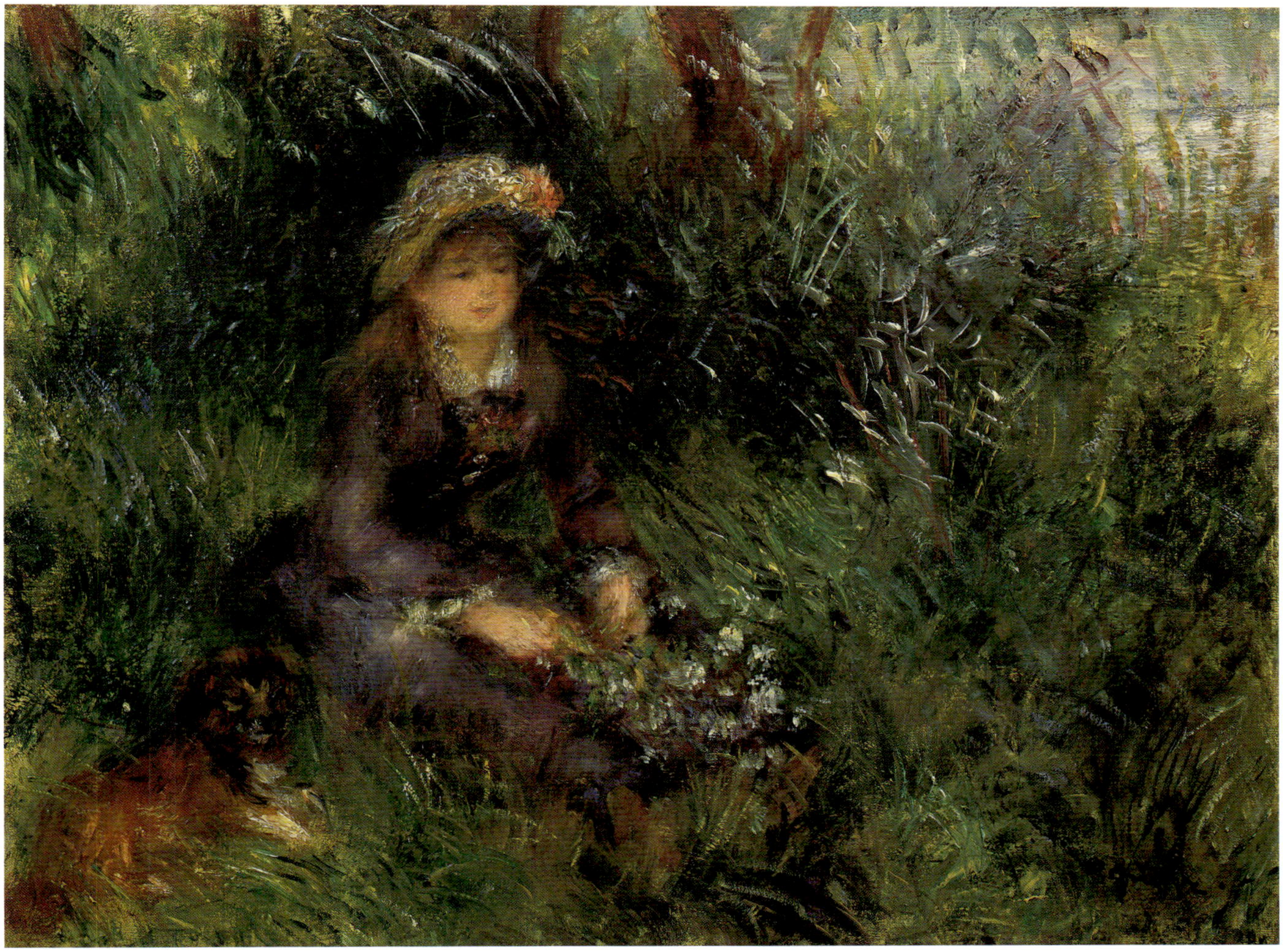

54 Arab Festival, 1881

Oil on canvas
73.5 × 92 cm; 28½ × 36½ in.
Musée d'Orsay, Paris. Gift of the Fondation Biddle in memory of Margaret Biddle 1957 (RF 1957-8)

PROVENANCE:
Bought from the artist by Durand-Ruel, 1892; Claude Monet, 1900; Durand-Ruel; Margaret Biddle

LITERATURE:
Kahn 1888, pp. 544–6; Rey 1931, p. 53; Alazard 1946, pp. 125–33; Rewald 1961, pp. 454, 462; Daulte 1971, p. 45; Fezzi 1972, no. 462; Gaunt and Adler 1982, no. 37; London 1984, no. 109; White 1984, pp. 105, 109; House and Distel 1985, pp. 99, 226–7; Tucker 2001, no. 23, pp. 224–5; Benjamin 2003, pp. 58–60; Guégan 2003, pp. 213–5, 230–1

Arab Festival is an extravagant and complex picture that weds elements of Impressionist landscape painting to Orientalist imagery, particularly in its reference to the paintings of Eugène Delacroix from the 1830s and 1840s. It is at once thoroughly self-conscious and impetuously expressive, capturing a public performance – the nature of which no one has been able adequately to define[1] – on the ruins of the ramparts behind the city of Algiers. In the centre of this crumbling amphitheatre is a group of musicians dressed mostly in white, playing tambourines and flutes. The movement of their garments demonstrates that they are dancing along to the music, while the audience, dressed in both European and varieties of North African dress, looks on. This lively spectacle, seen here from a distance, is exactly the kind of activity that inspired Renoir in Montmartre, where he created his panorama of the *Ball at the Moulin de la Galette* (Musée d'Orsay, Paris), but the painting is closer in scope to his images of the streets of Paris (see cats. 12, 29, 30), recording scenes of modern life in their infinite variety of costumes and architecture. On his first trip to Algeria, Renoir produced only landscapes (owing to his difficulty obtaining native models), and this scene from the outskirts of Algiers stands out among these as his only image of a public display. By undertaking such a painting, Renoir was taking on his hero Delacroix, whose images of the Aïssaoua festivals of Tangiers (see fig. 105) would have been known to him from the posthumous retrospective of Delacroix's work held at the Ecole des Beaux-Arts in 1864.[2]

When Delacroix was in Morocco in 1831–2, he had the opportunity to witness numerous public events as the escort to the French ambassador, the Comte de Mornay. One of the more bizarre exhibitions he witnessed were the devotional practices of the *Aïssaouas*, a sect who demonstrated their spiritual ardour by abandoning normal conventions of public behaviour. Delacroix's representations of these ceremonies, long titled the *The Aïssaouas of Tangiers,* allowed Europeans and others visual access to this devotional practice and, in the description of the work in the catalogue of the Salon of 1838, the artist explained some of the strange convulsions of the figures he had depicted as an emergence from prayer.[3] The Aïssaoua practice was a kind of public event but one that reflected a search for spiritual truth among its adherents.

While Renoir similarly experienced the Orient at first-hand, the subject of his imagery is different. In *Arab Festival* he offered an image of dancing, musical Arabs merely as one of the entertainments of life in the colony available to tourists, even though he borrowed heavily from Delacroix's bright palette, juxtaposing intense reds and whites with the blue water of the Mediterranean in the background. In addition he communicated a sense of movement through his energetic brushwork. Renoir's image is a long view seen from above ('a cliché of Impressionist pictorial composition', in the words of John House)[4] and, indeed, it follows another Impressionist cliché in being composed primarily of small strokes of vivid colour – but in no way

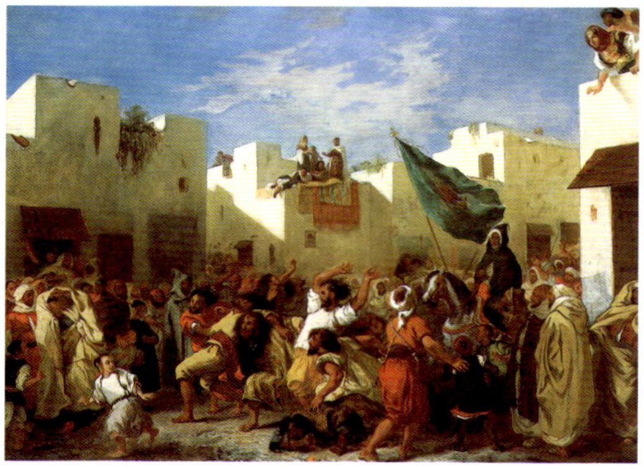

FIG. 105 Ferdinand-Victor-Eugène Delacroix (1798–1863), *The Aïssaouas of Tangiers,* 1838. Oil on canvas, 95.6 × 128.6 cm; 37⅝ × 50⅝ in. The Minneapolis Institute of Arts, Minnesota. Bequest of J. Jerome Hill (73.42.3).

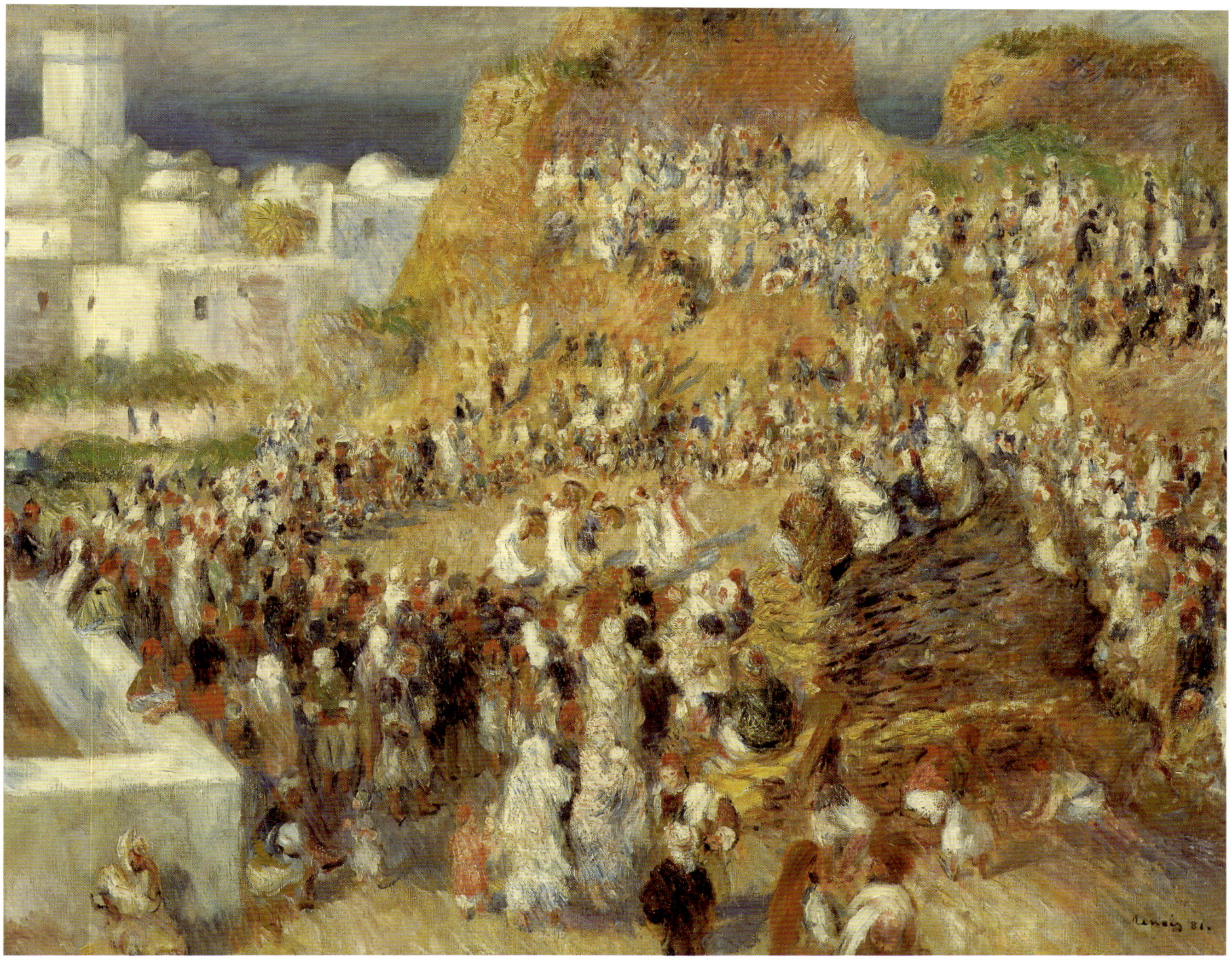

is this painting typical of Renoir's Impressionist style. In fact, *Arab Festival* is as forceful and audacious as any landscape he produced, a notion reinforced by the fact that its eventual buyer was Claude Monet. Renoir's use of a loaded brush and a palette knife to push masses of paint around the canvas has resulted in thick encrustations of pigment that appear almost incomprehensible from up close. From a distance, however, the image coheres into a robust and energetic representation of colourful modern life in Algeria, at that moment a distant and exotic province of France. JZ

1 Roger Benjamin has put considerable effort into ascertaining the details of both the location and the nature of the performance but concludes: 'The nature of the Arab festival represented seems to defy precise definition'; Benjamin 2003, pp. 58–60.

2 In 1875, Renoir made a to-scale copy of Delacroix's *Jewish Wedding in Morocco* (Musée du Louvre, Paris).

3 Lee Johnson, *The Paintings of Eugène Delacroix, A Critical Catalogue*, Oxford 1986, III, p. 171.

4 House and Distel 1985, p. 226.

55 Field of Banana Trees Near Algiers, 1881

Oil on canvas
51.5 × 63.5 cm; 20¼ × 25 in.
Musée d'Orsay, Paris (RF 1959-1)

PROVENANCE:
Sold by the artist to Durand-Ruel, April 1881, for 200 francs; comtesse de Brécey [sic], Paris; acquired by the Musée du Louvre, Paris, 1959

LITERATURE:
Alazard 1946, pp. 125–33; Daulte 1971, p. 45; Fezzi 1972, no. 461; Callen 1978, p. 71; White 1984, pp. 105, 109; Benjamin 2003, pp. 14, 72–3; Guégan 2003, pp. 232–3

Writing to his dealer Durand-Ruel from Algiers in March 1881, Renoir stated: 'I have remained distant from all the painters, in the sun, in order to think about what I am doing'.[1] Indeed, none of Renoir's contemporaries, nor any previous painters of Algiers, took on a landscape subject so pedestrian as a section of banana palms blocking a distant view of the city of Algiers. In a location where French artists had represented the significant scenic monuments and views for 50 years, Renoir seems to have found a composition that no other artist would have dreamed of approaching. Yet what a fantastic demonstration of his skills as a painter this is! The banana palm-fronds, each emerging from a central shoot yet interlacing with one another, become the subject of a vegetal frieze. Whether Renoir knew it or not, the banana palms were just as foreign to the Algerian terrain as he was. A more typical view of the vegetation around Algiers can be seen in a watercolour completed at the very beginning of the French occupation of Algiers (fig. 106). Rather than provide an image of the colony that would be familiar to French viewers (and collectors), Renoir instead focused upon a grove of banana palms and found there an unprecedented source of visual interest.

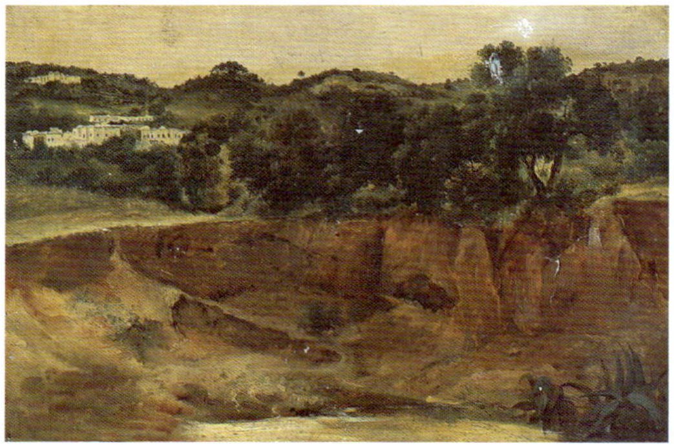

FIG. 106 Jean-Charles Langlois (1789–1870), *Gardens in the Algiers Countryside*, 1832. Oil on paper mounted on canvas, 33.5 × 48 cm; 13¼ × 18⅞ in. Musée des Beaux-Arts, Caen (2005.1.90).

In his *Grammar*, penned in about 1883, Renoir repeatedly called on decorative artists to observe nature and learn to imitate natural forms as a source of inspiration.[2] This painting seems to be an example of this kind of activity that he would later counsel others to follow. Rather than plan an artificial landscape composition, Renoir has simply looked and responded to visual stimuli with an incredible painterly facility. For an artist who was just then being hounded by his Impressionist contemporaries for his participation in the annual, state-sponsored Salon (the main thrust of his letter to Durand-Ruel mentioned above is a defence of this action on financial grounds), he certainly generated an atypical landscape composition. The eye of the viewer is met with an array of colours – reds, ochres, yellows and countless shades of green – that mingle and intertwine but nevertheless hang together as a depiction of a corner of the world. The picture was shown at the Impressionist exhibition of 1882 (at the behest of Durand-Ruel and against the will of the artist), where it impressed Eugène Manet, who singled it out in a letter to his wife Berthe Morisot, finding it 'highly successful'.[3] JZ

1 Alazard 1946, p. 131.
2 Herbert 2000, pp. 122–53.
3 Callen 1978, p. 71.

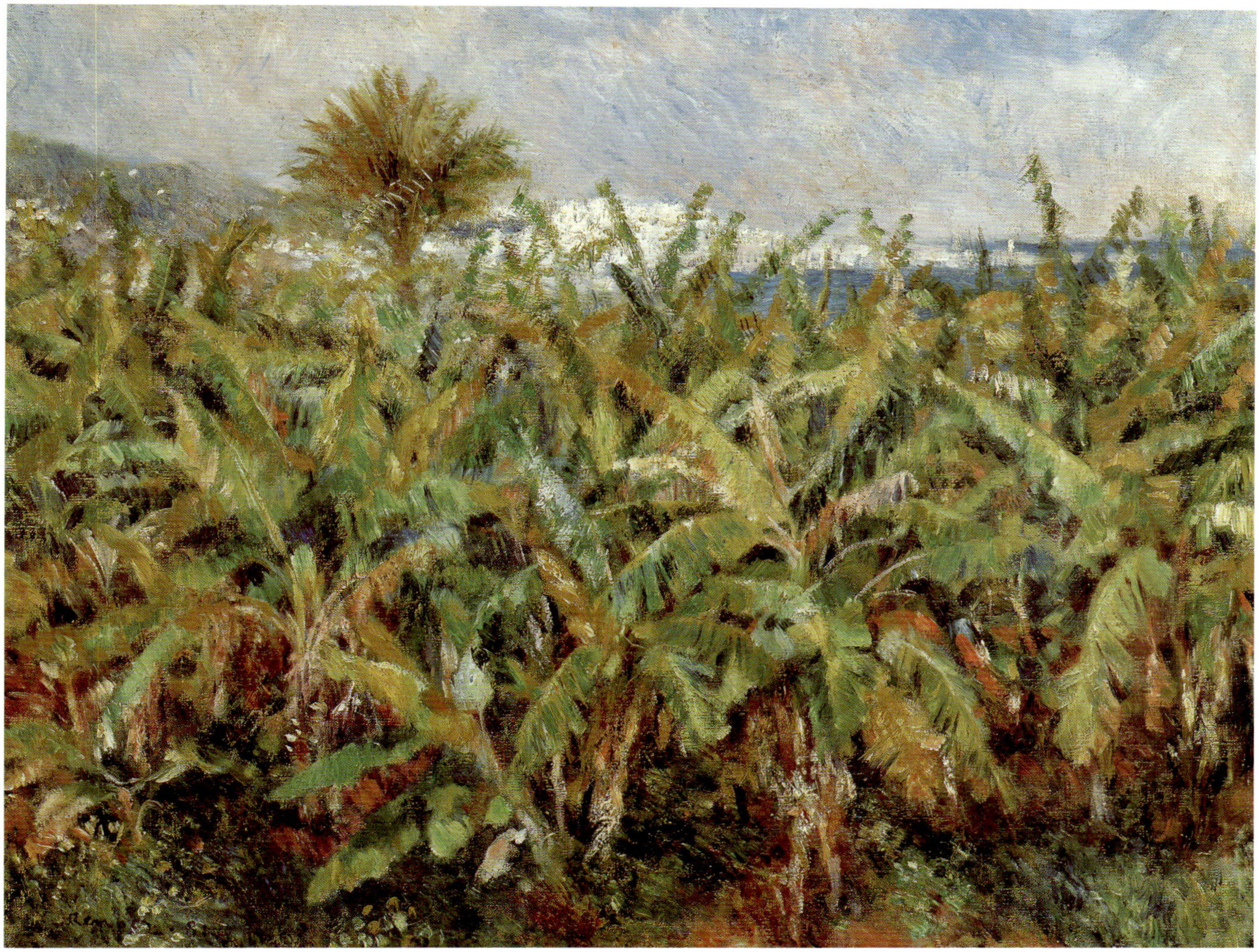

56 The Jardin d'Essai, Algiers, 1881

Oil on canvas
80 × 65 cm; 31⅞ × 25⅝ in.
MGM MIRAGE Corporate Collection (157)

PROVENANCE:
Sold by the artist to Durand-Ruel, April 1881, for 700 francs; sold to G.W. Vanderbilt II, 1892; Bellagio Gallery of Fine Art, 1999

LITERATURE:
Alazard 1946, pp. 125–33; Fezzi 1972, no. 514; Tucker 1999, p. 70; Tucker 2001, no. 22, pp. 224–5; Benjamin 2003, pp. 5, 14, 64–70; Guégan 2003, pp. 215, 220–1

While it bears some similarities in handling to *Arab Festival* (cat. 54), one's impression before this painting is that a quiet scene has been brought to life through an apparently wild technique. Examined more carefully, there are subtleties in this style which reveal Renoir's mastery of landscape painting. The composition is an absolutely standard view down an *allée* of palms of varying heights, with figures promenading into the distance, a pair of Algerians and a pair of Europeans behind them – a postcard (fig. 107) showing just such a view even features an artist rendering the scene.[1] The lush tropical garden, planted by the French colonial government to serve both science and recreation, was a well-known sight in Algiers. Thus, in concept, the work mimics earlier paintings Renoir and his companions had made in the suburbs of Paris, depicting leisure as an essential aspect of modern life. Renoir would also paint predominantly postcard views when he travelled to Italy later in the year (see cats. 62–5). However, although in this way the *Jardin d'Essai* is the most conventional of all the scenes Renoir painted in Algiers in the spring of 1881, in formal terms the painting is explosive, a sensually overpowering image of exotic natural forms. Paul Tucker has written of the palm fronds as similar to 'fireworks',[2] and indeed the taller date palms in the top half of the composition appear like arrows of colour emanating from a central core. One perceives greens and browns but also purple, gold and red tones against a lush blue sky. In the lower register, the shorter palms send out fronds that resemble many vegetal hands lining the path. The ground itself is brushed on in slick blond and violet tones, not unlike the effect in *Landscape at Wargemont* (cat. 43), but generally with thicker paint, laid on very dry. Renoir did not build up the impasto in layers, but seems rather to have dragged the loaded brush across the canvas to produce elongated strokes. The paint is swirling, globby, coagulated. It is not that the painter is communicating to the viewer through paint. Rather, the visual field of pigment, the wild acrobatics of strokes delineating forms of dizzying complexity – the structure of innumerable palm fronds that both describe and interrupt the spatial sense of the picture – produces a feeling of being in the lush terrain of the painting. The viewer experi-ences the sensual world the artist felt transformed into the lasting flesh of pigment. The painting was packed and sent back to Paris; later it was relined, which ought to have reduced the vivid appearance of the pigment. Yet the freshness of the surface remains. JZ

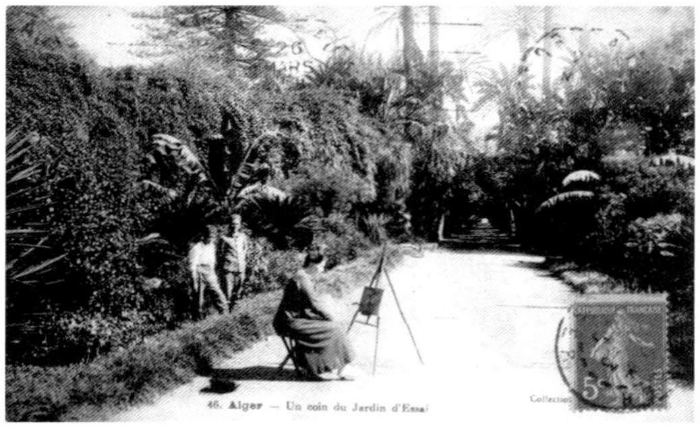

FIG. 107 *Algiers – A Corner of the Jardin d'Essai*, about 1904. Postcard, Centre des Archives d'Outre-Mer, Aix-en-Provence (Archives Nationales, 60 Fi/I).

1 This postcard was originally reproduced in Benjamin 2003, p. 64.
2 Tucker 1999, p. 71.

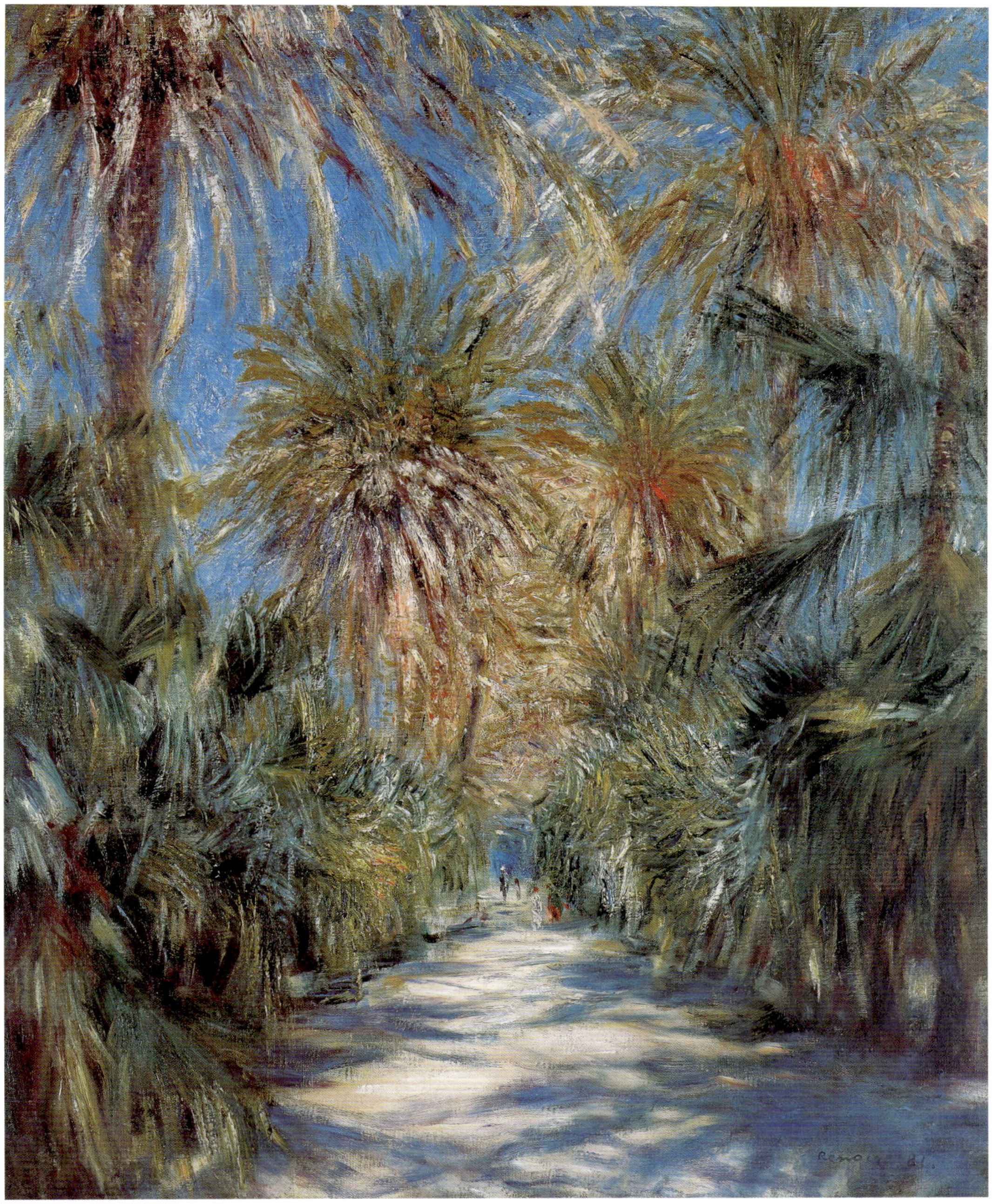

57 Algerian Landscape, 'The Ravine of the Wild Woman', 1881

Oil on canvas,
65 × 81 cm; 25½ × 31⅞ in.
Musée d'Orsay, Paris (RF 1943-62)

PROVENANCE:
Sold by the artist to Durand-Ruel, April 1881, for 200 francs; Bernheim, 1909; J.-B. Stang, Oslo; purchased by Musée du Louvre, 1943

LITERATURE:
Alazard 1946, pp. 125–33; Bazin 1946, pp. 6–10; Daulte 1971, p. 45; Fezzi 1972, no. 502; Callen 1978, pp. 78–9; House and Distel 1985, pp. 98, 225–6; Rouart 1985, p. 64; Benjamin 2003, pp. 76–8; Guégan 2003, pp. 216, 234

Despite the provocative title, this painting appears entirely without anecdote. Rather, it is an exercise in pure visual sensuality, for which Renoir is justly famous. Here it is not one of the numerous nudes Renoir painted throughout his career, but the luxuriant foliage of a ravine outside Algiers that allows the viewer to feel the material beauty of the external world. The artist seems to have consciously eschewed the picturesque exoticism of previous depictions of the Algerian landscape – with the exception of the spiky aloes in the fore-ground – drawing instead on the natural beauty of the world and the jewel-like palette of earlier artists such as Titian, Rubens and Delacroix.

This colourful and luxuriant landscape bears comparison with the finest landscape Renoir created while staying with the Berards at Wargemont, *Landscape at Wargemont* (cat. 43). Both works are notable for their loose modelling and rich colours, and their viewpoints, looking out across an open space filled with vegetation and revealing little of the sky, are quite similar. In a letter to Madame Berard, Renoir explicitly compared the landscapes of Normandy to those he was witnessing in Algiers.[1] In *Algerian Landscape*, however, in comparison to the lightly brushed character of the earlier landscape, Renoir used more densely applied paint, without allowing the surface become too thick. As a result, there is no light reflected off the white ground, leading to a perception of a richer, denser texture of the foliage. The modelling is also highly animated and the painting remains a monument to a dramatic performance executed in pulsating strokes of vivid pigment.

Germain Bazin described this picture as representing a shift from an Impressionist to a 'fauve' style on Renoir's part, a deliberately ahistorical description which nevertheless does much to illuminate this picture.[2] Not only is it quite possible to perceive a direct line from this image to Matisse's Moroccan landscapes, such as *Periwinkles/Moroccan Garden* (fig. 108), but, in Renoir's hands, the colonial landscape becomes a Mediterranean site of pure viewing pleasure. The memories of colonial violence and the effects of colonial development are edited out, though this landscape would become a suburb of Algiers in just a few years.[3] Instead, the ravine seems like a lush and exquisite natural world in which the painter can find inspiration and the viewer can admire the artful tactics Renoir employed to transform it into a sensuous, bright and idealised escape from the prosaic world. JZ

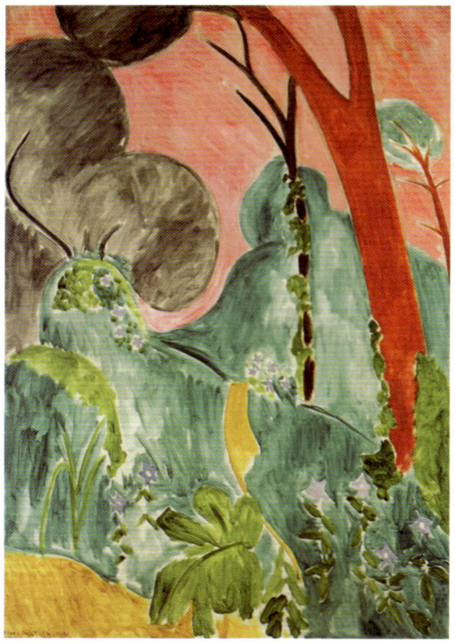

FIG. 108 Henri Matisse (1869–1954), *Periwinkles / Moroccan Garden*, 1912. Oil, pencil and charcoal on canvas, 116.8 × 82.5 cm; 46 × 32½ in. Museum of Modern Art, New York. Gift of Florence M. Schoenborn (341.1985).

1 Reprinted in Benjamin 2003, p. 144.
2 Bazin 1946, p. 10.
3 Benjamin 2003, p. 78.

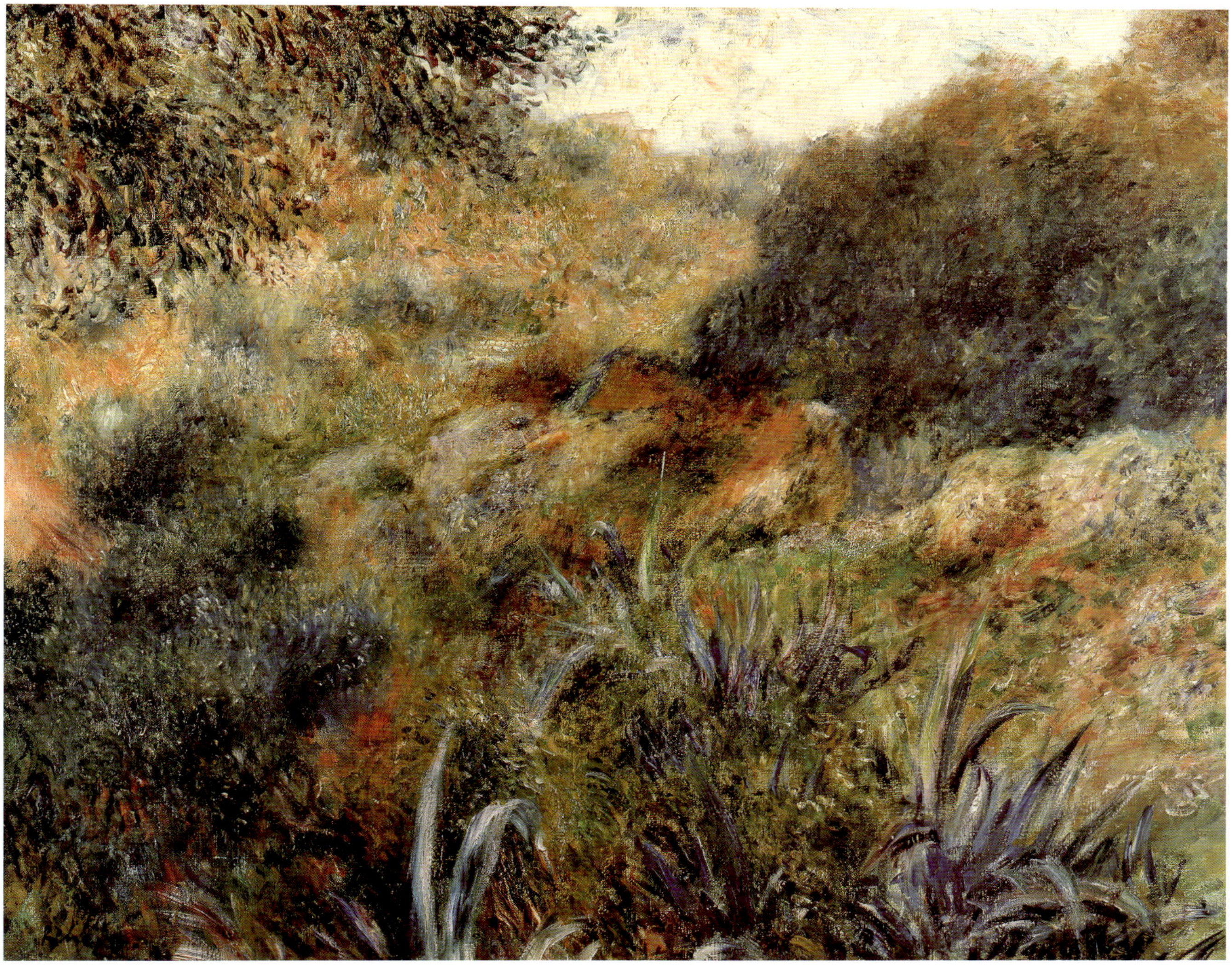

58 The Seine at Chatou, 1881

Oil on canvas
73.3 × 92.4 cm; 14⅛ × 29⅛ in.
Museum of Fine Arts, Boston. Gift of Arthur Brewster Emmons (19.771)

PROVENANCE:
Durand-Ruel, Paris, 25 August 1891; Mrs Blair, New York, 26 January 1900; Mr Sehley, New York, by 1901; Durand-Ruel, New York, 4 March 1901; Arthur Brewster Emmons, Newport and Boston, 5 March 1906; given by Arthur Brewster Emmons to the Museum of Fine Arts, Boston, 1919

LITERATURE:
New York 1937, no. 28; Florisoone 1938, p. 120; Fezzi 1972, no. 443; House and Distel 1985, no. 57; Moffett 1985, pp. 379–81; Langdon 1986, no. 7; House 1995, no. 98; Rathbone 1996, cat. no. 37; Tucker 2001, no. 21; Boston 1999, no. 56

Renoir visited Chatou, a small town near Bougival to the west of Paris, in April and May of 1881. He had painted there before, in a broad and liquid manner, in about 1871 (cat. 9). Now, however, he was a more experienced painter in fuller control of his technique and with a renewed interest in experimentation. He had only recently returned from Algeria, an eye-opening trip that had provoked a rich vein of creativity in him. As the present picture attests, the painterly animation that characterises his Algerian works did not desert him back on native soil. Indeed, the effulgence of the North African scene may have compelled him to seek out scenes in the French countryside of equal animation and variety. In this way he could maintain the painterly energy that foreign vistas had provoked in him only a few months before. Chatou provided him with such fulsome motifs. Here, he depicts a river bank bursting with early bloom. The canvas can hardly contain it. Tall grasses, flowering bushes, trees, water and a sky billowing with clouds fill the picture with movement. A young girl laden with freshly picked flowers has made her way towards the river through the sun-dappled grasses in the foreground. She gazes down at the swift-moving water and the red pleasure boats on it, absorbed by the panoply of nature in springtime, and adroitly absorbed into its ambient atmosphere by the painter's brush. In the distance, houses dot the country landscape, some low down on the plane by the river, others in the hills that roll away, a reminder of the keen pleasure that Renoir took, and felt should be taken, in living in intimate proximity to nature.

Everywhere Renoir evokes the myriad details of the natural world. To do so he employs several different types of brushstroke. The paint is applied unevenly, in some places thickly, in others, such as around the flowering tree in the left foreground with its thousand tiny dots of colour, thinly enough so that the weave of the canvas is visible. Longer brushstrokes render the tall grasses. A lighter, more feathery touch evokes the young leaves of the green trees. The water is an interweaving pattern of white and blue strokes, further animated at lower left by licks of cobalt blue. It is as if Renoir is responding to each detail in turn, finding the touch and density of paint that will most convincingly capture the freshness and the specificity of each particular motif. This is an exercise in painterly improvisation in which we see the artist striving to find, as quickly as possible one imagines, an equivalency between an object in nature and the response it evokes in his mind and eye as his hand moves across the canvas and the springtime sun warms him. CR

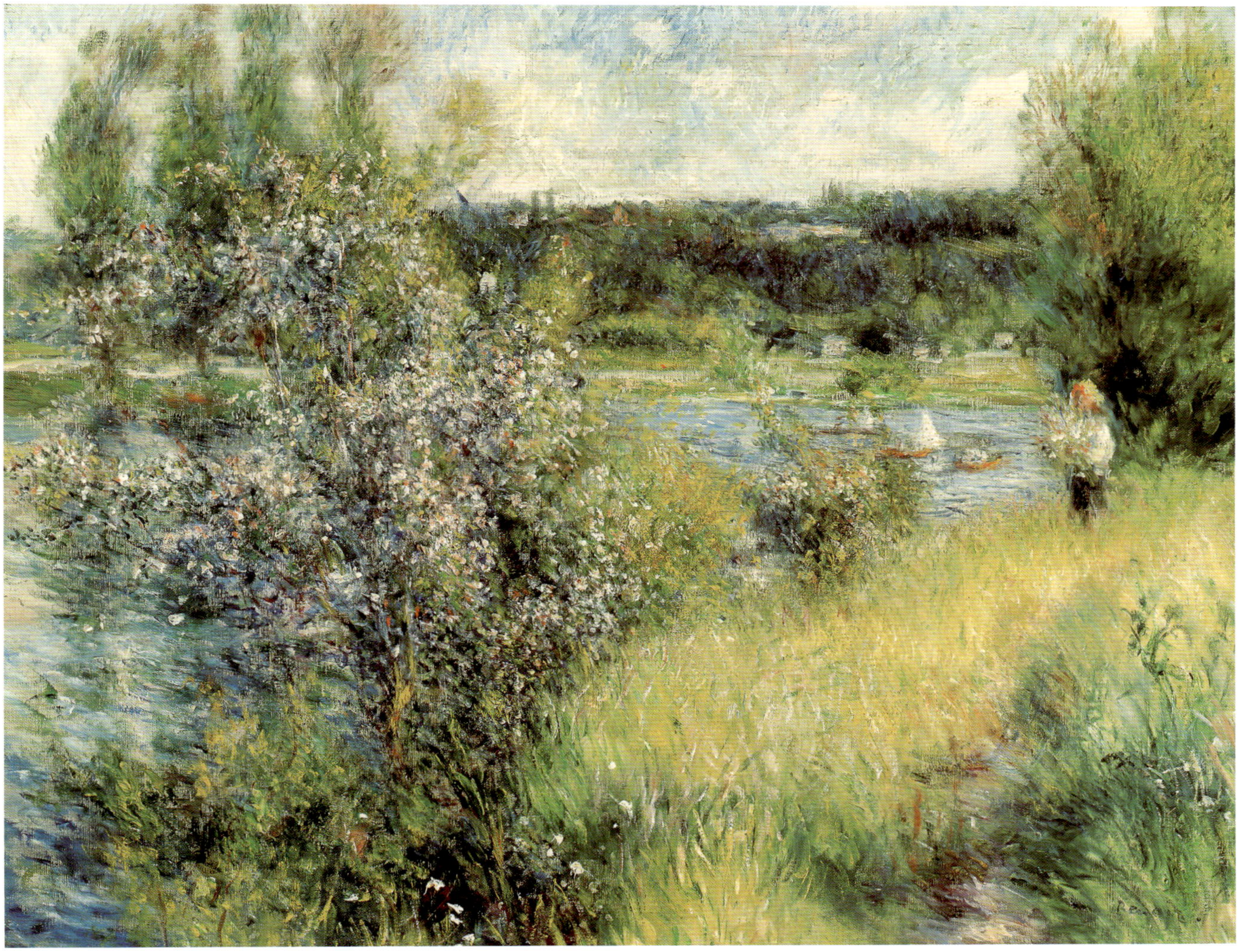

59 Banks of the Seine, about 1881

Oil on canvas
53 × 64 cm; 19¾ × 24 in.
Private collection

PROVENANCE:
Bought from the artist by Durand-Ruel by 25 July 1891; Galerie Bing, Paris; Freud Art Galleries, New York; Knoedler & Co., New York; Moritz Gutman, New York; the Hon. Mrs Michael Astor; sold Sotheby's, London, 23 March 1983, lot 11

This picture, previously described as being painted near Argenteuil in 1875, is in fact much closer to the paintings Renoir made in the summer of 1881 near Chatou (see cats. 58, 60, 61). Indeed the picture must have been made on the same island as *The Seine at Chatou* (cat. 58), though a bit further down the path, because the set of four poplars visible in that painting behind the flowering tree at left are further away, in the middle distance of *Banks of the Seine*. The season also seems a little later, as the trees are no longer in full bloom and the heat seems to hang beneath the vaporous sky. The green and yellow pigments in the foreground are vigorously applied, providing a decorative screen of lush tones that seem to hover on the lower half of the canvas. The background is rendered in feathery strokes while the sky is thick and white with highlights of pink and yellow mixed in, which create a sense of a thick atmosphere. In brief, the painting is a carefully structured composition of visual sensations and painterly improvisation in line with Renoir's recent experience painting landscapes in Algeria (see cats. 54–7).

This painting has been seen in a public institution only when it was on deposit at the National Gallery, London, from 1972 to 1982, and it has never been in a Renoir exhibition or publication on the artist. The present exhibition provides an opportunity to evaluate it anew and to place it in its proper context in the development of Renoir's career. This bright and sensual landscape provides a testament to the artist's immersion in the landscape subject and his unique ability to communicate a sense of his own vivid impressions of the natural world through the techniques of Impressionist painting. Renoir employed individual strokes of colour and the layering of pigments to suggest visual transitions such as masses of foliage that overlap, or the multiple reflections in the river.

The period between 1878 and 1882 has been described as the point when Impressionism reached a crisis.[1] While it is undoubtedly true that the cohesiveness of the group of artists that gave birth to the Impressionist exhibitions was beginning to come apart by this point, the visual language of the Impressionist technique persisted and was reinvented by these artists and many others. Looking at the evidence of this painting and others Renoir made at this time demonstrates that the artist himself was not experiencing any artistic crisis but was, in fact, making some of the finest landscapes of his career, employing methods first developed in the mid-1870s, albeit pushed to productive extremes. The incredible density of surface in both the foreground and sky of this painting produces a decorative effect, of visual patterns that are perceptible across the surface of the painting. *Banks of the Seine* points the way forward towards a new approach to painting – an experiment with decorative surface effects – that the artist would not achieve for years to come. JZ

1 Isaacson 1980. However, the author acknowledges Renoir's persistent use of Impressionist technique in Venice in 1881 (p. 182).

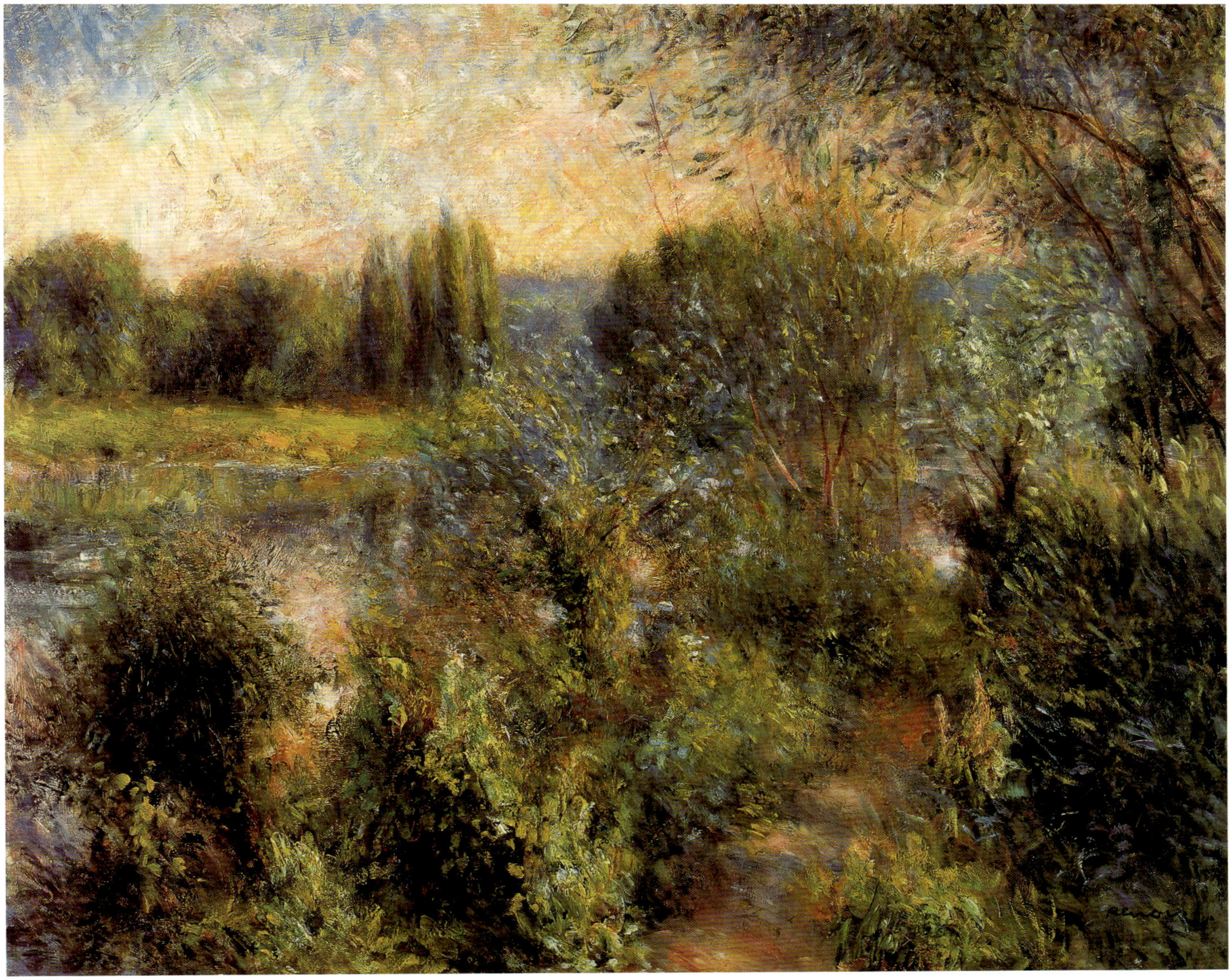

60 Chestnut Trees in Bloom, 1881

Oil on canvas
71 × 89 cm; 27 × 35 in.
Nationalgalerie, Staatliche Museen, Berlin (A I 975)

PROVENANCE:
Sold by Renoir to Durand-Ruel on 6 July 1881 for 500 francs; acquired from Durand-Ruel by the Nationalgalerie in December 1906 for 13,500 francs, as a gift of Elise Koenigs

LITERATURE:
Barnes and De Mazia 1935, pp. 77–82, 403–4; Paul 1993, pp. 192–4, 368; von Hohenzollern and Schuster 1996, pp. 114–15

Like the related *The Railway Bridge at Chatou* (cat. 61), *Chestnut Trees in Bloom*, one of the artist's largest and most ambitious 'pure landscapes',[1] was worked on in Chatou in the spring of 1881, shortly after Renoir had returned from his first visit to Algeria. It was delivered to Durand-Ruel, along with three other Chatou pictures, on 6 July of that year, and acquired for the modest figure of 500 francs.[2] Durand-Ruel included *Chestnut Trees in Bloom* ('*Marronniers en fleurs*') among the 25 Renoirs he lent to the seventh Impressionist exhibition in March 1882, at which it was mentioned briefly, but favourably, by three reviewers.[3] By the time the dealer sold the landscape to Hugo von Tschudi (1851–1911), the energetic director of Berlin's Nationalgalerie, Renoir's stock had risen considerably. After a year and a half of negotiations, *Chestnut Trees in Bloom* was acquired in December 1906 for 13,500 francs, 27 times its price of purchase a quarter of a century earlier.[4]

We are exceptionally well informed about the circumstances in which *Chestnut Trees in Bloom* was conceived. Having left Algeria around 3 April, Renoir seems to have settled almost immediately in Chatou, and it was from this 'prettiest of Parisian suburbs' that he wrote to Théodore Duret in London on Easter Monday (18 April) announcing the recent visit of James McNeill Whistler.[5] Duret had been responsible for the introduction, having just published an article on Whistler in the *Gazette des Beaux-Arts*, which Renoir had read.[6] Whistler and Renoir lunched together, presumably at the restaurant La Fournaise: 'I am really very happy to have been able to spend a little time with this great artist,' wrote Renoir.[7] As he had to Whistler, Renoir apologised to Duret for postponing yet again his visit to London: 'I am struggling with trees in bloom, women and children, and can see no further than that at the moment.'[8]

Although blossoms were a subject beloved of the American artist, *Chestnut Trees in Bloom* has nothing of Whistler's *japonisant* ethereality. It is a solidly constructed, spatially complex landscape, in which the flickering, mobile brushwork and high chromatic scale create an intense luminosity. Renoir's subject is the splendid chestnut tree in full flower, at the foot of whose trunk a pair of straw-hatted gardeners in blue trousers and rolled-up shirtsleeves are hard at work tending the lawn. The trees appear to be situated at the edge of an elevated garden terrace enclosed by a stone wall, of which the curvilinear form echoes the path that leads to the river at right. Although nothing else of the property is indicated, Renoir's setting might well be one of the 'elegant villas that have replaced the little rustic houses' and as such bears witness to the gentrification of the village.[9] Rowing aside, Chatou was also esteemed for its agreeable situation on the Seine: 'It is surrounded by several beautiful villas … from which one enjoys the most delicious views of the surrounding countryside'.[10] On the path bordering the river at right in *Chestnut Trees in Bloom* we note the diminutive presence of an elegantly attired mother and daughter, both dressed in white. The realities of leisure in the suburbs are attended to with the greatest subtlety and discretion.

Renoir's handling in this grand, asymmetrical vista is at once unfettered and tightly controlled. Over a creamy beige ground, which is visible particularly in the lower foreground and in the sky above, he applies calligraphic, feathery strokes of blue, pink, and white to suggest the mobility of the dazzling sunlight. His touch changes in the description of the trees, whose leaves and flowers are painted in dry nodules of pink and green that

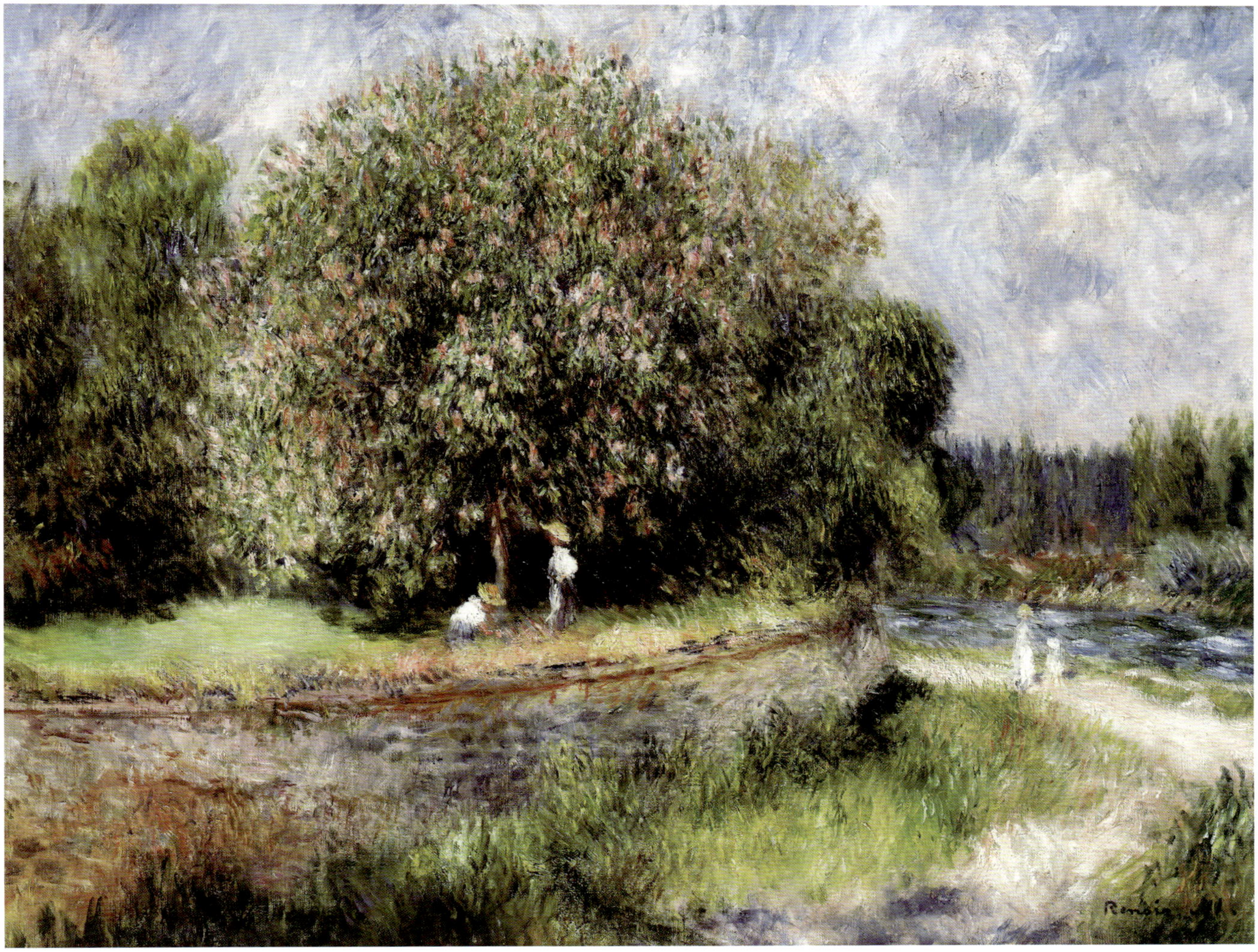

almost replicate the materiality of the blossoms and foliage themselves. The river at right is rendered in summary strokes of blue, white and green, and the rare shadows in the grass and pathway in the foreground appear etched in inky blue-black.

Renoir captures the effect of direct sunlight in a scene that is absolutely assured in its structure. The wide sweep of the foreground grass and incoming path leads the eye to the river and the poplars, standing to attention in the distance, but without diverting attention from the majestic trees in bloom, the absorbed gardeners, the peerless green lawn (no sign of struggle here!). Anticipating his collaboration with Cézanne at L'Estaque the following year, *Chestnut Trees in Bloom* is among Renoir's most rigorously 'constructed' landscapes, of which the formal concentration was best articulated (somewhat unexpectedly) by Barnes and De Mazia: 'The total effect of this landscape,' they wrote, 'is that of a rich, multicoloured bouquet floating upward in a clear, cerulean atmosphere.'[11] CBB

1 The canvas is not a standard stretcher size, and is considerably larger than the related *Railway Bridge at Chatou*, a size 15.

2 Archives Durand-Ruel, Stockbook, 6 July 1881: 'no. 1156, *Marronniers en fleurs*, 500 francs' (purchased from Renoir). The other pictures acquired the same day are '1154, *La Seine à Chatou* (*effet de soir*), 500 francs; 1156, *Les Canotiers*, 400 francs; 1157, *Les Bords de la Seine*, 300 francs'.

3 Berson 1996, I, p. 377: *Catalogue de la 7eme exposition des artistes indépendants*, no. 155, *Maronniers en fleurs*. '*Renoir a jeté sur ses marronniers en fleurs et sur sa poignée de géraniums toutes les ardeurs chatoyantes de son coloris*; A. Hepp, *Le Voltaire*, 3 March 1882, Berson 1996, I, p. 394. '*Ce qu'il y a de plus singulier, c'est que M. Renoir n'est pas le premier venu, témoin son* Bouquet de Lilas *et ses* Marronniers en fleurs *qui, vus de loin, donnent un impression de fraîcheur charmante*'; Nivelle, *Le Soleil*, 4 March 1882, *ibid.*, I, p. 406. '*Je veux citer aussi ses marronniers en fleurs, ses géraniums, et ses pivoines*'; Robert, *La Petite Presse*, 5 March 1882, *ibid.*, I, p. 429.

4 Paul 1993, p. 368. Durand-Ruel sent the painting on approval to Berlin in April 1905, offered Tschudi a discounted price (down from 15,000 francs) on 10 November 1906, and received payment in June 1907; see the correspondence between Georges Durand-Ruel and Hugo van Tschudi in the Zentralarchiv, Staatliche Museen zu Berlin, letters of 10 November 1906 (no. 2173) and 6 June 1907 (no. 1223).

5 Renoir to Duret, '*Lundi de Pâques 81*'; Florisoone 1938, p. 40. Whistler spent the week of 14–21 April in Paris, much of it with the American dealer George A. Lucas, in whose company he visited the sixth Impressionist exhibition, boycotted by Renoir and Monet, on the day of his arrival. Whistler had brought over his recent etchings of Venice, which he took with him to Chatou; see L.M.C. Randall, *The Diary of George A. Lucas, an American Art Agent in Paris, 1857–1909*, 2 vols., Princeton 1979, II, pp. 518–19.

6 '*Sans vous je ne lui eusse certainement pas adressé la parole, car j'ai commence par lui parler de votre article de la revue*'; Florisoone 1938, p. 40.

7 '*Je viens de voir Wistler* [*sic*], *il a été bien charmant, il est venu déjeuner avec moi à Chatou et je suis vraiment bien heureux d'avoir passé quelques instants avec ce grand artiste . . . Je déjeune demain avec lui*'; *ibidem*, p. 40.

8 *Ibidem.*

9 Herbert 1988, p. 247, citing an article in *L'Illustration* of 22 May 1869.

10 Larousse 1865–90, III, p. 1090.

11 Barnes and De Mazia 1935, pp. 403–4.

61 The Railway Bridge at Chatou, 1881

Oil on canvas
54 × 65.5 cm; 21¼ × 25¾ in.
Musée d'Orsay, Paris. Caillebotte Bequest 1894 (RF 3758)

As the flowering trees confirm, *The Railway Bridge at Chatou* was painted at the same season as *Chestnut Trees in Bloom* (cat. 60); the canvases were worked on in Chatou between mid-April and early July 1881.[1] A circular lawn is common to both compositions as well, but here it has a more constrained, even shabby appearance. Robert Herbert has identified the site as on the Ile de Chiart, south of Chatou (the village was situated on the west bank of the Seine by the road bridge; see cat. 32), and has suggested that Renoir's view is from a private fenced garden or the courtyard of a café.[2] There is little here of the opulence and expansiveness of the property portrayed in *Chestnut Trees in Bloom*.

With the road bridge far behind him, Renoir paints the view south towards Croissy, where the railway bridge crossed the island to link Chatou and Reuil. There were stations in both villages, part of the Chemin de fer de l'Ouest inaugurated in August 1837.[3] Rebuilt after its destruction by arsonists in February 1848, the railway bridge served the St-Germain line that originated in the Gare St-Lazare and enabled Parisians to reach this picturesque fishing village in well under an hour.[4] As Herbert has also noted, the bridge is 'so generously enveloped in foliage that it makes a graceful capriole, not a dynamic industrial leap'.[5] Yet comparison with an early photograph of the bridge confirms that Renoir was scrupulous in his delineation of industrial architecture, and that he rendered this arched construction of steel and stone in painstaking detail (fig. 109).[6]

The deliberation of Renoir's handling in *The Railway Bridge at Chatou*, with its tight brushwork and encrusted surfaces, is also consistent with that of *Chestnut Trees in Bloom*. Even on a reduced scale, Renoir creates a compact, structured composition that is complex in its spatial organisation. From the grassy garden, at the open fence of which stands a straw-hatted villager, arms reddened from the sun, the eye is led to the grand chestnut trees in full flower at the edge of the property and from them to the river and bridge beyond. The arch and its stone facing, resolutely inscribed in white at left, appears larger and with greater clarity than the section of the bridge that traverses the river itself, just glimpsed between the two red-flowering chestnut trees at right. In this way Renoir suggests the distance travelled from one bank to the next, yet any openness in the vista is blocked by the vertical poplars and white and pink chestnuts massing in the background; they form an impenetrable frieze that obliges the eye to attend to the quivering grasses in the foreground. If Renoir 'struggled' with the flowering trees (to recall a phrase he used in a letter to Théodore Duret; see cat. 50), he has emerged the victor in this seemingly 'uncomposed' landscape, 'irregular' in layout and vibrant in its evocation of dazzling sunlight.

Signed and dated in purple-blue at lower right, in a manner consistent with finished works of the period, *The Railway Bridge at Chatou* resembles the type of picture Renoir was producing for Durand-Ruel in the months following his return from Algeria.[7] Yet this was not a dealer's picture,

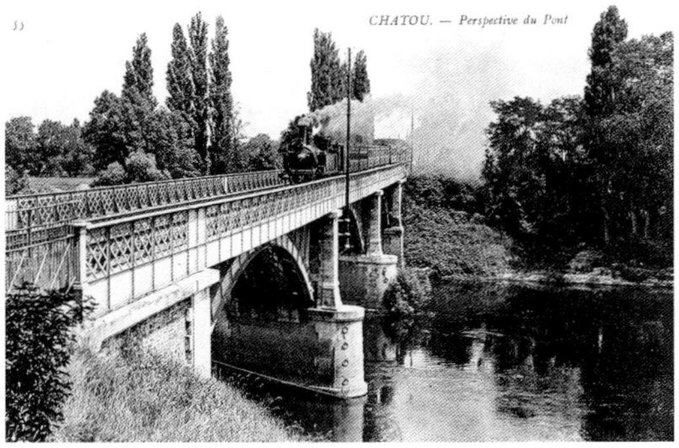

FIG. 109 *Chatou, Perspective of the Bridge*, nineteenth century. Photograph. Bibliothèque nationale de France, Paris.

PROVENANCE:
Sold by Renoir to Gustave Caillebotte (1848–1894) by 1883; among the forty works bequeathed by him to the state in 1896; Paris, Musée du Luxembourg, 1896–1933; Musée du Louvre, Jeu de Paume, 1933–1986; Musée d'Orsay

LITERATURE:
Herbert 1988, pp. 246–9; Compin, Lacambre and Roquebert 1990, II, p. 395; Bumpus 1990, no. 36; Distel 1995, pp. 64–5

for the landscape entered the collection of Renoir's great friend and patron Gustave Caillebotte, who would own four landscapes by the artist, three of which are in the current exhibition (see cats. 31, 36).[8] Caillebotte generously supported several Impressionists financially in the 1870s – Renoir paid off a four-year-old debt of 5,500 francs in June 1881 – but acquired their paintings for modest sums.[9] He rarely paid more than 300 francs for Monet's landscapes and Renoir's *Railway Bridge at Chatou* it is unlikely to have cost him much more.[10] We do not know when this landscape entered Caillebotte's collection – shortly after its completion, no doubt – but it was certainly in his possession by early 1883, when it was among the five works lent to Durand-Ruel's ill-fated Renoir retrospective of March of that year.[11] There it was exhibited under the title '*Les Marronniers roses*' and, while not singled out in any review, was denigrated by association. As I have noted in my essay in this catalogue, Renoir's recent landscapes solicited surprisingly negative opinion from the very critics who had formerly numbered among the chief supporters of his work.[12]

The landscape changed title when it was inventoried with the other '*Tableaux légués à l'Etat*' in Caillebotte's studio in his mansion at Petit Gennevilliers on 8 March 1894. The notary appraising the work described it as 'a painting by Renoir in its gilded frame (representing) the île de Croissy'.[13] Less than a fortnight later, Gustave Geffroy moved the landscape's location upstream, publishing the work as showing the bridge at Chatou ('*Le Pont de Chatou*'), and this is the title that it has retained ever since, with clarification as to the sort of bridge portrayed.[14] CBB

1 Renoir informed Duret on 18 April 1881 that he was 'struggling with flowers in bloom'; he delivered a group of four Chatou landscapes to Durand-Ruel on 6 July 1881. These documents establish the period in which *Railway Bridge at Chatou* was conceived and completed; see further cat. 50.

2 Herbert 1988, p. 248.

3 Joanne 1881, p. 140.

4 *Ibidem*, pp. 144–5: '*Chatou est pour les pêcheurs, ce qu'est Asnières pour les canotiers, leur lieu de prédilection.*' On Monet and Renoir's paintings that incorporate the St-Germain line, see Crosnier-Leconte 1990, pp. 12–19.

5 Herbert 1988, p. 248.

6 Rathbone 1996, pp. 90–2.

7 For reasons that are not altogether apparent, the signature on this painting is repeatedly catalogued as having been '*ajoutée postérieurement par Renoir*'; see Compin and Roquebert 1986, IV, p. 175, and Compin, Lacambre and Roquebert 1990, II, p. 395.

8 See Anne Distel's illustrated inventory of Caillebotte's collection in Distel 1994, pp. 63–5.

9 See 'Gustave Caillebotte, peintre, mécène et collectionneur' and the chronology in Distel 1994, pp. 21–30 and 351–5. On 22 June 1881, Renoir acquitted a debt contracted in 1877, perhaps related to an ill-fated joint venture to manufacture Mac Lean cement; see *Pierre-Auguste Renoir, 1841–1919, Personal Artefacts and Archives Collection*, Hantman's, 14 May 2005, lot 17.

10 It should be noted that Renoir's *The Bridge at Chatou* (cat. 32) had sold to de Bellio for 42 francs in the disastrous Hoschedé sale of 5 June 1878; Bodelsen 1968, p. 340.

11 On the third of Durand-Ruel's one-man shows, held in rented premises at 9 boulevard de la Madeleine, see Ward 1996, pp. 616–18.

12 Renoir himself was more concerned about securing figure paintings from Caillebotte's collection for this retrospective; see his undated letter to '*Mon cher Caillebotte*', in which he delicately enquired about the *Nude in the Sunlight*, 1875 (Musée d'Orsay, Paris), which Caillebotte decided not to lend; Berhaut 1994, p. 277.

13 '*Un tableau de Renoir avec cadre doré "île de Croissy"*: *Inventaire après le décès de monsieur Gustave Caillebotte;* Distel 1994, p. 31.

14 Geffroy's article, 'La Collection Caillebotte', appeared in *Le Journal* on 19 March 1894; when the bequest was finally exhibited at the Musée du Luxembourg in February 1897 the work was entitled *Le Pont de chemin de fer à Chatou;* Distel 1994, pp. 64–5.

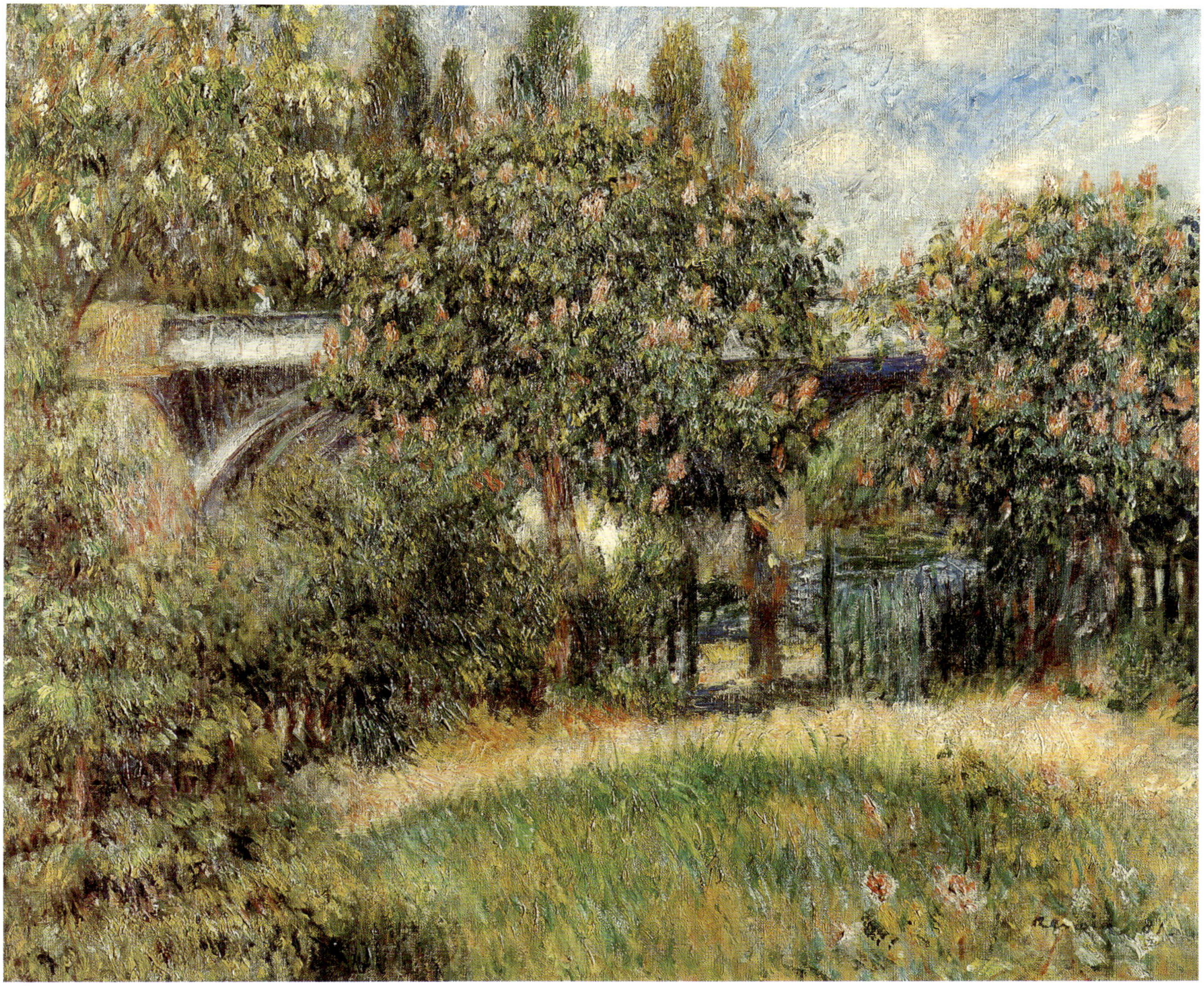

62 Venice, the Doge's Palace, 1881

Oil on canvas
54.3 × 65.3 cm; 21⅜ × 25⅞ in.
Sterling and Francine Clark Art Institute, Williamstown, Massachusetts (1955.596)

PROVENANCE:
Probably bought by Durand-Ruel from Renoir, 12 May 1882; E. Oppenheim sale, Paris, Hôtel Drouot, 11 May 1897, bought by Durand-Ruel; sold by Durand-Ruel to Sterling Clark, 3 March 1933

LITERATURE:
White 1969, pp. 337–9, 341–3, 345–7; Callen 1978, p. 74; White 1984, pp. 112, 121; House and Distel 1985, p. 231; Berson 1996, I, pp. 381, 388, 394–6, 400–2, 405–6, 410, 413, 416 (reprinting reviews of the 1882 group exhibition), and II, pp. 211, 230; Kern 1996, pp. 77, 78, 80, 83

Renoir's primary motive in travelling to Italy in 1881–2 was to study the work of the Old Masters, and notably to see the work of Raphael[1] – an unexpected interest for an Impressionist painter, and one that stands as a clear marker of Renoir's dissatisfaction with the informality and lack of draughtsmanship in his own recent work. However, his first major stop in Italy was in Venice, in late October and early November 1881. The fluent painterly qualities of Venetian sixteenth-century painting, notably of Titian and Veronese, would have been far closer than Raphael to his own previous interests, but neither his letters from Venice nor his later reminiscences suggest that his experience of their paintings in Venice was a revelation to him; he had studied their work closely in the Louvre;[2] it was the art of Tiepolo and Carpaccio that aroused his interest.[3]

His main focus in Venice was the place itself, and he painted a sequence of canvases of the standard tourist sites – the Grand Canal, the Lagoon, the gondolas (see cats. 62, 63) and the Doge's Palace. *Venice, The Doge's Palace* is one of the two most highly finished of these canvases; the other represents the Grand Canal. It seems very likely that these were the two Venetian views that Durand-Ruel included in the seventh Impressionist group exhibition in March 1882.[4] Together, they present the most stereotypical view of Venice, sites that had been represented by the city's most celebrated painters, by Canaletto, Turner and many others. As he wrote to Charles Deudon, 'I have painted the Doge's Palace seen from San Giorgio; that has never been done before, I think. There were at least six of us queuing up to paint it.'[5]

Venice, the Doge's Palace is a fascinating attempt to combine topographical specificity with Impressionist facture. The brushwork is busy and variegated throughout, and the forms of the buildings are suggested by coloured touches rather than linear contours. Their shadowed sides are richly coloured, predominantly in a full blue, picking up the colour of the sky, and set off against the dominant cream, yellow and soft orange hues that define their sunlit façades. The same colours are repeated in the water, with the addition of rich green strokes. At the centre of the composition, the green, white and red flag acts as a pivot around which the predominant blue-orange contrast of the rest of the composition revolves (the house in *The Bridge at Chatou*, cat. 32, fulfils a very similar function). The darker tones of the shadowed sides of the buildings also help to structure the composition. Typically for Renoir, the reflections in the water are only approximately indicated – the reflection of the Campanile, for instance, is wider than the tower itself; unlike Monet, Renoir never notated such effects precisely.

Within this array of coloured touches, a remarkable amount of information is conveyed about the details of the buildings. Though not precisely defined, the superimposed arcading of the Doge's Palace and the fenestration of the Zecca to the left are indicated in considerable detail; the upper level of arcading on the Palace façade appears even to have the correct number of arches (34), and the orb and cross that top the principal dome of San Marco can be clearly seen above the Palace roof.

Critical response to the Venice canvases at the 1882 exhibition was largely negative. Several reviewers compared them to the work of Félix Ziem, renowned for his endlessly repeated hot-toned Venetian views; Jacques de Biez described them as 'the ugliest fireworks',[6] while Paul Leroi saw them as 'the most outrageous series of ferocious daubs that a calumniator of Venice could possibly imagine'.[7] Louis Leroy was

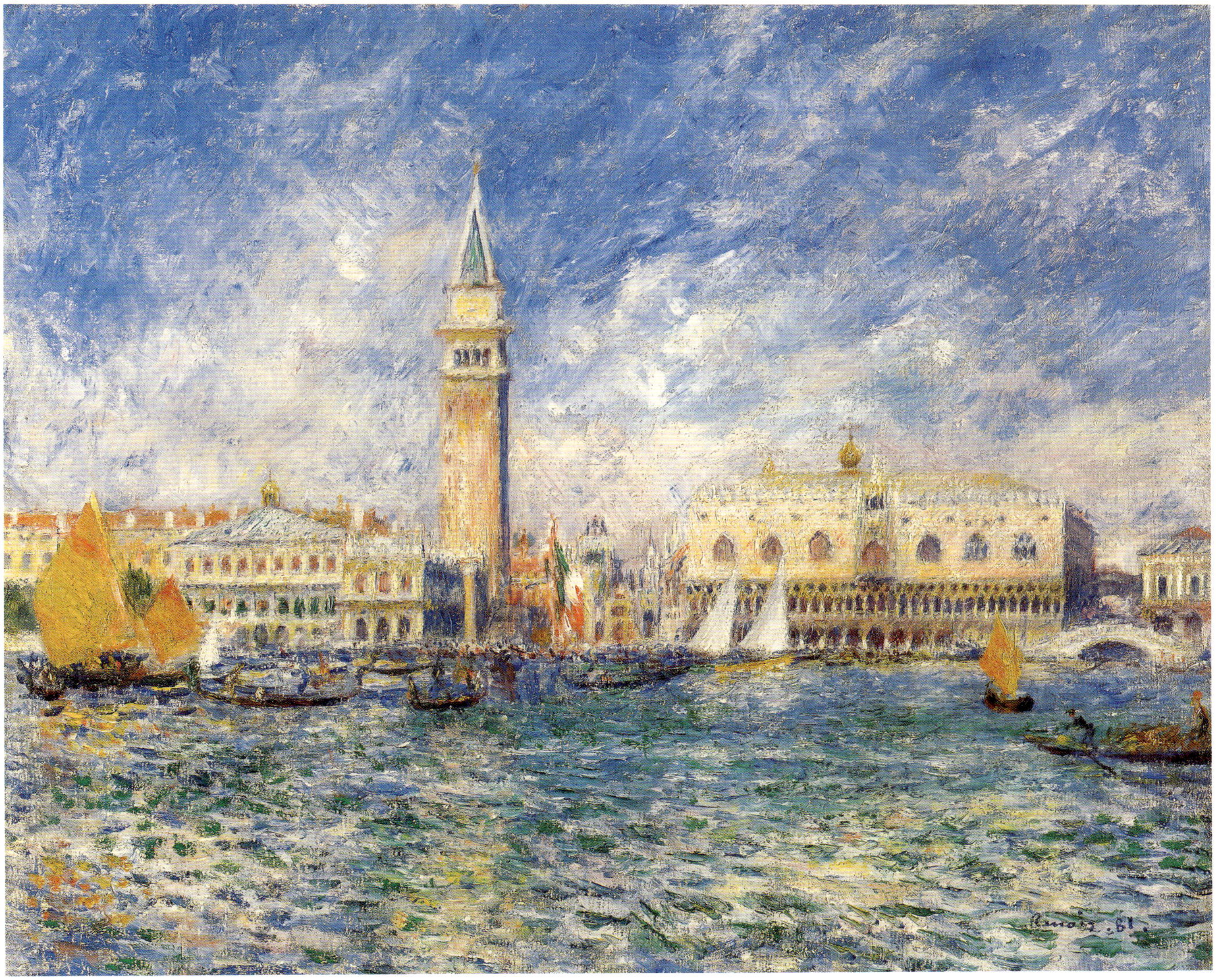

particularly critical of the treatment of the water: 'The painter has posed himself this problem: to create water that is . . . solid, on which gondolas on wheels can roll, without it being possible to interpret this hatched, striped, spotty surface as any sort of dry land. He has admirably mastered this difficulty. It resembles nothing in the known world.'[8] JH

1 See letter from Renoir to Madame Charpentier, n.d., from Venice, in Florisoone 1938, p. 36.
2 *Ibidem.*
3 *Ibid.*, for mention of his discovery of Tiepolo; Vollard 1938, p. 201, for his discovery of Carpaccio.
4 Durand-Ruel registered two Venetian views, one of them subtitled '*G. Canal*', in his stockbook on 30 November 1881; this entry was erased and the pictures re-entered in the stockbook on 12 May 1882, presumably when the purchase was completed. These must have been the two Venice views included in the seventh group exhibition in March 1882, since all the Renoirs exhibited came from the dealer's stock, and they were the only Venice views in his hands by this date. The '*G. Canal*' picture can be securely identified as the painting now in the Museum of Fine Arts, Boston (cat. 63). For many reasons, it is highly probable that the other canvas was *Venice, The Doge's Palace*: the two are the same size; they are very similar in execution, and markedly different from Renoir's other Venice views; the reviewers consistently discussed them as a pair; and in a letter to Charles Deudon from Venice, Renoir mentioned that he had sent two canvases to Durand-Ruel, immediately following this by describing the view of the Doge's Palace, implying that it was one of the two; letter from Renoir to Charles Deudon, n.d., from Venice, in Schneider 1945, pp. 96–7.
5 Letter from Renoir to Charles Deudon, n.d., from Venice, as cited in note 4.
6 Jacques de Biez, 'Les Petits Salons: les Indépendants', *Paris*, 8 March 1882, reprinted in Berson 1996, I, p. 381.
7 Paul Leroi, 'Salon de 1882', *L'Art*, 29, 1882, p. 98, reprinted in Berson 1996, I, p. 401.
8 Louis Leroy, 'Exposition des impressionnistes', *Le Charivari*, 17 March 1882, reprinted in Berson 1996, I, p. 402.

63 The Grand Canal, Venice, 1881

Oil on canvas
54 × 65.1 cm; 21¼ × 25¾ in.
Museum of Fine Arts, Boston, Massachusetts. Bequest of Alexander Cochrane (19.173)

Scenes of the Grand Canal had been a staple of Venetian *veduta* or view painting since Carlevarijs, Canaletto and Bellotto invented the genre and carried it to its highest achievements in the eighteenth century. They were second in popularity perhaps only to scenes of the Doge's Palace (cat. 62). Even more than depictions of the palace as seen across the waters of the wide Bacino, however, such canal views insistently revealed the essential strangeness of Venice, for there the buildings that lined both sides as they would a city street rose straight up out of the water instead. It was this magical incongruity that had long enthralled visitors to the Serenissima, and art buyers too. Renoir would have known it when he painted the present view; if not, his dealer, Durand-Ruel, might well have reminded him what a saleable Venetian scene would be.

Unlike the earlier great exponents of *veduta* painting, who rendered each building with painstaking accuracy in order that viewers could identify each one, Renoir was more interested in the general effect of sunlight shimmering on water and glinting off richly textured stone façades.[1] It is not immediately apparent which stretch of the Grand Canal we are looking at, so subsumed are the buildings in the rich atmospheric effects Renoir captures. The two rows of *palazzi* that blend into each other in the distance seem like a golden caesura across the centre of the canvas between blue sky above, tinged with scudding clouds, and the blue water below, flecked with shimmering reflections. The wideness of the canal at the point Renoir depicts it, however, and the commanding façade of the *palazzo* at far left suggest that it is the heavily trafficked stretch running from the magnificent Ca' Foscari towards the Rialto bridge. 'The view from Palazzo Foscari at the Volta del Canal back to the Rialto Bridge, a distance of some 800 metres, is one of the most splendid that Venice has to offer and Canaletto painted it several times … making it one of the canonical images of the city' (fig. 110).[2] Renoir was interested here in experiencing for himself what so many other visitors to Venice had experienced before him, and what so many fellow artists had painted; he was producing tourist art of a very high order.

PROVENANCE:
Sold by the artist to Durand-Ruel, Paris, 1882; Durand-Ruel, New York, 1889; Alexander Cochrane, Boston; Bequest of Alexander Cochrane to the Museum of Fine Arts, Boston, 1919

LITERATURE:
Drucker 1944, no. 73; Fezzi 1972, no. 482; Wildenstein 1972, no. 28; Tucker 2001, no. 23; House 2004, pp. 187–8

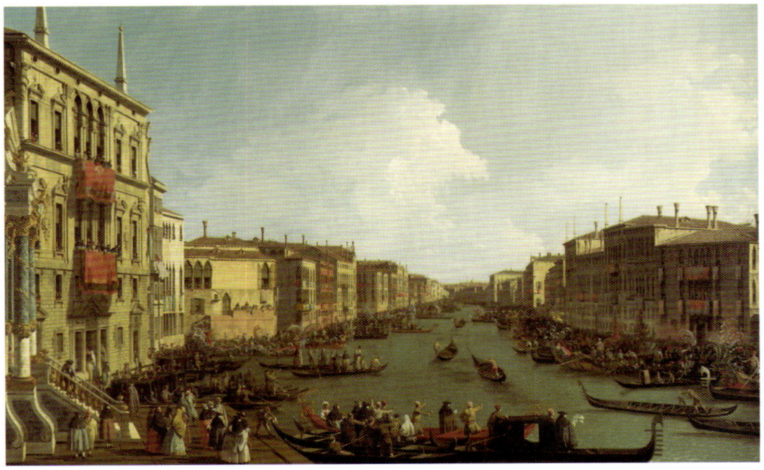

FIG. 110 Canaletto (1697–1768), *Venice: A Regatta on the Grand Canal*, about 1735. Oil on canvas, 117.2 × 186.7 cm; 46 × 73½ in. The National Gallery, London, 1876 (NG 938).

The pomp and splendour of the regattas that had once made this stretch of the canal an irresistible lure for *veduta* painters and their patrons were largely a thing of the past by the time Renoir visited. Nonetheless the scene is richly animated by the black-hulled gondolas, so distinctive of the city, and the striped mooring poles that jut out of the water.[3] Edouard Manet had painted beguiling views of Venice featuring both when he visited in 1874, works that Renoir might well have known.[4] Renoir does not use black paint to depict the gondolas, however, but deep purples and blues that suggest the play of light reflected off the water, as he instinctively understood that the interaction of water and sunlight and the transformations they wrought on the physical world were the key to Venice's deep and abiding charm. Soon after Renoir's return to Paris, Durand-Ruel included the painting in the seventh Impressionist Exhibition of 1882. CR

Shown in Philadelphia only

1 This is not to say that Canaletto and his contemporaries did not alter the spatial relationships among buildings and otherwise re-arrange reality in their Venetian paintings; they manipulated the laws of perspective with great subtlety to do so. But individual *palazzi* and *chiese* could always be identified. On this subject, see D. Bomford and G. Finaldi, *Venice through Canaletto's Eyes*, exh. cat., National Gallery, London, 1998.

2 *Ibidem*, p. 28.

3 Renoir could not have painted his picture on 1 or 2 November 1881, as the gondoliers were on strike on those days, according to Grieve in A. Grieve, *Whistler's Venice*, New Haven and London, 2000, p. 20.

4 Manet's Venetian scenes of 1875 were not exhibited until later, but one was owned by Tissot and another by the collector and singer Fauré, both known to Renoir.

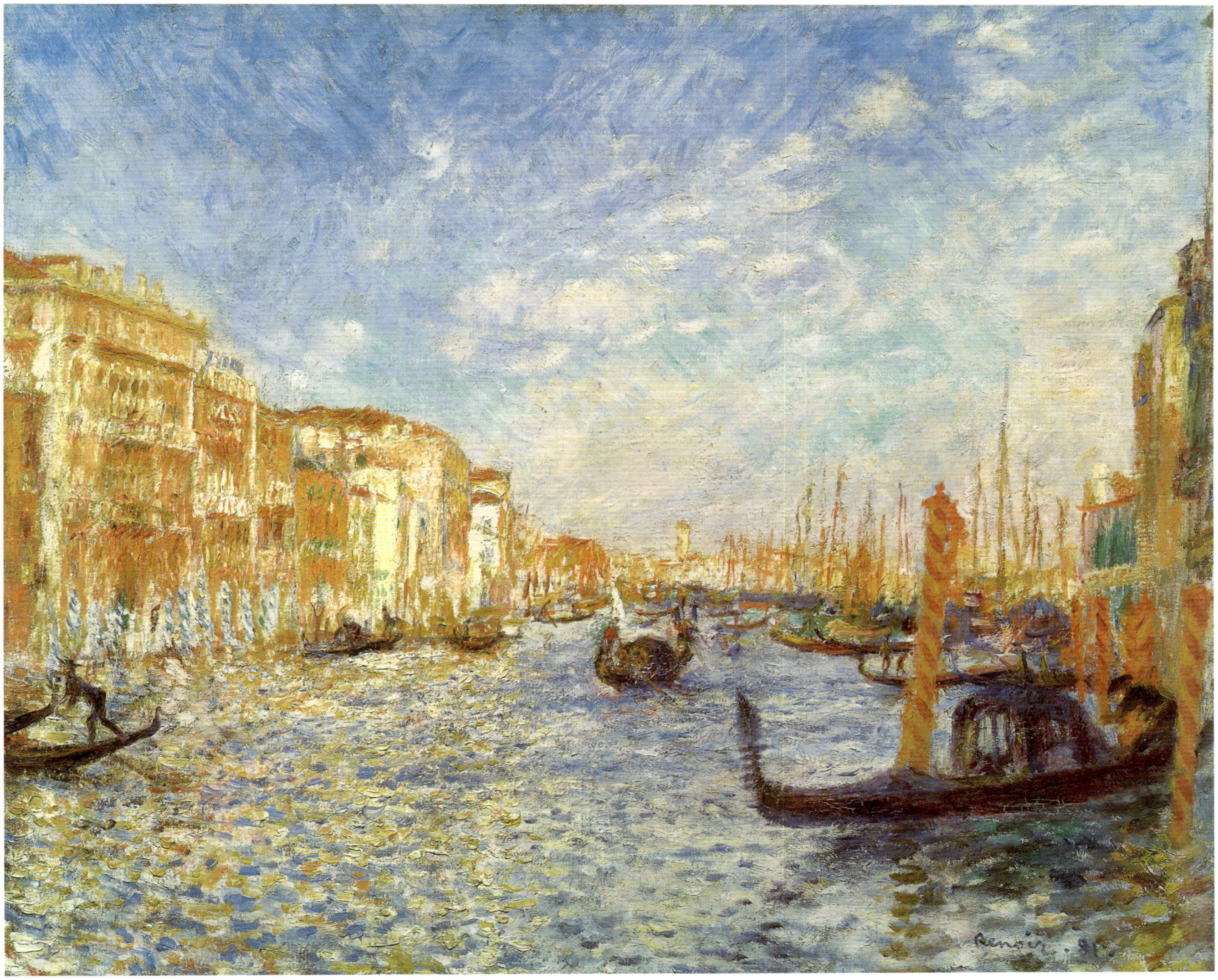

64 Piazza San Marco, Venice, 1881

Oil on canvas
65.4 × 81.3 cm; 25¾ × 32 in.
The Minneapolis Institute of Arts, Minnesota. The John R. Van Derlip Fund (51.19)

PROVENANCE:
Robert de Bonnières, Paris, before 1892; Ambroise Vollard, Paris; Hugo von Tschudi, Munich, 1910; bequeathed by Tschudi to the Pinakothek (Staatsgalerie), Munich, by 1912; de-accessioned 1942; Sam Salz, Inc., New York, by 1951; acquired by the Minneapolis Institute of Arts, 1951

LITERATURE:
Vollard 1918, vol. 1, no. 66; Meier-Graefe 1929, p. 156, pl. 142; Drucker 1944, p. 72, pl. 66; White 1969, pp. 345–6, no. 4 and letter 1; Minneapolis Institute of Arts, 1970, pp. 284–5, no. 151; Fezzi 1972, no. 484; Isaacson 1980, no. 49; Schneider 1985, p. 54; House and Distel 1985, no. 61; Gerstein 1989, no. 73; Brettell 2000, p. 184, fig. 129

Perhaps because he knew such pictures would be saleable commodities, Renoir made a point of painting the most familiar and popular sites of Venice. The Doge's Palace (cat. 62) had been depicted by generations of artists before him. Meanwhile contemporaries like Félix Ziem made such views their lucrative stock-in-trade. However, Renoir would be harshly criticised in avant-garde circles in Paris for the conventionality of his Venetian scenes: Eugène Manet called the works mentioned above 'detestable'[1] when Durand-Ruel included them in the seventh Impressionist Exhibition in 1882.

Renoir's spirited *Piazza San Marco* differs from his other perhaps too predictable and more fully resolved Venetian views. It is not finished but a sketch with much white priming still visible. The freedom of execution – an approach not likely to attract conventional Parisian collectors at the time – further animates the work and imbues it with a palpable sense of personal engagement on the part of the artist. The spatial complexity of the piazza is downplayed. Neighbouring monuments such as the Campanile at right, which figures prominently in *Venice, the Doge's Palace*, are only summarily indicated here, and without detail. The square is populated by pigeons and several strollers at left, each little more than a quick lick of paint. Rather, Renoir focuses attention on, indeed provides a vivid 'portrait' of, the basilica itself. There, the rich play and counter-play of architectural forms, the deep recesses of portals, the arcades and bundled columns advancing and retreating in space, the domes and cupolas, all shimmering in gold like a celestial vision, predominate. The façade is touched with flecks of red and blue as well, evoking the dull lustre of antique mosaics with which the basilica is encrusted. This 'gloriously frenzied representation'[2] is marked, then, by an intensity of observation and economy of rendering that suggest Renoir approached the motif with more complex considerations in mind than those he brought to bear elsewhere in Venice.

By 1881 Renoir was passionately involved in thinking and writing about questions of architecture and architectural ornament, and in the comparison of modern, machine-made architecture with far more characterful ancient and medieval works. He had published two essays on the matter in 1877 and soon would begin assembling notes for more ambitious statements on the role of individual imagination and craft in the shaping of buildings. In about 1883, he would praise San Marco specifically as a telling example of that formal irregularity, in emulation of nature itself, which he considered the highest achievement of architecture: 'San Marco, regular to the eye, in its totality not a single matching detail. The regularity of the eye being the only acceptable one, [the builders] rejected the regularity of the compass'.[3] Such thinking, as Robert Herbert has shown, was influenced by the writings of John Ruskin, a passionate champion of medieval Venice and its architecture. 'No document survives that shows Renoir's awareness of Ruskin,' he comments, 'but his writings of

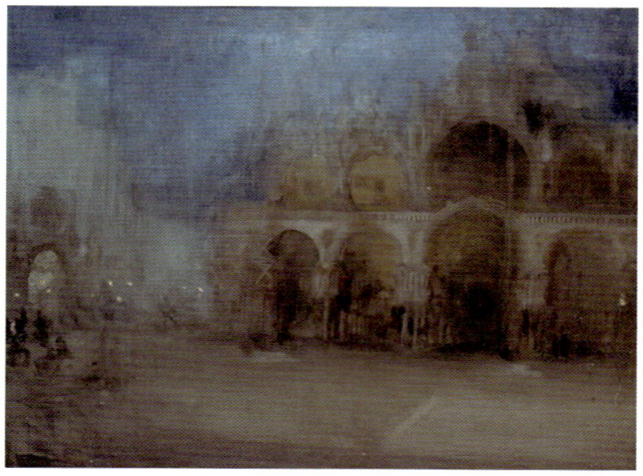

FIG. 111 James Abbott McNeill Whistler (1834–1903), *Nocturne: Blue and Gold – St Mark's, Venice*, 1880. Oil on canvas, 44.5 × 59.7 cm; 27½ × 23½ in. National Museums Wales (NMW A 210).

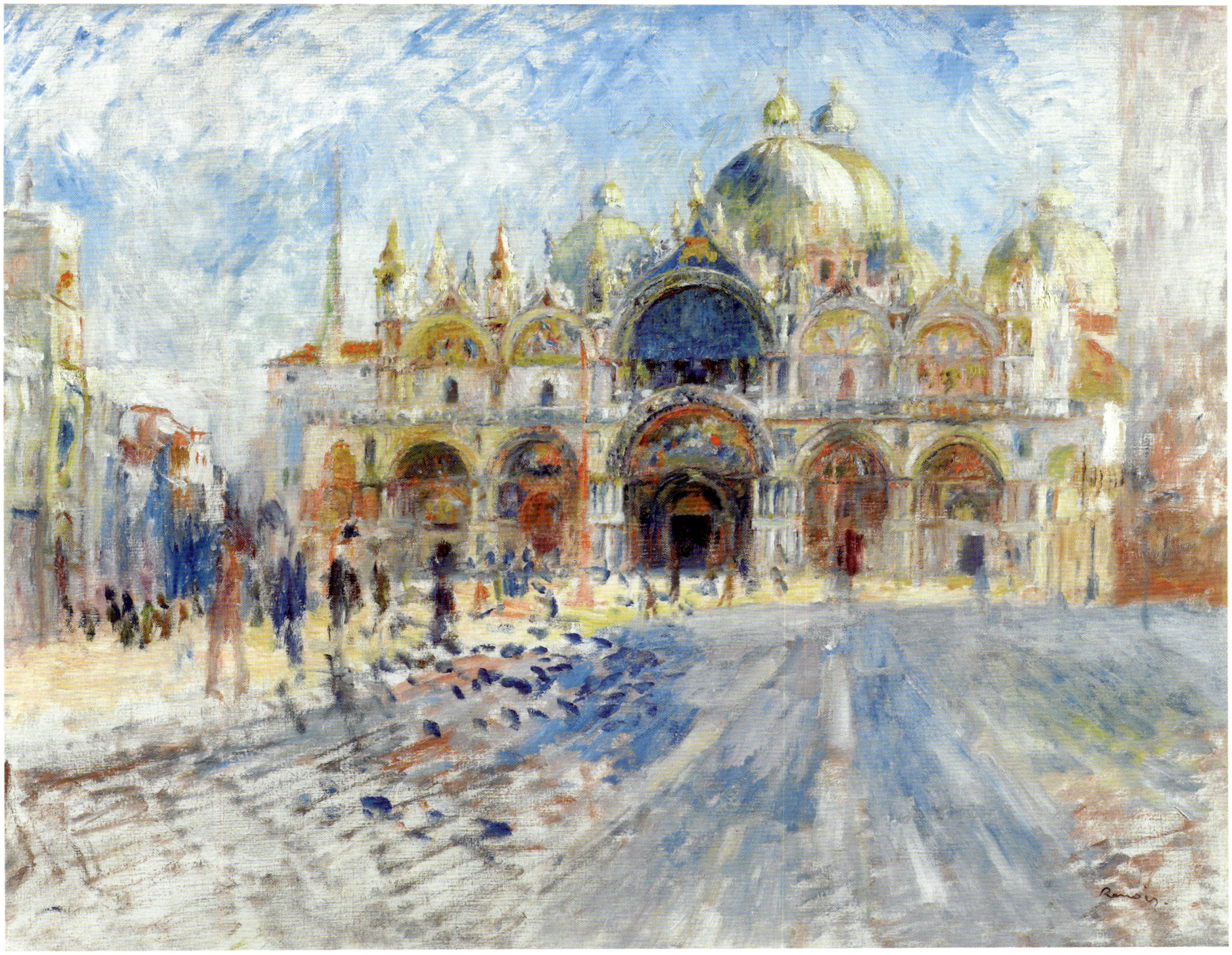

1883–4 . . . are surprisingly full of notions generally attached to the British critic.'[4] Herbert goes on to trace in detail the connections between the two men's thought. If Renoir was indeed coming to fashion himself a disciple of Ruskin, as he approached San Marco in 1881 he would have known that the basilica had only recently been the subject of intense international controversy, and that Ruskin had been at the centre of the storm.

Several years earlier an ill-judged restoration of the basilica had been undertaken that saw medieval mosaics replaced by jarringly modern substitutes; further barbarisms had been perpetrated on parts of the extensive marble cladding which, not being structural, need not have been discarded but were; much original detailing was irrevocably lost. More recently, it had been decided that the entire west façade facing the piazza should come under restoration as well. By the time Ruskin arrived in Venice in 1876 some of the scaffolding was already in place for work to begin. Ruskin, generally opposed to the restoration of early architecture and specifically committed to the preservation of San Marco, swung into action. He wrote articles on the desecration, successfully urged William Morris and others in Britain to take up the cause – some 30 articles critical of the restoration appeared in the British press alone in the final months of 1879[5] – and supported the publication in 1877 of an Italian-language book by the Venetian nobleman Conte Alvise Zorzi vehemently opposing the project. The British critic contributed a typically impassioned foreword.[6] The controversy was at its height in 1879 when Whistler visited Venice. His depiction of the Piazza San Marco in the gas-lit glow of evening, painted at that time, shows part of the west façade still under scaffolding (fig. 111).[7] Early in 1880 The Fine Art Society urged Whistler to make more Venetian images as a way of cashing in on the controversy.[8]

Ruskin was victorious. Because of the controversy he had provoked, an inquiry was launched and the restoration of the west façade was in the end cancelled. By the time Renoir arrived in Venice all scaffolding had disappeared; the masterpiece of medieval architecture was saved. It was a proof and demonstration that activism in defence of architecture – an activism that some four years earlier Renoir had urged on artists in order to save Paris from the perils of modernisation[9] – could indeed yield results. Renoir may have conceived the present painting, then, as more than another typical Venetian scene. It was perhaps a deeply felt private celebration of the principles he was coming to espouse about architecture, and by extension of the zealous and indefatigable critic on the basis of whose thought he was formulating his own. Having captured the character of the basilica so deftly, he saw no reason to bring the sketch to a higher finish. CR

1 Quoted in House and Distel 1985, no. 60, p. 202.
2 Brettell 2000, p. 184.
3 Renoir, 'Grammar, 1883–1884, F 12', in Herbert 2000, p. 124.
4 Herbert 2000, p. 25–6. He also remarks (p. 27, note 4) that Ruskin was 'a kind of local hero in Venice' by 1881 and that 'Renoir may well have been reminded of the British writer' when he came to paint the present picture; I wish to push that suggestion further here.
5 A. Grieve, *Whistler's Venice*, New Haven and London, 2000, p. 172.
6 On the San Marco controversy, see R. Hewison, *Ruskin a Venezia/Ruskin in Venice*, Venice 1983, pp. 62–5, and J. Unrau, *Ruskin and St Mark's*, London 1984.
7 Whistler and Renoir had lunch together at Chatou in the spring of 1881, soon after the former artist returned from Venice (see cat. 60). Lisa R. Leavitt has suggested that he may have urged Renoir to visit Venice on his forthcoming Italian trip (see *Impressionism Abroad: Boston and French Painting*, exh. cat., Royal Academy of Arts, London 2005, p. 121). Though no friend of Ruskin's – his lawsuit against the critic had driven him into bankruptcy – Whistler may also have discussed the San Marco controversy and his own images of the church and city with Renoir. Renoir's moody, tonal painting *Venice, Fog* (Kreeger Museum, Washington, DC; fig. 50, p. 69), reminiscent of Whistler's paintings, shows that the American artist was indeed on the French painter's mind in Venice.
8 A. Grieve, *Whistler's Venice*, New Haven and London, 2000, p. 120.
9 On which, see my essay in this catalogue, pp. 33–49.

65 The Bay of Naples (Morning), 1881

Formerly known as *The Bay of Naples (Evening)*
Oil on canvas
59.7 × 81.3 cm; 23½ × 32 in.
The Metropolitan Museum of Art, New York. Bequest of Julia W. Emmons, 1956 (56.135.8)

Renoir reached Naples late in 1881 and stayed for two months, departing in the second half of January 1882. As Venice had done earlier in his Italian sojourn, but Rome failed to do, the crumbling but endlessly vibrant southern metropolis inspired Renoir to paint. Primarily, he devoted himself to the female figure and produced such ambitious canvases as *Mother and Child* (fig. 49, p. 69; Barnes Foundation, Merion, PA) and *Blonde Bather I* (fig. 47, p. 68; Sterling and Francine Clark Art Institute, Williamstown, MA), both of which evince the impact that the art of Raphael, recently studied in Rome, had had upon him. During his stay he also travelled in the vicinity of Naples, to Sorrento and Capri, and as far as Palermo in Sicily, where he gained access to Richard Wagner and sketched his portrait (Musée d'Orsay, Paris). He also found time for landscape, especially cityscape painting, as Naples abundantly lived up to its picturesque reputation. Like Algiers earlier in the year, where brilliant sunlight and the city's proximity to the sea dazzled him, at Naples Renoir was struck by the gradations of the light and by the city's imposing location on a sweeping bay overlooking the Mediterranean. Towering over the scene was the distinctive profile of Vesuvius, universal symbol of nature's force.

Renoir painted two closely related views of the bay with its ships and bustling quay and the volcano beyond – the present work in New York and a second in Williamstown (fig. 112). It has become common to ascribe times of day to the two pictures, the Williamstown picture usually being seen as a depiction of morning, the New York painting one of evening.[2] However, John House, currently cataloguing the rich collection of Renoirs at Williamstown, has realised that at some point in their history the subjects of the two pictures were confused with one another: the geographical orientation of Naples and the angles of sunlight in the paintings establish that the present work must in fact be a morning view and the Williamstown painting an evening scene.[3] Colin B. Bailey remarks of a recent visit, moreover, that the reflections on the water of the bay are indeed more dramatic in the morning, as in the New York painting, and more generalised in the late afternoon and evening, as in the Williamstown work.[4]

Like the earlier *Venice, the Doge's Palace* (cat. 62), the choice of motif in both Neapolitan scenes is essentially conventional. Renoir has positioned himself at a window or on a balcony above the north-eastern end of the quay at the Piazza Municipio, perhaps at the Hotel Trinacaria where he lodged.[5] He looks down and across at the most instantly recognisable features of the site, the semi-circular bay and looming volcano. Such a familiar image, he might have hoped, would surely attract Parisian collectors. This was also a modest attempt at series painting, structured on the changing light. Renoir distinguishes between the morning shadows of the present painting, which are puddles of blue on the inland side of the carts, and the shadows of evening which stretch out in front of or behind the carts moving

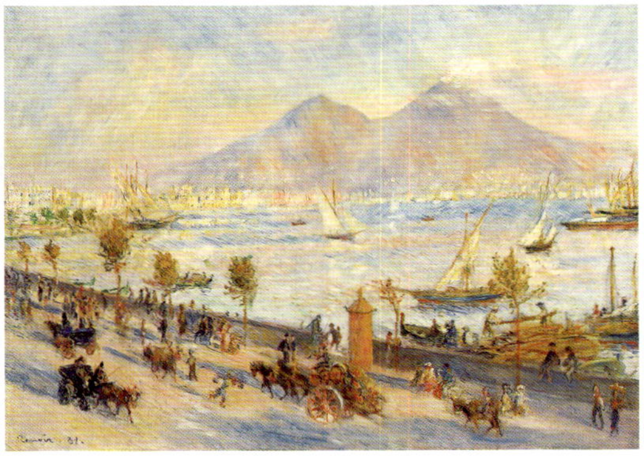

FIG. 112 *The Bay of Naples*, 1881. Oil on canvas, 57.9 × 80.8 cm; 22⅞ × 31⅞ in. Sterling and Francine Clark Art Institute, Williamstown, Massachusetts (1955.587).

PROVENANCE:
Sold by the artist to Durand-Ruel, 22 May 1882; bought by Inglis, 1 May 1883; bought by Boussod & Valadon, Paris, 18 July 1888; bought by Durand-Ruel, 24 December 1891;[1] Potter Palmer, Chicago, in 1894; Durand-Ruel Gallery, New York, 1894–1911; Arthur B. Emmons, New York and Newport, 1911–23; Mrs Arthur B. Emmons, 1922–56; The Metropolitan Museum of Art, New York, bequest of Mrs Arthur B. Emmons, 1956

LITERATURE:
Wildenstein, New York, 1958, no. 33; Sterling and Salinger 1967, p. 154–5, illus.; White 1969, pp. 333–51; Fezzi 1972, no. 491; Ann Arbor 1977, no. 46; Baetjer 1980, I, p. 152; White 1984, pp. 116, 122; Shone 2002, p. 51, illus.

FIG. 113 The Bay of Naples in the morning, photograph by Colin B. Bailey, August 2006.

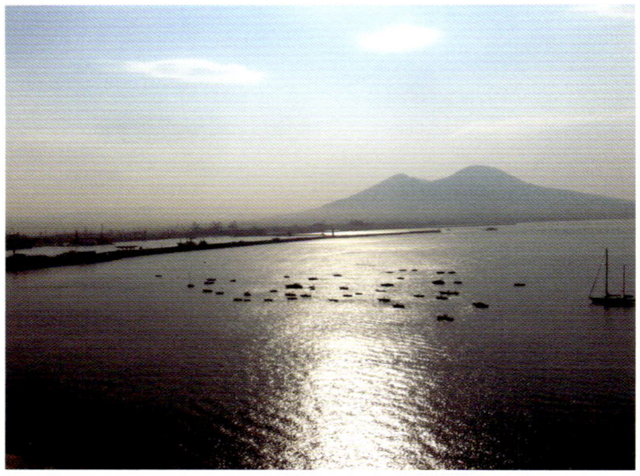

along the quay at lower left. The present picture, however, is somewhat more panoramic than the one at Williamstown. The sweep of the bay is broader and more detailed, the Neapolitans populating the quay smaller. Sky takes up a greater proportion of the canvas. The artist also provides more information about his own location, as at the lower left the edge of a walled terrace can be seen, on or just above which he would have positioned his easel.

Renoir was deeply impressed by the ancient Roman frescoes from Pompeii, over which he lingered in the national museum at Naples, admiring the sense in them of permeating light. Their influence has been detected in the subdued, pastel palettes of these pictures.[6] Certainly, the muted tonal unity he achieves in the Naples views recalls the effect of fresco. But he is working in oils, and the way he achieves that effect is necessarily different: it is effected in part by careful parallel brushstrokes, particularly in the sky of the present painting, which lacks almost altogether the complementary pink tones that animate the Williamstown painting and has a more general blue tonality. Those parallel strokes are wittily rhymed by the diagonal lines of the furled sails of the boats in the harbour, which set up an agitated linear rhythm across the centre of the canvas.

Renoir knew that his old friend Cézanne had been involved for several years in painting another bay, at L'Estaque, and that his art was making great advances as he examined and re-examined that not dissimilar Mediterranean motif. Perhaps it was as he painted the Bay of Naples that Renoir resolved to visit Cézanne at L'Estaque on his way home from Italy, and to work with him there (see cats. 66, 67). CR

1 For the painting's early provenance, see Rewald, 'Theo van Gogh as art dealer', in *Studies in Post-Impressionism*, London and New York 1986, pp. 32, 96, 109 (footnote 60); with thanks to Martin Bailey for drawing attention to this source.
2 It is not yet clear when this temporal distinction was first introduced.
3 John House in communication with the author, 14 July 2006; full details of this important correction will appear in House's forthcoming catalogue of the Clark Renoirs. The author was initially sceptical but a photograph of the Bay of Naples in the morning recently taken by Colin B. Bailey (fig. 113), consultation with colleagues Dawson Carr and Larry Keith, both knowledgeable about Naples, and reference to Google Earth, quickly confirmed the correctness of House's observation.
4 Colin B. Bailey in communication with the author, 13 September 2006.
5 Néret 2001, p. 155. Bailey reports that no trace of the hotel is to be seen today.
6 White 1984, p. 115; Kern 1996, p. 80.

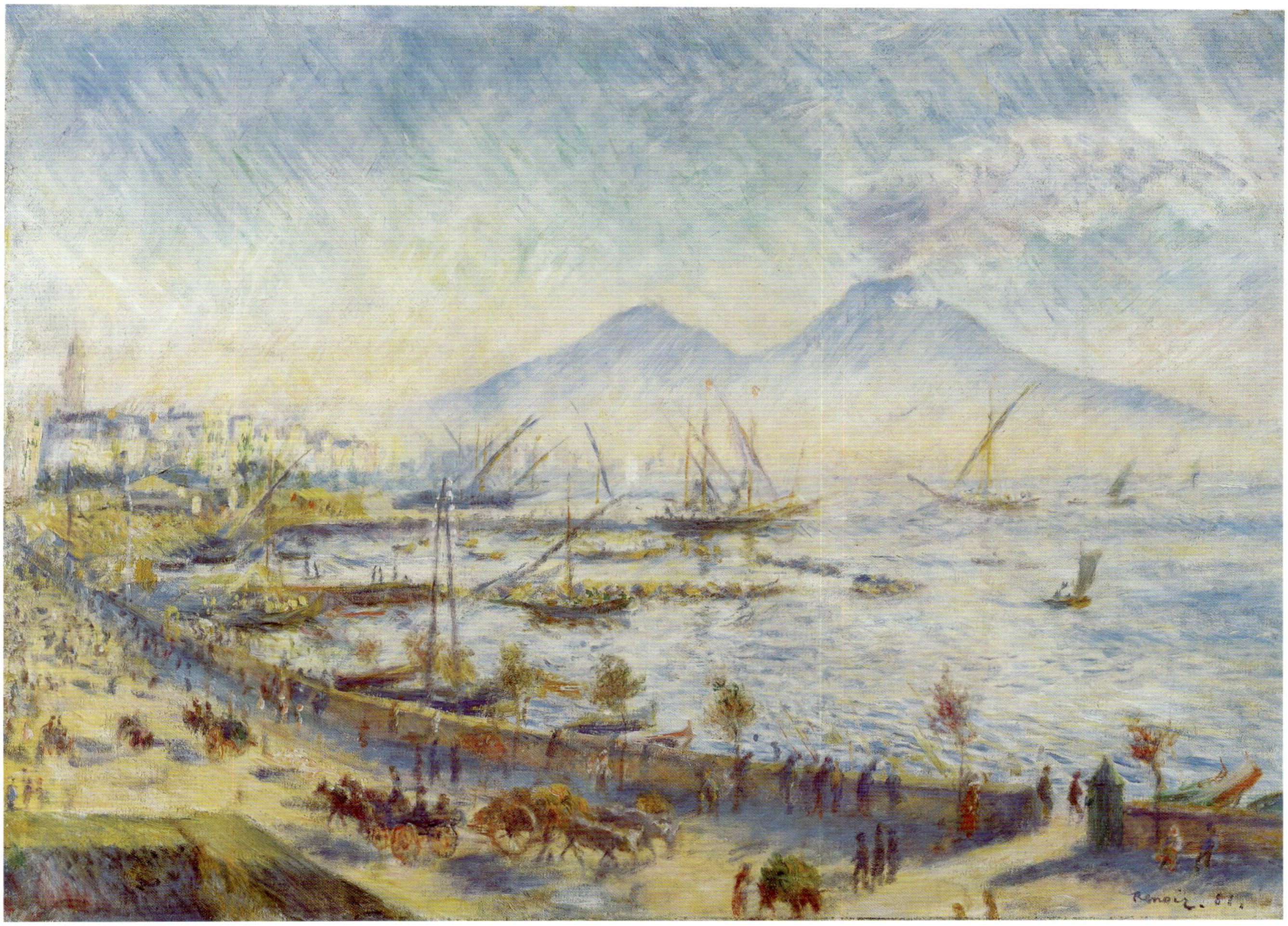

66 Rocks at L'Estaque, 1882

Oil on canvas
32.2 × 40.3 cm; 12⅝ × 15⅞ in.
Private collection

PROVENANCE:
Galerie Durand-Ruel, Paris; Sotheby's, New York, 15 November 1989, lot 318; Sotheby's, London, 24 June 1996, lot 32; private collection, London

LITERATURE:
Fezzi 1972, no. 509; Fezzi 1985 no. 487; Tucker 2001, no. 24

On his return from Italy in January 1882, Renoir passed through Provence, staying at the Hôtel des Bains in L'Estaque, a small fishing village on the Mediterranean, north-west of Marseilles. 'It would really be a shame to leave this lovely countryside without bringing something back,' he noted in a letter to Paul Durand-Ruel, his dealer, referring to the works he intended to paint there.[1] He went on, almost as an afterthought, 'What's more, I met Cézanne there and we're going to work together.' There is something disingenuous in Renoir's tone here, as if the meeting with Cézanne were mere chance, though of course he would not be the first artist to hide his true motives from a dealer or patron. Renoir would have known that L'Estaque played a major role in Cézanne's life and work. His old friend had summered there as a child, felt deeply drawn to the place, and had painted assiduously at L'Estaque from the late 1860s. Indeed, it was the site where his art can be said to have reached its maturity.[2] The intense admiration that Renoir and his colleagues were coming to feel for Cézanne's art derived in part from the audacious works he had made in and around the town and looking across its bay. In their monumentality and architectonic clarity these canvases were unlike anything they themselves had yet attempted. Renoir, returning from Italy, would have diverted to L'Estaque recognising the site to be central to Cézanne's achievement and with the firm intention of meeting his friend there. (Whether Cézanne knew in advance he was coming is not certain.) The paintings Renoir executed at L'Estaque – four of them, including the present work and *Rocky Crags at L'Estaque* (cat. 67), and there might have been more if he had not been felled by a serious attack of pneumonia – testify to the influence Cézanne exerted on the slightly younger artist, and to the alacrity with which Renoir sought out and absorbed the lessons Cézanne taught. Perhaps he did not want Durand-Ruel to know that, now past 40, he was still quite so willing to put himself in the position of student to a contemporary.

Like *Rocky Crags at L'Estaque*, the present painting, too, takes as its subject the shrub-covered hills above the village. Unlike that picture, and as the much larger scale of the trees indicates, this is more a close-up view of the motif, nearer the top of a hill. The motif corresponds, more or less, to the upper left quadrant of *Rocky Crags at L'Estaque* – this is not to say that it is necessarily the same motif, but that its extent is about a quarter that of the more panoramic Boston picture, the scale of individual objects about four times larger. The present work is also more fully detailed, with greater attention paid to the shrubbery, and less to the bare rock face that gives the Boston picture such monumentality. In some areas, including the grass and sky, Renoir uses small parallel brush strokes derived from Cézanne's example, though elsewhere he follows the contours of forms in a manner more consistent with his own earlier painting style. He wrote from L'Estaque to another patron, Madame Charpentier, of his painting there, 'I have ended up by not bothering any more with the small details.'[3] In comparison to *Rocky Crags* this picture does, however, bother with small details and more closely resembles complex works of the previous year, teeming with incident, like *Arab Festival* (cat. 54). This fact, combined with the more intimate view of the landscape, suggests that Renoir may have painted this picture relatively early in his stay. Subsequently, he reverted to the grander and more panoramic vision of *Rocky Crags* which, as has long been recognised, more fully assimilates

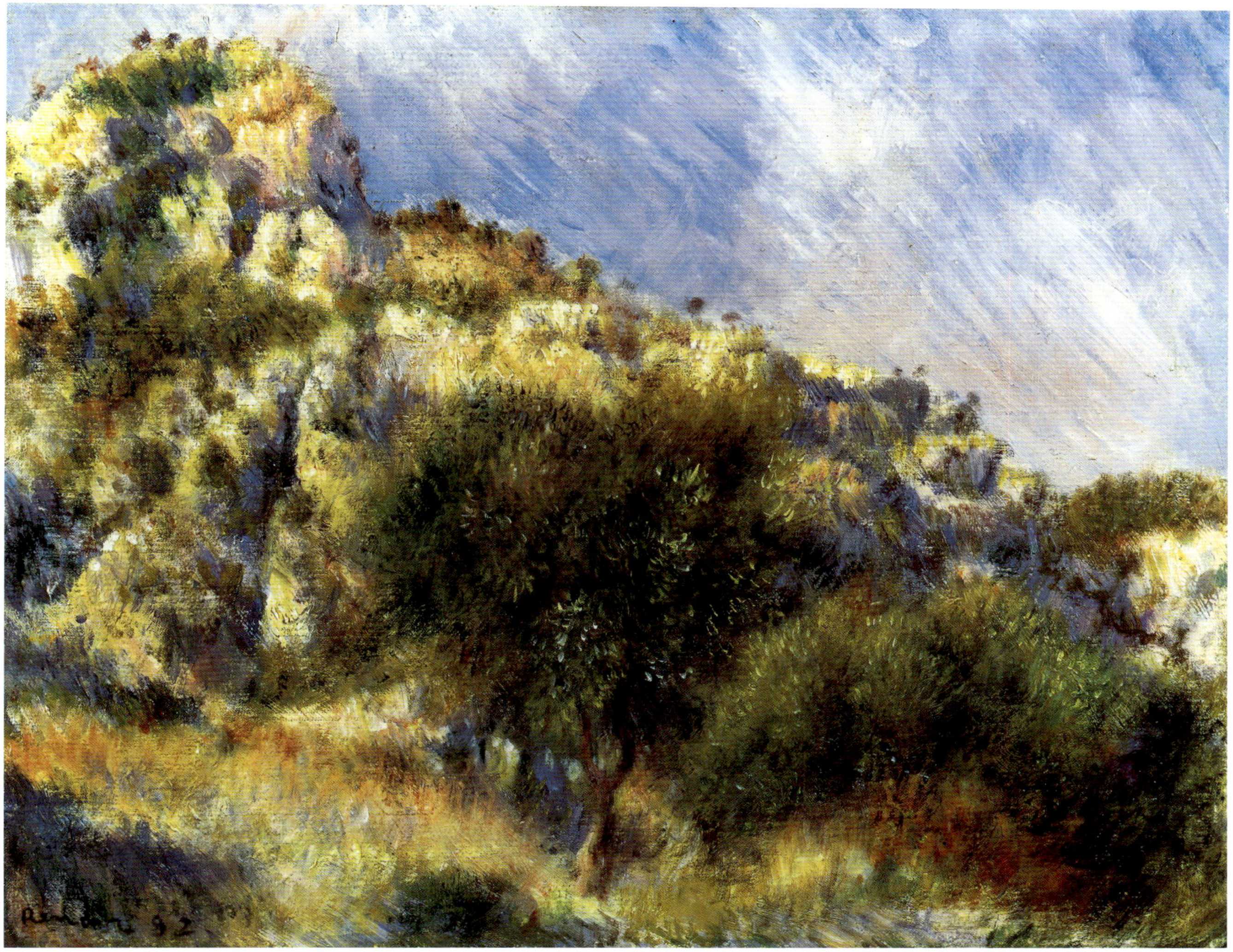

Cézanne's simplified and architectonic vision of the place, as seen in paintings like his *Rocks at L'Estaque* (Museu de Arte de São Paulo, Assis Chateaubriand). Renoir also told Madame Charpentier in the wake of his visit to Italy and to L'Estaque, 'I shall, I believe, have acquired the simplicity and grandeur of the ancient painters.'[4] For a second time, Renoir writes to Paris downplaying the role in the transformation of his art of his reclusive contemporary, no less simple and grand, whom he had sought out on his native ground. CR

Shown in London only

1 Letter of 23 January 1882 to Paul Durand-Ruel; Venturi 1939, I, p. 118.
2 On the importance of L'Estaque for Cézanne see most recently V. Serrano in *Cézanne in Provence*, exh. cat., (National Gallery of Art) Washington, DC 2006, pp. 124–36.
3 Quoted in Shackelford and Wissman 2000, no. 57, p. 134.
4 *Ibidem.*

67 Rocky Crags at L'Estaque, 1882

Oil on canvas
60 × 82 cm; 23⅝ × 32¼ in.
Museum of Fine Arts, Boston, Massachusetts. Juliana Cheney Edwards Collection (39.678)

PROVENANCE:
Sold to Durand-Ruel in 1891; sold to Catholina Lambert, 25 February 1892; Robert J. Edwards, Boston, by 1915; Hannah Marcy Edwards, Boston; by inheritance to her sister, Grace M. Edwards, Boston; bequest of Hannah Marcy Edwards, 1939

LITERATURE:
Boston 1939, no. 48; Venturi 1939, I, p. 61; Rewald 1946, p. 363; Fezzi 1972, no. 510; Boston 1973, no. 77; Callen 1982, pp. 118–21; White 1984, pp. 120, 123; House and Distel 1985, pp. 108, 233; Schneider 1985, p. 54; House and Murphy 1988, pp. 216, 239; Czynmek 1990, no. 151; Zafran and Boardingham 1992, p. 222; Thomson 1994, pp. 65–8; Wissman 2000, p. 134; Shackelford and Wissman 2002, pp. 171–2, 268; Cogeval and Vial 2005, pp. 126–7

This painting was created during Renoir's brief sojourn in L'Estaque after his return from Italy in the winter of 1882. It is probably the work that was exhibited in his 1883 retrospective exhibition at the Galerie Durand-Ruel in April 1883, under the title *Campagne de L'Estaque.*[1] A letter from Renoir to Durand-Ruel, dated 23 January 1882, states that he had met up with Paul Cézanne (see further cat. 66) and that they were planning to work together.[2] This painting probably emerged from such a shared excursion and is comparable to another work by Cézanne, *Viaduct at L'Estaque* (fig. 114), also dated to 1882. As many authors have pointed out, Cézanne's technique is quite dissimilar to Renoir's, with the former artist interested in visual structure derived from geometric forms and the latter more interested in the appearance of the scene and the visual impact of the surface of the canvas. Comparing these two representations of the outskirts of L'Estaque, it is quite clear that Renoir is a tourist on Cézanne's territory but, as always, it is Renoir's endless adaptability that makes his landscapes compelling.

Renoir's technique is very distinct here from his practice both in Algeria in 1881 and on his recent trip to Italy. There is a range of tones in evidence, but gone are the bright colouristic flourishes that characterise his paintings on these recent sojourns. When he was painting in Algeria and Venice, Renoir's canvases reflected an array of deep cool hues and golden highlights, but here he is much more restrained, removing almost all of his red tones and making do with a more limited palette of blues, greens and tans. There are many layers of paint, suggesting multiple reworkings. Traces of previous brushwork are covered over and thin layers of wash add final details, creating visual interest across the surface of the canvas. The bright blue sky suggests none of the changeability of the artist's northern landscapes, whether in the outskirts of Paris or on the coast of Normandy. Anthea Callen, who has made the most careful study of the artist's technique in this work,[3] finds traces of Cézanne's signature parallel brushstrokes in the foreground, but Renoir is in no way systematic in his representation of this mountainous ravine. Though this panoramic landscape is more structured than much of his landscape painting of this period, the inherent geometry of the composition has been overlain with flourishes of colour

JZ

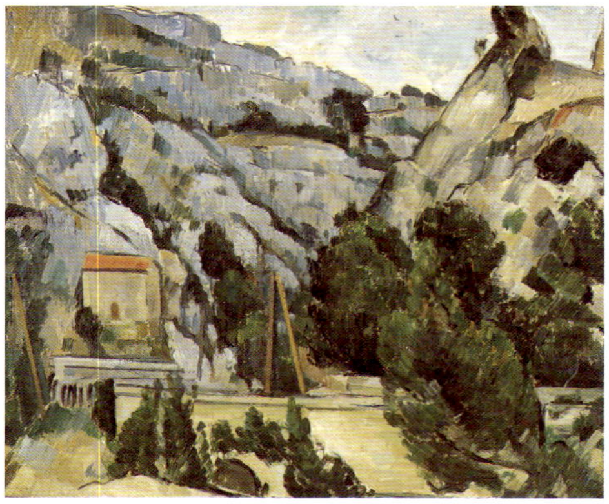

FIG. 114 Paul Cézanne (1839–1906), *Viaduct at L'Estaque*, 1882. Oil on canvas, 46.5 × 55.6 cm; 18⅝ × 21⅞ in. Oberlin College, Ohio, Allen Memorial Art Museum, R.T. Miller, Jr. Fund and Mrs F.F. Prentiss Fund, 1950 (1950.3).

1 House 1985, p. 233.
2 Venturi 1939, I, p. 118.
3 Callen 1982, pp. 118–21.

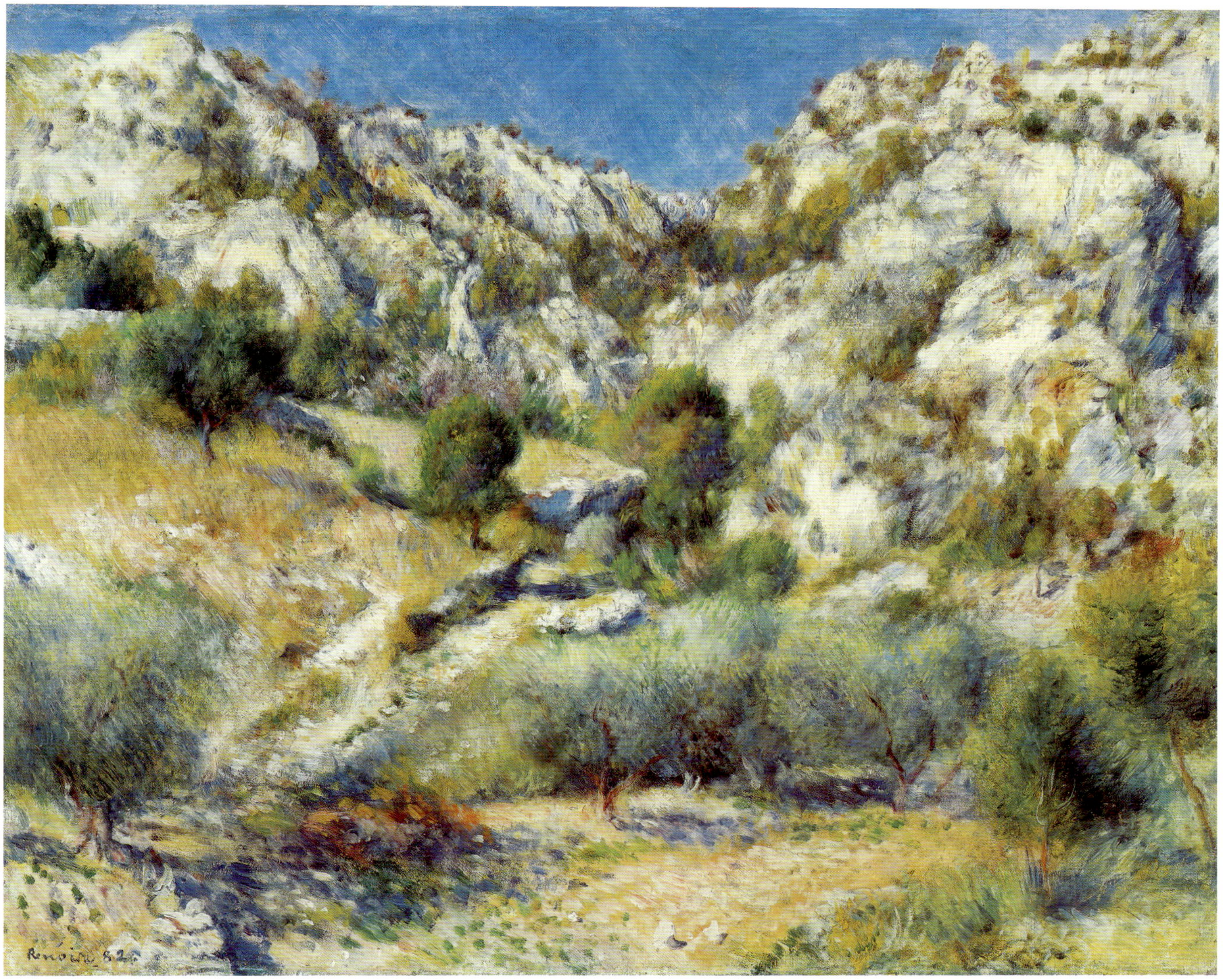
Renoir 82

68 The Wave, 1882

Oil on canvas
53.3 × 63.5 cm; 21 × 25 in.
Collection of the Dixon Gallery and Gardens, Memphis, Tennessee. Museum purchase from Cornelia Ritchie and Ritchie Trust No. 4. Provided through a gift from the Robinson Family Fund (1996.2.12)

PROVENANCE:
Galerie Durand-Ruel, Paris; Van Diemen-Lilienfeld Galleries, New York; Montgomery H.W. Ritchie, 1949; Cornelia Ritchie; Dixon Gallery and Gardens, 1996

LITERATURE:
Fezzi 1972, no. 548; Fezzi 1985, no. 526; Brettell 2000, pp. 67, 186–7; Tucker 2001, pp. 114–15; Goldin 2002–3, pp. 191, 498; Wilson-Bareau and Deneger 2003, p. 244, 249, pl. 118; Leighton 2004, pp. 68, 70

Lionello Venturi noted of this jewel-bright depiction of a wave crashing to the shore that it showed '*Renoir en folie*'.[1] The phrase suggests something of the dynamism with which the artist invested the image, the sense that his rapid application of paint in roiling cascades of colour had something in it of frenzied possession. If artists of legend lashed themselves to the mast to experience the full force of the sea, here Renoir is in no less danger of a pummelling by the elements as the foam the wave has churned up rushes towards the Norman coast where he painted the work in the summer of 1882.[2] It is one of his most immediate statements about the forces of nature. Tiny ships glimpsed along the horizon at upper left signal the puniness of man in comparison. Indeed, the very application of paint, full of energy and improvisation, mimics such natural forces and anticipates the 'overall' quality of 'action' painting in the following century. So thick is the impasto that it is possible paint was pressed directly from the tube on to the canvas.[3] The sea is less frightening here, however, than it is dazzlingly beautiful. Brushstrokes are thickly applied, especially in the left foreground, with reds, greens and blues flashing out of the spume. Colours are more thinly applied and blended in the more distant, green-tinged sea. Wispy white tips of foam which have liberated themselves from the surging wave dance with Rococo abandon at top; Renoir's confrontation with raw nature is tempered by his innate appreciation of its decorative and delicate grace.

The summer of 1882 was not the first time Renoir had painted waves. Three years earlier, in 1879, he had taken up the motif, painting works that include a more monochromatically blue canvas (cat. 45). Various reasons can be suggested for his return to wave painting now. Monet had executed wave paintings in 1881 at Fécamp and Renoir often kept a close eye on what his friend was doing, testing himself against it. In May 1882 he would also have seen wave paintings by Courbet, the most famous practitioner of this sub-genre, in a retrospective exhibition of the late artist's work at the Ecole des Beaux-Arts in Paris.[4] He might well have recalled the impact that Courbet's *Waves*, painted at Etretat in 1869, had on him when he first saw them a generation earlier at the Salon of 1870. He would have been reminded, too, of the ways in which Courbet invested such images with a tragic sense of human destiny. Renoir's aspirations for his own *Waves* were less exalted, however. As John House has noted, he treated the subject 'with far greater delicacy and lightness of touch; he seems to have been more concerned with the visual spectacle before him than with any weightier significance in the theme'.[5] CR

1 Quoted in Fezzi 1985, no. 526.
2 Sheila K. Tabakoff has suggested that the work 'must have been painted in either July or August [1882] in Pourville, where Renoir spent these months with Monet and his family'; Dixon Gallery curatorial archives, letter of 20 December 1995.
3 The suggestion is Colin B. Bailey's.
4 Brettell 2000, p. 186.
5 House 1994, p. 76.

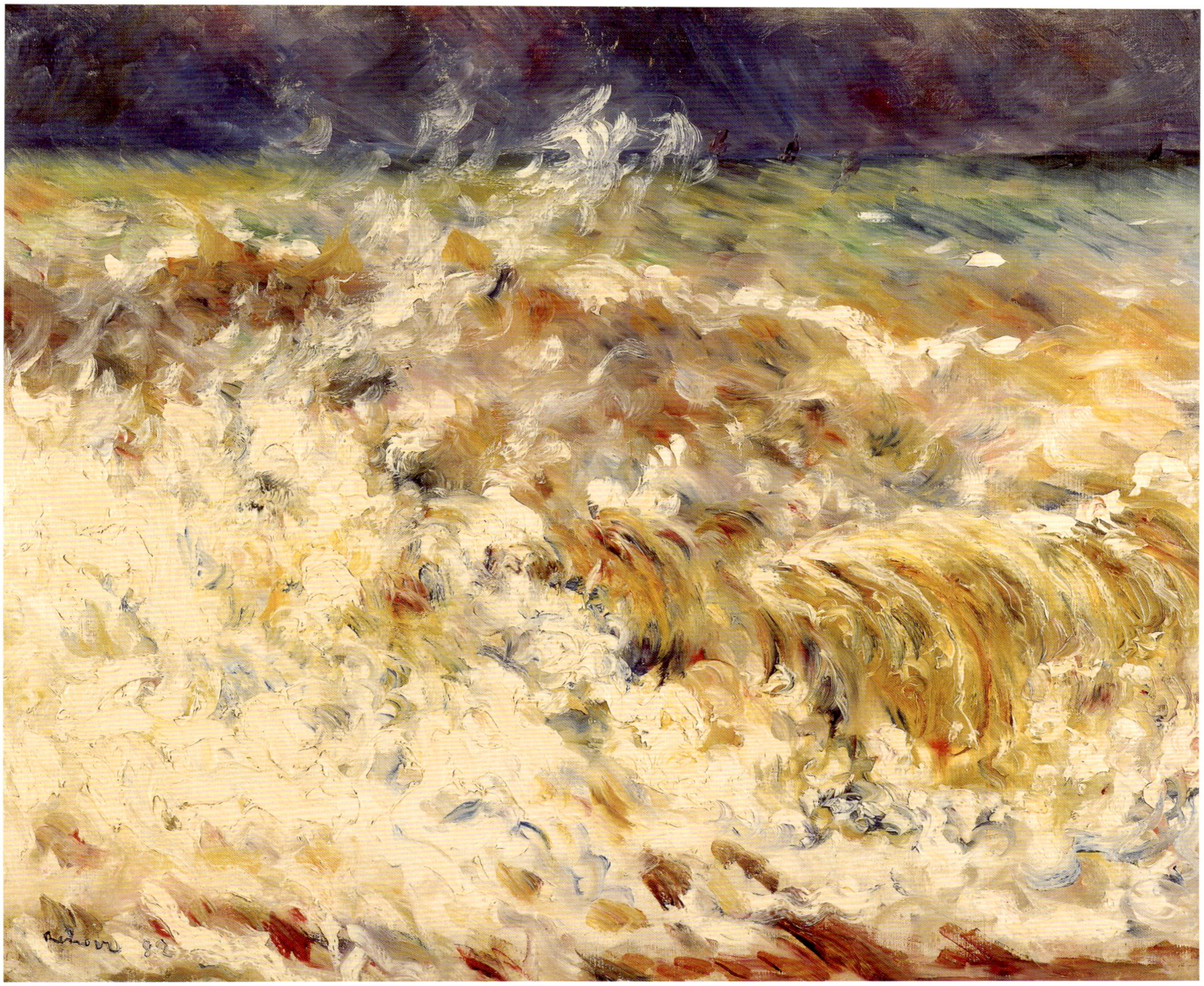

69 Hills around the Bay of Moulin Huet, Guernsey, 1883

Oil on canvas
46 × 65.4 cm; 18⅛ × 25¾ in.
The Metropolitan Museum of Art, New York. Bequest of Julia W. Emmons, 1956 (56.135.9)

PROVENANCE:
Sold by the artist to Durand-Ruel, Paris, 15 December 1883 or 12 March 1884; A.B. Emmons, 29 December 1911

LITERATURE:
Meier-Graefe 1929, p. 157; Sterling and Salinger 1967, p. 155; Fezzi 1972, no. 578; House 1988, pp. 6, 8, 10, 16, 18, 24; House 1994, p. 21

This small painting is one of the four that Renoir sold to Durand-Ruel shortly after his return from a trip to the island of Guernsey,[1] and the fact that the painting is dated and that it sold so quickly suggests that Renoir perceived a market for his landscapes by this date, despite all the adverse critical reception of his recent landscapes in the press (see the essay by Colin B. Bailey in this catalogue, pp. 50–81). Durand-Ruel included the present work in an important early exhibition of Impressionism in London in 1905 at the Grafton Gallery; when it did not sell, it was transferred to the New York office of Durand-Ruel and sold there.

The landscape itself is luminous and full of an impressive array of foliage, supported by the island's unique climate. The painting was made from the hills above Moulin Huet Bay, the most beautiful spot on the island, frequented by tourists, and where Renoir stayed. It is an unlikely choice for a landscape view because the cliffs and sea which constitute the scenic element are distant and obscured by the foliage and the hill in the foreground. In this case Renoir was evidently resisting the postcard view, in contrast to *Fog on Guernsey* (cat. 70), made on the same trip. The pigment has been laid on thick; various colours seem to converge, to interact and to disperse on the canvas. Yet the colour seems to transmit, as opposed to absorb, light. This magic is achieved by layering daubs of pigment on top of light and dark areas and creating zones of light and colour through blending on the surface of the canvas. This style of painting could be classed as exuberant, not only in terms of its rich and complex palette but also in the sense that the paint seems to be playing across the surface of the canvas with a vibrating effect, similar to the sensation of wind blowing through the rushes.

Renoir's unique sensitivity to the shimmering, sensual effects of the material world is here translated into a diminutive but extravagantly rich and luminous painting. The visual structure of the landscape is supplanted by the sensual effect of inhabiting it. But this kind of painting was not sustained by Renoir. His manner of translating his vision into landscapes had by this point outpaced his Impressionist experiments, while the technical complexities of this new style were soon to be abandoned for a more synthetic and indirect method of representing the external world. JZ

1 House 1988, p. 8.

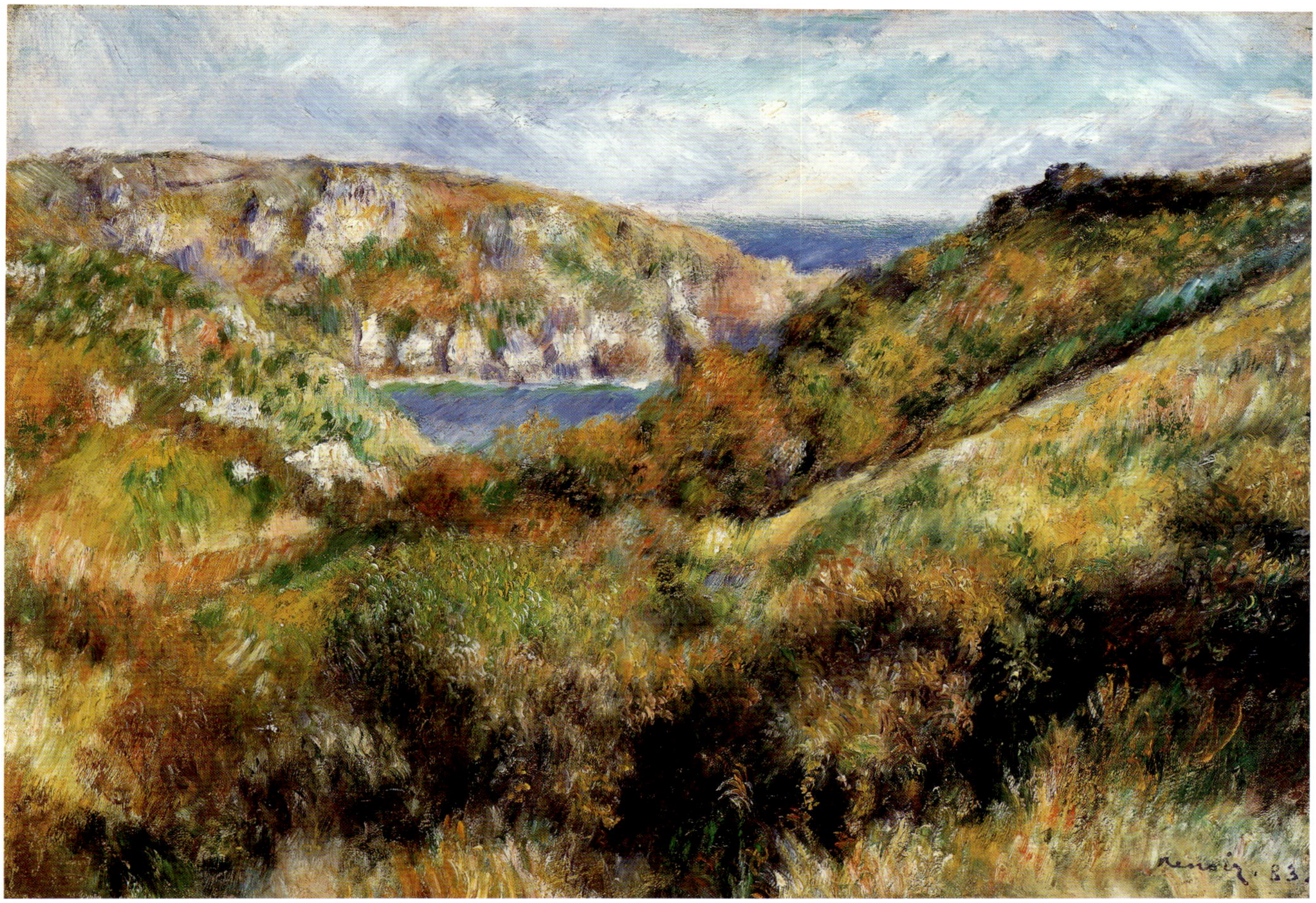
Renoir. 83.

70 Fog on Guernsey, 1883

Oil on canvas
54 × 65 cm; 21¼ × 25⅝ in.
Cincinnati Art Museum, Ohio. John J. Emery Endowment and the Edwin and Virginia Irwin Memorial (2004.46)

PROVENANCE:
Sold by the artist to Galerie Durand-Ruel, Paris, December 1883; Lillie P. Bliss, New York, 1913; her estate 1931–3; Museum of Modern Art, New York, 1933–43, bequest of Lillie P. Bliss; Durand-Ruel Gallery, New York, and Paul Rosenberg, New York, 1943–*c.*1949; private collection; Sotheby's, London, 6 December 1978, lot 221; private collection; Hirschl & Adler Galleries, New York; Cincinnati Art Museum, acquired November 2004

LITERATURE:
Fezzi 1972, no. 580; House 1988, pp. 8–10

Renoir spent more than a month on the Channel Island of Guernsey in the late summer and early autumn of 1883. During that time he painted some 15 canvases showing various aspects of the Moulin Huet Bay near St Peter Port, a popular tourist destination on the south coast of the island. He concentrated on three principal motifs: the bay from the hill top track winding down to the sea, the picturesque rocks jutting out of its waters, and the bathers who frequented the beach. Some of the works are small and sketch-like and were probably painted *en plein air*. Others are larger and more highly finished and were probably worked up in the artist's Paris studio. Writing to his dealer Durand-Ruel, Renoir described his delight in the place, adding that 'in spite of the small quantity of things I'll be able to bring back, I hope to give you an idea of these charming landscapes'.[1]

The trip, and its implications for Renoir's artistic development, has been studied most fully by John House.[2] He points in particular to the four highly finished landscapes, of which the present work is one, that show views looking down over the bay from the west. As House points out, all four are consistent in their high degree of finish and are signed and dated *Renoir 83*, unlike Renoir's other Guernsey canvases.[3] Moreover, they seem to have been sold to Durand-Ruel soon after Renoir's return. In them, Renoir was most interested in capturing the changing light effects and the constantly shifting view of the bay as one moved downwards and towards it. In the present picture, complementary touches of reddish-orange and blue-green, applied in quick, small brushstrokes, animate the foreground. The more brilliant orange of the cottage roof and the blue of the water at right are the high point of colour. All of these tones are picked up in the hills across the bay, but in a more subdued and pastel palette. Here, too, longer, more blended brushstrokes in the upper reaches of the picture serve to evoke the blurring effect of fog, an ambient veil of humidity soon to be burned off by the morning sun.

Superficially at least, the motif Renoir explores here, a cottage perched on a hilltop with water far below, resembles Monet's various depictions of a customs house, or fisherman's cottage as he sometimes identified it, clinging to the edge of a cliff at Varengeville. Monet painted his pictures in 1882 and exhibited at least three of them with Durand-Ruel early in 1883, when Renoir would have seen them.[4] Is this another example of Renoir keeping a close eye on a colleague's experiments and then trying his hand at something similar? If so, the result eschews the sublime power of Monet's view of nature in favour of a more pastoral conception of landscape, swathed in beneficent moisture.
As House points out, Renoir, unlike his colleague, was not one to be clambering over isolated and dangerous cliff tops in search of dramatic motifs. He would have passed this cottage – its ruins still stood as recently as 1988 – as he sauntered from his nearby hotel along a much-frequented path down to the sea.[5] CR

1 Letter of 27 September 1883, quoted in White 1984, p. 133.
2 House 1988, p. 3; see also House's remarks in *Renoir: Master Impressionist* 1994, nos. 22 and 23.
3 By way of comparison, a *plein-air* sketch depicting rocks jutting out of the water at Moulin Huet Bay in the National Gallery (NG 6204) is signed at lower left but not dated. The large *Children on the Seashore, Guernsey* (Museum of Fine Arts, Boston), painted back in the Paris studio, is also signed but not dated. The careful combination of name and date on these four landscapes alone establishes that Renoir considered them a group separate from the other Guernsey paintings.
4 Wildenstein 1974–91, nos. 733, 736, 743.
5 House 1988, p. 8.

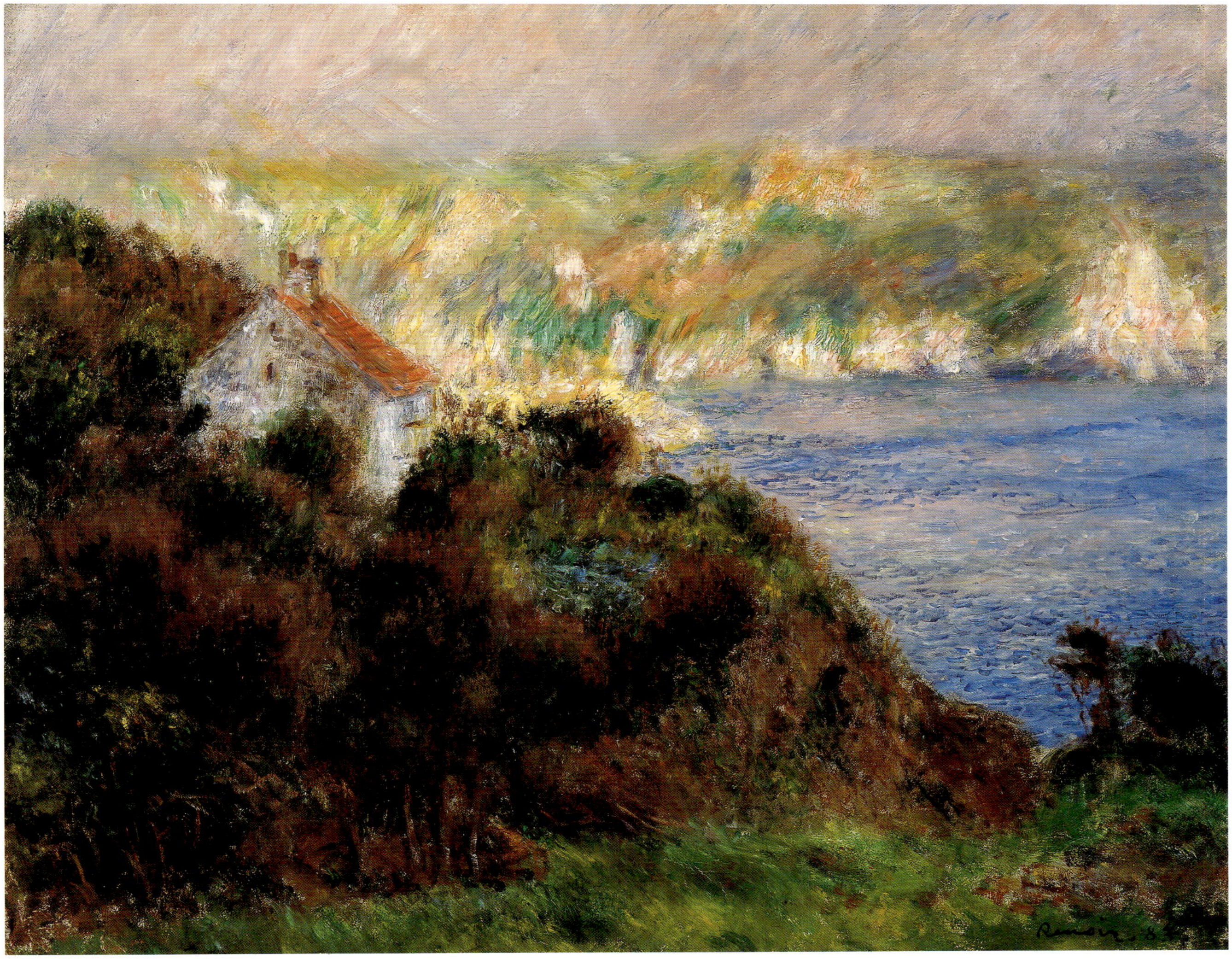

71 Mediterranean Landscape, 1883

Oil on canvas
53.7 × 65.3 cm; 21 × 25¾ in.
Neue Pinakothek Bayerische Staatsgemäldesammlungen, Munich (14217)

PROVENANCE:
Durand-Ruel, Paris; Justin K. Tannhauser, Berlin; Elly Koehler, Gauting; bequeathed, 1971

LITERATURE:
Fezzi 1972, no. 592, p. 115; Keller 1987, pp. 148, 156; Benjamin 2003, p. 110

This painting of lush undergrowth has been variously dated by Renoir scholars, from 1883 to 1893. On stylistic grounds, it is more likely to date from the early 1880s, given the very rich surface of the canvas built up with a wide array of divergent brushstrokes that trace a bright gold and green universe of foliage. There is an erratic character to the brushwork that is not present in Renoir's landscapes of the early 1890s. If the dating is uncertain, so also is the location of the site that has been painted, since there is little visual information that could confirm any topographical identification. Certainly, the density of the flora and the colour of the sky in the background suggest that the picture is set somewhere in the Mediterranean basin but, in the early 1880s, Renoir's travels took him to Algeria, Italy, L'Estaque and also along the Côte d'Azur on a trip with Monet. Rather than making a claim that one of these locations is represented here, it seems more sensible to address the fact that none of these locations is, in fact, depicted but rather the corner of a nondescript wood or orchard.

What can this tell us about Renoir's interests as a landscape painter? In the years 1882–4, Renoir was preparing his *Grammar*, a tract on the arts and how they could best be preserved in the modern world. Renoir elaborated his ideas on the relationship between nature and art in this crucial work. In his first draft, the artist wrote, 'The greatest of all artists is he who has admired nature the most',[1] and by the final draft he had taken this idea even further: 'Any individual wishing to make art must be inspired solely by works of nature . . . She alone can give us the variety of composition, design and colour necessary to make art.'[2] As also in a number of other unconventional paintings (cats. 36, 55), Renoir avoided all traditional conventions of landscape depiction in order to study nature. Despite the arrival of the Industrial Revolution, the expansion of the suburbs, and the general decline of traditional agriculture, Renoir apparently employed the word 'nature' without any irony whatsoever. In fact, it is clear from the text that he perceived nature as the antidote to much of what was wrong not only with the arts but with modern society in general. Whatever one might think of this late-nineteenth-century pantheism, it certainly led the artist to observe the world carefully and render even the most humble landscapes movingly.

In this painting, there is a dark cavity at the centre of the picture in which a path seems to continue under the brush. A single barren tree emerges from the undergrowth on the right hand side and extends horizontally across the canvas. A mosaic-like surface of impasto brushstrokes communicates the density and variety of the foliage. The source of light is clear from the form of the tree, but Renoir seems more interested in the local colours that appear to emanate from the shrubs and grasses represented through fleshy, multi-layered strokes of pigment. There is a very slight sense of depth suggested in this painting by the diagonal path that leads from the lower left towards the centre, but the overall impression is one of a vibrant, fluctuating surface of tones, vividly rendered and immediately perceived. JZ

Shown in London only

1 Herbert 2000, p. 103.
2 *Ibidem*, p. 122.

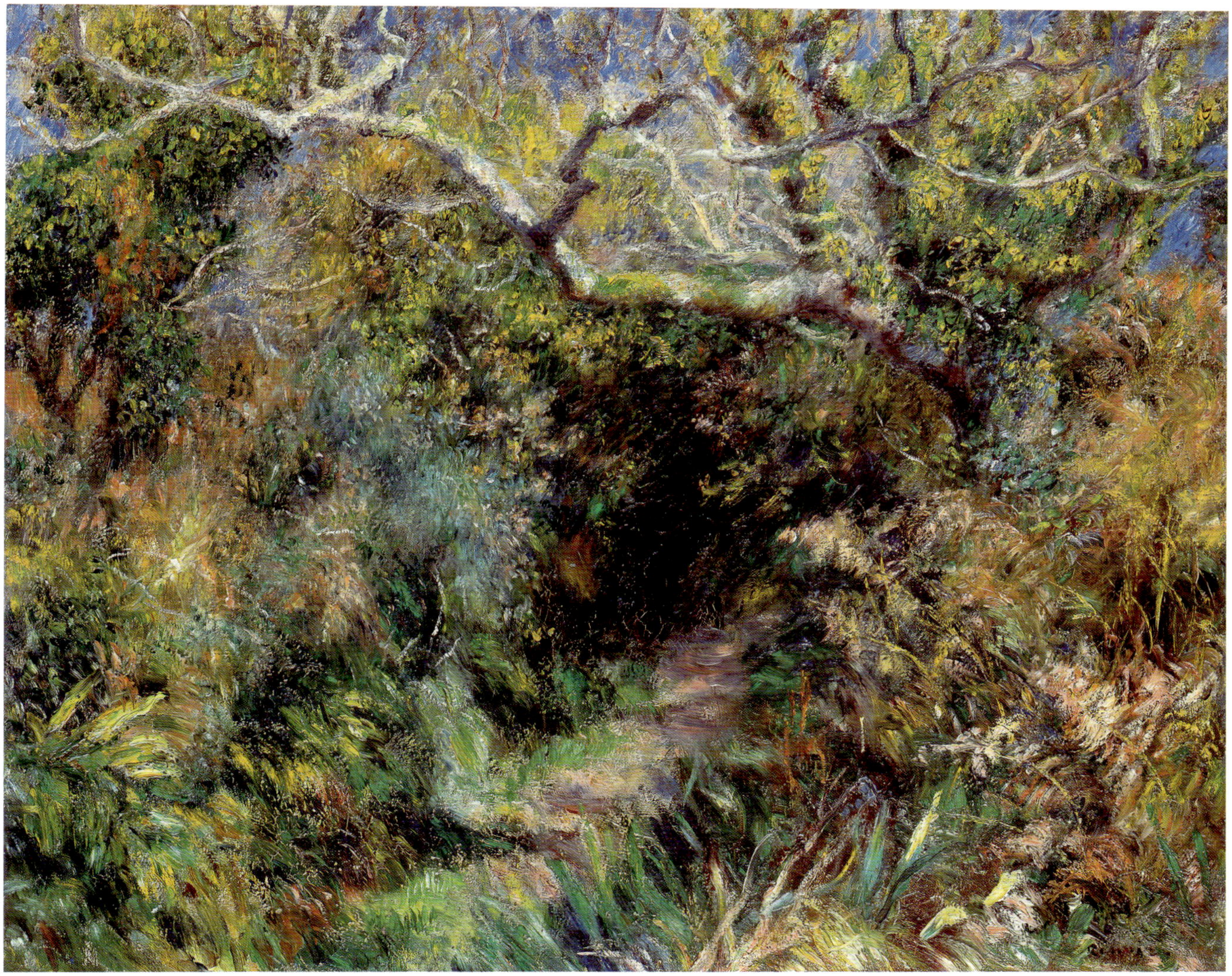

72 Landscape Near Menton, 1883

Oil on canvas
65.8 × 81.3 cm; 26 × 32 in.
Museum of Fine Arts, Boston, Massachusetts. Bequest of John T. Spaulding (48.596)

PROVENANCE:
Acquired from the artist in 1884 by Durand-Ruel; sold to the Prince de Wagram, Paris, by 1918; bought by Durand-Ruel after his death; sold to John T. Spaulding, Beverly, Mass., December 1924; bequeathed by him to the Museum of Fine Arts, 3 June 1948

LITERATURE:
Meier-Graefe 1929, p. 194; Boston 1931, no. 105; Barnes and De Mazia 1935, pp. 83, 455; Boston 1948, p. 18; Boston 1955, p. 54; Fezzi 1972, no. 591; Boston 1973, no. 80; White 1984, p. 135; House and Distel 1985, pp. 109, 239; Murphy 1985, p. 240; Wadley 1987, p. 228; Updike 1989, p. 83; Boston 1999, no. 52; House 1995, no. 105; Shackelford and Wissman 2002, pp. 168, 172–3, 268

Landscape Near Menton is an unexpected composition, with Renoir focusing on a group of trees by the coastline, rather than the view of the Mediterranean sea that can also be seen from this point. During a trip in which Renoir and Monet sought to develop studies of scenery for future compositions (see cat. 71), Renoir instead created this picture of apparently wild nature; a landscape composed of twisting trees and windswept undergrowth. Throughout his career, Renoir redefined landscape to suit his tastes, rarely making a scenic landscape view organised in a traditional manner. In part, he was rejecting academic principles of composition – Renoir was not inclined to construct a classical, stylised landscape in the tradition of Poussin, as he would have been taught at the studio of Charles Gleyre. Instead, he is more interested in immersing himself in nature, charting its irregularity and its fascination with charming alacrity.

This composition is a flurry of visual perceptions, both directly rendered and suggested through painterly effect. There is a sincerity in Renoir's approach to representing the natural world which suggests that he didn't invent these scenes or slavishly record every detail – rather, he translated them; the play of light on the foliage is a stylistic development that moves beyond his Impressionist technique and points forward towards decorative painting – a tradition that reached its apogee in France in the eighteenth century, but was resurrected by avant-garde artists in the 1890s. This landscape connects to the traditions of Watteau and Boucher, even as it augurs the next generation's pictorial discoveries. *Landscape Near Menton* was created to appeal to the senses of the viewer. Lavish, curving brushstrokes transmit a release from the confines of society and modernity, a retreat into a more vividly colourful world.

Elsewhere, nature may have been losing ground to the ravages of modern transportation and urban growth, but in this image the world is pure and this landscape was designed to offer the simple pleasure of viewing. JZ

Shown in Ottawa and Philadelphia only

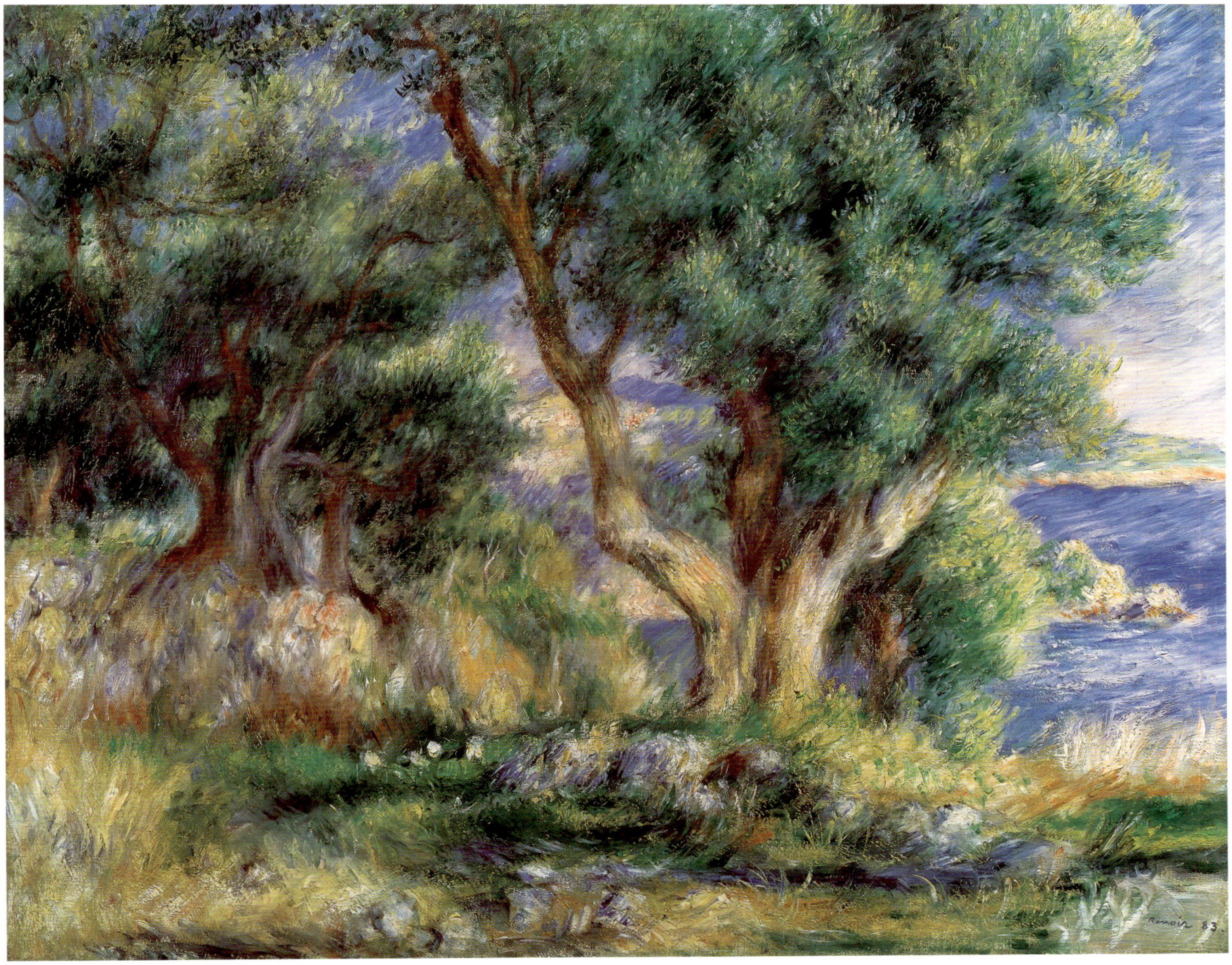

73 View from Cap Martin at Monte Carlo, 1883

Oil on canvas
66 × 81 cm; 26 × 32⅛ in.
Corcoran Gallery of Art, Washington, DC. Edward C. and Mary Walker Collection (37.45)

PROVENANCE:
Bought by Durand-Ruel, probably from Renoir, 8 September 1887 (stockbook 1884/90, no. 1190, stock no. 1460); sold to Durand-Ruel, New York, 1897 (no. 1849); E. Milliken, 23 March 1893; Milliken sale, New York, bought by Durand-Ruel, 1902 (no. 2784); Edward C. and Mary Walker, 1907; bequeathed to Corcoran Gallery, 1937

LITERATURE:
Venturi 1939, I, pp. 126–7; Robinson 1983, pp. 67–9; Fezzi 1972, no. 512; White 1996, p. 103; Cogeval and Vial 2005, pp. 116–7, 259

This little-known and rarely exhibited landscape is one of only three landscape paintings to emerge from a trip Renoir took with Claude Monet in December 1883 to the Riviera, from Marseilles to Genoa. While Monet returned to the area again soon after his return to Paris and began to paint landscapes at Bordighera, Renoir did not return to the Mediterranean for many years. On the basis of a letter from Renoir to Durand-Ruel,[1] Barbara Erlich White has asserted that this painting must have been made not during the trip but upon the artist's return from Paris in the studio.[2] However, while the picture was perhaps not finished on Renoir and Monet's joint 'vacation', it is likely that the canvas was begun in front of the motif, and this work is in many ways similar to such paintings Renoir had completed the year before on his trip to Italy (cats. 62–5).

Like his Italian works, the present painting features a prominent tourist view, in this case the Tête de Chien (dog's head) rock towering above the city of Monte Carlo, as seen from the Cap Martin. The Côte d'Azur of Renoir's time was nothing like the tourist attraction it has become today, but, then as now, guidebooks directed visitors to all the most important sites. Renoir and Monet were not merely enjoying these sites but speculating on them. They sought locations that would make for spectacular paintings appealing to the new élite bourgeois clientele that Durand-Ruel was recruiting as customers for Impressionist art.[3] This painting is an unapologetic postcard view, like Renoir's renditions of Venice or the Bay of Naples. Monet must have perceived its potential as well, for he made several paintings of this same site (see fig. 115), which were finished and signed in 1884 when he returned to the Mediterranean alone. Although the two artists spent 18 days together and talked of coming back together, Monet set off for the Mediterranean less than a month after their return to Paris without telling Renoir. Monet protested to his dealer that he needed to work alone,[4] but it also seems likely that he felt the competition from Renoir and he must have wanted to stake out this new territory on his own.

While Monet's view focuses upon visual structure, and the road to the right leads the viewer's eye towards the mountain in the background, Renoir's painting somewhat obscures the view with foreground trees and a hill on the right. By representing these foreground elements, the artist positions the viewer in his landscape. The bright pastel tones of the water and the sky in the background are balanced by the dark blues of the foreground foliage; the movement of the brush across the surface of the canvas catches the eye and draws attention to the artist's process of making the work. This is a fundamental characteristic of Impressionist painting, but Renoir's technique has changed from the mid-1870s. In this work the pigment is thick and glossy, sometimes even mixed on the surface of the painting, with highlights of thick pigment that sit on the surface of the canvas. JZ
Shown in Ottawa only

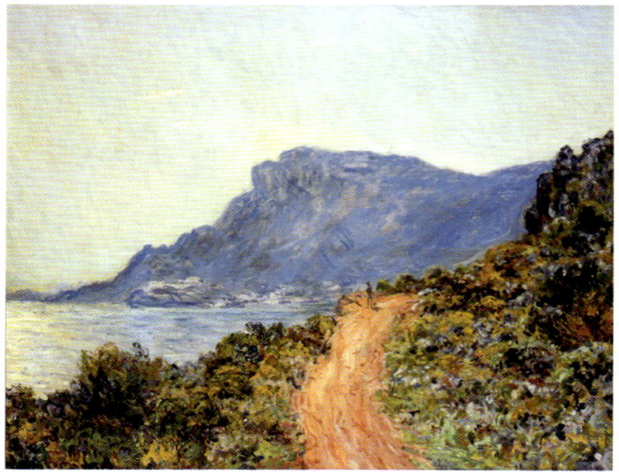

FIG. 115 Claude Monet (1840–1926), *The Monaco Corniche*, 1884. Oil on canvas, 74 × 92 cm; 29⅛ × 36⅛ in. Stedelijk Museum, Amsterdam (B554).

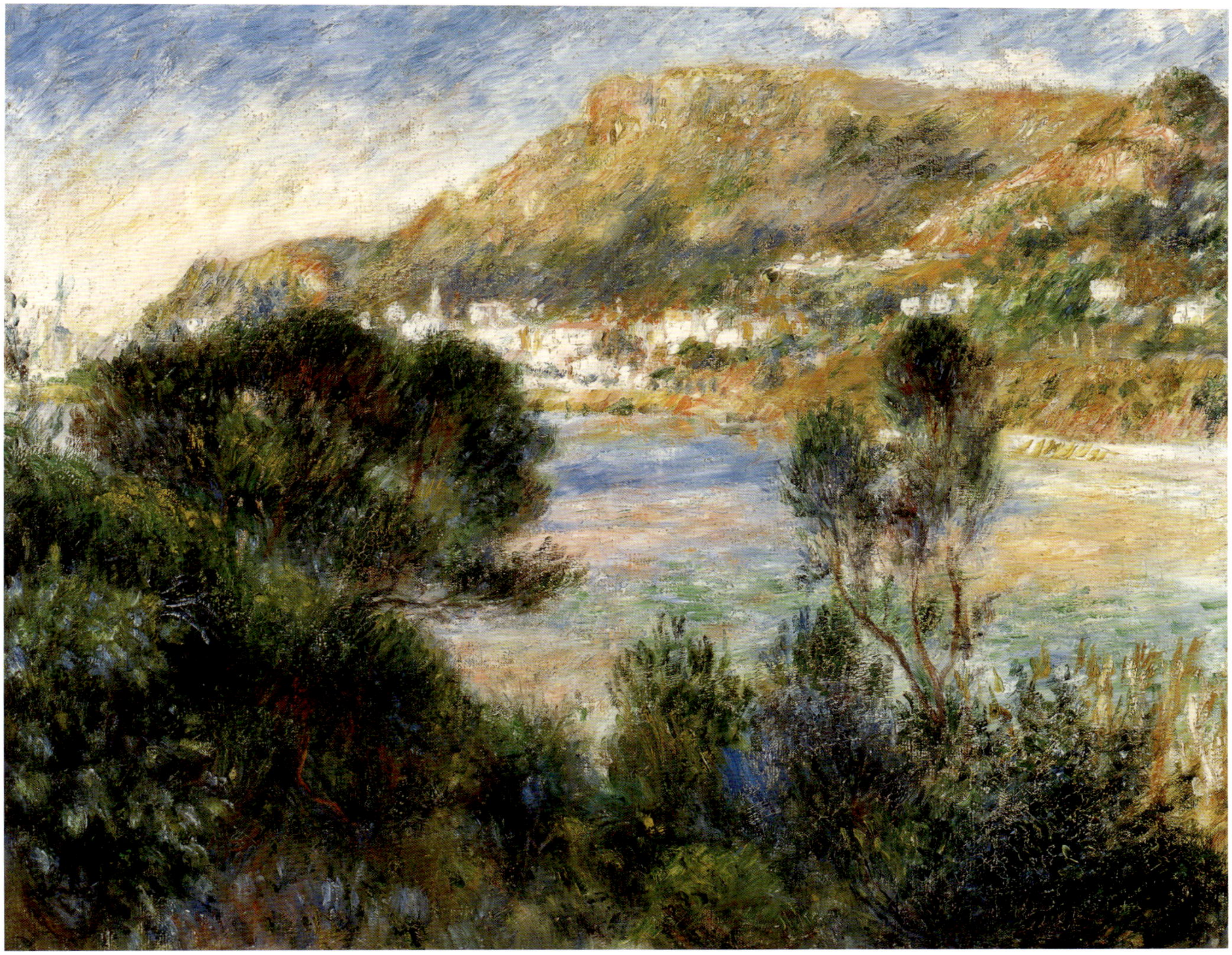

1 Venturi 1939, I, pp. 126–7.
2 White 1996, p. 103.
3 Adler in House 1994, pp. 29–39.
4 Letter to Durand-Ruel, 12 January 1884; Venturi 1939, I, pp. 267–8.

TOPOGRAPHICAL CHRONOLOGY 1860–1883

ROBERT McDONALD PARKER

This topographical or site chronology tabulates the places Renoir lived, visited and painted during the period 1860 to 1883. Previously published information, such as the excellent chronology provided in House and Distel 1985, has been re-verified, with emphasis on the sites that inspired Renoir's landscapes. For the notes of Renoir's portraiture during the period I have relied on Bailey 1997. Priority has been given to unpublished information. Careful examination of Renoir's movements has made it possible to re-evaluate and re-date some of his landscapes of this period. Since this chronology focuses on the identification of the places visited and the landscapes painted by Renoir, alone and in the company of other Impressionists, the career and related landscape paintings for this same time period, particularly of Monet, Sisley and Pissarro have also been recorded.

Unless otherwise indicated, addresses are those of Paris; *arrondissements* are those of today. Modern addresses are given whenever possible, although in smaller places, such as Louveciennes, streets were often not numbered until the late nineteenth century.

AUTHOR'S NOTE

Paintings by Renoir are identified by their Daulte (D) catalogue raisonné numbers; works not catalogued by Daulte are identified by the numbers in the catalogue of Fezzi and Henry (F/H); some further works are noted as uncatalogued.

F. Daulte, *Auguste Renoir: Catalogue raisonné de l'œuvre peint. I. Figures 1860–1890*, Lausanne 1971

E. Fezzi and J. Henry, *Tout l'œuvre peint de Renoir, période impressionniste, 1869–1883*, Paris 1985

Works by other artists are identified by reference to the following catalogue raisonnés:

DS: F. Daulte, *Alfred Sisley: Catalogue raisonné de l'œuvre peint. I. Figures 1860–1890*, Lausanne 1971

P/S: J. Pissarro and C. Durand-Ruel Snollaerts, *Pissarro: Catalogue critique des peintures*, 3 vols, Paris 2005

S: M. Schulman, *Frédéric Bazille*, Paris 1995

W: D. Wildenstein, *Claude Monet: Biographie et catalogue raisonné*, 5 vols, Lausanne and Paris 1974–1991

ACKNOWLEDGEMENTS

The author would like to acknowledge the following persons for their contributions to this text, particularly those who provided information hitherto unpublished and presented here for the first time: M. and Mme Jacques Läy (for Louveciennes); M. Claude Féron (for Pourville), M. François Guého (for Berneval and Wargemont), Mlle Séverine Drigeard (for St-Cloud), M. Marc Le Coeur (for Berck, Marlotte, Palaiseau, Pau and Ville d'Avray, in addition to his published information, as cited), M. Pierre Wittmer (for Petit-Gennevilliers and Caillebotte), M. Raphaël Gerard (for Montmartre and the rue Corot) and Isabelle Guignard (for Champrosay). An asterisk (*) by the location denotes their contribution of information.

For the visual comparatives, I would like to thank the staffs of the relevant institutions for allowing me to review and reproduce images from their collections, and in particular Mme Bernard Billaud at the Bibliothèque historique de la ville de Paris, M. Christophe Léribault (formerly) at the Musée Carnavalet, Paris, and M. Pascal Lagadec at the Médiathèque Jean Renoir, Dieppe.

I would like to thank the staff at the Bureau de Documentation and the Bibliothèque du Musée d'Orsay and, in particular, M. Dominique Lobstein for his generous aid, and Mlle Brigitte Lainé at the Archives de la ville de Paris for her enlightened perceptions and active participation in my research quests.

For sharing both her vast knowledge of the Impressionist painters and her personal archives, I would like to thank Marina Ferretti-Bocquillon. Monique Nonne's comprehensive unpublished materials on the Belgian artists and their agents for the Parisian salons proved invaluable in studying Renoir's colour suppliers. Benoît Noël kindly provided me with names and contacts in Bougival, Croissy-sur-Seine and Chatou. I am grateful to Elizabeth A. Williams, Elizabeth A. Barone and Helena Boyden Lamb for their enthusiastic support and infallible assistance throughout this project.

1841 25 FEBRUARY
Renoir is born at 35 boulevard Ste-Catherine (today, 71 boulevard Gambetta) in Limoges, the sixth of seven children of Léonard Renoir (1799–1874), a tailor, and Marguerite Merlet (1807–1896), a dressmaker.

1845 The Renoirs move from Limoges to Paris, where they first live near the Temple de l'Oratoire (I *arrondissement*, today).

In Paris, Renoir begins studies at the Ecole de dessin et des arts décoratifs, a drawing school on the rue des Petits-Carreaux (II *arrondissement*, today). Emile-Henri Laporte (1841–1919) is a fellow student.

1855 (or earlier)
Renoir's parents move to 23 rue d'Argenteuil (I *arrondissement*, today), where his father is listed as a tenant on the fifth floor in 1855 and on the sixth in 1858. This is frequently given as the artist's address until 1865. [Archives de la ville de Paris: (rue d'Argenteuil, 1852) D1P4/ 42] The father's tailoring business, however, is not recorded at this address in the commercial registry from 1855 until 1865. [*Annuaire du commerce*, Paris, rue d'Argenteuil 1855–65]

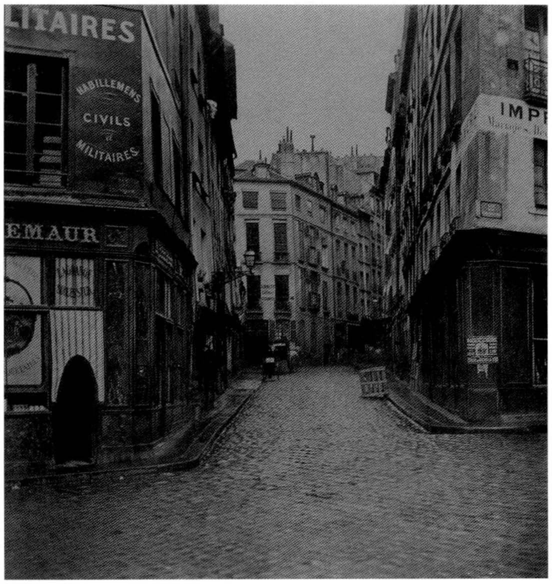

FIG. 116 Charles Marville (1816–*c*.1879), *Rue d'Argenteuil*, about 1864. Photograph. Bibliothèque historique de la ville de Paris (BhvP: GP III 27).

1860 24 JANUARY
Renoir is listed in a register of art students who requested permissions and received cards authorising them to work in the Louvre; he gives his address as 23 rue d'Argenteuil. [Archives des Musées Nationaux: *LL16, Enregistrement des cartes des permissions de travail, 1860–5]

1861 5 MARCH
Renoir is again listed as an art student, at the same address, with permission to work in the Louvre. [Archives des Musées Nationaux: *LL16, Enregistrement des cartes des permissions de travail, 1860–5]

In November Renoir is registered as a pupil and studies with Charles Gleyre (1806–1874) in the master's studio.

8 NOVEMBER
Gleyre writes a letter of introduction to the curator of the Cabinet des Estampes of the Bibliothèque nationale asking permission for Renoir to consult works on paper. [Bibliothèque nationale de France: Rés. Ye 118, tome 1 (A–L), under Gleyre]

1862 21 JANUARY
Renoir again receives permission to study and copy works in the Louvre; his noted address remains 23 rue d'Argenteuil. [Archives des Musées Nationaux: *LL16 Enregistrement des cartes des permissions de travail, 1860–5]

APRIL
Renoir is admitted to the Ecole des Beaux-Arts. His address, 29 place Dauphine (I *arrondissement*, today), is also that of Emile-Henri Laporte, his friend and fellow student in Gleyre's atelier. Laporte's father runs a business on the fourth floor of the same building as a *gainier*, making a variety of leather linings for fur clothing. [Archives de la ville de Paris: (place Dauphine, 1862) D1P4/ 331; *Annuaire du commerce*, Paris, place Dauphine, 1861–4]

1 OCTOBER–31 DECEMBER
Renoir does military service.

AUTUMN–WINTER
Alfred Sisley (1839–1899), Frédéric Bazille (1841–1870) and Claude Monet (1840–1926) join Gleyre's studio. Artists such as Vicomte Lepic (1839–1889) and J.A.M. Whistler (1834–1903) also studied with the Swiss-born teacher.

1863 21 MARCH
Renoir ranks 20 out of 80 participants after the figure-drawing examinations at the Ecole des Beaux-Arts. By October, he will figure in 28th position in his class.

EARLY SPRING
Monet and Bazille leave Gleyre's studio to work in Chailly-en-Bière, a small village near Barbizon frequented by Théodore Rousseau (1812–1867) and Jean-François Millet (1814–1875). They stay at Père Paillard's Hôtel du Cheval-Blanc. Renoir and Sisley are believed to have joined them at Easter (5 April).

9 APRIL
Renoir again receives permission to study works at the Louvre, giving his address as 23 rue d'Argenteuil. [Archives des Musées Nationaux: *LL16 Enregistrement des cartes des permissions de travail, 1860–5]

1 MAY
In preparation for the annual Salons, Renoir begins to concentrate on large-scale figure paintings for much of the next decade. His painting, *A Nymph and a Faun*, inspired by Diaz de la Peña's genre painting, is refused; Renoir, supposedly, destroys the work.

15 MAY
The Salon des Refusés opens in an annexe of the Palais de l'Industrie on the Champs-Elysées.

1864 5 JANUARY–5 MARCH
Renoir begins military training.

5 APRIL
At the Ecole des Beaux-Arts Renoir is placed tenth among the 106 candidates vying for the limited admissions of drawing and sculpture students.

SPRING
Gleyre closes his studio; he dies ten years later.

APRIL–MAY
Monet and Bazille return to Fontainebleau and again stay at Hôtel du Cheval-Blanc in Chailly-en-Bière. Monet paints *Le Pavé de Chailly-en-Bière* (W19), a large open landscape depicting the road from Chailly to Fontainebleau.

1 MAY
The Salon of 1864 opens on the Champs-Elysées. Renoir gives his address as 23 rue Argenteuil, and exhibits one work (no. 1618, *Esméralda)*, inspired by Victor Hugo's *Notre-Dame de Paris.*

1 JUNE
Renoir is again given permission to work in the Louvre, giving his address as 23 rue d'Argenteuil. [Archives des Musées Nationaux: *LL16 Enregistrement des cartes des permissions de travail, 1860–5]

SUMMER
Renoir's portraits of Sisley (D37) and of his father, William Sisley (D11), are now believed to have been painted at this time. He also executes portraits of Laporte (D9) and his sister Marie-Zélie (D10), probably in their apartment on the place Dauphine, Paris.

1865 FEBRUARY–APRIL
Renoir, Sisley and Jules Le Coeur (1832–1882), an architect turned painter, are in Fontainebleau and in *Marlotte, 75 kilometres south-east of Paris, where Jules Le Coeur rents a house on the rue de la Cheminée blanche (today, 30 rue Delort). The house will become a meeting-place for the three artists and their friends.

MAY–JUNE
At the Salon of 1865, Renoir has two works accepted (nos. 1802, 1803 respectively); one is the portrait of Sisley's father (D11), the other the lost landscape entitled *Soirée d'été*. The catalogue lists Renoir's address as 43 avenue d'Eylau (today, avenue Victor-Hugo, XVI *arrondissement*), which is also the address of Jules Le Coeur. [*Annuaire du commerce*, Paris, avenue d'Eylau, 1865, 1866; Le Coeur in São Paulo 2002, p. 198]

3 JULY
Renoir gives his Paris address as Sisley's residence at 31 avenue de Neuilly (XVI *arrondissement*, today), in a letter inviting Bazille on a boat trip to Rouen and Le Havre to watch the regatta with Sisley and Léon Grange, another young artist. Renoir also invites Bazille to join Sisley and himself in the forest of La Celle-St-Cloud, where Renoir probably painted *A Clearing in the Woods* (F/H9, cat. 2), which was previously thought to depict Fontainebleau.

WINTER
Renoir and Sisley spend part of winter in Marlotte. Sisley's landscape views of Marlotte (dated 1866, but probably painted in late 1865 to early 1866) will be accepted for the May 1866 Salon – *Village Street in Marlotte* (DS3); *Village Street in Marlotte – Women going to the Woods* (DS4). Renoir's scenes are not specifically identifiable as of Marlotte; these landscapes (uncatalogued; see cat. 1 *Landscape with two Figures*) recall the sketch-like, naturalist manner of the Barbizon painters, such as Camille Corot (1796–1875) and Narcisse Diaz de la Peña (1809–1876). While in Marlotte, Jules Le Coeur executes a portrait of Renoir.

1866 16 JANUARY–15 MARCH
Charles-Clément Le Coeur (1805–1897), first curator of the art museum in *Pau and founder of the Société des Amis des Arts de Pau, invites Renoir to exhibit three landscapes (nos. 211–213) at the third annual winter exhibition. One of these is *La Mare aux fées* (no. 212), possibly identified as *Outing in a Rowing-boat* (uncatalogued). The exhibited paintings are offered for sale; *La Mare aux fées* is listed at 800 francs. The catalogue also lists Renoir's address in Paris as 20 rue Visconti (VI *arrondissement*, today), a studio shared with Bazille, and later with Monet.

FEBRUARY
Renoir, Sisley and Jules Le Coeur hike through the forest of Fontainbleau and stay at Mère Antony's inn at Marlotte (today, 37 rue Murger); they also go to Milly-la-fôret and Courances. Renoir paints *Jules Le Coeur and his Dogs walking in the Forest of Fontainebleau* (F/H11, cat. 3).

MARCH–APRIL
Renoir stays in Marlotte with Sisley and Jules Le Coeur. Lise Tréhot (1848–1922) first models for his portraits and landscapes; she will remain a favourite subject for the next six years.

EARLY SUMMER
In Marlotte, Renoir paints *The Inn of Mère Antony* (D20), a large-scale indoor scene.

15–31 AUGUST
Renoir and Sisley travel to *Berck and visit Charles Le Coeur (1830–1906), who has rented a house there. Renoir sells a landscape, probably *Outing in a Rowing-boat* (uncatalogued), to an unnamed German banker. [Le Coeur in São Paulo 2002, no. 90, p. 220]

1867 SPRING
Renoir and Bazille continue to share a studio in Paris at 20 rue Visconti (VI *arrondissement*, today); the building had numerous ateliers. [Archives de la ville de Paris: (rue Visconti, 1852) D1P4/ 1222] Bazille paints two portraits of Renoir, one is posed unconventionally with his feet on a chair (S30) and another is a more traditional pose (S31).

30 MARCH
The works of the future Impressionists (Renoir, Bazille, Monet, Sisley, Pissarro, Cézanne and Manet) are all rejected at the annual Salon, including Renoir's *Diana the Huntress* (D30).

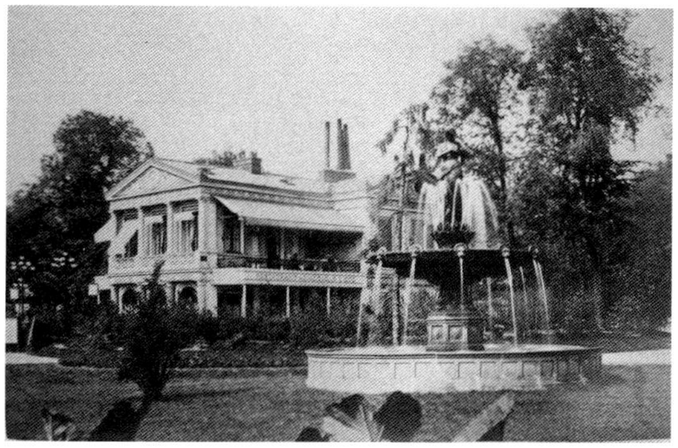

FIG. 117 E. Fiorillo (active 1879–1920), *Restaurant de l'Alcazar d'été sur Champs-Elysées*, mid-1800s. Photograph. Bibliothèque historique de la ville de Paris (BhvP: Paris Album 4°1, no. 221). Renoir painted this restaurant in his view of the Champs-Elysées during 1867 Universal Exhibition (F/H 19, see fig. 26).

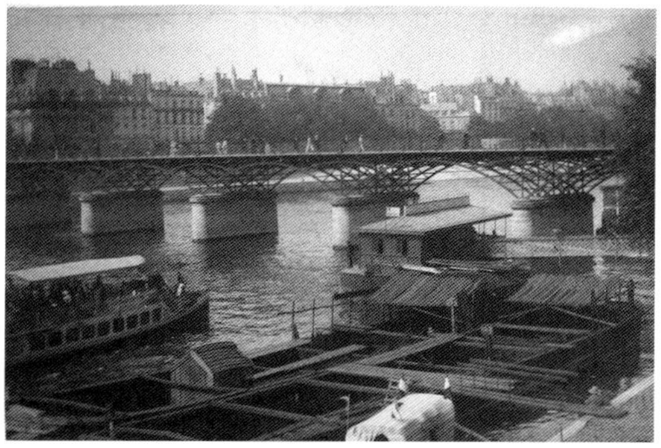

FIG. 118 Hippolyte Blancard (1843–1924), *Untitled*, 1860s or 1870s. Photograph. Bibliothèque historique de la ville de Paris (BhvP: Paris Album 4°18, p. 192, cliché 1369). In *Le Pont des Arts* (F/H 27, see fig. 27), Renoir depicts one of the boats and a floating barge of Paris;s 'Compagnie des bateaux express', a passenger transportation service on the Seine, accessed from the *quai* by gangplanks.

APRIL
The Universal Exhibition opens on 1 April in Paris and will last until 3 November. Gustave Courbet (1819–1877) and Edouard Manet (1832–1883) exhibit their paintings in special pavilions on the place d'Alma. Meanwhile, Renoir works on the *The Champs-Elysées during the Fair of 1867* (F/H19, figs 26 and 117) and paints a view of the Pont des Arts from the left bank of the Seine (F/H27; figs 27 and 115). Monet moves to Paris: he paints the church of St-Germain-Auxerrois (W84), the quai du Louvre (W83) and the Jardin de la Princesse of the Louvre (W85). In May, Monet writes that he and Renoir are working on their cityscapes of Paris [Wildenstein, vol. v, p. 188, letter 2687].

SUMMER
Renoir paints a full-length portrait of Tréhot in the forest of Fontainebleau at Chailly-en-Bière (*Lise with a Parasol*, D29). The work was perhaps a response to Monet's full-length portrait of Camille Monet in a green dress (W65) that was highly praised at the Salon of 1866.

AUGUST
Renoir visits Chantilly, where he paints two additional versions of Tréhot standing in the forest, wearing a hat and a white dress with a long ribbon-sash and holding a bouquet of flowers (D31, 32).

NOVEMBER
In Bazille's studio, Renoir begins to paint *Fréderic Bazille painting 'The Heron'* (D28). In the background, hanging on the wall of the studio, Renoir has rendered Monet's *Snowy Road at Honfleur* (W82). The still life of a heron on Bazille's easel (*Still Life with Heron*, DS35) and a version of the same subject by Sisley (*Still Life with Heron*, D5) confirm the strong artistic camaraderie between the four artists (Renoir, Bazille, Monet and Sisley), working and painting together.

LATE DECEMBER
Paris is subjected to a period of intense cold weather in the final days of the year. Bazille and Renoir leave the atelier at 20 rue Visconti at the end of December 1867.

1868 JANUARY
The bitter winter continues. The Seine freezes and, in Paris, the river is frozen for 11 consecutive days. Renoir paints skaters on a lake in the Bois de Bologne (F/H28, cat. 4) and a snowy landscape (uncatalogued, Christie's, New York, 10 November 1987, lot 4).

WINTER OR EARLY SPRING
Renoir shares a studio that Bazille has rented in the Batignolles district, west of Montmartre, at 9 rue de la Paix (re-named rue de La Condamine at the end of 1868). In the catalogue of the Salon of May 1868 Sisley also gives this as his address. The third floor studio was located between the courtyard and a garden; the building's entrance is today at 7 rue de La Condamine. [Archives de la ville de Paris: (rue de La Condamine, 1862) D1P4/ 592]

SPRING
By the agency of Charles Le Coeur, Renoir begins preparatory watercolours (one study is in the Von der Heydt-Museum, Wuppertal) for the ceiling decorations of the Hôtel Bibesco (22 boulevard de Latour-Maubourg, now destroyed), the Parisian home of the Prince Georges Bibesco (1834–1902); construction of the building begins in 1869, and is completed in the summer of 1872. [Le Coeur in São Paulo 2002, pp. 211–14, illus. p. 49]

APRIL
During a visit to Chailly-en-Bière Renoir executes what is considered a genre painting, a double portrait of Sisley and Lise Tréhot (*The Engaged Couple*, D34), in a softly focused outdoor setting.

1 MAY
At the Salon, Renoir exhibits (no. 2113) his full-length portrait *Lise with a Parasol* (D29). His address is given as 9 rue de la Paix, Batignolles.

JUNE
Renoir's parents move to *Voisins-Louveciennes, where the family lives at 14 (or 16) rue de Voisins in a house with a garden owned by François Joseph Leclercq, a local merchant.

AUGUST–SEPTEMBER
Renoir and Jules Le Coeur go to *Ville d'Avray (38 rue de St-Cloud, today) with their pregnant mistresses, Lise and Clémence Tréhot. Both women give birth on 14 September. Renoir's mistress, Lise Tréhot, gives birth to a boy, of an 'unknown' father. The child is named Pierre Tréhot; Renoir and Jules Le Coeur sign the birth certificate as witnesses. Nothing is known of the child's life or of his fate. [Le Coeur in São Paulo 2002, pp. 203–5]

1869 1 MAY
Renoir has one work (*En été*, no. 2021, D33), for which the model is Tréhot, accepted at the Salon of 1869 and gives his address as 9 rue de la Paix, Batignolles.

SPRING
Pissarro moves to Louveciennes, renting from M. Retrou a house at 22 route de Versailles.

JULY–SEPTEMBER
While living at his parent's house in Voisins-Louveciennes, Renoir paints a stern portrait of his father, Léonard (D44). He frequently visits the Monets in nearby Saint-Michel, a hamlet of Bougival. The two artists work side by side and paint similar views of the people and activities of the bathing houses around Croissy-sur-Seine, known as La Grenouillère. Renoir's bathing scene (F/H34, cat. 6) and Monet's (W134) are from the same viewpoint.

Renoir and Monet take a brief boat trip along the Seine to Normandy. Both paint barges along the Seine: Monet's little-known work (uncatalogued in Wildenstein) was exhibited in Treviso, 2001–2, no. 4. Renoir's work is *Chalands sur Seine* (F/H33).

OCTOBER
Renoir exhibits recent works at the shop of Marie-Charles-Edouard Carpentier (1830–1883), a colour supplier located at 8 boulevard Montmartre (IX *arrondissement*, today) who had acquired the business from Armand Deforge (1802–1886), his former partner, in 1865 [Archives de la ville de Paris: 5mi3 / 1199, acte 756]. Among the works are two outdoor portraits: *Lise with a Parasol* (D29) and *The Engaged Couple* (D34).

1870 Bazille's *The Artist's Studio, 9 rue de la Condamine* (S56) depicts the studio he had rented and, periodically, shared with Renoir and Sisley since 1867. Bazille is at the centre, leaning against an easel. Louis-Edmond Maître (1840–1898), with whom Bazille shared a passion for music, especially Wagner, plays the piano. Manet is present. The three other figures may be either Renoir, Sisley, Monet, Jules Le Coeur or the critic Zacharie Astruc.

In preparation for the Salon, Fantin-Latour finishes *A Studio in the Batignolles Quarter* (Musée d'Orsay, Paris), a homage to Manet, who is depicted at his easel surrounded by friends and artists such as Renoir, Bazille, Monet and Louis-Edmond Maître. The painting depicts Manet's atelier at 86 rue Guyot (rue Médéric, XVIII *arrondissement*, today).

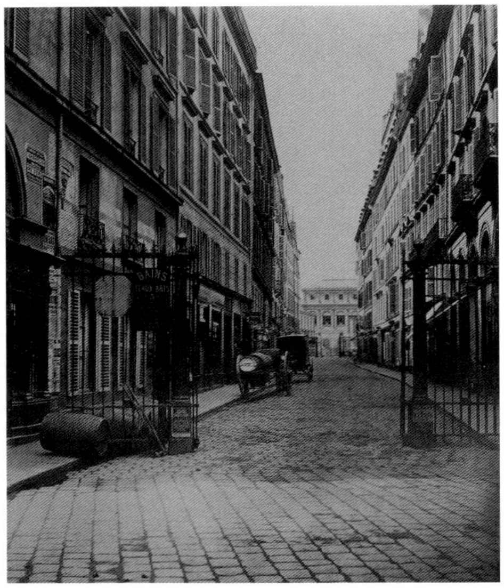

FIG. 119 Charles Marville (1816–*c*.1879), *Rue des Beaux-Arts*, about 1868. Photograph. Bibliothèque historique de la ville de Paris (BhvP: GP XXIV13).

1 MAY
Renoir has two works accepted at the Salon, a landscape with women, including a nude, beside a river (no. 2405, D54), and an Algerian woman reclining or 'odalisque' (no. 2406, D48). The catalogue of the 1870 Salon lists Renoir's address as 'chez M. Bazille, rue des Beaux-Arts, 8' (VI *arrondissement*, today). Renoir shares the apartment/atelier with Bazille, who has rented it since April. It is in the building where Fantin-Latour has had his atelier since 1867 (see fig. 116).

Pissarro continues to paint scenes of Louveciennes, Bougival and Marly-le-Roi, including a spring view of Louveciennes and its aqueduct (P/S158). Renoir will paint the same road in *Louveciennes (today, rue du Général de Gaulle and rue de Voisins) with the aqueduct in the distance (uncatalogued, cat. 8). Monet paints scenes of Bougival and the Seine and surrounding areas (W150–3).

In and around Chatou, Renoir depicts Tréhot outdoors, either in a boat or along the banks of the Seine (D51, 57–60).

JUNE
Renoir stays with Maître at 5 rue Taranne (VI *arrondissement*; the street no longer exists, having been absorbed into the present-day boulevard St-Germain) with Maître.

18 JULY
The Franco–Prussian War commences

21 JULY
In Paris, in his absence, Renoir's mistress Lise Tréhot gives birth to a girl, Jeanne Marguerite (1870–1934), in a municipal health establishment (today, Hôpital Fernand Widal, 200 rue du Faubourg Saint-Denis, X *arrondissement*). [Gélineau in São Paulo 2002, p. 224]

Renoir visits Charles Le Coeur and his family in *Palaiseau, 20 kilometres south of Paris, where the family had been living since April 1870 to refuge from the war [Le Coeur in São Paulo 2002, pp. 210–11]. Here, he paints two portraits of the architect Charles Le Coeur (D99, 100), once thought to have been executed at the family property in Fontenay-aux-Roses in 1874.

26 AUGUST
Renoir is called up to the fourth platoon of the 10th Chasseurs à Cheval in Libourne, a town approximately 575 kilometres south-west of Paris. Bridges are blown up in Bougival, Croissy-sur-Seine and Chatou to prevent the advance of the Prussians. Prussian soldiers destroy property in Bougival and Louveciennes; Sisley and Pissarro lose much of their artistic production to date.

2 SEPTEMBER
Napoléon III surrenders.

19 SEPTEMBER
The Siege of Paris begins.

1871 JANUARY
During his military duty, Renoir becomes gravely ill from dysentery while serving in Vic-en-Bigorre, in the region of the Pyrenees near Tarbes. His uncle brings him to Bordeaux for treatment. Following the armistice on 28 January 1871, Renoir rejoins his regiment in Vic-en-Bigorre. He spends two months in the Hautes-Pyrénées with Captain Edouard Bernier (1822–1880) and his wife, Marie Octavie Bernier (1838–1920), and paints their portraits (D70, 69 respectively).

10 MARCH
Renoir is demobilised, but does not return to Paris until April.

18 MARCH
The Commune in Paris begins.

Thanks to a permit obtained from Raoul Rigault (1846–1871), Prefect of Police and Member of the Commune, later shot in Versailles, Renoir is able to travel during the Commune between Paris and Louveciennes, where his parents are living. During the height of the Commune, Renoir returns to Paris and rents a room on the rue du Dragon (VI *arrondissement*, today). Maître and his companion Rapha were living nearby at 5 rue Taranne, in an apartment Maître had shared with Renoir during the summer of 1870. Renoir paints a full-length portrait of Rapha Maître (D66) in April 1871 and will, during the year, execute another portrait of her (D68) as well as Maître reading (D72).

16 MAY
In Paris, Courbet participates in the destruction of the Vendôme column – a symbol of Bonapartisme – for which he will be imprisoned for six months.

21–28 MAY
The Commune ends in bloodshed

END OF JUNE
Pissarro returns to Louveciennes from England, where he had taken refuge during the Franco-Prussian War and the Commune, and begins to paint scenes around Louveciennes and Bougival. He paints a view of the Seine at Bougival (P/S204) that Monet will also paint (W236).

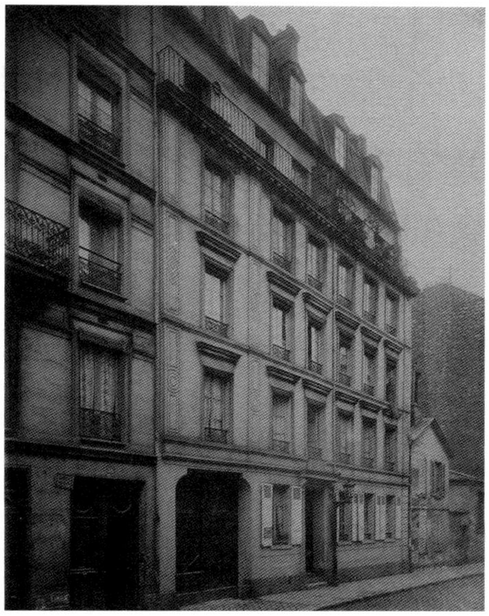

FIG. 120 Union Photographique française, *34, Rue Notre-Dame-des-Champs*, January 1903. Photograph. Bibliothèque historique de la ville de Paris (BhvP: GP XXIII 65).

Renoir spends a few days at *Marlotte with Jules Le Coeur (today, 30 rue Delort). By the end of summer he will have finished the ceiling paintings for the Hôtel Bibesco in Paris. [Le Coeur in São Paulo 2002, p. 198]

SEPTEMBER
Renoir rents one of the numerous ateliers at 34 rue Notre-Dame-des-Champs (VI *arrondissement*; the building no longer exists, see fig. 117); Courbet and Whistler had studios in the same street. Renoir will work here until he takes a studio in the IX *arrondissement*, on the rue St-Georges, probably in 1873.

1872 JANUARY
Renoir lives in Paris and paints urban subjects. Meanwhile, Sisley has been staying with the Monet family in Argenteuil. Sisley and Monet work side by side painting the boats and bridges along the Seine (D26 and W197).

Renoir continues to paint scenes of Paris. His view of Pont Neuf (F/H74; cat. 12) is similar to Monet's version of the same subject (*The Pont Neuf*, W193, see fig. 66, p. 114).

AUTUMN
Sisley moves to Louveciennes, 2 rue de la Princesse, a few streets away from Renoir's parents; he will live here until 1875.

AUTUMN 1872 (TO EARLY 1873)
Renoir works on his largest canvas to date, *Riding in the Bois de Boulogne* (D94), probably executed in the Salle des fêtes of the Ecole Militaire in Paris. The work was submitted to the Salon of 1873 and rejected.

1873 SPRING
Sisley and Renoir paint the same view in Louveciennes (Sisley, *Enfants jouant dans la Prairie*, DS63; Renoir, *Country Road in Springtime* [uncatalogued, Christie's, New York, 2 May 2006, lot 20; Rewald 1973, p. 287]). Both artists also depict the house in *Voisins-Louveciennes where Renoir's mother will later live (Renoir, uncatalogued, Piasa, Paris 6 November 1999, lot 75; Sisley, DS 33). This same area of *Voisins-Louveciennes (now place Fernand Guillaume at intersection of the rue de Voisins and the avenue Saint-Martin) was painted from different perspectives by Sisley and Pissarro in 1871 and 1872: their views of the rue de Voisins are similar (DS18; P/S208). Pissarro also painted the village of Voisins from the avenue St-Martin (P/S235).

Renoir paints scenes of Bougival (F/H41; cat. 17) and of rural villages in the vicinity.

SUMMER
Renoir visits Charles Le Coeur at *Fontenay-aux-Roses and paints a view of the garden there (F/H126). The friendship between the Le Coeur family and Renoir ends, probably because of Renoir's presumed advances toward Marie, Le Coeur's 15-year-old daughter. [Le Coeur in São Paulo 2002, pp. 214–15]

Renoir spends time in Argenteuil with Claude Monet and his wife, who had rented a villa known as the Maison Aubry, at 2 rue Pierre Guienne, from the Realist painter Théodule Ribot (1823–1891). Renoir and Monet worked closely together: as Monet is recording his garden on canvas (W287), Renoir paints *Claude Monet painting in his Garden in Argenteuil* (D131; cat. 19). Both depict a duck pond (Renoir cats. 20, 21; Monet, W289) and the railroad bridge at Argenteuil (Renoir, uncatalogued, private collection, Japan; Monet, W279). In 1873–4, Renoir will also execute *The Reader*, a portrait of Monet (D87).

Renoir continues to explore the areas west of Paris. It is probably at this moment that he travels to La Celle-St-Cloud, staying at the Maison de la Treille, 9 rue St-Pierre (today, rue de la République) near Bougival and Louveciennes. *In the Parc de St-Cloud* (uncatalogued, cat. 14) is probably painted along the Seine between the bridges of *St-Cloud and Sèvres.

AUTUMN, PROBABLY OCTOBER
In Paris, Renoir rents an apartment and a modest fourth-floor studio at 35 rue St-Georges (IX *arrondissement*, today), where he will work primarily on portraits and nudes. [Archives de la ville de Paris: (rue St. Georges, 1876) D1P4/ 1013]

27 DECEMBER
In Renoir's studio, a group of artists, including the future Impressionists, form the Société Anonyme des Artistes.

1874 15 APRIL–15 MAY
The first Impressionist exhibition is held in Nadar's studio at 35 boulevard des Capucines (II *arrondissement*, today). The exhibition attracts approximately 3,500 visitors. 30 participants and 165 works are listed in the catalogue. Renoir gives his address as 35 rue St-Georges (IX *arrondissement*, today): he exhibits seven works, including *The Harvesters* (I–144, F/H96 cat. 16). Sisley lists his address as 2 rue de la Princesse, Voisins-Louveciennes and exhibits paintings of Louveciennes, Port Marly, and Bougival. Pissarro exhibits five landscapes. Among Monet's works are the famous *Impression, soleil levant* (W263), a landscape (W132/274), a seascape (W126/296), and a painting of the boulevard des Capucines (W292/293).

SUMMER
Renoir visits Monet in Argenteuil, where Manet, Monet and Renoir paint together in July. Manet paints *The Monet Family in their Garden at Argenteuil* (The Metropolitan Museum of Art, New York); Monet paints *Manet painting in Monet's Garden at Argenteuil* (W342); and Renoir paints *Madame Monet and her son, Jean* (D104, fig. 35). On 1 October 1874, the Monet family will move to another villa in Argenteuil, at 5 boulevard St-Denis (today, 21 boulevard Karl-Marx). Renoir paints sailing boats on the Seine at Argenteuil (F/H94, cat. 23; F/H114, cat. 24).

17 DECEMBER
The Société Anonyme is dissolved in Renoir's studio at 35 rue St-Georges. During the winter, Renoir continues to live in Paris.

22 DECEMBER
Renoir's father Léonard dies in Voisins-Louveciennes. Two of his sons witness his death certificate; Auguste was living in Paris at 35 rue St-Georges; Edmond, at 5 rue Guy-Patin (X *arrondissement*, today).

1875 WINTER
Like Sisley and Monet, Renoir paints a snowy landscape (F/H142, cat. 35).

SPRING 1875
Renoir paints city views of the neighbourhood near his studio on the rue St-Georges; these include the Place St-Georges (uncatalogued; cat. 31), the Grands Boulevards and streets near the Opéra (F/H181, cat. 30) and the recently built Eglise de la Trinité (F/H622, cat. 29), designed by the architect Théodore Ballu (1817–1885).

24 MARCH
Works by Impressionist artists Monet, Morisot, Renoir and Sisley are sold at the Hôtel Drouot, the Paris auction house. At least ten of Renoir's 20 works are landscapes. Among the lots are two views of the Institut de France on the Quai Malaquais (uncatalogued, cat. 25, F/H90). Georges Charpentier, a publisher of Naturalist writers, acquires his first Renoir, *Pêcheur à la ligne* (D103), at this sale.

SPRING–SUMMER
Renoir returns to the Ile de Chatou, where in 1874 he had executed a view of the Seine (F/H113). He spends several short visits at the restaurant and boarding-house of the family of Alphonse Fournaise (1823–1905) and paints landscapes along the Seine (*Wash-house at Bas Meudon*, F/H182; *The Bridge at Chatou*, F/H146, cat. 32; *The Skiff*, F/H364, cat. 33) as well as portraits of Alphonse Fournaise (D158) and his daughter, Alphonsine (1846–1937), over the next five years. In 1875, Monet will paint a near identical version of *The Bridge at Chatou* (W367).

Probably in the late months of 1875, while Monet was working on *Camille Monet in Japanese Costume* (W387), which was finished, signed and dated in 1876, Renoir paints *Claude Monet Painting* (D132, signed and dated 1875) in Monet's villa at 5 boulevard St-Denis in Argenteuil. Both paintings would be among the eighteen works exhibited by Monet and Renoir in the second Impressionist exhibition in April 1876 (Monet, II–153; Renoir, II–220).

1876 6 JANUARY–6 MARCH
In *Pau, at the twelfth annual exhibition of the Musée des Beaux-Arts, several young Impressionist artists – including Degas, Manet, Morisot, Pissarro and Renoir – exhibit portraits and landscapes. Both of Renoir's submissions are of women (no. 280, *Couseuse*; no. 281, *Jeune fille jouant avec un chat*).

Renoir paints *The Artist's Studio, rue St-Georges* (D188).

MARCH–OCTOBER
Perhaps hoping to paint outdoors, Renoir rents a house with a garden in *Montmartre, at 12–14, rue Cortot (today, portions of the building at 14 rue Cortot, XVIII *arrondissement*, today). He will continue to live at 35 rue St-Georges. Renoir's portraiture, commissioned by wealthy patrons, should have given him some financial relief and had perhaps motivated him to rent additional studio space; however, in the following years, particularly in 1877 and 1878, he is again short of money.

11 APRIL–9 MAY
The second Impressionist exhibition is held at 11 rue Le Peletier (IX *arrondissement*, today) at the premises of one of the Durand-Ruel galleries. The catalogue lists 19 participants and 252 works. Renoir's submissions are dominated by figures and portraits. Among his 18 noted works (17 oil paintings, one pastel) the majority are loaned by the artist's friend and collector Victor Chocquet. *Luncheon at La Fournaise* (D305, cat. 34) is listed in the catalogue (II–221) as *Déjeuner chez Fournaise*. Renoir also exhibits (II–220) a portrait of 'M. M . . .', perhaps one of the two portraits of Monet in the Jean Dollfus collection (D87, 132), and his famous portrait of Bazille *Frédéric Bazille Painting 'The Heron'* (II–224, D28), which was lent by Manet. Renoir's address is given as 35 rue St-Georges. Sisley exhibits landscapes of Louveciennes and Marly-le-Roi. Several views of the Seine at Argenteuil, including a painting of the railroad bridge (possibly, W279) and one of the famous bathing houses of La Grenouillère (W134/136), are among Monet's exhibited works. Pissarro shows several snow scenes of Pontoise, as well as agricultural scenes.

Renoir paints a portrait of Alfred Sisley (D117) in the second home of Monet in Argenteuil; the work will be shown in 1877 at the third Impressionist exhibition (III–190).

LATE SPRING
In Montmartre, Renoir paints *plein-air* studies and portraits in which he concentrates on the effects of sunlight and shadows. He works in the garden (*Garden in the rue Cortot, Montmartre*, D193, cat. 39) or perhaps in one of a series of gardens behind buildings which adjoin the property as well as painting outdoors nearby at the Moulin de la Galette. His monumental canvas *The Ball at the Moulin de la Galette* (III–186, D209) will be one of his most important works presented at the third Impressionist exhibition in April 1877.

SEPTEMBER
Renoir goes to *Champrosay to see Alphonse Daudet (1840–1897), the Realist novelist and playwright who he had met at the Charpentiers', and visits the writer's residence (today, 22 rue Alphonse Daudet, one of several addresses he had there). He paints a portrait of Mme Daudet (Julia Allard Daudet, 1847–1940) (D163) and *The Seine at Champrosay* (F/H252, cat. 36).

OCTOBER
Charpentier commissions Renoir to decorate his apartment in Paris at 11–13 rue de Grenelle (VII *arrondissement*, today). Renoir also paints a portrait of the Charpentiers' daughter Georgette (D178) and probably begins a commission for the first portrait of *Mme Georges Charpentier* (D226); both will be presented at the third Impressionist exhibition in April 1877 (III–188, III–187, respectively).

1877 Monet paints scenes of the Gare St-Lazare (W438–49).

APRIL
The third Impressionist exhibition is held at 6 rue Le Peletier (IX *arrondissement*, today), near the Durand-Ruel gallery at 11 rue Le Peletier. The catalogue lists 241 works, 21 are by Renoir. Five are landscapes: of his urban genre scenes, *The Ball at the Moulin de la Galette* (III–186, D209) is perhaps the most spectacular; *The Seine at Champrosay* (III–195, F/H252, cat. 36) and *The Dahlias* (III–204), which is now thought to be the *Garden in the rue Cortot, Montmartre* (D193; cat. 39). One of his most remarkable cityscapes, *Le Coucher de soleil* (III-197), is now believed lost. Charpentier lends portraits of his wife (D226) and of his daughter (D178).

Sisley's 17 submissions are dominated by views of Marly-le-Roi. Monet's urban scenes of Parisian parks and the Gare St-Lazare account for the majority of his 30 works. Pissarro exhibits 22 landscapes, mostly of Pontoise or along the banks of the Oise river.

28 MAY
45 Impressionist paintings are sold by auction at the Hôtel Drouot. The average price attained per work is 169 francs. Renoir places two landscapes, depicting autumn (lot 29) and spring (lot 30) in the sale; neither has been identified.

Renoir paints the first two portraits of Jeanne Samary (1857–1890, D228, 229), an actress from the Comédie-Française; he will depict her at least twelve times over the next three years.

1878 25 MAY
Renoir's *Le Café* (D272 as '*La tasse de chocolat*') is accepted at the Salon of 1878 (no. 1883), his first work in eight years to be exhibited. His address is listed as 35 rue St-Georges.

OCTOBER
Renoir finishes *Madame Charpentier and her Children* (D266) in October 1878 for the Salon of 1879. He will also paint a full-length portrait of Samary (D263). Both paintings are exhibited in the following year at the Salon of 1879 (no. 2527, D266; no. 2528, D263).

1879 WINTER
Monet paints scenes of Vétheuil and Lavacourt in the snow (W505–15).

10 APRIL–11 MAY
The fourth Impressionist exhibition is held at 28 avenue de l'Opéra (II *arrondissement*, today) from 10 April until 11 May. Renoir and Sisley are not among the 16 known exhibitors. 29 works are exhibited by Monet, nearly all *plein-air* works depicting landscapes in different seasons and atmospheric conditions. Pissarro, too, shows a record 38 works, mostly landscapes. The catalogue lists 246 works. A total of 15,400 visitors is recorded.

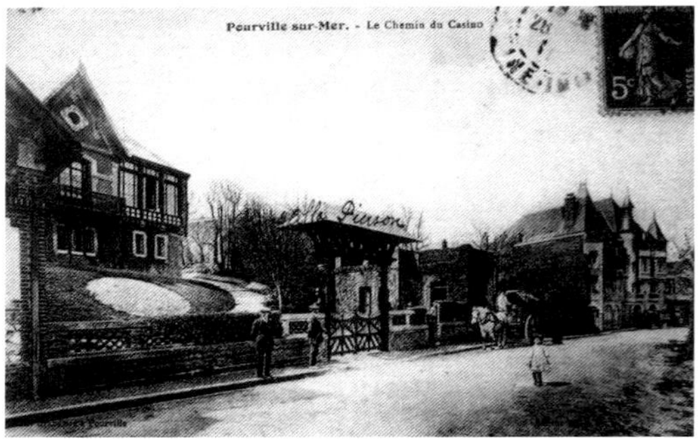

FIG. 121 *Blanche Pierson's Villa, Pourville, c.1900.* Postcard. Collection Claude Féron.

12 MAY
At the Salon, Renoir's *Madame Charpentier and her Children* (no. 2527, D266) is highly praised. It is one of four works by Renoir accepted (nos. 2527–8, 4476–7).

19 JUNE
A solo exhibition of Renoir paintings and pastels at the gallery La Vie Moderne at 7 boulevard des Italiens (II *arrondissement*, today) is organised.

SUMMER
Renoir executes numerous works along the Seine near Bougival and Chatou, where he will begin to paint with more frequency (F/H360, cat. 50). These river scenes and related subjects and activities will replace the depictions of Montmartre. He will paint several portraits of the Fournaise family at Chatou.

AUGUST–SEPTEMBER
Renoir visits the coast of Normandy as a guest at the château and estate in *Wargemont (Derchingny-Graincourt) of the Protestant banker Paul Berard (1833–1905) for the first time. He paints the rose garden on the Berard estate (*La Roseraie de Wargemont*, F/H355) and *Landscape at Wargemont* (F/H356, cat. 43), now identified as a view of the nearby fields south of the château, bordered by the trees of the Bois de St-Quentin and the Rideaux de Sauchay-le-Bas. He begins the first of 14 family portraits that Berard will commission over the next few years. The artist explores the surrounding countryside, visiting Martin-Eglise, Ancourt and Sauchay and writing of their charms in an undated letter to Madame Charpentier [Florisoone 1938, p. 37]. He chooses the coastline and beaches along the English Channel near *Berneval as inspiration for several paintings, including *Cliffs at Berneval* (F/H350, cat. 47), once thought to be a view of Pourville but now believed to represent the cliffs of Berneval looking north-east toward Penly, and *Musselfishers at Berneval* (D292, fig. 44). Other works executed during this stay are *The Wave* (F/H348, cat. 45), and *The Mussel Harvest* (F/H405, cat. 46, formerly *The Vintagers*).

SEPTEMBER
Renoir visits Jacques-Emile Blanche (1861–1942) and his mother in Dieppe. Here he paints decorations (D313, 315–18) on the theme of Wagner's *Tannhaüser* for the dining room of their house, a châlet located on the Bas-Fort Blanc (now destroyed). Between late summer and early autumn Renoir is believed to have executed views of neighbouring *Pourville, painting the cottage of the actress Blanche Pierson (F/H351; see fig. 118), today 22 rue Léonce Grau, and another landscape (F/H319).

From the end of 1879 to the beginning of 1880 one of the coldest winters of the century is recorded in France. Snow falls over most of the country during the first ten days of December.

1880 As the terrible winter ends, the Seine thaws. On 3 January, as the ice begins to break, a portion of the Pont des Invalides in Paris collapses. Monet paints the frozen Seine and winter scenes of the icy river in Vétheuil and Lavacourt (1879, W552–3; 1880, W554–77). Sisley paints views of the Seine, the subsequent floods in Moret (DS337–40) and snow scenes (DS342, 343, 345–8).

Renoir concentrates on urban scenes and begins studies of a woman with a hat (D323–5) for a painting of the Place de Clichy (D326).

1–30 APRIL
The fifth Impressionist exhibition is held at 10 rue des Pyramides (I *arrondissement*, today). The catalogue lists 232 works and 19 participants. Renoir, Sisley, Monet and Cézanne do not participate. Pissarro exhibits 11 paintings, the majority being landscapes, and a series of etchings of rural scenes.

1 MAY
At the Salon, Renoir exhibits two works (*Pêcheuse de moules à Berneval, côte normande*, no. 3195; *Jeune fille endormie*, no. 3196), the first of which represents mussel fishers on the coast of Normandy at Berneval (D292). The work was purchased by Durand-Ruel in November 1880, an indication that that Renoir's 'subject' or genre pictures were beginning to find their market.

JUNE–JULY
Renoir visits the Berards at Wargemont and paints views of the Normandy coast in *Harvest at Berneval* (F/H405, cat. 51), which is now believed to depict the English Channel between *Berneval and Belleville from the fields at Val du Prêtre, and another unlocated vista of the sea near Wargemont (F/H402, cat. 52). Through the Berards he meets the banker Georges Grimpel (1838–1910) and paints portraits of the Grimpel children (D335–7).

JULY–AUGUST
Through the critic and collector Charles Ephrussi (1849–1905) Renoir paints portraits of Thérèse Prascovia Ephrussi (1851–1911) and of her mother Madame Eugène Fould (1812–1888).

Renoir begins to paint *Luncheon of the Boating Party* (D379, fig. 89, p. 170) on the Ile de Chatou at the Restaurant Fournaise. Towards the end of the summer, Renoir writes to Berard about the expenses of painting and hiring models [Berard 1968, pp. 4–5].

LATE SUMMER
Renoir stays with the Fournaises during his painting campaigns at Chatou in August–September 1880 and continues to accept portrait commissions that will help to subsidise his ambitious undertakings such as *Luncheon of the Boating Party* (D379).

NOVEMBER
Between 16 and 26 November, winter temperatures in France drop below -6° C twice. Ice remains in the city streets and surrounding countryside from late November and throughout December.

1881 JANUARY–FEBRUARY
Monet, still interested in atmospheric conditions, paints the floods at Vétheuil (W638–9, 641–2.)

In *Louveciennes, Renoir's mother moves from 23 rue de Voisins, Voisins-Louveciennes, to 10 rue du Pont, Louveciennes, where she lives until 1886. Renoir's sister Elisa (Marie-Hélène Elisa Renoir, 1833–1901) and her husband Charles Leray rent a house nearby in the Enclos de la Machine, place Bellevue, Louveciennes, from 1881 until 1886.

After having finished a portrait of their eldest daughter Irène, Renoir paints a double portrait of Alice and Elisabeth Cahen d'Anvers (D361) – all the children of the composer Albert Cahen d'Anvers (1846–1903) – at the family's residence in Paris, at 66 avenue Montaigne (VIII *arrondissement*, today). He will finish the double portrait before leaving for Algeria; the work will be presented at the Salon of 1881 in May.

FEBRUARY
Durand-Ruel begins to make regular purchases of paintings from Renoir.

4 MARCH–17 APRIL
Renoir abandons the idea of a trip to London organised by Théodore Duret (1838–1927), and travels to Algeria with Paul-Auguste Lhote (1851–*c.*1891/2), who will also accompany him to Italy, later in the year. Eugène-Pierre Lestrinquez and Frédéric Cordey (1854–1911) are also present. Renoir looks for a house in 'Mustapha inférieure' along the coast south of the port [Benjamin 2003, p. 144]. He paints scenes of Arab life (F/H441, cat. 54), *The Mosque of sidi Abd-er-Rahman* (F/H493) as well as views of the Jardin d'Essai (F/H492, cat. 56), and the abundant natural vegetation (F/H440, cat. 55; F/H480, cat. 57).

2 APRIL–1 MAY
The sixth Impressionist Exhibition is again held at 35 boulevard des Capucines (II *arrondissement*, today). Renoir, Monet and Sisley are not among the 13 participants. Pissarro exhibits paintings and gouaches, a total of 28 works, mainly rural landscapes of Pontoise. The catalogue lists 170 works; this is the smallest of the eight Impressionist exhibitions.

7 APRIL
Durand-Ruel purchases five Algerian views from Renoir (including F/H492, cat. 55; F/H440, cat. 56; F/H480, cat. 57).

Upon returning from Algeria, Renoir paints at Chatou (F/H424, cat. 58; F/H449, cat. 61).

18 APRIL
Renoir has lunch with Whistler, a former student from Gleyre's atelier, at Chatou.

LATE SPRING
Renoir rents a room, perhaps for a studio or for storage, at 18 rue Norvins (XVIII *arrondissement*, today), a few streets away from the rue Cortot studio.

2 MAY–JUNE
Renoir exhibits two portraits of the Cahen d'Anvers children at the Salon of 1881 (nos. 1986, 1987).

20–27 JULY
Renoir travels to Dieppe. During his visit Madame Blanche receives him with reticence. He stays at Wargemont at the Berards' château; this is Renoir's third summer at Wargemont.

SEPTEMBER
Renoir is once again at Wargemont, where he paints the portrait of Albert Cahen d'Anvers (D362) at the Berards' residence; the work is signed and dated *Renoir / Wargemont, 9.Sbre.81*. He also paints *Studies of the Children of Paul Berard* (D365).

OCTOBER–NOVEMBER
Renoir leaves for Italy at the end of October. He is probably accompanied by his mistress Aline Victorine Charigot (1859–1915), who has modelled for him since 1879. On 1 November, Renoir is in Venice, where he paints the Piazza San Marco (F/H462, cat. 64), the Doge's Palace (F/H461, cat. 62) and the Grand Canal (F/H460; cat. 63, and F/H458, 458a, 459, 461). Probably with Charigot, Renoir visits Padua and Florence and travels to Rome, where, at the Vatican, he particularly admires Raphael's frescoes. The couple stay in Naples, at the Albergo de la Trinacria, one of several small hotels on the Piazza del Municipio near the Castel Nuovo and Palazzo Reale, by the port [K. Baedeker, *Italie Méridionale*, 7th edn., p. 24, Leipzig 1883]. Renoir writes to his dealer Durand-Ruel on 21 November about the Pompeiian frescoes in the Naples museum [according to Baedeker 1883, the Pompeiian frescoes were exhibited in seven ground-floor galleries in the Museo Nazionale. *Ibidem*, pp. 62–6]. He paints views of the bay of Naples at different times of day (F/H468, fig. 112; F/H469, cat. 65). He and Charigot visit Pompeii and Sorrento, depicted in two landscapes (F/H466, 471).

DECEMBER
Renoir visits Calabria and paints a landscape (F/H489). At the end of the year he is in Capri, where he stays at the Hôtel du Louvre, one of several hôtels on the shore west of the port [Baedeker 1883, p. 164], and paints the sea and waves (F/H465).

1882 JANUARY
Renoir tries to get a letter of introduction to see Richard Wagner (1813–1883), who is in Palermo working on his opera *Parsifal*, which will open in Bayreuth in July. While waiting to meet the composer, Renoir visits Monreale. Wagner receives him in Palermo (Hôtel des Palmes) on 14 January and Renoir paints his portrait (D394).

17 JANUARY
Renoir paints the landscape in the vicinity of Naples (F/H470), and anticipates returning to France via Marseilles.

23 JANUARY
Renoir stays in L'Estaque (Hôtel des Bains) and works close to Cézanne. He paints several landscapes of the rocky coast of L'Estaque (F/H487, cat. 66; F/H488, 67; also F/H489).

FEBRUARY
Renoir writes to Durand-Ruel to express his refusal to participate in the seventh Impressionist exhibition [Venturi 1939, vol. I, pp. 120–1].

MARCH
The seventh Impressionist exhibition is held in the Salons du Panorama de Reichshoffen at 251 rue St-Honoré (I *arrondissement*, today). Of the eight Impressionist exhibitions the seventh has the fewest participants. The catalogue lists nine artists and 203 works. Despite Renoir's opposition, Durand-Ruel lends 25 of his paintings, including the artist's monumental *Luncheon of the Boating Party* (VII–140, D379), one of the exhibition's highlights. 10 of the works are landscapes, such as his views of Venice (VII–146, F/H460, cat. 63; VII–147, either F/H459 or F/H461, cat. 62) and those from his first trip of Algeria (*Field of Banana Trees near Algiers*, VII–143, F/H440, cat. 55; *The Jardin d'Essai, Algiers*, VII–157, F/H492, cat. 56). Other Renoir landscapes exhibited were *Chestnut Trees in Bloom* (VII–155, F/H453, cat. 60) and numerous views of the Seine, notably VII–151 and 154, which are thought to be *Rowers at Chatou* (D307, F/H 360, cat. 50) and *The Seine at Chatou* (F/H424, cat. 58).

Monet exhibits 35 paintings, both still lifes and landscapes. Sisley shows 27 paintings, mainly landscapes of the villages along the Seine and Loing rivers near Moret; most are owned by Durand-Ruel. Pissarro exhibits 36 works, scenes of the landscapes and rural life in and near Pontoise.

MARCH–APRIL
Renoir remains in the south of France to paint. In early March he is diagnosed with pneumonia. Following the advice of a doctor, he and Charigot leave Marseilles and travel on the steamship *Moeris* to Algeria, where their arrival is noted in *L'Akhbar*, a local newspaper, on 11 March 1882; in Algiers, they rent lodgings at 30 rue de la Marine, near the Djamâ al-Kabir or Grand Mosque, and stay there until their return to France in late April [Benjamin 2003, pp. 40, 43]. In contrast to the scenes of colourful vegetation and festivities he painted on his first trip to Algeria in 1881, Renoir's second stay in Algiers is devoted primarily to portraits and genre subjects.

1 MAY
Renoir exhibits a portrait of Yvonne Grimpel (no. 2268, D335) at the Salon of 1882.

JUNE
Renoir begins a portrait of Marie Henriette Valentine Billet Clapisson (1849–1930) (D428), wife of the avid collector of Impressionist painting Léon Clapisson (1836–1894). He depicts her sitting on a bench surrounded by the flowering garden of their home in Neuilly at 48 rue Charles-Laffitte. The portrait is rejected by the sitter.

SUMMER
Renoir returns to the Seine-Maritime region of Normandy and is probably the Berards' guest in Wargemont. He visits Monet and the Hoschedés, who are staying in Pourville at the Villa Juliette.

MID-JUNE–EARLY OCTOBER
Monet paints the cliffs, beaches, and boats at Pourville (W751–92).

Renoir depicts the churning waves of the sea in a nearly abstract canvas (F/H526, cat. 68), similar to Monet's views of the Normandy beach of Les Petites-Dalles in 1880 (W623–4) and in 1881 (W661–3).

AUGUST
Renoir is invited to Dieppe for the month with Paul Durand-Ruel (1831–1922) and his family, and often visits Jacques-Emile Blanche. Durand-Ruel commissions Renoir to paint various portraits of his five teenage children (D408–11).

1883 JANUARY–APRIL
These months are generally considered one of the most productive periods in Renoir's career. Suzanne Valadon (1865–1938) and Paul-Auguste Lhote pose for *Dance in the City* (D440) and *Dance at Bougival* (D438). Lhote and Renoir's future wife Aline Charigot pose for *Dance in the Country* (D441). Renoir and Charigot will marry seven years later, on 14 April 1890. In an effort to please his sitter, Renoir attempts a second portrait of Marie Henriette Valentine Billet Clapisson, this time in evening gown with gloves and jewellery (D433).

1–25 APRIL
An exhibition of 70 paintings by Renoir, including some of his 'most masterful narrative works', is held at the Galerie Durand-Ruel on 9 boulevard de la Madeleine (VIII *arrondissement*, today). 14 canvases are landscapes.

15 APRIL–20 JULY
In London, Renoir is among the Impressionists whose works are exhibited with Dowdeswell & Dowdeswell, Grovesnor Gallery, at 133 New Bond Street. He has nine paintings there.

MAY–JUNE
The portrait of Madame Clapisson (no. 2031, D433), Renoir's sole submission to the Salon of 1883, is overlooked by the critics.

LATE SUMMER
Renoir goes to Petit-Gennevilliers, a suburb approximately 10 kilometres west of Paris, to the home of Gustave Caillebotte (1848–1894). He paints a portrait of Caillebotte's mistress, Charlotte Berthier (D432).

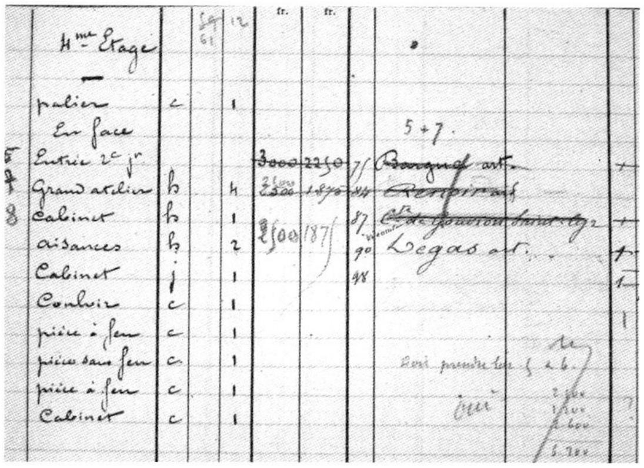

FIG. 122 Archival fiscal records for 37 rue Laval in 1876 and later, as indicated, denoting occupants Renoir and Degas [Archives de la ville de Paris: (rue Laval, 1876) D1P4/1200].

AUGUST
While in Normandy, Renoir paints a view of Yport (F/H540) at low tide as well as portraits of Charigot (D446) and Robert Nunès (D447). He stays at the Maison Aubourg, rue de l'Eglise, Yport. He will also execute a portrait of Lucie Berard (1880–1977), *Child in a White Dress* (*Lucie Berard*) (D449), around the time of her third birthday on 10 July, probably at Wargemont.

EARLY SEPTEMBER–9 OCTOBER
Renoir goes to Jersey and Guernsey in the company of Charigot and Lhote. In Guernsey, they stay for a little more than a month in a lodging house (then no. 4, George Road, St Peter Port) within a short walking distance of the Bay of Moulin Huet at the island's south-eastern tip [House 1988, p. 3]. Renoir executes about 15 paintings in this vicinity – seascapes and scenes of figures and bathers on the Guernsey coast (F/H547; F/H549; F/H550, cat. 69; F/H552, cat. 70), which are noted for their open and colourful brushwork and abundance of white pigment. [House 1988, p. 3]

OCTOBER
Renoir rents a large fourth-floor studio at 37 rue Laval (today, rue Victor-Massé) until, probably, October 1886. The studio is later occupied by Degas. [Archives de la ville de Paris: (rue Laval, 1876) D1P4/1200; see fig. 122.]

16 DECEMBER
Renoir and Monet travel along the Riviera to sketch and to paint. Travelling from Marseilles to Genoa, they pass through French and Italian cities such as Hyères, St-Raphaël, Monte Carlo and Bordighera (F/H490). Renoir paints a landscape near Menton (F/H563, cat. 72). Before returning home, the two painters visit Cézanne in Aix-en-Provence. In a letter to Berard (sale Hôtel Drouot, Paris, 16 February 1979, lot 76) written from Hôtel du Parc et de la Méditerranée, Monte Carlo, Renoir explained: 'But it is more for seeing than for working that I have come'.

LANDSCAPES IN THE SALON

A number of studies, this survey among them, have emphasised the decisive role played by landscape in the history of French painting. One of the ways of gauging its importance is to study landscape painting from the point of view of the critics: they were keen to praise or to condemn this type of painting, which underwent significant development in the nineteenth century. Authors such as Théophile Thoré-Bürger, Théophile Gautier, Charles Baudelaire, Champfleury, Emile Zola and Jules-Antoine Castagnary made declarations about landscape in the Salon in particular. In a critique of 1873 Castagnary speaks of the 'army of landscape painters' whose 'battalions are decimated by the jury every year',[1] but whom nothing could deter, not even the obstacles set in their way by the State and its official institutions. One may ask exactly how many landscape painters managed to surmount such obstacles and to shoulder their way into the Salon. Fortunately, the catalogue issued each year to accompany the exhibition provides an approximate answer.

Presented here are figures for the years 1861 to 1880. Of course, the catalogues have their limitations, one of which is that they provide only titles: in the absence of a reproduction of the work in question we often cannot be certain whether it was a landscape subject or not. Nevertheless, reading these booklets is very revealing, and enables us to draw a number of conclusions. In order to make the basis of our results clear, we have identified landscapes according to the following indications in the titles given in the catalogues:

General
View, recollection, plain, heathland, mountain, meadows, road, outskirts, entrance to a village, footpath, glade, stream, lake, pool, marsh, river, pond, bay, seasons, stormy weather, rain, evening, morning, sunset, forests, under the trees, ravines, cliffs, rocks, gardens terrace, mills.

Seascapes
Sea, scenes involving boats of any kind (including battles, shipwrecks), fishing and fishermen (titles such 'Return of the Fishing Fleet'; 'Fishermen resting on the Shore, Evening'; 'Preparation for fishing, at Célans'), harbours, quays.

Streets
For example, 'A street in Constantine'.

Historical and mythological landscapes
For example, 'Dance of the Nymphs'; 'Wood Nymphs'; 'Rinaldo and Armida in the Enchanted Forest'; 'Dancing Fauns'; 'The Huntress'.

Hunting scenes
For example, 'The Hunters' Rest'; 'Battle of the Stags'; 'Departure / Return / Meet'; 'Hunters / Poachers'.

Figures in a landscape
For example, 'Woman at the Well; Landscape in the Black Forest'; 'Woman bathing'; 'Women bathing by Moonlight'.

Animals in a landscape
For example, 'Pasture / Leaving for the Pasture / Leaving the Pasture'; 'Herd of Sheep / Cattle'; 'Wild Horses in the Meadows'.

We have excluded paintings of peasants (for example, paintings by Millet) from this overview as they would be better classified as rural genre paintings.

1 Jules-Antoine Castagnary, *Salons: 1857–1879*, Bibliothèque Charpentier, Paris 1892, vol. 1, p. 78.

COMPILED BY NELDA DAMIANO

ANALYSIS OF THE SALON CATALOGUES

	1861	1862	1863	1863	1864	1864	1865	1866	1867	1868	1869
		No Salon		*Salon des Refusés*		*Salon des Refusés*					
Paintings catalogued	3146		1915	680	1995	282	2264	1998	1581	2587	1196
Of which landscapes	644		502	183	642	99	680	638	477	798	348
	(20%)		(26%)	(27%)	(32%)	(35%)	(30%)	(32%)	(30%)	(31%)	(29%)
Categories of landscape											
General	505		402	157	535	81	582	532	383	672	282
Seascapes	55		34	10	32	5	40	43	36	46	31
Streets	5		6	1	9	0	5	9	6	4	4
Historical/mythological	5		1	0	4	0	2	5	7	1	0
Hunting scenes	23		15	1	22	2	21	15	12	23	14
Figures in a landscape	4		6	2	7	3	4	5	10	9	6
Animals in a landscape	47		38	12	33	8	26	29	23	43	11

	1870	1871	1872	1873	1874	1875	1876	1877	1878	1879	1880
		No Salon									
Paintings catalogued	2974		1231*	1242**	1852	2019	2095	2192	2330	3040	3957
Of which landscapes	1002		403	362	545	608	624	598	629	781	1059
	(34%)		(33%)	(29%)	(29%)	(30%)	(30%)	(28%)	(27%)	(26%)	(27%)
Categories of landscape											
General	850		346	292	439	489	529	497	520	636	873
Seascapes	62		25	29	54	67	38	54	64	92	109
Streets	14		4	7	8	13	12	6	9	15	17
Historical/mythological	1		1	1	1	2	2	1	1	1	5
Hunting scenes	20		5	14	14	7	13	10	7	11	13
Figures in a landscape	15		0	3	3	6	5	4	5	3	6
Animals in a landscape	40		22	16	26	24	25	26	23	23	36

* out of 1536 items which include drawings, watercolours, pastels, enamels, miniatures, porcelain, ceramics.
** out of 1491 items which include drawings, watercolours, pastels, enamels, miniatures, porcelain, ceramics.

BIBLIOGRAPHY

Adams 1994
S. Adams, *The Barbizon School & the Origins of Impressionism*, London 1994.

Adhémar and Dayez-Distel 1979
H. Adhémar and A. Dayez-Distel, eds, *Catalogue du Musée du jeu de paume*, Paris 1979.

Adriani 1996
G. Adriani, *Renoir*, Cologne 1996.

Alazard 1946
J. Alazard, 'Les séjours d'Auguste Renoir à Alger' in *Études d'Art du Musée des Beaux-Arts d'Alger*, Algiers 1946.

Albert-Montémont 1859
Guide Universel et complet de l'Etranger dans Paris, Paris 1859.

Alexandre 1892
A. Alexandre, preface in *Exposition A. Renoir*, exh. cat., Paris (Galeries Durand-Ruel) 1892, pp. 3–36.

Angrand 1968
P. Angrand, 'L'Etat mécène. Période autoritaire du Second Empire (1851–1860)', *Gazette des beaux-arts*, vol. 71 (1968), p. 303–45.

Ann Arbor 1977
Pompeii as a Source of Inspiration, exh. cat. Ann Arbor (University of Michigan Museum of Art) 1977.

Arcangeli 1989
F. Arcangeli, *Monet*, Bologna 1989.

Arnaldo 2004
J. Arnaldo, *Carmen Thyssen-Bornemisza Collection*, trans. L. Suffield, Madrid 2004.

Art Institute of Chicago 1961
Paintings in the Art Institute of Chicago. A Catalogue of the Picture Collection, Chicago 1961.

Art Institute of Chicago 1973
Paintings by Renoir, exh cat., Chicago (Art Institute of Chicago) 1973.

Atlanta 1984
The High Museum. The Henry P. McIlhenny Collection: Nineteenth Century French and English Masterpieces, Atlanta 1984.

Auffret 2004
F. Auffret, *Johan Barthold Jongkind, 1819–1891. Héritier Contemporain and Précurseur. Biographie Illustrée*, Paris 2004.

Baedeker 1878
K. Baedeker, *Paris and its Environs*, Leipzig 1878.

Baetjer 1878
K. Baetjer, *European Paintings in the Metropolitan Museum of Art by Artists born in or before 1865*, 3 vols, New York 1980.

Bailey 1997
C.B. Bailey *et al*, *Renoir's Portraits: Impressions of an Age*, exh. cat., Ottawa (National Gallery of Canada), Chicago (The Art Institute of Chicago) and Fort Worth (Kimbell Art Museum), New Haven and London 1997.

Bailey 2003
C.B. Bailey, 'Renoir and Algeria: Williamstown, Dallas and Paris', *The Burlington Magazine*, vol. CXLV (2003), pp. 682–4.

Bailey and Rishel 1989
C.B. Bailey and J.J. Rishel, *Masterpieces of Impressionism & Post-Impressionism: the Annenberg Collection*, Philadelphia 1989.

Bailly-Herzberg 1980
J. Bailly-Herzberg, *Correspondance de Camille Pissarro*, 5 vols, Paris 1980.

Barnes and De Mazia 1935
A. Barnes and V. De Mazia, *The Art of Renoir*, New York 1935.

Baudelaire 1992
C. Baudelaire, *Critique d'art suivi de Critique musicale* (1859), ed. Claude Pichois, Paris 1992.

Baudot 1949
J. Baudot, *Renoir: ses amis, ses modèles*, Paris 1949.

Bazin 1946
G. Bazin, 'Musée du Louvre. Un tableau de Renoir: Le Ravin de la femme sauvage', *Bulletin des Musées de France*, vol. 10 (1946), pp. 6–10.

Bellony-Rewald 1976
A. Bellony-Rewald, *The Lost World of the Impressionists*, London 1976.

Benjamin 2003
R. Benjamin, *Renoir and Algeria*, exh. cat., Williamstown (Sterling and Francine Clark Art Institute) and Dallas (Dallas Museum of Art), New Haven and London 2003.

Berard 1956
M. Berard, 'Un diplomate, ami de Renoir', *Revue d'histoire diplomatique*, July–September 1956, pp. 239–46.

Berard 1968
M. Berard, 'Lettres à un ami', *Revue de Paris*, December 1968, pp. 54–8.

Berhaut
M. Berhaut, *Caillebotte: catalogues raisonne des peintures et pastels*, Paris 1949, p. 238.

Berson 1996
R. Berson, ed., *The New Painting: Impressionism, 1874–1886. Documentation*, 2 vols, exh. cat., San Francisco (Fine Arts Museums of San Francisco) and Washington 1996.

Blanc 1866
C. Blanc, 'Salon de 1866 (2e article)', *Gazette des beaux-arts*, 1 July 1866, pp. 28–71.

Blanche 1921
J.-E. Blanche, 'La technique de Renoir', *L'Amour de l'Art*, II: 2 (February 1921), p. 33–40.

Blanche 1927
J.-E. Blanche, *Dieppe*, Paris 1927.

Blanche 1931
J.-E. Blanche, *Les arts plastiques*, Paris 1931.

Blanche 1937
J.-E. Blanche, *Portraits of a Lifetime*, London 1937.

Blanche 1949
J.-E. Blanche, *La Pêche aux souvenirs*, Paris 1949.

Bodelsen 1968
M. Bodelsen, 'Early Impressionist Sales, 1874–94 in the Light of Some Unpublished "Procès Verbaux"', *The Burlington Magazine*, CX (1968), pp. 331–49.

Boime 1971
A. Boime, *The Academy and French Painting in the Nineteenth Century*, London and New York 1971.

Boime 1995
A. Boime, *Art and the French Commune: Imagining Paris after War and Revolution*, Princeton 1995.

Bomford 1990
D. Bomford *et al*, *Art in the Making: Impressionism*, exh cat., London (National Gallery) 1990.

Boston 1915
Robert Dawson Evans Memorial Galleries for Paintings (opening exhibition), exh. cat., Boston (Museum of Fine Arts) 1915.

Boston 1931
'Exhibition of French Paintings Lent by Mr. John T. Spaulding', *Bulletin of the Museum of Fine Arts, Boston*, vol. 29 (June 1931), p. 53.

Boston 1939
Juliana Cheney Edwards Collection, exh. cat., Boston (Museum of Fine Arts) 1939.

Boston 1948
The Collections of John Taylor Spaulding, exh. cat., Boston (Museum of Fine Arts) 1948.

Boston 1955
The Collections of John Taylor Spaulding, exh. cat., Boston (Museum of Fine Arts) 1955.

Boston 1973
The Collections of John Taylor Spaulding, exh. cat., Boston (Museum of Fine Arts) 1973.

Boston 1973a
Impressionism, French and American, exh. cat., Boston (Museum of Fine Arts) 1973.

Boston 1999
The Collections of John Taylor Spaulding, exh. cat., Boston (Museum of Fine Arts) 1999.

Boston 1999
Monet, Renoir and the Impressionist Landscape, exh. cat., Boston (Museum of Fine Arts) 1999.

Braun 1932
'L'Impressionnisme et quelques précurseurs', *Bulletin des Expositions* (Galerie d'Art Braun), III, 1932.

Brenneman 2002
D.A. Brenneman, *Paris in the Age of Impressionism: Masterworks from the Musée d'Orsay*, exh. cat., Atlanta (High Museum of Art) and Houston (Museum of Fine Arts), New York 2002.

Brettell 1995
R.R. Brettell, *Impressionist Paintings, Drawings, and Sculpture from the Wendy and Emery Reves Collection*, Dallas 1995.

Brettell 2000
R.R. Brettell, *Impression: Painting Quickly in France, 1860–1890*, exh. cat., Williamstown (Sterling and Francine Clark Art Institute), New Haven and London 2000.

Brettell and Schaefer 1984
R.R. Brettell and S. Schaefer, *A Day in the Country: Impressionism and the French Landscape*, Los Angeles (Los Angeles County Museum of Art), Chicago (Art Institute) and Paris (Galeries nationales du Grand Palais), Los Angeles 1984.

Brunner 1980
M.-A. Brunner, 'Bibliographie des expositions de province, 1815–50', *Gazette des Beaux-Arts*, May–June 1980, pp. 198–212.

Bumpus 1990
J. Bumpus, *Impressionist Gardens*, Oxford 1990.

Burty 1867
P. Burty, *Notice des Etudes Peintes par M. Théodore Rousseau. Exposée au Cercle des Arts, Paris, June 1867*, Paris 1867.

Burty 1875
P. Burty, preface to the *Catalogue des Tableaux et Aquarelles par Claude Monet, Berthe Morisot, A. Renoir, A. Sisley*, Paris 1875.

Burty 1875a
P. Burty, *Exposition de l'Oeuvre de Corot à l'Ecole Nationale des Beaux-Arts*, Paris 1875.

Cabanne 1970
P. Cabanne in M. Robida *et al*, *Renoir*, exh. cat., New York (Durand-Ruel Gallery) 1970.

Cachin 1983
Cachin *et al*, *Manet, 1832–1883*, exh. cat., Paris (Galeries nationales du Grand Palais) and New York (The Metropolitan Museum of Art), New York 1983.

Cahiers d'aujourd'hui 1921
'L'Éternel jury', *Les Cahiers d'aujourd'hui*, 2 (1921).

Callen 1978
A. Callen, *Renoir*, London 1978.

Callen 1982
A. Callen, *Techniques of Impressionists*, London 1982.

Callen 2000
A. Callen, *The Art of Impressionism: Painting Technique & the Making of Modernity*, New Haven and London 2000.

Camesasca and Bardi 1989
E. Camesasca and P.M. Bardi, *The São Paulo Collection: from Manet to Matisse*, exh. cat., Amsterdam (Rijksmuseum Vincent Van Gogh), Amsterdam and Milan 1989.

Carstairs 1929
C. Carstairs, 'Renoir', *Apollo*, vol x, no. 55 (July 1929), pp. 34–5.

Castagnary 1892
J. Castagnary, *Salons: 1857–1870*, 2 vols, Paris 1892.

Catinat 1952
M. Catinat, *Les Bords de la Seine avec Renoir et Maupassant*, Chatou 1952.

Champa 1973
K.S. Champa, *Studies in Early Impressionism*, New Haven and London 1973.

Champa 1991
K.S. Champa, *The Rise of Landscape Painting in France: Corot to Monet*, exh. cat., Manchester, New Hampshire (Currier Gallery of Art) 1991.

Champfleury 1861
Champfleury, *Grandes Figures d'hier et d'aujourd'hui. Balzac, Gérard de Nerval, Wagner, Courbet*, Paris 1861, pp. 245–63.

Chamson 1949
A. and L. Chamson, *Renoir*, Lausanne 1949.

Galerie Charpentier 1943
Les Jardins de France, exh. cat., Paris (Galerie Charpentier) 1943.

Galerie Charpentier 1945
Paris 1944–1945, exh. cat., Paris (Galerie Charpentier) 1945.

Chillaz 1997
V. de Chillaz, *Inventaire Général des Autographes. Musée du Louvre, Département des Arts Graphiques*, Paris 1997.

Chu 1996
P.-D. Chu, ed., *Correspondance de Courbet*, Paris 1996.

Clark 1935
K. Clark, 'A Renoir Exhibition', *The Burlington Magazine*, LXVII (1935), pp. 3–7.

Clark 1984
T.J. Clark, *The Painting of Modern Life: Paris in the Art of Manet and his Followers*, Princeton 1984.

Clark 1985
T.J. Clark, *The Painting of Modern Life: Paris in the Art of Manet and his Followers*, London and New York 1985.

Clarke and Thomson 2003
M. Clarke and R. Thomson, *Monet: the Seine and the Sea 1878–1883*, Edinburgh (National Galleries of Scotland) 2003.

Cogeval and Vial 2005
G. Cogeval and M.-P. Vial, eds, *Right under the sun: landscape in Provence from classicism to modernism, 1750–1900*, exh. cat., Montreal (Montréal Museum of Fine Arts) 2005.

Cognat 1950
R. Cognat, *La Peinture française au temps des impressionistes*, Paris 1950.

Collins 2001
J.B. Collins, 'Seeking l'esprit gaulois: Renoir's *Bal du Moulin de la Galette* and Aspects of French Social History and Popular Culture', Ph.D. thesis, McGill University, Montreal 2001.

Compin and Roquebert 1986
I. Compin and A. Roquebert, *Catalogue sommaire illustré des peintures du musée du Louvre et du musée d'Orsay. Ecole française*, 5 vols, Paris 1986.

Compin, Lacambre and Roquebert 1990
I. Compin, G. Lacambre and A. Roquebert, *Musée d'Orsay. Catalogue sommaire illustré des peintures*, 2 vols, Paris 1990.

Constable 1955
W.G. Constable, ed., *Summary Catalogue of European Paintings*, Boston (Museum of Fine Arts) 1955.

Cooper 1954
D. Cooper, *The Courtauld Collection. A Catalogue and Introduction*, London 1954.

Cooper 1959
D. Cooper, 'Renoir, Lise and the Le Coeur Family. A Study of Renoir's Early Development', *The Burlington Magazine*, CI (1959), May pp. 163–71 and September/October p. 322–8.

Copenhagen 1996
Impressionists in Town, exh. cat., (Ordrupgard) Copenhagen 1996.

Crosnier Leconte 1990
M.-L. Crosnier Leconte, *La naissance des gares*, Paris 1990.

Crow 1986
T. Crow, 'Renoir: a Symposium', *Art in America*, vol. 74 (1986), pp. 117–19.

Czynmek 1990
G. Czynmek, *Landschaft im Licht: Impressionistische malerei in Europa und Nordamerika 1860–1910*, exh. cat., Cologne (Wallraf-Richartz-Museum) and Zurich (Kunsthaus Zurich) 1990.

Daulte 1952
F. Daulte, *Frédéric Bazille et son temps*, Geneva 1952.

Daulte 1964
F. Daulte, *Chefs-d'oeuvre des collections suisses*, Lausanne 1952.

Daulte 1959
F. Daulte, *Alfred Sisley. Catalogue raisonné de l'œuvre*, Lausanne and Paris 1959.

Daulte 1971
F. Daulte, *Auguste Renoir: catalogue raisonné de l'œuvre peint*, Lausanne and Paris 1971.

Daulte 1973
F. Daulte, *Renoir*, London 1973.

Daulte 1977
F. Daulte, *Monet et ses amis: le legs Michel Monet, la donation Donop de Monchy*, exh. cat., Paris (Musée Marmottan) 1977.

Davenport 1983
N. Davenport, 'Armand Auguste Deforge, an Art Dealer in Nineteenth-Century Paris and "La peinture de fantaisie"', *Gazette des beaux-arts,* February 1983, pp. 81–8.

D'Ayala Valva 2005
M. d'Ayaya Valva, *Les Classiques d'art Renoir*, Paris 2005.

De Andia 1991
B. de Andia, ed., *Le 16è: Chaillot, Passy, Auteuil: métamorphoses des trois villages*, Paris 1991.

Delécluze 1850
E. Delécluze, 'Exposition de 1850', *Journal des Débats*, 25 February 1851.

Devriès and Lesure 1988
A. Devriès and F. Lesure, *Dictionnaire des éditeurs de musique français, volume II: de 1820 à 1914*, Geneva 1988.

Distel 1989
A. Distel, 'Charles Deudon (1832–1914), collectionneur', *Revue de l'art*, 86 (1989), pp. 58–65.

Distel 1990
A. Distel, *Impressionism: The First Collectors, 1874–1886*, New York 1990.

Distel 1993
A. Distel, *Renoir, 'il faut embellir'*, Paris 1993.

Distel 1994
A. Distel *et al*, *Gustave Caillebotte 1848–1894*, exh. cat., Paris (Galeries nationales du Grand Palais) 1994.

Distel 1995
A. Distel, *Gustave Caillebotte, Urban Impressionist*, exh. cat., Paris (Musée d'Orsay) and Chicago (The Art Institute of Chicago), New York 1995.

Drucker 1944
M. Drucker, *Renoir*, Paris 1944.

Drucker 1955
M. Drucker, *Renoir*, Paris 1955.

Druick 1997
D.W. Druick, *Renoir*, London 1997.

Drutt 2001
M. Drutt, ed., *Thannhauser: the Thannhauser Collection of the Guggenheim Museum*, New York 2001.

Du Camp 1859
M. Du Camp, *Le Salon de 1859*, Paris 1859.

Du Camp 1867
M. Du Camp, *Les Beaux-Arts a l'Exposition Universelle et aux Salons de 1863, 1864, 1865, 1866 & 1867*, Paris 1867.

Dumas and Shapiro 1998
A. Dumas and M.E. Shapiro, *Impressionism: Paintings Collected by European Museums*, exh. cat., Atlanta (High Museum of Art), Seattle (Seattle Art Museum) and Denver (Art Museum), New York 1998.

Durand-Ruel 1873
Galerie Durand-Ruel. Recueil d'Estampes Gravées à l'eau-forte, introduction by Armand Silvestre, Paris 1873.

Durand-Ruel 1958
Galerie Durand-Ruel, *Hommage à Renoir*, Paris 1958.

Durand-Ruel 1969
Galerie Durand-Ruel, *Renoir intime*, Paris 1969.

Durand-Ruel 1974
Galerie Durand-Ruel, *Hommage à Paul Durand-Ruel: Cent ans d'Impressionisme*, Paris 1974.

Duranty 1876
E. Duranty, *La Nouvelle Peinture*, Paris 1876.

Duret 1867
T. Duret, *Les Peintres Français en 1867*, Paris 1867.

Duret 1870
T. Duret, 'Salon de 1870', *L'Électeur libre*, 16 June 1870 (reprinted with introduction by Denys Riout in *Critique d'avant-garde. Théodore Duret*, Paris 1998).

Duret 1924
T. Duret, *Renoir*, Paris 1924.

Duret 1998
T. Duret, *Critique d'avant-garde* (1885), Paris 1998.

Edgell 1949
G.H. Edgell, *French Painters in the Museum of Fine Arts: Corot to Utrillo*, Boston (Museum of Fine Arts) 1949.

Faison 1973
S.L. Faison Jr., 'Renoir's hommage à Manet' in *Intuition und Kunstwissenschaft. Festschrift für Hanns Swarzenski*, ed. Peter Boch, Berlin 1973, pp. 571–8.

Fechter 1910
P. Fechter, in *Kunst und Kunstler*, 1910, pp. 21, 24.

Feist 1961
P.H. Feist, *Auguste Renoir*, Leipzig 1961.

Fernier 1978
R. Fernier, *La vie et l'œuvre de Gustave Courbet: catalogue raisonné*, 2 vols, Geneva and Lausanne 1978.

Fezzi 1972
E. Fezzi, *L'Opera completa di Renoir nel perioda impressionista 1869–1883*, Milan 1972.

Fezzi 1985
E. Fezzi, *Tout l'œuvre peint de Renoir: période impressionniste 1869–1883*, ed. J. Henry, Paris 1985.

Florisoone 1938
M. Florisoone, *Renoir*, Paris 1938.

Forgione 2005
N. Forgione, 'Everyday Life in Motion: the Art of Walking in Late Nineteenth-Century Paris', *The Art Bulletin*, 87 (2005), pp. 664–87.

Fosca 1961
F. Fosca, *Renoir. L' homme et son oeuvre*, Paris 1961.

Fox 1953
M.S. Fox, *Renoir*, New York 1953.

Fried 1986
M. Fried, 'Renoir, a Symposium', *Art in America*, 74, 3 (1986), pp. 117–19.

Gaunt 1952
W. Gaunt, *Renoir*, London 1952.

Gaunt and Adler 1982
W. Gaunt and K. Adler, *Renoir*, Oxford 1982.

Gautier 1856
T. Gautier, *Les Beaux-Arts en Europe. 1855*, 2 vols, Paris 1856.

Gautier 1858
T. Gautier, 'La Rue Laffitte', *L'Artiste*, 3 January 1858, pp. 10–13.

Gautier 1861
T. Gautier, *Abécédaire du Salon de 1861*, Paris 1861.

Gautier 1992
T. Gautier, *Exposition de 1859*, eds W. Drost and U. Henninges, Heidelberg 1992.

Geffroy 1922
G. Geffroy, *Claude Monet, sa vie, son oeuvre*, Paris 1922.

Gerstein 1989
M.S. Gerstein, *Impressionism: Selections from Five American Museums*, New York 1989.

Gimpel 1963
R. Gimpel, *Journal d'un collectionneur, marchand de tableaux*, Paris 1963.

Godfroy 1992
C. Durand-Ruel Godfroy, P. Durand-Ruel and A. Sisley, *Sisley*, Paris 1992.

Godfroy 1995
C. Durand-Ruel Godfroy, *Correspondance de Renoir et Durand-Ruel, lettres réunies et annotées*, 2 vols, Lausanne 1995.

Goncourt 1855
E. and J. de Goncourt, *La Peinture à l'Exposition Universelle de 1855*, Paris 1855 (reprinted in *Études d'Art*, Paris 1893).

Goldin 2002
M. Goldin, *L'impressionismo e l'eta di Van Gogh*, Treviso 2002.

Grafton Galleries 1905
Pictures by Boudin, Manet, Pissarro, Cézanne, Monet, Renoir, Degas, Morisot, Sisley, exh. cat., London (Grafton Galleries) 1905.

Green 1989
N. Green, 'Circuits of production, circuits of consumption: the case of mid-nineteenth-century French art dealing', *Art Journal*, spring 1989, pp. 29–34.

Grégoire 1993
S. Grégoire, *Plein air: les impressionnistes dans le paysage*, Paris 1993.

von Groschwitz 1966
G. von Groschwitz, 'Renoir's Garden in Montmartre', *Carnegie Magazine*, March 1966, pp. 77–9.

Guégan 1992
S. Guégan, *Regards d'écrivains au Musée d'Orsay*, exh. cat., Paris (Musée d'Orsay) 1992.

Guégan 2003
S. Guégan, ed., *De Delacroix à Renoir. L'Algérie des peintres*, exh. cat., Paris (Institut du Monde Arabe) 2003.

Haskell 1976
F. Haskell, *Rediscoveries in Art: Some Aspects of Taste, Fashion and Collecting in England and France*, Ithaca NY 1976.

Heilbrun 1986
F. Heilbrun, *Les paysages des impressionnistes*, Paris 1986.

Heilbrun 1989
F. Heilbrun *et al*, *L'invention d'un regard (1839–1918): cent cinquantenaire de la photographie, XIXe siècle*, Paris 1989.

Henriet 1854
F. Henriet, 'Le Musée des Rues, I. Le marchand de tableaux', *L'Artiste*, 15 November 1854, pp. 113–15, and 1 December 1854, pp. 133–5.

Herbert 1988
R.L. Herbert, *Impressionism: Art, Leisure, and Parisian Society*, New Haven and London 1988.

Herbert 1994
R.L. Herbert, *Monet on the Normandy Coast: Tourism and Painting, 1867–1886*, New Haven and London 1994.

Herbert 1995
R.L. Herbert, *Peasants and 'primitivism': French prints from Millet to Gauguin*, exh. cat., South Hadley MA (Mount Holyoke College Art Museum) 1995.

Herbert 2000
R.L. Herbert, *Nature's Workshop: Renoir's Writings on the Decorative Arts*, New Haven and London 2000.

High Museum of Art 1984
The Henry P. McIlhenny Collection: Nineteenth-Century French and English Masterpieces, exh. cat., Atlanta (High Museum of Art) 1984.

Hillairet 1963
J. Hillairet, *Dictionnaire historique des rues de Paris*, 2 vols, Paris 1963.

von Hohenzollern and Schuster 1996
J.G.P. von Hohenzollern and P.-K. Schuster, *Manet bis Van Gogh: Hugo von Tschudi und der Kampf um die Moderne*, Munich and New York 1996.

Holland and Hart-Davis 2000
M. Holland and R. Hart-Davis, *The Complete Letters of Oscar Wilde*, New York 2000.

Hoog 1984
M. Hoog, *Catalogue de la collection Jean Walter et Paul Guillaume*, Paris 1984.

House 1974
J. House, *Impressionism: its Masters, its Precursors, and its Influences in Britain*, exh. cat., London (Royal Academy of Arts) 1974.

House 1985
J. House, *Renoir*, London 1985.

House 1986
J. House, *Monet: Nature into Art*, New Haven 1986.

House 1988
J. House, *Renoir, 1841–1919, Artists in Guernsey*, exh. cat., Guernsey (Guernsey Museum and Art Gallery) 1988.

House 1992
J. House, 'Renoir's "Baigneuses" of 1887 and the politics of escapism', *Burlington Magazine*, CXXXIV (1992), pp. 578–85.

House 1994
J. House, *Renoir, Master Impressionist*, exh. cat., Brisbane (Queensland Art Gallery), Melbourne (National Gallery of Victoria) and Sydney (Art Exhibitions Australia Ltd), Brisbane 1994.

House 1995
J. House *et al*, *Impressions of France: Monet, Renoir, Pissarro and their Rivals*, exh. cat., London (Hayward Gallery) and Boston (Museum of Fine Arts), Boston 1995.

House 1997
J. House, *Pierre-Auguste Renoir: La promenade*, Los Angeles 1997.

House 2004
J. House, *Impressionism: Paint and Politics*, New Haven and London 2004.

House and Distel 1985
J. House and A. Distel, *Renoir*, exh. cat., London (Hayward Gallery), Paris (Galeries nationales du Grand Palais) and Boston (Museum of Fine Arts), Paris 1985.

House and Murphy 1988
J. House and A. Murphy, *Renoir Retrospective*, exh. cat., Nagoya (Nagoya City Art Museum) 1988.

Houth 1972
M. and E. Houth, *Bougival et les rives de la Seine: des anciens vignerons aux impressionnistes*, Saint-Germain-en-Laye 1972.

Howard 1991
M. Howard, *The Impressionists by Themselves*, London 1991.

Isaacson 1980
J. Isaacson, *The Crisis of Impressionism: 1878–1882*, exh. cat., Ann Arbor (University of Michigan) 1980.

Isaacson 1982
J. Isaacson, 'Impressionism and Journalistic Illustration', *Arts Magazine*, 56 (1982), pp. 95–115.

Jean-Aubry and Schmit 1968
G. Jean-Aubry and R. Schmit, *La Vie et l'œuvre d'après les lettres et les documents inédits d'Eugène Boudin*, Paris 1968.

Joanne 1856
A. Joanne, *Les environs de Paris illustrés*, Paris 1856.

Joanne 1881
A. Joanne, *Les environs de Paris illustrés*, Paris 1881.

Kahn 1888
G. Kahn, 'Exposition des impressionisistes', *Revue indépendante*, June 1888, pp. 544–6.

Keller 1987
H. Keller, *Auguste Renoir*, Munich 1987.

Kelly 1999
S. Kelly, 'The Landscapes of Theodore Rousseau and their Market' in A. Burmester, C. Heilmann and M. Zimmermann, eds, *Barbizon: Malerei der Natur – Natur der Malerei*, Munich 1999, pp. 419–36.

Kelly 2003
S. Kelly in *Soil and Stone: Impressionism, Urbanism, Environment*, in F. Fowle and R. Thomson, eds., Aldershot 2003, pp. 398–401.

Kendall 1993
R. Kendall, *Degas Landscapes*, New Haven 1993.

Kern 1996
S. Kern *et al*, *A Passion for Renoir: Sterling and Francine Clark Collect, 1916–1951*, exh. cat., Williamstown (Sterling and Francine Clarke Institute), New York 1996.

Keyzer 1995
K. De Keyzer, *From Manet to Gauguin: Masterpieces from Swiss Private Collections*, exh. cat., (Royal Academy of Arts) Ghent 1995.

Kostenevich 1995
A. Kostenevich, *Hidden Treasures Revealed: Impressionist Masterpieces and other Important French Paintings Preserved by the State Hermitage Museum*, St Petersburg and New York 1995.

Laclotte 1989
M. Laclotte, *Les donateurs du Louvre*, Paris 1989.

Lagrange 1866
L. Lagrange. 'Bulletin Mensuel. Mars. 1866. Exposition du Cercle de l'Union Artistique', *Gazette des Beaux Arts*, 1 April 1866, pp. 398–401.

Langdon 1986
H. Langdon, *Impressionist Seasons*, London 1986.

Laprade 1956
J. Laprade, *L'impressionnisme*, Paris 1956.

Larousse 1865–90
P. Larousse, *Grand dictionnaire universel du XIXe siècle : français, historique, géographique, biographique, mythologique, bibliographique, littéraire, artistique, scientifique, etc.*, Paris 1865–90.

Lassalle 1992
C. Lassalle, *Croissy-sur-Seine: les impressionistes à la Grenouillère*, Croissy-sur-Seine 1992.

Lay 1993
J. and M. Lay, 'Rediscovering La Grenouillère: ars longa, vita brevis', *Apollo*, 137 (1993), pp. 281–6.

Le Coeur 1996
M. Le Coeur, *Charles Le Coeur (1830–1906), architecte et premier amateur de Renoir*, Paris 1996.

Le Coeur 1996a
M. Le Coeur, 'Le Salon annuel de la Société des amis des arts de Pau. Quartier d'hiver des impressionnistes de 1876 à 1879', *Histoire de l'art*, 35/36 (1996), pp. 57–70.

Le Coeur 1998
M. Le Coeur, 'A Drawing of Renoir in 1866', *The Burlington Magazine*, CXL (May 1998), pp. 319–22.

Leighton 2004
J. Leighton, *Edouard Manet: Impressions of the Sea*, Amsterdam 2004.

Léri 1983
J.-M. Léri, *Montmartre*, Paris 1983.

Leymarie 1955
J. Leymarie, *Impressionism; biographical and critical study*, trans. James Emmons, 2 vols, Geneva 1955.

Llorens and Llombart 2002
T. Llorens and F.V. Garin Llombart, *Il Trionfo del Colore. Collezione Carmen Thyssen-Bornemisza*, exh. cat., Rome (Palazzo Ruspoli), Milan 2002.

Lochnan 2004
K. Lochnan, *Turner, Whistler, Monet,* exh. cat., London (Tate) and Ontario (Art Gallery of Ontario), London 2004.

Los Angeles County Museum of Art 1955
Pierre-Auguste Renoir: Paintings, Drawings, Prints and Sculpture, exh. cat., Los Angeles (Los Angeles County Museum of Art), 1955.

Los Angeles-Chicago-Paris 1984–5
L'impressionnisme et le paysage français, exh. cat., Los Angeles (Los Angeles County Museum of Art), Chicago (Art Institute of Chicago) and Paris (Galeries nationales du Grand Palais), Paris 1985.

Loyrette and Tinterow 1994
H. Loyrette and G. Tinterow, *Impressionnisme. Les origines 1859–1869*, exh. cat., Paris (Galeries nationales du Grand Palais) and New York (The Metropolitan Museum of Art) 1994.

Luxenberg 1998
A. Luxenberg, 'Creating Desastres: Andrieu's photographs of urban ruins in the Paris of 1871', *The Art Bulletin,* vol. 80 (March 1998), pp. 113–37.

Manet 1979
J. Manet, *Journal (1893–1899)*, Paris 1979.

Martini 1978
A. Martini, *Renoir*, New York 1978.

Marly-le-Roi 1984
De Renoir à Vuillard: Marly-le-Roi, Louveciennes, leurs environs, exh. cat., Marly-le-Roi (Le Musée) 1984.

Mauclair 1905
C. Mauclair, *L'Art et la coueur. Les Maîtres contemporains*, 4 vols, Paris 1905.

Maxon 1970
John Maxon, *The Art Institute of Chicago*, Chicago 1970.

Maxon 1973
J. Maxon, *Paintings by Renoir*, Chicago 1973.

McCauley 1994
E.A. McCauley, *Industrial Madness: Commercial Photography in Paris, 1848–1871*, New Haven 1994.

Meier-Graefe 1911
J. Meier-Graefe, *Auguste Renoir*, Munich 1911.

Meier-Graefe 1912
J. Meier-Graefe, *Auguste Renoir*, Paris 1912.

Meier-Graefe 1929
J. Meier-Graefe, *Renoir*, Leipzig 1929.

Milner 1988
J. Milner, *The Studios of Paris: the Capital of Art in the Late Nineteenth Century*, New Haven 1988.

Minneapolis 1970
Catalogue of European Paintings in the Minneapolis Institute of Arts, Minneapolis 1970.

Moffett 1985
C. Moffett *et al*, *The New Painting: Impressionism 1874–1886*, exh. cat., San Francisco (The Fine Arts Museum) 1985.

Moffett 1986
C. Moffett *et al*, *The New Painting: Impressionism 1874–1886*, Geneva 1986.

Moffett 1998
C Moffett *et al*, *Impressionists in Winter: effets de neige*, Washington, DC 1998.

Monneret 1980
S. Monneret, *Renoir*, trans. E. Read, London, 1990.

Monneret 1989
S. Monneret, *Renoir*, Paris 1989.

Moreau-Nélaton 1926
E. Moreau-Nélaton, *Manet raconté par lui-même*, 2 vols, Paris 1926.

Morel 1883
H. Morel, 'P.-A. Renoir', *Le Réveil*, 2 July 1883, pp. 1–2.

Munro 2003
J. Munro, *French Impressionists*, Cambridge and New York 2003.

Murphy 1985
A. Murphy, *European Painting in the Museum of Fine Arts, Boston.* Boston (Museum of Fine Arts), 1985.

Murray 1854
J. Murray, *A Handbook for Travellers in France*, London 1854.

Musée de l'Orangerie 1946
Les chefs-d'œuvre des collections privées françaises retrouvés en Allemagne, exh. cat., Paris (Musée de l'Orangerie) 1946.

National Gallery of Art 1991
Art for the Nation: Gifts in Honor of the 50th Anniversary of the National Gallery of Art, Washington (National Gallery of Art) 1991.

Néret 2001
G. Néret, *Renoir, Painter of Happiness 1841–1919*, Cologne 2001.

New York 1932
Exhibition of Masterpieces by Pissarro and Auguste Renoir, exh. cat., New York (Durand-Ruel Gallery) 1932.

New York 1937
Renoir: A Special Exhibition of his Paintings, exh. cat., New York (The Metropolitan Museum of Art) 1937.

Noël and Hournon 2004
B. Noël and J. Hournon, *Les Arts en Seine. Le paradis des impressionnistes*, Paris 2004.

Novotny 1960
F. Novotny, *Painting and Sculpture in Europe, 1780–1880*, London 1960.

Pach 1973
W. Pach, *Auguste Renoir: Leben und Werk*, Cologne 1973.

Pantazzi, Pomarède and Tinterow 1996
M. Pantazzi, V. Pomarède and G. Tinterow, *Corot*, exh. cat., New York (The Metropolitan Museum of Art), Ottawa (National Gallery of Canada) and Paris (Galeries nationales du Grand Palais), New York 1996.

Paris 1978
Pont-Neuf, 1578–1978: exposition organisée par le Musée Carnavalet et la Délégation à l'action artistique de la ville de Paris, Paris 1978.

Paris Guide 1867
Paris guide par les principaux écrivains et artistes de la France, 2 vols, Paris 1867.

Paris-New York 1974
Centenaire de l'impressionnisme, exh. cat., Paris (Galeries nationales du Grand Palais) and New York (The Metropolitan Museum of Art), Paris 1974.

Patin 1986
S. Patin, *À la campagne*, Paris 1986.

Paul 1993
B. Paul, *Hugo von Tschudi und die moderne französische Kunst im Deutschen Kaiserreich*, Mainz 1993.

Pelloquet 1867
T. Pelloquet, 'Salon de 1867', *Le Monde Illustré*, Paris 1867.

Pickvance 1984
R. Pickvance, 'La Grenouillère' in eds J. Rewald and F. Weitzenhoffer, *Aspects of Monet: a Symposium on the Artist's Life and Times*, New York 1984, pp. 38–51.

Pissarro 1997
J. Pissarro, *Monet and the Mediterranean*, exh. cat., Fort Worth (Kimbell Art Museum) and New York 1997.

Pissarro and Durand-Ruel Snollaerts 2005
J. Pissarro and C. Durand-Ruel Snollaerts, *Pissarro: Critical Catalogue of Paintings*, 3 vols, Milan, Paris and New York 2005.

Pomarède 2002
V. Pomarède, ed., *L'École de Barbizon. La Peinture de plein-air avant l'Impressionisme*, Lyon 2002.

Pope 1930
A. Pope, 'French paintings in the collection of John T. Spaulding', *The Art News*, (28, 26 April 1930) pp. 97, 121.

Portland 2004
Monet to Matisse, Homer to Hartley: American Masters and their

European Muses, (Portland Museum of Art) Portland 2004, pp. 54, 62.

Poulain 1932
G. Poulain, *Bazille et ses amis*, Paris 1932.

Proust 1897
A. Proust, *Edouard Manet: Souvenirs*, Paris 1996.

Rabinow 2000
R. Rabinow, 'Modern art comes to the Metropolitan: the 1921 exhibition of Impressionist and Post-Impressionist paintings', *Apollo* (October 2000) pp. 3–12.

Rathbone 1996
E.E. Rathbone *et al*, *Impressionists on the Seine: A Celebration of Renoir's Luncheon of the Boating Party*, Washington, DC 1996.

Reff 1982
T. Reff, *Manet and Modern Paris*, exh. cat., Washington, DC (National Gallery of Art) 1982.

Reinhard-Felice 2003
M. Reinhard-Felice, *Sammlung Oskar Reinhart 'Am Römerholz', Winterthur: Gesamtkatalog*, Basle 2003.

Renoir 1879
E. Renoir, 'Cinquième exposition de La Vie Moderne. P.-A. Renoir', *La Vie Moderne* (19 June 1879) pp. 174–5.

Renoir 1962
J. Renoir, *Renoir, my Father*, trans. R. and D. Weaver, Boston 1962.

Renoir 1981
J. Renoir, *Pierre-Auguste Renoir, mon père*, Paris 1981.

Rewald 1945
J. Rewald, 'Auguste Renoir and His Brother', *Gazette des Beaux-Arts*, XXVI, 3 (1945), pp. 171–88.

Rewald 1946
J. Rewald, *The History of Impressionism*, New York (Museum of Modern Art), 1946.

Rewald 1950
J. Rewald with L. Pissarro, *Camille Pissarro: lettres à son fils Lucien*, Paris 1950.

Rewald 1961
J. Rewald, *The History of Impressionism*, New York 1961.

Rewald 1973
J. Rewald, *The History of Impressionism*, New York 1973.

Rewald 1978
J. Rewald, *Paul Cézanne, correspondance*, Paris 1978.

Rewald 1980
J. Rewald, *The History of Impressionism*, New York 1980.

Rewald 1986
J. Rewald, *Histoire de l'impressionnisme*, Paris 1986.

Rey 1931
R. Rey, *La Renaissance du sentiment classique*, Paris 1931.

Rice 1997
S. Rice, *Parisian Views*, Cambridge MA 1997.

Riopelle 1990
C. Riopelle, 'Renoir: The Great Bathers', *Bulletin: Philadelphia Museum of Art*, Philadelphia 1990.

Riout 1989
D. Riout, *Les écrivains devant l'impressionnisme*, Paris 1989.

Rivière 1877
G. Rivière, 'L'exposition des impressionistes', *L'Impressioniste* I, 6 April 1877, reprinted in Venturi 1939, vol. II.

Rivière 1921
G. Rivière, *Renoir et ses amis*, Paris 1921.

Robaut 1905
A. Robaut, *L'œuvre de Corot: Catalogue raisonné et illustré. Précédé de l'Histoire de Corot et de ses œuvres par Etienne Moreau-Nélaton, ornée de dessins et croquis originaux du maître*, 5 vols, Paris 1905.

Robinson 1983
L.F. Robinson, *La vie moderne: Nineteenth-Century French Art from the Corcoran Gallery*, exh. cat., Washington, DC (The Gallery) 1983.

Roos 1988
J.M. Roos, 'Within the "zone of silence": Monet and Manet in 1878', *Art History*, XI/3 (1988), pp. 374–407.

Rouart 1951
D. Rouart, *Correspondance de Berthe Morisot avec sa famille et ses amis Manet, Puvis de Chavannes, Degas, Monet, Renoir et Mallarmé*, Paris 1950.

Rouart 1985
D. Rouart, *Renoir*, Geneva 1985.

Roy 1985
A. Roy, 'The Palette of Three Impressionists', *National Gallery Technical Bulletin, vol 7*, London 1985, pp. 15–16.

Sabatier-Ungher 1851
F. Sabatier-Ungher, *Salon de 1851*, Paris 1851.

São Paulo 2002
Renoir: O Pintor da Vida, exh. cat., São Paulo (Museu de Arte) 2002.

Sapporo 1999
Renoir: Modern Eyes, exh. cat. (Kawamura Memorial Museum of Art, The Miyagi Museum of Art, Hokkaido Museum of Modern Art), Sapporo 1999.

Schneider 1945
M. Schneider, 'Lettres de Renoir sur l'Italie', *L'Age d'or*, I (1945), p. 95–9.

Schneider 1985
C.P. Schneider, 'Renoir: Le peintre des figures comme paysagiste', *Apollo*, July 1985, pp. 49–56.

Schulman 1999
M. Schulman, *Théodore Rousseau, 1812–1867: catalogue raisonné de l'œuvre peint*, Paris 1999.

Sensier 1881
A. Sensier, *La Vie et L'Œuvre de J-F. Millet*, Paris 1881.

Shackelford and Wissman 2000
G. Shackelford and F.E. Wissman, *Monet, Renoir, and the Impressionist Landscape*, exh. cat., Ottawa (National Gallery of Canada) 2000.

Shackelford and Wissman 2002
G.T.M. Shackelford and F.E. Wissman, *Impressions of Light: the French Landscape from Corot to Monet*, Boston 2002.

Shiff 1999
R. Shiff, 'Natural, Personal, Pictorial: Corot and the Painter's Mark' in *Barbizon. Malerei der Natur. Natur der Malerei*, Munich 1999, pp. 120–38.

Shimada 1985
N. Shimada, *Renoir*, Tokyo 1985.

Shone 1992
R. Shone, *Sisley*, New York 1992.

Shone 2002
R. Shone, *The Janice H. Levin Collection of French Art*, exh. cat., New York (The Metropolitan Museum of Art) 2002.

Signac 1978
P. Signac, *D'Eugène Delacroix au néo-impressionnisme* (1899), ed., F. Cachin, Paris 1978.

Silvestre 1857
T. Silvestre, *Histoire des Artistes Vivants Français et Etrangers. Etudes d'après Nature*, Paris 1857.

Silvestre 1873
A. Silvestre, *Recueil d'estampes gravées a l'eau forte*, Paris and London 1873.

Silvestre 1926
T. Silvestre, *Les artistes français*, 2 vols, Paris 1926.

Skeggs 1987
D. Skeggs, *River of Light: Monet's impressions of the Seine*, London 1987.

Solnit 2000
R. Solnit, *Wanderlust: A History of Walking*, London 2000.

Spadoni 2006
C. Spadoni, *Turner, Monet, Pollock: From Romanticism to Informal Art,* Milan 2006.

Spate 1992
V. Spate, *Claude Monet: Life and Work*, New York 1992.

Sterling and Salinger 1967
C. Sterling and M. Salinger, *Metropolitan Museum of Art, French Paintings*, III (XIX–XX centuries), New York 1967.

Stevens 1984
M. Stevens, *The Orientalists*, exh. cat., London (Royal Academy of Arts) 1984.

Stevens 1992
M. Stevens, ed., *Alfred Sisley*, exh. cat., London (Royal Academy of Arts), Paris (Musée d'Orsay) and Baltimore (Walters Art Gallery), New Haven 1992.

Stevenson 1992
L. Stevenson, *Manet*, Fort Worth 1992.

Stolwijk 1999
C. Stolwijk, *Theo Van Gogh*, exh. cat., Amsterdam (Van Gogh Museum) 1999.

Stuckey 1995
C.F. Stuckey, *Claude Monet, 1840–1926*, exh. cat., Chicago (The Art Institute of Chicago), New York 1995.

Stuckey and Scott 1987
C.F. Stuckey and W.P. Scott, *Berthe Morisot, Impressionist*, New York 1987.

Sullivan and Meyer 1995
E.J. Sullivan and R. Krueger Meyer, *The Taft Museum, European and American Paintings*, New York 1995.

Tabarant 1947
A. Tabarant, *Manet et ses œuvres*, Paris 1947.

Thomson 1982
R. Thomson, '"Les Quat Pattes": The image of the dog in late nineteenth-century French art', *Art History,* September 1982, 5, pp. 89–107.

Thomson 1994
R. Thomson, *Monet to Matisse, Landscape Painting in France 1874–1914*, exh. cat., Edinburgh (National Gallery of Scotland) 1994.

Thoré 1870
T. Thoré, *Salons de W. Bürger, 1861 à 1868, avec une preface par T. Thoré*, 2 vols, Paris 1870.

Tinterow and Lacambre 2003
G. Tinterow and G. Lacambre, *Manet/Velázquez: the French Taste for Spanish Painting*, exh. cat., New York (Metropolitan Museum of Art), London and New Haven 2003.

Tucker 1982
P.H. Tucker, *Monet at Argenteuil*, New Haven and London 1982.

Tucker 1995
P.H. Tucker, *Claude Monet. Life and Art*, New Haven and London 1995.

Tucker 1999
P.H. Tucker, *The Bellagio Gallery of Fine Art: European and American Masters*, Las Vegas 1999.

Tucker 2000
P.H. Tucker, *The Impressionists at Argenteuil*, exh. cat., Washington (National Gallery of Art) and Hartford CT (Wadsworth Atheneum of Art) 2000.

Tucker 2001
P.H. Tucker, *Renoir: From Outsider to Old Master 1870–1892*, exh. cat., Nagoya (Bridgestone Museum of Art and Nagoya City Art Museum) 2001.

Updike 1989
J. Updike, *Just Looking: Essays on Art*, New York 1989.

Vail 1886
G.E. Vail, *L'Art du patinage*, Paris 1886.

Vaisse 1995
P. Vaisse, *La Troisième République et les peintres*, Paris 1995.

Vallès-Bled and Sanfo 2002
M. Vallès-Bled and V. Sanfo, *Renoir e la luce dell'impressionismo*, Milan 2002.

Vatuone 1992
D. Vatuone, *Frédéric Bazille: correspondance recueillie, présentée et annotée*, Montpellier 1992.

Venturi 1939
L. Venturi, *Les Archives de l'Impressionnisme*, 2 vols, Paris 1939.

Vollard 1918
A. Vollard, 'La jeunesse de Renoir', *La Renaissance de l'art français et des industries de lux*, III (May 1918), pp. 16–24.

Vollard 1918a
A. Vollard, *Tableaux, pastels et dessins de Pierre-Auguste Renoir*, 2 vols, Paris 1918.

Vollard 1919
A. Vollard, *La vie et l'oeuvre de Pierre-Auguste Renoir*, Paris 1919

Vollard 1925
A. Vollard, *Renoir: An Intimate Record*, trans. H.I. Van Doren and R.T. Weaver, New York 1925.

Vollard 1938
A. Vollard, *En écoutant Cézanne, Degas, Renoir*, Paris 1938.

Vollard 1989
A. Vollard, *Pierre-Auguste Renoir. Paintings, Pastels and Drawings* (1918), San Francisco 1989.

Wadley 1987
Nicholas Wadley, ed., *Renoir: a Retrospective*, New York 1987.

Wagner 1981
A.M. Wagner, 'Courbet's Landscapes and their Market', *Art History*, 4, 4 (1981), pp. 410–31.

Waldmann 1930
E.Waldmann, *La Collection Oscar Schmitz*, Paris 1930.

Walter 1966
R. Walter, 'Les maisons de Claude Monet à Argenteuil', *Gazette des beaux-arts*, LXVIII (1966), pp. 333–42.

Ward 1991
M. Ward, 'Impressionist Installations and Private Exhibitions', *Art Bulletin*, LXXVI, 4 (1991), pp. 599–622.

Ward 1996
M. Ward, *Pissarro, Neo-Impressionism, and the Spaces of the Avant-Garde*, Chicago and London 1996.

Washington-Montreal-Yokohama-London 1990
The Passionate Eye: Impressionist and Other Master Paintings from the Collection of Emil G. Bührle, exh. cat., Washington (National Gallery of Art), Montreal (The Montreal Museum of Fine Arts), Yokohama (Yokohama Museum of Art) and London (Royal Academy of Arts), Zurich 1990.

Wattenmaker 1993
R.J. Wattenmaker *et al*, *Great French Paintings from the Barnes Foundation: Impressionist, Post-impressionist, and Early Modern*, New York 1993.

Weber 1976
E. Weber, *Peasants into Frenchmen: the modernization of rural France, 1870–1914*, Stanford CA 1976.

Weinberg 1981
B. Weinberg, 'Nineteenth-Century American Painters at the Ecole des Beaux-Arts', *American Art Journal*, XII (1981), pp. 66–84.

Weisberg 1993
G.P. Weisberg, *The Independent Critic: Philippe Burty and the Visual Arts of Mid-Nineteenth-Century France*, New York 1993.

Wheldon 1975
K. Wheldon, *Renoir and his Art*, New York 1975.

White 1969
B.E. White, 'Renoir's Trip to Italy', *Art Bulletin*, LI (1969), pp. 333–51.

White 1984
B.E. White, *Renoir, His Life, Art and Letters*, New York 1984.

White 1996
B.E. White, *Impressionists Side by Side. Their Friendships, Rivalries and Artistic Exchanges*, New York 1996.

Whitfield 1990
S. Whitfield, *Impressionismus und Postimpressionimus: Sammlung Thyssen-Bornemisza*, exh. cat., Villa Favorita (Lugano), Milan 1990.

Wildenstein 1936
Wildenstein and Company, *La Collection Oscar Schmitz*, Paris 1936.

Wildenstein 1950
Wildenstein and Company, *A loan exhibition of Renoir for the benefit of the New York Infirmary*, exh. cat., New York 1950.

Wildenstein 1958
Wildenstein and Company, *Renoir: Loan Exhibition for the Benefit of The Citizen's Committee for Children of New York City*, New York 1958.

Wildenstein 1972
Venice Rediscovered: A Loan Exhibition in aid of The Venice in Peril Fund, New York 1972.

Wildenstein 1974
D. Wildenstein, *Renoir: The Gentle Rebel*, exh cat., New York (Wildenstein Galleries) 1974.

Wildenstein 1974–91
D. Wildenstein, *Claude Monet: biographie et catalogue raisonné*, 5 vols, Lausanne 1974–91.

Wildenstein 1996
D. Wildenstein, *Monet*, Cologne and Paris 1996.

Willett 1992
J. Willett, *The Dieppe Connection: the Town and its Artists from Turner to Braque*, London 1992.

Willsdon 2004
C.A.P. Willsdon, *In the Gardens of Impressionism*, New York 2004.

Wilson-Bareau and Deneger 2003
J. Wilson-Bareau and D. Deneger *et al*, *Manet and the Sea*, exh. cat., Philadelphia (Philadelphia Museum of Art) 2003.

Wissman 2000
F.E. Wissman, *European Vistas: Cultural Landscapes*, Detroit 2000.

Wolohojian 2003
S. Wolohojian, ed., *A Private Passion: 19th-Century Paintings and Drawings from the Grenville L. Winthop Collection, Harvard University*, exh. cat., New York (Metropolitan Museum of Art), New Haven 2003.

Wood 1999
P. Wood, ed., *The Challenge of the Avant-Garde*, New Haven and London 1999.

Wrigley 1993
R. Wrigley, *The Origins of French Art Criticism: from the Ancien Régime to the Restoration*, Oxford 1993.

Zafran and Boardingham 1992
E. Zafran and R.J. Boardingham, *Crosscurrents: European and American Impressionism*, exh. cat., Boston (Museum of Fine Arts) 1992.

Zola 1991
E. Zola, *Ecrist sur l'art*, J-P Leduc, ed, Paris 1992.

LENDERS

Berlin
Staatliche Museen, Nationalgalerie

Boston, Massachusetts
Museum of Fine Arts

Cambridge, England
The Fitzwilliam Museum

Chicago, Illinois
The Art Institute of Chicago

Cincinnati, Illinois
Cincinnati Art Museum

Dallas, Texas
Dallas Museum of Art

Detroit, Michigan
The Detroit Institute of Arts

Fukushima
Morohashi Museum of Modern Art

Hartford, Connecticut
Wadsworth Atheneum Museum of Art

Las Vegas, Nevada
MGM Mirage Corporation Collection

London
The National Gallery

Los Angeles, California
The J. Paul Getty Museum

Madrid
Museo Thyssen-Bornemisza

Memphis, Tennessee
The Dixon Gallery and Gardens

Milwaukee, Wisconsin
Milwaukee Art Museum

Minneapolis, Minnesota
Minneapolis Institute of Arts

Moscow
Pushkin State Museum of Fine Arts

Munich
Neue Pinakothek, Bayerische Staatsgemäldesammlungen

New York, New York
The Metropolitan Museum of Art

Paris
Musée de l'Orangerie
Musée d'Orsay

Philadelphia, Pennsylvania
Philadelphia Museum of Art

Pittsburgh, Pennsylvania
Carnegie Museum of Art

Portland, Maine
The Portland Museum of Art

Portland, Oregon
Portland Art Museum

Providence, Rhode Island
Museum of Art, Rhode Island School of Design, Private Collection

São Paulo
Museu de Arte de São Paulo, Assis Chateaubriand

Stockholm
Nationalmuseum

Toledo, Ohio
The Toledo Museum of Art

Tokyo
The National Museum of Western Art

Toronto
Art Gallery of Ontario

Washington, DC
The Corcoran Gallery of Art
National Gallery of Art

Williamstown, Massachusetts
Sterling and Francine Clark Art Institute

Zurich
Kunsthaus

Wendy and Leonard Goldberg

Joseph Hackmey, Israel

Carmen Thyssen-Bornemisza

And all those lenders and private collectors who wish to remain anonymous

PHOTOGRAPHIC CREDITS

Aix en Provence
© Centre des Archives d-Outre-Mer, Aix en Provence: fig. 107

Amsterdam
© Stedelijk Museum, Amsterdam: fig. 115

Berlin
Nationalgalerie
© Staatliche Museen zu Berlin. Bildarchiv Preussischer Kulturbesitz: cat. 60. Photo: Jörg P. Anders: fig. 24

Bordeaux
Musée des Beaux-Arts
© RMN, Paris. Photo A. Danvers: fig. 6

Boston, Massachusetts (MA)
© Museum of Fine Arts, Boston, Massachusetts: cats. 26, 58, 63, 67, 72; figs. 34, 64.

Caen
© Musée des Beaux-Arts, Caen: fig. 106

Cambridge
© Fitzwilliam Museum, Cambridge: cat. 13

Cardiff
© National Museum Wales: figs. 69, 111

Chatou
© Les Amis de la Maison Fournaise: fig. 101

Chicago, Illinois
© The Art Institute of Chicago, Illinois: cats. 45, 49; fig. 102. Photo by Robert Hashimoto: cat. 34; fig. 38

Cincinnati
© Cincinnati Art Museum, Ohio: cat. 70
© Taft Museum of Art, Cincinnati, Ohio: fig. 14

Dallas, Texas
© Dallas Museum of Art, Texas: cat. 21; fig. 66

Detroit, Michigan
© The Detroit Institute of Arts: cat. 2

Hartford, Connecticut
© Wadsworth Atheneum Museum of Art, Hartford, Connecticut: cat. 19

Karlsruhe
Staatliche Kunstalle: fig. 73

Las Vegas
© MGM MIRAGE Corporate Collection: cat. 56

Liverpool
© Walker Art Gallery, National Museums Liverpool: fig. 11

London
© The National Gallery, London: cats. 33; figs. 8, 16, 40, 61, 62, 97, 110

Los Angeles, California
© The J. Paul Getty Museum, Los Angeles, California: cat. 7

Madrid
© Copyright Museo Thyssen-Bornemisza, Madrid: cats. 37, 44; fig. 8

Memphis, Tennesse
© Collection of the Dixon Gallery and Gardens, Memphis, Tennessee: cat. 68

Merion, Pennsylvania
© Photograph reproduced with permission from The Barnes Foundation, Merion Pennsylvania: figs. 39, 44, 49, 99

Milan
© Photo Courtesy of the owner
cat. 10

Milwaukee, Wisconsin
© Milwaukee Art Museum, Wisconsin. Photo by John R. Glembin: cat. 17

Minneapolis, Minnesota
© Minneapolis Institute of Arts: cat. 64; fig. 105

Montreal, Quebec
© Collection Centre Canadien d'Architecture/Canadian Centre for Architecture, Montreal: figs. 25, 71

Moscow
Pushkin State Museum, Moscow
© Photo Bridgeman Art Library, London
cat. 5

Munich
Neue Pinakothek, Bayerische Staatsgemäldesammlungen, Munich
© Bayer & Mitko – Artothek: cat. 71

New York
© Colin B. Bailey fig. 42, 75, 93, 96, 103, 113. © The Metropolitan Museum of Art, New York: cats. 8, 52, 65, 69; figs. 10, 48, 67, 84

The Museum of Modern Art, New York
© 2006, The Museum of Modern Art/Scala, Florence, © Succession H. Matisse/DACS 2007: fig. 108

Northampton
© Smith College Museum of Art, Northampton, Massachusetts: fig. 74

Oberlin
© Oberlin College, Allen Memorial Art Museum: figs. 23, 114

Oslo
© Nasjonalgalleriet, Oslo. Photo: J. Lathion: fig. 22

Paris
Archives de la Ville de Paris © Robert McDonald Parker: fig. 122. **Bibliotheque historique de la Ville de Paris** © Robert McDonald Parker: figs. 81, 116, 117, 118, 119, 120. © Bibliothèque Nationale de France, Paris: figs. 13, 20, 59, 70, 109. **Musee Carnavalet, Histoire de Paris** © Mairie de Paris, Photothèque des Musées de la ville de Paris. Photo Pierrain: fig. 87. © The Art Archive: fig. 17. © Robert McDonald Parker: figs. 58, 65, 91, 92. **Musée d'Orsay, Paris** © Art Archive, London: figs. 2, 31, 55, 72, 77, 88. © RMN, Paris: cat. 18; figs. 5, 21, 28, 33, 54, 76. Photo Hervé Lewandowski: cats. 36, 54, 55, 57; fig. 1. Photo René-Gabriel Ojéda: cat. 61. **Musee national de l'Orangerie** © RMN, Paris: cat. 35. **Petit Palais, Musée des Beaux-Arts de la Ville de Paris** © Photothèque des Musées de la Ville de Paris: fig. 56.

Pasadena, California
© The Norton Simon Foundation, Pasadena, California: fig. 27.

Philadelphia, Pennsylvania
© Philadelphia Museum of Art, Pennsylvania: cat. 30; figs. 15, 104.

Pittsburgh, Pennsylvania
© Carnegie Museum of Art, Pittsburgh: cat. 39; fig. 41

Portland, Maine
© Portland Museum of Art, Maine. Photo Meyersphoto.com: cat. 27

Portland, Oregon
© Portland Art Museum, Portland, Oregon: cat. 23

Prague
© National Gallery in Prague: fig. 85.

Private collection
© Photo courtesy of the owner: cats. 1, 10, 14, 15, 16, 20, 22, 28, 31, 40, 42, 51, 59, 66; figs. 26, 32, 43, 45, 46, 51, 68, 79, 98.© The Art Archive: fig. 19. © Photo Bridgeman Art Library, London: cat. 4. © Photo courtesy Galérie Michèle Chomette, Paris: fig. 18. © Courtesy Christie's Images, London: figs. 57, 63, 80, 82, 90, 94. © Courtesy of Durand-Ruel et Cie: cat. 53. © Robert McDonald Parker: fig. 121. © Courtesy Nathan Fine Art Berlin/Zürich: cat. 47. © Photo courtesy Alain Renoir: fig. 29. © Courtesy the owner/ Museum of Art, Rhode Island School of Design. Photo Cathy Carver: cat. 29. © Courtesy Galérie Schmit, Paris: cat. 25. © Photo Sotheby's/akg-images: fig. 86. © Tajan, Paris: figs. 36, 83.

Richmond, Virginia
© Virginia Museum of Fine Arts, Richmond, Virginia. Photo Travis Fullerton: fig. 9

São Paulo. Museu de Arte de São Paulo Assis Chateaubriand, São Paulo, Brazil
© Photo Bridgeman Art Library, London: cat. 3; fig. 4.

Stockholm. Nationalmuseum, Stockholm
© The National Art Museums of Sweden: cat. 6

Tokyo
© National Museum of Western Art, Tokyo: cat. 41; fig. 30.

Toledo, Ohio
© Toledo Museum of Art, Toledo, Ohio: cat. 43; fig. 12

Toronto, Ontario
© Art Gallery of Ontario, Toronto: cat. 9

Vienna, Oesterreichische Galerie Belvedere, Vienna
© Art Resource: fig. 7

Washington DC
© The Kreeger Museum: fig. 50. © Corcoran Gallery of Art, Washington, DC: cat. 73. © National Gallery of Art, Washington, DC. Image 2005 Board of Trustees: cats. 12, 24, 38, 46, 50; figs. 35, 78. © ARS, NY and DACS London 2007: fig. 95. © The Phillips Collection, Washington, DC: fig. 89

Williamstown, Massachusetts
© Sterling and Francine Clark Art Institute, Williamstown, Massachusetts, USA: cats. 32, 62; figs. 3, 47, 52, 53, 112

Wintherthur
© Oskar Reinhart Collection 'am Römerholz', Winterthur: figs. 37, 60.

Yoma-Gun, Fukushima-ken
© Morohashi Museum of Modern Art, Japan: cat. 11

Zürich
© 2006 Kunsthaus Zürich. All rights reserved: cat. 48

INDEX

Academy, The 126
Adriani, Götz 62, 120, 180, 206
After the Storm (*c.* 1872) 116, *116*, 117
Algeria/Algiers 33, 48, 65, 66, 67, 69–70, 72, 222–9, 254, 277–8
Algerian Girl (1870) 94
Algerian Landscape, 'The Ravine of the Wild Woman' (1881; cat. 57) 67, 228, *229*, 277
Allée in the Woods (*c.* 1878–9; cat. 42) 190, *191*
Almond Trees in Flower (*c.* 1875) 157
Andrieu, Jules: *Désastres de la guerre; St-Cloud..* 120, *120*
Arab Festival (1881; cat. 54) 48, 67, 222–3, *223*, 252
Argenteuil 53, 55, 56, 57–8, 62, 117, 132–49 *passim*, 166, 172, 273–5
At the Coast (1883) 73
auctions *see* Hôtel Drouot, Paris
Ayer, Winslow B. 147

Baldus, Edouard (photographer)
Church of St-Germain l'Auxerrois 42, *43*
Destruction of the Grande Galérie 45, *45*
Tuileries Palace, Paris 36, *36*
Ball at the Moulin de la Galette, The (1876) 59, 61, 164, 170, 176, 182, 222, 275
Ballu, Roger 13
Ballu, Théodore 42, 46, 274
Banks of the Seine (*c.* 1881; cat. 59) 232, *233*
Barbizon School 19–25, 26, 27, 28, 52, 54, 84, 108, 118, 127, 188
Barnes, A. and de Mazia, V.: *The Art of Renoir* 114, 130, 236
Barron, Louis 166
Bather with a Griffon (1870) 12, 94
Bathers: Essay in Decorative Painting (1887) 11
Baudelaire, Charles 25
Bay of Moulin Huet through the Trees, The (1883) 73–4, 279
Bay of Naples, The (1881) 249, *249*, 250, 277
Bay of Naples (Morning), The (1881; cat. 65) 48, 68, *68*, 249–50, *251*, 277
Bazille, Frédéric 37, 38, 42, 52, 87, 94, 269–72, 275
portrait (Renoir, 1867) 92
Studio in the rue de la Condamine 12, 84, *84*, 272
Bazin, Germain 228
Bellio, Georges de 59, 167
Berard, Alfred: *Portrait of Alfred Berard with his Dog* (Renoir, 1881) 220, *220*
Berard, Paul 62, 66, 67, 69, 74
Renoir's visits 15, 63, 65, 192, 194, 199, 206, 215, 228, 276–8
Béraud, Jean: *Les Boulevards* 162, *162*
Bernadille (critic) 13
Berneval-sur-mer (Normandy) 63, 65, 204, 206, *207*, 215, *215*, *217*, 276
Berson, Ruth 58
Biez, Jacques de 240
Blancard, Hippolyte: untitled photograph of Paris *271*
Blanche, Jacques-Emile 63, 64, 65, 192, 194, 199, 206, 276, 278
Blonde Bather I (1882) 68, *68*, 249
Boat at Chatou (*1871*) 106, *106*
Bodelsen, Merete 57
Boucher, François 154, 264
Boudin, Eugène 24, 25
On the Beach, Sunset 24, 24–5
Bougival 128, *128*, *129*, 130, *130*, 134, 272–4
Bracquemond, Félix 126
Brame, Hector 24, 27
Brettell, Richard 118
Bridge at Chatou, The (*c.* 1875; cat. 32) 58, 59, 166–7, *167*, 240, 274
Burty, Philippe 23, 27, 29*n*36, 70, 71–2, 126, 200
By the Water (1879–80; cat. 49) 65, 210, *211*

Cadart, Alfred, and Luquet, Jules: gallery 25
Cahen d'Anvers, Albert 65, 66, 277
Cahen d'Anvers, Irène 66
Caillebotte, Gustave 49, 59, 71, 142, 164, 238, 278
Callen, Anthea 116, 254
Callot, Jacques: *The Pont Neuf and the Tour de Nesle* 39, *39*
Canaletto (Antonio Canale) 240
Venice: A Regatta on the Grand Canal 243, *243*
Venice: The Doge's Palace 34, 35, 240
Carpentier, Marie-Charles-Edouard 54, 100, 272
Celle-St-Cloud, La 86, *86*, 110, 130, 270, 274
Cercle des Arts, Paris 27
Cézanne, Paul 55, 72, 77*n*21, 88, 108, 270, 279
with Renoir at L'Estaque 11, 71, 236, 250, 252–3, 278
paintings:
Rocks at L'Estaque 253
Viaduct at L'Estaque 254, *254*
Champa, Kermit 84, 86
Champfleury, Jules 25
Champrosay 13, 174, *175*, 275
Champs-Elysées during the Fair of 1867, The (1867) 42–3, *43*, 53–4, 271
Charigot, Aline *see* Renoir, Aline
Charpentier, Georges 57, 62, 63, 274–5
Charpentier, Mme 62, 63
Mme Charpentier and her Children (Renoir, 1878) 63, 275–6
Renoir's letters to 67, 194, 252, 253
Château and its rose garden (1879) 64, *64*
Chatou 58, 59, 65, 71, 106, *107*, 157, *159*, 166–70, 212, *213*, 220, 230, *231*, 234–9, 272–4, 276–7
Chestnut Trees in Bloom (1881; cat. 60) 65, 234, *235*, 236, 239, 278
Children's Afternoon at Wargemont (1884) 75
Chocquet, Victor 59, 65, 168, 275
Clapisson, Léon 70, 278
Clapisson, Mme: portrait (Renoir, 1882) 66–7, 70, 81*n*156, 278
Clearing in the Woods, A (1865; cat. 2) 86–7, *87*, 270
Cliffs at Berneval (1879; cat. 47) 206, *207*, 208, 276
Colombes, near Argenteuil 132
Confidences (*La Tonnelle*) (*c.* 1874; cat. 27) 57, 154, *155*, 156
Cooper, Douglas 90, 168
Coquart, Antoine, and Lucas, Claude (after Louis Bretez): *Le Plan Turgot* 35, *35*
Corot, Jean-Baptiste-Camille 19, 20
influence on Renoir 28, 75, 84, 104, 108, 130, 270
sales 23, 24, 25, 29*n*31
paintings:
The Banks of a Canal near Rotterdam 23–4, *24*
Le Concert 26
Effet de matin 29*n*29
The Evening Star 29*n*26, *n*31, 30*n*55
Port of La Rochelle 28, 75
Solitude, Souvenir de Vigen, Limousin (1866) 22, *22*–3
Souvenir of Mortefontaine 23
Coucher de soleil, Le (1877) 59–60, 275
Country Road near Marlotte (*c.* 1865–6; cat. 1) 84, *85*
Courbet, Gustave 19, 20, 25, 271, 273
influence on Renoir 28, 37, 52, 88
sales 24
paintings:
Demoiselles de Village 20, *20*
Entrance to the Puits-Noir Valley; Twilight Effect
Low Tide at Trouville 25, *25*
Seascape 199, 200
Waves 256
Courvoisier: *Vue de la terrassee du Parc de St-Cloud 119*, 120

Daubigny, Charles-François 19, 20, 23, 24, 28, 29*n*29, 114, 119, 134
The Banks of the Oise (1859) 20–1, *21*
The Harvest 124, *124*
Le Printemps 29*n*29
La Vanne d'Optevoz 29*n*29
La Vue de Château de St-Cloud 120*n*5
Daudet, Alphonse 174, 275
Daudet, Mme: portrait (Renoir, 1876) 174, 275
Deforge, Armand-Auguste 54, 272
Degas, Edgar 55, 275, 279

Delacroix, Ferdinand-Victor-Eugène 48, 52, 174, 222
The Aïssaouas of Tangiers 222, *222*
Delécluze, Etienne 22
Descubes (critic) 13
Deudon, Charles 63, 65, 67, 240
Diana, the Huntress (1867) 12, 270
Diaz de la Peña, Narcisse-Virgile 23, 25–6, 28, 52, 90, 269–70
Forest of Fontainebleau 26, *26*
View of Diaz's Studio 26, *26*
Distel, Anne 61, 84
Doria, Count Armand 157
Duc, Joseph Louis: Palais de Justice 46
Du Camp, Maxime 19
Duck Pond, The (1873; cats 20, 21) 55, 138–9, *140*, *141*, 142, 274
Dupré, Jules 24, 27
Durand-Ruel, Paul 63, 65, 66, 243, 266
exhibits Courbet's *Seascape* 200
and Monet 11, 53, 54, 260
organises Renoir retrospective (1883) 16, 71, 24, 238, 254
as Pissarro's dealer 66
as Renoir's dealer 12, 15, 33, 54, 56, 66, 67, 68, 69–70, 71, 73, 75, 114, 115, 147, 157, 180, 192, 194, 196, 203, 212, 214, 218, 234, 258, 260, 277–8
Renoir's letters to 66, 70–1, 73, 74, 252, 260, 266
as Rousseau's dealer 24, 27
see also Impressionist exhibitions, 2nd, 7th
Duranty, Edouard: *New Painting* 117, 139
Duret, Théodore 19, 22, 23, 277
on Renoir 16, 58, 62, 63, 71
Renoir's letters to 51, 118, 120, 234, 237

Engaged Couple (1868) 100, 271–2
'*Environs of Pourville*' (1879) *203*, 204
Ephrussi, Charles 65, 277
Estaque, L' 65, 69, 71, 74, 250, 252–3, *253*, 254, *254*, *255*, 278
Evènement illustré, L' 95
Expositions Universelles, Paris 1855 26, 37
1867 19, 27, 37–8, 41, *41*, 43, *43*, 271

Fantin-Latour, Henri: *Atelier in the Batignolles* 53, *53*, 272
Féder, Jules 196
Fichot, Charles: *Exterior View of the Grands Magasins de la Belle Jardinière* 112, *112*
Field of Banana Trees Near Algiers (1881; cat. 55) 14, 47, 67, 224, *225*, 262, 278
Fiorillo, E. (photographer)
Restaurant de l'Alcazar d'été sur Champs-Elysées *271*
Sailing Boats on the Seine 146, *146*
Fisherman, The (1874) 57
Fishing (1874) 157
Flor, Charles 196
Fog on Guernsey (1883; cat. 70) 73–4, 258, 260, *261*, 279
Fontainebleau, forest of 19, 26, *26*, 27, *27*, 28, 52, 84, 86, 88, *89*, 90, 270
Fournaise, Alphonse: portrait (Renoir, 1875) 166, 274
Fournaise, Alphonsine (*later* Papillon) *210*
portrait (Renoir, 1875) 166
Fournaise, Jules-Alphonse 210, *210*
Fragonard, Jean-Honoré 102, 119
La Fête à St-Cloud 120*n*5
Franco-Prussian War 46, 100, 110, 120, *120*, 272–3
Friedrich, Caspar David 206

Garden at Fontenay-aux-Roses (1873) 57, *57*, 274
Garden (in the Park), The (1875–6) *61*, 61–2
Garden in the rue Cortot, Montmartre (1876; cat. 39) 13, *60*, 60–1, 62, 180, 182, *182*, *183*, 184, 185, 275
Garnier, Charles: L'Opéra, Paris 37, 38, 46
Gautier, Théophile 21, 23
Geffroy, Gustave 72–3, 238
Gimpel, René 115
Girl with a Cat (1880) 66, 70
Gleyre, Charles 52, 76*n*14, 264, 269–70
Goncourt, Edmond and Jules 19
Grammar (Renoir manuscript) 47, *47*, 224, 262
Grand Canal, Venice, The (1881; cat. 63) 15, 48, 68, 243–4, *245*, 277–8
Grands Boulevards, Les (1875; cat. 30) *32*, 46–7, 160, 162–3, *163*, 274
Grenouillère, La 95, 166, 272–5 *and see below*
Grenouillère, La (1869; cat. 5) 54, 94, 95–7, 96, 272
Grenouillère, La (1869; cat. 6) 54, 94, 95–6, *97*, 97–9, 292
Grenouillère, La (1869) 54, 95, 97–9
Guého, Francis 194
Guernsey 73, *73*, 74, *74*, 258, *259*, 260, *261*, 279
Gust of Wind, The (*c*. 1872; cat. 13) 14, 116–18, *117*, 122

Hartmann, Frédéric 23
Hartmann, Georges 55, 126
Hartmann, Mme: portrait (Renoir, 1874) 55, *55*, 126
Harvest at Berneval (1880; cat. 51) 215–16, *217*
Harvesters, The (1873; cat. 16) 12–13, 55, 124–7, *125*, 196, 274
Haussmann, Baron Eugène-Georges/'Haussmannisation' of Paris 33–4, 36–7, 38, 43, 45–7, 48–9, 91, 112, 114, 161
Hazard, Nicolas 115
Henriot Family, The (*c*. 1874) 154
Herbert, Robert L. 34, 39, 42, 46, 94, 102, 212, 237, 246
Hills around the Bay of Moulin Huet, Guernsey (1883; cat. 69) 74, 258, *259*
Hokusai: *Great Wave* 200
Hoschedé, Ernest 59, 61, 167, 184, 278
Hôtel Drouot, Paris: auctions 14, 25–6, 56–7, 146–7, 126, 150, 275
House, John 62, 100, 102, 106, 117, 136, 168, 222, 249, 256

Impressionist exhibitions
1st (1874) 12–13, 53, 126, 127, 139, 142, 274
2nd (1876) 13, 58, 170, 275
3rd (1877) 12, 13, 59–60, 61, 62, 71, 164, 174, 275
4th (1879) 276
5th (1880) 276
6th (1881) 277
7th (1882) 14, 66, 69, 70–71, 196, 212, 244, 246, 224, 234, 240
Impressioniste, L' (journal) 38
In the Forest of Fontainebleau (1866) 88
In the Parc de St-Cloud (*c*. 1873) 119–20, *121*
In the Rosegarden (1882) 67, *67*
In the Woods (*c*. 1877; cat. 41) 31*n*70, *50*, 62, 188, *189*
Inn of Mère Antony, The (1866) 90, 270
Institut au quai Malaquais, L' (*c*. 1874) 57, *57*, 150, *150*
Italy 65
see Naples; Venice

Jardin d'Essai, Algiers, The (1881, cat. 56) 14, 48, 67, 226, *227*, 277–8
Jongkind, Johann-Barthold 40, 134
The Seine and Notre-Dame de Paris 40, *40*
Jourdain, Roger: *Summer* (*Au Bal des Canotiers de Bougival*) 130, *130*

Kern, Steven 142

Lagrange, Léon 27
Landscape at Wargemont (1879; cat. 43) 64, 192, *193*, 194–5, 208, 228, 276
Landscape Near Menton (1883; cat. 72) 75, 264, *265*, 279
Landscape with Two Figures (1865–6) 84
Langlois, Jean-Charles: *Gardens in the Algiers Countryside* 224, *224*
Latouche, Gaston 91
Laundry-boat on the Seine, Near Paris (1871; cat. 11) 110, *112*
Leaving the Conservatory (1876) 176
Le Coeur, Charles Clément 270–1, 273–4
Le Coeur, Jules 53, 54, 84, 88, 270, 272–3
Jules Le Coeur and his Dogs walking in the Forest of Fontainebleau (Renoir, 1866; cat. 3) *18*, 88, *89*, 90, 188, 270
Le Coeur, Marc 90
Le Coeur, Marie 84, 274
Le Gray, Gustave: *Interior of 1852 Salon . . . 20*
Lepine, Stanislas 40
Leroi, Paul 15, 240
Leroy, Louis 240, 242
Lhote, Paul 73, 277–9
Lise with a Parasol (1867) 12, 53–4, 100, 271–2

Loge, La (1874) 12
Loge at the Opera, A (1881) 70
Lopez, Nini 62, 186
Louveciennes 100, *103*, 103–4, *104*, 106, 108, *108*, *109*, 134, 157, 272–6
Lovers, The (1875) 154, *154*, 156
Low Tide at Yport (1883) *72*, 73
Luncheon, The (1875) 58, *59*
Luncheon at La Fournaise (1875; cat. 34) 58, *58*, 59, 142, 168, 170, *171*, 210, 275
Luncheon of the Boating Party (1880–81) 15, 66, 70, 166, 170, *170*, 210, 220, 277–8

Mallarmé, Stéphane 53
Manet, Edouard 37–8, 52, 65, 110, 142, 270, 272
cityscape painting 33, 41, 114
influence on Renoir 53, 56, 130, 274–5
paintings:
Déjeuner sur l'Herbe 154, 156
The Monet Family in their Garden in Argenteuil 152, *152*, 274
Music in the Tuileries Gardens 92
View of Paris at the Time of the Universal Exhibition of 1867 41, *41*, 43, 53
Manet, Eugène 70, 224
Mare aux Fées, La (1866) 54, *54*, 77*n*27, 270
Marine, Guernsey (1883) 74, *74*
Marlotte 52, 53, 84, 86, 88, 270, 273
Marville, Charles (photographer)
Rue d'Argenteuil 269
Rue des Beaux-Arts 272
Matisse, Henri 212
Periwinkles/Moroccan Garden 228, *228*
Maupassant, Guy de
Le Père 130
Un Vie 200
Mediterranean, the 262–7
see also Estaque, L'
Mediterranean Landscape (1883; cat. 71) 262, *263*
Menzel, Adolph 41
Meryon, Charles (engraver) 40
Le Pont-au-Change 41, 49*n*8
Le Pont Neuf and the Samaritaine 40
Millet, Jean-François 20, 21, 23, 24, 31*n*66, 114, 138, 269
The Gust of Wind 118, *118*
November 22
Scène champêtre, gardeuse de vache 29*n*29
Winter 21, 21–2
Molins, Auguste de 116, 117
Monet, Camille 55, 94, 136, 152, 271, 273–5
Camille Monet and her son Jean (Renoir, 1874) 56, *56*, 274
Monet, Claude 16, 37, 49, 51, 52, 53, 62, 71, 72, 200, 223, 269–79
cityscape painting 33, 41–2, 91, 271, 275
and Durand-Ruel 11, 53, 54, 260
influence on Renoir 53, 55, 58, 75, 87, 98–9, 108, 127, 182, 184
on painting trips with Renoir 11, 52, 54, 55, 74, 94–5, 98, 134, 142, 144, 172, 262, 264, 272
plans first Impressionist exhibition with Renoir 53, 139, 142
sales 13, 54, 150
stylistic comparisons with Renoir 99, 132, 135, 136, 138, 142, 146, 148, 166, 240, 260, 272, 274
Claude Monet Painting in his Garden at Argenteuil (Renoir, *c.* 1873; cat. 19) 55, 135–6, *137*, 142, 182, 274
paintings:
The Artist's Garden in Argenteuil 135, 135–6
Boulevard des Capucines 48–9
The Bridge at Argenteuil 166, *166*
Cart on the Road to Honfleur, Snow 92
Les Dindons 61
Duck Pond 138, *138*, 142, 274
Frost 172, *172*
The Garden of the Princess 42, *42*
La Grenouillère 97–9, *98*, 166, 272
The Monaco Corniche 266, *266*
On the Bank of the Seine, Bennecourt 142
The Pont Neuf 114, *114*, 273
Poppies at Argenteuil 57
Regatta at Argenteuil 148, *148*
Rowers at Argenteuil 144, *144*, 146
St-Germain l'Auxerrois 42, *42*
The Seine at Argenteuil 132, *132*
The Seine at Bougival 128, *128*, 273
View of the Argenteuil Plain 132, *134*
Monet, Jean 94
Montmartre, Paris 49, 60, 176, *176*, 177, *177*, 275
see also Garden in the rue Cortot, Montmartre
Morisot, Berthe 29*n*27, 51, 55, 57, 100, 130, 150, 224, 274–5
Mosque at Algiers, The (1882) 70, *70*
Mother and Child (1881) 68, 69, 249
Musselfishers at Berneval (1880) 12, 63, *63*, 66, 204, 276
Mussel Harvest, The (1879; cat. 46) 203–4, *205*, 276
Musset, Alfred de 29*n*26

Nadar (Gaspard-Félix Tournachon) 41, 125, 127
Naples/Bay of Naples 33, 48, 67, *68*, 68–9, 72, 249–50, *251*, 277
Napoléon III, Emperor 23, 33, 34, 36, 37, 42, 45, 46, 273
Naturalist movement 19, 126
Near the Lake see By the Water
'New Painting' 53, 62, 71, 117, 139
Nini in the Garden (*c.* 1875–6) 62
'Nymphe se mirant dans l'eau' (1864) 77*n*27

Orchard at Louveciennes (1875) 157
Ostade, Isaac van: *Canal gelé avec couple patinant* 92 *and n*13
Paris 19, 33, 35, 39–47, 57, 58, 110, 112–15, 150, 160–5, 269, 272–3
'Haussmannisation of' *see* Haussmann, Baron Eugène-Georges
Turgot map 35, *35*
see also Expositions Universelles; Hôtel Drouot; Montmartre; Salons
Parker, Robert McDonald 194
Path rising through Tall Grass (1873) 14, *15*, 57–8
Pelloquet, Théodore 19, 21–2
Petit, Georges 11
Piazza San Marco, Venice (1881; cat. 64) 48, 246, *247*, 248, 277
Picking Flowers (1875–6; cat. 38) 62, *179*, 180–1
Pickvance, Ronald 128
Pissarro, Camille 51, 52, 55, 88, 108, 139, 270, 272–8
and Durand-Ruel 54, 66
influenced by Corot 29*n*27
and Renoir's paintings 70
sales 13
paintings:
A Morning in June 126, 127
View from Louveciennes 103, *103*, 104
Place de la Trinité, La (1875; cat. 29) 46, 160–1, *161*
Place de la Trinité, La (1875) 46, 160, *160*
Place St-Georges, La (1875; cat. 31) 13, 59, 164, *165*
Pollock, Jackson: *Lavender Mist* (*Number 1*) 188, *188*
Pont des Arts, Le (1867) 13–14, 43, *44*, 44–5, 54, 114, 150
Pont Neuf, The (1872; cat. 12) 45–6, 56, 110, 112, *113*, 114–15, 119, 275
Porcheron, Emile 58
Portrait of Bazille (1867) 92
Portrait of Alfred Berard with his Dog (1881) 220, *220*
Portrait of Mme Clapisson (1882) 66–7, 70, 81*n*156
Portrait of Mme Daudet (1876) 174
Portrait of Alphonse Fournaise (1875) 166
Portrait of Alphonsine Fournaise (1875) 166
Portrait of Madame Hartmann (1874) 55, *55*, 126
Portrait of Mlle Samary (1878) 63
Presles, Raoul de 95
Promenade, La (1870; cat. 7) 100, *101*, 102, 104

Quai Malaquais, Le (*c.* 1874; cat. 25) 57, 150, *151*, 274

Railway Bridge at Chatou, The (1881; cat. 61) 65, 234, 237–8, *239*
Raphael (Raffaello Sanzio) 67, 68, 249, 277
Rathbone, Eliza 168
'*Ravine of the Wild Woman, The*' *see Algerian Landscape*
Reader, Springtime, The (1872) 136

Regatta at Argenteuil (1874; cat. 24) 55, 134, 148, *149*, 274

Renoir, Aline (*née* Charigot) 65, 66, 68, 70, 73, 200, 277–9
Madame Renoir with a Dog (Renoir, 1880; cat. 53) 220, *221*
Renoir, Jean 35, 39
Renoir, Victor-Edmond 56, 71, 102, 112, 114, 176–7, 274
Ribot, Théodule 135
Riding in the Bois de Boulogne (1873) 12, 54, 55, 273
Rivière, Georges 13, 59–60, 61, 119, 164
Renoir et ses amis 52, 119, 134, 176, 177, 182
Road in Louveciennnes (1870; cat. 8) 103–4, *105*, 108
Robert, Hubert 39–40
Rochelle, La 28, 75
Rocks at L'Estaque (1882; cat. 66) 252–3, *253*
Rocky Crags at L'Estaque (1882; cat. 67) 71, 252–3, 254, *255*
Roevens, E.: *Le Club des Patineurs* 92, *92*
Roos, Jane Mayo 45
Rousseau, Théodore 19
influence on Renoir 28, 52, 269
one-man show (1867) 27
patrons and sales 23, 24, 25, 26
Salon exhibits 20, 22
painting:
Fontainebleau 27, *27*
Rowers at Argenteuil (*c.* 1873–4, cat. 22) 142, *143*
Rowers at Chatou (1880–1; cat. 50) 65, 212, *213*, 214, 278
Rowers' Lunch, The see Luncheon at La Fournaise
Ruskin, John 39, 246, 248

Sabatier-Ungher, François 22
St-Cloud 119–20, *120*, *121*, 134
Salon des Refusés (1873) 12, 55, 270
Salons, Paris 11, 20, *20*, 21, 22, 25, 38, 52–3, 54, 55, 84, 94, 269–75
Samary, Mlle: portrait (Renoir, 1878) 63, 275
Sardou, Victorien 103
Seated Bather (1883) 73
Seine, River 40, *40*, 44, *44*, *45*, 91, 110, 128, *128*, *129*, 232, *233*, *272*, 276
see also Argenteuil; Chatou; Grenouillère, La; *and below*
Seine at Argenteuil, The (*c.* 1873; cat. 18) 132, *133*, 134
Seine at Argenteuil, The (1874; cat. 23) 55, 56, 134, 142, 144, *145*, 146–7, 274
Seine at Champrosay, The (1876; cat. 36) *10*, 13, 71, 164, 174, *175*, 262, 275
Seine at Chatou, The (1871; cat. 9) 106, *107*, 108, 110, 230
Seine at Chatou, The (1881; cat. 58) 14, 230, *231*, 232, 278
Silvestre, Armand 70
Sisley, Alfred 29*n*27
relationship with Renoir 52, 53, 86, 88, 142, 269–74, 276–8
sales 13, 54, 150
Alfred Sisley and his Wife (Renoir, 1868) 54
paintings:
The Avenue of Chestnut Trees in La Celle-St-Cloud 86, *86*
Bougival 128
Early Snow at Louveciennes 108, *108*
The Seine at Argenteuil 132
Skaters in the Bois de Boulogne (1868; cat. 4) 43, 91–2, *93*, 271
Skiff, The (1875; cat. 33) 58–9, *59*, 168–9, *169*, 274
Snowy Landscape (*c.* 1875; cat. 35) 91, 171, *172*, 274
Société anonyme 55, 126, 274
Soirée d'été, La (*c.* 1865) 52
Solnit, Rebecca 37
Springtime (in Chatou) (*c.* 1875; cat. 28) 157–8, *159*
Steinbart, Carl 194
Still Life with Peonies and Poppies (*c.* 1872) 114
Studies for Musselfishers at Berneval (*c.* 1880) 204, *204*
Study (*Nude in Sunlight*) (1876) 182
Swing, The (1876) 164, 176, 182

Terral, Abel 76*n*14
Thomas, Gabriel 57
Thomson, David Croal 29*n*8
Thoré, Théophile 19, 26
Tinterow, Gary 104
Tréhot, Lise 102, 106, 270–2
Troyon, Constant 23, 24
Tschudi, Hugo von 234
Tucker, Paul 148, 226
Turner, J. M. W. 126, 240
Two Sisters (*On the Terrace*) (1881) 65, 70, *212*, 214

Universal Exhibitions *see* Expositions Universelles

Velde, Adriaen van de: *Rivière glacée avec patineurs . . . 92 and n*13
Venice 15, 33, *34*, 35, 48, 67, 240–8, 254, 277
see also below
Venice, Fog (1881) 69, *69*, 277–8
Venice, The Doge's Palace (1881; cat. 62) 15, 48, 240, *241*, 242, 246, 249
Venturi, Lionello 256
Vernet, Joseph 40
View at Guernsey (1883) *73*, 73–4
View from Cap Martin at Monte Carlo (1883; cat. 73) 266, *267*
View of Bougival (1873, cat. 17) 120, 128–31, *129*
View of the Coast Near Wargemont (1880; cat. 52) 204, 215, 218, *219*
Village Street (*Louveciennes*) (*c.* 1871–2; cat. 10) 108, *109*
Vintagers, The see Mussel Harvest, The
Vollard, Ambroise 75, 90, 91, 134, 176, 177, 200

Ward, Martha 27
Wargemont (Normandy) 63–4, 65, 71, 192, *192*, *193*, 194, *194*, 218, 279
Watering-place, The (1873; cat. 15) 31*n*66, 57, 122, *123*, 128
Watteau, Antoine 102, 154, 161, 264
Le Faux Pas 102, 130
La Finette 102
Wave, The (1879; cat. 45) 65, 199–200, *201*, 202, 256, 276
Wave, The (1882; cat. 68) 65, 71, 256, *257*, 278
Wheatfield (1879; cat. 44) 196, *197*, 198
Whistler, James Abbott McNeill 48, 65, 206, 234, 269, 273, 277
Nocturne: Blue and Gold – St Mark's, Venice *246*, 248
White, Barbara 98, 266
Wilde, Oscar 65, 204
Winter Landscape (1868) 91
Woman at the Seaside, Seascape (1879–80; cat. 48) 208, *209*
Woman gathering Flowers (*c.* 1874) 15, *16*
Woman with a Parasol and a Small Child on a Sunlit Hillside (1874; cat. 26) 56, *56*, 152–3, *153*
Woman with a Parasol in a Garden (1875–6; cat. 37) 62, 177, *178*, 180–81
Women bathing (*c.* 1866) 53
Women in a Garden (*c.* 1876; cat. 40) 62, 185–6, *187*

Young Trees in the Forest (1866) 88, *88*
Young Woman seated in the Garden (*c.* 1876) *185*, 186
Yport (Normandy) 65, *72*, 73, 279
Ziem, Félix 15, 70, 240, 246
Zola, Emile 58, 78*n*38, 110
L'Assommoir 110
La Faute de l'abbé Mouret 186
Zorzi, Conte Alvise 248